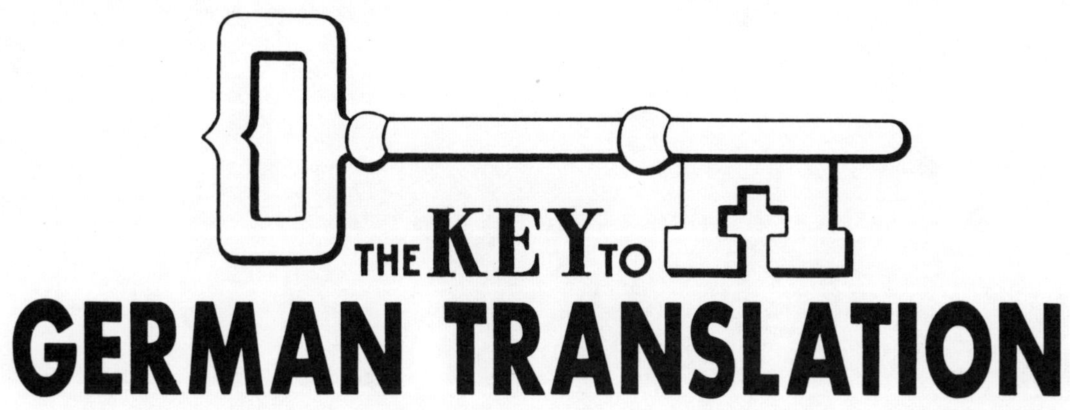

EIGHTH EDITION

The analytical approach to German translation based upon *the capitalized noun* and ELEVEN MAJOR RULES

By the late

C. V. POLLARD, LL.D.

Associate Professor of Germanic Languages
The University of Texas

Published By

THE UNIVERSITY COOPERATIVE SOCIETY, INC.
Austin, Texas

1963

TO MY WIFE
KALEI JACOBSEN POLLARD
Who had a share in the
pleasure and labor of this work

In the earliest periods of civilization, translators have been the agents of propagating knowledge from nation to nation, and the value of their labours has been inestimable; but in the present age, when so many different languages have become the depositories of the vast treasures of literature and of science which have been accumulating for centuries, the utility of accurate translation has greatly increased, and it has become a more important object to attain perfection in the art.

Roget, *Thesaurus*, Introduction

Die Erlernung der Sprachen führt zu tausendfaltiger Berührung mit der Denk- und Anschauungsweise des fremden Volkes: jedes Wort, jede Wendung enthält ein Stück seines nationalen geistigen Lebens.

Friedrich Paulsen

INTRODUCTION

The purpose of this book is to facilitate German translation. That this has been done by the rules discussed in this text, is attested by graduate and undergraduate students in this and other universities in the country. The book is intended for students who have had one or two semesters of German grammar. However, graduate and research students who need German and who have not had courses in formal grammar will find the method easy to understand.

In order to make it possible for students to plunge earlier into mature texts in their major fields of study, it has been found expedient and profitable to forego some of the linguistic advantages of prolonged grammar drill. Since it is generally true that students in American colleges and universities have limited time to devote to the study of language, it is the considered opinion of the author that the time spent in mastering grammar forms should be limited so that it will be possible for students to delve into the wonderful materials—literary and scientific—that may be read in German. The teacher who may disagree with this opinion is still free to spend as much time as he chooses in discussing and teaching any grammatical points which he feels merit fuller discussion. Indeed, he is just as free to spend time on grammar in this as with any other text.

The one basic feature that distinguishes this book from other texts dealing with German is the non-grammatical approach. This method emphasizes the logical arrangement of the words in the sentence and teaches the student how to analyze the sentence on the basis of a few simple formulae. Grammar becomes then a "functional" matter. The difficulties which it presents are taken care of on the spot where and when they are encountered. Thus grammar is taught, but only functionally. The rules outlined and illustrated in this text are aimed to "set" and "fortify" the grammar that students have spent so much time in their first semester to acquire. The ease with which sentences unfold by the rules clears up much of the grammar that is otherwise obscure and difficult for them to understand. Classes which have used the method have stressed this time and again both to the author and to other teachers who have used it. The most frequent question that must be answered is: "Why haven't we been taught the rules earlier"?

This simplified approach to German translation focuses the student's attention upon certain "key points" in the German sentence that lead him to a smooth, rapid and accurate translation. These points are impressed forcefully upon his mind by ample model sentences which help him to realize and visualize at a glance that German sentences fit certain patterns. These points have not been discussed in a descriptive manner in previous texts dealing with German. The author is not acquainted with any other text that gives the student a condensed, but thorough approach to the study of complicated German.

By use of the very simple, logical and easily applied rules set forth in this book, the student soon forms in his mind a set of habits which rarely need to be broken in translation work. The simple manner and the certainty with which sentences unfold stimulate and encourage the student to further reading and study of German. Instead of spending valuable time in learning the intricacies of German grammar, he is free to acquire a vocabulary in his own field of study. A knowledge of the rules and of the vocabulary makes the reading of the most complicated type of German a pleasure. The mastery of one sentence creates a desire to see how the next sentence will unfold. Students in classes where the method has been used do not find it overly burdensome to write out as much as 150 lines of translation in one assignment. Furthermore, it is just as easy to teach a class as to teach an individual. After the teacher has used the method one semester, he will find himself at home in it, and the results and enthusiastic attitude of the students will prompt him to use it again and again.

The method presented in this text was offered originally in the author's two other books: *German—The Easy Way,* Hardin College, 1945 and *The Key to Rapid Translation of German,* Hardin College, 1947. These two books were made possible by the very excellent and much appreciated cooperation of Dr. James B. Boren, President of Hardin College, Wichita Falls, Texas. The success of these books and the welcome they received among graduate and undergraduate students in all parts of the country emboldened the author to hope that in this new and more perfect presentation this book may attract many new friends for the study of German. The author has benefited greatly by his own experience in using the book both with graduate students and in classes since 1945. He has also appreciated and benefited by the suggestions of other teachers both in this and other universities who have used the book in class.

The author has sought to give in this new text much better and more carefully chosen model sentences and also more vocabulary aid. The text material is more up to date due to the kindness of German publishers in permitting use of copyright material. This was not possible in the other books, for these publications went to press during the war at which time permission to use foreign material was unobtainable. The new text also includes a great deal more material for classroom purposes with greater emphasis on social science topics.

A chapter has been added on the "insertion of clauses, phrases etc." which is not found in other German texts. Here the student is shown graphically how to interweave clauses, phrases, appositives and the like in a clear and easily comprehensible manner. A chapter on word formation and vocabulary building will greatly aid the student in developing a vocabulary. The text also includes an appendix which gives a more careful discussion of the "catchy" points of German grammar and German words that offer trouble to the American student. Cross references are made constantly to the appendix throughout the reading material. Exact and ample illustrations are given here to show the use of such things as **"werden"**, the troublesome **"es"**, the **reflexive constructions**, the **subjunctive**, and a few of the more bothersome terms as **indem, selbst, wenn-auch, je-umso, zufolge, da, derselbe, derjenige, um-willen, gegenüber** and others. When difficulty arises in the text material, cross references are made to these points. In fact, there are so many references to certain points that students will gradually stop referring to them.

Each of the pages contains about 600 to 700 words. There are about 500 words of text material and between 100-150 words of vocabulary. The total amount of reading material in the book can be best realized if the reader will remember that each page contains about three pages of material found in ordinary texts used in German classes. This has been made possible by the wider page of the book. Instead of giving the vocabulary and notes at the bottom of the page or in the back of the book, the author has been able to offer all of this on the right side of the page, while keeping the page intact for the text material. The handy references to the notes and vocabulary on the side of the page aid greatly in translation and are appealing to the student.

The book offers a wide selection from various fields. It is intended to give a goodly amount of reading material in several fields so that a student in almost any branch of study may become well enough acquainted with vocabulary and sentence structure, word order, etc., that he will find reading in his own major field profitable and interesting. Reading selections are divided into groups as follows: 1. Social Sciences—history, anthropology, economics, psychology, philosophy, government and literature. 2. Biological Sciences—anatomy, bacteriology, sex determination and heredity, and botany. 3. Physical Sciences— geology, chemistry, physics and mathematics. The attempt has been made to choose those materials that may be read with profit by students in any of these or allied fields of study. Thus a student of medicine may derive equal benefit by reading any of the selections on bacteriology, sex determination and heredity, anatomy, botany and even the articles on chemistry and psychology. A student of literature or history will find material in his own field or in philosophy, anthropology, psychology or the first part of the section on mathematics. A student of chemistry may derive equal benefit by reading material in physics, geology, mathematics or even some of the biological sciences.

Students who have covered this material will have gained sufficient acquaintance with constructions common to this type of literature. With familiarity in the application of the rules, with acquisition of a vocabulary in his field of study, they should be in a position to read and consult with facility and satisfaction articles in texts and journals in their branch of study.

The reading selections are usually divided as follows: 1. The first part of the reading selections contains superior numbers for each rule involved in the sentence. 2. The second part will have an asterisk (*) indicating where certain rules are involved. 3. In some sections both numbers and asterisks are intentionally omitted and the reader is left on his own. All selections are accompanied by a rather large vocabulary which the teacher may use or not just as he sees fit. The student who is using the book by himself, or the classroom student who is studying at home, will gain much benefit from the vocabulary and notes in the margins. The author wishes to state that the limitations of space often dictated the choice of definitions given for any particular word. The aim was, however, to give the meaning most often used for the particular word. To give the student practice in recognizing plural forms, the definition of many nouns that are plural in the German text is given in the singular.

The student or teacher may feel free to begin the reading at any point in the text. The reason for repeating some notes and comments again and again is that students may not follow the reading from the first page to the last, but may choose to skip around. If some notes and comments should appear too numerous or even unnecessary to suit some teachers or students, bear in mind that the author has had those students in mind who are studying German alone and perhaps for the first time. He also wanted to aid those students who are rather poorly prepared to do reading of such difficulty. Many of these make up a goodly portion of the class in this type of reading.

Procedure in Discussing and Learning the Rules

Students or classes that have had one or more semesters of German should begin immediately with the discussion of the rules. Clear and ample illustrations are given for each rule, but it is not absolutely necessary to go over **all** illustrations or model sentences. Here the student and the teacher may be guided by how rapidly and thoroughly the rules are understood. It may be found that half of the illustrations are sufficient to understand fully some of the rules. Other model sentences may be left for review or for drill work with slower students. A translation of the model sentences is given immediately after the discussion of the rules. As will be emphasized in the discussion of the rules, it is a good plan to have someone read these sentences in English while the German word order is followed, for in this way the student is better able to see the application of the rules and watch the sentence unfold. The sentences are translated in such a way as to show the application of the rules and there is no intention of giving them in perfect English style.

The sequence in which the rules are presented is of paramount importance. The author has found it advantageous to take up the rules in groups or divisions. Certain groups should be kept together as units. The rules dealing with NOUNS on the breaks constitute one group, while those rules dealing with VERBS on the breaks constitute another. The plan suggested here has been followed also with individual candidates for advanced degrees who have used the method in acquiring a reading knowledge of the language. Classes here at the University of Texas have followed this same procedure. The author recommends that the rules be presented in this order:

1. **Rule 1** should be thoroughly discussed and learned, for it is with this rule that the student learns the full value of the **capitalized** noun and how it is used as a guide or pivot point in reading German. Section 1-D of rule 1 is very important and should be carefully noted, for here the verb appears before the subject. After rule 1 is carefully studied, then the student should go on to

2. **Rule 2.** This rule illustrates the second part of speech that may be found on the break. Sufficient illustrations are given to master this rule in a short time. Except for the prefix (and little words that may be found to the left of it) the student should know that he is still following **rule 1.** It is advisable to refer the student to the diagram on the inside cover of the book. The prefix is the first element that is not in English word order and must be removed from the end position. After the student has become sufficiently acquainted with rule 2 (and rule 1), he should then take up

3. **Rule 3.** Though this is a difficult feature of the German language, and is usually left in grammars to the very last, this rule fits in perfectly at this time in the presentation of the rules. Study carefully the introductory remarks. Go over carefully, either individually or with a class, the "Discussion and Analysis" of the rule. When this discussion is thoroughly understood, it is not difficult to follow the various types. The student should then take up type 1a. NO ATTEMPT SHOULD BE MADE TO TAKE UP ALL OF THE TYPES OF THE "3" CONSTRUCTION AT ONE TIME. Take up **Type 1a** first and then before going on to **type 2**, take up

4. **Rules 4, 5, 6.** These rules are used **to remove verbs from the end position.** It should be the aim to keep these three rules together as a unit. After they have been thoroughly understood and the student has acquired skill in **shifting to pick up the verb,** and he has learned to work back to the noun, he should then take up **type 2** of the "3" construction. Whenever a new type of the "3" construction is discussed, the other types of this construction should be reviewed, thus keeping the entire construction together as a unit. When type 2 of the "3" construction is well understood, take up then

5. **Rules 7** and 8 (the last of the verb rules). Go over as many sentences and illustrations as necessary to fully understand the application of these rules. Constant reference should be made to the diagram on the inside cover of the book to show how to remove elements, in this case verbs, that are found on the right side of the double line in this diagram.

After rules 7 and 8 are completed, a careful review should be made of rules **4, 5, 6.** A review of all of the verb rules should then be made, namely rules 4, 5, 6, 7 and 8.

At this point, type 3 of the "3" construction may be added. After this third type is perfectly clear, then all three types of the "3" construction should be reviewed.

NOTE: Some teachers and students may prefer to leave C-1, C-2 and C-3 of the "3" construction for later discussion. In some respects this may be advisable, for these three types are not as common as the others. The three main types of the "3" construction are 1, 2, 3. A discussion of these irregular types becomes imperative in this book to make the treatment of the participial construction thorough and complete. Reference will be made to these irregular types when difficulty arises in the text material.

6. When rules 4, 5, 6, 7, and 8 are perfectly clear, rules 9, 10 and 11 should be discussed before taking up the reading material. When these last three rules are explained and sufficient drill work has been done with them, the other rules should be reviewed again and again in order to keep the entire system together as a unit. The auxiliary verbs in rule 6 should be constantly reviewed, in particular the uses of "werden". The discussion of the auxiliaries in the appendix (section 7) will prove to be helpful here.

It is helpful to remind students at all times that they are following fundamentally **Rule 1.** Reference should be made repeatedly to the diagram on the inside cover of the book. **THE IMPORTANCE OF THE BOLD-FACE OR CAPITALIZED NOUN SHOULD BE STRESSED AT ALL TIMES.**

BEGINNERS

How to Start Your Study of German

The suggestions in this section are intended primarily for graduate and research students who have not had courses in German, but who need German for this work and for their degrees. These first steps may also be helpful for all other students for review purposes. The procedure or approach is approximately the same as the author has used in introducing scores of Ph. D. candidates to the reading of complicated German in their various fields of study. The small amount of time spent in learning these points or tables will save the student much of the confusion and embarrassment usually encountered in the study of a new language.

It is recommended to begin your study of German in the following order:

1. Refer to section 6, page 3 of the appendix and study carefully all of this section. The results here will be gratifying, for after practicing on this section there should be no difficulty in looking up a troublesome verb. The more skill you acquire in looking up verbs, the more time you will save in actual translation. It is often true that much time is lost in searching for irregular verb forms. By following the hints given in this section, you should be able to look up a troublesome verb form in about 15 seconds. The verb list at the end of this book will be of high value to you in this practice work.

2. Refer to page 1 of the appendix and master the declension (and meanings) of the definite article and note the similarity of this declension with all other "der" words, e. g.: **dieser, jener, jeder, solcher, welcher, mancher.**

3. Inasmuch as the relative pronouns (appendix section 3 page 2) are similar to the definite article, learn these relative forms. Study the comments below the declension of them.

4. Learn the declension of the indefinite article (appendix section 2, page 2) and note the similarity of this declension with the declension of the definite articles in section 1. Except for the three bold-face forms, the endings are like those in the definite article table.

5. Learn the personal pronouns (appendix section 4, page 2). It is especially important to know the personal pronouns for the third person, for your reading will be almost entirely in the third person of the verb. Note that **er sie es** can all mean "it".

6. The possessive adjectives for the third person of the personal pronouns are listed in the appendix, section 4, page 2, 3. Study the declension of the possessive adjectives as they are listed in section 5 of the appendix. Note that the declension is the same as the declension of the indefinite article listed in the appendix section 2, page 2.

7. Become thoroughly familiar with the auxiliary verbs (appendix section 7, page 5ff). The verb "werden" must be thoroughly learned. A better understanding of it will be gradually acquired as you read.

8. A study should be made of the main points you should know about verbs (appendix section 8—page 7).

NOTE: Part Two of the appendix should not be learned at this time. This section is really intended for reference purposes after reading has been started. There is no objection, however, if you care to take up each division and thoroughly learn it as you go along. Sections 11, 12, and 14 may prove to be very helpful.

After you have learned these 8 divisions, refer to the discussion of the rules immediately following the introduction. Begin your study of the rules in the order recommended in this section.

The discussion of WORD FORMATION (appendix pages 18 and 19) and HOW TO MULTIPLY YOUR VOCABULARY (appendix pages 20 and 21) may be started either before all of the rules are studied or immediately afterward. Care should be used not to take up too many of these rules at one time.

The discussion of COMPOUND NOUNS will prove to be very helpful early in your study of German. (appendix pagc 21.)

It was the author's original intention to show the definitions of the words on the same line as the text material. However, due to the printing exigencies, it was not possible for the linotypist to adhere rigidly to this plan. In some cases the definitions appear one line above or below the line where they should appear. The author is trusting to the indulgence of those for whose benefit the definitions are given.

In a work of this nature and of such magnitude imperfections may appear. Notwithstanding the pains put forth by the author and his worthy colleagues, occasional errors may be found. This is especially true in respect to the vocabulary on the sides of the pages. Due to the short line, it is quite impossible to give the shades of meaning that might seem necessary and advisable. If you are using the book as teachers, you may discuss with your students the various meanings, synonyms, etc. that might be used for some of these definitions. In some instances, the author tried to keep close to the text in order to show how the word is made up and thus to help students to learn the vocabulary more easily.

Acknowledgements

I wish to take this opportunity to express my sincere gratitude and appreciation to all those teachers and students who have offered suggestions. My grateful acknowledgments are also due to my colleagues who were, at all times, ready to aid me with their kind advice, suggestions and helpful criticism in preparing this edition. I am especially indebted to Dr. Charles H. Holzwarth, Dr. Stanley Werbow and Dr. Leroy R. Shaw for their careful reading of the text material. Dr. George Schulz-Behrend deserves special mention for his careful reading of the text and the new material that has been added to this edition.

I feel indebted to Mr. Ed Rather, manager of the University Co-op and to Mr. C. W. Swenson for their high interest in the work and for the aid they gave during the printing operations and for doing everything in their power to make this a more perfect volume.

It is my pleasure to express my appreciation to the sources from which the selections were taken, especially to Gustav Fischer Verlag, Jena; Springer Verlag, Berlin; Gebrüder Bornträger Verlag, Berlin; A. Meiner Verlag, Berlin; Johann Aloysius Barth, Leipzig; Rascher Verlag, Zürich; B. G. Teubner Verlag, Leipzig; Ferdinand Enke, Verlagsbuchhandlung, Stuttgart; George Westermann Verlag, Berlin. To the authors indicated in the various articles, I owe a great deal of gratitude.

C. V. POLLARD

TABLE OF CONTENTS

TABLE OF CONTENTS—(Continued)

TABLE OF CONTENTS—(Continued)

TABLE OF CONTENTS—(Continued)

APPENDIX

Word Formation

The Capitalized German Noun

Americans have read since early childhood straight forward to the end of the sentence. In this reading process, they have failed to observe one of the most significant features of the English language—the fact that a noun usually ends the sentence. English teachers have not called their students' attention to this phenomenon, for the reason that grammars do not mention it.

Since this word order is normal for the English-speaking student, the words follow each other in logical sequence. There is no need to bring light to bear on the noun or any other part of speech that may come at the end of the English sentence. However, in learning German, it is the **end word** that gives some hint as to the relationship of the words in the sentence and how they may be best put into English word order.

In German also the noun is frequently found at the end of the sentence and in translation work the American reader may follow with absolute confidence the regular English word order directly toward that noun. Furthermore, the noun in German is very conspicuous, for it is always written with a capital letter. (Rarely is there an exception to this rule). The German noun will constitute the major point—the key or pivot point of the sentence in this entire system, and the rules of the system will be constructed around this point. American readers will find it of tremendous psychological advantage to be able to rearrange the German sentence in such a way that it will end with a noun. Once this is done, translation becomes automatic and enjoyable.

The final word in the German sentence determines how the sentence is to be translated. If the noun is at the end, the student is to follow one procedure. If the verb is at the end, he follows another procedure. The only parts of speech that may be found at the end of the sentence in German are: Nouns, pronouns, verbs, adverbs, adjectives and prepositions. Since there are only six parts of speech that can possibly end a German sentence, it follows that there should be only six different approaches in the translation of any German sentence. For the time being, the following table shows the four major types of sentences usually encountered in the reading of a text:

			Rule
TYPE ONE	..........NOUN		1
TYPE TWO a)	..........NOUN	Prefix (prep. or adv.)	2
b)	..........NOUN	NOUN	9
TYPE THREE (a)	..........NOUN	verb.	4 or
	..........NOUN	verb verb	5 or
	..........NOUN	verb verb verb	6 or
	..........NOUN	verb verb verb	7 or 8
b)	..........NOUN	predicate adjective.	6
TYPE FOUR	..........Pronoun, adjective, adverb		1

(See also comments on type four on inside cover of this book.)

From this table it will be seen that the noun is the PIVOT POINT in the sentence. All words on the left side of the double lines are in English word order. The object is then to learn how to remove elements that may be found on the right side of the noun or double line in this table. The numbers on the right side of the page indicate the rules which will be used in removing these elements. The process resolves itself into a forward and backward movement TOWARD A NOUN. In other words, translation is made directly forward to the noun as in this illustration:

——————————→ NOUN.

Or when the student gets a signal to pick up an element that is not in English word order, such as prefixes, predicate adjectives or verbs, he then moves backward to the first noun and then resumes his forward movement to the noun as in this illustration:

←——————

Wir können //..........NOUN adverb verb verb verb.

THE STUDENT PROGRESSES EITHER FORWARD OR BACKWARD TO A PIVOT POINT—**THE NOUN.**

Rule 1

THE NOUN RULE

Illustrations:

————————————————————→NOUN.[1]

————————————————————→NOUN,[1] ——————→NOUN,[1] ——————→NOUN.[1]

————————————————————→NOUN, ——————————————→NOUN?

In the diagram you will note nouns on certain points which will be called "breaks" in this entire book. These breaks may be any of the punctuation marks such as periods, semi-colons, colons, commas, question marks and even **parentheses. Subsequently it will be shown that even the coordinating** conjunctions may constitute **breaks, for they also break the thought.**

Before any attempt is made to translate a German sentence, make a close examination **of the breaks in it. Watch carefully what type of word is found** immediately **in front of the breaks.** Certain **very definite cues are given on the breaks which will aid you to translate smoothly and** accurately. **If you find a noun in front of the break, you adopt one procedure. If you find a verb in front of the break, you** follow another procedure. **Numerous illustrations will be given to show you what to do** no matter **what part of speech comes at** the **end of the sentence.**

The accuracy and confidence which result from strict **adherence to the rules of the method will act as a stimulant to further reading and study of German. The** grammar forms **that you have learned in** former courses **will be impressed forcibly on your mind by the rules.**

OBSERVE CAREFULLY WHAT TYPE OF WORD OR WHAT PART OF SPEECH IS FOUND IN FRONT OF THE BREAK.

RULE 1.

IF YOU FIND A NOUN RIGHT IN FRONT OF THE BREAK (period or semi-colon) YOU ARE TO TRANSLATE FORWARD WORD FOR WORD.

The noun is the safety signal to go right ahead just as you would do in English word order. **Proceed directly toward it. If you should have any trouble in coming** forward to the noun, you will be taken care of in the pages **that follow. For the time being,** remember this major rule: WHEN THE NOUN IS ON THE BREAK, PROCEED **DIRECTLY TO THAT NOUN.** You will not make an error.

A

Comments and Suggestions on the Drill Sentences

In the drill sentences for rule 1 (and also for all other rules), the sentences themselves will be given on the left hand side of the page. On the right side will be found the translations of as many words as space permits. Some helpful hints on troublesome points will be given, as well as references to difficulties that are more fully discussed and illustrated in the appendix or in the discussion of some of the rules.

In order to impress the rules more forcibly on your mind, go over them again and again. **If it is possible to have some other student, friend, wife or teacher** read the translated sentences back to you while you follow **the German text, you will find it tremendously helpful, for in this way you** can focus your attention upon the breaks and watch the **sentence unfold.**

It is suggested not to work on the vocabulary in these model sentences. They may not be words that you would **expect in your field of study. For the present time, you should** aim to acquire skill in the application of the rules. **Learn the theory of translation and the** various formulae and you will find later that many of the words which would **not mean anything to you in isolation will carry full** meaning when used in the sentence. In this connection, you will **profit a great deal if you will acquaint yourself** with a few rules on the development of a vocabulary **in the back part of this book.**

A literal translation of many model sentences is given on **p. 51/2 ff.**

B

The pivot nouns in these model sentences are in bold-face type. IF THE NOUN IS IN FRONT OF THE BREAK, YOU ARE TO TRANSLATE WORD FOR WORD.

1. **Und mit der Schönheit des Landes geht auch seine Fruchtbarkeit Hand in Hand.**[1]

S. beauty d. of the g. goes s. its
F. fertility

2. Die philosophischen Ansichten tragen in doppeltem Sinne den **Namen der Philosophie der Aufklärung.**[1]

A. views t. carry d. double
S. sense A. enlightment

3. Das aktive Verhalten bei der Erweiterung unserer Kenntnisse und Einsichten hat aber noch in dieser Hinsicht besonderen **Wert.**[1]

V. behaviour E. broadening
K. knowledge E. views
H. respect b. special W. value

4. **Der Charakter des griechischen Geisteslebens zur Zeit seiner höchsten Blüte war die unmittelbare Hingebung des Subjekts ans Objekt.**[1]

g. Greek G. intellectual life
Z. time B. bloom, flourish u. immediate, direct
H. devotion

5. Lamarcks **Philosophie Zoologique** war der erste wissenschaftliche **Entwurf** einer wahren Entwicklungsgeschichte der Arten, einer "natürlichen Schöpfungsgeschichte" der **Pflanzen,** der Tiere **und des Menschen.**[1]

w. was e. first
w. scientific E. sketch w. true A. species
E. development-history S. history of creation
P. plants T. animals M. man

6. **Hand** in Hand mit dem allgemeinen Entwicklungsgange der **Scholastik** ging die Entwicklung des Gegensatzes zwischen **Nominalismus und Realismus.**[1]

a. general E. development course
g. went E. development G. contrast
z. between

Discussion: What do the bold face nouns in sentences 1-7 tell you to do?

7. **Der Stifter** der realistischen **Entwicklungsreihe,**[1] **der Vater des modernen Empirismus und Materialismus,** ist der Engländer **John Locke.**[1]

S. founder E. evolutionary series
V. father
E. Englishman

8. **Es gibt** nach seiner Auffassung keinen wesentlichen Unterschied zwischen lebendiger und lebloser **Natur,**[1] **die** ganze Natur **ist** eine einzige zusammenhängende **Erscheinungswelt,**[1] und dieselben Ursachen sind wirksam auch allein in der lebendigen **Natur.**[1]

E. g. there is n. according to
A. conception w. essential U. difference
g. entire e. single
z. connected E. world phenomenon
U. causes w. effective a. alone

9. **Diese** Ursachen sind die atmosphärischen **Einflüsse,**[1] das **Wasser** in seinen verschiedenen **Formen,**[1] als Schnee und **Eis, Nebel und Regen,** der fliessende Strom und die Brandung des **Meeres,**[1] endlich die vulkanischen **Erscheinungen.**[1]

U. causes E. influences
v. different S. snow
N. fog R. rain f. flowing S. stream
B. surf E. phenomena

Discussion: Note the breaks in the sentence and the nouns on these breaks. Notice also how these nouns lead **you** forward in each instance point to point. TRANSLATE FORWARD WORD FOR WORD TO THE NOUN.

C

THE CO-ORDINATING CONJUNCTIONS ARE ALSO BREAKS

These are **und, aber, oder, denn, sondern.** If a noun is found in front of one of these words, YOU ARE TO PROCEED JUST AS IF THE NOUN WERE IN FRONT OF A PERIOD OR SEMI-COLON. The noun is still the pivot point in the sentence—**WORK DIRECTLY TOWARD IT:**

1. **Die** philosophischen Ansichten tragen in doppeltem Sinne den **Namen** einer Philosophie der **Aufklärung**[1] **und** sind als solche **zugleich Ausdruck des Geistes der Zeit.**[1]

A. views t. carry
d double S. sense
A. enlightenment s. such z. at the same time
A. expression G. spirit

2. Wir **kennen** die **Grundzüge** des tektonischen **Aufbaues** der **Erde**[1], aber wir weisen gleichzeitig **auf** die Beziehungen zur heutigen Oberflächengestaltung der **Erde.**[1]

k. know G. basic features
A. structure w. refer g. at the same time
B. relations h. present O. surface formation
E. earth

3. Wir **stehen** heute ganz im Anfang dieser **Entwicklung** und die **Erforschung** dieses ungeheueren Gebietes ist die lohnende **Aufgabe** und das glänzende Ziel der zukünftigen **Physik.**[1]

s. stand g. altogether A. beginning
E. development E. study u. enormous
G. field l. profitable A. task
g. brilliant Z. goal z. future

4. Der bedeutendste Vertreter, Boileau, predigte die Oberherrschaft des Verstandes über die Literatur und bewunderte dennoch so unverständige und unglaubliche Erzählungen wie die homerischen Epen; er **empfahl** dem Dichter Wahrscheinlichkeit und Einfalt.

b. most important V. representative
p. preached O. predominance V. reason
b. admired u. unreasonable u. incredible
E. tales
e. recommended D. poet W. probability
E. simplicity, naivete

Discussion: Progress point by point to each noun on the break. This is after all English word order. **Note the nouns in sentences 1-3 which are in bold-face type. What nouns should be bold-faced in sentence 4? Underline these nouns.** Note that 'des' or 'der' or words with 'es' or 'er' endings mean 'of'. See app. 1, a.

5. Aber **Beobachtungen** **schliessen** **zweierlei** in **sich,**[1] **Auffassung** der **Erscheinungen** und Beschreibung der **Erscheinungen;**[1] d. h. klare und lebendige **Erfahrung** und ein Bericht über diese Erfahrung in Worten oder **Formeln.**[1]

B. observations s. include z. two things
A. comprehension E. phenomena
B. description of the phenomena
E. experience B. report E. experience
F. formulae

6. Die **Kraft** zweier **Punktladungen** **aufeinander** im materiefreien **Raum ist** proportional dem Produkt der **Ladungen**[1] und umgekehrt proportional dem Quadrat der **Erde.**[1]

K. force P. point-charges a. upon one another
m. matter-free R. space
L. charges u. inversely

Discussion: The nouns are bold faced for definite purposes. They tell you to translate directly to them. **The habit of reading** forward to a noun may be carried over to the reading of any text. Learn to focus your attention **on the break. If a noun is there,** work directly to it.

Review the declension of the definite and indefinite articles. See app. 1 and 2. What does 'dem' mean in sentence 6? der? zweier?

7. Die **Paraffine** **finden sich** in grösserer oder kleinerer **Menge** wohl in allen **Erdölen,**[1] und sie bilden sogar die **Hauptmasse** der meisten **Öle;**[1] besonders bezeichnend sind sie für die pennsylvanischen **Öle.**[1]

f. s. are found g. larger
k. smaller M. quantity
b. form s. even H. main mass Ö. oils
b. especially b. characteristic

D

THE VERB OFTEN APPEARS BEFORE THE SUBJECT

This is commonly known as inverted word order. It is much more common in German than in English. The treatment of the sentence with the noun at the end is the same as any other sentence in rule 1. The sentence may, however, sound stilted or awkward if the verb is left in front of the subject. There are times when the sentence will sound satisfactorily if the verb and the subject are left as they are. If the sentence should sound too stilted, rephrase it, putting the verb in its normal position as it would appear in English. The subject is also bold-faced on this page. Do not overlook the bold-faced noun on the end, for this is the signal to go ahead.

1. In diesem Falle unterscheidet **er** praktische und theoretische **Wissenschaft.**[1]

F. case u. distinguishes
W. science

2. Als Frucht derselben veröffentlichte er nach zehn Jahren sein berühmtes Werk über die Entwicklungsgeschichte der Tiere— "Beobachtung und **Reflexion**".[1]

F. fruit v. published n. after z. ten
J. years b. famous E. evolutionary-history
T. animals B. observation

Discussion: Since the subject 'er' follows the verb in these two sentences and you see that you could not possibly leave the subject in this position, rephrase the sentence and put the subject and predicate in English word order. Note that you still follow rule 1.

3. Trotzdem erwuchs im Verlaufe der nächsten Jahrhunderte **eine ungeheure Literatur** über die Person des Dichters.[1]

T. nevertheless V. course n. next
J. centuries u. vast, enormous ü. over, about

4. Unter dem gegebenen Titel erschienen in den Zeitschriften vom Jahre 1916 **meine ausführlichen und illustrierten Artikel** über die **Bacon-Frage.**

g. given e. appeared
Z. magazines a. detailed, extensive
F. question The verb must be in "second" position

The context of the sentence will tell you sometimes which is the subject — the material before the verb or the material after the verb. The grammar form may not tell you, for the feminine and the neuter forms are the same in the nominative and accusative.

5. Eine grosse Rolle spielt **die Konvektion** in den **Winden.**[1]

6. Ein direkter Beweis dieser anonymen oder pseudonymen Tätigkeit ist das Northhumberland **Dokument.**

s. plays (cf. page 3 sentence 4; also see discussion of this sentence page 3 sentence 4)

Keep in mind that the verb occupies the "key" position. The subject will be found on either side of it. As you proceed in normal word order toward the noun on the break, rephrase the sentence if it should sound stilted or paradoxical. In this way you will be able to see where the subject belongs in English.

7. Neben Wasser waren tätig auch noch andere Kräfte an der Veränderung der **Erdrinde.**[1]

W. water t. active a. other K. forces
V. change E. earth-crust

One (or more) dependent clauses may begin the sentence. If this happens, the subject will be found after the verb in the main clause. See sentences 2, 6, page 21; 10, 11, page 22; 7, 9, page 37. These model sentences should be studied after you have learned to shift to pick up verbs in rules 4, 5, 6, 7, 8.

See also the discussion of "es, das, dies" section 10 of the appendix.

8. Eine wichtige Bedeutung gewinnt endlich die Scheidung der Gebiete nach den Zwecken in der praktischen **Philosophie.**[1]

w. important B. meaning g. gains
S. separation G. fields n. according to
Z. purposes

E

MORE PRACTICE SENTENCES FOR RULE 1

A close scrutiny of your reading material will disclose that a good many of the sentences end with nouns. You are now becoming familiar with Rule 1 which tells you what to do when the sentence ends with a noun. Practice on these sentences and if at all possible have them read back to you after they have been translated into English. You may prefer to check your translations with the translations in another section of this book.

For the sake of practice and drill, underline the nouns that should be bold faced on this page.

1. Die Formationskunde ist nur ein Teil der ausgedehnten Wissenschaft der Geologie, d. h. der Lehre von der stofflichen und zwar **besonders mineralischen Zusammensetzung, dem Bau und der** Bildungsgeschichte des Erdkörpers.

F. formation science T. part a. extensive
W. science L. theory
s. material z. to be sure
Z. composition B. formation history
E. globe

2. Unter der Regierung der Königin Elizabeth, also über achtzig Jahre nach der Entdeckung des nordamerikanischen Kontinents durch die Cabots, unternahm der Glänzendste, der Fähigste der **Edlen** am englischen Hofe Sir Walter Raleigh, den ernsthaf**testen Kolonisationsversuch.**

R. government
a. eighty E. discovery
u. undertook
G. most brilliant F. most capable
E. nobles H. court e. most serious
K. attempt of colonization

3. Beispiele von diesen Vorgängen sind das Fallen eines Steines auf die Erde, die Vermischung zweier Gase oder mischbarer **Flüssigkeiten, die Diffusion und Auflösung fester Stoffe in einem Lösungsmittel und vor allem die unzähligen chemischen Prozesse.**

B. examples V. processes
S. rock V. mixing
m. mixable F. liquids
A. dissolution S. materials L. solvent
v. a. above all u. countless

4. In dem gemeinsamen Denken der Enzyklopädisten vollzog sich Schritt für Schritt der Umschwung vom Empirismus zum Sensualismus, vom Naturalismus zum Materialismus, vom Deismus **zum Atheismus, von der enthusiastischen zur egotistischen Moral.**

g. common D. thinking
v. s. was accomplished S. step by step
U. change
What do the nouns tell you to do?
Underline the pivot nouns.

5. Es gibt nach seiner Auffassung keinen wesentlichen Unterschied **zwischen lebendiger und lebloser Natur**; die ganze **Natur ist eine** einzige zusammenhängende Erscheinungswelt, und dieselben **Ursachen sind wirksam auch allein in der lebendigen Natur. Das Leben ist nur ein physikalisches Phänomen.** Alle **Organismen, alle Pflanzen, Tiere und an ihrer Spitze der Mensch, erklären** sich in ihren innern und äusseren Formverhältnissen ganz ebenso **wie die Mineralien und alle leblosen Naturkörper nur durch** mechanische Ursachen, ohne zwecktätige Ursachen. Dasselbe **gilt von der Entstehung der verschiedenen Arten.**	E. g. there is A. conception U. difference l. living l. lifeless g. entire e. single z. connected E. appearance-world. U. causes a. alone Continue to focus your attention on the end nouns—these indicate rule 1. P. plants T. animals S. top M. man e. s. explain themselves, see app 11, 4, a F. form conditions l. lifeless U. causes z. purposeful g. is true E. origin v. different, various
6. **Nur die Versuche von Hertz, nach einem etwa halben Jahrhundert,** zeigten die volle Berechtigung der Faradayschen Anschauungen durch zwei neue Erfahrungen, nämlich die Erkennntnis **des Vorhandenseins elektrischer Kräfte im materiefreien Raum ohne Ladungen und die Erkenntnis der endlichen Ausbreitungs**geschwindigkeit der elektrischen Vorgänge.	V. experiments e. approximate, per chance B. justification A. views E. experiments, discoveries E. recognition, knowledge V. existence K. forces R. space L. charges E. knowledge A. speed of spreading V. processes

Rule 2

THE PREFIX

A

This rule deals with the second part of speech that may be found on the break. This is the preposition (or adverb) used as prefixes to verbs.

The most common prefixes are:

an	at, on, to	ein	into	unter	under	heim	home
auf	on, upon, open	fort	away	um	around	hinter	**behind**
aus	out, out of	hin	thither	vor	before	entgegen	**toward**
bei	**with** See also app. 18, 1.	her	hither	zurück	back	dazwischen	**between (them)**
		mit	with	zusammen	together	statt	
da (dar)	there	nach	to, toward	nieder	down, low	(on use of 'nach' see also app. 15, 1)	
durch	through	über	over	wieder	again	teil	

Except for a few of those in the last two columns, the prefixes are generally 'little' words. These prefixes may be separated from the main verb and if so, stand at the end of independent clauses. Rule 2 deals with the prefix when it stands at the end of the clause or sentence. Once in a while a prefix may be found inside of the **clause or sentence, but this is not common.**

Illustrations for rule 2:

Er steht/..NOUN[1]	‖	auf.[2]
Wir gingen/..NOUN[1]	‖	hindurch.[2]
Er kommt/..NOUN[1]	‖	adv adv hin.[2]
Wir nehmen/..NOUN[1]	‖	adv adv zusammen.[2]

(Compare also diagram—inside cover—Type Two a)

In these illustrations you find "little" words on the breaks. These are prefixes that belong with the verbs. The German says: "I get in the morning at half past six up." In other words, he will try to put the prefix at the end in independent clauses.

A close examination of the illustrations will show how this rule is to be treated. Strictly speaking, you are still following rule 1, for you are to work straight forward to the noun. The only difference is that in this instance you must "stop" when you reach the verb to pick up the prefix before resuming your forward movement to the noun. In these illustrations, you would stop on 'steht' and look up 'aufstehen'; stop on 'gingen' and look up hindurchgehen; stop on "kommt" and look up "hinkommen"; stop on 'nehmen' and look up "zusammennehmen".

A sentence and discussion of it:

An der pazifischen Küste tauchen die alten	K. coast a. old
Gesteine nach den vorliegenden Berichten zuerst	G. rocks n. according to v. existing
in dieser Provinz wieder unter den jüngeren	B. reports w. again j. more recent
Bildungen auf.[2]	B. formations

What is the importance of the bold faced noun "Bildungen"? What do you do with "auf"? Where do you stop as you progress toward the noun?

Note that you are still following rule 1. The only difference being that you stop on the verb in order to attach the prefix to the verb. Then look up the verb in the dictionary in that form. You may then resume normal word order to the noun as rule 1 directs you to do.

In the last two illustrations above, you will note that the noun is not in front of the prefix as in the first two. Therefore, when you stop to pick up the prefix, remove all elements back to the first noun. When it becomes necessary to shift to pick up any element that is not in English word order, PICK UP SUCH AN ELEMENT AND AT THE SAME TIME ALL OTHER WORDS BACK TO THE FIRST NOUN. This is rule 1 again—which gives you the signal to go right straight ahead.

In order to impress more forcibly the application of rule 2, cover up the words on the right side of the double line. These words are automatically removed by rule 2. DO NOT FORGET TO STOP ON THE VERB AS YOU COME FORWARD IN THE SENTENCE.

B

DRILL SENTENCES FOR RULE 2—THE PREFIX RULE

The presence of a prefix on the break is cause for alarm. In all reading material of this book, you will be cautioned to "flag" those lines on which a prefix is found. It is best to recognize the prefixes before attempting the translation, for if prefixes are on the breaks the verbs to which these prefixes belong will not be complete. The purpose of the "flag" idea is to warn you that you must be more careful than otherwise to pick up the prefix at the right time. It is of tremendous psychological advantage to attack a paragraph with the prefixes "flagged" or (a paragraph without a prefix,) for then you know that you should not make an error in translation.

Put a "flag" out to the left hand side of the line where prefixes are located. As you translate forward, be more careful when you see these flags. Survey the situation and see if you are bringing in the prefix with the right verb.

	1. Diese Truppendivision setzte am nächsten Tage ihre	n. next s.f.—fort-setzen continue
——	vorrückende **Bewegung** fort.[2]	T. day v. advancing B. movement
	2. Daher weisen sie wie die chemischen Elemente gewisse	d. therefore w.a. show (note position of verb)
——	**Eigenschaften** auf.[2]	g. certain E. qualities.
	3. Auf diese Weise schliesst das Verhältnis zwischen	a. d. W. in this manner V. relation
——	Philosophie und Religion verschiedene **Momente** ein.[2]	z. between v. different
		M. features s.e. includes
	4. Im Gegensatz hierzu hebt wiederum Hebard die Notwendigkeit einer vorbereitenden Arbeit der übrigen Wissen-	G. contrast w. again (note position of the verb.)
		N. necessity v. preparatory
——	**schaften** hervor[2] und gibt die Bearbeitung der Begriffe als	ü. remaining W. sciences h.h. stresses
——	die wesentliche Aufgabe der **Philosophie** an.[2]	B. treatment B. concepts w. essential
		A. task a. designates

DISCUSSION: Explain why certain lines are 'flagged'. Why are certain nouns bold faced? Note that prefixes may be found on any number of breaks. Spot these prefixes before you begin.

——	5. Er geht von einer isolierten **Volkswirtschaft** aus[2] und	V. political economy
	fasst den Grundprozess des Wirtschaftslebens als einen	G. basic process W. economic life
	kontinuierlichen Kreislauf von produktiven Aufwendungen	K. cycle
	einerseits und konsumtiven Verwendungen anderseits inner-	A. expenditures e. on the one hand
——	halb einer **Wirtschaftsperiode** auf.	V. uses a. on the other hand i. within
		auffassen— comprehends

	6. Da schwimmen am Abend ganze Flotten von kleinen	A. evening g. entire
——	Segelbooten hinaus; dort werfen sie die Netze für die Nacht	S. sail boats w. throw
——	aus. Sie segeln schon beim Sonnenaufgang hinaus und	N. night S. sun rise
——	dann holen sie am nächsten Morgen die Heringe und	n. next
——	Aale ab.	h.a. go to get, fetch

DISCUSSION: What are the verbs in this sentence? Why are four lines 'flagged'? What nouns should be bold **faced?** Underline them. Where would you put a "2"?

	7. Auf diese Weise schliesst das Verhältnis zwischen	V. relation z. between
——	Philosophie und Religion verschiedene **Momente** ein,[2] bietet	v. different M. factors s.e. includes
——	sozusagen verschiedene **Seiten** dar[2].	d. offers v. different

	8. Bei Verdun fand im Jahre 1915 eine Schlacht zwischen	S. battle What is the verb?
——	den Deutschen und den **Franzosen** statt.[2]	f.s. took place

C

WHAT TO DO IF THE WORD IN FRONT OF THE PREFIX IS NOT A NOUN

If it becomes necessary to move out of line to pick up a prefix, pick up the prefix and any other **words or elements back to the first noun.** You are then ready to move forward as rule 1 tells you to do. If the subject should follow the verb, rearrange the subject and predicate. Continue to "flag" the lines on which the troublesome prefixes are located.

	1. Dies tritt namentlich auf **Sonnenphotographien** ganz	n. especially S. photographs of the sun
——	deutlich hervor.[2]	g. quite d. clearly h. stands out

Since the prefix is on the break, stop when you reach the verb. Do not resume forward movement until the prefix is picked up and **with it any other words** or **elements back to the first noun.**

	2. Galilei teilte von der ganzen **Beobachtung** öffentlich	mit-t. reported g. entire B. observation
——	zunächst gar nichts mit.[2]	ö. publicly z. at first g. at all n. nothing
	3. Zwei zusammenstossende Moleküle prallen also, viel-	z. colliding a. rebound
——	leicht ähnlich wie zwei elastische **Bälle,** voneinander ab.[2]	v. perhaps ä. similarly w. as
		v. from one another What does 'ab' go with?
	4. Dies stimmt mit den Bestimmungen von **Hess** wesentlich	ü. agrees B. provisions
——	sehr gut überein.[2]	w. essentially
	5. Solche Abweichungen kommen in der bestehenden	A. deviations b. existing v. occur
——	**Tauschwirtschaft** ziemlich häufig vor.[2]	T. exchange, barter-economy z. rather
	6. Sein Vater und seine Mutter wirkten schon in der früh-	e. acted, influenced
——	esten **Jugend** wohltätig auf ihn ein.[2]	f. earliest J. youth w. kindly.
	7. Die wesentliche Verschiedenheit der dauerhaften Güter	w. essential V. difference d. permanent
	einerseits und der Nutzungen derselben anderseits tritt in	G. goods e. on the one hand N. use
	diesen Fällen langer **Dauerhaftigkeit** besonders deutlich	a. on the other hand h. stands out
——	und klar hervor.[2]	D. durability d. clearly

DISCUSSION: Why is the noun "Dauerhaftigkeit" in bold face type? What does 'hervor' go with? What other words are picked up before resuming normal word order?

	8. Darum fiel für Bacon das Einteilungsmerkmal von	E. classification characteristic.
——	**Aristoteles** von vornherein hinweg.[2]	h. fell away v. v. from the outset
	9. Die einzelnen Teilungen treten unter sehr günstigen	e. individual T. divisions
	Ernährungsbedingungen ausserordentlich rasch und stetig	g. favorable E. nutritional conditions
——	nacheinander auf.[2]	r. rapidly s. constantly n. after one another
		a. appear
	10 Über die Kernteilung selbst gehen die **Untersuchungser-**	K. nuclear division s. itself
——	**gebnisse** allerdings ziemlich stark auseinander.	U. investigation results a. of course
		z. rather a. go apart, diverge, separate
	11. Doch weichen die gesamten Kosten für das Studium	What goes with 'weichen'? g. total
——	eines Faches an gleichartigen **Hochschulen** nicht wesentlich	F. subject g. similar type
	von einander ab.[2]	a. deviate w. essentially

If after the translation is made, you find the order stilted, adjust the subject and predicate so that they will fall into English word order. **IF A STOP IS MADE TO PICK UP A PREFIX, TRANSLATE ALL WORDS AND ELEMENTS BACK TO THE FIRST NOUN**—your signal to go ahead.

Rule 3

THE PARTICIPIAL CONSTRUCTION

The participial construction represents one of the greatest difficulties for the American student of German. Having no parallel in English, many students find the word order of this construction completely foreign to them and frequently unmanageable. The reason may well be the fact that grammars give inadequate attention to it. Many grammars limit their discussions of it to a half dozen lines with no more than two or three brief illustrations. The author is convinced that this construction can be understood and mastered only by careful study supported by numerous examples. No one denies that it is one of the most important rules for the reading of involved German. It is absolutely essential for the student to get a thorough knowledge of this construction if he wants to acquire facility and accuracy in reading scientific German.

This construction gets its name from the two participles—present and past—which are used to modify nouns. The difficulty lies in the fact that words modifying the participles are placed in front of the participles whereas in English they follow. Compare the English "The facts known at that time." Or, "The cannon standing near the city." Frequently the word that introduces this construction is removed one, two or several lines from the noun it modifies.

Although to a degree somewhat more complicated than rules 1 and 2, rule 3 fits in right at this time in this system of reading. The reason for discussing it this early in the presentation of the rules will become clear in the course of this discussion. It is not advisable to attempt to understand fully all of this construction at one time. The construction is divided into several sections and should be studied division by division.

In rules 1 and 2 translation was made straight forward to the noun. It will be seen by diagrams and adequate model sentences that only the participial construction can block a student's progress as he progresses toward the noun. Thus rule 3 is the next step in this method. Once learned, it unfolds with ease and accuracy.

CHARACTERISTICS OF THIS RULE

1. Two kinds of participles are used—hence the term participial construction.

   a) Present participle.

      These are formed by adding a **d** to any German infinitive. For example:

      gehen-gehend, singen-singend, tanzen-tanzend, betteln-bettelnd.

   b) Past participle.

      gesehen, gemacht, gelassen, gegeben.

2. The present participle denotes an action which is going on. The past participle indicates an action which is completed.

   a) Present participles are used actively. That is, they indicate what the noun they modify does. For example:

      Der singende Mann, die sprechenden Studenten, das tanzende Mädchen.

   b) Past participles are usually used passively. This means that the subject suffers the action of the verb. For example:

      Der geschriebene Brief, das gekaufte Auto, das gelesene Buch.

   A few past participles may be used actively. For example: Der gefallene Soldat.

3. Both present and past participles may be used as adjectives. In this case they will always end with one of these endings: e en er es em. There are no other adjective endings.

   For example. Present participles: der singende Mann, mit dem lachenden Knaben.
   Past participles: ein gestohlener Brief, der geschriebene Satz.

4. Modifiers may be placed between the introductory word and the present or past participles. This is where the difficulty arises for the American student. Follow each step carefully:

   a)

Das Mädchen	the girl
Das singende Mädchen	the singing girl
Das jetzt singende Mädchen	the now singing girl
Das in der Schule singende Mädchen	the in the school singing girl.

German		English	
b) Das Geld		the money	
das	gestohlene Geld	the	stolen money
das gestern	gestohlene Geld	the yesterday	stolen money
das von dem Studenten	gestohlene Geld	the by the student	stolen money

5. An adjective may be used just like a participle.

a) Das für den Körper nötige Nahrungsmittel war frei.

The——————————food which was necessary for the body was free.

b) Es gibt einige für die Wirtschaft im allgemeinen sehr wichtige Erscheinungen.

There are some————————————————phenomena

which are very important generally for the economy.

RULE 3

DISCUSSION AND ANALYSIS

The statement has been made in rules 1 and 2 that if you proceed straight forward toward the noun on the break, you would not make an error. This is very true, however, there is ONE exception to this rule. The illustration below demonstrates that there is one chance for an error, namely rule 3.

1.

————3/ stop
————————————————NOUN.[1]
————3/ stop
————————————————NOUN;[1]
————3/ stop
————————————————NOUN[1] auf.[2]

IF A NOUN IS IN FRONT OF A PERIOD OR SEMI-COLON, THEN THE ONLY CHANCE FOR ERROR IS RULE 3.

If the noun is on a period or semi-colon you may work forward word for word to that noun and know that unless you encounter a "3" construction on the way you will not make an error. The same applies if a noun is present after a prefix is removed as in the third illustration above.

It is highly important to watch the punctuation marks. The period and semi-colon are extremely important and valuable, for you may work directly to them if you find nouns at these points. Some difficulty may arise in case the noun is on a comma due to the fact that the comma does not indicate the end of the thought. If a comma is used, there may be reason to shift past the comma to pick up a needed element beyond the comma. This would not happen if the period or semi-colon were the breaks. But on the way toward a comma, you may not only be "stopped" by rule 3 as in the illustrations above, but also by rules 4, 5, 6. Note this illustration:

2. Da er/[4]—————— NOUN, —————— NOUN[1] unmöglich so vertraut gewesen sein konnte,

Since he/ ←————————————————

NOUN, NOUN impossibly so familiar been have could

Note that the subject and predicate are connected together, and that then the translation is back to the noun. Here rule 1 gives the safety signal to go on forward.

Had there been a period or semi-colon after the first noun, no shift would have been necessary. On the way toward a comma, you must be more careful, for you may need to shift not only because of rule 3, but also rules 4, - 5, - 6. Each rule will be explained later.

Every step in this construction is carefully and adequately discussed. There are sufficient illustrations and model sentences to enable you to acquire a clear understanding of each point. It is recommended that you study and understand thoroughly each division before proceeding to another division. Inasmuch as you may be studying by yourself, it is hoped that you will benefit by the drill questions asked on the right side of the page and in the discussion. Some things are said over and over again primarily for drill purposes. If at all possible to have someone read the translated sentences to you, by all means do so, for then you are better able to focus your attention upon the shifts necessary for smooth translation. Take up as many of the model sentences as you think are necessary in your particular case.

RULE 3—ILLUSTRATIONS FOR PRACTICE

1. a) Die.. Partikeln enthalten lebende **Keime.**[1]
The———————————— particles contain living germs.

b) Die.. suspendierten Partikeln enthalten lebende **Keime.**[1]
The———————————— suspended particles contain living **germs.**

NOTE THAT YOU ARE FOLLOWING RULE 1, WORKING DIRECTLY FORWARD WORD FOR WORD TO THE NOUN.

c) Die in der Luft suspendierten Partikeln enthalten lebende **Keime.**[1]
The in the air suspended particles contain living germs.

Another element has been inserted between the article and the participle form. This is where **rule 3 will aid you** in translation.

2. a) Die.. Strahlen erzeugen **Phosphoreszenz.**[1]
The rays produce phosphorescence.

b) Die.. **angehörenden Strahlen** erzeugen **Phosphoreszenz.**[1]
The related or belonging rays produce phosphorescence.

NOTE THAT YOU ARE ACTUALLY FOLLOWING RULE 1, YOU ARE WORKING STRAIGHT AHEAD TO THE NOUN ON THE BREAK.

c) Die dem violetten Teile des Spektrums angehörenden Strahlen erzeugen **Phosphoreszenz.**[1]
The————————————————————Rays belonging to the violet part of the spectrum produce phosphorescence.

Another element has been inserted between the article and the participle form.

RULE 3—HOW TO RECOGNIZE IT

WHEN TWO WORDS OCCUR IN GERMAN THAT CANNOT BE CONSECUTIVE IN ENGLISH—YOU ARE ENTERING A "3" CONSTRUCTION.

This is a major point that must not be forgotten, for it applies to all types of the "3" construction.

Note the combinations of two words that commonly occur in German which cannot be consecutive in English.

die dem (see 2-c) above	bekannten von	einer in
die in (see 1-c) above	in aus	vorhandene auf
das auf	ein in	einige für

IF TWO WORDS OCCUR IN GERMAN THAT CANNOT BE CONSECUTIVE IN ENGLISH, STOP AND SURVEY THE SITUATION. The construction will unfold according to the **five types** now to be explained.

A

TYPE ONE OF RULE 3—THE "DER" WORD CALLING FOR A NOUN

In this type of the "3" construction the noun will be called for by der, die, das (in any form of the declension) or by any of the "der" words. (see app. page 1).

IF THE "DER" WORD CALLS FOR A NOUN, THE NOUN WILL FOLLOW A WORD ENDING WITH E OR EN.

1. Die[3] dem violetten Teil des **Spektrums**[1] angehörenden Strahlen erzeugen **Phosphoreszenz.**[1]
A D C B E F

The noun on the break is—as always—your signal to go right to this noun. However, the article "die" **cannot be** followed by "dem" as these **two words cannot be consecutive.**

1. Shift to pick up the noun—IT WILL FOLLOW A WORD ENDING WITH E OR EN. (A to B)
2. Make a "which" clause out of the word that has the "e" or "en" on it. (C)
3. Work back to the next noun (Spektrums)
4. Go right on forward in normal word order. (D, then E and F)

NOTE THE IMPORTANCE OF THE "PIVOT" NOUNS—They are bold faced.

2. Die/in der **Luft** suspendierten Partikeln enthalten lebende **Keime.**[1]
A D C B E F G

DISCUSSION: When a noun is called for by an article (or der word) take the following steps:

1. Shift to pick up the noun—it will follow a word ending with **e** or **en.**
2. Make a "which" clause out of the word that precedes the noun, or has the **e** or **en** on it.
3. With this "which" clause, work back to the next noun—in this sentence "Luft".
4. Go back into normal word order and go directly to the nouns "Luft" and then "Keime".

YOU WILL BE ABLE TO TELL BY THE "WHICH" CLAUSE WHETHER OR NOT YOU HAVE PICKED UP THE RIGHT NOUN.
If the "which clause" is not clear you have very probably picked up the wrong noun.

3. Die[3] in den ersten Jahrzehnten der **Eisenbahnentwicklung** erbauten Bahnen waren von lokalem **Charakter.**[1]

DISCUSSION: What does the noun "Charakter" tell you to do? What prevents you from going directly to this noun? Since "die" is a "der" word, what letters must your noun follow? Out of which word do you make the "which" clause? What are the "pivot" nouns? Indicate where you would insert A B C D etc. as has been done in sentences 1 and 2.

4. Columbus beschrieb die[3] im **Westen** liegenden Wunderländer in den glühendsten **Farben.**[1]

b. described l. which lie
W. wonder-lands g. warmest F. colors

5. Die[3] am 9. und 10. August westlich von **Verdun** erfolgten Kämpfe führten zu keinem positiven **Resultat.**[1]

w. west
e. which took place (why which?) K. battles

6. Die Gesamtheit der[3] die **Bedürfnisbefriedigung** ermöglichenden Tätigkeiten bildet die **Wirtschaft.**[1]

G. totality B. want satisfaction
e. which make possible W. economy

DISCUSSION: Give reasons for the position of "3" and "1" in sentences 4, 5, 6. Indicate also why certain nouns are in bold face type. After you have translated sentence 6, you will note that the subject follows the verb. (See app. 9,b.)

7. Die[3] aus **Zellulose** bestehende Membran der Zelle höherer Pflanzen gilt als total permeabel für die verschiedenen **Lösungen.**[1]

b. which consists (be sure to take all of the subject)
h. of higher P. plants g. is considered, is valid
v. different L. solutions

8. Die auf die Masseneinheit an einem Punkte des **Raumes** ausgeübte Kraft ist ein Mass für die Stärke des Feldes an dieser **Stelle.**

M. mass unit R. space
a. which is exerted K. force
S. strength S. place

DISCUSSION: Where would you insert a "3"? a 1? Show why certain nouns are bold faced. Bear in mind that you are entitled to go forward word for word unless you encounter a "3" construction on the way. This, of course, stops you inasmuch as another shift is now necessary—this time for a noun that is not in English word order.

9. Die durch die Sonderung der Mathematik gewonnene Vereinigung aller realen Wissenschaften führt direkt zu einer besonderen wichtigen **Frage.**[1]

d. thru S. separation g. which is gained
V. combination W. sciences f. leads
b. special w. important

DISCUSSION: When it becomes necessary to shift to pick up a noun, be sure to take all of the noun. This time the noun is **Vereinigung aller realen Wissenschaften.**

Where would you put a "3" in this sentence? Why? Why do you make a "which" clause out of "gewonnene"? Why would you write "Mathematik" with bold face type? Frage?

10. Die Menge der[3] vom **Körper** emittierten Strahlungsenergie hängt von seiner **Temperatur** ab.[2]

M. quantity e. which are emitted S. ray energy
a. depends v. on.

Cite reasons for the numbers 2 and 3. Also indicate why certain nouns are bold faced. What do you do with "ab"? What are your "pivot" nouns?

11. Auf der durch diese metaphysischen und naturphilosophischen Voraussetzungen gegebenen Grundlage lösen sich nun für Leibnitz **zugleich** die Hauptprobleme der **Psychologie.**[1]

d. thru, by
V. presuppositions g. which is given
l. s. are solved (app. 11, 4, a)

DISCUSSION: Where would you insert a "3" in this sentence? Why? What two nouns would then become the "pivot" nouns? What word becomes a "which" clause?

12. Diese vom Körper emittierte Strahlungsenergie ist gleich der vom Körper absorbierten **Strahlungsenergie.**

K. body e. which is emitted S. ray energy
g. equal a. which is absorbed

Note that you could have two -or even more- "3" constructions in the same sentence. You will be able to tell when a "3" construction is involved, for there will be present two words that cannot be consecutive. You would put a "3" in two places in this sentence. Where? and why?

13. Dieser Körper absorbiert nur einen ganz bestimmten Teil **dieser**[3] **ihm zugestrahlten Energie.**[1]

K. body
b. definite T. part z. which is radiated

14. **Der**[3] **für uns noch hauptsächlich in Betracht** kommende Typus **ist das Inlandeis.**[1]

h. chiefly B. consideration
k. which comes I. inland ice

15. Der[3] für die weitere Entwicklung der **Theologie** so ausserordentlich wichtig gewordene Beweis entsprang aus diesem **Bedürfnis.**[1]

w. further E. development B. proof
a. extraordinary w. important g. which had become (why which?) B. proof B. need

16. **Nur die**[3] **in den Fluss von den Siedlungen kommenden Ströme führen neben reichlichen Bakterienmassen auch eine erhebliche** Menge toter Substanz **zu.**[2]

F. river S. settlements
k. which come S. streams r. plentiful
e. considerable M. quantity t. of dead
z. supply

DISCUSSION: Take note of the application of each rule. You may also recognize how one rule dovetails with another and how necessary rule 3 is after learning rules 1 and 2.

Give reasons for the numbers in sentences 17-20. Also show why it is necessary to bold face certain nouns.

17. **Dies war unwahrscheinlich nach den**[3] vom österreichischen **Konsulate** eingelaufenen **Nachrichten.**[1]

u. improbable n. according to the
e. which came in N. reports

DISCUSSION: The first indication you have that you are entering a "3" construction is the two words **den vom** which obviously cannot be consecutive. The object is to find a noun which follows an "e" or "en". The first noun that follows one of these letters is "Konsulate". Pick up this noun and try to make a "which" clause out of the word preceding this noun. As a general rule, you will always be able to tell by the "which" clause" whether or not you have found the right noun. Other nouns may be present following one of these letters. Thus in this sentence, try first the adjective "österreichischen" as a "which" clause and since that will not be possible, try the next word that has the ending "en".

What are the two "pivot" nouns in this sentence? What word may now be made into a **which** clause?

18. **Man beschreibt tatsächlich die**[3] **bis jetzt in der Weise besprochenen Tatsachen.**[1]

b. describes t. actually
b. which were discussed T. facts

19. **Jede**[3] **in einem Körper** innewohnende Wärme besteht in einer **schwingenden Bewegung seiner Moleküle und Atome.**[1]

K. body i. which is inherent W. heat
b. consists s. vibrating B. movement

Explain why a "3" is placed over "jede".. Over "die" in sentence 18. Give reasons why certain nouns are bold faced.

20. **Die**[3] von den verschiedenen **Abwässern** stammenden Verbindungen geben einen[3] in grosser **Verdünnung** noch brauchbaren Nährboden ab.[2]

v. different A. waste waters
s. which come (why which?) V. compounds
V. dilution b. which is usable a. furnish

DISCUSSION: More than one "3" construction may appear in the same sentence, often one inside of another. As you work forward and backward to your noun, keep constantly in mind that you may translate word for word forward unless you encounter a "3" construction. In each instance here you have two words that cannot be consecutive.

Note how "Abwässern" and "Verdünnung" actually become rule 1, for these are the pivot nouns you work forward to after the "3" construction has been taken care of.

21. Mit dem oben beschriebenen Stadium erreichten bei den mit Lungen atmenden Tieren dieser ganze Apparat und die ihm gehörigen Gefässe den Höhepunkt der **Entwicklung.**

o. above b. described S. stage e. reached
a. which breathe T. animals g. entire
g. which belong G. vessels
E. development

DISCUSSION: Where would you put a "3" in this sentence? Why two of them? What nouns would you bold face in this sentence? What words cannot be consecutive?

22. Bei der **Konvektion** bewegt sich der[3] die **Wärme** tragende Körper selbst von einem Orte zum **Anderen.**[1]

b. s. is moved, see app. 11, 4, a. W. heat
t. which carries s. itself O. place

23. Die[3] in der **Mundhöhle** gelegenen Organe sind die Zähne, die Zunge und die[3] den **Speichel** absondernden **Speicheldrüsen.**[1]

M. mouth cavity g. which are situated
Z. teeth Z. tongue S. saliva
S. salivary glands a. which secrete

DISCUSSION: How do you recognize the "3" constructions in this sentence? **What are your pivot nouns in sentences 22 and 23? Which words become the "which" clauses?**

24 Die[3] für die Preisbildung massgebenden Prinzipien leiteten wir **im vorigen Kapitel** als notwendige Konsequenzen des allgemeinen **wirtschaftlichen Prinzips** her.[2]

P. price formation m. which are decisive
v. foregoing n. **necessary**
a. general w. economic l.h. derived

Give reasons for each of the numbers—2 and 3. Indicate why certain nouns are bold faced.

25. Im August erfolgte die Vereinigung mit der[3] schon am Tage vorher in **Berlin** eingelangten Hauptkolonne der **Infanterie.**[1]

e. took place V. combination, junction
v. before e. which arrived

Be sure to pick up the entire noun when you shift. This includes any other nouns following "des" and "der" or words with "es. or "er" endings. (see app. 1, a) Account for the numbers 3 and 1 in this sentence. Explain why "Berlin" is really the end of the sentence.

TYPE TWO OF THE "3" CONSTRUCTION

In rule 3 a shift to pick up a noun may be called for by

1. An indefinite article (ein, eine) in any form of the declension, or any word declined like "ein", namely mein, dein, sein, ihr, unser, euer or kein. (See App. 2)

THE RULE: If the introductory word in this construction is an indefinite article or any word declined like "ein", look for a noun following not only an **e** and **en** as in type 1, but also **er** and **es.**

TYPE ONE

der word——} e / en

TYPE TWO

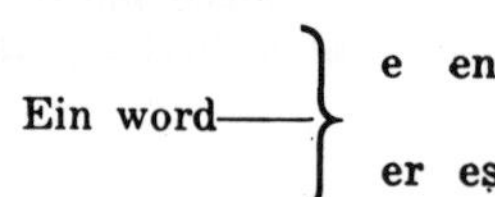

2. YOU HAVE THE SAME SIGNAL FOR THE "3" CONSTRUCTION. When two words in German follow each other that cannot be consecutive, you are entering a "3" construction.

3. The noun which you want will have before it a word with an e, en, er, es, ending. Do the same as you did in type 1, namely, make a "which" clause out of the word that precedes the noun. Then work back immediately to the next noun—your signal to go straight ahead again. The "which" clause will help you to determine whether or not you have picked up the right noun. If you find that the word with one of these endings on it will not admit of a "which" clause, try the next noun that follows one of these endings.

B

DRILL SENTENCES FOR TYPE 2 OF THE "3" CONSTRUCTION

1. Ein[3] im Jahre 1824 erlassenes Gesetz erhöhte den Gewinn auf gewissen **Manufakturen.**[1]
A D C B E —**and straight forward to the noun.**

A ———————————law **which was issued** in the year 1824 increased the profit on certain manufactured **goods.**

The process of translation in type 2 is exactly the same as in type 1. The only difference is that there is a different "call" that is made for the noun. In type 2 it is the "EIN WORD".

2. Sie enthalten eine[3] über die verschiedenen **Lehrgebiete** angekündigte Vorlesung mit Angabe des Namens des **Lehrers.**[1]

e. contain v. different L. fields
a. which was announced (why which?)
A. specification L. teacher V. lecture

DISCUSSION: What signal does the noun "Lehrers" give you? How are you told that you are entering a "3" construction? Why do you make a "which" clause out of **angekündigte** and not "verschiedenen". Why is now **Lehrgebiete** bold faced?

3. Das Gleiche gilt für eine[3] in den meisten Bakterien in gewissen **Entwicklungszuständen** auftretende **Substanz.**[1]

G. same g. is true m. most
g. certain E. stages of development
a. which appears (why which?)

DISCUSSION: Where would you put a "3" in this sentence? a 1? What nouns become now your bold face nouns? What two words cannot be consecutive? What word becomes the "which" clause

4. Ein teilweise mit flüssiger schwefeliger Säure erfülltes Glasrohr befindet sich in einem mit Paraffin beschickten **Probierrohre.**[1]

t. partially f. liquid S. acid
e. which is filled G. glass tube
b. which is coated, loaded P. test tube

DISCUSSION: It would be possible to put a "3" in two places in this sentence. Where? What words occur that cannot be consecutive? Now what words become the "which" clauses? the pivot nouns?

5. Ein[3] in neuerer **Zeit** vielfach gebrauchtes Verfahren besteht in dem Betupfen der Wundränder und ihrer Umgebung mit **Jod.**[1]

n. more recent g. which is used V. method
b. consists B. dabbing W. wound edges
U. vicinity J. iodine

How are you told that you are entering a "3" construction? Why is "Zeit" not the noun that goes with "ein"? Out of what word do you now make the "which" clause?

REVIEW:

The "3" construction is so far introduced in two (2) different ways. First by the "der" word and second by the "ein" word. In either case you will find two words that cannot be consecutive. When this occurs, a shift is made to pick up a noun. Here again you know which noun to pick up, for it will follow either an **e** or **en** in type 1 and **e, en, er, es,** in type 2. Out of the word that has one of these endings, make a "which" clause and with this "which" clause work back to the next noun. If this word cannot be made into a "which" clause, try the next one.

C

TYPE 3 OF THE "3" CONSTRUCTION

In Rule 3 a noun may be called for by

1. An Adjective.

   THE RULE: If the introductory word for a "3" construction is an adjective, you are told by the ending of the **first adjective** what the noun must follow. You will have as an ending of the adjectives either an **e, en, er, es, em.**

2. You have the same signal in this type of a "3" construction as in types 1 and 2. TWO WORDS MAY OCCUR IN GERMAN THAT CANNOT BE CONSECUTIVE IN ENGLISH. This is the signal for the "3" construction. Note these combinations:

   Wichtige in — nötige an — Verschiedene auf — dichtes zum — folgendes von

DRILL SENTENCES FOR TYPE 3 OF THE "3" CONSTRUCTION

1. Die Wirtschaft ist eine vorbereitende,[3] auf die Ermöglichung einer künftigen **Bedürfnisbefriedigung** gerichtete **Tätigkeit.**[1]

W. economy v. preparatory
E. making possible k. future B. want satisfaction g. which is directed T. activity

DISCUSSION: What is the significance of the "e" on "vorbereitende"? gerichtete? What would you do if this ending were "er"? "es"? "en"? "em"?

2. Wir schliessen daraus auf wichtige[3], nach dem **Erdmittelpunkt** gerichtete **Kräfte.**

s. conclude d. from that w. important
E. earth-center-point g. which are directed

DISCUSSION: Why is **Kräfte** bold faced? Erdmittelpunkt? why is the "e" on **wichtige** so important? on **gerichtete?**

3. Es ist ein eigentümlicher[3] aber auf die intellektuelle Entwicklung jener Zeit ein helles **Licht** werfender **Umstand.**[1]

e. peculiar Why a "3" here?
E. development h. bright L. light
w. which throws (why which?)

4. Wahrscheinlich haben vorhandene in den oberflächlichen Schichten des Platins eingeschlossene Gase einen wesentlichen **Einfluss.**[1]

W. probably v. existing o. upper
S. layers e. which are enclosed
w. essential E. influence

DISCUSSION: Where would you insert a "3"? What noun would you then bold face? Why is "Schichten" not the noun that goes with "vorhandene"?

5. Unter der Haut bildet es an vielen Stellen ein dichtes, zum Schutze tiefer gelegener Gebilde dienendes Polster.

H. skin S. places
d. thick t. g. of the deeper lying
S. protection P. pad d. which serves

What is the importance of "es" on dienendes? Why is "Gebilde" not the noun you want?

6. Beide **Arten** von **Antworten** kennzeichnen eine besondere[3] im alltäglichen **Leben** nur selten vorkommende **Anpassungsart.**[1]

A. types A. answers k. mark
b. special a. every day Why a "3" here?
v. which occurs (why which?)

7. Das Verhältnis zweier[3] zum gleichen **Drucke** gehöriger Siedetemperaturen ist hier keineswegs konstant, sondern steigt **mit der Temperatur** an.[2]

V. relation g. identical D. pressure
g. which belong (why which?) k. in no way
a. rises

Observe the ending "zweier". What is the significance of the "er" ending? What other ending could this be? What do you do with "an"? Why are certain nouns bold-faced?

C—1

THE "3" CONSTRUCTION WITH MORE THAN ONE ADJECTIVE

The "3" construction may have one or more adjectives modifying the same principal noun. This type of construction is introduced in the three ways that have been discussed, namely 1. by a definite article (type 1), 2nd. by an indefinite article (type 2) and 3. An adjective (type 3). No matter which type introduces the "3" construction, there may be more than one adjective modifying the same principal noun. Analyze carefully the following illustrations:

Das[3] vom **Verfasser** angegebene und von **Voller** ausgearbeitete Verfahren ist von grosser **Bedeutung.**[1]
A D C F E B G and straight ahead.

The———————————————————————procedure
which was indicated by the author and which was worked out by Voller is of great importance.

DISCUSSION: The two words **das vom** is your signal that you are entering a "3" construction, for these words cannot be consecutive. The construction is introduced by a "der"word, hence the noun must follow an **e** or **en.** As you move along the line, you encounter "angegebene", an adjective which is calling for a noun. Since the ending of this adjective is an **e,** the noun must follow an **e,** for the noun must follow the ending indicated **by the first adjective.**

Let **X** be inserted where the noun should be after "angegebene", and let this X stand for the noun "Verfahren" which should actually follow "angegebene". There will be as many X's as there are adjectives. In translation make a "which" clause out of each adjective, but be sure to take the adjectives in their order. Repeat the above translation several times and note why the letters A B C D E F G are placed as they are. Now practice with the following sentences:

1. Folgendes[3] vom **Verfasser** angegebenes X und von **Voller** ausgearbeitetes Verfahren ist von **Bedeutung.**[1]

f. following a. which was indicated
a. which was worked out V. method

DISCUSSION: How are you told that you are entering a "3" construction? In other words, what two words follow each other that cannot be consecutive?

Give your reasons for the position of the numbers 1 and 3 and also for the bold face nouns. What two words are made now into "which" clauses? Which one first? Why? Why the **X?**

2. Man träufelt einige Tropfen in ein[3] von **Lichtstrahlen getroffenes** X, und mit **Wasser** gefülltes **Gefäss.**[1]

t. pours T. drops L. light rays
g. which is struck g. which is filled
G. vessel

DISCUSSION: What two words warn you that you are entering a "3" construction? Why is there an X after getroffenes? The author suggests that you make a "which" clause out of "getroffenes" first. Why? Show why certain nouns are in bold face type.

3. Man beschreibt die[3] bis jetzt **besprochenen** und in diesem **Abschnitt** behandelten **Tatsachen.**[1]

b. describes b. which are discussed
A. section b. which were treated T. facts

Where would you insert an X? Why? Why do you make a "which" clause out of "besprochenen" before you do "behandelten"? Go over the sentence again and again.

4. Nichtsdestoweniger ist es ein[3] durch hundertfältige wiederholte **Erfahrungen** bestätigter, sich alle **Tage** stets bewährender **Satz.**[1]

N. nevertheless h. hundred fold
w. repeated E. experiments b. which is confirmed
b. which holds true, is verified

What two words indicate that you are entering a "3" construction? What significance do you attach to the "er" on "bestätigter"? Why would you insert an X after this word? Give your reason why certain nouns are bold faced.

5. Die Amide sind im allgemeinen die den **Hefen** zuträglichsten und von ihnen am besten und leichtesten assimilierbaren **Stickstoffverbindungen.**[1]

i. a. in general H. yeasts
z. which are most useful l. easiest
a. which are assimilatable

DISCUSSION: As you translate forward to the last noun, you encounter the two articles **die den.** This is immediately the signal that you are entering a "3" construction. Since the noun is called for by one of the "der" words, it must follow an **e** or **en.** The first adjective has an **en** ending and this of course indicates that the noun will now follow a word with an **en** ending. In this sentence there should be two "Stickstoffverbindungen", since there are two adjectives. Supply an X for the missing noun. Be sure to make a "which" clause out of the first adjective. Then the second and so on. Check the translation in another section of this book.

6. Die im Jahre 1876 ausgearbeiteten und später im Jahre 1877 erlassenen Gemeindeverordnungen machten einen verschiedenen Entwicklungsgang durch.[2]

a. which were worked out. s. later
J. year e. which were issued m. made
d-machen passed through, went through
v. different E. developmental — course

DISCUSSION: Where would you insert a "3"? an X? a 2? Why in each instance? Why is it so necessary to make a "which" clause out of "ausgearbeiteten" first? What do you do with "durch"?

7. Es bildet sich ein neuer, in der älteren theologischen Form des Ontologismus noch nicht zureichend von dem Gebiet des demonstrativen Erkennens geschiedener Begriff: der des intuitiven Erkennens.

b.s. is formed (app. 11, 4, a) ä. older
n. n. not yet
z. sufficiently G. field
E. recognition g. which was separated
B. concept, E. recognition

DISCUSSION: What is the importance of the "er" on "neuer"? on "geschiedener"? What nouns should now be bold faced? Note the two articles—that of . . .

8. In der Grafschaft und Stadt konzentrierte sich die früher auf viele Zweckverbände verteilte X, in grosser **Unordnung** zersplitterte **lokale Verwaltungstätigkeit.**

G. county S. city k. s. was concentrated
f. earlier Z. purpose-units v. which was distributed z. which was broken up
V. administrative activity.

DISCUSSION: What two words appear in this sentence that cannot be consecutive? What is the importance of the "e" on verteilte? What does the X stand for? Give reasons for all of the bold face nouns. If an adjective appears as "lokale", use it as an adjective and not a "which" clause.

9. Die Form der Anschauung war auch die ursprüngliche, nämlich in Analogie zu den bereits gut untersuchten Gravitationserscheinungen **gebildete,** und bis ins letzte Viertel des vergangenen Jahrhunderts **herrschende (Form).**

A. view u. original
b. already u. investigated
G. gravitation-phenomena g. which was formed
v. past J. century h. which prevailed

DISCUSSION: There should be a noun following three adjectives in this sentence. Which adjectives? What is the first indication that you are entering a "3" construction? What is the importance of the "e" on **ursprüngliche? gebildete?** herrschende? It is recommended to put an X after gibildete? why? An X would be placed after "herrschende" if the noun "Form" were not there.

***NOTE: Some teachers may prefer to leave C-1, C-2 and C-3 for a later date. These three groups may be taken up after D and E are studied or after some of the verb rules are taken care of, namely rules 4, 5, 6, 7, 8. Students may also find it advisable to leave these three groups until later since these three types are not as common as other types of the "3" construction.**

Review

Review two or three sentences for each of the types of the "3" construction.
What is the signal that tells you that you are entering a "3" construction?
What letters will your noun follow in type 1? type 2? type 3?

Give a complete discussion of two or three sentences in which more than one adjective modifies the same principal noun. Go to the board and point out the movements that must be made for smooth translation of a sentence of this type.

C—2

WHAT TO DO IF THE GUIDE NOUN IS MISSING

The "3" construction may at times be complicated by the fact that the noun which should be expected after an adjective may not be given. In case the noun does not follow the word which expects a noun, supply X for this noun and let X stand for the noun which should be present. In translation use the word "one", "ones", "those," "that which". The illustrations will clarify this point more fully. Go over these sentences until this type of the "3" construction is thoroughly understood.

ILLUSTRATION:

Es gibt wenige Gesetze von solcher Fruchtbarkeit wie das[3] in **Gleichung D** enthaltene.

DISCUSSION: The two words "das in" indicate that you are entering a "3" construction, for they cannot be consecutive. Since the "das" is a "der" word, the noun must follow an "e" or "en". When you see that there is no noun after the "e" on **enthaltene,** substitute an X for the understood noun. (Gesetz). Translate the X with the words "the one", "that one". Continue to make a "which" clause out of the word preceding the noun—in this case "which is contained".

1. Die[3] von ihm ausgesprochenen Anschauungen sind die[3] von den **Dichtern** seiner **Zeit** in **Anwendung** gebrachten X.

a. which were expressed A. views
D. poets Z. time A. application
g. which were brought

DISCUSSION: How are you told that you are entering a "3" construction? Note that after you dispose of one "3" construction another one is encountered. In both instances you have two words that CANNOT BE CONSECUTIVE.

What does the X stand for? What is the importance of the "en" on **ausgesprochenen?** on **gebrachten?** Why are certain nouns bold faced? Supply the words "the ones" for the X. Then make a "which" clause out of the word "gebrachten". Study this sentence carefully.

2. Diese Form der Philosophie war auch die ursprüngliche, und bis ins letzte Viertel des vergangenen Jahrhunderts herrschende.

a. also
b. till l. last V. quarter v. past
J. century h. which prevailed

DISCUSSION: What significance do you attach to the "e" on ursprüngliche? herrschende? Where would you insert an X? Why?

3. Der Ursachenzusammenhang ist niemals der einseitige, nach einer bestimmten Wirkung wirkende.

U. causal connection n. never e. one-sided
b. certain N. effect w. which acts

DISCUSSION: Explain why the 'e' on einseitige is important for translation purposes. What does "wirkende" modify? In other words, where would you insert an "X"? What would you make out of "wirkende"?

You could put the word **one** or **ones** after "gebraucht en" in sentence 1, or **herrschende** in sentence 2 or after "wirkende" in sentence 3. Why?

C—3

THE WORD THAT EXPECTS A NOUN MAY ITSELF BE CAPITALIZED

This capitalized word performs the function of a noun and adjective simultaneously. This type is not as often used as the others, but should be learned so that if reference is made to it in the reading material of this book it will be understood. This type of sentence is treated in about the same way as those in section C-2. The only difference is that the word that should be the adjective (in that it has the adjective ending on it) may itself be capitalized.

1. Mit gleichem Interesse umfasst er das[3] in der Natur,[1] in der **Geschichte,** und im Innern des Menschen selbst **Gegebene.**

g. same u. embraces, included
G. history s. himself
G. given, that which is given.

DISCUSSION:

The following points must be kept in mind:

a) You will still have two words that cannot be consecutive in English,—your signal that you are dealing with a "3" construction. Note **das in** in this sentence.

b) the noun will follow the same letters the various types call for: 1. type 1, the noun will follow **an e or en.** 2. type 2, the noun will follow an **e, en, er, es.** 3. type 3—the noun will follow the ending indicated by **the first adjective**—either e, en, er, es, em.

c) THE WORD THAT BEARS ONE OF THESE ENDINGS MAY ITSELF BE CAPITALIZED. Out of this word make a "which" clause by saying: "that which", "those which", "that something which" or "the thing which". In this sentence you would say "that which is given".

What would the following expressions mean?

das vorher Gesagte, das Bestehende das jetzt Bekannte der dadurch Erzeugte
das zu jeder Zeit Hervorgerufene, die öfters Vorherrschende, das Gelesene

D

TYPE 4 OF THE "3" CONSTRUCTION

A "3" construction may be called for by a preposition.

This will be indicated again by the fact that there will be two words that cannot follow each other consecutively. This is the case in all types of the III construction. The method of treating a sentence where a preposition is calling for a noun is the same in all other types of the "3" construction. Simply make a "which" clause out of the word that precedes the noun, then work back to the next noun—your signal to go ahead again.

1. Es besteht aus[3] durch die **Krone** ernannten **Senatoren.**[1]

b. consists a. of e. who are appointed
why who?

2. Bei höherem Erwärmen zerfällt es in Chlor und in mit **Chlor** gesättigtes **Wasser.**[1]

h. higher E. heating z. decomposes
Why a "3" here? g. which is saturated

3. Man machte die bedeutsame Beobachtung an[3] für die **Untersuchung** besonders günstigen Eiern.

b. significant B. observation E. eggs
g. which are favorable U. investigation

4. Das Gemeindegesetz vom 20 August 1870 bleibt weiter in Kraft mit[3] in den folgenden **Bestimmungen** enthaltenen Abänderungen.

G. community law b. remains
w. further K. force f. following B. provisions
w. which are contained (why which?) **A. changes**

5. Die Schilddrüse entwickelte sich hier zu einem relative grossen Organe mit[3] für die **Lebenstätigkeit** äusserst wichtigen Funktionen.

S. thyroid gland e. s. developed
L. life activity
a. extremely w. which are important

Give reasons for bold face nouns in these sentences; also for the position of the numbers.

E

A NUMERAL MAY ALSO CALL FOR A NOUN

When a numeral calls for a noun, you are to follow the same cues as heretofore, namely two words will follow one another in German that cannot be consecutive in English. When this happens, shift to pick up the noun and then work back word for word to the next noun. You may then resume normal word order from the point at which you skipped to pick up the noun.

1. Wir setzen auf den Apparat zwei[3] aus Schwarz und **Weiss** zusammengesetzte **Scheiben.**[1]

s. set z. two S. black
W. white z. which are composed **S. discs**

2. Von den 105[3] mit Newport im Frühjahr **1607** herübergekommenen Männern waren nur 12 gewöhnliche **Arbeiter.**[1]

F. Spring h. who came over
g. ordinary A. workers

3. Vier[3] in die Höhe geworfene Bälle kommen nach einigen Sekunden wieder zur **Erde** zurück.[2]

g. which are thrown i. d. H. upward
e. a few w. again z. come back

4. Man führte hier fünf[3] in allen **Einzelheiten** vollständig ausgeführte **Arbeitstheorien** vor.[2]

f. five E. details v. completely
a. which were carried out A. labor theories

DISCUSSION: Cite reasons for the position of the numbers and indicate why certain nouns are in **bold face type.** Which words become now the "which" clauses?

F

THE "HIDDEN" 3-CONSTRUCTION

In the other types of the "3" construction there is a **definite call** for the noun. These "calls" are 1. the **der** word; 2. the **ein** word; 3. the **adjective**; 4. the **preposition**; 5. the numeral. There are times when there is NO definite call for the noun. This is a rare construction.

Points to remember:

1. The noun appears with an adjective modifier — usually a **present** or **past participle.**

2. The adjective immediately preceding the noun is the only adjective modifying that noun. Otherwise it would be in one of the other types of the "3" construction. Usually the adjective will end with either **e** or **en.**

3. This construction usually occurs when the plural of a noun is used **without an article.** (See discussion of the noun, page 27 of appendix).

   Example: singular eine Zelle plural Zellen
   singular stehende Zelle plural stehende Zellen

4. As in all types of the "3" construction, the attributive adjective does not have to be a participle.
   Example: eine bisher noch gültige Antwort bisher noch gültige Antworten

Illustrations of the "Hidden" 3 construction:

In voller **Entwicklung stehende** Zellen werden durch äussere Bedingungen verändert. Cells (which stand) in complete development are changed by outer conditions.

Durch pathologische **Prozesse** hervorgerufene Veränderungen sind natürlich zu berücksichtigen.

Changes which are produced by pathological processes are of course to be considered.

You will note that neither **Zellen** nor **Veränderungen** are called for as is the case with other types of the "3" construction. The modified noun suddenly appears. It is necessary in translation to **begin** with the noun, make a "which" clause out of the adjective that precedes it, work back to the next noun and then go back into normal word order.

Rule 4

THE SUBJECT APPEARS WITHOUT A VERB

The two principal types of words that are found on the breaks in German sentences are NOUNS and VERBS. A glance at any German text will reveal how often this is the case. You have been studying up to this time what to do when nouns come at the end of the sentence. You will now be concerned with verbs that appear at the end of the sentences. Rules 4, 5, 6, 7 and 8 tell you what to do when a verb is found at the end of the sentence (or clause).

About 80 percent of the verbs at the end of the sentence are removed from the end position by the application of rules 4, 5, 6. The other 20 percent are taken care of by rules 7 and 8. It is not infrequent to find that rules 4, 5, 6 take care of nearly all the verbs that may appear at the end of a clause or sentence. It is extremely necessary to become thoroughly familiar with these rules. There is practically no exception to the verb rules.

RULE 4—THE SUBJECT MAY APPEAR WITHOUT A VERB FORM.

Illustration:

Wenn wir[4] die Hand in sehr heisses Wasser tauchen,

If we/———————— NOUN dip the hand in very hot water,

WHENEVER A SUBJECT APPEARS WITHOUT A VERB FORM, MAKE A SHIFT, i.e. go immediately to the other "breaks" in the sentence to find the verb that goes with the subject. When you shift to pick up a verb, pick up all other words and word units back to the first noun, and then begin translating again from the point where you stopped to shift.

Thus you will see that you are working forward to a noun as you learned to do in rule 1, or you find it necessary to shift to pick up a verb at which time you work backward to the first noun, your signal to go ahead again. As a general rule, the American reader does not want to go backward in the sentence as this is contrary to English word order. This is precisely where the difficulty arises in translation, for the reason that a number of adjustments are necessary to bring the word order into line.

Another diagram of rule 4:

←————————————————

Es ist klar, dass er[4] ————————————NOUN viel poetisch tätig gewesen sein muss.

It is clear, that he ————————————→NOUN much poetically active been have must.

The complete sentence in German:

1. Es ist klar, dass er[1] in der Zeit bis zu seinem 46. **Lebensjahr** viel poetisch tätig gewesen sein muss.

k. clear Z. time
L. life-year t. active

2. **Da Muller**[4] vorher den normalen **Genprozess** quantitativ genau **untersucht** hatte, veröffentlichte er sogleich seine **Resultate.**[1]

d. since v. previously
g. exactly u. investigated v. published
s. right away, at once.

3. Die drei Gruppen enthalten dann eine Reihe von **Enzymen,**[1] wie **sie**[4] **für die** verschiedenen **Umsetzungen** als spezifisch bezeichnet **werden können.**

e. contain R. series
w. as v. different U. decompositions
a. s. as specific (a word unit) b. designated

DISCUSSION: Cite the reasons for the position of each of the numbers. Show why certain nouns are in bold faced type. How far back do you go when you shift to pick up a verb?

Your aim is to move forward as much as possible in normal order. If a shift is called for — as in rule 4 — make the shift to pick up the verb. Then work back in normal order and as you do pick up all words (or word units) back to the first noun. You are then back to rule 1—YOUR SIGNAL TO GO ON FORWARD IN NORMAL WORD ORDER.

Note the expression "as specific". Do not break up a unit of this kind by saying "specific as", for these words are kept together as an adverbial unit.

4. **Es folgt** daraus, **dass** eine besondere Wertlehre[4] für die ökonomische **Wissenschaft** zum mindesten vollständig unnötig ist.

f. follows d. from this W. value theory
W. science z. m. at least (a word unit)
v. completely u. unnecessary

DISCUSSION: It is the subject "Wertlehre" that is calling for the verb. Pick up the verb and work then word for word back to the first noun. Note that "zum mindesten" are kept together as a unit. If you are not satisfied with the order of the words beyond the noun, rearrange these words to suit yourself. It may be necessary to rearrange adjectives and adverbs.

5. Es war nicht nur in dem **Sinne,**[1] dass **er**[4] die Handlungen und Personen seiner **Dichtungen** frei erfunden und meisterhaft komponiert hatte.

S. sense What does 'er' call for?
H. actions D. poetic works
e. invented m. masterfully

What do you do when a **noun** is on the break? a verb? How far back do you go when you pick up the verb? What are the two "pivot" nouns?

6. **Während** für die festen Körper die Lage der Elementarteilchen[4] **gegeneinander** im wesentlichen unveränderlich ist, sind die Moleküle leicht gegeneinander verschiebbar in den **Flüssigkeiten.**[1]

W. while K. bodies f. solid L. position
E. particles of elements g. one against the other
i. w. in the main u. invariable
l. easily v. displaceable F. liquids

DISCUSSION: When a shift is called for by a subject, be sure to take "all of the subject". The subject may be followed by a number of "of" constructions. Usually a "des" or "der" or words with es or er endings following another noun have the meaning "of". See app. 1, 1a.

7. Wir schliessen daraus, dass **wir**[4] die Dauer der Bewegung der **Kugel**[1] noch weiter verlängern können.

s. conclude d. from that D. duration
B. movement K. ball, sphere v. lengthen

Be constantly mindful of the numbers. These are important to train you to watch for the shifts necessary for smooth translation. When you understand the sentence, try to disregard the numbers.

8. Man wusste nicht, dass der Monitor[4] aus einem Kampfe mit **seinem furchtbaren Gegner** wiederum siegreich hervorgehen würde.

w. did not know (why rule 4?)
K. battle f. terrible G. opponent w. again
g. victoriously h. go forth w. would
henceforth the **ly** will be for you to supply.

DISCUSSION: Why is the noun "Gegner" actually the end of the sentence and rule 1? After you get back to this noun, rule 3 could appear, but since it does not appear you may work forward to the noun.

9. Die Oberfläche ist gekrümmt, da die Schwererichtungen[4] an **verschiedenen, weit voneinander entfernten Punkten der Oberfläche** nicht mehr als parallel angesehen werden können.

g. curved S. directions of gravity
v. different w. far e. removed
O. surface n. m. no longer
a. w. k. can be regarded (see app. 7, 6)

DISCUSSION: How far back is it necessary to go when you shift to pick up the verb? If you are not satisfied with the word order of these end words, rearrange them to suit your desires. It would not sound correct to say—can be regarded as parallel no more—, but at least you know that you must shift to pick up the verb and that you must work back to the first noun. The question of wording this clause is then left for you to decide.

10. Wenn auch der Präsident[4] auf diese **Pläne** nicht eingehen zu **können glaubte, gab er dem General den Befehl, dass er[4] Mc Dowell auf der Fredericksburg-Richmond Linie** vorgehen lassen **sollte.**

w. a. even though
e. to enter in g. believed z. k. to be able
B. command
v. go forward l. let

DISCUSSION: Show why the 4's are placed in these positions. Indicate also why certain nouns are bold faced. Rearrange the sentence to suit yourself. Note that you are working forward and backward to a **PIVOT NOUN.**

11. Wenn wir[4] alle bisherigen Kenntnisse über den Bau und die **Erscheinungen der Erdrinde, die Untersuchungen der Geophysik,** der Astronomie und alle anderen **Vermutungen** zusammenfassen dürfen, so gewinnen wir folgendes Annäherungsbild vom Schalenbau **der Erde.**[1]

b. previous K. knowledge B. structure
E. phenomena E. earth crust U. investigations
a. other V. suppositions
z. combine g. gain f. following
A. approximate picture S. shell structure

DISCUSSIONS: Why is it not possible to go directly to "Bau"? How many breaks do you pass up on your way to find the verb? What are now the two "pivot nouns"? Do not forget that on the way to the noun "Vermutungen" a "3" construction could stop you again. It does not occur this time, but could occur. Cite reasons for the position of the numbers.

NOTE THIS DEPENDENT CLAUSE:

12. Da er[4] sonst mit dem gesellschaftlichen **Anstande,**[1] der **verfeinerten** Denkweise, und dem staatlichen und höfischen **Zeremoniell unmöglich** so vertraut gewesen sein konnte, so . . .

s. otherwise g. social A. behaviour
v. refined D. manner of thinking
h. courtly u. impossibly v. familiar
g. s. k. could have been

DISCUSSION: This clause illustrates the importance of the comma as a "break", as opposed to a period or semi-colon. (See also first page of discussion of rule 3—diagram number 2.)

If the punctuation mark after "Anstande" were a period or a semi-colon, no shift would be necessary and you would be entitled to work straight forward word for word to this noun. Then only rule 3 could stop you on the way. However, when the comma constitutes the break, more care must be used, for on the way to this comma you may encounter a subject without a verb. Note how in this clause the subject "er" stops you. Shift to each successive break in search for the verb. As soon as you find the verb, pick it up and work back to the next noun and begin the translation again from the point from which you shifted. Initially your pivot noun is "Anstande", but because of the shift "Zeremoniell" becomes the pivot noun. Why should there be a period after this noun?

13. Wenn man[4] nach der Anordnung von **Abb. 553 das Ende** eines **Metalstabes** von 50cm Länge und 1cm Querschnitt durch eine[3] darunter gesetzte Flamme erwärmt, so zeigen die[3] in gleichen Abständen in den **Stab eingesetzten** Thermometer gewisse **Temperaturerhöhungen an.**[2]

A. arrangement
M. metal rod L. length
Q. cross section g. which is placed
darunter under it g. like A. distances
e. which are set g. certain
T. temperature—increases a. indicate

DISCUSSION: Note each of the steps necessary for smooth translation.

1. Rule 4 indicates a subject "calling for a verb"—erwärmt.

2. As you start forward again toward "Flamme", the "eine" stops you, for this is a "3" construction.

3. There is a prefix on the next break—hence you must stop on the verb to attach this prefix to the verb "zeigen". Then look up the verb in the dictionary in this form.

4. As you translate toward "Temperaturerhöhungen", you encounter "die in"—two words that cannot be consecutive. A shift is now made to pick up the noun that "die" calls for—Thermometer.

5. When you pick up the noun Thermometer, make a "which" clause out of the word preceding the noun as rule 3 directs you to do. When you get back to the first noun "Stab" you are back to rule 1 again—your signal to go on forward. Now check the translation in another part of this book. Go over the sentence several times if necessary until each point is thoroughly understood.

Review of rule 4—

Rule 4 is the first of the five rules that call for verbs. In rule 4 the subject appears without a verb—if it does make a shift to the next break or breaks to find the verb. When the verb is picked up, pick up also all other words and word units **back to the first noun.**

The subject may be a personal pronoun or a noun. If the subject is a noun, BE SURE TO USE ALL OF THE NOUN. Attached to this noun may be a number of "of" constructions. Observe carefully any "es" or "er" forms, for these may be the genitive form or "of".

Rule 5

THE RELATIVE PRONOUNS

If you have not had courses in German, learn thoroughly appendix section 3. It would be advisable to review the declensions of the relative pronouns even if you have had courses in German.

Relative pronouns "call" for verbs.

ILLUSTRATION OF RULE 5:

was[5]
welcher
———————————NOUN,[1] der ———————NOUN[1] adv. verb verb verb.

Note that relatives are usually preceded by a comma—see appendix 3a.

1. Er verwandte Glasflaschen mit engen **Hälsen,** {die[5] / welche[5]} nach **Füllung**[1] luftdicht verschlossen werden konnten.

Note that the German sentence is exactly like the diagram. The noun on the first break indicates that you may translate directly to this noun. On the next break you find a verb which is now removed from the end position by rule 5—the relative pronoun. When you shift to pick up the verb, work in normal order back to the first noun as you were instructed to do in rule 4. In fact, rule 5 is the same as rule 4 except that in rule 5 it is the relative that is calling for the verb.

THE NOUN IS STILL YOUR PIVOT POINT. When a shift becomes necessary, make the shift and work back as quickly as possible to the first noun. Except for rule 3, you would be entitled to go forward then right to the noun. Strictly speaking, your aim is to GET BACK TO THE NOUN whenever a shift is made to pick up a needed element as for example: A prefix in rule 2; a noun in rule 3 and a verb in rules 4 and 5.

Follow carefully the shifts in these sentences. If possible, have someone read the translated sentences back to you as you follow the German word order. Rule 4 will be stressed now along with rule five because very often a subject follows the relative and then it is the subject that is removing the verb and not the relative pronoun.

2. Es diente auch zur Auffindung einer Menge neuer **Tatsachen,**[1] welche[5] ohne diesen Durst nach **Gold** vielleicht noch länger verborgen geblieben wären.

d. served A. discovery M. quantity
T. facts o. without D. thirst n. for
v. perhaps v. concealed g. remained

DISCUSSION: What is the reason for the shift in this sentence? How far back do you go when you do shift?

3. Kant zeigt, dass die religiöse Weltanschauung nicht auf **Begriffen** beruht, die nach bestimmten logischen und empirischen **Kriterien** genau und sinngemäss definiert werden können.

z. shows W. world-philosophy
B. concepts b. certain
g. accurately s. sensibly

DISCUSSION: How many verbs must now be removed from the end position? What rule takes out the first verb? the second? How far back are you supposed to translate when you shift to pick up a verb? Where would you put a 4? a 5? Why in each case? Why the two bold face nouns?

The relative pronoun may be two words instead of one. Furthermore, the SUBJECT may follow the relative. This subject would then be calling for the verb and **not the relative pronoun.**

4. Zu diesem Zweck zeigt man eine Reihe von anatomischen **Präparationen,**[1] an welchen ein Röntgengramm[1] besonders anschaulich und verständlich demonstriert werden kann.

Z. purpose z. shows R. series
R. X-ray gram a. clearly
v. understandably

The verb on the end of the sentence must obviously be removed from this position. You have the choice here of letting the "relative" **an welchen** take out the verb or the "subject" whichever sounds best to you. The best advice is to **try** the relative first and then if it is apparent to you that the **subject** is calling for the verb, restate the sentence with the subject (4) picking up the verb. You do know that either rule 4 or rule 5 will remove the verb. How far back do you go when you do pick up the verb?

5. In der Hefezelle finden wir dann eine Reihe von **Enzymen,**[1] über die wir[1] uns schon bei der Besprechung der Bakterienenzymen genauer orientiert haben.

H. yeast cell R. series
ü.d. concerning which B. discussion
o. informed g. more exactly

DISCUSSION: It is apparent in this sentence that "wir" calls for the verb and not "über die".

6. Von dem **Eindruck,** den die Aufsätze[4] als **Ganzes** auf uns machen, wenden wir also unser **Augenmerk** ab[2] und richten es auf die einzelnen **Gedanken,**[1] die in den einzelnen **Arbeiten** vertreten sind.

E. impression A. essays G. whole
a. turn away A. view, aim r. direct
e. individual G. ideas A. works v. represented.

DISCUSSION: Give reasons for each of the numbers, and each of the bold face nouns. In line one **den** is a relative pronoun—why doesn't it call for the verb? Why a 2 in line two? a 5 in line 3?

7. Chemische **Syteme,** die[5] von der stabilen **Form** weit entfernt sind, verändern sich häufig bei **Temperatursteigerung,**[1] wenn diese[4] nämlich der Geschwindigkeit, mit der sie[4] dem Gleichgewichts**zustande** zustreben, einen hinreichenden **Wert** gibt.

w. far e. removed
v. s. are changed T. temperature increase
G. velocity G. state of equilibrium z. strive for

There are 3 relative pronouns in this sentence. Why does "diese" in line 2 call for "gibt" and not "zustreben"? Note that "sie" in line 3 calls for "zustreben" and not the relative "mit der."

8. Dies ist eine allgemeine **Erscheinung,**[1] **deren Wichtigkeit**[4] für den Verlauf der chemischen Umsetzung und **deren Bedeutung**[4] für die Existenz der sogenannten "stürmischen **Reaktionen"** alsbald einleuchten wird.

a. general E. phenomenon W. importance
U. transformation B. importance s. so called
s. violent e. be evident a. immediately

Note that "deren" in lines 1 and 2 are the genitive form of the relative and mean "whose". Also note that "deren Wichtigkeit and deren Bedeutung" call for the verb einleuchten wird.

RULE 5

B

A "wo" plus a preposition may be substituted for a relative pronoun. Or a preposition may be combined with a relative. Both of these types must be observed, for the German uses both types. Illustrations:

Der Stuhl, auf dem (or worauf—upon which) er jetzt sitzt, ist alt.
Die Stadt, in der (or worin—in which) er jetzt lebt, ist gross.
Der Wald, durch den (or wodurch—thru which) er jetzt fährt, ist grün.

1. Marshall beginnt vom Begriff des **Sozialkapitals,** worunter er[4] das Kapital vom Standpunkt eines ganzen **Volkes** versteht.

B. concept w. by which
S. standpoint g. whole v. means

2. Der zweite Abschnitt, mit dem (or womit) wir uns jetzt beschäftigen wollen, dauert genau ein Jahrhundert, nämlich bis zum Erscheinen des Darwinschen Werkes über den Ursprung der Arten, welche die gesamte Biologie umgestaltete.

A. section w. with which
b. occupy, concern g. exactly
E. appearance U. origin
A. species u. transformed

As in the case of the relative pronouns **der** and **welcher** the subject may follow the "wo" words. Note "er" in number 1. Also "wir" in number 2. In both sentences 1 and 2 it would be permissible to use "worunter or unter dem" or womit or mit dem.

RULE 5

C

You have become more or less familiar with the shifts necessary to pick up verbs that are found on the end of the sentence. When you made such shifts, you were instructed to work back to the next noun before resuming forward translation. Some difficulty may arise in case the noun that you work back to is not present. This noun may have been recited already in the early part of the sentence and it may not be repeated.

IF A SHIFT IS MADE TO PICK UP A VERB, WORK BACK TO THE FIRST NOUN. However, in working backward to the first noun DO NOT GO BACK PAST A WORD THAT CAN MODIFY A NOUN, i.e. any word with an adjective ending on it that **can take a noun.** These endings are **e, en, er, es, em.**

Study carefully the following sentences, for they will be referred to from now on whenever any difficulty of this kind arises. Fortunately it does not occur often.

1. Auf früheren Kulturstufen ist nämlich die sehr natürliche Vorstellung vorherrschend[1], dass sehr wertvolle Güter[4] nicht gegen wesentlich niedriger geschätzte ausgetauscht werden können.

f. earlier K. cultural levels n. namely
V. idea, conception v. dominant
w. valuable G. goods w. essentially
g. valued (ones) a. exchanged

Discussion: Since "vorherrschend" is not a verb, you are permitted to translate straight forward to this word and is thus rule 1. The subject "Güter" calls for the verb on the break. At this time you are supposed to work back directly to the noun. However YOU MUST NOT WORK BACK PAST A WORD THAT HAS ON IT AN ADJECTIVE ENDING. You would not make sense if you tried it. Here the adjective "geschätzte" expects a noun, hence stop here and continue on from "Güter".

2. Hier sind es nun zwei **Gesichtspunkte,**[1] die[5] sich zwingender als die einzig **möglichen** herausgestellt haben.

s. e. there are (see app. 10, 3, g) G. view points
z. more forcefully e. only m. possible (ones)

DISCUSSION: Why do you shift on "die"? How far back are you supposed to go? Why do you have to stop on the word "möglichen" this time? Note that you could supply an X after the word "möglichen" and let X stand for the noun. Translate the "X" then by the words "the ones". What other endings could there be on "möglichen" that could stop you from going back any farther? Note how impossible it would be to make sense beyond the point at which the noun is expected.

3. Die Geschichte der exakten Wissenschaften lehrt uns,[1] dass man[4] auf zwei wesentlich verschiedenen Wegen zur Entdeckung eines neuen **Naturgesetzes** gelangen kann, von denen wir[4] den einen als den empirischen, den zweiten als den **theoretischen** bezeichnen können.

G. history W. science l. teaches
w. essentially v. different W. ways
E. discovery N. natural law g. come
v. d. of which d. e. the one b. designate

DISCUSSION: Pay close attention to the rules that "call" for verbs. When the shift is made to pick up a verb, work back to the first noun. However DO NOT WORK BACK PAST A WORD THAT EXPECTS A NOUN. Firstly, it will not make sense if you do, and secondly you must assume the noun follows any of the adjective endings. Why then is "theoretischen" bold-faced in this sentence?

RULE 5

D

Practice Sentences for Rule 5

In case you have understood thoroughly rule 5 up to this point, it may not be necessary to go over these additional sentences. If you feel, however, that you do need more illustrations of the application of rule 5, you may be amply repaid for your efforts.

1. Im Jahre 1859 entdeckte Pflucker merkwürdige **Strahlen,**[1] die[5] in stark evakuierten Röhren von der **Kathode** ausgehen und die[5] deshalb allgemein als **Kathodenstrahlen** bezeichnet werden.

J. year e. discovered m. remarkable S. rays
s. strongly, highly R. tubes
d. therefore a. generally
b. designated w. are (app. 7, 5, a)

DISCUSSION: Cite the reasons for the position of the numbers. Note that a relative may be used after "und" (or any other coordinating conjunction—oder, sondern, denn, aber) without a comma before it. What nouns become now the "pivot" nouns?

2. Columbus sandte einen Brief an die **Königin,**[1] worin er[4] seine Empfindungen über die unwürdige **Behandlung** ausdrückte.

s. sent B. letter K. queen
w. in which (could also be "in dem")
u. undignified, improper B. treatment
a. expressed

DISCUSSION: Note the use of "worin". This might just as well be "in dem". Why rule 1? rule 4?

3. **Der absolute Gegensatz zum Kostenprinzip ist das Gratisprinzip,**[1] **wonach**[5] wirtschaftliche Güter[4] den Konsumenten ohne spezielles **Entgelt** dargeboten werden müssen.

G. opposite, contrast
w. according to which w. economic G. goods
K. consumers E. recompense d. offered
w. m. must be (see also appendix 7, 6)

DISCUSSION: Why is there a 1 on the first break? A "5" is placed intentionally over "wonach" to show that this word may be used to "take out" the verb. Rephrase the sentence, this time, let the subject "wirtschaftliche Güter" take out the verb and not the "wonach". Which do you now prefer?

4. Das wirtschaftliche Streben geht dann auf Herstellung einer gewissen Gleichmässigkeit der Versorgung der verschiedenen Bedürfnisse aus,[2] wobei auch die verschiedenen Bedürfnisse gewissermassen beschränkt werden müssen.

w. economic S. endeavor d. then
H. production g. certain G. uniformity
V. supply v. different B. wants a. proceeds
w. in which case v. different
g. to a certain extent b. limited

DISCUSSION: Where would you put a "2" in this sentence? why? Two nouns should be written in bold face type. Which nouns? The "wobei" may be used as a relative form to remove the verb. Or you may choose to let the subject "die verschiedenen Bedürfnisse" take out the verb. Very often this is left entirely up to you. Try both and see which you prefer. Obviously one of the rules 4 or 5 will take out the verb. Since rule 3 does not now appear you may work forward to the noun.

5. Zu Beginn des 16. Jahrhunderts finden wir auch als Namen für die Körper, welche angeblich die Gärung verursachen, das Wort "Ferment", womit man im weitesten Sinne des Wortes jeden Stoff bezeichnete, welcher irgendwelche chemische Reaktion auszulösen imstande ist.

Z.B. at the beginning J. century
ang. allegedly, ostensibly
G. fermentation v. cause w. with which
w. broadest S. sense S. material
b. designated i. in any way a. induce i. able.

DISCUSSION: There are five nouns that should be bold faced. Which nouns are these? What rules do you use to remove the verbs? Where would you insert a 5? a 4? a 1?

6. **Der** obere Teil der **Halbinsel,** worauf[5] die Hauptstadt der Konföderation und das Operationsobjekt **McClellans** liegt, wird durch den **Fluss** durchschnitten.

o. upper T. part H. peninsula H. capital
w. upon which
w.—d. is intersected

Let the "wo" word take out the verb **liegt.** If you are then not satisfied, let the subject "die Hauptstadt der Konföderation" take it out.

Rule 6

AUXILIARIES—THE "STOP" VERBS

Rule 6 is extremely important in reading German. It deals with the auxiliary verbs which in this text are called "stop verbs". A rather large percentage of German sentences are connected in some way with one of these verbs.

Students with some grammar training have an advantage here, for they have studied the conjugation of these verbs and should know the meanings of them in the various tenses. In case you have not had courses in German, your progress will be at the outset to some extent retarded. You should, however, proceed with rule 6 and be learning on the side the tense forms of these verbs. It is encouraging to know that the use of these words will become clearer and more understandable with each day. In case difficulty arises in your reading, you may always refer to the forms given in the appendix. (See app. 7:1-8)

Section 7:3, 4, 5 and 6 of the appendix are extremely important, for these deal with the verb "werden" which is most confusing to American students of German. The use of this verb will become manageable with practice. Reference is made to these sections constantly in the reading material of the text. Although the auxiliary or stop verbs are listed in the appendix, it seems still practical to add a few of them here.

Haben—to have		**Sein**—to be	
er hat	he has	er ist	he is
er hatte	he had	er war	he was
er hat —gehabt	he has had	er ist —gewesen	he has been
er hatte —gehabt	he had had	er war —gewesen	he had been
er wird —haben	he will have	er wird —sein	he will be
er würde —haben	he would have	er würde —sein	he would be
er würde—gehabt haben	he would have had	er würde —gewesen sein	he would have been
(see also appendix 7-2)		(See also appendix 7-1)	

ON USE OF "WERDEN" study carefully appendix 7-3 — WERDEN meaning **to become.**

"WERDEN" MAY ALSO BE USED WITH AN INFINITIVE TO FORM THE FUTURE TENSE—SEE APP. 7:4.

"WERDEN" MAY BE USED WITH THE PAST PARTICIPLE — It is then used "passively". See app. 7, 5.

OTHER STOP VERBS

er, sie, es	kann	muss	will	darf	soll	mag	lässt	bleibt	(present)
wir, sie	können	müssen	wollen	dürfen	sollen	mögen	lassen	bleiben	
er, sie, es	konnte	musste	wollte	durfte	sollte	mochte	liess	blieb	(past)
wir, sie	konnten	mussten	wollten	durften	sollten	mochten	liessen	blieben	
	gekonnt	gemusst	gewollt	gedurft	gesollt	gemocht	gelassen	geblieben	(Past parti-
	*können	müssen	wollen	dürfen	sollen	mögen	lassen		ciples)

Note: These infinitives may appear instead of a past participle when another verb is expressed. For example: er hat ihn gesucht—Er hat ihn **suchen** wollen. Er hat nicht **schlafen** können. **Haben** Sie die Sätze schreiben können? Ja, ich habe **gekonnt.**

ANY OF THE VERBS ON THIS PAGE MAY BE USED WITH ANOTHER VERB FORM.

A

RULE 6:

Whenever you encounter any of these verbs (in any tense), you must **stop.** Be careful NOT TO MOVE FORWARD ANOTHER WORD until you have ascertained whether or not there is another verb form used with one of these verbs.

If you encounter in your reading "ist", "kann", "wird", "darf", "lässt", etc. be conscious of the fact that on some other break in the sentence there may be another verb form used with these verbs. If there is no other verb, there will be a noun there which will be the signal to go on forward in the sentence.

Illustrations for rule 6:

	1	←
1. Er hatte[6]/ (see if there is a verb used with "hatte")	NOUN	verb verb.
2. Er ist[6]/ (see if there is a verb used with "ist")	NOUN	No verb.
3. Er kann[6]/ (see if there is a verb used with "kann")	NOUN	← adverb verb verb
4. Er ist[6]/ (Forms of "sein" may take out a pred. adj.) (compare also with diagram on page 1)	NOUN	Predicate Adjective

A sentence involving a "stop" verb:

Wir müssen[6] die Tätigkeit des Lehrers und ihre Wirkungen auf das **Schulkind**[1] zuerst genau wissenschaftlich analysiert haben.

A diagram of this sentence:

Wir müssen[6]..NOUN[1]
adv. adv. adv. verb verb.
←

The translation of it by rule 6:

We must[6] ——— have analyzed scientifically accurately first— the activity of the teacher and its effects upon the school child.

Observe the following Points:

There is a great deal of similarity in rule 6 and rules 4 and 5. In fact all of them "call" for verb forms. If a shift is made to pick up a verb because of one these "stop verbs", make the shift and then work back to the next noun just as you have been doing with rules 4 and 5.

The noun is still your pivot point. This is rule one (1) and permits you to go forward word for word. Only rule 3 could stop you on the way.

DO NOT GO BACK PAST A WORD THAT COULD MODIFY THE NOUN. See more on this point in rule 5-C.

Learn to STOP ON THE CUE. A shift will be necessary in case you encounter:

A subject without a verb—rule 4
A relative without a verb—rule 5
An auxiliary or stop verb is calling for another verb form—rule 6.

No matter what the reason for the shift is, work back to the first noun (or to an adjective that expects a noun) and then go back into normal word order.

YOUR OBJECT IS TO REMOVE ANY ELEMENTS FOUND ON THE RIGHT HAND SIDE OF THE DOUBLE LINE IN THE ABOVE DIAGRAM. Once these elements are removed, you may proceed with confidence toward the noun.

B

DRILL SENTENCES FOR RULE 6

In the sentences of this book, both in the model sentences and in much of the reading material, there will be found a "6" above one of these stop verbs. This indicates that it is the "stop verb" that is calling for another verb form. However, a subject may follow this stop verb and it will be then necessary to rearrange the subject and predicate as you were told to do in rule 1—D.

1. Wir werden[6] daher vieles aus dem **Buch** als unbrauchbar beiseite lassen.

w. shall (app. 7, 4) B. book
a. u. as unusable b. aside l. leave

2. Sie dürfen[6] auch deshalb mit demselben **Recht** allerdings zusammen genannt werden.

d. may d. therefore d. the same (app. 14, 1)
R. right a. of course z. together g. named

3. Wir wollen[6] die obigen allgemeinen **Andeutungen** noch etwas näher zu erklären versuchen.

w. want to o. above a. general A. suggestions
e. somewhat n. nearer e. explain v. attempt

DISCUSSION: Give reasons for the position of "6" in these three sentences. How far back do you go when you do shift to pick up the verb? Justify the bold face nouns.

4. Die folgenden Methoden sind[6] in dieser **Weise** bisher mehr oder weniger eingehend benutzt worden.

f. following s. have i.d. W. in this way
b. hitherto e. thoroughly b. used

DISCUSSION: You are stopped in this sentence by the verb "sind". Make the shift that is called for by rule 6. For the use of sind—benutzt worden, see app. 7, 5, c. What noun becomes now the "pivot" noun? Note how far you go back in this sentence.

5. Man kann in diesem Falle etwa folgendermassen verfahren.

F. case e. perhaps f. as follows
v. proceed

6. Im folgenden sollen die Rorschachschen Theorien in der Reihenfolge zuerst im einzelnen besprochen werden.

f. following s. are to
R. series, sequence z. first i. e. in detail
b. discussed w. be

DISCUSSION: Where would you put a "6" in sentence 5? sentence 6? Why? What nouns in these sentences would you then bold face? why? Note the expression **are to be discussed.**

7. Die Theorie der Temperatursinne kann zu dieser Zeit noch nicht richtig gegeben werden.

T. temperature senses d. this
Z. time n. n. not yet g. w. be given

Where would you insert a "6"? why? Then what noun becomes the "pivot" noun?

8. Wir wollen[6] zunächst einmal klar zu machen suchen, was[5] denn eigentlich eine chemische **Verbindung** ist.

z. first of all k. clear s. seek
e. really V. compound

9. Die verschiedenen Fälle der Genmanifestierung können[6] bezüglich der **Symmetrieverhältnisse** folgendermassen theoretisch genau klassifiziert werden.

v. different F. cases G. gene manifestation
b. with regard to S. symmetry conditions
f. as follows g. accurately
k. w. be classified (see app. 7, 6)

10. Vom Gesichtspunkt einer Einzelwirtschaft oder eines speziellen Produktionszweiges müssen[6] die Produktionskosten eines **Gutes** ganz natürlich als gegeben erscheinen.

G. viewpoint E. individual economy
P. branch of production
G. good, commodity g. quite
a. g. as given, known e. appear

C

DO NOT GO BACK PAST A WORD THAT CAN MODIFY A NOUN

(See also Rule 5-c)

1. Die Wirkung dieser Enzyme scheint[6] eine sehr **komplizierte** zu sein.

W. effect s. seems (to what?)
k. complicated one

DISCUSSION: When you shift to pick up the verb "zu sein", do not go back any farther since an adjective appears which should modify a noun. When the noun is not present, do not go back beyond that point where the noun should be. In order to make it more clear, put an X down after the adjective "komplizierte" and let the X stand for the noun.

2. **Zwar kann**[6] eine wirtschaftliche Klassifizierung niemals die Schärfe einer **mathematischen** erreichen.

Z. indeed w. economic
n. never S. sharpness e. reach

DISCUSSION: Why is "mathematischen" bold faced even though it is not a noun? Note how impossible it would be to work back beyond the point where the noun is expected.

3. Nach diesem grossen Kometen ist[6] zwar 1787 noch ein ähnlicher **wichtiger** erschienen, der[5] der **Sonne** etwas näher gekommen ist.

g. great z. indeed
ä. similar w. important (one) e. appeared
S. sun n. closer e. somewhat

DISCUSSION: What does "ist" call for? When you pick up the verb, why do you not work back to 1787? What other adjective ending could warn you that a noun is "expected"?

4. Man wird[6] dennoch jenen Vorgang bei der Abtretung von Helgoland nicht als einen **exceptionellen** bezeichnen.

w. will (app. 7, 4) V. process A. surrender
e. exceptional (one) b. designate

DISCUSSION: Note that "werden" plus an infinitive forms the future tense. When you shift to pick up "bezeichnen" why do you not work back to Helgoland? What other adjective ending could stop you? Where could you supply an X?

5. Die Testobjekte müssen[6] dem Desinfektionmittel so ausgesetzt sein, dass die Einwirkung unveränderlich eine gleichmässige und **vollkommene** ist.

D. d-medium, means
a. exposed E. effect u. invariably
g. uniform v. complete (one)

It is customary for me in this book to bold face the noun in front of verb forms. Why is "vollkommene" bold-face even though it is not a noun? What other adjective endings could stop you on the way back? Cite reasons for the numbers. See also rule 5-C, 7-D on this point.

D

Additional Practice Sentences for Rule 6

1. Der andere Grund ist durch die Veröffentlichung des lange erwarteten zweibändigen Lebens des Dichters von seinem Sohne, dem jetzigen Lord Tennyson, gänzlich und glücklich beseitigt.

a. other G. reason V. publication
e. expected z. two volume L. life
S. son j. present
g. entirely b. put or set aside

2. Wichtige Hinweise auf die geheime Dichterschaft Bacons, auf seine geheime Doppelrolle, sind aber in zahlreichen Titelblättern und den alten Originalausgaben der Werke Bacons und seiner Pseudonyme, besonders Shakespeares, zahlreich enthalten.

W. important H. references g. secret
Di. authorship Do. dual role
z. numerous T. title pages
W. works
z. numerously e. contained

3. Diese Auffassung des Sparens ist mit der fortdauernden Wirtschaft, die allen unseren Betrachtungen zugrunde liegt, notwendig eng verknüpft.

A. conception S. saving f. continuous
W. economy B. considerations
z. l. lie at the base of n. necessarily
e. closely v. connected

DISCUSSION: Where would you put a "6" in these sentences? a "5" in sentence 3? What nouns should then be bold faced? Have someone read the translated sentence to you and watch it unfold.

E

RULE 6—THE PREDICATE ADJECTIVE

Illustration: (See also page 1—type Three-b)

Pope war[6] mit den Resultaten der Kämpfe dieses **Tages** vollständig zufrieden.

Diagram of this sentence:

Pope war/..NOUN adverb predicate adjective

The translation:

Pope was—satisfied completely—with the results of the battles of this day.

With forms of **sein** (sometimes **werden**) stop and pick up predicate adjectives. If such a shift is made, work right back to the next noun as you have been doing in all of rule 6—as well as in rules 4 and 5.

Predicate adjectives are usually easy to recognize. As a rule they do not have verb endings. Note these predicate adjectives: feststellbar, nötig, gemeinsam, möglich, abhängig, nah.

1. Dazu sind[6] auch die entsprechenden physikalischen Zustände der **Umgebung** notwendig.

D. for that e. corresponding
Z. conditions U. environment n. necessary

2. Der erste dieser Faktoren ist[6] natürlich allen philosophischen Systemen einer bestimmten **Periode** gemeinsam.

e. first a. to all
b. certain
g. common

3. Das Magnesium, besonders im Magnesiumsulfat, ist[6] dem **Wachstum** ebenfalls unumgänglich notwendig.

b. especially e. likewise
W. growth u. unavoidably n. necessary

4. So sind[6] die Begriffe der Bewegung, der Materie, der Kraft oder Energie den verschiedenen **Naturwissenschaften** gemeinsam.

B. concepts B. movement
K. power d.v. to the different (Why to?)
g. common

DISCUSSION: Show why a "6" is placed above certain words in these four sentences. What nouns become now the "pivot" nouns?

5. Die Kraft ist[6] dem Produkt aus den beschleunigten Massen und den[3] ihnen erteilten **Beschleunigungen** proportional.

K. force b. accelerated
e. which are given B. accelerations

6. Gerade die osmotischen Verhältnisse bei den Bakterien sind für die richtige Erkenntnis und praktische Beurteilung von Gärungsvorgängen wichtig.

G. exactly V. conditions
r. correct E. recognition w. important
B. judgment G. fermentation processes

7. Die individuelle Nachfrage eines Gutes ist[6] im allgemeinen von den Preisen sämtlicher Güter, oder jedenfalls sämtlicher Güter, die für die betreffende Einzelwirtschaft eine Bedeutung haben, abhängig.

N. demand G. good, commodity
a. general v. on s. of all
j. at any rate b. concerned
E. individual economy B. importance
a. dependent

8. Ohne Zweifel ist[6] diese Einteilung schon gegenüber der[3] in der platonischen Akademie ausgeführten Sonderung der wissenschaftlichen Arbeiten unvollständig.

Z. doubt E. division, classification
g. with respect to a. which was carried out
S. separation w. scientific A. works
u. incomplete

DISCUSSION: In the sentences 5–8 insert a "6" where certain predicate adjectives are called for. Underline all nouns that should be bold faced. Why is there a "3" in sentences 5 and 8? a 5 in sentence 7?

If at all possible to have some one read these sentences to you, do so, for then you will be better able to focus your attention on the "key" points in the sentence. They are translated in the section following the discussion of the rules.

F

Three Other Stop Verbs — lassen, sich lassen, bleiben

There are a few other verbs that may be classified as "stop" verbs of which **lassen** and "sich lassen" are the most important. **Bleiben** may also call for another verb form. **Scheinen** may also belong in this group, but it usually calls for "zu" which is taken up in rule 7. The verbs "lehren and lernen" may also call for another verb form. (Wir lernen ihn kennen)

1. Bacons anerkannte Werke lassen[6] uns den Dichter, namentlich **den Dramatiker,** deutlich erkennen.	a. recognized W. works l. let, permit n. especially d. clearly e. recognize
2. Viele Bestimmungen bleiben[6] in der Verfassung der Vereinigten **Staaten** bestehen.	B. provisions V. constitution V. United S. States b. existing
3. Der Offizier liess[6] die Soldaten an diesem Tage zwei **Stunden ruhen.**	S. soldiers T. day S. hours r. rest (let the soldiers rest)

DISCUSSION: Show why rule 6 is involved in these three sentences. Why are the bold face nouns important?

NOTE THAT BLEIBEN MAY TAKE OUT A VERB OR AN ADJECTIVE (as in the case of "sein")

4. Wir bleiben[6] lange in dem Zimmer sitzen.	Z. room s. sitting
5. Die Studenten blieben[6] dem Studium der **Mathematik** gleichgültig.	S. study b. remained g. indifferent
6. Dabei blieb[6] der Gegensatz zwischen der sensualistischen Associationspsychologie und den nativistischen Theorien verschiedenen Ursprungs für die **Entwicklung** massgebend.	G. contrast z. between v. of different U. origin E. development m. decisive

Note how in sentences 4, 5, 6, the verb "bleiben" takes out both predicate adjectives and verbs. Reference will be made to these sentences if difficulty should appear in the reading material of this text.

SICH lassen can be, may be

This verb is frequently used as a substitute for the passive.

es lässt sich sagen	it can (or may) be said	es lässt sich nicht verstehen
es liess sich sagen	it could be said	it cannot be understood

7. Dieses Naturgesetz lässt sich[6] in folgender **Weise** formulieren.	f. following W. manner
8. Die Grösse der Moleküle hat sich[6] auf verschiedenen **Wegen** bestimmen lassen.	G. size v. different W. ways b. determined l. been
9. Die Inhalte des Gesetzes lassen sich in folgende **Sätze** zusammenfassen.	I. contents G. law s. l. can be f. following S. statements z. summarized
10. Die[3] im vorstehenden **Abschnitt** entwickelten Sätze lassen sich[6] kurz folgendermassen aussprechen.	v. foregoing A. chapter e. which were developed (Why which?) f. as follows a. expressed

DISCUSSION: Justify the presence of certain numbers in sentences 7-10. Why is there a "3" in sentence 10? In sentence 8 note the translation: has — been defined.

Rule 7

A

THE "ZU" VERB RULE

RULE 7 DEALS WITH VERBS USED WITH "ZU" or "to" in English.

1. Note the following verbs and the position of the "zu".

a) zu hoffen — zu ändern — aufzugehen — anzunehmen
zu betrachten — zu kommen — vorzukommen — emporzukommen

The "zu" is placed to one side of the verb or inside of it. A verb with "zu" attached is not a "zu" verb. Note the following verbs:

b) zugibt	zugab	zugegeben	these are verbs coming from **zugeben.** "Zu" is a prefix.
zuordnen	zuordnete	zugeordnet	these are verbs coming from **zuordnen.** "Zu" is a prefix
zunimmt	zunahm	zugenommen	these are verbs coming from **zunehmen.** "Zu" is a prefix.

2. English and German are almost identical in the use of "to" or "zu" in German. That is to say when the English calls for a "to", the German will call for a "zu".

In this rule certain English expressions help you understand the German. Note the following illustrations:

It is necessary .... to	We are obligated .... to
I am inclined .... to	He is authorized .... to
They have tried .... to	The tendency is .... to
This type permits .... to	It would be possible .... to

These illustrations show the type of words that call for "to" in English. This same type of words and expressions calls for a "zu" in German. Be conscious of this in your reading. LEARN TO "FEEL" THE "ZU". You will do well to acquire the habit of shifting the minute the break in the thought occurs, i.e., where there is **a distinct call** for an infinitive with **zu.** You would not say for example: These students are required—this work. You may say: These students are required **to do** this work. The difficulty that arises here is that the German places the verb with "zu" at the end of the phrase or sentence, often many breaks or far away from where it would be expected in English.

In the discussion of rules 4, 5, 6, you were cautioned to observe the breaks in a sentence or paragraph and if verbs were on the breaks to remove the verb with these rules. In the use of rules 4-5-6 there is a definite and distinct "call" for the verbs inasmuch as you will have in 4. a Subject without a verb; 5. A relative calling for a verb; 6. A Stop verb that may expect another verb form.

The "call" that is made for the "zu" verb is often not too clear. It will take a great deal more skill to handle rule 7 than it does the other three verb rules. In order to acquire facility and to avoid any possibility of overlooking the "zu" verb and in order to keep the translation smooth and continuous, it is suggested to put a "flag" out to the left hand side of the margin on the line where a "zu" is located. This is done (as also in rule 2) to warn you that there is cause for caution in that line. Word the translation so that you will "come out" with a **"to".** Prefixes should also be "flagged" for they often offer difficulty. A few seconds time spent in "flagging" the prefixes and "zu" verbs in a paragraph will save much time in actual translation, for you have "located" the places where an error might be made. If prefixes are present, the verbs will not be complete. If "zu" verbs are present, you may overlook the "call" that is made for these verbs. A warning to be careful is helpful.

If you have carefully scrutinized a paragraph and you do not find a prefix or a "zu" verb, you may then work confidently toward the noun and by that is meant either forward toward the noun or backward to the noun after a shift is made. The object is to REMOVE any element beyond the noun—beyond the double line in the diagram on page 1. This has been emphasized many times in the discussion of the model sentences up to this point.

In order to become skillful and accurate in reading technical material—either scientific or literary—it is imperative to understand fully the application of this rule. It will be seen in the course of the discussion how important the removal of the "zu" verb is for the reading of German. As a general rule, grammars give very little attention to this point and many times the translation becomes totally unmanageable because of the inability of the translator to find the troublesome "zu" verb. Students who have used the rules find it very helpful to "flag" these verbs before the translation is begun and to be extra cautious in the neighborhood of the flags.

Illustrations of a "zu" verb construction:

1. Es ist auch notwendig,[7] die verschiedenen Begriffe It is also necessary .... NOUN	im einzelnen zu untersuchen. to investigate in detail the different concepts
2. Sie sind jetzt imstande[7], die Berichte in der Zeitung You are now able .... NOUN	leichter und verständlicher zu lesen. to read more intelligently and more easily the reports in the newspaper.

Other illustrations of rule 7:

3. Wir müssen versuchen,[7] ________ NOUN[1] We must try NOUN	zu verstehen, to understand.
4. Der Präsident ist befugt, ________ NOUN[1] The president is empowered NOUN	zu erlassen. to issue.
5. Es ist auch möglich ________ NOUN[1] It is also possible NOUN	hervorzurufen. to produce.

B

DRILL SENTENCES FOR RULE 7

1. Wir müssen versuchen,[7] eine Beziehung zwischen Reiz —— und Empfindung in chemischen **Begriffen** festzustellen.	v. try B. relation z. between R. stimulus E. sensation B. terms f. to establish
2. Es ist auch möglich,[7] die Druckempfindungen von ver- —— schiedenen **Intensitätsgraden** hervorzurufen.	m. possible D. pressure sensations v. different h. to produce

DISCUSSION: Why is there a "7" on line 1? Why is there a "flag" out in these two sentences? Justify the bold face nouns.

3. Viele Substanzen haben die Eigenschaft[7], nur die Bildung —— eines oder mehrerer **Enzyme** zu hemmen.	E. attribute, quality, characteristic B. formation m. several h. inhibit
4. In diesem Falle wäre es besser[7], die Empfindung und Vorstellung als Unterklassen einer besonderen Art seelischer —— **Elemente** zu betrachten.	F. case w. would be E. sensation V. idea U. sub-classes b. special s. psychic A. kind b. consider

DISCUSSION: What is the expression that "calls" for the "zu"? What noun becomes now the pivot noun? What is the expression in sentence 3 that calls for the zu? Which one of the definitions best admits of a "to"? When the "zu" is on the break, word the translation so that the "zu" will come in at the right time.

5. In Erwiderung gab man ihm die Ermächtigung,[7] einige Regimenter der Besatzung auf Fort **Monroe** an sich zu —— ziehen.	E. reply Erm. authority (to what?) e. some B. garrison a. s. to himself z. z. to draw

Indicate why "Monroe" should be bold faced and why a "7" should be on line 1.

6. Neue, sehr bedeutende Schwierigkeiten entstehen durch die Aufgabe,[7] alle angewandten **Masstäbe** möglichst genau —— miteinander zu vergleichen.	b. significant S. difficulties A. task a. used, applied M. standards m. as possible g. accurately v. compare

DISCUSSION: What is the word or expression that calls for "zu"? What is the importance of the flag? the bold face noun?

7. Unter dem Einfluss der ersten dieser Bedingungen suchte[7] die Philosophie die führende Stellung in Leben und —— **Wissenschaft** zu erobern.	E. influence B. conditions s. sought f. leading. S. position W. science e. conquer

DISCUSSION: Why is there a "7" on suchte? Note that you may have to rearrange the subject and predicate if they are not in English word order. It would be incorrect to put a"7" on "Philosophie", for it is the verb "seek" that is calling for the verb—NOT the subject.

8. Ein Versuch,[7] das ganze Gebiet der **Psychologie** systematisch zu überblicken, ist[6] nicht nur von den Grundanschauungen über die Aufgabe der **Psychologie** abhängig, sondern auch von dem Stande der psychologischen **Einzelforschung.**[1]

V. attempt. g. entire G. field
ü. to survey
G. basic views A. task
a. dependent v. on S. state
E. detail-study

DISCUSSION: Give reasons for the position of the numbers 1, 6, 7. Also show why certain nouns are in bold face type. Line 2 is flagged—why?

9. So pflegt[7] man bei der Aufstellung eines Bakteriensystems die morphologischen Eigentümlichkeiten in erster Linie zur Gruppierung der **Pilze** zu benutzen.

p. is accustomed (to what?) A. setting up
E. peculiarities
b. use Why a bold face noun here?

10. Es war in diesem Falle erforderlich[7], ihren Rückzug nach dem **Einschiffungspunkte** unbelästigt bewerkstelligen zu können.

F. case e. necessary R. retreat
E. embarkation point u. unmolested
b. begin, put to work z. k. to be able

11. Traube gebührt das Verdienst[7], das Thermometer am Krankenbette zur **Fieberbestimmung** wieder eingeführt zu haben.

g. is due V. credit (to what?)
K. sick bed F. determination of fever
e. introduced

12. Denning glaubt[7] jedoch kürzlich einen hellen Fleck auf dem **Ringe** genügend verfolgt zu haben.

g. believes (to what?) k. recently
F. spot g. sufficiently v. followed up

13. Es erschien völlig unmöglich[7], die verschiedenen Probleme, die[5] vom 16. und 17. Jahrhundert in der Mechanik, der Optik, Geographie, und bald auch in der Chemie, Physiologie und Tierkunde auftauchten, alle unter dem **Begriffe** zusammenzufassen.

e. appeared v. completely u. impossible
Why rule 5? rule 7?
b. soon
T. zoology a. arose
B. concept z. combine What calls for this zu verb?

14. Vor allem werden wir versuchen[7], der poetischen Bedeutung des Dichters in seinem Verhältnis zur Vergangenheit, in seinen Beziehungen zur Gegenwart und in allen seinen charakteristischen **Eigenschaften** gerecht zu werden.

v. a. above all v. try (to what?)
B. importance D. poet V. relation
Verg. past B. relations G. present
E. attributes
g. z. w. to do justice (What calls for this zu verb?

15. Das Röntgenverfahren gibt auch die Möglichkeit[7], den Arzt und den Studenten durch direkten Vergleich des anatomischen Präparates mit dem **Röntgenbild** besser zu unterrichten.

M. possibility
A. doctor V. comparison
R. x-ray picture
u. instruct (what calls for this verb?)

C

THREE GERMAN EXPRESSIONS THAT CALL FOR "ZU"

If the "zu" is not removable with the English expressions, then the "zu" verb in German is taken out by three German expressions.

Um—zu in order to — Er geht in die Stadt, um Fleisch und Gemüse zu kaufen.
He goes to the city **in order to** buy meat and vegetables.

ohne—zu without plus an "ing" in English:
Die Studenten lernen Deutsch, ohne in die Schule zu gehen.
The students learn German without **going** to school. Note **ing.**

anstatt—zu instead plus an "ing" in English:
Sie geht in die Stadt, anstatt zu Hause zu bleiben.
She goes to the city instead of **remaining** at home. Note **ing.**

1. Es entwickelt sich auch, ohne[7] eine so schwere **Krankheit** hervorzurufen.

e. develops, is developed o. without
K. illness h. producing (why "ing"?)

2. Ohne[7] auf die interessante geschichtliche Entwicklung der alkoholischen Gärung einzugehen, können wir letztere den enzymatischen Vorgängen zuzählen.

O. without g. historical E. development
G. fermentation e. entering in, going into
l. latter V. processes z. ascribe to

3. Um[7] das Preisbildungsproblem für den hier betrachteten **Fall** zu lösen, brauchen wir[7] also nur die n Preise
—— als die Unbekannten des **Problems** zu betrachten.

U-zu in order to P. price-formation-problem
b. considered z. l. to solve b. need
U. unknowns b. consider

—— 4. Teils um[7] diese grossen **Scharen** auseinander zu halten, teils um[7] den weiteren Vormarsch gegen die **Drina**
—— einzuleiten, erteilte Baron Phillip der Truppendivision
—— den **Auftrag**[7], über den **Fluss** vorzurücken, um[7] sich der[3] nach **Rogatio** führenden Strasse bis in die Gegend dieses
—— **Ortes** zu versichern.

T. partially S. groups a. apart
w. further V. advance
e. to induce, start ert. issued
A. order v. advance u-zu in order to
f. which leads S. highway G. region
v. assure O. place

DISCUSSION: Why are there four "flags" out in this sentence? Explain why a "7" is found over certain words. What are now the pivot nouns? why rule 3 in line 4?

5. Um die Messungsergebnisse, also die Masszahlen der Längenmessung auch dann vergleichen zu können, wenn die Messungen von verschiedenen Personen ausgeführt worden sind, ist man übereingekommen, allerorts dieselbe Längeneinheit zugrunde zu legen.

M. measuring-results M. measuring numbers
L. length measurement v. compare
M. measurements v. different a. carried out
ü. agreed a. everywhere
L. length unit z. z. l. to take as a basis'

Where would you put a flag in this sentence? a 7? a 4? What nouns become now the bold face nouns?

D

1. Wir tun besser,[7] die Farbstoffe einfach in wasserlösliche und **wasserunlösliche** zu trennen.

b. better F. color-materials e. simply w. water soluble t. separate w. water insoluble

2. Es ist eine alltägliche Aufgabe des organischen Chemikers[7], neu aufgefundene Substanzen durch einige einfache Bestimmungen mit bereits **bekannten** zu vergleichen.

a. every-day, commonplace A. task
n. newly a. found e. some
e. simple B. determinations b. already
v. compare b. known (ones)

DISCUSSION: When a shift is made to pick up a verb with "zu", work back to the next noun—OR TO A WORD THAT CAN MODIFY A NOUN. Note how in these two sentences you are not able to go back farther than the adjectives which should modify nouns. See also Rule 5-C and Rule 6-C on this point.

What other adjective endings could there be on "wasserunlösliche" and "bekannten" that would stop you on the way back?

E

THE "DA" WORDS MAY CALL FOR "ZU"

If a "da" word calls for a "zu" verb, remove the **da** or **dar** and make out of the "zu" verb an "ing" form in English.

A "da" word such as darin, darauf, dadurch, dazu, in one part of the sentence may call for a "zu" in another. If there is a "zu" with a verb on the break, a "da" word could be sufficient call for it. (See also discussion of "da" words—appendix 23:3.) The following sentences illustrate more fully what is meant by "da" words and how they "call" for an infinitive with "zu".

1. Der Nutzen einer guten Hypothese besteht also wesentlich darin[7], unsere Erkenntnis der **Naturerscheinungen** zu vertiefen und zu erweitern.

N. utility b. consists
w. essentially d. in-doing What?
v. intensifying e. broadening

2. Bis vor kurzem beschränkte man sich darauf[7], durch Betupfen mit antiseptischen Flüssigkeiten die eingewanderten Erreger abzutöten.

v. k. until recently d. to (what?)
B. dabbing F. liquids e. invading
E. exciters, germs a. killing off

3. Besonders in früherer Zeit begnügte man sich meistens damit[7], aus zugänglichen Durchschnittszahlen die quantitative Zusammensetzung der Kost einfach zu berechnen.

B. especially f. earlier b. m. s. one was content
d. there with (to what?) D. average numbers
Z. composition b. computing

DISCUSSION: Give reasons for the "7" in sentences 1, 2, 3. Note how the "da" word calls for the "zu". Frequently the "to" is avoided in English by the use of the present participle. The first sentence could then read: "The utility of a good hypothesis consists essentially in intensifying and broadening our knowledge of the natural phenomena. How then would you translate sentences 2 and 3. While it is not incorrect and might even be preferable to use the present participle, for the time being try to use the "to" in order to get the habit of taking care of the "zu" verb. Continue to flag the line on which the "zu" verb is located. The "da" word may be the call for it.

4. **Trotz** all dieser **Bewegungen** in den Kolonien zur **Erhaltung** der **Freiheit** dachte niemand im Ernst daran[7], das Band zwischen **England und den Kolonien zu** lösen.

T. in spite of B. movements E. preservation
F. freedom n. no one E. seriously
d. there-on (to what?) z. l. of dissolving

5. **Aristoteles** ging nur darauf[7] hinaus[2], die logischen Tatsachen in **Beziehung** auf **Satzbildung** und **Schlussverfahren** zu sammeln.

h. proceeded d. there-to (to what?)
T. facts B. relation S. proposition formation
z. s. to gather
S. process of reasoning, conclusion

6. **Wir** legen keinen **Wert** darauf[7], näher auf diese Frage von der geheimnisvollen Zusammenstellung dieser **Gebilde** einzugehen, ehe wir das Wesen der **Schwerkraft** kennen gelernt haben.

W. value d. there-upon (to what)
g. mysterious Z. composition G. structures
e. to go in W. nature S. gravity

DISCUSSION: Cite reasons for the position of the numbers in sentences 4, 5, 6. Also indicate why certain nouns are bold faced and where you would put a flag. Note how the "da" word calls for "zu".

F

SOME SPECIFIC VERBS MAY CALL FOR "ZU"

Scheinen, brauchen, pflegen, (seem, need, to be accustomed to) may call for "zu". Usually the same verbs which call for "to" in English will call for "zu" in German.

1. Die Moleküle scheinen[7] in diesen verdünntesten aller bekannten **Medien** so weit voneinander entfernt zu sein, dass keines[4] die Anziehung eines **andern** spürt.

s. seem (to what?) v. most dilute
b. known e. removed
A. attraction a. other sp. feels, senses

2. Der Preis braucht[7] nur auf dieser Knappheit zu beruhen, ist[6] keineswegs notwendig als eine Bedingung des Angebots des betreffenden **Produktionsmittels** aufzufassen.

b. needs (to what?) K. scarcity
b. depend k. in no way n. necessary
B. condition A. supply b. concerned
a. to be interpreted, conceived

See also sentences 7, 9, 12 (B) for other verbs commonly used with "zu".

Rule 8

WHEN SHIFTS ARE CALLED FOR BY
und, aber, oder, sondern, denn, wie, etc.

Illustration:

Das Oregongebiet wurde[6] .... NOUN[1] beansprucht und[8] .... NOUN[1] festgestellt.

DISCUSSION: Rule 8 is the last of the five rules used to remove verbs from the end position. The verbs on the two breaks in this sentence must now be removed. Rule 6 applies in the first case, since "wurde" is a stop verb. Rule 8 removes the last verb. This rule has certain characteristics which distinguish it from other verb rules. Again it is necessary to focus your attention on the nouns in front of the verbs, for these nouns give you the signal to go ahead after the verbs are removed.

A

RULE 8.

If after the coordinating conjunctions the subject and predicate do not follow, check the next break or breaks to see if there is another verb form that might be used with the already indicated subject. This rule applies almost always when a **subject** and **predicate** do not follow "und, aber, oder, denn, sondern ". If a verb form is present, pick it up and work back again to the first noun—your signal to go on forward. Check carefully these illustrations:

1. Das Oregongebiet wurde[6] auf Grund der Entdeckung und **Besiedlung** beansprucht und[8] schliesslich durch Vertrag mit Grossbritannien am 15. Juni 1846 zur Nordgrenze der Vereinigten **Staaten** festgestellt.

O. Oregon territory G. basis E. discovery
B. settlement b. claimed s. finally
N. northern boundary
V. S. United States f. established.

DISCUSSION: The two bold-face nouns are actually on the two breaks in this sentence. The verbs come out automatically by the application of the rules 6 and 8 respectively. Since after "und" you do not have a subject and predicate, check the next break to see if there is **another verb** used with the same subject. If there is, pick it up after "und" and then work straight ahead to the noun.

2. Man muss[6] aus diesem Umstande die **Konsequenz** ziehen und[8] die ganze sogenannte Wertlehre vollständig aus der ökonomischen **Wissenschaft** ausmustern

U. circumstance
z. draw g. entire s. so called W. value theory
v. completely a. eliminate

DISCUSSION: Why is there a "6" on **muss**? an "8" on **und**? Why these two bold face nouns?

3. Nun wollen wir einen zweiten Reiz von derselben Grösse nehmen und allmählich seine Intensität um sehr kleine Beträge wachsen lassen.

R. stimulus d. the same (app. 14, 1)
G. size n. take a. gradually u. by
B. amounts w. grow l. let

DISCUSSION: Where would you put a "6"? an "8"? Why in each case? Underline the nouns that should then be in bold face type. If a subject and predicate followed "und", there would be no cause for a shift and you would be permitted to go straight ahead, or go ahead at least until a shift is called for.

4. McDowell erhielt sofort den Befehl,[7] das Vorgehen gegen **Richmond** zu unterlassen und[8] mit den beiden anderen nach dem Schenandoah **Tale** zu marschieren.

e. received B. command (to what?)
z. u. to discontinue and what?
T. valley Why rule 7? rule 8?

5. Lemonier will[6] nicht nur Land und **Leute** beschreiben, sondern[8] **auch** in die Seele des Volkes und des **Landes** eindringen.

b. describe Le. people
s. but (what?) S. soul
e. penetrate

DISCUSSION: Give the reason for each of the numbers on this page. Show also why certain nouns **appear in bold face type.** If in doubt, go over the sentence again and again in order to become more familiar with the **rules. Your object** is to remove elements on the right side of the **noun.**

6. Wenn wir[4] ablenkende **Einflüsse** ausschalten, und[8] die Aufmerksamkeit auf eine einzelne **Empfindung** konzentrieren, so steht diese klar und deutlich vor **uns.**[1]

a. distracting E. influences a. eliminate
A. attention e. individual E. sensation
d. distinctly

7. Einzelne Bemühungen hervorragender Denker[7], sich von diesem zu befreien und[8] zu einer natürlichen **Auffassung** zu gelangen, blieben hoffnungslos.[1]

e. single B. efforts h. of outstanding
b. liberate A. conception
g. come b. remained h. hopeless

8. **Wenn** die Berechnung[4] nicht möglich ist, so misst man den **Rauminhalt** eines **Körpers**[1], indem man[4] ihn in **Wasser** eintaucht und[8] **das** Volumen der verdrängten Wassermenge mittels einer **der angegebenen Methoden** misst.

B. computation m. measures
R. space-content K. body i. (in that), by—ing
e. immerse u. and (what) v. displaced
W. water quantity m. by means of a. stated

9. **Die Materialien,** die[5] von uns nicht produziert werden können, **oder**[8] **jedenfalls zur Zeit** nicht produziert werden, weil sie[4] leichter **direkt aus der Natur** zu haben sind, nennen wir Rohmaterialien im eigentlichen **Sinne.**[1]

v. u. by us Why rule 5?
j. at any rate Why rule 8?
w. because Why rule 4? z. h. to be had (app. 12, 1) R. raw materials e. real

B

OPTIONAL

PRACTICE SENTENCES FOR RULE 8

The sentences in this section are intended for drill and practice. The use of them is left entirely to the wishes of either teachers or individuals. Some teachers may feel that their classes are well enough familiar with rule 8, while others may find that they need more drill. The same applies to individuals. In either case, the sentences offer good examples of certain types of sentences encountered in reading complicated German.

The time spent in working with these extra sentences may prove to be very profitable. These illustrations are very long and often involve many of the rules now familiar to the reader. It is interesting to see how one rule dovetails with another in the unraveling of a complicated sentence. If you choose to go over them, answer also the questions asked in the margin. They are intended also for drill purposes. Give reasons for each of the numbers.

1. Kant hat[6] allerdings diesen **Standpunkt** bisweilen verlassen und[8] namentlich an einigen sehr merkwürdigen **Stellen,** die ich[4] in meiner natürlichen **Schöpfungsgeschichte** ausführlich besprochen habe, sich in ganz entgegengesetztem **Sinne** ausgesprochen.

a. of course b. at times
v. abandoned n. especially m. noticeable
S. places S. creative-history
a. extensively b. discussed
e. opposite S. sense a. expressed

2. Er machte seine Studien von 1810 bis 1814 in **Dorpat**[1] und ging **dann nach Würzburg**[1], wo Dollinger[4] ihn nicht allein in die vergleichende **Anatomie** einführte, sondern[8] auch durch seine naturphilosophische **Richtung** höchst befruchtend und anregend auf **ihn**[1] wirkte.

m. pursued why rule 1? rule 4?
a. alone, only v. comparative s. but (what?)
R. direction, trend h. highly
b. fruitfully a. stimulatingly
w. act, effect

DISCUSSION: Review the diagram on the inside cover of the book or on page 1. The object is to remove elements on the right side of the double line—or the bold face noun. Note that "ihn", a pronoun, stops you from going back just as does a noun. You would also not go back farther if you encounter a word that could modify a noun. See Rule 5-C, also rules 6 C and 7 D.

3. Die Behandlung der Diphtheritis beschränkte sich darauf,[7] durch Betupfen mit antiseptischen Flüssigkeiten die eingewanderten **Erreger** abzutöten und[8] die Kräfte des Patienten durch reichen **Weingenuss** hochzuhalten und[8] das Fieber durch Bäder und **Medikamente** zu bekämpfen und[8] schliesslich durch **Luftröhrenschnitt der Erstickungsgefahr** vorzubeugen.

B. treatment b. s. was limited (app. 11, 4a)
d. there-to (to what?) B. dabbing
e. invading E. germs, exciters a. killing off
K. energies, strength r. rich h. keeping up
F. fever B. baths z. b. combating
s. finally L. incision of the trachea
v. obviate E. danger of suffocation

DISCUSSION: Show why rules 7 and 8 are involved in this sentence. On a separate sheet, draw a diagram of this sentence according to the diagram on page 1. What importance do you attach to the bold face nouns?

4. Wir sind nun zur Zeit im Besitze einiger Erfahrungsgesetze **und Hypothesen,**[1] die[5] von weitgehender Anwendbarkeit zwar für jeden Zweig der **Naturforschung** sind und[8] demgemäss einer didaktischen Behandlung jedes **Zweiges** vorangestellt zu werden verdienen, aber[8] ganz besondere Berücksichtigung bei der Darlegung des gegenwärtigen Standes der theoretischen **Chemie** verlangen.

Z. time B. possession E. experimental laws
w. far-reaching A. applicability
z. indeed Z. branch N. natural science
d. accordingly e. d. to a didactic
v. z. w. v. deserve to be place ahead of
B. consideration D. presentation g. present
S. state v. demand. Why rules 1, 5, 8?

5. Er war es, der[5] die Philosophie nach **Athen,** von jetzt an Mittelpunkt des geistigen Lebens in **Griechenland,** verpflanzte, und[8] namentlich durch seine persönliche Beziehung zu Perikles, Euripides und anderen bedeutenden Männern, auf die damalige Zeitbildung einen entscheidenden **Einfluss** übte.

e.w.e. it was he Why rule 5?
M. center g. intellectual L. life
v. transplanted What does "und" call for?
B. relation b. significant
d. then e. decisive
ü. exercised E. influence

6. Dies bedeutet, dass das Prinzip der Knappheit[4] nicht allein **ausreicht,** um[7] die **Preisbildung** zu bestimmen, sondern[8] durch gewisse supplementäre Prinzipien, welche[5] neue Bedingungen der **Preisbildung** darstellen und[8] die Unbestimmtheit des **Problems** aufheben, ergänzt werden muss.

b. means K. scarcity (why rule 4)
a. suffices u.z.b. in order to determine
s. but —why rule 8? Connect with **muss.**
B. conditions d. represent
U. uncertainty a. remove e. supplemented

DISCUSSION: What are your pivot nouns? What rules help you to "remove" the verbs? Note how "sondern" calls for "muss' as the other verbs are in their own clauses. When you shift to pick up "muss" and you work back to the noun, do not go back past a comma, for then you may become involved in another clause.

7. Um[7] das Preisbildungsproblem für den hier betrachteten **Fall zu lösen,** brauchen[7] wir also nur die n Preise als die Unbekannten **des Problems** zu betrachten und[8] dieselben nach der gewöhnlichen mathematischen **Methode** vorläufig als gegeben anzunehmen.

P. price-formation-problem b. considered
z. l. solve b. need
U. unknowns b. consider
g. ordinary v. tentatively a.g. as given
a. to assume. Why rules 7 and 8?

8. Die Energie bewährt sich hier als eine gute **Dienerin,**[1] indem sie[4] uns nicht nur den Überblick über das **Tatsachenmaterial** erleichtert, sondern[8] uns auch gleichzeitig häufig die unmittelbaren Ergebnisse der **Beobachtungen** erweitern und vertiefen hilft.

b.s. proves itself
i. in that Ü. survey T. fact material
e. facilities s. but (what?) Note: **help us to**
u. immediate E. results e. broaden and
v. intensify

9. Wir können[6] also das **Prinzip** aufstellen, dass für den hier betrachteten Fall unbestimmter Produktionskosten der Preis gleich der Quote zwischen Gesamtkosten und Nachfrage bei diesem **Preis** sein muss und[8] durch die gleichförmige Verteilung der **Gesamtkosten auf die Nachfrage** bestimmt sein muss und[8] folglich mit den so berechneten **Durchschnittskosten** übereinstimmen muss.

a. formulate
b: considered u. indefinite
g. equal G. total costs N. demand
g. uniform V. distribution
G. total costs N. demand b. determined
f. consequently b. computed D. average costs
ü. agree.

DISCUSSION: Give reasons for each of the numbers. Indicate why certain nouns are bold faced. Draw a diagram on a separate sheet similar to the one on page 1 and show how each division ends with a noun.

10. Niemand kann ohne mannigfache Veranstaltungen die topographischen Grundlagen für den Flächeninhalt des Landes mit seinen Gebietsabteilungen und für die Lage der Berge und Flüsse gewinnen oder Volks—und Viehzählungen vornehmen, oder Geburten, Trauungen und Todesfälle notieren und die Culturflächen an Acker, Wiese, Weide und Wald feststellen oder die Einfuhr und Ausfuhr der verschiedenen Waaren in den verschiedenen Grenzen ermitteln, oder öffentliche Einnahmen und Ausgaben kennen.

N. no one m. various V. preparations
G. basis F. area-content
G. regional divisions L. location
B. mountains F. rivers g. win, gain
v. undertake G. births T. weddings
A. acre W. meadow W. pasture W. forest
f. determine E. import A. export
W. commodities v. different G. borders
e. ascertain ö. public E. income
A. expenditures k. know

DISCUSSION: There should be five "8"s in this sentence. Locate the position for each one. A "6" would be placed above "kann", why? What nouns should now be bold faced? Have someone read the sentence to you and observe in particular rule 8.

11. Er würde[6] dann die **Wahl**[7] gehabt haben, entweder auf dem Nordufer des Jamesfluss gegen **Richmond** vorzugehen oder[8] durch Übergang auf das Südufer gleichzeitig gegen die Verbindungen der Hauptstadt mit dem übrigen Teil der **Konföderation** zu operieren, oder[8] die Verbindung mit dem **Yorkfluss** momentan preiszugeben und[8] kühn gegen Richmond vorzugehen, um[7] im Falle eines ungünstigen Ausgangs des erwarteten Kampfes nach dem **Jamesfluss** zurückzuziehen.

W. choice (to what?) e. either
N. north-bank v. to proceed
Ü. transfer S. south bank V. communication
H. capitol ü. remaining T. part
o. or (what?)
p. abandon k. boldly
F. case u. unfavorable A. outcome
e. expected K. battle z. to withdraw

a) DISCUSSION: Note how one rule interlocks with the other to form a coherent whole. Note how it is possible to follow two main rules in the translation of this sentence. Draw a diagram as is shown on page 1 to indicate how all of the verbs in this sentence are removed—back to the next noun.

b) Rule 8 will also apply in case verbs continue to fall in front of successive breaks even though "und, aber, oder, sondern" are not present. Repeat this sentence leaving out "oder" and "und" and note how rule 8 is still applicable.

C

OTHER "LITTLE" WORDS THAT MAY CALL FOR VERBS

These are usually the following:

wie as, than, how	also therefore, hence	doch still, however	ja to be sure, indeed
als as, than, when	somit therefore, consequently	d. h. that is, i.e.	sowie just as, so as

1. Wie[8] aus der **Zusammenstellung** hervorgeht, bestehen bei den einzelnen Arten beträchtliche Unterschiede hinsichtlich der Temperaturkardinalpunkte der **Sporenbildung.**[1]

wie as h. follows Z. table
e. individual A. types b. considerable
U. differences h. with regard to

DISCUSSION: The word "wie" often calls for a verb as in this case even though the subject may not have been announced. Continue to watch the pivot nouns as heretofore.

2. Durch diese Bedingung wird[6] der **Einheitspreis** im allgemeinen bestimmt, d. h.[8] in den Preisen der mitwirkenden **Produktionsmittel** ausgedrückt und[8] somit in die Unbestimmtheit der **Produktionskosten** gehoben.

B. condition E. unit-price
b. determined d. h. that is (what?)
a. expressed m. cooperating
U. indefiniteness g. raised

3. Die Kompressibilität ist anfänglich grösser, als[8] dem Boyleschen **Gesetze** entspricht.

a. initially a. than (what?)
G. law e. corresponds

4. Viele Offiziere scheinen[7] lieber die Kräfte unserer Soldaten durch **Überanstrengung** abzunutzen, als[8] die Hülfe farbiger Menschen zur Arbeit an den **Verschanzungen** anzunehmen.

s. seem (to what?) l. rather, prefer K. strength
Ü. over-exertion a. to wear out
H. aid f. colored M. people V. trenches
a. to accept What calls for this verb?

DISCUSSION: Keep in mind that these little words may often call for verbs. If they do, pick up the verbs and work back to the noun as you have been doing in rules 4, 5, 6, 7.

D

ADJECTIVES MAY BE PICKED UP

just as verbs in rule 8. These adjectives may be located on successive breaks. The same words which call for verbs on the breaks, e.g., **und, aber, oder, denn, sondern,** and the little words mentioned in section C, may also call for adjectives. Follow these illustrations:

1. Die Bewegungsgeschwindigkeit der Bakterien ist[6] bei den einzelnen **Arten** verschieden und[8] bei ein und derselben Art von einer **Reihe** äusserer **Einflüsse** abhängig.

B. motion-velocity
e. individual A. types v. different
R. series ä outer, external E. influences
a. dependent

DISCUSSION: What does **"ist"** call for? **und?** Why are the two nouns bold faced?

2. Dieser Student ist[6] dem Lehrer zu jeder **Zeit** behilflich, doch[8] **der deutschen Sprache** vollständig gleichgültig.

b. helpful
d. still S. language v. completely
g. indifferent

DISCUSSION: Give reasons for the position of 6 and 8. Show why these two nouns are bold faced. Note that both **behilflich** and **gleichgültig** are adjectives and they are removed by the rules. Read the sentence several times until you do not need the numbers. See diagram page 1—three b.

3. Von einer bestimmten Belastung an ist,[6] wie[8] bereits auf Seite 183 ausgeführt worden ist, die Verlängerung eines **Drahtes** stärker, als[8] der **Proportionalität** entsprechen würde.

b. certain, definite B. load, charge a. on
v. already a. stated, carried out
V. elongation D. wire s. greater
e. correspond

DISCUSSION: Rule 8 aids in removing verbs from the end position. Give reasons why this rule is applicable on two occasions in this sentence. Also show why certain nouns are bold faced. Note that "ist" can take out a predicate adjective and that **"wie"** and **"als"** may call for verbs.

E

What to do if the Auxiliary verb is missing

In many sentences it frequently happens that the auxiliary verb is missing with some participles and infinitives. This is especially the case with rule 8.

The auxiliary verbs **haben, sein, werden** (discussed in rule 6) may be used with two or more participles or infinitives. Compare the following sentences in English:

These songs have been written, published and sold in Germany.

The students will read, write and study their German assignment.

Just as in English, the German may choose not to repeat the auxiliary verbs with each participle or infinitive. It would not be necessary to say, for example: These songs have been written, **have been** published and **have been** sold. The only difficulty that should arise in the German text is that the auxiliary verb would be placed at the end of the sentence. It would be necessary to **"borrow"** an auxiliary from the last break in the sentence if other participles are found on successive breaks **without an auxiliary verb.** Study carefully these model sentences:

1. Dieses Prinzip muss[6]..................NOUN aufgegeben X oder[8]..................NOUN angenommen werden.

DISCUSSION: Here an X is placed where the first auxiliary verb is expected. The verb "werden" (to be) may be repeated as many times as there are participles that need an auxiliary verb.

This principle must.......... **be** given up or[8] **be** accepted. (Note the "be" for each participle form.) Rule 8 is usually involved in this type of construction.

When the shift is made to pick up the verb (and you have to borrow an auxiliary) GO BACK TO THE FIRST PARTICIPLE. In other words, take the participles in their order. Note how you would pick up "aufgegeben" in this sentence before you do "angenommen".

2. Weiterhin muss[6] die **Erscheinung** beobachtet werden, d. h. ihr Verlauf muss[6] sofort festgestellt X und auf messbare **Grössen** zürückgeführt werden.

W. further E. phenomenon b. observed d. that is V. course f. established m. measurable G. factors, magnitudes

DISCUSSION: Cite reasons for the position of 6 and the X. Show why the two nouns are in heavy print. See also appendix 7, 6 for use of muss—zurückgeführt werden.

3. Eine Wissenschaft besteht aus einer grossen Gruppe von **Beobachtungen,**[1] die[5] zueinander in **Beziehung** gesetzt X und[8] unter allgemeine **Gesetze** geordnet sind.

W. science b. consists B. observations z. to one another B. relation a. general G. laws g. arranged

DISCUSSION: What does the X stand for? What does "die" call for? und? Why two bold face nouns?

4. Wir dürfen[6] auch mit **Recht** annehmen, dass zahlreiche Farbstoffe[4] als Leukoverbindung aus der **Zelle** ausgeschieden X und[8] dann zur gefärbten **Verbindung** oxydiert werden.

d. may R. justice a. assume z. numerous F. dyes Z. cell a. extracted g. colored V. compound

DISCUSSION: Give reasons for each of the numbers. Why is there an X in this sentence.

5. Ein intensiver Fortschritt geschah im Jahre 1783,[1] in welchem die Zellentheorie[4] begründet X und[8] auch für die Entwicklungsgeschichte plötzlich ein neues Gebiet der **Forschung** eröffnet wurde.

F. progress g. occurred Z. cell theory b. founded E. evolutionary history p. suddenly G. field F. research e. opened

DISCUSSION: What verb does "Zellentheorie" call for? why not "begründet"? Why the X?

6. Voltaire ist der grosse **Schriftsteller,**[1] welcher[5] nicht nur dieser Sache den beredtesten **Ausdruck** gegeben X sondern[8] auch die positiven Momente der **Aufklärung** nachdrücklich vertreten hat.

S. writer d. S. this matter b. most eloquent M. factors A. enlightenment n. emphatically v. represented

DISCUSSION: Which verb does "welcher" call for? sondern? What does the X stand for? Why these bold face nouns? When you pick up the auxiliary BE SURE TO GO BACK TO THE FIRST PARTICIPLE.

7. Die Methode der Selbstbewegung des Begriffs aber vervollkommnet **Hegel,**[1] indem er[4] zunächst an dem Begriff des Seins jene **Gegensätze,** nachzuweisen X und[8] dann dieselben auch auf alle anderen **Begriffsstufen** anzuwenden sucht.

S. self-movement B. concept a. however v. perfects i. in that z. first of all B. concept S. existence G. contradiction n. to show B. concept-stages, levels a. to apply s. seeks

DISCUSSION: Observe that "er" actually calls for "sucht" and that this is now first used with **"nachzuweisen"** —NOT ANZUWENDEN. Note how rule 8 is now involved, in that the "und" calls for the verb **"sucht"** again. Explain why each of the three nouns is bold faced.

8. Die Bakterientoxine sind kompliziert gebaute Gifte von grösster **Wirksamkeit,**[1], die[5] von der **Bakterienzelle** gebildet und[8] entweder als Endotoxine in der lebenden **Zelle** zurückgehalten oder[8] als Ektotoxine in das umgebende **Substrat** abgegeben werden.

g. formed G. poisons g. greatest W. effectiveness g. formed e. either z. held back u. surrounding a. given off

DISCUSSION: Cite reasons for the position of each of the numbers. Note that "die" calls for "werden" and that this verb is used with several participles. Borrow this "werden" and then go back to the first participle, the second, the third and as many others as there may be. Now show why certain nouns are bold faced. Draw a diagram of the sentence similar to that given on page 1. Show what rules you use to remove elements beyond the double line.

F

ALS, WIE

Als and **wie** may be classed as breaks, for oftentimes you may find prefixes, predicate adjectives and verbs in front of these two words. If you find need to shift to pick up one of these words, (particularly verbs) and it is not on the "break" as you expect it to be, see if it is in front of **"als"** or **"wie"**. No confusion should arise in your mind on this point, if you will keep in mind that these two words may be classed as breaks just like **und, aber, oder, denn, sondern.**

1. Meistens werden[6] aussen immer niederere Drucke herrschen als im Innern der **Bakterienzelle.**[1]

m. mostly w. will (app. 7, 4) n. lower D. pressures h. prevail I. inside

DISCUSSION: You are still following rule 1 and you should be able to translate directly to the last noun. However, you are stopped on "werden" (a stop verb—rule 6). Note that the verb that goes with "werden" appears in front of **"als"**—now one of your breaks.

2. Das Gesetz sagt, dass die ausgestrahlte Wärmemenge[4] sich genau so verhält wie die vierte Potenz der absoluten Temperatur des strahlenden **Körpers.**[1]

G. law a. exradiated W. heat quantity
v. g. behaves itself
s. radiating R. body

DISCUSSION: Why is it that you cannot proceed directly to the noun on the break as rule 1 tells you to do? Where is the verb this time? If it helps you to see more clearly the verb form, put a comma in front of "wie". Some older German books used to have a comma here.

3. Die elektromotorische Kraft wird[6] mit Hilfe eines Ohmschen Gesetzes definiert als die Spannung an den Enden eines **Leiters.**[1]

K. power H. help, aid W. is (see app. 7, 5, a)
G. law S. tension, voltage
L conductor

DISCUSSION: Give reasons for each of the numbers. Where are the "breaks" in this sentence? Why is it impossible to translate directly to **"Leiters"?**

4. Auf unsere Sprache und Literatur hat Luthers Bibel einen so weitreichenden Einfluss gewonnen wie kein anderes Buch.

S. language
w. far-reaching E. influence g. gained
a. other

DISCUSSION: Where would you insert a "6" why? a "1"? Where are the breaks in this sentence? Do not forget that "als" and "wie" may be breaks. What nouns would you now bold face?

5. Es hat[6] sich noch weit später unter viel grösseren Schwierigkeiten entwickelt als ihre natürliche **Schwester,**[1] die **Keimesgeschichte.**[1]

s. later g. greater
S. difficulties e.h.s.e. it has been developed
(note app. 11, 4, d) S. sister
K. germinal history

DISCUSSION: Why is it not possible to translate directly toward the noun "Schwester"? Where are the "breaks" in this sentence? Give reasons for the numbers 1 and 6.

6. Die Bodenbenutzung nimmt im Preisbildungsprozess prinzipiell dieselbe Stellung ein wie die anderen **Produktionsfaktoren.**[1]

B. use-of-land What goes with "nimmt"?
S. position e. occupies

DISCUSSION: With the noun on the end, you should be able to go right to this noun according to rule 1. What is the other break in the sentence? Note that a prefix could appear in front of "als" and "wie" just as a verb does.

7. Die Kenntnis der deutschen Literatur ist[6] für den Studenten ebenso lehrreich wie die Kenntnis der englischen **Literatur.**[1]

K. knowledge
S. student l. instructive

DISCUSSION: Note that prefixes (as in sentence 6), verbs (as in sentences 1-5) may be found in front of als and wie. Sentence 7 shows that adjectives may also appear in front of "als" and "wie". Note "lehrreich" in this sentence.

Rule 9

THE DOUBLE NOUN RULE

A

WHEN TWO NOUNS ARE ON THE BREAK (and the last noun is not preceded by "des" or "der") PICK UP THE LAST NOUN WITH THE VERB. Compare also the diagram on page 1—Type 2-b.

Illustration:

Delegaten nahmen / .... **Friedens-Kongress**[1] Teil.[9]

Delegaten aus allen Teilen der Union nahmen an den Versammlungen des **Friedens-Kongress** Teil.[9]
Delegates from all parts of the union took .... part in the assemblies of the peace congress.

DISCUSSION: Some writers would not capitalize "teil" and would use it as a prefix. Hence rules 9 and 2 are similar in that in both instances the verbs are not complete. Either a prefix may go with a verb and change its meaning or a noun may go with it.

1. **Luther hatte sowohl mit Humanismus wie mit der Mystik Fühlung.**[9] — s-w. both as; F. contact

DISCUSSION: Why is "Mystik" bold faced and not "Fühlung"? Note that "Fühlung" goes with "hatte" just as much as a prefix would be used with a verb.

2. Lincoln nahm von seinen Freunden in **Washington** Abschied.[9] — **F. friends; A. leave Why rule 9? Why the bold faced noun?**

3. Plotin lehrte seit seinem vierzigsten Jahre in **Rom** Philosophie.[9] — **v. fortieth J. year; Why rule 9?**

4. **Die Lehrsätze der Thermodynamik verlangen bei der wissenschaftlichen Untersuchung jeder einzelnen Naturerscheinung Beachtung.**[9] — L. theorems v. demand; w. scientific U. investigation; N. natural phenomenon B. respect

DISCUSSION: What calls for this last noun? Under what conditions would it not be permissible to pick up this noun?

5. **Die Unabhängigkeitserklärung des Jahres 1776 nahm auf die Verletzung derartiger Rechte Bezug**[9] **und stellte selbst eine Reihe unäusserlicher Rechte auf.**[2] — **U. independence declaration n. took; V. violation d. of such R. rights; s. itself R. series u. inalienable; Bezug (regard)**

DISCUSSION: What goes with "nahm"? why? What is the pivot noun? Compare this sentence now with the diagram on page 1, type two b. The "Bezug" is just as much a part of the verb nahm as auf is a part of "stellte". Observe that you always remove the "last" noun with the verb.

6. **In neuerer Zeit kommen bei wissenschaftlichen und auch bei vielen technischen Messungen immer mehr die elektrischen Thermometer in Gebrauch.**[9] — **n. more recent w. scientific; M. measurements; i. G. in use (why rule 9?)**

7. **Man macht von der Trennung der Holzzellen auch bei der Darstellung der**[3] **als Papierstoff verwendeten Holzzellulose Gebrauch.**[9] — **T. separation H. wood cells**; D. production P. paper material; **v. which was used G. use**

DISCUSSION: Show why rule 9 is involved in this sentence. Also rule 3. Two nouns should be written with bold face type, which nouns? NOTE THAT YOU PICK UP THE "LAST" NOUN WITH THE VERB IN RULE 9.

B

Since verbs are found on the end of the clause or sentence, it is necessary to use rules 4, 5, 6, 7 and 8 to remove these verbs. When such shifts are made, work back word for word to the next noun. This is your signal to move straight forward again from the position from which the skip was made.

WHEN YOU SHIFT TO PICK UP THE VERB AND YOU HAVE WORKED BACK TO THE NOUN, AND YOU FIND TWO NOUNS CLOSE TOGETHER, PICK UP ONE OF THESE NOUNS WITH THE VERB. Hence no matter whether you are moving forward as in the sentences under A or backward to the noun, IT IS ALWAYS THE LAST NOUN THAT COMES OUT WITH THE VERB.

DO NOT PICK UP A NOUN IF IT IS PRECEDED BY DES OR DER OR WORDS WITH ES OR ER ENDINGS. You may pick up one, two or even three words with the verb.

Very often you have some choice in rule 9. You may choose to pick up the last noun and then again you may decide not to do so. It is a good plan to try to "pick up" a noun to the left of the verb when verbs are removed from the end position. Frequently an idiom is involved in Rule 9 and for the most part you will be taking care of the idiom without knowing that you are dealing with an idiom.

Illustration:

Wir wollen[6] .... **NOUN**[1] ‖ **Aufschluss**[9] **suchen.**

Compare with diagram, page 1—2b

Wir wollen auf Grund klarer Überlegung über die Probleme des Daseins ‖ **Aufschluss**[9] **suchen.**
We will—seek information—on the basis of clear consideration concerning the problems of existence.

Additional diagrams:

1. **Er hat**[6] .... **NOUN**[1] ‖ **NOUN**[9] **verb verb.**
2. **Das Gesetz kann**[6] .... **NOUN**[1] ‖ **in Beziehung**[9] **verb verb.**
3. **Henry Clay war es, der**[5] .... **NOUN**[1] ‖ **Grenzen verb verb verb.**

Compare these illustrations again with the diagram on page 1. Note that your object or aim in translation is to remove the elements on the right side of the double line. Rule 9 tells you now to pick up the last noun WHEN TWO NOUNS ARE CLOSE TOGETHER AND THE LAST NOUN IS NOT PRECEDED BY "DES" OR "DER".

4. Die amerikanische **Regierung** würde[6] wohl nur unter ganz abnormen **Umständen** in Versuchung[9] kommen. — R. government w. indeed, probably U. circumstances i. V. in temptation

DISCUSSION: Cite the reasons for the position of the numbers. Why is "U" bold-faced and not "V"?

5. Henry Clay war es, der[5] 1820 durch das sogenannte **Missouri** Kompromiss der weitern Ausbreitung der **Sklaverei** Grenzen[9] zu setzen suchte. — W. es. it was Why rule 5? s. so called d. w. a. to the further spread G. limits s. sought

DISCUSSION: When you shift to pick up the verb, how far back do you go? What noun becomes now the "pivot" noun? Why is rule 9 involved?

6. Was[5] hier ausgeführt wird, soll für jede **Wirtschaftsform** Geltung haben. — a. carried out, stated s. is said to G. validity W. economic form

DISCUSSION: Where would you put a 6? why? a 9? why? What noun becomes now the pivot noun? Draw a diagram of the sentence to show how it corresponds with the diagram page 1, type two b.

7. Eine grosse Zahl von **Bakterienarten** vermag[7] unter geeigneten Bedingungen und in der freien Natur Licht[9] zu entwickeln. — Z. number v. is able g. appropriate B. conditions e. develop Why is this noun bold-faced?

8. Lincoln sah sich genötigt,[7] von seinem Recht als **Präsident** und Chef der Land- und Seekräfte der **Union** [9]Gebrauch zu machen. — g. necessitated R. right S. sea forces G. use Why is this noun picked up?

9. So erklärte er, dass Literatur[4] nicht in technischer Geschicklichkeit, sondern in der ganzen **Lebensanschauung** ihre Wurzeln hatte. — e. explained Why rule 4 here? G. skill L. life philosophy W. roots (Why do you pick up this noun?)

10. Der Weg eines Körpers wird seine Bahn genannt, wenn man nur auf die Form des Weges Rücksicht nimmt. — K. body W. way B. path g. called R. regard Where would you put a 6? 9?

11. Vor allem in diesen praktischen Anwendungen kommt der konziliatorische Charakter der Leibnitzschen **Philosophie** [9]zur Geltung. — v. a. above all A. applications Why is this noun bold faced? G. value (Why rule 9?)

12. Wir können[6] sie erörtern, ohne[7] auf die **Qualität** Rücksicht[9] zu nehmen. — e. discuss w. without Why rule 7? R. regard (Why rule 9?)

13. In diesem ersten Kapitel wollen[6] wir unsere Untersuchungen auf die **Vorgänge** beschränken, die[5] für jede **Wirtschaft** in Betracht kommen und[8] somit für die Wirtschaft im allgemeinen eine wesentliche Bedeutung haben. — K. chapter U. investigations V. processes b. limit W. economy B. consideration s. consequently w. essential B. importance

DISCUSSION: All verbs on the right hand side of the nouns in these sentences are removed by the rules which are now familiar to you. Justify the position of each of the numbers in this sentence. No matter how many elements make up the structure of the sentence, each of the elements is taken care of by the rules. Note how "und" calls for "haben". Inasmuch as "Bedeutung" is far away from "Wirtschaft", do not pick up this noun.

14. Er gab von neuem seinem Zweifel in die Weisheit des[3] von McClellan vorgeschlagenen Präparationsplanes Ausdruck. — v. n. anew Z. doubt Why rule 3? v. which was proposed (why which?) Why rule 9? What is the pivot noun?

15. Der[3] mit der Pazifizierung dieser **Gegenden** betraute Rheinländer beschloss daher,[7] noch einmal einen kräftigen Schlag gegen diesen letzten Versuch der **Aufständischen** zu führen. — b. who was entrusted G. regions b. resolved d. therefore n. e. once more S. blow g. against V. attempt A. rebels f. lead, direct

DISCUSSION: Indicate why certain nouns are bold-faced. What calls for the "zu" verb? Give the reasons for the numbers. Why is it not permissible to pick up "Aufständischen" according to rule 9?

16. Die Kreuzzüge dienten,[7] die chemischen Kenntnisse und Ansichten der Araber nach Europa überzuführen, wo bei der mystischen Richtung jenes Zeitalters besonders die Lehre von der Metallverwandlung[4] ungemeinen **Eingang** fand und[8] teils auch die **Alchemisten** erweckte, welche[5] so mühselige als fruchtlose **Versuche** anstellten,[7] aus unedlen **Metallen** Gold[9] zu erhalten. — K. crusades d. served (to what?) A. views ü. to transfer R. trend Z. age b. especially L. theory M. metal transformation E. entrance Why rule 4? rule 8? t. partially e. awakened a. made f. fruitless V. attempts (to what?) e. obtain

Rule 10

WHAT TO DO WHEN THE VERB STARTS THE SENTENCE

A

When you begin to translate, intending perhaps to go directly ahead to the noun on the first break, and you find at the beginning of the sentence a **verb form,** survey the situation according to the steps now to be discussed.

Continue to focus your attention on the FIRST BREAK, for this gives you a signal how to approach the translation. If a noun is there, work directly to it. If on the way to the noun you get a signal to move out of line to pick up a needed element, make the shift and work back then to the next noun, your signal to go back into normal word order.

RULE 10.

WHEN THE VERB APPEARS FIRST IN THE SENTENCE LOOK FOR THE LITTLE WORD "SO" or "DANN" ON SOME SUBSEQUENT BREAK. (You may have to go several breaks before you find the so or dann.) IF YOU FIND THE "SO" (or dann), THEN YOU HAVE SOLVED THE PROBLEM OF TRANSLATION. The "so" is a signal that you are dealing with an "if" clause. The sentence will then unfold if you take the following steps.

1. Say "if" for the verb.

2. Pass up the verb and take the sentence word for word until you get the subject.
(care must be used to be sure to take "all of the subject".)

3. Drop back for the verb.

4. Follow the rules you have learned up to this point, i.e. if you have a noun on the break, follow rule 1. If another verb is to be removed, use rules 4, 5, 6, 7, 8 to remove the verbs.

ILLUSTRATIONS FOR RULE 10:

(if) subject
1. verb man .... NOUN[1] so .... NOUN[1].

10-6
2. (if) subject
verb wir .... NOUN[1] verb, so- or dann .... NOUN[1] verb.
(A "10" would appear because the verb is first, and a"6" would appear because it is a stop verb)

German sentence for illustration Number 1:

[10]Besitzt **eine Strömung** überall gleiche Richtung und **Geschwindigkeit**[1], so nennt man sie eine homogene **Strömung.**[1]

If a current—possesses everywhere equal direction and speed, so one calls it a homogeneous current. (you may leave out the "so" in translation.) Compare with illustration number 1.

German sentence for illustration Number 2:

[10]Wollen **wir** nun zu einer Wissenschaft der **Geschichte** gelangen, so müssen[6] wir diese sozialen **Gruppen** betrachten. (Compare with illustration number 2.)

If **we** will—come now to a science of history, we must consider these social groups.

Observations on rule 10:

The "so" will be found always on the "break" **after a comma.** A "dann" may also be used instead of "so", but either of them may be omitted in translation. The "so" or "dann" may be found many breaks away—don't be alarmed if you have to go several lines before you find it.

The author has intended to offer a good many illustrations for rule 10 inasmuch as there is so much interweaving of the other rules. However, some teachers and individuals may prefer not to take up all of the sentences at one time. Some of the sentences may be left for practice later. Follow carefully the discussion of each sentence.

3. [10]Beschränken wir uns auf das südamerikanische **Festland,**[1] so sehen wir die charakteristischen Eigentümlichkeiten aus dieser **Periode.**[1]

B. if we limit (Why if?) s. South American
F. continent E. peculiarities
Why rule 1? rule 10?

4. [10]Ist[6] ein fremdes **Gas** vorhanden, so findet die Bildung von Dampf in gleicher **Weise** statt,[2] bis sein Partialdruck[4] dem Dampfdruck gleich geworden ist.

f. foreign v. present B. formation
D. vapor g. W. same manner s. takes place
D. vapor pressure

DISCUSSION: Give reasons for each bold face noun and the position of each number.

5. [10]Ist nun die Verfassung nicht vollkommen genau auf diesen **Punkt,**[1] so kann[6] der Kongress sie nach Belieben ändern.

V. constitution v. perfectly g. exact
P. point Why rule 1? rule 10?
ä. change Bring in the subject when the verb precedes as does "kann".

6. [10] Dividiert man diesen Wert durch das **Molekulargewicht,**[1] so kann[6] man mittels dieser Zahl das spezifische Volumen mit einer Genauigkeit von 2% berechnen.

W. value M. molecular weight
m. by means of Z. number
G. accuracy b. compute Why rule 10? rule 6?

7. [10]Will[6] man sich schnell über das Röntgenspektrum eines gegebenen **Stoffes,**[1] z. B. für analytische **Zwecke,** orientieren, so wird[6] man vorteilhaft einen Spektographen mit kleinerer Dispersion und entsprechend kürzerer **Expositionsdauer** benutzen.

s. quickly R. X-Ray spectrum
g. given S. substance Z. purposes
w. will (app. 7, 4) v. advantageously
e. correspondingly k. shorter b. use.

DISCUSSION: Why is it not possible to go right to "Stoffes" according to rule 1? When you find the verb first, what must you then look for? Why are there two rules—10 and 6—at the very first of this sentence. What calls for "benutzen"? DO NOT GO BACK PAST A COMMA OR A NOUN.

8. [10]**Wird** nun durch Evakuieren der Gefässe der Druck[4] erniedrigt, **so kann**[6] man wie gewöhnlich durch Erhitzen des Gefässes **a** die Substanz zum **Sieden** bringen.

G. vessels D. pressure
e. lowered g. ordinarily E. heating
Si. boiling

DISCUSSION: Why is there a "10" on the first word? a "4" on Druck? a "6" on "kann"? Observe how far you must go before you pick up the subject. Do not be alarmed if you have to go far into the sentence before you encounter the subject. When you do pick up the subject, drop back for the verb and take care of the verb by your rules.

9. [10]Wirken auf denselben Massenpunkt gleichzeitig zwei Kräfte, **so stört** erfahrungsgemäss die eine nicht die **Wirkung** der anderen.

W. act, effect g. simultaneously
K. forces s. disturbs e. by way of experience
d. e. the one W. effect

DISCUSSION: Why a "10" on Wirken? How far do you now go before you encounter the subject? Why is it impossible to go directly to the first noun? Rearrange the last clause so that the subject comes in before the verb.

10. [10]Untersuchen wir beide Stücke genau, d. h. [10]bestimmen wir die[3] für **sie** charakteristische Eigenschaften, wie Farbe, Elastizität, **Dichte,** so finden wir, dass diese[4] dieselben sind, wie die des ursprünglichen **Drahtes.**

U. investigate S. pieces g. accurately
b. determine E. qualities c. which are characteristic F. color D. density
d. the same (app. 14, 1) u. original D. wire
d. des those of

DISCUSSION: There may be one, two, three or more verbs on successive breaks. No matter how many you find, repeat the "if" as many times as you have verbs first. Justify each of the numbers and the bold face nouns. Note in the last line **die des,** those of the original wire.

11. [10]Machen wir denselben Versuch mit grössern **Steinen,** mit Metallstücken oder Holzstücken verschiedener **Grösse** oder[10-6] lassen wir mehrere derartige Körper von verschiedenem **Gewichte** gleichzeitig fallen, so kommen alle **Körper** gleichzeitig unten an[2].

Why rule 10? V. attempt, experiment
S. stones M. pieces of metal H.p. of wood
G. size l-f. let fall m. several d. such
v. different G. weight g. simultaneously
a. arrive u. down below g. at same time

DISCUSSION: Give reasons for each of the numbers in this sentence. Justify each bold face noun. Why do you go back to "Körper" when you pick up "an"?

12. Ist die Berechnung nicht möglich, so misst man den Rauminhalt eines Körpers, indem man ihn in Wasser eintaucht, und[8] das Volumen der verdrängten Wassermenge mittels einer der angegebenen **Methoden** misst.

B. calculation m. possible m. measures
R. space content i. by —ing e. immerse
v. displaced W. quantity of water
m. by means of a. stated

DISCUSSION: Where would you put a 10? a 4? a 1? Explain what nouns should then be bold faced?

13. [10]Wird durch die Beschränkung der individuellen Arbeitsleistung die gesamte dargebotene Arbeitsmenge[4] nicht vermindert, sondern[8] nur auf eine grössere Zahl von **Individuen** verteilt, so können[6] offenbar die Knappheit der Arbeit und der Preis derselben nicht von der **Veränderung** beeinflusst werden.

B. limitation Why rule 10?
A. work performance g. entire d. offered
v. diminished s. but (what?) Z. number
v. distributed o. obviously
K. scarcity V. change b. influenced
w. be (app. 7-6)

DISCUSSION: How far is it necessary to go into the sentence before you encounter the subject? The **rule** (10) states specifically: IF THE VERB STARTS THE SENTENCE—LOOK FOR SO—IF YOU FIND THE "SO", SAY "IF" FOR THE VERB, take the sentence word for word **until you encounter the subject, then drop back for the verb.** You are then entitled to follow the rules you have learned up to this time.

14. [10]Sehen wir von diesen Ungleichmässigkeiten der Volksvermehrung ab[2] und[10] betrachten wir die Volksvermehrung in ihrem Ganzen als Ausdruck für das Angebot von **Arbeitern**[1], so haben[6] wir in erster Linie unsere Aufmerksamkeit auf das Verhältnis zwischen dieser Volksvermehrung und der gleichzeitigen Vermehrung der übrigen Produktionsfaktoren, also des Bodens und des **Kapitals,** zu richten.

U. dissimilarities V. population increase
a. disregard, look away from b. consider
G. entirety A. expression A. supply
A. attention i. e. L. primarily
V. relation V. population increase
g. simultaneous V. increase ü. remaining
B. soil r. to direct

DISCUSSION: Justify the bold face nouns in each sentence. Show also why the numbers are placed over certain words. Note in particular rules 2 and 10 in this sentence. How many verbs could appear in rule 10? Note how far "so" is in this sentence. It might be 10 lines away.

15. [10-6]Werden arbeitssparende Maschinen in einem verhältnismässig kleinen **Produktionszweig** eingeführt, und[10] ist die Expansionsfähigkeit dieser Industrie nicht besonders gross, so wird[6] wenigstens für die nächste Zukunft die Nachfrage nach der betreffenden **Arbeit** vermindert.

a. work saving machines v. relatively
e. introduced Why rule 10 again?
E. e-ability b. especially
w. at least n. nearest Z. future
N. demand n. for b. concerned

B

WHAT TO DO IF THERE IS NO "SO" OR "DANN"

1. The "so" or "dann" should be present if the "if" clause is intended. However, once in a while these words may be left out if it can be clearly seen that an "if" clause is meant. If a verb starts a sentence and **there is a "result" clause,** you are still entitled to say "if".

2. If there is no "so" or "dann", look for the question mark at the end of the sentence. Naturally if a question mark is present, you are dealing with a question. Treat the sentence then according to the rules you now know, i.e. go forward to the noun or remove a verb from the end position and then move backward to the first noun. **Rule 1 tells you** then to resume normal word order.

3. If there is no question mark, and there is also no "so" or "dann", make a command out of the verb, i.e. supply let him, let us, let them, let her, etc.

(this part of rule 10 is very important in mathematics and physics)

Usually the subject follows immediately after the verb.

4. See D below.

C

Drill Sentences—When "so" and "dann" are absent

1. [10]Betrachten wir die Lehrer in den verschiedenen Schulen dieses **Gebietes.**

B. w. let us consider v. different
G. district Why "let us"?

2. [10]Halten wir eine **Untersuchung,** ob nicht gewisse Tatsachen der Geschichte und Erfahrung[4] diese Vermutung bestätigen.

H.w. let us make U. investigation
g. certain T. facts G. history E. experience
V. supposition b. verify

3. [10]Stellen wir jetzt unsere Kurven für die relative Goldmenge und für das allgemeine Preisniveau auf ein besonderes **Diagramm** zusammen.[2]

j. now
G. quantity a. general P. price level
z. combine together (use let us - Why?)

D

Inversion may also be used for greater emphasis. Such inversions precede adverbs, e.g. doch, wohl, nun, erst, etc. It is recommended to begin the sentence with the adverb and then follow the rules you have learned. In sentences of this type, there will be no "so" or "dann" and of course no question mark.

1. [10-6]Hat doch der grösste Dichter, Grillparzer, den Vorzug seiner **Werke** erklärt.

g. greatest D. poet
V. preference, advantage e. explained

2. [10-6]Hat doch der viel geschäftige Bahr selber die Übersicht solchen Austauschens nord- und süddeutscher **Dramen** erleichtert.

v. very g. busy s. himself
Ü. survey A. exchange
e. facilitate

DISCUSSION: In these two sentences, begin with "still" and then take care of the verb. Substitute any of the other words, e.g. ja, zwar, nun, erst, and let them begin the sentence. Let the emphasis be as strong as possible and supply whatever adverb you care to make this possible.

Rule 11

A

PARTICIPLES USED AS ADVERBS

Both the present and past participles may be used in phrases. When so used these two participles are found generally at the beginning or end of the phrase. In following the rules of this system, no difficulty should arise in translation if the participles are found within the phrase.

You are to continue to focus your attention on the breaks as you have been instructed to do in all of the rules so far discussed. When you go to the break and you find either of these two participles at that point, there is cause for caution. Usually on the break you will find a noun or a verb. You may find a participle, if so, this particular participle may be used as an adverb.

This construction has certain very definite characteristics which distinguish it from all other constructions in which the participles are used. Heretofore, the present and past participles were discussed in rule 3. They were then used as adjectives—modifying nouns, in which case they have as an ending one of the adjective endings e en er es em. The participles in rule 11 do not have **an adjective ending.** Study carefully the diagram, the sentences and the discussion of them.

Illustration:

..........NOUN[1] abweichend,[11] muss[6] man..........NOUN[1] verb.

A sentence conforming to this diagram:

pres. p.

1. Vom gewöhnlich vorgenommenen **Verfahren** abweichend,[11] muss[6] man das methodologische von dem logischen **Problem** sondern.

While deviating from the ordinarily undertaken procedure, one must separate the methodological from the logical problem.

RULE 11:

If the **present participle** (or the past participle) appears either at the beginning or end of the phrase, BEGIN THE TRANSLATION OF THAT PHRASE WITH THAT WORD. Supply a word like "while" or "when", or "on", in order to make an adverbial phrase out of the participle.

In the above illustration, the present participle "abweichend" is found on the break. It must be remembered that this participle could just as well appear at the very first of the sentence. No matter whether it is first or last in the phrase, BEGIN THE TRANSLATION OF THAT PHRASE WITH THE PARTICIPLE and if at all possible supply **when, while.** Thus you may start the sentence with "while deviating" and then go straight ahead as rule 1 tells you to do—to the noun.

2. [11]Rechnend auf die Entmutigung der Potomac **Armee,** entschloss sich Lee zur **Offensive.**[1]

R. while calculating
E. discouragement e. decided

3. Auf die Methodik der **Versuche** etwas näher eingehend,[11] wollen[6] wir kurz eine Übersicht über die **Hauptresultate** geben.

V. experiments e. somewhat n. closer
e. while going in (Why while?) k. briefly
H. main results

DISCUSSION: Why do you begin both sentence 2 and 3 with "while"? What nouns become now the "pivot" nouns? Continue to observe the breaks, if present participles are found on them apply rule 11. When the participles are picked up, work back to the first noun.

4. Im frühen Alter, sich eines hohen Rufes als tüchtiger **Advokat** erfreuend,[11] wurde[6] Lincoln als Mitglied der **Staatslegislatur** erwählt.

f. early A. age R. reputation t. efficient
e. while enjoying (Why while?) M. member
e. chosen

DISCUSSION: In what two places do you usually find the present participle? Why is "Advokat" in bold-face type? Justify the position of each of the numbers.

5. Einen grösseren Teil seines Lebens am königlichen **Hofe** verbringend, kam Tennyson später an die Universität in Cambridge.

T. part k. royal
H. court v. after spending s. later
Where would you insert 11? 1? Why?

6. Am 10. März 1492 ging Columbus unter **Segel,**[1] seinen Bruder **als Stellvertreter** zurücklassend.[11]

S. sail Why rule 1?
B. brother S. representative z. while leaving behind

7. Der Ehrlichschen **Terminologie** folgend,[11] heisst der Giftkomplex **toxophore Gruppe und der bindende Komplex haptophore Gruppe.**[1]

f. while following
G. poison complex
Why rule 11? rule 1?

8. Im wesentlichen auf lokaler Initiative und **Selbstbestimmung beruhend,**[11] **ist**[6] die Schulverwaltung in höherem Grade zentralisiert.

i. w. essentially Now why rule 11?
S. self-determination b. while resting
Schv. school administration h. higher

9. **Alles** unter den Gesichtspunkt unmittelbar sittlicher **Förderung stellend,**[11] fand Sokrates in der "vernunftlosen" Natur so wenig ein würdiges Objekt des **Studiums,**[1] dass er[4] sie vielmehr als äusserliches Mittel für äussere **Zwecke** aufzufassen wusste.

G. viewpoint u. immediate s. ethical
F. advancement s. while placing
v. unreasonable w. worthy
v. rather ä external
M. means Z. purposes a. to conceive

DISCUSSION: Give reasons for the positions of the numbers. Justify each bold-face noun. Note how one rule interlocks with the other. Focus your attention on the pivot nouns.

B

ADDITIONAL PRACTICE SENTENCES FOR RULE 11

If additional drill and practice is needed for this rule, examine carefully these extra sentences. These sentences are longer and contain some divisions that are used with other rules.

1. Immer an Hand des Gegebenen vom Einzelnen zum **Einzelnen** vorwärts schreitend,[11] fasst er jedes Gebiet des **Wirklichen** für **sich**[1] und macht es zum Gegenstande einer besonderen **Schrift.**[1]

a.H. d. by use of G. given **E. detail**
v. forward s. while progressing
W. real G. object
b. special S. article

DISCUSSION: What type of word do you find on the first break? Where else could this verb appear? How do you start the translation? Justify each number and each bold-face noun.

2. Er betätigte sich nicht aktiv im Dienste der **Kirche,**[1] sondern widmete sich, seiner angeborenen Neigung zur Naturwissenschaft und **Forschung** folgend,[11] Experimenten und Untersuchungen und dem **Lehramt.**[1]

b. was occupied D. service
w. devoted a. inborn N. tendency
N. natural science F. research f. while following L. teaching profession

DISCUSSION: Note the inserted phrase (While following his inborn tendency to natural science and research). Translate the sentence without this phrase and then repeat the sentence with it. Note that when the present participle is on the end or the beginning of a phrase, **begin the translation of that phrase with that word.** Note the present participle in this next sentence:

3. Von Würzburg kam Baer nach Berlin,[1] und dann, einer Aufforderung des Physiologen Burdach folgend,[11] nach Königsberg,[1] wo er[4] mit einigen Unterbrechungen bis 1834 Vorlesungen über Zoologie hielt und[8] seine wichtigsten **Arbeiten** dort vollendete.

k. came
f. while following A. request
e. some U. interruptions
V. lectures why rule 8? 11? 4?
w. important A. works v. completed

4. In seinem Gefängnis in Fort **Warren,**[1] und im Hafen von Boston über die Vernichtung seiner **Regierung** nachdenkend,[11] seine Amtsgenossen als umherirrende Vagabonden oder als **Verbrecher** angeklagt wissend,[11] welch bittere Ironie muss[6] dies später für den grossen Redner von **Georgia** gewesen sein.

G. prison H. harbor
V. destruction n. while meditating
A. office comrades umh. roaming
V. criminals a. accused w. while knowing
R. orator g. s. have been

DISCUSSION: Examine carefully each sentence before you translate. Observe the breaks in it and be conscious of what you find on these breaks. If you have examined this sentence, you have very probably noticed the two present participle forms on the breaks. The rule stipulates that you begin these phrases with the respective participles. Give reasons for the numbers and the pivot nouns.

5. Amerika ist ein **Reich,**[1] welches,[5] im Westen bis an das stille **Weltmeer** reichend[11], und im Norden und Süden sich fast von dem Pol zu den **Tropen** erstreckend,[11] mit seinen Millionen von Einwohnern einen stolzen Platz unter den Völkern der **Erde** einnimmt.

R. realm
W. ocean r. while reaching
S. south s.e. while extending
E. inhabitants s. proud P. place, position
e. occupies E. earth

C

PAST PARTICIPLE USED ADVERBIALLY

Past participles may be used in the same way as the present participles discussed under A. It is still **advisable** to use "while" or "when" in translating such participles. With respect to the past participles, observe these **points to** determine whether or not this is the type of construction you are dealing with:

Ask yourself these questions:

1. Is there a subject and predicate in the phrase?
2. Does the past participle have an auxiliary verb?
3. Does the participle come at the beginning or end of the phrase?

If there is NO subject or predicate in the phrase, and if the participle does not have an **auxiliary verb and** it does come at the end or beginning of the phrase, you are very probably entering an "11" construction. Note the diagram and the sentences that follow:

Illustration:

.... NOUN beraubt,[11] .... **NOUN.**[1]

A German sentence conforming to this diagram: (See also diagram on inside cover of book, Type 6-b)

1. Frühzeitig seiner **Eltern** beraubt[11], kam er im siebzehnten Jahre nach **Athen**[1].
While robbed at an early time of his parents, he came in his seventeenth year to Athens.

2. Nach der **Wellenlänge** gemessen,[11] unterscheidet man zweckmässig folgende Arten von **Strahlen.**[1]

g. when measured (Why when?) u. distinguishes
z. expediently f. following S. rays

DISCUSSION: Why do you start with "when measured"? What nouns become now the pivot nouns? Where else might this participle appear? Draw a diagram of this sentence as on inside cover Type six-b.

3. In drei **Teilen** eingeteilt,[11] gingen sie dann an die Geschütze und erwiderten das feindliche **Feuer.**[1]

T. parts e. while or when divided g. went
G. cannons e. replied f. enemy F. fire

DISCUSSION: Give reasons for the numbers and also show why certain nouns are **bold faced**. Where could you put "eingeteilt"? What other kind of participle might this be? Draw a diagram of the sentence.

4. Unter der Administration Pierce bereits zu einem **beunruhigenden Zerwürfnis** gediehen, übernahm Buchanan ein schlimmes **Vermächtnis.**[1]

b. already
b. disturbing Z. dissension g. while having proceeded
(Why while?) ü. took over V. legacy

DISCUSSION: Where would you insert an "11"? why? Why do you start the translation with "while having proceeded"? Where else could "gediehen" appear? What are your pivot nouns? (The participle is, of course, dangling.)

5. Sobald der Tag graute, legten die Schiffe an[2] und Columbus bestieg, in scharlachrote **Admiralsuniform** gekleidet,[11] und das königliche Banner von **Castillen** schwingend,[11] das neuentdeckte **Land.**[1]

g. dawned a. lay to Why rule 2?
b. ascended (what) s. scarlet red
g. While clothed Why rule 11?
s. while swinging n. newly discovered

6. In **Isabella** krank und erschöpft angelangt,[11] fand Columbus seinen energischen Bruder Bartolomeo mit Lebensmitteln aus **Spanien** vor.[2]

a. while or on arriving e. exhausted
What does "vor" go with?
L. food supplies v. find present

7. In jeder **Weise** gründlich vorbereitet,[11] in vielen Sätteln gerecht,[11] und sich bereits eines nationalen **Rufes** erfreuend,[11] trat Franklin 1754 in eine neue **Politik** ein.[2]

g. v. while thoroughly prepared why rule 11?
g. while fit for anything u. and (what?)
e. while enjoying (Why while?) Why rule 2?
e. entered in

8. **Eine Tonne, auf dem Äquator genau abgewogen**[11] **und**[8]**nach den** Polen transportiert,[11] würde[6] dort um etwas mehr als **3 kg** schwerer **gefunden werden.**

a. when weighed (Why when?) g. exactly
t. when transported (Why when?) w. would
s. heavier

9. Sowohl lebende als auch tote **Bakterien,**[1] **in Flüssigkeiten** auf-geschwemmt,[11] zeigen diese **Bewegung.**[1]

l. living t. dead F. liquids
a. when inundated z. show B. movement

DISCUSSION: As you work forward to Bakterien and then to Bewegung, insert the phrase, "when flooded in liquids". What are the pivot nouns?

10. Auf diese Weise zumeist an der Unterfläche des **Gletschers** gelagert,[11] bilden sie die Hauptbestandteile der **Grundmoräne.**[1]

a. d. W. in this way z. mostly U. under surface g. when deposited
H. main components G. ground moraine

11. Von Gicht und **Augenleiden** schwer **heimgesucht,**[11] und[8] für den Unterhalt der **Mannschaft** bekümmert,[11] steuerte er nordwestlich und erreichte am 10. August die **Insel.**[1]

G. gout A. eye trouble h. while afflicted
b. while worried U. maintenance, support
s. steered e. reached
I. island

DISCUSSION: Give reasons for the bold faced nouns. Why is it that actually the nouns are on the end of these phrases? Begin each phrase with the participle and if possible supply "when" or "while". Remember also that these participles may appear at the **first** or **last** of the phrase.

12. Darauf sandte **Jackson,**[1] vom Kongress mit grösserer Macht **betraut,**[11] General Scott mit Truppen nach **Charleston.**[1]

d. thereupon g. greater
M. power b. while entrusted

Here is the skeleton of this sentence:

Darauf sandte Jackson—General Scott mit Truppen nach **Charleston.**[1]

Now insert the phrase **"while entrusted** by congress with greater authority". Repeat the entire sentence with the inserted "11" construction. Taking this model, how would you show in skeleton form sentences 5, 8, and 9.

Translation of Model Sentences

It is the object in this section to offer a literal translation of most of the model sentences used in the discussion of the rules. This seems expedient and desirable, for by comparison of the translation with the model sentences the reader is able to progress much faster in the study of the rules and thus take up at an earlier date the reading material in his field. It should not be the reader's purpose to learn the vocabulary in the model sentences. His main goal should be at present to master the rules and to acquire facility in the application of them.

The translations should aid in particular a student who is studying the book by himself, for they serve as a means of "checking" his own translations. If he is fortunate enough to have some other person read the translated sentences to him in English as he follows the German, this will prove to be extremely effective, for in this way he may focus his attention so much better on the breaks and watch the sentence unfold.

The sentences are translated as near as possible to the text. They are almost literal, word for word translations and no attempt has been made to put them into good English style. The object is to translate strictly by the rule. After the idea which is conveyed in the sentence is clearly understood, the student is free to put it in his own words. Follow the word order just as these sentences are translated even if they sound at the moment somewhat stilted. In some words a hyphen is placed to show how words are divided. Pay attention to such words. In some sentences a blank space is left intentionally in order to show that at this point a **shift** is necessary. Let your eye, therefore, make the shift to pick up the needed element that is out of line with respect to English word order. Refer constantly to the inside cover of the book to see types of sentences usually encountered in reading a German text.

In accordance with the suggestions and wishes of some students, some sentences are left untranslated. The student, if he cares to, may translate these sentences for practice.

It may not be necessary to take up as many sentences as have been supplied. Take up only as many as you think you need to understand perfectly the rule involved. In classes, teachers may find that half of the illustrations are enough to understand the rule. The sentences are at least given to aid the student to see more clearly how to apply the rules.

RULE 1-B

1. And with the beauty of the land also its fertility goes hand in hand.

2. The philosophical views carry in double sense the name of the philosophy of the enlightenment.

3. The active behaviour with the widening of our knowledge and views has however still in this respect special value.

4. The character of the Greek intellectual life at the time of its highest bloom was the immediate devotion of the subject to the object.

5. Lamarcks **Zoological Philosophy** was the first scientific sketch of a true evolutionary history of the species, of a natural history of creation of plants, animals and man.

6. There is according to his concept no essential difference between living and lifeless nature; the whole nature is a single coherent world-appearance and the same causes are effective also alone in the living nature.

RULE 1-C

1. The philosophical views carry in double sense the name of a philosophy of enlightenment and are as such simultaneously (the) expression of the spirit of the time.

2. We know the basic-features of the tectonic structure of the earth, but we point at-the-same-time to the relations with the present surface-formation of the earth.

3. We stand today altogether at the beginning of this de**velopment and the study of this vast field is the profitable task and the brilliant goal of the future physics.**

4. The most significant representative, Boileau, preached predominance of the mind over literature and admired such nevertheless unreasonable and unbelievable tales as the Homeric epics; he recommended to the poet probability and simplicity.

RULE 1-D

1. In this case he distinguishes practical and theoretical science.

2. As (a)fruit of the same he published after ten years his famous work over the development-history of animals "Observation and Reflexion."

3. Nevertheless grew up in the course of the next centuries a vast literature about the person of the poet. (now rearrange the sentence putting subject and predicate where they ought to be in English)

4. Under the given title appeared in the magazines of the year 1916 my extensive and illustrated articles about the Bacon question. (Rearrange for smooth and better English.)

5. A great role plays the convection in the winds. (Rearrange; note position of the subject.)

6. A direct proof of this anonymous or pseudononymous activity is the Northhumberland Document.

7. Along with water were active also still other forces in the change of the earth-crust.

RULE 1-E

1. (The) formation-science is only a part of the extensive **science of geology, i.e. the theory of the material and indeed especially the mineral composition, the structure and the formation-history of the earth-body.**

2. Under the government of Queen Elizabeth, hence over 80 years after the discovery of the north-american conti**nent by the Cabots, the most brilliant, the most capable of the nobles at the English court, Sir Walter Raleigh, undertook the most serious attempt-of-colonization.**

3. Examples of these processes are the falling of a rock upon the earth, the mixing of two gases or mixable fluids, the diffusion and dissolution of solid materials in a solvent and above all the countless chemical processes.

4. In the common thinking of the encyclopedists was accomplished (app. 11, 4, b) step by step the change from empirism to sensualism, from naturalism to materialism, from deism to atheism, from the enthusiastic to the egotistical moral.

RULE 2-A

Model—On the pacific coast arise the old rocks according to the present reports first in this province again under the more recent formations.

RULE 2-B

1. This troup-division continued on the next day its advancing movement.

2. Therefore they show as the chemical elements certain qualities.

3. In this way the relation between philosophy and religion includes different factors (features).

4. In contrast here-to Hebard emphasizes again the neces**sity of a preparatory work of the remaining sciences and** designates the treatment of (the) concepts as the essential **task of philosophy.**

5. He proceeds from the isolated political-economy and comprehends the basic-process of the economic-life as a continuous cycle of productive expenditures on the one side and consumer use on the other side within an economic-period.

RULE 2-C

1. This stands out quite clearly especially on photographs-of the sun.

2. Galileo reported nothing at all nearly publicly of the entire observation.

3. Two colliding molecules rebound from one another therefore, perhaps similarly as two elastic balls.

4. This agrees very well essentially with the determinations of Hess.

5. Such deviations occur rather frequently in the existing barter-economy.

6. His father and his mother acted upon him kindly even in the earliest youth.

7. The essential difference of the durable goods on the one hand and the utility of the same on the other hand stands out clearly and distinctly especially in these cases of long durability.

RULE 3-A

1. The rays which belong to the violet part of the spectrum produce phosphorescence.

2. The particles which are suspended in the air contain living germs.

3. The roads which were built in the first decades of railway-development were of local character.

4. Columbus described the wonder-lands which lie in the west in the warmest colors.

5. The battles which took place on the 9th and 10th of August west of Verdun led to no positive result.

6. The totality of the activities which make possible the satisfaction-of-wants forms the economy. (the subject is following the verb)

7. The membrane of the cell of higher plants (this is the entire noun) which consists of cellulose is valid (or is considered) as totally permeable **for the** different solutions.

11. Upon the basis which is given by these metaphysical and nature-philosophical suppositions are solved (app. 11, 4a) now for Leibnitz at the same time the main problems of psychology.

13. This body absorbs only a quite definite part of this energy which is in-radiated to it.

15. The proof which has become so extraordinarily important for the further development of theology arose from this need.

16. Only the streams which come into the river from the settlements supply along with plenty (of) bacteria-masses also a considerable amount of dead material.

19. Each heat which is inherent in a body consists in a vibrating motion of its molecules and atoms.

20. The compounds **which** come from the different waste waters give off a nutrient-base **which** is still usable in great dilution.

21. With the above described stage reached with the **animals** which breathe with lungs this whole apparatus and the vessels which belong to it the high-point of the development.

23. The organs **which** are situated in the mouth-cavity are the teeth, the tongue, and the salivary glands **which secrete** the saliva.

RULE 3—Type 2-B

2. They contain a lecture (reading) which is announced about the different fields of instruction with the indication of the name of the teacher.

3. The same is true for a substance which appears in most bacteria in certain stages of development.

4. A glass tube which is filled partly with liquid sulphuric acid is found (app. 11, 4a) in a test-tube which is loaded with paraffine.

RULE 3-C Type 3

1. (The) Economics is a preparatory activity **which** is directed to the making possible of a future want-satisfaction.

2. We conclude from that upon (or as to) important forces which are directed to the center point of the earth.

4. Probably have existing gases which are enclosed in the superficial layers of the platinum an essential influence.

5. Under the skin it forms on many places a thick cushion (pad) which serves to the protection of deeper-lying forms.

6. Both types of answers mark a special type of adaptation which occurs only rarely in every day life.

7. The relation of two boiling temperatures which belong to the same pressure is here in no way constant, but rises with the temperature.

RULE 3 C-1

1. (The) following process which was indicated by the author and which was worked out by Voller is of importance.

2. One pours a few drops into a vessel which is struck by light rays and which is filled with water.

4. Nevertheless it is a principle which is verified by hundredfold repeated experiments (and) which holds true constantly every day.

5. The amides are in general the nitrogen-compounds which are most agreeable in general to the yeasts and **which** are assimilatable by them best and most easily.

8. In the county and city was concentrated the local administrative-activity which was distributed earlier to the many purpose-units and which was broken up in great disorder.

9. The form of the view (philosophy) was also the original one(form) which was formed namely in analogy to the already well investigated gravitation-phenomena and which prevails up to the last quarter of the past century.

RULE 3 C-2

1. The views which are expressed by him are the X(ones) which were brought by the poets of his time into application.

2. This form of philosophy was also the original one which prevailed up to the last quarter of the past century.

3. The causal-connection is never the one-sided one which acts according to a certain effect.

RULE 3 C-3

1. With the same interest he comprehends that which is given in nature, in history and in the interior of man himself.

RULE 3-D Type 4

1. It consists of senators who are chosen by the crown.

2. With higher heating it decomposes in chlorine and into Water which is saturated with chlorine.

3. One made the significant observation on eggs which were favorable especially for the investigation.

RULE 3-E

1. We set upon the apparatus two discs which are composed of black and white.

2. Of the 105 men who came over with Newport in the spring of 1607 were only 12 ordinary laborers.

RULE 4

2. Since Muller had investigated accurately quantitatively before the normal gene-process, he published immediately his results.

3. The three groups contain then a series of Enzymes, as they can be designated as specific for the different decompositions.

4. It follows from this that a special value-theory is unnecessary completely at least for the economic science.

5. It was not only in the sense that he had composed masterfully and invented freely the acts and persons of his poetic works.

6. While for the solid bodies the location of the element-particles is unchangeable in the main one-against-another, the molecules are easly one-against-another displaceable in the liquids.

9. The surface is curved, since the directions-of-gravity may be regarded as parallel no more on different far from-one-another removed points of the surface.

10. Even though the president believed to be able to enter in not upon these plans, he gave the general the command that he should let McDowell advance upon the Fredericksburg-Richmond line.

11. Make a translation of this sentence.

12. Since he could not possibly otherwise have been so familiar with the social behavior, the refined way of thinking and the stately and courtly ceremonial . . .

13. If one heats according to the arrangement of figure 553 the end of a metal-rod of 50cm length and 1cm cross-section by a flame which is placed under it so indicate the thermometers which are installed in equal distances in the rod certain temperature-increases.

RULE 5

1. He used glass-bottles with narrow necks which could be sealed air-tight after filling.

2. It served for the discovery of a quantity of new facts which—would have remained concealed longer still perhaps without this thirst for gold.

3. Kant shows that the religious world-philosophy rested not upon concepts which can be defined sensibly and exactly according to certain logical and empirical criteria.

4. To this purpose one shows a series of anatomical preparations, on which an X-ray gram can be demonstrated understandably and clearly particularly. (Now rearrange to make for smoother English.)

5. In the yeast-cell we find then a series of enzymes, over which we have informed ourselves more exactly already in the discussion of the bacterial-enzymes.

6. From the impression which the essays make upon us as a whole we turn away our view and direct it upon the individual thoughts which are represented in the individual works. (Rearrange if desirable.)

7. Chemical systems which are removed far from the stabile forms are changed frequently with increase of temperature if this gives namely to the velocity, with which they strive toward the equilibrium state, an adequate value.

8. This is a general phenomenon whose importance for the course of chemical transformation and whose importance for the existence of so-called 'violent' (explosive) reactions will be evident immediately.

RULE 5-B

1. Marshall begins from the concept of social capital by which he understands the capital from the standpoint of an entire people.

2. The second section with which we want to concern now ourselves lasts exactly one century, namely until the appearance of the Darwinian work concerning the origin of the species, which transformed all biology.

RULE 5-C

1. Upon earlier cultural-levels is namely the very natural conception predominant that very valuable goods can be exchanged not against lesser valued (ones).

2. Here there are now two viewpoints which have demonstrated themselves more forcefully as the only possible (ones).

3. The history of the exact sciences teaches us that one can come upon two essentially different ways to the discovery of a new natural-law of which we can designate the one as empirical, the second as the theoretical (one)

RULE 5-D

1. In the year 1859 Pflucker discovered remarkable rays which go-out in highly evacuated tubes from the cathode and which are designated therefore generally as cathode rays.

2. Columbus sent a letter to the queen in which he expressed his feelings over the improper treatment.

3. The absolute contrast to the cost-principle is the gratis-principle according to which economic goods must be offered to the consumers without special recompense.

4. The economic effort goes-out (proceeds) then to (the) production of a certain uniformity of supply of different wants in which case also the different wants must be limited somewhat.

5. At the beginning of the 16th century we find also as names for the bodies which cause ostensibly the fermentation the word "ferment", with which one designated in the broadest sense of the word every substance which is able to induce any chemical reaction.

6. The upper part of the peninsula upon which lies the capitol of the confederation and the Operation point of McClellan is intersected by the river.

RULE 6-B

1. We shall leave aside as unusable therefore much from this book.

2. They may be named together of course also therefore with the same right.

3. We want to try to explain closer somewhat still the above general suggestions.

4. The following methods have been used thoroughly more or less up to now in this way.

5. One can proceed as follows perhaps in this case.

6. In the following are to be discussed in detail first the Rorschach theories in sequence.

9. The different cases of gene-manifestation can be classified accurately theoretically as follows with regard to the symmetry-conditions.

10. From the viewpoint of an individual-economy or a special production-branch must appear as given quite naturally the production costs of a good.

RULE 6-C

1. The effect of these enzymes seems to be a very complicated (one).

2. Indeed an economic classification can reach never the sharpness of a mathematical (one).

3. After this great comet has appeared indeed in 1787 still a similar important (one) which has come closer somewhat to the sun.

4. One will designate nevertheless that process in the case of the surrender of Helgoland not as the exceptional (one).

5. The test-objects must be so exposed to the disinfectant-medium that the effect is invariably a uniform and complete (one).

RULE 6-D

1. The other basis is put aside happily and entirely by the publication of the long expected two-volume life of the poet by his son, the present Lord Tennyson.

2. Translate: shift on "sind".

3. This conception of saving is linked narrowly necessarily with the progressive economics which lies at the base of all our considerations.

RULE 6-E

1. For that are necessary also the corresponding physical conditions of the vicinity.

2. The first of these factors is—common naturally to all philosophical systems of a certain period.

3. Translate.

4. Translate—as in number 2.

5. The power is — proportional to the product from the accelerated masses and the accelerations which are given to them.

6. Translate-pick up "wichtig".

7. The individual demand of a good is — dependent in general on the prices of all goods or at any rate all goods which-have for the concerned individual economy a significance.

8. Without a doubt is —incomplete this classification already over-against the—separation of the scientific works which have been carried out in the platonic academy.

RULE 6-F

1. Bacon's recognized works permit us to recognize clearly the poet, especially the dramatist.

2. Many determinations (or provisions) remain "existing" in the constitution of the United States.

3. The officer permits the soldiers to rest two hours on this day.

4. Translate.

5. Translate as in number 2.

6. In this case remained - decisive the contrast between the sensualistic association-phychology and the nativistic theories of different origin for the development.

7. This natural law **can be** formulated as follows:

8. The size of the molecules **has been** defined in different ways.

10. The—principles which were developed in the foregoing section can be expressed as follows briefly.

RULE 7-B

1. We must try—to establish a relation between stimulus and sensation in chemical terms.

2. It is also possible—to produce pressure-sensations of different intensity-degree.

3. Many substances have the attribute—to check only the formation of one or more enzymes.

4. In this case, it **would be** better— to consider sensation an idea as sub-classes of a special type of mental elements.

5. In reply one gave to him the authority— to draw to himself some regiments of the garrison on F. M.

6. Translate: Watch the expression "task".

7. Under the influence of the first of these conditions philosophy sought —to conquer the leading position in life and science.

8. An attempt — to look-over systematically the entire field of psychology is—dependent not only on the basic-views over the task of psychology but also on the state of psychological detail-study.

9. So one **is accustomed**—to use in the setting-up of a bacteria-system the morphological peculiarities in the first place for the grouping of the fungi.

10. It was in this case necessary — to put-to-work unmolested their retreat to the embarkation point.

11. Traube is due the credit – to have introduced again the thermometer at the sick-bed to the (or for the) determination-of-fever.

12. Translate: Watch the expression "believes".

13. It appeared completely impossible—to summarize the different problems which – arose from the 16th and 17th century in mechanics, optics, geography and soon also in chemistry, physiology, and zoology, all under the term.

14. Above all we will try – to do justice to the poetic importance of the poet in his relation to the past, in his relation to the present and in all his characteristic qualities.

15. The X-ray-method gives also the possibility—to instruct better the doctor and the student by direct comparison of the anatomical preparation with the X-ray-picture.

RULE 7-C

1. It is developed (app. 11, 4a) also without-producing a so serious disease.

2. Without going-in to the interesting historical development of the alcoholic fermentation, we can count the latter to the enzymatic processes.

3. In order to-solve the price-formation-problem for the here considered case, we need—to consider therefore only the n prices as the unknowns of the problem.

4. Partially in order— to keep apart these large groups, partially in order — to introduce the further advance against the Drina, Baron Phillip issued to the troup-division the order – to advance over the river in order— to assure himself of the — highway which leads to Rogatio up to the region of this place.

RULE 7-D

1. We do better – to separate the color materials simply in water-soluble and water-insoluble.

2. It is a common-place task of the organic chemist— to compare newly found substances by some simple determinations with already known (ones).

RULE 7-E

1. The use of a good hypothesis consist thus essentially **in broadening** and **intensifying** our knowledge of the natural phenomena.

2. Up until recently one limited himself **to killing off** by dabbing with antiseptic liquids the invading exciters (germs).

3. Especially in more recent time one was content **with computing** simply from accessible average-numbers the quantitative composition of the diet.

4. In spite of all these movements in the colonies for the preservation of freedom no one thought earnestly **of dissolving** the bond between England and the colonies.

5. Aristotle went-out only there-to — to collect the logical facts in relation to proposition-formation and process-of reasoning.

6. We put no value thereupon— to enter more closely upon the question of the mysterious tabulation of these forms before we have learned to know the nature of gravity-force.

RULE 7-F

1. The molecules seem to be removed from one-another so far in these most dilute of all known media that none senses the attraction of another.

2. The price needs to depend only upon this scarcity, is in no-way to be conceived necessarily as a condition of the supply of the concerned production-means.

RULE 8

1. The Oregon-territory was—claimed on the basis of discovery and settlement and—established by treaty with Great Britain on the 15th of June 1846 to the northern-boundary of the United States.

2. One must—draw from this circumstance the consequence and eliminate the entire so-called value theory completely from the economic science.

3. Now we want to take a second stimulus of the same magnitude and—let increase gradually its intensity by very small amounts.

4. McDowell received immediately the command, to discontinue the plan against Richmond and—to march with the two others to the Shenandoah valley.

5. Translate: Two shifts are necessary.

6. If we—eliminate distracting influences and concentrate the attention upon a single sensation, then this stands clearly and distinctly before us.

7. Single efforts of outstanding thinkers—to liberate themselves from this and to come to a natural- conception remained hopeless.

8. If the calculation is not possible, then one measures the space-content of a body, by immersing it in water and —by measuring the volume of the displaced water-quantity by means of one of the indicated methods.

9. The materials which can – be produced not by us or —are produced not any rate at the time, because they **are to be** had more easily directly from nature, we call raw-materials in the real sense.

RULE 8-B

(try to use only for "checking" purposes)

1. Kant has abandoned at times of course this standpoint and—expressed especially on some very remarkable places which I have discussed in detail in my natural creative-history—himself in totally opposite sense.

2. He pursued his studies from 1810 to 1814 in Dorpat and and went then to Würzburg where Dollinger introduced him alone into the comparative anatomy, but acted also by his natural-philosophical trend highly fruitfully and stimulatingly upon him.

3. The treatment of diphtheria was limited there-to—to kill-off by dabbing with antiseptic liquids the invading exciters and –to keep high the strength of the patient by rich wine-consumption and –to combat fever by baths and medicines and to obviate finally by incision of the trachea the danger of suffocation.

4. We are now at the time in possession of some experimental-laws and hypotheses which are of far-reaching applicability to be sure for each branch of natural-science and deserve to be placed ahead accordingly of a didactic treatment of each branch but – require quite especial consideration in the presentation of the present state of theoretical chemistry.

5. He it was, who transplanted the philosophy to Athens, from now on the center-point of the intellectual life in Greece and exerted especially by his personal relation to Pericles, E. and other significant men upon the then time-culture a decisive influence.

6. This means that the principle of scarcity does not alone suffice in order — to determine the price formation but — must be supplemented by certain supplementary principles which represent new conditions of price-formation and abolish the uncertainty of the problem.

7. In order to solve the price-formation-problem for the here considered case we need to consider therefore only the n prices as the unknowns of the problem and to assume as given tentatively the same according to the general mathematical method.

8. (The) energy proves true here as a good servant in that it facilitates (for us) not only the survey over the factual-data, but — helps (us) to intensify and broaden also simultaneously frequently the immediate results of the observations.

9. We can set-up therefore the principle that for the here considered case of uncertain production-costs the price must be equal to the quota between total costs and the demand at this price and – must be defined by the uniform distribution of the total costs to the demand and must agree consequently with the so computed average-costs.

10. No one can – obtain without various preparations the topographical basis for the area-content of the land with its territorial-divisions and for the location of the mountains and rivers or -undertake census or cattle-countings or—note births, weddings ond cases-of-death and-determine the cultivation -surfaces in acre, meadow, pasture, and forest or ascertain the importation and exportation of the different goods in the different borders or know public income and expenditures.

11. He would have had then the choice – to proceed either upon the north-bank of the James-river toward Richmond or—to operate by transferring to the south-bank simultaneously against the connections of the capitol-city with the remaining part of the confederation or— to abandon momentarily the connection with the York-river and—to proceed boldly against Richmond, in order to withdraw in case of an unfavorable outcome of the expected battle to the James-river.

RULE 8-C

1. As – proceeds from the tabulation consist in the case of the single types considerable differences with regard to the cardinal-points-of temperature of spore-formation.

2. By this condition is – determined in general the unit-price, that is, expressed in the prices of the co-operating production-means and raised therefore into the indefiniteness of the production-costs.

3. The compressibility is initially larger than—corresponds to the Boyle law.

4. Many officers seem — to wear -out rather the strength of our soldiers by over-exertion than to take-on (accept) the aid of the colored men for the work in the trenches.

RULE 8-D

1. The velocity-of movement of the bacteria is different in the individual types and – dependent with one and the same type on a series of outer influences.

2. This student is—helpful to the teacher at any time, however indifferent completely to the German language.

3. From a certain load on is—stronger, as — has been stated already on page 183—the lengtening of a wire-than — would correspond to the proportionality.

RULE 8-E

2. Further the phenomenon must be observed, i.e. its course must — **be** established immediately and **be** traced back to measurable magnitudes.

3. A science consists of a large group of observations which **are** set to one another in relation and **are** arranged under general laws.

4. We must – assume also with justice that numerous dye-materials — **are** extracted as leuco-compound out of the cell and **are** oxydized then to the colored compound.

5. An intensive advancement occurred in the year 1783, in which the cell-theory **was** established and (there) was opened also for the developmental-history suddenly a new field of study.

6. Voltaire is the great writer who **has** given not only to this matter the most eloquent expression but **has** represented emphatically also the positive factors of the enlightenment.

7. The method of self-movement of the concept however Mr. Hegel perfects in that he **seeks** to use first of all in the concept of existence those contrasts and **seeks** to apply then the same to all other concept-levels.

8. The bacteria-toxines are complexly built poisons of the greatest effectiveness which **are** formed by the bacteria-cell and **are** held back either as endo-toxines in the living cell or **are** given off as ekto-toxines into the surrounding substratum.

RULE 8-F

1. Mostly will – prevail outside always lower pressures than on the inside of the bacteria-cell.

2. The law says that the exradiated heat quantity behaves itself exactly as the fourth power of the absolute temperature of the radiating body.

3. The electro-motor force is defined with the aid of an Ohm law as the voltage on the ends of a conductor.

4. Upon our language and literature Luthers bible has gained a so far-reaching influnece as no other book.

5. It has **been** developed still much later under much greater difficulties than its natural sister — the germ history.

6. The use-of-land takes -in (occupies) in the price-formation- process principally the same position as the other production-factors.

7. The knowledge of the German literature is for the student just as instructive as the knowledge of English literature.

RULE 9-A

1. Luther had (a) feeling both with humanism as with mysticism.

2. Lincoln took leave from his friends in Washington.

3. Plotin taught – philosophy since his 40th year (of life) in Rome.

4. The theorems of thermo-dynamics require consideration in the scientific investigation of each individual natural-phenomenon.

5. The independence-declaration of the year 1776 took —regard to the violation of such rights and set-up itself a series of inalienable rights.

6. In more recent time come—into use with the scientific and also with many technical measurements always more the electrical thermometers.

7. Man makes—use of the separation of wood-cells also with the production of the—wood-cellulose **which** was used as paper-material.

RULE 9-B

4. The American government would come in temptation indeed only under quite abnormal conditions.

5. Henry Clay it was who – sought to set limits-in 1820 by the socalled Missouri compromise to the further spread of slavery.

6. What – is carried out here is to have **value** for every economic-form.

7. A great number of bacteria-types is able – to develop **light** under appropriate conditions and free nature.

8. Lincoln saw himself necessitated – to make **use** of his right as president and chief of the land and sea-forces of the union.

9. So he explained that literature – had **its** roots not in technical skill but in the entire philosophy.

10. The way of a body is—called its path when one takes **regard** only to the form of the way.

11. Above all in these practical applications comes **to value** the conciliatory character of the Leibnitz philosophy.

12. We can discuss it, without taking **regard** to the quality.

13. In this first chapter we will limit our investigation to the processes which come into consideration for each economy and have therefore for the economy in general an essential importance.

14. He gave ——— expression anew to his doubt in the wisdom of the – preparation plan which was suggested by McClellan.

15. The — Rhinelander who was entrusted with the pacification of these regions resolved – to lead still once a powerful blow against this last attempt of the rebels.

16. The crusades served – to transfer to Europe the chemical knowledge and views of the Arabs whereby the mystical trend of that age especially the theory of metal-transformation found uncommon entrance and aroused partly also the alchemists who made just as fabulous as fruitless attempts to make Gold from non-precious metals.

RULE 10

3. **If** we limit ourselves to the South-American continent, we see the characteristic peculiarities from this period.

4. **If** a foreign gas is present, then the formation of vapor takes place in equal manner until its partial-pressure has become equal to the vapor pressure.

5. **If** now the constitution is not completely exact on this point, congress can change it according to desire.

6. **If** one divides this value by the molecular weight then one can compute by means of this number the specific volume with an accuracy of 2%.

7. Translate for practice.

8. **If** now by evacuation of the vessels the pressure **is** lowered, then one can bring as usual by heating of the vessel **a** the substance to boiling.

9. **If** upon the same mass-point simultaneously two forces act, then disturbs by way of experience the one not the effect of the other.

10. **If** we investigate both pieces exactly, i.e., if we determine the qualities which are characteristic for them, as color, elasticity, density, we find that these are the same as those of the original wire.

11. Translate for practice.

12. **If** the calculation is not possible, then one measures the space-content of a body in that one immerses it in

water and measures the volume of the displaced water-quantity by means of one of the indicated methods.

13. If by the limitation of the individual work-performance the entire offered work-quantity is not diminished, but distributed only to one larger number of individuals, then can be influenced obviously the scarcity of work and the price of the same not by the change.

14. If we look-away from these dissimiliarities of the population-increase and if we consider the population increase in its entirety as the expression for the supply of laborers, then we have to direct in the first place our attention to the relation between this population increase and the simultaneous increase of the remaining production-factors therefore of the soil and capital.

15. If work-saving machines are introduced in a relatively small production-branch and if the expansion-ability of this industry is not especially great, then is diminished at least for the nearest future the demand for the concerned work.

RULE 10-C

1. **Let us** consider the teachers in the different schools of this region.

2. **Let us** make an investigation if certain facts of history and experience verify this assumption.

3. Let us combine-together now our curves for the relative gold-quantity and for the general price-level upon one special diagram.

RULE 10-D

1. Still (however), the greatest poet, Grillparzer has explained the advantage of his works.

2. Still (however), the very busy Bahr himself has facilitated the survey of such an exchange of north and south-German dramas.

RULE 11-A

2. **While** calculating on the discouragement of the Potomac Army, Lee decided (to) on the defensive.

3. **While** entering closer somewhat upon the method of the experiments, we will give briefly a survey over the main results.

4. **While** enjoying in early age a high reputation as an efficient lawyer, Lincoln was elected as a member of the state legislature.

5. **After** spending a greater part of his life at the royal court, Tennyson came later to the university in Cambridge.

6. Translate for practice.

7. Translate for practice.

8. **While** resting in the main on local initiative, and self-determination, the school-administration is centralized in a higher degree.

9. While putting everything under the viewpoint of immediate ethical advancement, Socrates found in the "unreasonable" nature so little a worthy object of study that he knew to (or knew how to) comprehend it rather as external means for outer purposes.

RULE 11-B

1. While progressing forward always by use of the given from detail to detail, he combines each field of the real for itself and makes it a subject of a special article.

2. He was occupied not actively in the service of the church but devoted himself, **while** following his inborn talent for natural-science and research to experiments and investigations and the teaching profession.

3. From Würzburg Baer came to Berlin and then **while** following a challenge of the physiologist Burdach to Königsberg where he held (gave) with some interruptions until 1883 lectures about zoology and completed there his most important works.

4. **While** meditating in his prison in Fort Warren and in the harbor of Boston over the destruction of his government, while knowing accused his confederates as roaming vagabonds or as criminals, what bitter irony must this have been later for the great speaker from Georgia.

5. America is an empire, which, **while** reaching in the west up to the Pacific ocean and while extending on the north and south from the pole to the tropics, occupies with its millions of inhabitants a proud place among the peoples of the earth.

RULE 11-C

2. Translate for practice; follow vocabulary.

3. Translate; follow the vocabulary.

4. **While** prospering under the administration of Pierce already to a disturbing dissention Buchanan took over a bad legacy.

5. As soon as the day dawned, the ships lay to and Columbus ascended **while** clothed in scarlet-red admirals-uniform and while swinging the banner of Castilion, the newly discovered land.

6. While arriving exhausted and sick in Isabella, Columbus found his energetic brother Bartholomeo with foods from Spain.

7. While prepared thoroughly in every way, while fit in many saddles, and while enjoying already a national reputation, Franklin entered in 1754 into a new policy.

8-12. Do for practice.

How to Handle Inserted Elements

German sentences become frequently unwieldy due to the presence of inserted elements, such as qualifying clauses, phrases, appositives and the like. This feature of the language tends to confuse American students who attempt to read highly complicated material. It is extremely essential to acquire skill in handling sentences of this type, for the German is accustomed to write long and involved sentences, often with several inserted elements. The silence of grammars on the matter of inserted elements adds to the difficulty.

It is the purpose of this section to show a number of illustrations and to discuss step by step how the various elements fit into the sentence to make a complete thought. The punctuation plays, of course, an important role, for practically all inserted elements are set off by punctuation marks—usually commas.

Inasmuch as the German is so very careful in punctuating sentences, there is nothing alarming about these inserted elements, for at the end of each of them will be found a word—and it is this word that gives the signal how each division is to be treated. If the end word is a noun, rule 1 is the guide. If the end word is a verb, then rules 4, 5, 6, 7, 8 are involved. No matter how many divisions there are in the sentence, the end word gives the signal how each division is to be translated. In most cases a verb is found at the end of one of these divisions.

Follow carefully the discussion of each of these illustrations. Note how one part of the sentence is kept in abeyance while inserted elements (one, two or more) are taken care of. You must learn to keep the inserted elements separated from the main thought. In many cases, these inserted elements are no more than parenthetical statements. In the following illustrations **the main thought appears in bold faced type.** The inserted elements will be marked with capital letters. Go over the sentences several times after you have read the discussion. The sentences are also marked with the numbers of the rules you have learned.

A B A

1. **Bewusstsein ist,** (wie ein Blick auf ein Lexikon zeigt,) **ein sehr vieldeutiger Begriff.**[1]

The A in this sentence designates the MAIN THOUGHT and the B (or any additional capital letters) refer to inserted elements. The main thought is also in bold faced type.

A. Consciousness is (main thought) a very ambiguous term.

B. , as a glance at a dictionary shows,

C. Repeat the sentence, inserting B into A where the break in the thought occurs. Note that the comma after "ist" indicates the insertion of a parenthetical statement. Keep uppermost in your mind the first part of the main thought as you bring in the inserted clause.

A B A

2. **Der zweite Abschnitt,** (mit dem wir[4] uns jetzt zu beschäftigen haben,) **dauert ein Jahrhundert,**[1]

A. The second section (main thought) lasts a century.

B. , with which we have to concern ourselves now,

C. Repeat the sentence inserting B into A where the punctuation mark breaks the thought. Raise or lower your voice as you bring in the clause. After the clause is taken care of, resume normal order to the last noun, rule 1. Go over the sentence several times.

A B A

3. **Auf dem unabhängigen Wege führt,** (wie[8] weiter unten auseinandergesetzt werden wird,) **die kinetische Theorie der Gase zu der gleichen Annahme.**[1]

A. On the independent (direct) way , the kinetic theory of gases leads to the same assumption.

B. , as will be discussed further below,

C. Now repeat the sentence. Insert the clause immediately when the break in the thought occurs. Note that usually the verb is at the end of one of the inserted elements. Apply rules 4, 5, 6, 7, 8 to remove such verbs. The noun "Annahme" is the pivot noun and rule 1.

A B

4. **Die Theorie,** (welche[4] die freie Konkurrenz als Mittel zur Realisierung einer normalen Preisbildung betrachtet,) **setzt ferner die Existenz eines Marktes voraus**[2].

A. The theory (main thought) presupposes further the existence of a market.

B. , which considers the free competition as a means to the realization of a normal price formation,

C. Now repeat the entire sentence, this time holding the first part (the theory) in your mind as you bring in the dependent clause. Note the rules that are now involved in the sentence. You would have difficulty in translating the sentence if you attempt to finish the main thought before inserting the dependent clause., for in this case you would have the wrong antecedent for the relative "which". The antecedent for "which" is "theory" and not "market".

A B

5. **Unglücklicherweise hatte**[6] **Newton,** (von einer falschen **Voraussetzung** ausgehend[11],) **zu seiner Zeit bewiesen,** dass die Konstruktion eines Fernohres[4] eine theoretische **Unmöglichkeit** sei.

A. Unfortunately Newton had . . . proved at his time

B. , while proceeding from a false assumption,

C. that the construction of a telescope was a theoretical impossibility.

D. Repeat the sentence and as you do insert B into A where the break in the thought occurs. Learn to keep in your mind the first part as you insert this time an "11" construction.

A B

6. **Wir haben gefunden, dass diese Forderungen**[4] **in einer Preisbildung,** (die[5] von dem Prinzip der Knappheit und den supplementären Prinzipien der **Preisbildung** reguliert wird,)[9] **zum Ausdruck kommen.**

A. We have found that these requirements come to expression in a price-formation.

B. , which is regulated by the principle of scarcity and the supplementary principles of price formation,

C. Insert B into A and repeat the sentence. Note that this time you may keep the entire main thought in mind as you bring in the clause.

A B

7. **In solchen Fällen ist**[6], (um[7] eine zuverlässige Vorstellung von dem Kostmass des betreffenden **Individuums** zu erhalten,) **notwendig,**[7] **die Untersuchungen auf mindestens eine Woche auszudehnen.**

A. In such cases is . . . necessary

B. , in order to obtain a reliable idea of the amount of diet of the individual concerned,

C. to extend the investigations to at least a week.

D. Now repeat the sentence and insert B into A, then go ahead with the rest of the sentence. Note that the "zu" verbs are called for by 1. um— zu and 2. necessary—to. What is now the importance of Individuums and Woche?

A B

8. **Wir sagten, dass man**[4], (um[7] den Gegenstand der Physik und der **Psychologie** zu verstehen,) **die menschliche Erfahrung von entgegengesetzten Gesichtspunkten betrachten müsse.**

A. We said that one . . . must consider the human experience from opposite viewpoints

B. , in order to understand the subject of physics and of psychology,

C. Repeat the sentence and as you do insert B into A. Or you may choose to "hold" the first part in your mind as you bring in the infinitive phrase as follows:

We said that **one**—in order to understand the subject of physics and psychology—must consider the human experience from opposite points of view.

A B

9. **Daher können**[6] wir, (wenn wir[4] alle eben merklichen Unterschiede als gleich, alle kleinsten Empfindungsdistanzen als gleiche **Empfindungsdistanzen** betrachten)

die Ergebnisse unserer **Versuche** zusammenfassen.
A

A. Therefore we can . . . summarize the results of our experiments.

B. , if we consider all barely noticeable differences as equal, all very small sensation-distances as equal sensation distances,

C. Repeat the sentence, but this time translate as you were instructed to do in Number 8, namely hold "Therefore we can" in your mind as you bring in the clause, then resume normal order for the rest of the sentence. Which method do you prefer in this sentence?

SENTENCES WITH SEVERAL INSERTED ELEMENTS

A B C

1. **Ein Indianer,** (welcher[5] von einem **Lande** zu erzählen wusste,) (wo die Schiffe aus Gold gebaut würden) (Peru), **war Führer der Expedition.**

A. An Indian was a leader of the expedition.

B. , who knew to tell of a land,

C. , where the ships were built of Gold (Peru),

D. Now repeat the sentence inserting first B, then C into A. Note how the comma after "Indianer" indicates the insertion of one (or perhaps more) inserted elements. Learn to keep uppermost in your mind the first part as you insert the various inserted elements.

2. **Solche Grössen,** (die[5] einen einfachen **Zahlenwert** haben und (die[5] wie algebräische **Zahlen** behandelt werden,) **heissen Skalargrössen.**[1]

DISCUSSION: Analyze carefully the sentence before you translate it. Note the numbers of the rules which are indicated in this sentence.

Where would you put A to denote the main thought?

Where would you put B for the first inserted element? C for the second?

With these points well in hand, review the translation below.

A. Such magnitudes, , , are called skalar magnitudes.

B. which have the simple numerical value and

C. which are treated as algebraic numbers

D. Now repeat the sentence. Inasmuch as you have other clauses in the sentence, keep the first part namely "such magnitudes" uppermost in your mind as you bring in these clauses. When the clauses are taken care of, translate straight forward to the last noun—rule 1.

A

3. **Nun sind kleinste Entfernungen,** (da sie[4] kleinste mögliche Entfernungen sind,) (bei denen[5] Empfindungen unterschieden werden können)
notwendigerweise gleiche Entfernungen.[1]

A. Now are smallest distances . . . . . . (necessarily like distances.)

B. , since they are the smallest possible distances,

C. , in which sensations can be distinguished,

D. Repeat the sentence and as you do insert B and then C into A. Note that it would be more correct this time not to recite the last part until the clauses are inserted.

A B C

4. **Der Ort,** (an dem[5] sich ein **Körper** befindet,) (der[5] gleichzeitig an mehreren **Bewegungen** teilnimmt,) **wird**[6] durch **den Satz vom Parallelogram der Bewegungen gefunden.**

A. The place,

B. , at which a body is found,

C. , which takes part simultaneously in several movements,

D. is — found by the principle of the parallelogram of movements. Give reasons for each step.

5. **Der erste,** (welcher[5] das Vorhandensein eines grossen Meeres jenseits der Anden,) (von dem schon Columbus[4] auf seiner letzten Reise dunkle **Nachrichten** erhalten hatte ,) (feststellte) **war der spanische Ritter Balboa.**[1]

DISCUSSION: What is the main thought? What is the first inserted element? the second?

What does the "welcher" call for? why not "hatte"? With these points well in hand, review the translation below:

A. The first,

B. , who established the presence of a great ocean beyond the Andes,

C. , from whom Columbus had received on his last trip obscure reports,

D. was the Spanish Knight Balboa. Try to keep the first part in your mind as you bring in the various inserted elements, then finish the main thought.

A B C D

6. **Es kann**[6] **gesagt werden, dass wir,**[1] (da sie[1] **Elemente** sind,) (da sie[4] der **Analyze** widerstehen,) und[8] nicht auf etwas **einfacheres** zurückgeführt werden können,) **keine Möglichkeit haben,** sie anzuordnen.

DISCUSSION: How many inserted elements do you have in this sentence? What verb does "wir" call for? Why not "sind?" With these points in mind, review the following translation:

A. It can be said, that we,

B. since they are elements, C. since they resist analysis D. and can be reduced not to something more simple

E. have no possibility to arrange them.

Rearrange the sentence to suit your wishes. It has been translated here strictly according to rules. You may choose to take care of the entire main thought and then bring in the three other statements. Practice on this type of sentence, for such sentences occur frequently.

A B

7. **Es ist wichtig,**[7] die[3] in der Charakterisierung des elektrischen Zustandes durch die Erregung des **Äthers** niedergelegte

C D

Vorstellung, die Faraday in genialer Intuition, unverstanden von seinen **Zeitgenossen,** aufgebaut hatte,

A

deutlich zu machen.

A. It is important (the main thought minus the object) to make clear . . .

B. the . . . idea which was laid down for the characterization of the electric condition by excitation of the ether

C. which Faraday . . . had formulated with ingenious intention

D. not understood by his contemporaries,

Now repeat the entire sentence and as many times as you need to in order to bring in each of these elements. Note also the "3" construction that appears in this sentence. What is the importance of the noun "Äthers" and also why do you say "which was laid down"?

The following sentence contains several inserted elements. While the tendency is to get away from extremely long sentences of this type, there are still some fields that contain many sentences with one, two, three or more inserted elements. By following the plan outlined in the foregoing sentences, and also in this one, there should be no difficulty in arranging such sentences correctly. Glance over the following sentence and note the inserted elements enclosed in parentheses. Then follow the discussion point by point. The main thought is in bold-face type. The inserted elements are indicated with capital letters.

A B

8. **Vergleichen wir die Beziehung zwischen Philosophie und Religion,** (die[5] sich so aus der allmählichen geschichtlichen

A C

Entwicklung dieses **Verhältnisses** offenbart,) **mit jener anderen Beziehung,** (die[5] sich uns oben als diejenige ergab,)

D

(die[5] für das Verhältnis zwischen der Philosophie der Gesamtheit der **Einzelwissenschaften** massgebend sein muss,) (weil

E A A A

sie[4] einem fundamentalen Bedürfnis der heutigen **Wissenschaft** entspricht,) **so ist es augenfällig, dass ein Unterschied**

A

hier nicht mehr besteht, sondern dass sich lediglich die Religionswissenschaft[4] **der Gesamtheit der übrigen Wissenschaften einzuordnen hat.**

A. If we compare the relation between philosophy and religion

B. , which is revealed thus from the gradual historical development of this condition,

A. with that other relation

C. , which was demonstrated to us above as that one

D. which must be authentic (decisive) for the relation between philosophy and the totality of the individual sciences,

E. because it corresponds to a fundamental need of the present-day science,

A. it is obvious that a difference no longer exists here, but merely that the science of religion has to classify itself with the totality of the other sciences.

READING

Selections from the

SOCIAL SCIENCES

BIOLOGICAL SCIENCES

PHYSICAL SCIENCES

How to Approach the Translation of a German Paragraph or Page

1. "Spot" or locate all of the breaks—or punctuation marks in the paragraph.

You will save yourself much time, and perhaps much trouble, if you will take a few seconds and locate all of the breaks before you begin to translate. DO NOT BEGIN TO TRANSLATE UNTIL YOU HAVE LOCATED EVERY BREAK IN THE PARAGRAPH.

An illustration may be in place: A football quarterback takes a few seconds to look over his opposing backfield. During this time he surveys as hastily as possible the backfield on the opposing team. He locates the position of the fullback, the half backs, the quarterback and the ends. He then plans the attack and calls the signal where the play will be made.

You should do your own quarterbacking as a translator; i.e. you should be just as careful in locating the breaks so that you can plan your attack for translation. As you go over the paragraph, be conscious of the types of words you are finding on the breaks, e.g. verbs, nouns, pronouns, adverbs, adjectives and prepositions. Experience will show that nouns and verbs are on the breaks most of the time. The Rules, of course, tell you what to do no matter what part of speech comes at the end of the sentence, clause, or phrase.

The punctuation marks (the breaks) become by this method extremely important. It is at these points that you get the clue as to how to proceed in the sentence units. Reference should be made constantly to the page on the inside cover of the book in order to form a picture in your mind as to how you are supposed to translate. You are generally proceeding forward and backward to a pivot point—THE NOUN. Any elements found on the right side of the double line in the diagram on the inside cover page must be removed by the Rules indicated.

2. IN ORDER TO OBVIATE ANY FURTHER TROUBLE IN TRANSLATION—

1. "Flag" all prefixes before you begin to translate. As you scan the paragraph be especially careful to note the PREFIXES in it. Put a flag out to the left side of the margin where these words are located. As you approach the flag, be careful when you reach a verb form. The prefix which is now flagged and is on the break is very probably a part of the verb. Some little words that are not prefixes (and yet may be found on the break) are discussed in the Appendix—section 21. See also more on the flagging procedure in the discussion of Rule 2.

2. "Flag" all "zu"-verbs. Never translate a paragraph until this type of verbs is carefully checked and flagged. Again extreme care must be used as you approach the flag, for at these points there will be a "call" for a "zu"-verb and you must be prepared to pick up this verb at the right time. It is imperative to acquire skill in picking up a "zu"-verb. It is one of the major obstacles for the American reader, inasmuch as the "zu"-verb occupies a place in the sentence far removed from where it would be expected in English. (See also the discussion of Rule 7 and note how the model sentences for this rule are flagged.)

The use of "flags" in translation has a tremendous value. In the first place there is a psychological advantage in knowing what obstacles you may encounter before you begin. Experience has shown that prefixes and "zu"-verbs are two points where errors may be made. The second and perhaps the most important advantage in flagging a paragraph is the confidence-building feature of it. If no flags are out, you may depend entirely on the rules and know that you may proceed with full confidence FORWARD TO THE NOUN or BACKWARD TO THE NOUN. Rule 3 must of course be watched for at all times.

3. After a page or more has been translated, have someone read your translation back to you. In this way you will be able to follow the German word order better and watch the sentence unfold. This also aids in the development of vocabulary. When even more progress has been made, read off the German text to someone as that person follows the English word order. In case of difficulty, he may prompt you.

DO NOT BE DISCOURAGED IF YOU CAN TRANSLATE ONLY A FEW LINES PER HOUR at the beginning. The speed of your translation will increase as you become more familiar with the application of the Rules and after you have acquired more vocabulary.

4. When the translation work is begun, make use of the hints given in the back of the book on the development of vocabulary. Do not attempt to learn all of these rules in one sitting, but take them up gradually.

5. MASTER THE CHART ON THE VERY LAST PAGE OF THIS BOOK.

GESCHICHTE

Die Besiedlung Neu-Englands und die Pilgerväter und Puritaner †

Die gewaltige kirchliche **Umgestaltung,**[1] welche[5] im 16. Jahrhundert Deutschland und Frankreich in zwei grosse **Lager** spaltete, hatte[6] auch in England und Schottland eine "reformierte" **Partei** gebildet, welche[5] im Gegensatz zu dem[3] unter der Regierung der Königin **Elizabeth** festgestellten Episkopalsystem auf Unabhängigkeit der Kirche vom Staate und auf Freiheit der **Lehre** drang, sowie[8] die Einfachheit im Kultus nach dem Muster der ältesten apostolischen und der Schweizer Reformierten **Kirche** einführte. Die Anhänger dieser Partei erhielten unter Anspielung auf ihren Reinigungseifer den Namen **Puritaner.**[1]

g. powerful U. transformation
Note the numbers and indicate the reasons for them. s. split
g. formed G. opposition (Why Rule 3?)
f. which was established (Why which?)
U. independence F. freedom S. state
L. teaching d. pressed (Note Rule 8.)
E. simplicity M. pattern ä. oldest
e. introduced A. adherents
A. reference R. zeal-for-purity

Königin Elizabeth, die[5] sich ihnen widersetzte, erliess 1562 die sogenannte Uniformitäts-**Akte,**[1] ein Gesetz der kirchlichen **Gleichförmigkeit,**[1] durch welches[5] das Bekenntnis und die Unterschrift der neununddreissig Artikel, sowie die Teilnahme an den bisherigen kirchlichen **Gebräuchen** befohlen wurde. Diejenigen, welche[5] sich der Akte fügten, wurden[6] "Konformisten", die **Widerstrebenden** "Nonkonformisten", später **"Dissenters"** genannt,[8] mit Geld und **Gefängnis** bestraft,[8] ihrer **Ämter** entsetzt, und[8] vielfach verfolgt, die Geistlichen[4] sogar des Landes verwiesen.

w. opposed e. issued
G. law
G. uniformity B. confession
U. signing T. participation
b. previous G. usages b. commanded
D. those (App. 14, 2) s.f. conformed
W. opponents (Note Rule 8 B, sent. 11 b.)
Gef. prison b. punished e. removed
v. persecuted G. pastors v. banished s. even

Ihre eigentümlichen **Ansichten,**[1] welche[5] sich fast bloss auf die äussere **Kirchenverfassung** bezogen, während sie[4] den reformirten **Lehrbegriff,** besonders die calvinistische **Prädestinationslehre,** streng festhielten, bestanden namentlich in **Folgendem:** sie verwarfen die bischöfliche Kirchenverfassung als nicht nach göttlichem **Recht** bestehend, erklärten alle Diener der Kirche für völlig gleich,[1] wollten[6] die Kirche aus der engen Verbindung mit dem Staate herausreissen und forderten, dass jede einzelne Kirchengemeinschaft[4] durch Presbyterien, die ganze Kirche durch die Beschlüsse der[3] aus denselben gebildeten **Synoden,** geleitet werde; sie verwarfen, als spätere papistische Zutaten alle priesterliche **Kleidung,**[1] das Zeichen des **Kreuzes,**[1] das Neigen des Hauptes beim Namen **Jesu,**[1] das Knieen beim **Abendmahl,**[1] die Konfirmation,[1] die Gebete nach **Formularen,**[1] selbst **die kirchlichen** Feste und **Festzeiten.**[1]

e. peculiar A. views b. exclusively
s. b. are based K. church constitutions
L. teaching-concept, dogma s. strictly
f. maintained b. consisted v. rejected
a. b. as existing n. according to
D. servants v. completely g. equal
h. remove e. close V. connection
f. required e. single K. parish
B. decrees Why Rule 3?
g. which were formed g. conducted
Z. additions K. clothing
Z. sign K. cross N. bowing Note Rule 1.
G. prayer s. even (App. 13, 2a)

Bei dem schroffen Gegensatz gegen die herrschende Kirche wurden[6] die Verordnungen auf das **Strengste** gegen sie vollzogen, und als sie,[4] dadurch erbittert,[11] 1580 Satiren gegen die Königin und deren bischöfliche **Regierung** drucken liessen, wurden[6] einige hingerichtet und alle,[4] welche[5] einen Monat lang die bischöfliche **Kirche** nicht besuchten, vom Parlament mit zwanzig Pfund Sterling **Strafe** belegt. Ja, 1592, wurde[6] die Versäumniss des Kultus sogar mit Gefängnis und **Landesverweisung** bestraft,[8] ausserdem viele heimliche presbyterianische **Geistliche** abgesetzt.

s. rough G. opposition h. prevailing
v. accomplished V. ordinances
a.d.S. most severely Note Rule 11.
e. embittered d. l. had printed
h. executed M. month
bes. visited, attended bel. assessed
V. neglect G. prison K. worship
b. punished (Note rule 8 B, s. 11, b.)
a. dismissed G. clergymen

Nachdem sie[4] in den letzten Regierungsjahren Elizabeths einigermassen **Ruhe** gehabt hatten, wurden[6] sie unter **Jakob I.** wieder mehr bedrückt, weil er[4] ihr **Unabhängigkeitsgefühl** für politisch gefährlich hielt. Infolgedessen verliess 1607 ein Häuflein Puritaner aus Scrooby im nördlichen England unter Leitung ihres Geistlichen John Robinson die **Heimat**[1] und liess sich in dem duldsameren Holland in der Stadt **Leyden** nieder.[2] Sie hatten[6] indessen auch hier mit vielfacher **Not** zu kämpfen; als Fremde fanden sie keinen **Anklang**[1] und gingen der Gefahr entgegen,[2-7] in dem grossen **Menschenstrom** spurlos zu verschwinden.

n. after R. years of government
e. to some extent R. rest
b. oppressed U. independence-feeling
g. dangerous (h. held as) i. consequently
H. group
L. leadership G. pastor H. home
What goes with "liess"? d. tolerant
i. meanwhile k. fight, struggle
F. foreigners A. accord G. danger
e. approached (the danger to what?)
v. disappear s. without a trace

Da hörten sie von der neuen englischen Kolonie in **Virginien**[1] und kamen auf den **Gedanken,**[7] in jenen **Wildnissen**[9] ein Asyl zu suchen. Die Gefahren der Auswanderung und des Meeres er-

h. heard
G. thought (to what?)
G. dangers A. emigration M. sea

†G. A. Zimmermann, **Vierhundert Jahre amerikanischer Geschichte**

schreckten diese **Menschen**[1], die man[4] Pilgerväter nannte, weil sie[4] um ihrer **Religion** willen wanderten, und die[5] an Verbannung gewöhnt waren, nicht; und so schrieben sie nach **England**[1]: "Seit langer Zeit sind wir der zarten Milch unseres Mutter**landes** entwöhnt und[8] mit den Schwierigkeiten eines fremden **Landes** vertraut; das Volk ist arbeitsam und einfach; wir sind[6] miteinander als ein Körper durch einen **Vertrag** gebunden, den Gott[4] selbst geheiligt hat; wir würden[6] uns ein Gewissen daraus machen[7], ihn zu verletzen; wir halten uns tief verpflichtet,[7] uns allen das Wohl des Nächsten und der **Gemeinde** angelegen sein zu lassen. Wir sind nicht gleich **Menschen,**[1] die Kleinigkeiten[4] entmutigen können.

e. frightened M. people
u-w. for the sake of (App. 20, la, b)
g. accustomed Note position of nicht.
za. tender, delicate
e. weaned S. difficulties f. foreign
v. accustomed, entrusted a. industrious
K. body V. treaty, contract
g. sanctified G. conscience
v. violate
v. obligated (to what?)
a.s.z.l. to let ourselves be interested
d. whom K. trivialities e. discourage

Im Jahre 1620, am 17. September, schiffte sich ein Teil derselben nach einem feierlichen Gottesdienste und Fasten auf dem Schiffe "**Mayflower**" ein;[2] ihre Zahl betrug gegen **100,** Frauen und **Kinder** eingerechnet. Ihr Ziel war das Ufer des **Hudson,**[1] also die **Stelle,**[1] wo jetzt New York steht. Allein der Schiffskapitän brachte sie nach einer nahezu dreimonatlichen gefährlichen Fahrt weiter nördlich ans **Cap Cod,**[1] in eine Gegend,[1] die[5] nicht einmal mehr zu **Virginien** gehörte, sondern[8] an die **Nordgesellschaft** abgetreten war, mit der die "Pilgerväter"[4] keinen **Vertrag** abgeschlossen hatten. Ehe sie[4] am 11. **Dezember** landeten, versammelten sie sich in der Kajüte und verbanden sich gegenseitig,[1] weil man[4] nun auf einem **Boden** landen sollte, wo man[4] weder Eigentumsrecht, noch **Gerichtsbarkeit** hatte, durch einen schriftlichen **Vertrag,** der[5] noch erhalten ist und der[5] so lautet:

T. part f. solemn G. worship
e. embarked Z. number b. amounted
e. including Z. goal U. bank
A. but n. after nah. nearly
g. dangerous F. voyage G. region
g. belonged a. surrendered
V. treaty a. made, concluded
E. before v. assembled g. mutually
s. was to B. land w.–n. neither–nor
E. property right G. jurisdiction
V. contract e. preserved l. reads u. signed

"Im Namen Gottes, Amen Wir, deren Namen[4] unterschrieben sind, die loyalen Untertanen unseres **furchtbaren Königs Jakob,**[1] die wir[4] zur Ehre Gottes, zur Verbreitung des Christenglaubens, zum Ruhm auch unseres Königs und unseres **Landes**[9] eine Fahrt unternommen haben, um[7] die erste Ansiedlung in den nördlichen Teilen von **Virginia** zu gründen, wir vereinigen und verbinden uns kraft dieser Urkunde in Gegenwart **Gottes**[1] und eines jeden von uns vor dem anderen feierlich zu einem bürgerlichen **Gemeinwesen**[1], um[7] die **Ordnung** zu erhalten und alle **Mittel** aufzubringen, welche[5] zur Förderung der oben angegebenen **Absichten** dienlich sind. Zu diesem Zwecke werden[6] wir nach Erfordernis der Zeit und Umstände solche gerechte und billige Gesetze, Beschlüsse, Verfügungen und **Ämter aufstellen,** festsetzen und einrichten, welche[5] für das allgemeine Beste der **Kolonie** für nötig und passend erachtet werden und denen wir[4] hiermit allen gebührenden Gehorsam und alle pflichtmässige **Unterwerfung** geloben."

l. reads u. signed
U. subjects f. dread
E. honor V. spreading
R. fame
u. undertaken F. voyage A. settlement v. unite
k. by virtue of U. document G. presence
f. solemnly
b. civil G. commonwealth O. order
a. raise F. furtherance
a. indicated A. intentions Z. purpose
E. requirement U. circumstances
b. fair G. laws B. decrees V. command
f. establish e. arrange
n. necessary e. deemed p. fitting
g. due, proper G. obedience
U. compliance g. vow.

Sie landeten dann und entschlossen sich zur Niederlassung in einer **Örtlichkeit,**[1] welche[5] bei den **Indianern**[9] Patuzet hiess, die sie[4] aber zur Erinnerung an die letzte englische Stadt, welche sie[4] gesehen hatten,[9] New Plymouth nannten. John Carver wurde[6] zum Gouverneur erwählt. Mit unerschütterlichem Gottvertrauen ertrugen sie die Beschwerden des Hungers und der **Kälte**[1], und selten wohl gab es eine Schar sittlich festerer und fleissigerer **Leute**[1]. Schon im Monat Dezember starben sechs **Kolonisten**[1] und viele waren erkrankt. Der Gouverneur verlor seinen **Sohn**[1], neben welchem er und sein Weib selbst[4] bald zu **Grabe** gelegt wurden. Es gab eine **Zeit**[1], wo nur sieben Personen[4] nicht an das **Siechbett** gefesselt waren.

e. resolved N. settlement
Ö. locality b. with
h. was called E. memory
S. city
e. chosen, elected
u. unshakable G. trust in God e. bore
B. hardships g. e. was there
S. group s. morally f. more industrious
s. died (sterben)
e. ill v. lost n.w. beside whom
e. g. there was
Z. time g. bound, fetter

(If drill is necessary, give reasons for each number and the bold-faced nouns.)

Die Verfassung der Kolonie entwickelte sich von Anfang an völlig unabhängig vom **Mutterlande,**[1] zumal da die Ansiedler[4] in Plymouth niemals einen königlichen **Freibrief** erhielten und[8] ihnen erst volle zehn Jahre nach ihrer Landung von der Compagnie in England ein Rechtstitel auf das[3] in **Besitz** genommene **Land** zuerkannt wurde. Die ganze Gemeinde pflegte sich[7] zur **Beratung** zu versammeln und der Gouverneur leitete mit fünf, später sieben Beisitzern die öffentlichen **Angelegenheiten.**[1] Als 1639 die Zahl der Kolonisten[4] beträchtlich gestiegen war, richtete man ein Repräsentativsystem ein.[2] Das Volk machte seine Gesetze selbst und strafte nach **Willkür** die Verbrecher mit Geld, Haft oder dem **Tode.**[1]

V. constitution e. s. developed
v. completely **u. independent** z. especially
A. settlers n. never **F. charter**
e. received e. not until
R. legal title B. possession
g. which was taken z. acknowledged
p. was accustomed v. assemble
l. directed s. later B. assistants
A. affairs Z. number b. considerably
What goes with "richtete"?
G. laws s. penalized n. W. arbitrarily
V. criminals H. arrest

Der Nachschub aus England nahm mit den **Jahren** zu.[2] Immer noch litten dort die Puritaner unter dem Drucke religiöser **Intoleranz** und suchten Freiheit in der neuen **Welt.**[1] Die Plymouth-Compagnie gewährte ihnen einen neuen Landstrich an der Küste von **Massachusetts**[1], so dass sich 1628 John Endicott[4] mit 100 Anhängern auf den Weg nach **Amerika** machte. Lange durchstreifte man die **Umgegend**[1], ehe ein geeigneter Ort zur Ansiedlung[4] sich zeigen wollte. Zuletzt fiel ihre Wahl auf einen **Ort**[1], den die Indianer[4] Naumkeag nannten. Die Puritaner tauften ihn in **Salem** um[2].

N. recruits
z. increased (Why Rule 2?) l. suffered
D. pressure F. freedom
g. granted (Why Rule 1?)
Note that "sich" goes with "machte".
A. followers W. way
d. roamed U. region
g. suitable A. settlement Z. finally
W. choice n. called
u. re-christened

Im Jahre 1631 wurde[6] ein Gesetz erlassen, dass nur derjenige[4] ein **Stimmrecht** haben sollte, welcher[5] Glied einer Kirche der **Kolonie** sei. Da nun aber nur ein Viertel der Bevölkerung[4] aus **Gemeindegliedern** bestand, wurde[6] durch diese Massnahme die Mehrzahl von der **Regierung** ausgeschlossen. Überhaupt übten dieselben Puritaner, welche[5] hier eine Stätte der **Gewissensfreiheit** gesucht hatten, die ärgste **Tyrannei** aus.[2] Im Jahre 1635 verliess eine Schar Unzufriedener unter der Führung des Geistlichen Hooker das Gebiet von **Massachusetts,**[1] drang unter vielen Beschwerden bis an den Connecticut-Fluss vor[2] und gründete die Niederlassungen Windsor und **Hartford.**[1] Eine andere Kolonie wurde[6] 1638 durch Rev. John Davenport bei **New Haven** gegründet, welche[5] 1665 mit **Connecticut** vereinigt wurde.

w.e. was issued (App. 7, 5, b)
d. that one (App. 14,2) G. member
D. since (App. 25, 2) V. quarter
G. church members b. consisted
M. measure Meh. majority a. excluded
What goes with "übten"? welche?
G. freedom of conscience a. exercised
v. abandoned S. group U. dissatisfied
F. guidance G. pastor G. region
What goes with "drang"? B. hardships
v. pressed g. established
N. settlements w. g. was founded
(App. 7, 5, b) v. combined

Ziemlich gleichzeitig mit der Gründung der Kolonie Connecticut vollzog sich diejenige der östlichen Nachbarkolonie Rhode-**Island.**[1] In diesem[3] schon 1614 durch den holländischen Seefahrer **Block** entdeckten Gebiet unterhielten die Holländer einen einträglichen **Pelzhandel** und beanspruchten bald die Gerichtsbarkeit bis nach der Narragansett-Bai.[1] Da suchte in den Wäldern dieser Bucht Roger Williams von Salem eine Zufluchtsstätte vor der Verfolgung seiner eigenen **Glaubensbrüder.**[1] Er war Geistlicher an der Kirche zu **Salem.**[1] Bald aber erregten seine freisinnigen Ansichten über Gewissensfreiheit und den schädlichen Charakter einer Verschmelzung von Staat und **Kirche,**[1] wie sie[4] in **Massachusetts** tatsächlich bestand, bei den weltlichen und geistlichen Würdenträgern zu Boston grosses **Ärgernis**[1]. Immer kühner bestritt er auch die Rechtsgültigkeit des[3] von der obrigkeitlichen **Behörden** vertretenen königlichen **Privilegiums,**[1-7] indianisches Landgebiet mit Umgehung der käuflichen **Erwerbung**[9] in Besitz zu nehmen und sprach der bürgerlichen Gewalt die **Befugnis**[7] ab[2], Glauben und **Gottesdienst**[9] einem menschlichen **Individuum** aufzuzwingen. Die Verfechtung dieser Gesetze in Wort und Schrift zog ihm die Verbannung zu[2], welche[5] zu Ende des Jahres 1635 über ihn gehängt wurde.

z. almost g. at the same time
N. neighbor-colony (Why Rule 3?)
V. advocating
e. which was discovered (Why which?)
u. maintained e. profitable b. claimed
G. jurisdiction
d. Then, there (App. 25, 1)
Z. refuge place V persecution
e. own Gl. fellow believers
e. excited f. liberal-minded A. views
G. freedom of conscience s. harmful
V. fusion
b. existed t. actually
W. dignitaries A. anger
i. k. more and more boldly a. contested
R. legal validity v. which was represented
(Note the call here for a "to".)
B. possession Note Rule 9.
a. denied G. power B. authority
a. force upon (an individual) Verf. defense
V. banishment
z. incur g. imposed

If time permits, repeat the translation, this time ignoring the numbers as much as possible. Later an * will be placed where certain numbers should appear. Accustom yourself to the word order as outlined by the Rules. Your object is principally to remove elements on the right side of the noun.

Deutsche Ansiedler während der Kolonialzeit

(Give reasons for the numbers and the bold-faced nouns.)

Als, wie wir[4] in den vorigen **Kapiteln** gesehen haben, die Regierungen der west-europäischen Küstenländer[4] die Kolonisation der amerikanischen **Küstenstaaten** planmässig in Angriff nahmen, schauten sie sich um nach tüchtigen **Menschen,**[1] welche bereit waren,[7] die gefahrvolle Reise in die neue **Welt** zu unternehmen und[8] sich dort anzusiedeln. Der Markt, auf dem sie[4] solche **Kolonisten** warben, war— Deutschland.[1] Die Zustände unseres alten Vaterlandes waren ja damals höchst traurige[1] und[8] deshalb für den Ausbruch des **"Auswanderungsfiebers"** ausserordentlich geeignet. Der Dreissigjährige Krieg war vorüber. Er bildet den dunklen Hintergrund des düstern **Gemäldes,**[1] welches die deutsche Einwanderung der letzten Hälfte des 17. und 18. **Jahrhunderts**[4] unsern Blicken entrollt.

A. when w. as K. chapters
R. governments K. coast lands
p. systematically i. a. n. attacked
s. s. u. looked about n. for
b. ready (to what?) g. dangerous
u. undertake a. settle
w. recruited Z. conditions
d. at that time h. highly
d. therefore A. outbreak
a. extraordinary g. suited
H. background d. dismal
G. picture E. emigration H. half
e. unfolds u. B. to our views

Die erste Ansiedelung der neuen Welt ist ein grosses Bild des Grauens,[1] die Masseneinwanderung der Deutschen bis beinahe zur Hälfte unseres Jahrhunderts eine Geschichte von **Leiden.**[1] Deutschland war verwüstet. Viele Menschen hatten[6] den **Mut** verloren,[7] das Leben in der Heimat von **neuem** anzufangen. Hunderttausende blickten in die **Ferne,**[1] die Einen nach Osten, die Andern nach Westen, um[7] in der **Fremde** Hülfe[9] zu suchen. Zahlreiche Schriften erschienen für und gegen die Auswanderung nach diesen und jenen **Ländern.**[1] An den Höfen deutscher Fürsten begann die goldene Zeit der **Volksaussauger.**[1] Dabei hörten die Kriege nicht auf[2] und die ewigen Feindseligkeiten der kleinen Reichsstände unter einander. Dazu kamen die religiösen Wirren und **Bedrängnisse**[1] welche[5] den Auswanderern am ehesten den **Mut**[7] einflössten, den Gefahren der **Seereise** zu trotzen.

A. settlement Grau. horror
b. almost G. history
L. suffering v. devastated
M. courage (to what?) H. home country
a. begin F. distance
H. aid (Note Rule 9.)
Z. numerous S. articles
A. emigration
H. courts V. exploiter
a. ceased K. wars
e. eternal F. hostilities
W. confusions B. tribulations
e. instilled M. courage
t. defy G. dangers

Unter solchen Umständen fanden in Deutschland, welches[5] trotz aller Drangsale und Kriege, der Zahl nach, noch immer der Bienenkorb **Europas** war, Werber, Agenten für Schiffseigentümer, Landbesitzer und Andere, religiöse **Schwärmer,** welche[5] neue **Sekten** gründeten und[8] den schon bestehenden in der **Fremde**[9] neue Gläubige zuführen wollten, einen fruchtbaren **Boden,** ein willkommenes **Gehör.**[1] Die Rheder von Amsterdam, welche[5] den grössten Teil der Frachten nach **Indien** verloren, die englische Regierung, welche[5] ihre Kolonien bevölkern, die Gesellschaften, welche grosse Ländereien in der neuen **Welt** veräussern oder urbar machen wollten, sie alle warben auf dem deutschen Markte um Menschen,[1] um lebendige **Fracht.**[1] In diese Zeit fällt die erste deutsche Masseneinwanderung nach **Pennsylvanien**[1] und die Gründung von **Germantown,**[1] dann der Zug der Pfälzer nach London und von da nach New **York,**[1] die Einwanderung der Salzburger nach Carolina, Georgia und so weiter.[1]

U. conditions f. found (what?)
t. inspite of D. hardships
d. Z. n. in number B. bee-hive
W. recruiters S. ship owners
S. enthusiasts g. established
z. supply G. converts
f. fertile base w. welcome G. ear
R. ship owner, freighters F. freight
R. government
G. societies L. lands v. sell u. arable
w. recruited M. people
l. living F. freight
G. establishment

E. immigration

Allerdings gab es schon vorher einzelne Deutsche in **Amerika,**[1] welche[5] unter Holländer, Schweden und **Engländer** versprengt,[11] ihr Glück in der weiten **Welt** suchten. Aber ihre Fühlung mit dem aufgegebenen Vaterland war abgebrochen, sie zogen keine **Genossen** nach sich,[2] gründeten keine Niederlassung und blieben zufällige Bestandteile einer fremden **Bevölkerung.**[1] Erst mit der Gründung Germantowns (jetzt ein Teil der Stadt Philadelphia) beginnt die deutsche Ansiedlung in **Amerika.**[1] Der Führer dieser ersten Pilgerschaar war Franz Daniel **Pastorius.**[1] Am 26. September 1651 zu Sommerhausen in **Franken** geboren,[11] studierte er die Rechte und wurde dann der Hofmeister eines **Junkers,**[1] mit dem er[4] auf **Reisen** ging. Als er[4] wieder nach Deutschland zurückkehrte, erfuhr er, namentlich in Frankfurt

What rules have you used on the page?
A. of course g. e. there were
v. while dispersed
G. fortune, happiness
F. contact a. abandoned
G. confederates n. drew with them
N. settlement z. accidental
B. components f. foreign j. now
F. leader
P. pilgrim-group
g. born
R. law w. became (App. 7, 3, b)
z. returned

und **Krefeld,** dass Penn[4] auch am **Rhein** gepredigt und[8] eine Anzahl von Leuten für seine **Lehren** gewonnen habe. Mit diesen Quäkern und **Mennoniten,** die[5] sich zur Fahrt nach **Pennsylvanien** rüsteten, wurde Pastorius bekannt; er fand Gefallen an ihren Lehren und entschloss sich, "[7]in Gesellschaft dieser Gott fürchtenden Menschen nach der neuerdings erfundenen Provinz Pennsylvania, **an den Endgrenzen Americae in der Westwelt gelegen,**" überzusiedeln und[8] daselbst nebst ihren Freunden ein still und christliches **Leben** zu führen. Die Frankfurter Landgesellschaft, welche[5] die **Auswanderung**[9] ins Werk setzte, machte ihn zu ihrem **Agenten.**[1]

e. learned n. especially
g. preached (See Rule 8-E, sent. 1)
L. teachings
r. equipped F. journey G. pleasure
e. resolved (to what?) G. society f. fearing
n. recently e. discovered
E. end limits g. situated ü. to move to
u. and (to what?) **n. together with**
L. land company
A. emigration i.W.s. organized

Der erste Auswanderertrupp, der[5] aus Krefeldern und **Frankfurtern** bestand und[8] 13 Familien mit 40 **Köpfen** zählte, schiffte sich am 24. Juli auf dem[3] in London von einem Quäker gecharterten Schiff **Concord** ein. Am 6. Oktober 1683 betraten sie den amerikanischen **Boden** und schritten sogleich zum Aufbau ihrer **Wohnstätten,**[1] der ersten deutschen **Stadt,** die sich Deutsche[4] auf unserem **Kontinent** erbauten. Der erste Winter ist stets für neue Ansiedlungen die Zeit einer schweren **Prüfung** und nicht ohne Beschwerlichkeit brachten ihn die Krefelder und Frankfurter[4] **in der neuen Heimat zu.**[2] **Von Luxus war keine Rede; Penn selbst** war[6] kaum vor Jahresfrist nach der **Kolonie** gekommen; alles war[6] im Werden und **Entstehen** begriffen, und es fehlte in den Hütten selbst an **Lebensmitteln.**[1] Aber man ertrug die Leiden mit Geduld und **Humor,**[1] so dass Einige vorschlugen,[7] die Stadt nicht Germantown, sondern **Armentown** zu nennen.

What rules are you using to 'remove' verbs from the end position? b. consisted
g. which was chartered (Why which?)
eins. embarked B. soil
A. building up W. homes
e. built (for themselves)
s. always A. settlements
s. serious P. test B. hardship
z. spent (Note the subject.)
R. talk, discussion
k. scarcely w. i. b. was in the process of
e. f. there was lacking H. huts
L. foods e. endured L. suffering
G. patience v. proposed
What calls for the "zu" verb?

Der Ackerbau war in der ersten Zeit die Hauptbeschäftigung der **Ansiedler,**[1] denn der Boden musste[6] den **Pflanzer** ernähren und in kurzer Zeit trugen die Felder im Norden und Süden der Stadt Korn genug,[1] dass man[4] eigene **Bedürfnisse** befriedigen und[8] selbst nach auswärts **Getreide** abgeben konnte. Die[3] mit germantownschem **Korn** beladenen Schiffe gingen nach Barbados.[1] Auch der Handelssinn brachte Früchte.[1] Von den Indianern wurde[6] Pelzwerk gekauft und[8] nach **England** geschickt; Pennsylvanien war reich an Wild und der Eigentümer der Kolonie hatte[6] zum Zeichen seiner Abhängigkeit von England dem Könige alljährlich zwei Biberfelle als schuldigen **Tribut** zu entrichten.

A. agriculture H. main occupation
A. settlers m. had to
e. nourish t. carried
e. own B. needs (See Rule 8 E 1.) G. grain
a. export Why Rule 3? b. which were loaded
H. sense of trade
F. fruits P. hides, furs
g. sent W. game
E. property owner Z. sign A. dependence
a. annually B. beaver-hides s. indebted e. to pay

Aber noch eine ganz besondere Überraschung erwartete hier die Rheinländer.[1] **Auf den Bäumen** der Urwälder rankte ein[3] ihnen wohlbekanntes Gewächs empor:[2] es war die wilde Weinrebe,[1] an deren Veredelung sie[4] sich sofort machten. Der "Neue" mag[6] in den ersten **Jahren** recht sauer geschmeckt haben, aber er war besser als keiner. Ferner wurde[6] viel Flachs gebaut und gesammelt.

U. surprise
e. awaited B. trees
e. climbed up G. growth w. which was well known K. grape vine V. improvement through budding s.s. so.m. they started at once
g. tasted g. cultivated

Von Jahr zu Jahr kamen nun auf die Berichte der Erstangekommenen hin neue **Ansiedler,**[1] und schon im Jahre 1717 war die Einwanderung so stark[1], dass der damalige Statthalter[4] nachteilige Folgen davon befürchtete, wenn die Ausländer, d. h. die Deutschen,[4] entweder zu dicht bei einander wohnten oder[8] zerstreut unter den **Wilden** sich niederliessen. Die Verwüstung der herrlichen Rheinländer durch die **Franzosen**[1] und die religiöse Intoleranz trieb **Tausende,**[1] namentlich Anhänger von Sekten, Mennoniten, Mystiker, usw. nach **Pennsylvanien,**[1] wo sie[4] nach und nach die schönsten **Landesteile** besiedelten.

B. reports
E. first-arrivals h. (App. 21, 1)
E. emigration d. then
S. viceroy, governor n. disadvantageous
bef. feared z. d. too close
z. scattered W. Indians
n. settled V. devastation h. glorious
t. drove
A. adherents
n. u. n. by and by b. settled

Lutheraner und Reformierte fanden sich anfangs nur wenige ein.[2] Eine der ältesten lutherischen Ansiedelungen war die in Falkners Swamp (Neu-Hanover)[1], sogenannt nach ihrem Pastor Justus Falkner, der[5] 1703 zu Wicaco, jetzt Southwark in **Philadelphia,** ordiniert worden war.

What goes with "fanden"? a. initially
ä. oldest A. settlements
s. so named
j. now
o.w.w. had been ordained (App. 7, 5, d)

Sie befand sich im nordwestlichen Montgomery **County.**[1] Eine weitere Lutheraner-Niederlassung finden wir vor dem Jahre 1729 in Trappe (Neu-Providence) südlich von **Neu-Hanover.**[1] Es fehlte freilich der Sache der Lutheraner an fähigen **Predigern;**[1] erst als der junge, begabte,[3] in Göttingen und **Halle** ausgebildete Prediger Heinrich Mühlenberg[4] in Philadelphia **1741** eintraf und[8] mit energischer Hand sich der Sache der **Lutheraner** annahm, begann ein wirklicher **Aufschwung.**[1] Er sammelte die ratlosen **Lutheraner,**[1] organisierte sie und gab so der Kirche ein festes **Fundament.**[1] Ein Jahr nach seiner Ankunft baute er die Michaelskirche zu **Philadelphia.**[1] Mühlenbergs Tätigkeit liess[6] aber die Zahl der **Mitglieder** so anwachsen, dass zwanzig Jahre später eine neue — die Zionsgemeinde[4] — gegründet werden musste. Mühlenberg lebte abwechselnd an verschiedenen **Orten.**[1] Er brachte es dahin, dass 1763 schon 30 lutherische Gemeinden bestanden, und errichtete viele **Kirchen.**[1]

b.s. was found, was
w. further N. settlement
s. southward
S. cause f. capable P. preachers
g. gifted (Why Rule 3?)
a. who was trained (Why who?)
e. arrived u. and (what?)
a. took on, take charge of w. real
s. gathered r. disorganized
f. solid Note rule 1.
A. arrival T. activity l. caused Z. number
M. members a. increase
Z. Z. congregation a. alternately v. different
d. to the point G. congregations b. existed
e. erected

In all diesen verschiedenen deutschen Ansiedlungen gab sich auch geistiges Leben und **Streben** kund.[2] Diejenigen, welche kamen, um zu erziehen, und[8] eine gediegene **Bildung** mitbrachten, errichteten Bildungsanstalten in Bethlehem, Litiz und **Nazareth,**[1] die[5] bald zu den besten im **Staate** gehörten. Im Jahre 1738 wurde[6] in Germantown die erste deutsche Verlagsbuchhandlung und Druckerei von Christoph **Sauer** errichtet, nachdem schon vorher Benjamin Franklin[4] einige deutsche Schriften, freilich mit lateinischen Buchstaben, gedruckt hatte. Christoph Sauer druckte die erste deutsche **Bibel,**[1] ausserdem gab er und später sein Sohn und Nachfolger, im Laufe von 40 Jahren etwa 150 deutsche **Schriften** heraus.[2] Am 20. August 1739 erschien im Sauerschen Verlag der "Hoch-Deutsch Pennsylvanische **Geschicht-Schreiber**[1]," d. h. die erste Nummer der ersten deutschen Zeitung unseres **Landes.**[1] Auch errichtete Sauer eine Papiermühle, die erste Schriftgiesserei und eine Buchbinderei unter den **Deutschen.**[1]

v. different A. settlements
k. was manifested (App. 11, 4, b)
d. those (App. 14, 2) g. genuine, superior
B. training m. brought along e. erected
B. educational-institutions
g. belonged w. was (App. 7, 5, b)
V. book-publishing establishment D. printery
e. erected n. after
s. articles f. to be sure
B. letters g. printed
a. besides What goes with "gab"? N. successor
L. course h. published e. appeared
Note rule 2. V. publishing house
d. h. that is Z. newspaper e. erected
Note Rule 1.
u. among

Die ersten Anfänge der Freiheitsbewegung in den Kolonien

Ehe wir[4] die **Ereignisse** besprechen wollen, welche[5] zur Trennung der Kolonien von ihrem **Mutterlande** führten, ist es nötig,[7] erst einen kurzen Blick auf die Regierungsform in den einzelnen Kolonien am Ende der französischen **Kriege** zu werfen. Es gab nämlich damals drei verschiedene Formen der **Regierung,**[1]—ein "royal government", ein "charter government" und ein "proprietary government".[1] Was[5] unter diesen zu verstehen ist, wird[6] sogleich klar werden.

E. before E. events b. discuss
T. separation
n. necessary B. glance (Note Rule 7.)
e. individual K. war
w. throw e. g. there were
Note Rule 1.
w. what- z.v.i. what is meant
(App. 12, 1) w.w. will become

Die älteste Kolonie, Virginia,[1] hatte, nachdem die Virginia-Compagnie[4] aufgelöst worden war, die erstere der drei **Regierungsformen**[1], d. h. der König von England ernannte den **Gouverneur**[1] und billigte oder verwarf die **Gesetze,**[1] welche[5] von den **Kolonisten** angenommen wurden. New York war[6] einem Herzog von **York** gegeben worden und stand somit unter der dritten **Regierungsform;**[1] doch als dieser Herzog[4] als **Jakob II.** den englischen **Thron** bestieg, wurde New York auch eine königliche Provinz wie **Virginien.**[1] New Jersey wurde ebenfalls eine königliche **Provinz,**[1] nachdem der König[4] die Rechte der ersten Eigentümer gekauft hatte und Ost und West Jersey[4] vereinigt worden waren. Dasselbe war der Fall mit den beiden **Carolinas.**[1] Georgia wurde zuerst besiedelt unter der Leitung von 21 **Trustees**[1]; diese traten aber 1752 die Regierung auch an den **König ab.**[2]

n. after
a. dissolved
e. appointed
b. approved v. rejected G. laws
a. accepted w.g.w had been given (App. 7, 5, d)
H. duke
b. ascended w. became (why?)
e. likewise
n. after
E. property owners
v. united F. case d. the same
b. settled
L. leadership R. government
a. surrendered

(Underline the nouns that should be bold-faced.)

Im Jahre 1679 wurde[6] New Hampshire von Massachusetts getrennt und wurde auch eine königliche Provinz.[1] So gab es also nach 1752 sieben Kolonien,[1] welche[5] unter königlicher Regierung standen, nämlich Virginia, New York, New Jersey, Nord- und Süd-Carolina, Georgia und New Hampshire.[1] Drei Kolonien, Massachusetts, Connecticut und Rhode Island, dagegen hatten sogenannte charter- oder Freibrief-Regierungen,[1] d.h. sie konnten[6] sich nach dem[3] vom König ausgestellten Freibrief zum grossen Teil selbst regieren. Massachusetts erhielt allerdings, nachdem sein erster Charter[4] widerrufen worden war, einen[3] vom König ernannten Gouverneur, allein die Macht blieb tatsächlich in den Händen der Kolonial-Legislatur.[1] Maine war damals noch ein Teil von Massachusetts.[1]

Give reasons for the numbers where drill is necessary. g. separated g. e. there were
k. royal R. government (Note Rule 1.)
Note also all Rules that remove verbs.
d. three
d. on the other hand s. so-called (Why Rule 3?)
in this line? a. which was issued
r. rule, govern
a. of course n. after w. recalled
e. who was named a. but
t. actually
d. at that time T. part

Maryland war[6], wie wir gesehen, dem Lord Baltimore, Pennsylvanien William **Penn** geschenkt worden. Diese beiden Männer nannte man darum "proprietaries"[1], d. h. Eigentümer.[1] Ihre Erben übten infolgedessen in diesen beiden Kolonien etwa dieselbe Macht aus,[2] wie der König in den sieben königlichen Kolonien.[1]

w.g.w. had been given (App. 7, 5 d)
Note the use of the passive.
b. two d. therefore m. one
E. heirs i. consequently b. two
e. about a. exercised
What Rules are called for in the paragraphs?

Jede der genannten dreizehn Kolonien hatte eine gesetzgebende Körperschaft,[1] die[5] in zwei Teile oder Häuser geteilt war: das Unterhaus oder die Assembly, dessen Mitglieder[4] vom Volke gewählt wurden, und das Oberhaus, dessen Mitglieder[4] in den königlichen Kolonien vom König, und in den proprietary-Kolonien von den Eigentümern ernannt wurden. In den Charter-Kolonien wurde[6] der Gouverneur sowohl wie die Mitglieder des Council von der Assembly gewählt.

g. legislative K. body g. enumerated
g. divided U. lower house
M. members g. elected
K. king
e. chosen E. owners
w.g. was elected (App. 7, 5, b)
M. members

Um[7] ein Gesetz zu passieren, war es nötig, dass beide Häuser[4] dafür stimmten und der Gouverneur[4] es bestätigte, eine Einrichtung,[1] die[5] bekanntlich heute noch beibehalten ist. Denn unser Senat entspricht dem damaligen Council.[1] Freilich ein Unterschied ist vorhanden; heute nämlich erwählt das Volk die Gouverneure und die Mitglieder beider Häuser,[1] während beinahe in allen 13 Kolonien das Volk[4] keine Stimme in der Wahl derselben hatte. Das Volk konnte[6] damals also kein Gesetz gegen den Willen des Königs oder der Eigentümer annehmen; infolgedessen kam es fortwährend zu Reibereien und Streitigkeiten zwischen den Gouverneuren,[1] welche[5] unter den Instruktionen von England handelten und den Vertretern des Kolonialvolkes.[1]

G. law n. necessary
s. voted b. confirmed
E. arrangement b. retained
e. corresponds to d. then F. to be sure
U. distinction v. present e. elects
M. members b. of both
w. while b. almost
S. voice W. election d. of the same (App. 14, 1)
G. law a. adopt i. consequently
f. constantly R. friction S. disputes
h. acted
V. representatives

Da letzteres[4] keinen Einfluss bei der Wahl der Gouverneure hatte, so waren diese in der Regel unwürdige Personen.[1] Oft waren es Verwandte von Günstlingen am Hofe,[1] später wurde[6] ihre Wahl meist getroffen, um[7] irgend einem einflussreichen Manne, welcher[5] die Stimme eines Parlamentsmitgliedes kontrollieren konnte,[9] einen Gefallen zu erweisen. Einige von den Gouverneuren waren unwissend und tyrannisch, andere ausschweifend oder habgierig.[1] Lord Cornbury, z. B. ein Vetter der Königin Anna, verschwendete als Gouverneur von New York die Einkünfte der Kolonie,[1] liess[6] wen er wollte einsperren und gab sich überhaupt durch seinen unmoralischen Lebenswandel der Verachtung preis.[2] Andros, ebenfalls Gouverneur von New York[1] und von Neu-England,[1] war ein Tyrann in all seinen Massregeln.[1] Viele der Gouverneure hatten kein anderes Ziel im Auge,[1] als[7] ihre Macht dazu[7] zu verwenden, möglichst rasch für sich ein **Vermögen** zu erwerben, was[5] auch mehreren gelang. Gouverneur Fletcher von New York verkaufte für schweres Geld Lizenzen an Piraten.[1]

d. since E. influence W. choice
i. d. R. as a rule
u. unworthy w.e. they were (App. 10, 3, k)
V. relatives G. favorites g. made
e. influential S. vote, voice
G. favor (Note Rule 9.)
z. e. to show E. some u. ignorant
a. licentious h. avaricious, greedy
V. cousin
v. squandered E. income
l. e. had arrested w. whom
What goes with "gab"? L. mode of life
V. contempt p. exposed Note rules 1, 2, 6, 7.
M. measures
Z. goal i.A. in mind a. than (to what?)
v. use
V. wealth e. acquire
v. sold How many Rules have you used on this page?

(An asterisk * is placed immediately above the place where certain rules are involved. Indicate the rules if drill is needed at these points.)

Alle Gesetze, welche* den Handel zwischen den Kolonien und andern **Ländern** regulierten, wurden* ferner vom englischen **Parlament** gemacht, und gar oft wurden* die Kolonien wider ihren **Willen** gezwungen,[7] von englischen **Kaufleuten** gekaufte[9] Negersklaven zuzulassen; ebenso mussten* sie beinahe alle ihre Hauptprodukte zum Verkauf nach **England** senden. Sie durften[6] ferner keine anderen europäischen Waren, nur die **Englands** kaufen, und fremden Schiffen wurde* daher das Landen in den Häfen der **Kolonien** nicht erlaubt. Auch wurden* Gesetze gemacht, welche* die Kolonisten entmutigten,[7] irgend welche Waren, wie Eisen- und Wollen-**Waren**, herzustellen, die* in England fabriziert wurden. Die Kolonisten hatten viele **Pelze,*** konnten* also billige Hüte herstellen; allein kein Hutfabrikant durfte* seine Fabrikate von einer Kolonie in eine **andere** senden.

f. furthermore w.g. were made (App. 7, 5b)
g. even w. were
w. against g. forced K. merchants
z. admit g. which were bought
b. almost V. sale d. were allowed
d. those k. buy f. foreign
n. e. not permitted
G. laws e. discouraged (to what?)
i. w. any h. to produce
f. manufactured
P. hides h. produce b. cheap
d. was permitted
a. another (noun is expected here)

In allen wichtigen Hafenplätzen wurden* Zollhäuser errichtet und die Zollgebühren flossen in die Kasse des **Königs.*** Der Zweck dieser Einrichtung war aber nicht sowohl, um[7] eine weitere **Einnahme** zu erzielen, sondern um[7] die Kolonisten durch das Erheben eines Zolles auf fremde **Waren** zu zwingen,[8] ihren Bedarf von englischen Fabrikanten zu beziehen, und[8] die Zollbeamten in den **Stand** zu setzen,[7] überhaupt alle **Waren,** die* nicht aus England kamen, fernzuhalten. Die Kolonisten umgingen auf alle mögliche Weise diese lästigen **Bestimmungen,**[1] und der Schmuggelhandel blühte längs der ganzen **Küste.*** Waren wurden* heimlich in einsamen Bachmündungen auf Long Island oder in kleinen Buchten weiter südlich gelandet; auch wurden vielfach die Zollbeamten, ja selbst die **Gouverneure** bestochen. Tabak, **welcher* nur nach englischen Häfen ausgeführt werden durfte,** wurde* auf hoher See von amerikanischen auf holländische **Schiffe** verladen, oder[8] mittelst kleiner Boote von den Buchten am James-Fluss und der Chesapeake **Bai** hinausgebracht. Auf solche Weise gewöhnte sich natürlich das Volk daran,[7] die Gesetze des **Mutterlandes** zu missachten und durch die unklugen Gesetze des Parlaments wurden* die Kolonisten nach und nach mit dem Gedanken des Widerstandes gegen die englische **Autorität** vertraut gemacht.

w. important H. harbor places
e. erected Z. duties K. treasury
Z. aim E. arrangement
e. gain E. income
E. raising Z. tax f. foreign
z. force (Note Rule 8 B, 11, b.)
b. draw, get Z. toll officials
in d. S. in the position
f. to keep distant, away u. circumvented
l. troublesome B. provisions
b. flourished h. secretly e. isolated
B. bays v. frequently
Z. toll officials b. bribed
a. exported
d.w. was permitted to be (App. 7, 6)
m. by means of Note how Rule 8 helps to remove the last verb.
h. brought out g. accustomed
d. (there to) (App. 23, 3) G. laws
m. disrespect u. unwise G. laws
n. u. n.by and by G. idea W. resistance
v. familiar

Ein weiterer Grund, weshalb die Freiheitsbewegung[4] Wurzel fassen musste, war der, dass die meisten der Kolonisten[4] durch Akte der Tyrannei aus ihrem Mutterlande vertrieben,[11] sich eine **Stätte** bereiten wollten, wo sie ungehindert sich religiöser und politischer **Freiheit** erfreuen konnten.

w. wherefore, why F. freedom-movement
w. root d. this
Note Rule 11, "having been driven away"
b. prepare S. place
e. enjoy F. freedom

Die Ursachen der Revolution

U. causes

Trotz all dieser Bewegungen in den Kolonien **zur Erhaltung** der Freiheit dachte Niemand im Ernst **daran,**[7] das Band zwischen den Kolonien und **England** zu lösen. Im Gegenteil, gerade am Schlusse der französisch-indianischen Kriege hatte[6] das Gefühl der Dankbarkeit gegen das Mutterland im amerikanischen **Volke**[9] Platz gegriffen; man atmete endlich **auf**[2] und **sah** einer ruhigen, friedlichen **Zukunft** entgegen,[2] nachdem nun **die britische Flagge**[4] überall vom atlantischen Ozean bis zum Golfe, und vom Mississippi bis zur Hudsons **Bai** wehte und Frankreichs Herrschaft[4] endgültig gebrochen war. Eine Trennung vom Mutterlande würde[6] vielleicht dann eingetreten sein, wenn die Kolonien einmal so gross und bevölkert geworden wären, um noch länger abhängig sein zu können;[7] aber bis dahin wären[6] sicherlich noch zwei bis drei **Generationen** vergangen, wenn nicht die englischen Machthaber selbst[4] in ihrer Verblendung die[3] unter der Asche fortglimmende **Freiheitsbewegung** derart angefacht hätten, dass sie[4] in kürzester Frist zum **Bruch** führte.

T. in spite of B. movements
E. maintenance F. freedom thereof (See App. 23, 3.) G. on the contrary
g. just S. close K. war
G. feeling D. gratitude
P. g. taken hold
a. breathed freely e. looked toward
Note Rule 2. n. after
b. till, up to w. waved
H. domination e. finally T. separation
e. occurred
einmal sometime b. populous
a. dependent d. to that time, point
v. passed (vergehen) s. surely
M. authorities V. blindness
f. which continued to glow a. kindled
F. time B. break

Der[3] im Jahre 1760 zur **Regierung** gelangte Georg III. stand nämlich vollständig unter dem Einfluss seines **Staatssekretärs**, Earl von **Bute**[1], welcher[5] auch seine **Erziehung** geleitet hatte. Lord Bute aber schlug den Kolonien gegenüber eine **ganz** andere **Politik** ein[2], als sein genialer Vorgänger Pitt; er vertrat die Ansicht, dass die Kolonien[4], wenn nötig, mit Waffengewalt zur Unterwerfung unter das **Parlament** gebracht werden müssten. Die Freibriefe sollten[6] aufgehoben und die Bevölkerung der Kolonien der **Kronbesteuerung** unterworfen werden. Im Einverständnis mit dem König betraute er den Lord Cavendish mit der Verwaltung der **Kolonien** und der Ausführung dieser **Pläne**[1]. Cavendish ging alsbald an die **Arbeit**[1] und wurde[6] dabei von Lord **Grenville** unterstüzt, dessen Bestreben dahin ging,[7] die Navigationsakte, d. h. die bereits früher erwähnte Bestimmung, wonach nur britische Schiffe[4] in amerikanischen **Häfen** landen durften, sowie alle sonstigen Handelsbeschränkungen in schärfster **Weise**[9] zur Anwendung zu bringen.

g. who came (Why who?)
v. completely E. influence
E. education g. supervised, conducted
g. vis-à-vis (See App. 15, 3, c.)
e. adopted a. than
V. predecessor v. represented A. view
n. necessary W. force of arms
U. subjugation b. brought (App. 7, 6)
F. charters (Supply an X after "aufgehoben".)
Why? See Rule 8-E, sentences 1 and 2.)
Einver. agreement b. entrusted
V. administration A. execution
a. immediately w. u. was supported (App. 7, 5, b)
B. endeavor d. to that point (to what?)
b. already e. mentioned d. were permitted
s. other H. trade limitations
A. application Note Rule 9 and how the "zu"-verb is removed.

Ehe die neue Besteuerung[4] ins **Werk** gesetzt werden konnte, war[6] das Jahr **1763** halb vergangen und Lord Bute **hatte** resigniert. An seine Stelle trat Lord Grenville,[1] ein zwar rechtschaffener **Staatsmann**,[1] aber ohne besondere Begabung.[1] Da er[4] den Staatschatz leer fand und[8] die Staatsschuld durch die Kosten der letzten Kriege, um 700 Millionen **Dollars** vermehrt, kam auch er auf den naheliegenden Gedanken,[7] die Kolonien zur Besteuerung heranzuziehen. Im März nahm das Parlament seine Bill an,[2] welche[5] eine Abgabe auf Wein legte und[8] die Zollgebühren für Zucker erhöhte.

E. before B. taxation
w. v. had passed a. s. S. in his place
r. upright, honest b. special
B. talent D. since S. state debt d. by
v. increased n. near-lying, obvious G. idea
(to what?) h. draw on B. taxation
a. accepted A. duty
er. raised Z. duties Z. sugar

Noch grösser wurde aber die Erbitterung,[1] als Grenville[4] eine neue Abgabe in Gestalt einer Steuer auf Stempelpapier, die sogen. Stempelakte, vorschlug, deren Ertrag er[4] auf eine Million **Dollars** veranschlagte. In Boston war es namentlich Samuel **Adams**,[1] ein eifriger Puritaner, welcher[5] die **Opposition** leitete und[8] eine Bürgerversammlung einberief, die[5] entschieden Stellung gegen die **Stempelakte** nahm. In Massachusetts, Rhode Island, New York, Virginien, Carolina, Connecticut und anderen Kolonien berieten die Landesversammlungen Bittschriften gegen die geplante Beeinträchtigung der kolonialen **Wohlfahrt**.[1] Am Ende Oktober 1764 wurde[6] in Pennsylvanien der damals achtundfünfzig Jahre alte Benjamin **Franklin**, der Führer der[3] mit den Landeseigentümern in einer heftigen **Fehde** liegenden Volkspartei, trotz des heftigen Widerspruchs der Anhänger der **letzteren** gewählt, um[7] seine Heimat im **Mutterlande** zu vertreten.

E. bitterness
G. form S. tax S. stamp paper
v. proposed deren whose E. profit
v. estimated n. especially
e. zealous
l. led e. called together
e. decidedly S. position
b. advised, debated
L. assemblies B. petitions
B. impairment W. welfare d. at that time
Why Rule 3 here?
L. land-owners l. which was lying
F. feud t. in spite of W. opposition
g. elected v. represent

Jedermann setzte Vertrauen in seine Rechtschaffenheit, seine staatsmännische **Klugheit**, seine Kenntnis des amerikanischen **Volkes**.[1] Man versprach sich viel von dem Einflusse seines[3] auch in **England** wohlbekannten Namens. Bald nach seiner **Ankunft** wurde[6] er von Grenville, Pitt und anderen **Politikern** besucht, um[7] seine Meinung über die **Stempelsteuer** zu vernehmen. Franklin erklärte jedermann, dass die Amerikaner[4] sich niemals zu einer **Steuer** verstehen würden, die[5] ohne ihre **Zustimmung** ausgeschrieben sei, und dass der Versuch,[7] eine solche **Akte** durchzusetzen, die Einheit des **Reiches** gefährden würde.

V. confidence R. honesty
K. wisdom K. knowledge
v. promise oneself, expect
E. influence Why Rule 3?
A. arrival
b. visited M. opinion
v. to hear e. explained
n. never v. would agree S. tax
Z. approval, consent a. levied
V. attempt d. set or put through
g. endanger E. unity R. empire

(Note: In the remaining pages dealing with history, there will appear an * above the place where certain rules are involved. Only in extremely difficult sentences do the numbers still appear. If there is need for drill, give reasons for the numbers or the *. Also indicate what nouns should be in bold-face type.)

Die Besiedlung des Westens der Vereinigten Staaten

(In case drill is necessary, cite reasons for the numbers, the * and the bold-faced nouns.)

Mit der Einverleibung von Texas und der[3] von **Mexiko** abgetretenen Landstrecken hatte* das Gebiet der **Union** wieder gewaltig zugenommen, denn nun gehörten das heutige Texas, Kalifornien, Nevada usw. zu demselben und die pacifische Küste mit all ihrem Reichtum stand offen.[1] Schon vor dem mexikanischen Kriege hatte* man letztere zu erforschen unternommen. Wir wissen, dass schon im Jahre 1787 ein gewisser Kapt. Gray von Boston* nach der Küste des stillen **Ozeans** fuhr, um[7] **Pelzhandel** zu treiben; Er fuhr dann mit Pelzen nach **China** und brachte 1790 eine Ladung Tee zurück[2]. Im Jahre 1791 und 1792 fuhr er abermals nach dem stillen Ozean* und war der erste Weisse, welcher* die Mündung des mächtigen **Stromes** entdeckte, den er[4] nach seinem Schiffe **Columbia** nannte. Diese Entdeckungsreisen Grays sind darum wichtig, weil sich darauf der Anspruch der Ver. Staaten auf das ganze,[3] unter dem Namen Oregon-Land (Oregon war ein anderer Name für den Columbia-Fluss) bekannte, die heutigen Staaten Oregon, Washington, Idaho und einen Teil von **Montana** umfassende **Gebiet** stützte.

E. incorporation
a. which were surrendered G. region, area
z. increased g. powerfully g. belonged
K. coast R. wealth Note Rule 1 and the rules that remove the verbs.
u. undertaken e. explore w. know
g. certain
s. pacific P. fur trade t. carry on
P. hides
L. load (Note Rule 2.) z. bring back
a. once more W. white man
e. discovered M. mouth m. mighty
E. discovery-voyages
w. important What verb goes with "sich"?
A. claim Why rule 3? g. entire (what?)
a. another Why an X here? See Rule 3 C-1, discussion of model sentence and sentences **1,2,3,4.**
u. which embraces s. st. was supported

Lange Jahre nach Gray kamen nur vereinzelte Pioniere dorthin.[1] Im Jahre 1803 sandte Präsident Jefferson die Kapitäne Lewis und Clark den Missouri-Fluss hinauf,[2] um* über die Rocky Mountains nach dem Gebiet des Columbia-**Flusses** vorzudringen. Unter den fürchterlichsten Entbehrungen und Gefahren gelangten diese kühnen Pioniere nach ihrem **Ziele,*** verbrachten den ersten Winter am Mississippi,* gingen dann 1804 den Missouri bis zu seinen Quellen hinauf.[2] Lewis gab den drei Quellflüssen die Namen Jefferson, Madison und Gallatin.* Sie erreichten dann westlich den Kaskaskia River,* einen linken Nebenarm des Columbia,* dessen Mündung sie* am 15. November 1805 erreichten, nachdem sie* vom Zusammenfluss des Missouri und des Mississippi aus einen Weg von mehr als 4000 **Meilen** zurückgelegt hatten. Nachdem sie* den dritten Winter am südlichen Ufer des **Columbia** zugebracht hatten, kehrten sie zurück* und erreichten am 23. September 1806 glücklich St. Louis.* Der Kongress schenkte Lewis und seinen Begleitern für die geleisteten Dienste grosse Strecken Landes,* ausserdem wurde* Lewis, der[5] früher Privatsekretär **Jeffersons** gewesen war, zum Gouverneur des Territoriums **Missouri** ernannt. Von 1811 bis 1813 bestand an der Mündung des Columbia-Flusses die Ansiedlung Astoria von dem bekannten Johann Jakob **Astor***, welcher* dort den **Pelzhandel** im grossen betrieb.

v. individual, scattered
s. sent (senden) h. up
u. v. in order to penetrate G. region
f. terrible E. deprivations
G. dangers g. came k. bold
Z. goal v. spent what goes with "gingen"?
Q. sources
Q. source-rivers
Note rule 1 and the rules that remove the verbs.
e. reached w. westward
d. whose M. mouth e. reached
n. after Z. merging, juncture,
v. a. note (App. 21, la, b.) z. covered, traveled n. after
z. spent s. southern U. bank
z. came back e. reached
s. gave
B. companions g. accomplished D. service
S. areas a. besides g. w. had been
e. appointed, elected b. existed
M. mouth A. settlement
b. famous P. fur trade
b. carried on i. g. on large scale

Im Jahre 1810 schloss die Union mit England einen Vertrag ab,[2] wodurch die nördliche Grenze der Union festgestellt, aber das Oregon-Gebiet[4] den Bürgern und Untertanen beider **Mächte** offen erklärt wurde; Oregon gehörte also England und den Ver. Staaten vorläufig gemeinsam.[1] Als dann aber in den dreissiger und vierziger Jahren die Flut der Bevölkerung* sich nach dem Westen und **Nordwesten** zu wälzen begann, nachdem es[4] schon geschienen, als ob ein neuer Krieg mit England[4] deshalb ausbrechen würde beschloss der Kongress zu unterhandeln, und es gelang dem Staatssekretär Polks, Buchanan,[7] mit **England**[9] einen Vertrag abzuschliessen, worin der 49. Breitegrad[4] als Grenze anerkannt wurde, welche[5] heute noch die Grenze zwischen den Ver. Staaten und den britischen Besitzungen im **Nordwesten** bildet.

What goes with "schloss"?
a. concluded V. treaty G. boundary
f. established (See Rule 8-E. 1.)
b. both M. powers g. belonged
v. tentatively g. in common
F. tide
B. population z. w. to roll
n. after g. seemed (Note abs. of aux.)
a. break out z. u. to negotiate
g. succeeded (to what?)
a. conclude V. treaty (Note Rule 9.)
a. recognized G. boundary
B. possessions N. north west

Hauptplaneten†
Zahl und Epoche der Entdeckung

Von den sieben **Weltkörpern**, welche[5] seit dem höchsten Altertum durch ihre stets veränderte relative Entfernung unter einander von den,[3] gleiche Stellung und gleiche **Abstände** scheinbar bewahrenden, funkelnden Sternen des **Fixsternhimmels** unterschieden worden sind, zeigen sich nur fünf: Merkur, Mars, Venus, Jupiter und Saturn, sternartig. Die Sonne und Mond blieben, da sie[4] grosse Scheiben bilden, auch wegen der grösseren Wichtigkeit, die man[4] in Folge religiöser **Mythen** an sie knüpfte, gleichsam von den übrigen abgesondert. So kannten nach Diodor die Chaldäer nur 5 **Planeten**;[1] auch Plato, wo er[4] im Timäus nur einmal der **Planeten** erwähnt, sagt ausdrücklich, "um die[3] im Centrum des **Kosmos** ruhende Erde bewegen sich der Mond, die Sonne und fünf andere **Sterne**, welchen[5] der Name **Planeten** beigelegt wird; das Ganze also in **Umgängen**." Eben so werden[6] in der alten pythagorischen Vorstellung vom Himmelsgebäude nach Philolaus unter den 10 göttlichen Körpern "unmittelbar unter dem Fixsternhimmel" die fünf **Planeten** genannt; ihnen folgen dann Sonne, Monde und **Erde**. Selbst Ptolemäus redet immer nur noch von 5 **Planeten**.[1]

What does "welche" call for?
A. antiquity
What does "den" call for?
b. which preserve, keep f. sparkle
u. distinguished z.s. are shown
s. starlike
b. remained (what?) S. discs
W. importance
k. tied g. as it were
a. separated (What calls for "a"?)
e. make mention of (hence gen.) old, rare use of "erwähnen" here r. which rests b. move
S. stars w. to which
b. w. is given, attributed, assigned
U. loops, circuits
V. idea H. structure of heaven
g. divine u. directly, immediately
i. (after) them S. even r. speaks

Die Namen, durch welche die sternartigen 5 Planeten[4] bei den alten **Völkern** bezeichnet wurden, sind zweierlei **Art**: Götternamen, oder bedeutsame, beschreibende, von physischen Eigenschaften **hergenommene**. Was[5] ursprünglich davon den Chaldäern oder den **Agyptern** angehöre, ist nach den **Quellen**, die[5] bisher haben benutzt werden können, um so schwerer zu entscheiden, als die griechischen Schriftsteller[4] uns nicht die ursprünglichen,[3] bei anderen **Völkern** gebräuchlichen Namen, sondern nur in das **Griechische** übertragene, nach der Individualität ihrer **Ansichten** gemodelte **Aequivalente** darbieten. Was die Aegypter[4] früher als die **Chaldäer** besessen, ob diese[4] blos als begabte Schüler der **Ersteren** auftreten, berührt die wichtigsten aber dunklen Probleme der ersten Gesittung des **Menschengeschlechts**,[1] der Anfänge wissenschaftlicher Gedankenentwickelung am Nil oder am **Euphrat**.[1]

b. designated z. of two types G. divine names
bes. expressive (what?)
h. which were derived (Why is "h." bold-faced?)
u. so. s. all the more difficult z. e. to decide
S. writers (What does this subject call for?) ursp.?
g. which are original, common (Why which?)
ü. which have been carried over g. which are modeled (Why which?)
b. merely beg. gifted, talented ber. touches
w. most important G. civilization M. human race
G. thought development
A. striking, noticeable

Auffallend ist es, dass Plato und Aristoteles[4] sich nur der göttlichen Namen für die Planeten, die[5] auch Diodor nennt, bedienen: während später z. B. in dem[3] dem **Aristoteles** fälschlich zugeschriebenen Buche de Mundo schon ein Gemisch von beiden Arten von Benennungen, der göttlichen und der beschreibenden (expressiven) sich findet. Die beschreibenden **Benennungen**,[1] so alt und chaldäisch sie[4] zum Teil auch sein mögen, fanden sich bei griechischen und römischen **Schriftstellern**, doch erst recht häufig in der Zeit der **Cäsaren**.[1] Ihre Verbreitung hängt mit dem Einfluss der **Astrologie** zusammen.[2] Die Planetenzeichen sind, wenn man die Scheibe der Sonne und die Mondsichel auf ägyptischen **Monumenten** abrechnet, sehr neuen **Ursprungs**.[1]

g. divine
s. b. made use of
w. while z. which was ascribed (Why which?)
G. mixture b. both
B. names
s. f. is found (Why is?) s.a.un.ch. s. a.s. m. however old and Chaldean they may be S. writers h. frequently
V. distribution E. influence
z. connects, is connected
a. disregards s. n. U. of a very recent origin

Wenn sich die Zahl der sichtbaren Planeten[4] nach den frühesten Einschränkungen der Benennungen auf 5, später mit Hinzufügung der grossen Scheiben der Sonne und des Mondes auf 7 belief, so herrschten doch auch schon im Altertum **Vermutungen**,[1] dass ausser diesen sichtbaren Planeten noch andere, lichtschwächere, ungesehene, vorhanden waren. Diese Meinung wird[6] von Simplicius als eine **aristotelische** bezeichnet. "Es sei wahrscheinlich, dass solche dunkle **Weltkörper**,[4] die[5] sich um das gemeinsame **Centrum** bewegten, bisweilen Mondfinsternisse so gut als die **Erde** veranlassen." Artemidorus aus Ephesus, den Strabo[4] oft als **Geographen** anführt, glaubte an unzählige solcher dunkeln kreisenden **Weltkörper**.[1] Das alte ideale Wesen, die Gegenerde der **Pythagoreer**, gehört aber nicht in den Kreis dieser **Ahndungen**. Erde und Gegenerde* haben eine parallele, concentrische Bewegung, und die Gegenerde, ersonnen, um[7] der[3] sich planetarisch in 24 Stunden um das **Centralfeuer** bewegenden **Erde**[9] die Rotations-Bewegung zu ersparen, ist wohl nur die entgegengesetzte **Halbkugel**, die Antipoden-Hälfte unseres **Planeten**.

s. visible
E. limitations H. addition
S. discs b. amounted to
h. prevailed A. antiquity V. suppositions
l. weaker in light
v. present M. opinion
b. designated (Why is "aris." bold-faced?)
g. common
b. at times M. moon-eclipse v. cause
d. whom a. cites, mentions
k. circling
W. being G. counter-earth
A. notions (obs. for Ahnungen)
(*See **Ency. Brit.**, 14th ed., XVIII, 804.)
e. concocted (What does "um" call for?)
b. which moves e. save, spare
e. opposite H. half-sphere

†Alexander von Humboldt, **Kosmos**, 1869

Planeten

Allgemeine vergleichende Betrachtungen über eine ganze Klasse von Weltkörpern sollen[6] hier der Beschreibung der einzelnen **Weltkörper** vorangehen. Es beziehen* sich diese Betrachtungen[4] auf die 22 Hauptplaneten und 21 Monde (Trabanten oder Nebenplaneten), welche[5] bis jetzt entdeckt worden sind, nicht auf die planetarischen Weltkörper überhaupt,[1] unter denen die Cometen von berechneten Bahnen schon zehnmal zahlreicher sind. Die Planeten haben im ganzen eine schwache **Scintillation,** weil sie von reflectirtem **Sonnenlichte** leuchten und ihr planetarisches Licht[4] aus Scheiben emaniert. In dem aschfarbenen Lichte des **Mondes,**[1] wie in dem roten Licht seiner verfinsterten **Scheibe,** welches[5] besonders intensiv zwischen den **Wendekreisen** gesehen wird, erleidet das Sonnenlicht für den Beobachter auf der Erde eine zweimalige Änderung seiner **Richtung.**[1] Dass die Erde und andere Planeten, wie zumal einige merkwürdige Erscheinungen[4] auf dem[3] der **Sonne** nicht zugekehrten Teile der **Venus** beweisen,[8] auch einer eigenen, schwachen **Lichtentwickelung** fähig seien, ist[6] schon an einem anderen **Orte** erinnert worden.

v. comparative B. considerations g. entire
B. description
v. precede (See App. 10, 1, c.) b.e.s. refer
T. satellite
e. discovered ü. in general b. calculated, computed
B. orbits z. more numerous
S. twinkling
l. shine
S. discs a. ash-colored
r. red v. darkened
W. tropics
e. undergoes
z. double, two-time Ä. change R. direction
z. particularly m. peculiar E. phenomena
z. which faces (Why which?) b. prove
e. own, individual f. capable of
O. place e. called attention to
b. consider n. according to Z. sequence

Wir betrachten die Planeten nach ihrer **Zahl,**[1] nach der Zeitfolge ihrer **Entdeckung,**[1] nach ihrem **Volum,** unter sich oder[8] mit ihren Abständen von der **Sonne** verglichen; nach ihren relativen **Dichtigkeiten,** Massen, Rotations-Zeiten, und charakteristischer Verschiedenheit diesseits und jenseits der Zone der kleinen **Planeten.** Bei diesen Gegenständen vergleichender Betrachtung ist[6] es der Natur dieses **Werkes** angemessen,[7] einen besonderen Fleiss auf die Auswahl der numerischen **Verhältnisse** zu verwenden, welche[5] zu der Epoche, in der diese Blätter[4] erscheinen, für die genauesten, d. h. für die Resultate der neuesten und sichersten **Forschungen** gehalten werden.

E. discovery
A. distances v. compared
D. densities V. difference
diess. this side of
B. in the case of G. objects
a. appropriate, suitable (to what?) F. diligence
A. selection v. use
B. sheets, pages, f. as.
g. most accurate s. most sure F. studies

ANTHROPOLOGIE

Wesen und Aufgabe der Anthropologie†

Anthropologie ist,[6] wie verwandte Wissenschaften, besonders in letzter Zeit von der Tatsachenforschung immer mehr zur **Ursachenforschung** fortgeschritten, nicht weil sie[1] früher auf die letztere keinen **Wert** gelegt hätte, sondern weil erst ein Tatsachenfundament und neue Forschungsmethoden[1] gefunden werden mussten. Diese sind[6] zum Teil von benachbarten Wissenschaften, Zoologie und Botanik, bei denen die Ursachenforschung[4] auf geringere Schwierigkeiten stösst, ausgebildet worden. Von jeher hat[6] auch der anthropologische Forscher das Bedürfnis empfunden,[7] von der Kenntnis der fertigen Merkmale zur Erkenntnis ihrer Entstehung und ihrer **Ursachen** fortzuschreiten.

v. related W. sciences
l. recent T. fact-study
U. cause-study f. advanced
g. put W. value
T. fact-foundation F. research-m
m. had to be (App. 7, 6)
z. T. in part What does (sind)call for?
U. causal-study g. lesser S. difficulties
s. strikes, encounters a. formed
F. scientist e. sensed B. need
(to what?) K. knowledge f. finished
E. origin U. causes f. progress

Die Anthropologie hat daher die Aufgabe[7] alle[3] innerhalb der **Hominiden** vorkommenden ausgestorbenen und rezenten Formen hinsichtlich ihrer körperlichen **Eigenschaften** zu unterscheiden, zu charakterisieren und[8] in ihrer geographischen **Verbreitung** zu untersuchen, zunächst gleichgültig, ob es[4] sich dabei um Arten, Unterarten, Varietäten oder **Typen** handelt. Dann versucht sie,[7] die **Anthropogenese** zu rekonstruieren, indem sie[1] die verwandtschaftlichen Beziehungen sowohl innerhalb der Hominidengruppe als auch zu den genetisch nahestehenden **Formen** feststellt, und sie ist ausserdem bestrebt,[7] auch die **Ursachen** aufzudecken, welche[5] zu den verschiedenen **Formausprägungen** geführt haben. In letzterer Hinsicht ist es besonders wichtig,[7] durch familienbiologische Untersuchungen, die[5] gleichsam an die Stelle des **Experimentes** treten, einen Einblick in die erblichen Anlagen zu gewinnen.

A. task (to what?)
a. extinct v. which occur
h. in regard to k. physical E. qualities
u. distinguish
V. distribution u. investigate z. for the time being
g. indifferent A. types, species
e. h. s. u. it deals with v. tries
i. in that, by v. related, similar
B. relations i. within
n. near-standing
f. determine b. endeavouring (to what)
a. discover U. causes v. different
F. form-expressions H. respect
w. important (to what?) U. investigation
g. as it were (Note inserted clause.)
E. insight e. hereditary What rules call for verbs?

Die eben gegebene Definition der Anthropologie entspricht der modernen Auffassung unserer **Wissenschaft,**[1] denn der Terminus Anthropologie (von Anthropos-Mensch und Logos-Lehre) **bedeutet in wörtlicher Übersetzung nur Wissenschaft vom Menschen.**[1] Im Verlauf der wissenschaftlichen Entwicklung der beiden letzten Jahrhunderte hat[6] der Begriff "Anthropologie" aber mancherlei **Wandlungen** durchgemacht. Philosophen wie Kant, Fichte, u. a. haben[6] unter diesem Titel allgemein psychologische und pädagogische **Werke** publiziert, während für viele Naturforscher und **Mediziner,** wie Magnus, Wundt, Teichmayer u. a. der Ausdruck[4] synonym mit deskriptiver **Anatomie** war. Leider wird[6] oft noch in diesem ganz veralteten Sinne die[3] in den Mittelschulen gelehrte Anatomie des Menschen als **"Anthropologie"** bezeichnet.

e. corresponds **A. conception**
M. man
L. theory b. signifies w. literal
Ü. translation V. course
E. development b. two J. centuries
B. concept m. many W. changes
d. passed through, undergone a. generally
w. while u. a. among others
N. natural scientist
A. expression
L. unfortunately v. antiquated
S. sense g. which is taught (why which?)
M. high school b. designated

Der Begriff "Anthropologie" wird[6] aber auch heute noch öfters in doppelter Bedeutung, nämlich in einem weiteren und einem eingeschränkteren **Sinne verwendet.** Anthropologie im weiteren Sinne umfasst dann nicht nur, wie[8] oben angeführt, die Behandlung der Physis der **Menschheit,** sondern auch deren Psyche, d. h. der Gesamtäusserungen der sogenannten **"Völkerseele."**[10] Hält man an diesem umfassenden Begriffe fest,[2] so muss[6] man das ganze grosse Gebiet der **"Anthropologie im weiteren Sinne"** wieder trennen 1) in **"physische Anthropologie oder Rassenkunde"** und 2) in **"psychische Anthropologie oder Ethnologie bzw. Völkerkunde.**[1] Da für letztere Wissenschaft der Ausdruck Ethnologie[1] allgemein gebräuchlich geworden ist, so bezeichnet man auch die physische Anthropologie als "Anthropologie im engeren **Sinne.**[1]"

Beg. concept ö. often Bed. meaning
e. more limited S. sense, meaning v. used
a. cited B. treatment M. mankind
Ps. mind G. total-manifestations
Note Rule 10. u. comprehensive B. concept
f. hold-fast G. field
S. sense t. separate
R. science of races
d. since bzw. or
A. expression a. generally
g. customary b. designates
e. narrower S. sense

Eine derartige Verwendung desselben Ausdrucks ist aber unpraktisch und irreleitend,[1] und es empfiehlt sich daher in Zukunft[7] den Ausdruck "Anthropologie" stets nur im Sinne von "physischer **Anthropologie"** zu verwenden, wie es[1] auch in dem vorliegenden **Buche** geschehen ist.

d. such, of that type V. use
i. misleading e. s .is recommended (to what?)
A. expression
v. use
g. happened v. existing

Aus dem bisher Gesagten **geht hervor,**[2] dass die **Anthropologie**[1] innige Beziehungen zu einer Reihe anderer **Disziplinen** besitzt. Zunächst kommen[9] menschliche Anatomie, Zoologie und Vergleichende **Anatomie** in Betracht, dann Embryologie, Physiologie, Pathologie, Hygiene, besonders Sozialhygiene, ferner für

b. previously (See Rule 3, C-3, 1 c.)
i. close B. relations R. series
b. possesses Z. first of all Note Rule 9.
V. comparative B. consideration
Note Rule 1. b. especially

†Rudolf Martin, **Lehrbuch der Anthropologie**

bestimmte Fragestellungen Geographie, Ethnologie, Geologie und **Paläntologie.**[1] Die Beschäftigung mit anthropologischen Fragen setzt also die Kenntnis dieser Wissenschaften, insbesonders der drei erstgenannten, und zwar im Umfange des medizinischen Studiums, voraus,[2] doch sind[6] auch die übrigen Disziplinen in grösserem oder geringerem Grade in den Lehrgang der **Anthropologie** aufzunehmen. Dass sich bei anthropologischen Forschungen auch gelegentliche Beziehungen[4] zu anderen Wissenschaften, wie Linguistik, Nationalökonomie usw. herausbilden können, versteht sich von selbst.[1]

b. certain F. question(ing)
G. geology B. occupation
What goes with setzt? K. knowledge
i. especially z. what is more U. scope
v. presupposes U. remaining
G. degree L. systematic course
a. to be taken up (App. 12, 1)
F. studies g. occasional B. relations
h. formed
v. s. is understood

Historische Übersicht

Eine kurze historische Übersicht möge[6] den Leser mit den Namen derjenigen **Männer** vertraut machen, die[5] am meisten zur Entwicklung der Probleme der **Anthropologie** beigetragen haben. Einige Kenntnis von den Unterschieden der menschlichen **Varietäten,**[1] besonders soweit sie[4] äusserlich feststellbar waren, hatte schon das Altertum (Hippokrates um 400 v. Chr., Aristoteles 384-322 v. Chr.) und die menschlichen Darstellungen auf den Kunstwerken der Assyrer, Babylonier, Ägypter, Griechen und Römer* sind wertvolle Dokumente der **Rassenvergleichung.**[1]

Von einer eigentlichen Gewinnung wissenschaftlicher Daten und Materialien fremder Menschenrassen kann[6] man aber erst seit der Zeit der grossen **Entdeckungsreisen** sprechen, die,[5] mit Marco Polo **(1271-1295)** beginnend,[11] im 17. und 18. Jahrhundert grosse **Dimensionen** angenommen hatten. Das Studium der[3] von diesen **Reisen** stammenden Berichte und Sammlungen führte zu den ersten Anfängen einer menschlichen **Rassenlehre.**[1] So gering die gewonnenen Resultate[4] auch waren, so wurden sie doch bald allgemein bekannt, besonders dadurch, dass Linné und Buffon sie in ihren grossen und weit verbreiteten **Werken** verwendeten. Es ist auch das Verdienst dieser Autoren,[7] den Menschen in das zoologische **System** aufgenommen und[8] eine Klassifikation der **Menschenrassen** aufgestellt zu haben.

Die tierische Abstammung des Menschen und seine Ähnlichkeit mit den übrigen Primaten war[6] zwar schon viel früher mit grösserer oder geringerer **Überzeugungskraft** ausgesprochen worden. Man hatte[6] doch schon im Altertum zur Sektion und Präparation von **Affenleichen** gegriffen, um[7] die innere Organisation des **Menschen** kennen zu lernen. Aber erst im Jahre 1699 erschien die erste Abhandlung über die Anatomie eines Anthropomorphen von Edward **Tysen.** Auch die Frage des Polygenismus und **Monogenismus,** die[5] durch die sich immer mehrende Bekanntschaft mit fremden Völkern stets neue Anregung erhielt, wurde[6] im 18. und 19. **Jahrhundert** eifrig diskutiert, ohne aber zu positiven **Schlüssen** zu führen. Kants "Anthropologie in pragmatischer Hinsicht" war[6] nicht in biologischem **Sinne** zu verwerten.

U. survey
v. familiar Why Rule 6? 5?
E. development b. contributed
E. some K. knowledge U. differences
b. especially ä. outwardly s. so far as
f. determinable A. antiquity
m. human
D. presentations K. art works
w. valuable
R. race-comparison
e. real G. production
f. of foreign why of? M. human races
E. voyages of discovery
b. while beginning (Why while?)
a. taken on
s. which come (Why which?) B. report
S. collections A. beginnings
g. obtained so-auch. however slight
a. in general d. by the fact g. small
v. used
V. credit (to what?)
a. taken up u. and (to what?)
a. set up
A. descent
Ä. similarity ü. remaining, other
Ü. persuasive-force a. expressed (App. 7, 5, d)
A. antiquity
A. ape-bodies g. resorted to
Note Rule 7. e. not until
A. treatise
F. question
i. m. ever increasing
B. acquaintance f. foreign A. impetus
w. d. was discussed (App. 7, 5, b)
ohne-zu führen (rev. Rule 7) without leading
H. respect
v. to be utilized (App. 12, 1)

ANTHROPOLOGISCHE METHODEN

(Give reasons for the numbers. If a * appears, indicate what rule is involved at this point.)

Jede fruchtbringende anthropologische Arbeit hat[9] die genaue Kenntis der anthropologischen Methodik nach ihren verschiedenen **Richtungen hin** zur Voraussetzung. Zahlreiche mühsame und zeitraubende Erhebungen und Forschungen sind* für die **Anthropologie** wertlos geblieben, ja[8] schädlich geworden, einzig weil sie[1] ohne genügende methodische Kenntnisse unternommen wurden. Wie alle Wissenschaften erfordert auch die Anthropologie eine eingehende **Schulung,**[1] die* nur durch praktische Betätigung und **Übung** erworben werden kann. Leicht erscheint eine technische Manipulation nur dem Unerfahrenen;[1] die Schwierigkeiten erschliessen sich erst dem geübten und gewissenhaften **Beobachter,* die Schwierigkeiten der Verarbeitung und Interpretation der gesammelten Tatsachen meist nur dem Fachmann.***

f. productive A. work Note rule 9
g. exact K. knowledge n. according to
v. different R. directions V. prerequisite
m. laborious z. time consuming
Erh. inquiries w. value-less j. indeed
e. only g. sufficient
u. w. were undertaken (App. 7, 5b)
e. requires e. thorough
B. activity Ü. practice e. acquired
e. appears U. inexperienced
S. difficulties e. s. are disclosed
g. expert g. conscientious B. observer
V. processing g. collected
T. facts F. expert

METHODEN DER MATERIALGEWINNUNG

Das Material, das* sich dem Anthropologen zur **Untersuchung** darbietet, besteht entweder aus lebenden Individuen oder aus Leichen oder aus einzelnen **Körperteilen,*** die* sich in verschiedenem Zustande der Konservierung befinden können. Danach werden[6] auch die Vorschriften für die Materialgewinnung und Materialerhaltung verschieden sein müssen. Es sei[6] aber hier gleich betont, was[5] übrigens schon aus der früher gegebenen **Definition** hervorgeht, dass sich der Anthropologe* nicht auf das Sammeln menschlichen **Materials** beschränken darf, sondern dass er* seine Sammeltätigkeit auf die gesamte **Primatengruppe** ausdehnen muss, weil er für die Entscheidung wichtiger Fragen auf das Studium dieser **letzteren** angewiesen ist.

s. d. is offered (App. 11, 4a)
U. investigation b. consists
L. corpses e. individual
s. b. k. can be found v. different
D. according to that w. v. s. m. shall have to be different (App. 7, 4)
e. s. b. let it be stressed (App. 28, 1c)
w. h. which follows
S. collection m. human
b. limit d. must S. collecting-activity
g. total a. extend
E. decision
a. dependent l. latter

Lebendes Material

Die Untersuchung lebender menschlicher Individuen aller Altersstufen und beiderlei Geschlechts ist[6] heute in grösserem oder geringerem Umfange überall möglich und[8] nur da mit Schwierigkeiten verbunden, wo gesellschaftliche oder religiöse Vorstellungen entgegenstehen. In der Regel sind[6] nach gegebenen Aufklärungen und bei entsprechendem persönlichem Takt des Beobachters auch diese **Hindernisse** zu beseitigen. Die anthropologische Untersuchung weiblicher Individuen, besonders in Kulturländern,[1] kann[6] allerdings vielfach nur durch **Frauen** erreicht werden. Kaum eine andere Wissenschaft ist[6] so sehr auf die Mitwirkung der **Frau** angewiesen wie die **Anthropologie.***

U. investigation l. living
A. age-levels b. of both G. sex
U. extent m. possible (See Rule 6.)
S. difficulties (Note Rule 8.)
g. social V. ideas e. stand opposed
i. d. R. as a rule A. explanations
e. corresponding B. observer
b. to be removed
U. investigation w. female
a. of course v. frequently
e. attained k. scarcely
a. dependent (Note verb before "wie.")

Bei Naturvölkern hat das Vorbild grosse suggestive Kraft;* man versäume daher nicht,[7] die Untersuchung zuerst an sich selbst oder an einer vertrauten **Person** vorzunehmen. Dadurch zerstört man Furcht und Misstrauen* und wird[6] alsbald seine Beobachtungen auch an den zuerst scheuen **Eingeborenen** ausführen können.

Bei Kultur- and Halbkulturvölkern bieten diejenigen Institutionen das geeignetste Arbeitsfeld für den **Anthropologen,*** in denen eine grössere Anzahl von Individuen[4] angesammelt ist. Das sind in erster Linie die Schulen (Volks-Mittel- und Hochschulen, Privatinstitute) ferner Privatanstalten und Gefängnisse, die Krankenhäuser usw.*

b. in the case of V. example, model
K. force m. v. let one neglect (App. 28, 1a) (to what?) v. familiar
v. to undertake D. by that means
F. fear M. distrust w. will (App. 7, 4)
s. shy E. natives a. carry out
K. civilized b. offer
g. most suited A. working-field
A. number
a. collected d. s. those are (See App. 10, 3, k.)
f. further G. prisons K. hospitals

(Give reasons for the bold-faced nouns and for the position of the *. Explain why certain numbers appear.)

Die Möglichkeit,[7] in solchen Institutionen **Erhebungen vorzunehmen,** hängt immer von der Einwilligung der zuständigen **Behörde ab.**[2] Umfassende Untersuchungen dieser Art werden[6] am besten von **Gesellschaften** unternommen werden. Es sei[6] hier nur an die[3] von der Deutschen Anthropologischen Gesellschaft in den 70er Jahren des letzten **Jahrhunderts** ausgeführte Erhebung über die Farbe der **Haut,** der Haare und der Augen der Schulkinder, sowie an die geplante neue Untersuchung der physisch-anthropologischen Beschaffenheit der Bevölkerung des Deutschen **Reiches,** die[5] zunächst an **Rekruten** durchgeführt werden soll, und an die[3] von **München** ausgehenden Schulerhebungen seit dem Jahre **1921** erinnert. In kleinerem Umfange sind[6] solche Erhebungen aber auch dem **einzelnen** möglich. Ein dankbares Arbeitsfeld bietet die eigene Familie, die Verwandtschaft im weitesten Sinne und der **Bekanntenkreis,**[1] besonders da, wo es* sich um das Studium der so wichtigen **Vererbungsfragen** handelt. Die Errichtung anthropologischer **Büros,** wie solche[4] schon versuchsweise anlässlich grösserer **Ausstellungen** erfolgte, ist* bereits an verschiedenen **Universitäten** eingeführt worden.

E. inquiries
E. approval z. competent
B. authorities a. depend A. kind
w. u. w. will be undertaken (App. 7, 5e)
es sei-erinnert (App. 28, 1c)
a. which was carried out E. inquiry
F. color H. skin Ha. hair
g. planned U. investigation
B. nature B. population
d. carried out z. first
a. which proceed from (Why which?)
What calls for "erinnert"? U. scope
e. individual Note Rule 6.
A. working field V. relationship, relatives
w. broadest S. sense B. sphere of acquaintance
e. h. s. u. it is a matter of, deals with
w. important V. hereditary questions
E. erection v. experimentally
a. on occasion of A. exhibitions, fairs

Von lebenden Individuen suche[7] man auch stets **Haarproben** zu erhalten, hauptsächlich **Kopfhaare,*** aber auch Bart- und **Körperhaare.*** Es genügt in der Regel eine kleine Strähne oder Locke oder einzelne **Büschel,*** möglichst nahe der **Kopfhaut** abgeschnitten. Schlichte, straffe und wellige Haare sammelt man am besten in **Briefumschläge,*** krause in

s. m. let one seek (App. 28, 1a)
e. obtain h. chiefly
g. suffices i. d. R. as a rule
S. strand m. as much as possible
a. cut off S. smooth Str. taut
s. collects B. envelopes

kleinen Gläsern oder **Kartonschächtelchen.*** Man notiere möglichst genau: Geschlecht, Alter, Stand und eventuell auch Name des **Individuums,*** von dem* die Haare entnommen wurden.

kr. curly K. paste-board boxes
n. let one note (App. 28, 1a)
G. sex S. profession, class
e. were taken (App. 7, 5, 2)

ZWECK ANTHROPOLOGISCHER UNTERSUCHUNGEN

Die anthropologische Untersuchung bezweckt die möglichst genaue Feststellung der quantitativen und qualitativen Merkmale des menschlichen **Körpers,*** ihrer gegenseitigen **Beziehungen*** und ihrer Abhängigkeit von verschiedenen inneren und äusseren **Faktoren,*** z. B. Alter, Geschlecht und **Umwelt.**[1] Die Untersuchung selbst hat* an den einzelnen **Individuen** anzugreifen, aber ihr letztes Ziel ist nicht die Kenntnis des **Individuums,*** sondern der morphologischen Gruppen und deren Stellung zueinander.[1] Wenn auch die neuren Anwendungsgebiete der Anthropologie (Familienkunde, Eugenik, pädagogische Anthropologie, Sozialanthropologie) das **Einzelwesen** stärker berücksichtigen als frühere Zeiten,* so muss[6] es doch zur Gewinnung von Bewertungsmasstäben immer wieder in Beziehung zu der betreffenden morphologischen **Gruppe** gesetzt werden.

U. investigation b. aims
g. exact F. determination
M. characteristics g. mutual
B. relations A. dependence v. on
a. outer A. age G. sex
U. environment s. itself
a. attack Z. goal
K. knowledge Note Rule 1.
d. their (App. 22, 4, e) w. a. even though
A. fields of application
Note position of verb before als.
b. consider f. earlier
B. evaluation standards
i. w. again and again B. relation
b. concerned g. set
N. necessity

NOTWENDIGKEIT STATISCHER METHODEN

Zu diesem Zweck müssen* die gesammelten **Materialien** sachgemäss rechnerisch verarbeitet und graphisch dargestellt werden. Allein die statistischen Methoden liefern die geeigneten Daten (Zahlen, Parameter) zur Charakterisierung der einzelnen Aggregate und ihrer gegenseitigen **Beziehungen.*** Da aber nun alle diese Parameter* von den zufälligen Merkmalgrössen der untersuchten Einheiten **(Individuen)** abhängig sind, so wird[6] der Berechnung derselben die Wahrscheinlichkeitsrechnung zugrunde gelegt. Ihre genaue mathematische Begründung fällt in das Gebiet der höheren **Mathematik,**[1] ihre praktische Anwendung aber ist jedem möglich, der[5] eine gute Kenntnis der elementaren **Grundbegriffe** besitzt.

Z. purpose g. collected
s. appropriate r. mathematically
d. presented a. only l. yield
g. suitable
e. individual g. mutual
B. relations d. since (App. 25, 2)
z. accidental M. characteristic-sizes, magnitudes u. investigated
a. dependent z. g. is taken as a basis for
g. exact B. determination
G. field A. use
j. to each one K. knowledge
G. basic concepts b. has, possesses

ALLGEMEINE KÖRPERFORM DES MENSCHEN

(Underline the nouns that should be bold faced. Give reasons for the numbers or the *)

Der menschliche Körper unterscheidet sich von demjenigen der niederen Säuger,* im besonderen der übrigen Primaten durch eine grosse Reihe von Merkmalen,* die* den verschiedensten Organsystemen angehören und die[5] in den folgenden Abschnitten im einzelnen behandelt werden.

K. body u. s. is distinguished
d. that (App. 14, 2) S. mammals
R. series M. characteristics
a. belong to v. most different
b. treated f. following A. sections

Hier kann[6] nur auf die hauptsächlichsten morphologischen Chararkteristika der menschlichen **Körperform** aufmerksam gemacht werden, die* in dem aufrechten Gang, der mächtigen Entwicklung des Gehirnes und in der relativen Nacktheit der äusseren Körperbedeckung bestehen. Die Entwickelung dieser Merkmale reicht, wie Ontogenie und vergleichende Anatomie[4] lehren, weit in die Stammesgeschichte der Hominiden zurück.[2]

h. most principal
m. human a. g. w. be made attentive to (App. 7, 6) a. upright G. posture, gait
E. development G. brain
N. nakedness b. consist What calls for this verb? What goes with "reicht"?
v. comparative l. teach
S. ancestral history

Körperbau. Innere (vererbte) und äussere, peristatische Faktoren (Wohnverhältnisse, Lebensweise, Ernährung, besonders während des Wachstums) können* die menschlichen Körperformen stark beeinflussen. Ebenso ist der Einfluss des Geschlechts und des Alters von Bedeutung für den Körperbau und seine Veränderungen.* Darüber liegen heute eine grosse Zahl von Studien vor,[2] die[5] sich sowohl mit der normalen menschlichen Konstitution, wie auch mit der **krankhaften** befassen. Hier kann* nur der Körperbau des gesunden **Menschen**[9] in Betracht gezogen werden, trotzdem die grössten Untersuchungen der Konstitution des Menschen[4] in den letzten Jahren hauptsächlich **aus den Krankenhäusern hervorgegangen sind oder**[8] **doch zum** mindesten dort ihre Anregungen erhalten haben.

K. body structure
W. dwelling conditions L. mode of life
W. growth m. human
b. influence E. influence G. sex
A. Age B. importance K. body structure
v. changes D. concerning this
v. are present m. human
s. b. are concerned (a noun is expected here.)
i. B. g. w. can be drawn into consideration
t. even though
h. principally K. hospitals
h. s. have proceeded Note Rule 8.
A. impetus e. obtained

Kretschmer hat* die Körperbaulehre systematisch bei klinischen Untersuchungen angewendet und ist* zu ganz neuen

K. theory-of-body-structure
a. applied

Anschauungen gekommen. Vor ihm haben* aber schon eine Reihe von Autoren eine Einteilung in bestimmte menschliche Typen nach dem Körperbau vorgenommen.

A. views
R. series E. classification b. certain
v. undertaken

Die ganze Richtung verdankt aber in erster Linie Kretschmer eine wissenschaftliche Grundlage.* Zu seinen Beobachtungen verwendet er das Beobachtungsblatt für klinisch-psychiatrische Typenforschung,* dem[5] sich auch Henckel bei seinen anthropometrischen Erhebungen an **Geisteskranken** angeschlossen hat und durch welches versucht[7] wird, das Vorkommen bestimmter **Typen** als besonders charakteristisch festzulegen. Kretschmer benützt ausserdem für die optische Beschreibung ein grosses und ein abgekürztes Konstitutions-schema,* letzteres für den fortlaufenden klinischen Gebrauch.*. Auch Draper, Aschner versuchten, Disposition zu bestimmten **Krankheiten** festzustellen, ohne[7] die letzte **Konsequenz** zu ziehen, nämlich[8] wie Kretschmer, Bauer, u. a. die schulmässige anthropologische Messung bei der **Untersuchung** anzuwenden.

R. trend, direction v. owes i.e.l. primarily
w. scientific G. foundation
B. observations v. uses
T. type-study d. to which
E. inquiries G. mental-patients
a. joined, agree with v. tried
V. occurrence b. of certain
f. to determine b. uses a. besides
B. description a. abbreviated, short
f. continuous G. use
v. attempt (to what?)
b. certain
f. to determine o. without z. drawing
(why -ing?) s. classical M. measurement a. use

[10]Gelingt auch die erstere Methode bei besonders begabten Beobachtern, so entbehrt sie häufig der wissenschaftlichen Grundlage,* weshalb sie* für Lehrzwecke ausscheiden muss. Die neuere amerikanische Richtung hingegen hält die anthropometrische Untersuchung als Grundlage,* das Aufstellen von Schemata zur Typenbestimmung bei klinischen Beobachtungen für unerlässlich.[1] Wohl das eingehendste Beobachtungsblatt zur Erforschung der Konstitution stammt von Hanhart,* weshalb es* auch als Beilage diesem **Lehrbuch** beigegeben wurde.

g. (if) succeeds
b. talented B. observers e. lacks
G. basis w. wherefore a. eliminated
R. trend h. on the other hand
h. considers G. basis
A. formulation
B. observations f. u. as indispensable
e. most thorough E. study
s. comes w. wherefore B. supplement, appendix
b. added

KÖRPERGRÖSSE

Unter den messbaren Merkmalen der Körperform des lebenden Menschen steht die Körpergrösse,* d. h. die Längenausdehnung der Prinzipalachse in erster Linie.* Die Hauptachse des Körpers ist[6] von der ersten embryonalen Anlage bis zum Eintritt der Körperreife (Virilitas) in beständiger **Zunahme** begriffen, bleibt dann eine Zeit lang konstant*, um[7] im höheren Alter (durchschnittlich im 50. Lebensjahr) wieder um ca. 3 proz. abzunehmen. Diese letztgenannte Reduktion der Körpergrösse beruht auf Rückbildungsvorgängen*, hauptsächlich auf Schrumpfungsprozessen, auf Schwund und Kompression der Zwischenwirbelscheiben und auf Umgestaltung der Wirbelsäulenkrümmungen* und ist* als eine physiologische Erscheinung aufzufassen. Die wesentlichste Reduktion betrifft also den Rumpf*, während die untere Extremität,[4], in welcher die Knorpelgebilde[4] keinen so grossen Raum einnehmen, nur wenig zur Abnahme der **Körpergrösse** beiträgt. Im allgemeinen ist diese senile Grössenabnahme bei absolut Grossen beträchtlicher als bei Kleinen*, bei Frauen stärker als bei Männern.* Als Beispiel für die Körpergrössenabnahme absolut Grosser diene folgende Tabelle.*

U. among M. characteristics
l. living K. body-size s. occupies
i. e. L. (in) the first place
E. entrance b. constant Z. increase
i. b. in the process of A. rudiment
Note rule 7. h. advanced
A. age d. on the average
a. to decrease l. last named
b. depends R. degenerating-processes
S. shrinking process Z. inter-vertebral-discs
U. transforming W. vertebral-column-curvatures
a. to be conceived (App. 12,1)
b. concerns R. trunk K. cartilage
e. occupy R. space
b. contributes A. decrease
G. size-decrease b. more considerable
s. stronger B. example
d. let serve (App. 28, 1a)

Man kann* also hinsichtlich der Körpergrösse drei Perioden unterscheiden: Zunahme, Stillstand und Abnahme, wobei stets zu beachten ist, dass es sich um ein komplexes Mass handelt, das* sich aus der Länge des Stammes (Kopfhöhe und Wirbelsäule) und der unteren Extremität zusammensetzt und[8] daher naturgemäss durch die Entfaltung beider Abschnitte beeinflusst wird.

h. with regard to a. therefore
u. distinguish Z. increase
s. always z. b. i. is to be noted
L. length S. trunk
E. development A. sections s. z. is composed
b. influenced

Auf die[3] mit dem allgemeinen Körperwachstum zusammenhängenden Veränderungen der Grösse soll[6] in dem nächsten Abschnitt eingegangen werden. Hier handelt es sich zunächst um die Körpergrösse des ausgewachsenen Menschen,* die* im Laufe der Phylogenie rassenmässige Ausprägung erfahren hat.

z. which are connected
V. changes G. size
A. section z. first of all
a. adult L. course
e. undergone r. race-like A. expression

Aber auch bei den Menschen der Virilitätsperiode, Körperreife) und zwar innerhalb aller Rassen,* ist die Körpergrösse nicht absolut konstant,* sondern zeigt eine typische Tagesschwankung.* Diese besteht darin, dass der Körper am frühen Morgen nach einer längeren **Ruhelage** absolut grösser ist als

M. man
z. indeed w. within
z. shows
T. daily variation
M. morning R. resting-position

am späten Abend nach der Bewegung und Tätigkeit während des **Tages,* die*** vorwiegend eine vertikale Richtung der Prinzipalachse erfordern. Durch den Druck des Körpergewichts findet **eine Kompression** der Zwischenwirbelscheiben und der Gelenkknorpel der unteren Gliedmasse, sowie eine Abflachung des **Fussgewölbes statt,[2] die[5]** sich in ihrer Wirkung summieren und[8] im Laufe eines Tages den Betrag von durchschnittlich 30mm ausmachen. Auch ein Tiefersinken der Femurköpfe in die Beckenspanne ist[6] behauptet worden. Bei stundenlangem Stehen oder auch nach grossen Märschen und dem Tragen schwerer Lasten **ändern** sich auch die Krümmungen der Wirbelsäule* und es kann[6] die Grössenschwankung individuell einen Betrag von 50mm **erreichen.** Die grösste Abnahme tritt in den ersten Stunden der vertikalen Körperhaltung ein[2]; später wird dieselbe immer **geringer.** Dies ist[6] ausser bei Europäern auch bei Japanern beobachtet worden: die Abnahme beträgt bei letzteren bis morgens 11 Uhr 12 mm, bis 3 Uhr nachmittags 18 mm.[1] Bachmann hält **diese** Angaben für ungenau, weil es[4] nicht angegeben wurde, **wann** die Untersuchten[4] aufgestanden sind.

A. evening T. activity
v. predominately R. direction
e. require D. pressure
What goes with "findet"? G. joint cartilage G. limbs A. flattening out
F. arch of the foot
B. amount d. average
a. make up T. dropping
B. pelvic-socket b. claimed, maintained
T. carrying s. heavy L. loads
K. curvatures Note that "es" is not the subject.
G. size variation
A. decrease
K. body position
g. less
b. observed w. been (App. 7, 5, c)
n. afternoon
A. data u. inexact a. stated
U. investigated (persons) a. arisen

HAUTFARBE

Unter allen Eigenschaften,* welche die äussere Bedeckung des menschlichen Körpers darbietet, ist* die Hautfarbe am frühesten als Rassenmerkmal beachtet und beschrieben worden. Schon auf den Wandgemälden ägyptischer Gräber,* z. B. des Rekhmara-Grabes in Theben aus der 18. Dynastie,* erscheinen[6] die einzelnen Rassen scharf durch ihre verschiedene Färbung charakterisiert. Neben dem rotbraunen Ludu oder Rudu (Ägypter) sind[6] der schwarze Nasi (Neger), der gelbliche Amu (semitischer Asiate) und der hellfarbige Tamahu (Nord-Afrikaner) dargestellt. Viele Völkerbezeichnungen gehen auf die Hautfarbe zurück[2] und verhängnisvolle Urteile und Vorurteile knüpfen sich noch heute an die Begriffe des "Weissen" und "Farbigen."* Auch in allen Klassifikationsversuchen der Menschheit seit Linné, Blumenbach, Kant und Cuvier bildet die Hautfarbe eines der wichtigsten Unterscheidungsmerkmale.* Allerdings ist[6] mit einer Trennung in eine weisse europäische, braune asiatische, schwarze afrikanische **Rasse** heute nichts mehr anzufangen, weil die Verhältnisse der Hautpigmentierung[4] sehr komplizierte sind und[8] feinere Gruppierungen nötig machen.* Will man nur die Hauptunterschiede festhalten, so kann[6] man von weissen, gelbbraunen und braunschwarzen Varietäten reden; die rote Varietät ist[6] dabei in Wegfall gekommen, weil in der Tat die Hautfarbe der Indianer* ein Gelbbraun darstellt. Auch die **Bezeichnung** "weiss" sollte* in Zukunft vermieden werden, d. h.* durch "schwach pigmentiert" order "hellfarbig" ersetzt werden. Bei der grossen individuellen Variabilität der Pigmentierung und dem Mangel einer Korrelation mit anderen Körpermerkmalen ist überhaupt der systematische oder klassifikatorische Wert der Hautfärbung lange nicht so gross, wie[8] früher angenommen wurde.

Die Hautfarbe des Menschen beruht auf zwei Momenten:* 1. Auf der Anwesenheit eines körnigen Farbstoffes,* der* teils in den Zellen der Epidermis, teils im Corium (dermale Hülle), meistens in beiden Schichten zugleich eingelagert ist, und 2. in dem Durchschimmern des roten Blutfarbstoffs der feinen Hautgefässe durch die relativ durchsichtige[3] und an manchen Körperstellen sehr dünne Epidermis.* Aus der Kombination dieser beiden sehr verschieden entwickelten Elemente entsteht die reiche Skala der menschlichen Hautfarben.* Unter Umständen kann* auch der Serumgehalt der **Hautbedeckung**[9] eine Rolle spielen. Bei Naturvölkern kommt[9] gelegentlich als weiteres Moment noch die absichtliche oder unbeabsichtigte Verunreinigung der Hautoberfläche (auflagernder Schmutz, Drüsensekrete, aufgetragene Farbstoffe usw.), die[5] die Hautfarbe sehr verändern können,[9] in Betracht. Selbstverständlich ist[6] dieses Moment bei der Beurteilung der wahren Hautfarbe auszuschalten.

E. qualities ä. outer B. covering
(Note the subject.) d. offers H. skin-color
R. race characteristic
b. regarded b. described
G. grave e. appear (Note Rule 6.)
e. individual s. sharply v. different
N. along with
s. black g. yellowish
h. light colored
V. National designations, characteristics
v. disastrous V. prejudices
ank. tie on B. concepts
M. humanity K. classification attempts
b. forms
e. d. one of the U. distinguishing-characteristics
A. of course
i. a. is to be done
V. conditions
Note absence of noun. n. necessary
What calls for "machen"? What do you do when verb is first? festh. maintain
r. speak W. abolition
i. d. T. indeed
B. designation Z. future
v. avoided (App. 7, 6) d. h. that is
(Could call for verb; Rule 8) e. replaced
M. want of
K. physical characteristics
W. value H. skin color l. by far
a. assumed

M. man b. depends
M. factors A. presence F. pigment
t. partly
m. mostly b. both S. layers e. deposited
D. shining thru H. skin-vessels d. transparent
d. which is thin—why which?
v. differently e. developed
e. arises H. skin-colors
U. certain circumstances S. serum-content
N. primitive peoples (what goes with kommt?)
g. occasionally a. intended
V. impurification H. skin-surface
S. dirt a. put on
i. B. into consideration S. of course
B. judgment w. true
a. to be eliminated (App. 12, 1)

LANDWIRTSCHAFT

Die Kenntnis der natürlichen Grundlagen für organische Entwickelung auf der Erde ergibt häufig den Grund für das an bestimmten Orten daran geknüpfte verschiedene Kulturleben, nach Richtung, Mannigfaltigkeit oder Fortschritt. Will man deshalb die geographische Verschiedenheit einer Gegend und die wirtschaftliche Entwickelungsfähigkeit derselben durch Bodenkultur verstehen, so ist eine möglichst eingehende naturwissenschaftliche Orientierung über Luft und Klima, sowie über Boden und geologische Grundlage nicht zu entbehren. Und indem das animalische Leben die organische Arbeit der Pflanze zu seiner notwendigen naturgesetzlichen Voraussetzung hat, so sind die genannten Faktoren für viele Culturfragen, wie Population, Möglichkeit der Volksvermehrung überhaupt entscheidend.

Die Sonne ist das grosse mächtige Agens, welches für die Erwärmung der Erdoberfläche, für die Verteilung der wässrigen Niederschläge und die chemische Action auf der Erde von dem massgebensten Einfluss ist. Die Angabe der geographischen Breite macht es möglich, die Dauer und die Intensität der Sonnenwirkung in den verschiedenen Jahreszeiten während des Tages zu bestimmen, soweit es von dem Stande der Sonne zur Erdoberfläche im Weltraum bedingt wird.

Die Wirkung der Sonne auf die Erdoberfläche wird in hohem Grade modifiziert durch die Art und Weise, wie die feuchten Niederschläge auftreten, und das trockene kontinentale Klima im Innern vieler grosser Ländermassen unterscheidet sich in dieser Hinsicht sehr von dem feuchten und regnerischen Klima an vielen Meeresküsten.

Die Warmeverhältnisse sind stets in einem gewissen Zusammenhange mit der Licht- und chemischen Wirkung der Sonne und den Feuchtigkeitsverhältnissen einer Gegend aufzufassen, namentlich mit den feuchten Niederschlägen in gewissen Jahreszeiten und Monaten. Damit in den Pflanzen die chemische Action organischer Bildung aus unorganischen Stoffen vor sich gehe, damit die Culturpflanzen überhaupt existieren können und sich vollständig entwickeln, ist das gleichzeitige Zusammenwirken der genannten Faktoren und eine bestimmte Verteilung in den einzelnen Jahresabschnitten notwendig.

Während die Natur in manchen Gegenden Feuchtigkeit in Überfluss, jedoch zu wenig Licht und Wärme darbietet, als dass sich die Vegetation und manche Culturpflanzen noch zu entwickeln vermögen (hohe Gebirge, viele Polardistrikte), so wird in anderen Gegenden, in weit ausgedehnten Terrains, die überschüssige Licht- und Wärmeabgabe durch die Sonne nicht oder nicht genügend aktiv im Sinne organischer Bildung, weil die dazu notwendige Feuchtigkeit dahin durch die Luft nicht verbreitet wird. Sowie die Natur der Vegetation überhaupt, so ist auch die Zahl der anzubauenden Culturpflanzen, in gleichem Masse die Höhe und Sicherheit der Ernten grossenteils durch den Eintritt und die Stärke des Regenfalls in bestimmten Jahreszeiten bedingt, wie durch die Höhe des Jahresregens überhaupt. Sogar die Höhe des Schneefalles und die Art und Weise, wie der Winter mit viel oder wenig Feuchtigkeit in ein trockenes Frühjahr und einen heissen Sommer übergeht, ist in den Gegenden des sogenannten kontinentalen Klimas auf die Ernteerträge von Einfluss, wie man namentlich in der russischen Steppe deutlich erkannt hat.

Anthropologie, Ethnographie, und Urgeschichte

1. Anthropologie im weitesten Sinne umfasst die ganze Menschheit von dem ersten Auftreten menschlicher und menschenähnlicher Wesen bis auf den heutigen Tag. Im engeren Sinne des Wortes gliedert sie sich in drei Forschungsgebiete physische Anthropologie, Ethnographie, und Urgeschichte. Von diesen drei Disziplinen beschäftigt sich die Anthropologie hauptsächlich mit den körperlichen Eigenschaften der verschiedenen Rassen, die Ethnographie mit ihren geistigen, manuellen und anderen Leistungen und die Urgeschichte mit den Funden aus früheren, teilweise vorgeschichtlichen Zeiten der menschlichen Entwicklung.

2. Natürlich kann man von der Prähistorie alles, was sich auf die körperlichen Eigenschaften des Menschen bezieht, zur Anthropologie und alles andere zur Ethnographie rechnen. Aber eine derartige blosse Zweiteilung der Völkerkunde würde doch nur theoretischen Wert haben, da die Prähistorie ebensogut als selbständiges Forschungsgebiet zu gelten hat, als die physische Anthropologie und die Ethnographie.

3. Hingegen pflegt man meistens die gegenwärtigen und die alten Kulturvölker ganz aus dem Bereiche der Ethnographie auszuschliessen. Dies ist aus rein praktischen Gründen zweckmässig und auch theoretisch nicht anzufechten, solange man sich wenigstens darüber klar bleibt, dass eine scharfe Grenze zwischen Natur- und Kulturvölkern nicht besteht. Es gab eine Zeit, in der man nur die europäische oder auch nur die antikgriechische Kultur, und was mit dieser zusammenhing, als voll erkannte.

4. Aber wir kennen jetzt neben unserer sogenannten klassischen auch eine ägyptische, eine babylonische, eine indische, eine chinesiche, mehrere alt-amerikanische und sehr viele andere Kulturen, und je mehr unsere Kenntnisse auf dem Gebiete der Völkerkunde zunehmen, um so unsicherer erscheint uns die Grenze, die Natur- und Kulturvölker voneinander trennt. Tätsächlich erweisen sich alle Versuche, die verschiedenen Völker etwa nach ihrer Farbe oder nach ihrer Schönheit, nach dem Mehr oder Minder ihrer Bekleidung, nach dem Besitzen oder dem Fehlen von Schrift, nach dem Vorkommen von Menschenopfern oder nach anderen Kriterien irgendwelcher Art in hochstehende und minderwertige Rassen einzuteilen, als von vornherein durchaus verfehlt.

5. Deshalb ist es auch nicht leicht, den Begriff der Völkerkunde richtig abzugrenzen. In besonders drastischer Weise kommt dies auch in den ganz ungleichen Arbeitsgebieten der verschiedenen Museen zum Ausdruck. So ist sogar im Berliner Museum für Völkerkunde die ganz europäische Abteilung seit zwanzig Jahren weggepackt, und auch in vielen anderen Städten wird man die Ethnographie gerade des europäischen Menschen nur in den Museen für Kunstgewerbe , für Volkstrachten, für Hausindustrie oder auch gar nicht vertreten finden.

6. Selbstverständlich werden auch in den folgenden Betrachtungen die wirklichen Kulturvölker nicht in den Kreis der ethnographischen Untersuchung einzubeziehen sein; hingegen erscheint es mir nötig, das, was in den beiden früheren Auflagen dieses Handbuches auf prähistorische Untersuchungen beschränkt war, in dieser neuen* auch auf die grossen archäologischen Grabungen auszudehnen, die in den letzten Jahrzehnten, besonders in Vorderasien und in Ägypten, eine wissenschaftlich so hoch bedeutende Rolle zu spielen begonnen haben.

VÖLKERRECHT

Die Grundrechte in den amerikanischen Verfassungen

(Give reasons for the numbers. Also insert numbers where they have been intentionally omitted.)

Die Zusicherung einer Anzahl von Grundrechten bildet einen Bestandteil der Bundes- und sämtlicher **Staatsverfassungen.** Die Guarantien lassen sich[6] in ihrer grossen Mehrzahl auf Streitfragen und Errungenschaften englischer Verfassungskämpfe zurückführen und schliessen sich auch zum Teil im Wortlaut an.[2] Sie werden häufig kollektiv mit dem Namen "Bill of **Rights**" bezeichnet.

Z. assurance A. number G. **basic-rights**
B. component B. federal
S. state constitutions l. s. **can be**
S. disputes E. achievements **What goes with** "schliessen"? z. T. partly
W. wording, text w. b. are designated (App. 7, 5, a)

Wir finden derartige Erklärungen in den Gesetzen fast sämtlicher Kolonien aus dem siebzehnten **Jahrhundert.** Sie wiederholen die Worte der Magna **Carta,** die[5] Gerechtigkeit und gesetzliches **Verfahren** verbürgen, nahmen das Recht auf den Schwurprozess in Anspruch und verurteilten Steuern ohne **Volksvertretung.** Die Unabhängigkeitserklärung des Jahres 1776 nahm **auf** die Verletzung derartiger **Rechte**[9] Bezug und stellte selbst eine Reihe unveräusserlicher **Rechte** auf.

d. such E. declarations G. **laws**
s. all **Note rule 1 and the rules that 'remove'** the verbs G. justice
g. legal V. procedure v. **guarantee**
i. A. n. to claim v. condemned
V. popular representation U. **Independence** declaration Note Rules 9, 2.
V. violation u. inalienable

Die Bundesverfassung enthielt in ihrer ursprünglichen Fassung eine Anzahl von[3] auf solche **Rechte** bezüglichen **Bestimmungen;** sie sicherte das Recht auf Habeas Corpus und auf Geschworenenverfahren im **Strafprozess;** sie stellte den Tatbestand des **Hochverrats** fest, eine bedeutende Errungenschaft in der Geschichte des englischen **Rechts;** und verbot rückwirkende **Strafgesetze;** eine förmliche Bill of Rights **wurde** aber nicht aufgenommen.

B. federal constitution e. contained
F. version, wording A. number Why Rule 3?
b. which pertained
G. trial by jury S. criminal trial(s)
T. status, fact H. **high treason**
E. achievement G. history
S. criminal laws w. a. was taken up (App. 7, 5, b)
w. g. was censured A. **occasion**

Der Mangel einer solchen wurde[6] bei Anlass der Ratifikationsdiskussionen in den **Einzelstaaten** vielfach gerügt, und infolgedessen schlug der erste Kongress eine Bill of Rights in Form einer Anzahl von **Zusatzartikeln** vor, die[5] 1791 in die Verfassung **aufgenommen** wurden. Diese Zusatzartikel gelten als Beschränkungen der Regierung des Bundes und nicht der **Einzelstaaten,** während die Verbote der ursprünglichen Verfassung[4] sich zum Teil gegen den Bund, zum Teil gegen die **Staaten** richteten.

v. frequently
i. in consequence What goes with "schlug"?
A. number Z. **amendments**
V. constitution a. **taken up**
g. are considered B. limitations
E. individual states w. **while**
u. original z. T. **partly**
r. s. were directed (App. 11, 4, b)

Die Rekonstruktion nach dem Bürgerkrieg veranlasste weitere wichtige Schranken der **Bundesverfassung,** die[5] gegen den Missbrauch der Regierungsgewalt von seiten der **Einzelstaaten** schützen sollten, und die[5] die Bundesregierung nicht ausdrücklich binden.

B. civil war v. caused
w. important S. limitations
M. misuse R. governmental power
s. s. were to protect (Note the translation of "sollen".) a. expressly

Due Process of Law

Um[7] die[3] kurz zuvor von der **Sklaverei** emanzipierten Neger vor Benachteiligungen und Vergewaltigungen durch die Gesetzgebungen und Regierungen der **Südstaaten** zu schützen, wurde im **Jahre** 1868 ein weiterer Zusatzartikel in die **Bundesverfassung** aufgenommen, der den Staaten untersagte,[7] irgend einer Person Leben, Freiheit oder Eigentum ohne gehöriges **Rechtsverfahren** zu nehmen **und**[8] allen Personen in jedem Staat den gleichen Schutz der **Gesetze** zusicherte.

Why Rule 7? Rule 3? e. who were emancipated
B. disadvantages, discrimination V. violence
G. legislatures z. s. to protect What calls for the "zu"-verb? w. further
u. prohibited (to what?)
i. e. from any one E. property
g. due R. legal procedure Note Rule 8.
z. assured S. protection

Die Guarantie des gehörigen Rechtsverfahrens fand sich schon in den ersten **Zusatzartikeln** aber nur in Wirkung gegen die Bundesregierung selbst; sie fand sich auch in den meisten **Staatsverfassungen,** aber den Staaten gegenüber fehlte die **Bundessanktion.** Mit Annahme des vierzehnten Zusatzartikels wurde das gehörige Rechtsverfahren Grundrecht des gesamten **Landes** und drängte alle anderen Guarantien in den **Hintergrund.**

Das Wort "due process of law" findet sich in Sir Edward Cokes Kommentar zur Magna **Carta.** Einige amerikanische Verfassungen gebrauchen auch den Ausdruck "law of the land"

What rules are you using to remove the verbs?
W. effect
s. itself (See App. 13, 1) f. s. was found
g. opposite to (App. 15, 3, c)
A. acceptance
w. became (App. 7, 3, b) g. due
d. crowded H. back ground
f. s. is found (App. 11, 4, a)
E. some
g. use A. expression

(Insert numbers of the rules where they have been intentionally omitted.)

anstatt "due process." Die Wahl des Wortes ist belanglos, da die Bedeutung weit über den buchstäblichen **Sinn** hinausgeht.[10] Wäre alles, was das Gesetz bestimmt, "law of the land," so würde die Verfassungsguarantie nur gegenüber willkürlichen[3] nicht auf **Gesetz** beruhenden Akten der Verwaltung oder der Gerichte funktionieren können, und ihre Anwendung wäre von keiner **Wichtigkeit.** Die Gerichte haben es sorgfältig vermieden,[7] sich an irgend eine **Begriffsbestimmung** zu binden. Die am häufigsten zitierte Erklärung findet sich in einer der früheren Entscheidungen des **Oberbundesgerichts,** dass die Guarantie bezwecke,[7] den Einzelnen gegen eine willkürliche[3] an anerkannte Grundsätze privaten Rechts und **Gerechtigkeit** nicht gebundene **Regierungsgewalt** zu schützen.

W. choice b. irrelevant
d. since (App. 25, 2) b. literal
W. if everything (App. 28, 2, e)
V. constitutional-guarantee
w. arbitrary (Why Rule 3?) b. which rest
V. administration G. courts
w. would be W. importance
G. courts s. carefully v. avoided
B. definition a. h. most frequent
E. explanation f. s. is found (App. 11, 4a)
E. decisions O. federal supreme court
b. aims (to what?) Why Rule 3 now?
Gr. principles G. justice
g. which is bound (Why which?) s. protect

Mit Bezug auf Gesetzgebung muss "due process" bedeuten, dass ein Gesetz nicht willkürlich sein darf; jeder Akt der gesetzgebenden Gewalt muss sich als Äusserung einer vernunftgemässen **Rechtsordnung** rechtfertigen können. Mehr noch; nach dem Ausspruch eines höchsten Staatsgerichts verlangt die Verfassung Übereinstimmung des Gesetzes mit den hergebrachten Grundsätzen einer freien **Regierung.**

m. B. with respect G. legislation
b. mean G. law w. despotic, arbitrary
g. legislative G. power
r. justify A. expression v reasonable
A. expression
St. state court v. requires Ü. agreement
h. traditional G. principles
What rules are you using to remove verbs from the end position?

Das Wahlrecht

AKTIVES UND PASSIVES WAHLRECHT Da eine demokratische Verfassung[4] in der direkten Teilnahme der Bürger am **Staatsleben**[9] ihren **wirksamsten** Ausdruck findet, so nimmt das Wahlrecht im amerikanischen Staatsorganismus einen überaus wichtigen **Platz** ein. Der Bund überlässt einen Teil der Verfassung fast ganz und gar den **Einzelstaaten,** und in diesen hängt die Ausgestaltung des Rechts zum Teil von den Verfassungsurkunden z. T. von der **Gesetzgebung** ab.

W. suffrage d. since (App. 25, 2)
T. participation
i. w. A. its most effective expression
What goes with "nimmt"?
ü. very w. important P. place
ü. relinquishes f. almost E. single states
What goes with "hängt"? A. formation
V. constitutional documents a. depends on

Die Verfassungen bestimmen die Bedingungen des aktiven **Wahlrechts,** und lassen der Gesetzgebung in dieser Beziehung wenig oder gar keine **Freiheit,** sie verlangen häufig, dass die Wahl[4] vermittelst "ballot" vorzunehmen ist, und setzen den Wahltag für **Staatswahlen** fest. Die gesamte neuere Wahlreform beruht hingegen auf Gesetzesbestimmungen und beschäftigt sich mit **Punkten,** die von den Verfassungen offen gelassen sind.

b. determine B. conditions
W. suffrage G. legislation
B. respect F. freedom v. demand
v. z. is to be undertaken (App. 12, 1)
f. establish S. state elections
g. total W. election reform b. rests
G. legal-provisions b. is concerned
What calls for "sind"?

Die Verfassung der Vereinigten Staaten stellt nur das Abgeordnetenhaus auf direkte **Volkswahl,** während der Senat und der Theorie nach auch der Präsident[4] indirekt gewählt wird. In den Einzelstaaten findet das System der Volkswahl eine ungleich weitere Ausdehnung und umfasst, wie[8] sich aus der weiteren **Darstellung** ergeben wird, ausser der Legislatur die höchsten **Staatsämter,** die Richterstellen und die wichtigsten Ämter der **Lokalverwaltung.**

V. constitution
A. house of representatives
d. T. n. according to theory
g. chosen A. single states
A. extension u. embraces
w. e. w. as will be shown D. presentation
S. state offices
w. most important L. local administration

Das Recht zu wählen gilt nicht als eines der bürgerlichen **Grundrechte,** und wird[6] daher durch den vierzehnten **Zusatzartikel** nicht gewährleistet.

G. bill of rights z. w. to vote
g. guaranteed

Bis zum Bürgerkrieg überliess die Bundesverfassung die Bestimmung der aktiven Wahlqualifikation auch für Bundeszwecke den **Staaten.** Wer[5] nach einer Staatsverfassung an der Wahl der Mitglieder des zahlreicheren Teils der **Staatslegislatur** teilnehmen dürfte, sollte[6] damit auch für das Mitglied des Repräsentantenhauses in seinem **Bezirke** stimmen können. So kam es, dass in einzelnen Staaten Personen,[4] die[5] noch nicht naturalisiert waren, für Mitglieder des **Kongresses** stimmen konnten.

ü. relinquished B. federal constitution
B. determination
B. federal purposes
z. more numerous T. part
t. take part
M. member
B. district s. vote
Note the inserted clause.
s. vote

PHILOSOPHIE

Name und Begriff der Philosophie†

Unter Philosophie versteht der heutige Sprachgebrauch die wissenschaftliche Behandlung der allgemeinen Fragen von Welterkenntnis und **Lebensansicht.**[1] Diese unbestimmte Gesamtvorstellung haben[6] die einzelnen Philosophen je nach den **Voraussetzungen,** mit denen sie[4] in die **Denkarbeit** eintraten, und den Ergebnissen, die sie[4] dabei gewannen, in bestimmtere **Definitionen** zu verwandeln gesucht; diese gehen jedoch zum **Teil** so weit auseinander,[2] dass sie[4] sich nicht vereinbaren lassen, und dass die Gemeinsamkeit des Begriffs[4] zwischen ihnen verloren erscheinen kann. Aber auch jener allgemeinere Sinn ist schon eine Einschränkung und Umgestaltung der ursprünglichen **Bedeutung,** welche die Griechen[4] mit dem Namen **Philosophie** verbanden, und diese Wandlung ist[6] durch den ganzen Verlauf des abendländischen **Geisteslebens** herbeigeführt worden.

v. means by **S. speech usage**
B. treatment **a. general**
F. questions W. cognizance of the world
L. life view u. indefinite G. total
concept **See App. 9, l, b, e on position of the**
subject. D. thinking work
g. gained **b. more definite**
v. transform **z. T. partly**
auseinanderg. **diverge, separate**
s. v. l. cannot be reconciled G. communality, common ground v. lost
S. sense, meaning **E. limitation**
Um. transformation **u. original**
v. combined, associated
W. transformation **V. course** **a. western**
G. intellectual life **h. brought about**

Während das erste literarische Auftreten der Wörter **Philosophien** und Philosophia[4] noch die einfache und zugleich unbestimmte Bedeutung des "Strebens nach **Weisheit** erkennen lässt, hat[6] das Wort "Philosophie" in der[3] auf **Sokrates** folgenden Literatur und insbesondere in der platonisch-aristotelischen Schule den fest ausgeprägten **Sinn** erhalten, wonach es[4] genau dasselbe bezeichnet wie im Deutschen "Wissenschaft." Danach ist Philosophie im allgemeinen die methodische Arbeit des **Denkens,** durch welche[5] das "Seiende" erkannt werden soll; danach sind die einzelnen "Philosophien" die besonderen Wissenschaften,[1] in denen einzelne Gebiete des Seienden[4] untersucht und erkannt werden.

w. while A. appearance e. simple
z. at the same time u. indefinite
S. n. W. striving for wisdom
Note the position of the subject
Why is Sokrates bold faced?
a. pronounced e. obtained
b. designates (See Rule 7-F, 1, 2, 3 on position of the verb.)
S. existence e. recognized (See App. 7, 6, a, b on use of "werden".) e. individual G. fields
u. investigated e. recognized

Mit dieser ersten, theoretischen Bedeutung des Wortes Philosophie verband sich jedoch sehr früh eine zweite.[1] Die Entwicklung der griechischen Wissenschaft fiel in die Zeit der Auflösung des ursprünglichen religiösen und sittlichen **Bewusstseins**[1] und liess[6] nicht nur die Fragen nach der Bestimmung und den Aufgaben des Menschen mit der Zeit immer wichtiger für die wissenschaftliche **Untersuchung** werden, sondern[8] auch die Belehrung für die rechte Lebensführung als einen wesentlichen **Zweck,** schliesslich als den Hauptinhalt der **Wissenschaft** erscheinen. So erhielt die Philosophie in der hellenistischen Zeit die[3] schon früher bei den Sophisten und **Sokrates** angebahnte praktische Bedeutung einer Lebenskunst auf wissenschaftlicher Grundlage.[1]

B. importance
v. s. was combined (See App. 11, 4, abc.)
E. development A. dissolution u. original
s. ethical B. consciousness l. let
F. questions n. about B. destination
Aufg. tasks i. w. more and more important
w. become s. (liess) but let
B. instruction L. life conduct
w. essential Z. purpose H. main content
W. science e. appear
die the (what?) How are you told you are in Rule 3? a. which was pioneered
L. art of living G. basis

Infolge dieser Wandlung ging das rein theoretische Interesse auf die besonderen **Philosophien** über,[2] die[5] nun zum Teil die Namen ihrer besonderen, sei es historischen sei es naturwissenschaftlichen **Gegenstände** annahmen, während Mathematik und Medizin[4] weiterhin die Selbstständigkeit, welche sie[4] von Anfang an der Gesamtwissenschaft gegenüber besessen hatten, um so energischer bewahrten. Der Name der Philosophie aber **blieb**[6] an denjenigen wissenschaftlichen Bestrebungen haften, welche[5] aus den allgemeinsten Ergebnissen menschlicher Erkenntnis eine[3] das **Leben** bestimmende Überzeugung zu gewinnen hofften, und welche[5] schliesslich in dem Versuche des **Neuplatonismus**[7] gipfelten, aus

l. as result of W. change
b. special
Note Rule 2, and 5 s. be it
G. subjects, objects
a. took on w. while What verb does this first 4 call for? the second?
u. s. all the more b. preserved
b. h. remained attached (See rule 6, D, 3 and 4.)
A. most general Erg. results
b. which determines (Why which?)
Ü. conviction h. hoped s. finally
V. attempt (to what) g. culminated

†Windelband, **Lehrbuch der Geschichte der Philosophie**

solcher Philosophie heraus eine neue Religion an Stelle der alten verloren **gehenden** zu erzeugen.

V. attempt (to what?) g. culminated
aus-heraus (See App. 21.)
A noun should appear after **gehenden.**
See Rule 5c and Rule 6c.

An diesen Verhältnissen änderte sich zunächst wenig, als die Reste der antiken Wissenschaft[4] in die Bildung der heutigen Völker Europas als die intellektuell bestimmenden **Mächte** übergingen. Inhalt und Aufgabe desjenigen, was das Mittelalter[4] Philosophie nannte, deckte sich mit dem, was das spätere Altertum[4] darunter verstanden hatte. Jedoch erfuhr die Bedeutung der Philosophie eine wesentliche Veränderung durch den **Umstand,**[1] dass sie[4] ihre Aufgabe durch die positive Religion in gewissem **Sinne** bereits gelöst fand. Denn auch diese gewährte nicht nur eine sichere Überzeugung als Regel der persönlichen **Lebensführung,**[1] sondern auch im Zusammenhang damit eine allgemeine theoretische Ansicht über das **Seiende,** welche[5] um so mehr philosophischen **Charakters** war, als die Dogmen des Christentums[4] ihre Formulierung durchgängig unter dem Einfluss der antiken **Wissenschaft** erhalten hatte. Unter diesen Umständen blieb während der ungebrochenen Herrschaft der kirchlichen Lehre für die Philosophie in der Hauptsache nur die dienende Stellung einer wissenschaftlichen Begründung, Ausbildung und Verteidigung des **Dogmas** übrig.[2] Aber trotzdem trat sie mit immer deutlicher werdendem Bewusstsein in einen methodischen Gegensatz zur **Theologie,**[1] indem sie[4] dasselbe, was diese[4] auf Grund göttlicher **Offenbarung** lehrte, ihrerseits aus den Mitteln menschlicher **Erkenntnis** gewinnen und darstellen wollte.

V. conditions ä. s. was changed (App. 11, 4, a)
R. remnants W. science B. education
b. determining M. powers I. content
d. of that one (App. 14, 2)
d. s. coincided A. antiquity
v. understood j. however e. underwent
w. essential V. change U. circumstance
A. task g. certain S. sense b. already
g. guaranteed s. sure U. conviction
R. rule L. life conduct s. but
Z. connection a. general A. view
S. existence u. so m. all the more
Flag all lines where prefixes are found.
d. generally E. influence er. obtained
U. conditions What goes with "übrig"?
H. domination
d. subordinate, ancillary S. position
B. justification A. development
Vert. defense t. nevertheless
B. consciousness w. developing
G. contrast, opposition i. in that, by –ing
What verb goes with the first 4? the 2nd?
g. gain d. present

Die unausbleibliche Folge dieses Verhältnisses aber war, dass die Philosophie,[4] je freier das individuelle Denken[4] der Kirche gegenüber wurde, um so selbständiger auch die[3] ihr mit der **Religion** gemeinsame **Aufgabe** zu lösen begann,—dass sie[4] von der Darstellung und Verteidigung zur Kritik des **Dogmas** überging und[8] schliesslich ihre Lehre völlig unabhängig von den religiösen Interessen lediglich aus den **Quellen** herzuleiten suchte, die sie[4] dafür in dem "natürlichen Licht" der menschlichen Vernunft und **Erfahrung** zu besitzen meinte. Der methodische Gegensatz zur Theologie wuchs auf diese Weise zu einem sachlichen aus,[2] und die moderne Philosophie stellte sich als "Weltweisheit" dem **Dogma** gegenüber.[2] Dies Verhältnis nahm die mannigfachsten **Abstufungen** an,[2] es wechselte von anschmiegender Zustimmung bis zu scharfer **Bekämpfung;** aber stets blieb dabei die Aufgabe der "Philosophie" diejenige, welche ihr das Altertum[4] gegeben hatte: aus wissenschaftlicher Einsicht eine Welterkenntnis und eine **Lebensansicht** da zu begründen, wo die Religion[4] dies **Bedürfnis** nicht mehr allein zu erfüllen vermochte.

u. inevitable F. result V. condition
j. umso the – the (App. 26, 2)
D. thinking g. opposite to (App. 15, 3, c)
s. more independent
g. which is common (Why which?)
D. presentation V. defense v. completely
s. finally (Note Rule 8.)
u. independently l. solely h. derive
Note that subject follows the relative. V. reason
E. experience m. thought, supposed
G. contrast The noun is understood after "sachlichen"
g. opposite (App. 15, 3, c)
V. condition m. most varied A. gradations
w. changed Z. consent a. conforming
B. opposition s. always
Note that 'Aufgabe' calls for the 'zu'.
This 'zu' may be found beyond a colon.
E. understanding w. (world) cognizance
b. establish B. need
e. fulfill. v. was able (vermögen)

Caution: Flag all lines where prefixes and "zu"-verbs are found. Have someone read the page to you after it is translated and observe the application of each rule.

In der Überzeugung,[7] dieser **Aufgabe** gewachsen zu sein, sah es die Philosophie des 18. Jahrhunderts,[4] wie einst die der Griechen, für Recht und **Pflicht** an,[2] die Menschen über den Zusammenhang der **Dinge** aufzuklären und[8] von dieser Einsicht aus das Leben des Individuums wie der **Gesellschaft** zu regeln.

Ü. conviction (to what) g. equal to
Note the subject here.
d. d. that of R. right P. duty (to what?)
z. connection
u. and (to what?) E. knowledge (On use of "von aus" see App. 21, 1, a, b.) G. society

In dieser selbstgewissen Stellung wurde[6] die Philosophie durch **Kant** erschüttert, welcher[5] die Unmöglichkeit einer "philosophischen" (metaphysischen) Welterkenntnis neben oder über den einzelnen **Wissenschaften** nachwies und[8] dadurch Begriff und Aufgabe der **Philosophie** abermals einschränkte und veränderte. Denn nach diesem Verzicht engte sich das Gebiet der Philosophie als besonderer Wissenschaft auf eben jene kritische Selbstbesinnung der **Vernunft** ein, aus welcher Kant[4] die entscheidende **Einsicht** gewonnen hatte, und welche[5] nur noch systematisch auf die übrigen Tätigkeiten neben dem Wissen ausgedehnt werden sollte. Vereinbar blieb damit das, was Kant[4] den Weltbegriff der **Philosophie** nannte, ihr Beruf zur praktischen Lebensbestimmung.

s. self-assured S. position
e. shake up, stir U. impossibility
W. world knowledge e. individual
n. demonstrated, proved B. concept
a. once more e. limited v. changed
V. renunciation s. e. was narrowed
Geb. field b. special a. e. to just that
S. self-reflection V. reason
e. decisive E. understanding
ü. remaining T. activities
n. beside a. extended s. was to be
V. agreeable d. this W. world concept
B. calling L. life-determination, conduct

Freilich fehlt viel, dass dieser neue und wie es scheint abschliessende Begriff der Philosophie[4] sogleich zu allgemeiner **Geltung** gekommen wäre; vielmehr hat[6] die grosse **Mannigfaltigkeit** der philosophischen Bewegungen des 19. Jahrhunderts keine der früheren Formen der **Philosophie** unwiederholt gelassen, und eine üppige Entfaltung des "metaphyischen Bedürfnisses" hat[6] sogar zeitweilig zu der **Neigung**[7] zurückgeführt, alles menschliche Wissen in die **Philosophie** zurückzuschlingen und[8] diese wieder als **Gesamtwissenschaft** auszubilden.

F. to be sure f. is missing
a. conclusive B. concept
s. right away a. general G. validity, acceptance
v. rather M. variety
B. movements f. earlier
u. unrepeated g. left
ü. rich E. development B. need
z. led back s. even z. occasionally
N. tendency (to what?) W. knowledge
zurzusch. to revert back to, interweave
a. develop G. total science

Angesichts dieses Wechsels, welchen die Bedeutung des Wortes Philosophie[4] im Laufe der Zeiten durchgemacht hat, erscheint es untunlich,[7] aus historischer Vergleichung einen allgemeinen Begriff der **Philosophie** gewinnen zu wollen: keiner von denen, die man[4] zu diesem **Zwecke** aufgestellt hat, trifft auf alle diejenigen Gebilde der Geistestatigkeit zu,[2] welche[5] auf den **Namen**[9] Anspruch erheben. Schon die Unterordnung der Philosophie unter den allgemeinen Begriff der Wissenschaft wird[6] bei solchen Lehren, welche[5] einseitig die praktische **Bedeutung**[9] im Auge haben, bedenklich: noch weniger lässt[6] sich allgemeingültig bestimmen, was[5] Gegenstand und Form der Philosophie als besonderer Wissenschaft heissen soll. Die Aufgaben der Naturforschung füllen anfangs das Interesse der **Philosophie** fast allein aus,[2] bleiben dann lange Zeit in ihrem Umfang und scheiden erst in neuerer **Zeit** aus.[2] Die Geschichte umgekehrt ist[6] dem grössten Teile der philosophischen **Systeme** gleichgültig geblieben, um[7] erst verhältnismässig spät und vereinzelt als Objekt philosophischer **Untersuchung** aufzutreten. Die metaphysischen Lehren wiederum, in denen meist der Schwerpunkt der Philosophie[4] gesucht wird, sehen wir gerade an ihren bedeutsamen Wendepunkten entweder beiseite geschoben oder gar für unmöglich erklärt.

A. in face of W. change
B. significance L. course
d. passed through u. impractical (to what?)
V. comparison a. general B. concept
g. obtain d. those (See App. 14, 3.)
Z. purpose a. set up
G. forms G. intellectual activity
zut. applies A. claim e. raise
a. general B. concept
e. partial, biased wird becomes
B. importance b. questionable G. object
s. l. can be b. determined
h. s. is supposed to mean
a. initially On use of Rule 2, see Rule 2 C 1,2,3,4.
What goes with "füllen"? "scheiden"?
U. scope, extent G. history u. conversely
g. indifferent v. relatively v. isolated
a. appear What calls for the "zu"?
w. again S. center of gravity
g. sought b. significant W. turning points
u. impossible g. shoved aside

Anderseits ist[6] behauptet worden, die Philosophie behandle zwar dieselben Gegenstände wie die übrigen **Wissenschaften,**[1] aber in anderem Sinne und nach anderer **Methode:** allein auch dies spezifische Merkmal der Form hat keine historische **Allgemeingültigkeit.** Dass es[4] eine solche anerkannte philosophische **Methode** nicht gibt, würde[6] freilich kein **Einwurf** sein, wenn nur das Streben nach einer solchen[4] ein konstantes Merkmal aller **Philosophien** wäre. Dies ist jedoch so wenig der **Fall,** dass manche Philosophien[4] ihrer Wissenschaften den methodischen Charakter anderer Disziplinen, z B. der Mathematik oder der Naturforschung, aufdrückten, andere[4] aber von methodischer Behandlung ihrer **Probleme** überhaupt nichts wissen wollen und[8] die Tätigkeit der Philosophie in Analogie zu den genialen Konceptionen der **Kunst** setzen.

A. on the other hand i has
b. treats G. objects ü. remaining, other
a. different S. sense n. according to
al. but M. characteristic A. general validity
a. recognized
es gibt there is (See App. 10, 2, c, d.)
S. striving for M. characteristic
w. would be (See App. 28, 3, a.)
DO NOT FORGET TO FLAG PREFIXES AND "ZU"-VERBS, and to note the breaks.
a. stamp or imprint upon B. treatment
ü. at all T. activity **What does "und" call for?**
K. art

Aus diesen Umständen erklärt es sich auch, dass es[4] kein **festes,** allgemein historisch bestimmbares Verhältnis der Philosophie zu den übrigen **Wissenschaften** gibt. Wo die Philosophie[4] als **Gesamtwissenschaft** auftritt, da erscheinen die letzteren nur als ihre mehr oder minder deutlich gesonderten **Teile:** wo dagegen der Philosophie die Aufgabe[7] zugewiesen wird, die Ergebnisse der besonderen Wissenschaften in ihrer allgemeinen **Bedeutung** zusammenzufassen und[8] zu einer abschliessenden **Welterkenntnis** zu harmonisieren, da ergeben sich eigentümlich zusammengesetzte und verschränkte **Verhältnisse.**

U. circumstances **e.s. is explained**
f. fixed b. definable V. relation
ü. remaining, other
e. appear
g. separated T. parts d. on the other hand
z. assigned to wird. is (to what?)
E. results a. general
und (to what?) a. conclusive
W. world knowledge e. s. are shown
e. peculiarly z. composite v. interlaced
V. conditions

Zunächst zeigt sich eine Abhängigkeit der Philosophie von dem jeweiligen Stande der **Einsicht,**[1] die[5] in den besonderen **Disziplinen** erreicht ist: wesentliche Förderungen der Philosophie erwachsen aus den entscheidenden Fortschritten der Einzel**wissenschaften,** und zugleich ist[6] dadurch die Richtung und die **Grenze** bestimmt, worin die allgemeine Wissenschaft[4] jeweilig ihre **Aufgabe** zu lösen vermag. Umgekehrt aber erklärt sich daraus der Eingriff der Philosophie in die Arbeit der besonderen Wissen**schaften,** der[5] von diesen bald als Befruchtung, bald als **Hemmung** empfunden wird: denn die philosophische Behandlung der speziellen Fragen trägt zwar häufig vermöge des weiteren Gesichtspunktes und der kombinativen Richtung wertwolle Momente zur **Lösung** der **Probleme** bei,[2] in anderen Fällen jedoch stellt sie sich nur als eine **Verdoppelung** dar,[2] welche,[5] wenn sie[4] zu gleichen Resultaten führt, unnütz, wenn sie[4] aber andere **Ergebnisse** gewähren will, gefährlich erscheint.

Z. first of all **A. dependence**
j. actual S. state E. intelligence e. attained
w. essential F. advancements e. grow out
e. d. decisive F. progress
R. direction, trend
G. boundary b. limited j. for the time being
A. task v. is able U. conversely
E. encroachment
b. special bald – bald now – now B. productiveness
w. e. is sensed, felt B. treatment
h. frequently v. by virtue of
w. valuable M. factors
beitragen contribute (Note Rule 2.)
d. presents V. doubling, reduplication
g. same u. (erscheint) appears useless
E. results g. afford g. dangerous

Aus dem Gesagten erklärt sich ferner, dass die Beziehungen der Philosophie zu den sonstigen **Kulturtätigkeiten** nicht minder nahe sind als zu den **Einzelwissenschaften.** Denn in das Weltbild auf dessen Entwurf die metaphysisch gerichtete Philosophie hinzielt, drängen sich neben den Errungenschaften wissenschaftlicher Untersuchung überall auch die **Auffassungen** hinein,[2] welche[5] dem religiösen und sittlichen, dem künstlerischen Leben entstammen.

G. stated (See Rule 3 C 3 1.)
B. relations
s. other m. less (Why is K. bold-faced?)
W. world picture
E. draft, sketch, g. directed
h. aims n. along with E. achievements
U. investigation
hineind. are crowded in s. ethical
k. artistic e. come from

EINTEILUNG DER PHILOSOPHIE UND IHRER GESCHICHTE†

Es kann* hier nicht die **Absicht** sein,[7] eine systematische Einteilung der Pilosophie vorzutragen, denn eine solche würde* in keinem Falle historische **Gemeingültigkeit** besitzen können. Die Verschiedenheiten, welche* in der Bestimmung des Begriffs, der Aufgabe und der Gegenstände der Philosophie im Laufe der geschichtlichen **Entwicklung** obwalten, ziehen einen Wechsel auch der **Einteilung** so notwendig und selbstverständlich nach sich,[2] dass dies* keiner besondern **Erläuterungen** bedarf.

An * is placed where a certain rule is involved; indicate the Rule. **Watch the bold-face nouns.**
B. determination **Beg. concept A. task**
G. objects **L. course**
E. development o. prevail **W. change**
E. division n. necessarily s. self-evidently
n. s. z. entails **E. explanation**

Die älteste Philosophie kannte überhaupt noch keine **Gliederung.** Dem späteren Altertum war* eine Einteilung der Philosophie in Logik, Physik und **Ethik** geläufig. Im Mittelalter und noch mehr in der neueren Zeit werden* vielfach die beiden ersten als theoretische **Philosophie** zusammengefasst und* der praktischen gegenübergestellt. Seit Kant beginnt sich[7] eine neue Dreiteilung in logische, ethische und ästhetische **Philosophie** durchzusetzen. Doch hängen diese verschiedenen Einteilungen viel zu sehr von dem sachlichen Gange der Philosophie **selbst** ab,* als dass es sich verlohnte,* sie hier im einzelnen **aufzuzählen.**

k. knew
G. organization d. to the A. antiquity
E. classification g. familiar M. middle ages
w. are (See App. 7, 5, a.) b. two, both the
z. grouped together g. juxtaposed
b. begins (to what?)
D. triple division
d. assert What goes with "hängen"? v. z. s. much too much G. course
s. itself (App. 13, 2, f)
a. enumerate (What calls for the "zu"?)

Dagegen empfiehlt es sich,* der historischen Darstellung wenigstens eine Übersicht über den ganzen Umfang derjenigen **Probleme** voranzuschicken, welche* überhaupt, wenn auch in noch so verschiedenem Masse und verschiedener Wertung, Gegenstand der **Philosophie** gewesen sind,—eine Übersicht also, für die* keine systematische Geltung in Anspruch genommen wird, sondern nur der Zweck vorläufiger Orientierung* massgebend ist.

D. on the other hand e. s. is recommended
(to what?) D. presentation w. at least
Umf. scope v. send on before, preface
What does "welche" call for? ü. at all
wenn auch even if W. evaluation G. object
Ü. survey
für die for which G. value A. claim
Z. purpose v. preliminary
m. decisive

1. Theoretische Probleme nennen wir alle **diejenigen,** welche* sich teils auf die Erkenntnis der Wirklichkeit, teils auf die Untersuchung des Erkennens selbst beziehen. In der Erkenntnis der Wirklichkeit aber werden* die allgemeinen Fragen, welche* die Gesamtheit des **Wirklichen** betreffen, von denjenigen unterschieden, die* nur einzelne Gebiete der **Wirklichkeit** angehen. Mit den ersteren, den höchsten Prinzipien der Welterklärung und der* auf ihnen beruhenden allgemeinen **Weltansicht** beschäftigt sich die Metaphysik, von Aristoteles erste, d. h. **grundlegende Wissenschaft genannt[11] und[8] mit dem jetzt üblichen Namen nur wegen der Stellung bezeichnet, welche sie[4] in der antiken Sammlung der aristotelischen Werke "nach der Physik" einnahm. Vermöge seiner monotheistischen Weltanschauung nannte Aristoteles diesen Wissenszweig auch Theologie* Spätere haben* die rationale oder natürliche Theologie auch als Zweig der Metaphysik** behandelt.

d. those See app. 14, 2. t. partly
W. reality t. partly E. recognition
b. s. refer
What does "werden" call for? "welche"?
b. concern u. distinguished
e. isolated, individual G. fields
a. pertain to
W. world explanation b. which rests
W. world view b. s. is concerned
Note Rule 11 (while named or called)
Note how "und" calls for the other 11.
b. designated S. collection
V. by virtue of
W. world view W. branch of knowledge
S. later (ones)
Z. branch What calls for "behandelt"?
b. treated

Die besonderen Gebiete der Wirklichkeit sind die Natur und die **Geschichte.*** In der ersteren sind* äussere und innere Natur zu unterscheiden: die Probleme, welche die äussere Natur* **der Erkenntnis** darbietet, bezeichnet man als kosmologische oder speziell als naturphilosophische,* auch wohl als physische.* Die Erforschung der inneren Natur, d. h. des Bewusstseins und seiner

G. fields W. reality
What is the subject here?
s. z. u. are to be distinguished (See App. 12, 1.)
E. cognition d. offers
w. indeed
e. study **d. h. that is, i. e.**

†Windelband-Heimsoeth, **Lehrbuch der Geschichte der Philosophie**

Zustände und Tätigkeiten ist Sache der **Psychologie.*** Die philosophische Betrachtung der Geschichte gehört in den Rahmen der theoretischen Philosophie formell,* sofern das Wesen historischer Forschung* methodologisch und erkenntnistheoretisch untersucht wird, materiell dagegen nur insoweit als sie* auf Erforschung der* im historischen Leben der **Völker** obwaltenden **Gesetze** gerichtet sein soll: da aber die Geschichte* das Reich zweckmässiger Handlungen der **Menschen** ist, so fallen die Fragen der Geschichtsphilosophie,* sofern sie* den Gesamtzweck der historischen Bewegung und seine Erfüllung zu ihrem **Gegenstande** machen will, unter die praktischen **Probleme.***

B. consciousness **Z. conditions**
S. matter **Indicate the rule where the * appears.**
"Flag" Rules 2 and 7 R. realm W. nature
F. study e. epistemological
u. investigated w. is (App. 7, 5a)
E. Study d. of the (what?) so. is to be
L. life o. which prevail (Why which?)
G. history R. realm **z. expedient, appropriate**
H. acts
Note how "sie," the subject, calls for the verb.
G. total purpose B. movement
E. fulfillment G. subject, object
Have you "flagged" prefixes and "zu" verbs?

Die* auf die Erkenntnis **selbst** gerichtete Untersuchung wird im allgemeinen Sinne des Wortes **Logik** genannt.[10] Beschäftigt sie sich mit der Art, wie das Wissen* tatsächlich zustande kommt, so fällt diese psychogenetische Betrachtung in den Bereich der **Psychologie.**[10] Stellt man dagegen die Normen auf,* nach denen der Wahrheitswert der Vorstellungen* beurteilt werden soll, so nennt man diese die logischen **Gesetze*** und bezeichnet die* darauf gerichtete Untersuchung als Logik im engeren **Sinne.*** Als angewandte Logik erscheint die **Methodologie,** welche* die Vorschriften für die planmässige Einrichtung der wissenschaftlichen Tätigkeit mit Rücksicht auf die verschiedenen Erkenntniszwecke der einzelnen **Disziplinen** entwickelt. Die Probleme endlich, welche[5] sich aus den Fragen über die Tragweite und die Grenze der menschlichen Erkenntnis und ihr Verhältnis zu der[3] ihren **Gegenstand** bildenden **Wirklichkeit** erheben, machen die Aufgaben der Erkenntnistheorie aus.*

What does "die" call for? s. itself See App. 13, 2, f. wird gen. is called
B. sie s. if it is concerned (Why Rule 10?)
z. k. comes about B. consideration B. realm
Why Rule 10? a. sets up
Note how subj. comes in after the relative.
beu. judged G. laws
b. labels g. which is directed (Why which?)
e. narrower S. sense **a. applied**
p. methodical V. rules
E. arrangement T. activity
R. regard v. different E. purposes of cognition
e. develops
Note how Rule 5 is used. T. scope
G. limit V. relation
Why Rule 3? b. which forms W. reality
e. s. are raised (See App. 11, 4, a.) m. a. comprise
E. epistemology ausm. make up

2. Praktische Probleme heissen im allgemeinen diejenigen, welche* aus der Untersuchung der zweckbestimmten Tätigkeit des Menschen erwachsen. Auch hier ist* eine psychogenetische **Behandlung** möglich, welche* Sache der Psychologie ist. Dagegen ist diejenige **Disziplin,*** welche* das Handeln des Menschen unter dem Gesichtspunkte der sittlichen **Normbestimmung** betrachtet, die Ethik oder **Moralphilosophie.** Dabei pflegt[7] man unter Moral im engeren Sinne die Aufstellung und Begründung der sittlichen **Vorschriften** zu verstehen. Da sich aber alles sittliche Handeln[4] auf die **Gemeinschaft** bezieht, so schliesst sich an die **Moral** die Philosophie der Gesellschaft (für welche sich der unglückliche Name Soziologie[4] auf die **Dauer** doch durchzusetzen scheint,) und die **Rechtsphilosophie.*** Insofern weiterhin das Ideal menschlicher Gemeinschaft[4] den letzten Sinn der **Geschichte** ausmacht, erscheint, wie oben erwähnt, auch die Geschichtsphilosophie in diesem **Zusammenhange.*** Zu den praktischen Problemen im weitesten Sinne des Wortes gehören endlich auch diejenigen, welche* sich auf die Kunst und **Religion** beziehen. Für die philosophische Untersuchung über das Wesen des Schönen und der Kunst ist* seit dem Ende des 18. Jahrhunderts der Name Ästhetik eingeführt.

h. are called
d. those (App. 14, 2) U. investigation
z. purpose-determined T. activity
e. grow out B. treatment m. possible
Note how "ist" takes out "möglich".
H. action
G. viewpoint e. ethical b. considers D. in this connection p. one is accustomed (to what?)
S. sense A. formulation B. justification
s. ethical v. understand
s. moral, ethical G. society
s. b. refers s. s. is joined u. unfortunate
d. assert a. d. D. in the long run
R. philosophy of law
m. human G. society
a. makes up e. mentioned
Z. connection w. broadest S. sense
g. belong d. those
s. b. refer
W. nature K. art
i. ist eingeführt (What Rule is this?)

Die Deutsche Philosophie

Eine glückliche Vereinigung mehrfacher geistiger Bewegungen hat* zu Ende des 18. und zu Anfang des 19. Jahrhunderts in Deutschland eine Blüte der Philosophie hervorgebracht, welche* in der Geschichte des europäischen Denkens nur mit der grossen Entfaltung der griechischen Philosophie von Sokrates bis **Aristoteles** zu vergleichen ist. In einer intensiv und extensiv gleich mächtigen Entwicklung hat* der deutsche Geist während der kurzen Spanne von vier Jahrzehnten (1780 bis 1820) eine Fülle grossartig entworfener und allseitig ausgebildeter Systeme der philosophischen **Weltanschauung** erzeugt, wie sie* auf so engem **Raume** nirgends wieder zusammengedrängt sind und in allen diesen schürzen sich die gesamten Gedanken der vorhergehenden Philosophie zu eigenartigen und eindrucksvollen **Gebilden** zusammen.* Sie erscheinen in ihrer Gesamtheit als die reife Frucht eines langen **Wachstums,*** aus der* die Keimungen einer neuen **Entwicklung** spriessen sollen.

FLAG PREFIXES AND "ZU"-VERBS. m. of various B. movements A. beginning
J. century B. bloom, flourishing
h. brought forth (What calls for the verb?)
D. thinking, thought E. unfolding
What calls for the verb "ist" z. v.?
z. v. ist. is to be compared (App. 12, 1, a)
m. powerful E. development G. mind, spirit
w. during What does "hat" call for?
g. brilliantly e. sketched al. on all sides
a. developed, constructed
W. world view e. produced
n. nowhere z. compressed
What goes with "schürzen"? g. total
v. preceding e. peculiar e. impressive
G. forms e. appear
G. totality r. ripe F. fruit W. growth
a. d. from which (Let the relative aid to clear the verb out.) s. germinations

Diese glänzende Erscheinung hatte ihre Ursache in der unvergleichlichen Lebendigkeit des **Geistes,*** womit die deutsche Nation[4] damals die Kulturbewegung der Renaissance, die[5] in ihr durch äussere **Gewalt** unterbrochen war, mit neuer **Kraft** wieder aufnahm und* zur Vollendung führte. Sie erlebte—ein Vorgang ohne gleichen in der **Geschichte***—den Höhepunkt ihrer innerlichen Entwicklung zu derselben **Zeit** * wo ihre äussere Geschichte* den niedersten **Stand** erreichte. Als sie* politisch machtlos darniederlag, schuf sie ihre weltbezwingenden Denker und **Dichter.*** Die siegreiche Kraft aber lag gerade in dem Bunde zwischen Philosophie und **Dichtung.*** Die Gleichzeitigkeit von Kant und **Goethe,*** und die Verknüpfung ihrer Ideen durch **Schiller**—das sind die entscheidenden Züge jener **Zeit.** Durch diese Gemeinschaft der höchsten **Kulturarbeit,** in der[5] sich Dichtung und Philosophie gegenseitig zu glänzenden **Schöpfungen** förderten, ist* das deutsche Volk von neuem zu einer **Nation** geworden: hierin hat* es die Substanz seines **Geistes** wiedergefunden; aus ihr sind* die intellektuellen und die moralischen **Kräfte** geflossen, durch die es* im Laufe des folgenden Jahrhunderts in den **Stand**[7] gesetzt wurde, diese seine neu gewonnene Nationalität auch in der **Aussenwelt** zur Geltung* zu bringen.

g. brilliant E. phenomenon U. cause
u. incomparable L. vivacity G. mind, spirit
w. with which (See Rule 5.) d. at that time
What does 4 call for? 5?
u. interrupted K. strength. a. took up
V. completion e. experienced V. process
H. high point ä. outer
e. reached n. lowest
s. created W. world mastering
D. thinkers D. poets S. victorious
B. union What do the bold-face nouns tell you to do? G. simultaneousness
V. connection d. s. those are (App. 10, 3, n)
e. decisive Z. features G. community
D. literature, poetry g. mutually
S. creations f. s. were furthered
v. n. anew What does "hat" call for?
w. found again s. have (why?)
K. forces g. flown
L. course f. following
S. position (to what?)
g. gained A. outside world
z. G. b. assert What calls for this "zu"?

Die Geschichte der Philosophie ist* deshalb an dieser Stelle auf das engste mit derjenigen der allgemeinen **Literatur** verflochten, und die Beziehungen und Anregungen laufen zwischen beiden fortwährend hin und her.* Dies tritt charakteristisch in der gesteigerten und schliesslich entscheidenden **Bedeutung** hervor,* welche* in diesem Zusammenhange den ästhetischen Problemen und **Begriffen** zufiel. Für die Philosophie eröffnete sich damit eine neue **Welt,*** die sie[4] bisher nur mit gelegentlichen **Ausblicken** gestreift hatte.

(Did you flag it?) d. therefore
S. place a. d. e. in the closest way
v. interwoven (What calls for this verb?)
A. impulse, stimulation l. run
h. u. h. to and fro What goes with "tritt"?
s. ultimately e. decisive B. importance
Z. connection
B. concepts z. devolve upon
ö. was opened (App. 11, 4, b) d. therewith
g. touched A. outlook, prospect

Immanuel Kant†

Immanuel Kant wurde[6] zu Königsberg in Preussen den 22. April **1724** geboren. Sein Vater, ein rechtschaffner **Sattlermeister,** und seine Mutter, eine verständige fromme **Frau,** wirkten schon in der frühesten **Jugend** wohltätig auf ihn ein.[2] Im **Jahr** 1740 bezog er die Universität, wo er* vorzugweise Philosophie, Mathematik und Physik, als Fakultätswissenschaft aber die **Theologie** studierte. Seine schriftstellerische Laufbahn begann er im 23. **Jahre,** 1747, mit einer Abhandlung "Gedanken von der wahren Schätzung der lebendigen **Kräfte.**" Durch seine äusseren Verhältnisse war er genötigt,[7] einige Jahre hindurch **Hauslehrer** bei mehreren Familien in der Nähe von Königsberg zu werden. Im Jahr 1755 liess er sich als Privatdozent an der **Universität** nieder[2] und hielt nun Vorlesungen über Logik, Metaphysik, Physik und **Mathematik,** später auch über **Moral,** Anthropologie und physische **Geographie,** meist im Sinne der Wolfschen **Schule,** jedoch frühzeitig Zweifel gegen den **Dogmatismus** äussernd.[11]

w. g. was born (App. 7, 5, b)
r. upright, honest
v. reasonable, understanding
f. pious What goes with "w"? f. earliest
w. beneficent v. preferably
s. literary L. career
A. treatise G. thoughts
w. true S. estimation, evaluation l. living
V. conditions g. necessitated (to what?)
m. several e. some
N. vicinity What goes with "liess"?
n. settled V. lectures
s. later
m. mostly S. sense
j. however Z. doubt
ä. manifesting (Note Rule 11.)

Er war[6] zugleich seit der Herausgabe seiner ersten Dissertation unermüdlich als **Schriftsteller** tätig, obgleich sein entscheidendes Hauptwerk, die Kritik der reinen Vernunft,[4] erst in seinem 57. Lebensjahre, 1781, seine Kritik der praktischen Vernunft 1787, seine Religion innerhalb der Grenzen der reinen Vernunft erst 1793 erschien.

z. at the same time H. publication
u. untiringly S. writer
t. active (Note Rule 6, predicate adj. come out with forms of "sein".) V. reason
L. year of life i. within G. limits
e. appeared

Im Jahre 1770, ein 46 jähriger **Mann,** wurde er ordentlicher Professor der Logik und Metaphysik;[1] er blieb dies in ununterbrochener Lehrtätigkeit bis zum Jahre **1797,**[1] von wo an Alterschwäche[4] ihn daran hinderte. Berufungen nach Jena, Erlangen und Halle schlug er aus.[2] Bald strömten aus ganz Deutschland die Edelsten und Wissbegierigsten nach **Königsberg,** um[7] zu den Füssen des Königsberger **Weisen** zu sitzen. Einer seiner Verehrer, der Professor der Philosophie, Preuss aus **Würzburg,** der[5] sich nur kurze Zeit in **Königsberg aufhielt,** trat mit den Worten zu ihm ins **Zimmer:** er komme 160 Meilen weit her, um[7] ihn, **Kant** zu sehen und zu sprechen. In den letzten Jahren seines Lebens besass er ein kleines Haus mit einem Garten in einer geräuschlosen Gegend der **Stadt,** wo er[4] seine stille und regelmässige **Lebensweise** ungestört fortsetzen konnte. Sein Leben war äusserst einfach, nur auf einen guten Tisch hielt er etwas. Kant ist[6] nie aus der Provinz, nicht einmal bis nach **Danzig** gekommen. Seine grössten Reisen hatten[9] Landgüter in der **Umgegend** zum Ziel. Dennoch erlangte er durch Lesen von Reisebeschreibungen die genaueste Kenntnis der **Erde,** wie namentlich seine Vorlesungen über physische Geographie zeigen. Er war von kaum mittlerer **Grösse,** fein gebaut, von blauem **Auge,** immer gesund, bis er[4] endlich im hohen **Alter** kindisch wurde. Verheiratet war er nie. Strenge Wahrheitsliebe, grosse Redlichkeit und einfache Bescheidenheit bezeichnen seinen **Charakter.**

o. full professor
u. uninterrupted L. teaching work
A. weakness of age
B. calls
a. declined s. streamed
E. most noble W. most desirous of learning
u. z. in order (to what?)
V. admirers
How are you told this is a relative?
a. was staying
Have you "flagged" the "zu" verbs?
s. speak b. possessed
g. quiet G. region, part
r. regular u. undisturbed
f. continue a. extremely e. simple
T. table i. has (what?) n. e. not even
R. trips z. Z. h. had for a goal
e. acquired L. reading
g. most exact K. knowledge
n. especially V. lectures
z. show m. medium
g. healthy
v. married S. strict
W. love of truth R. honesty, uprightness
B. modesty b. characterize

†Albert Schwegler, **Geschichte der Philosophie im Umriss**

Übergang auf die Nachkantische Philosophie

Die Kantische Philosophie gewann in Deutschland bald eine fast unbedingte **Herrschaft.** Die imponierende Kühnheit ihres Standpunkts,* die Neuheit ihrer Resultate,* die Unabwendbarkeit ihrer Prinzipien,* der sittliche Ernst ihrer **Weltanschauung,*** vor allem der Geist der Freiheit und moralischen Autonomie,* der* in ihr wehte und der* den Strebungen jenes Zeitalters kräftigend entgegenkam, verschafften ihr ebenso begeisterten als ausgebreiteten Beifall. Sie bewirkte eine* unter allen gebildeten **Ständen** sich verbreitende,[3] in solchem Masse noch bei keinem Volke zum **Vorschein** gekommene Teilnahme an den philosophischen **Forschungen.*** In kurzer Zeit hatte* sie sich namentlich eine zahlreiche **Schule** herangezogen: es gab bald wenige deutsche **Universitäten,*** auf denen sie* nicht talentvolle **Vertreter** gehabt hätte, und in allen Fächern der Wissenschaft und **Literatur,*** namentlich in der Theologie und im Naturrecht, auch in den schönen Wissenschaften (Schiller) begann sich ihr Einfluss zu äussern.

Indicate what rule is involved where the * appears.
H. dominance **u. unconditional**
K. boldness N. novelty
U. inevitability What do these nouns tell you to do? **s. ethical E. seriousness**
F. freedom d. which
d. which (App. 3, a) S. endeavors
k. forcefully e. came to meet
v. procure **a. widespread B. acclaim**
[3]See Rule 3 C 1, sentences 2, 3, 4.
v. which spread itself **g. which came**
F. studies
h. attracted
e. g. there were
V. representatives a. d. See Rule 5B.
F. subjects
N. law of nature
b. began (to what?)
ä. express

Die meisten* in der Kantschen **Schule** hervorgetretenen Schriftsteller haben* sich auf eine erläuternde oder auch populäre Ausführung und Anwendung des empfangenen **Lehrbegriffs** beschränkt, und selbst die talentvollsten und selbständigsten unter den Verteidigern oder Verbesserern der kritischen Philosophie (Reinhold, Schulze, Beck, Fries) waren* nur darauf bedacht,[7] teils dem* von ihnen angenommenen Kantschen Lehrbegriff eine festere **Unterlage zu geben,** teils[7] einzelne[3] von ihnen bemerkte Mängel und Lücken zu beseitigen, teils[7] den Standpunkt des transcendentalen **Idealismus** reiner und folgerichtiger durchzuführen. Eine hervorragende,[3] durch wirklichen Fortschritt philosophisch epochemachende Stellung nehmen unter den Fortsetzern und Fortbildern der Kantschen Philosophie nur zwei Männer ein* (Fichte und Herbart); unter den Gegnern des Kantschen Kritizismus (z. B. Hamann, Herder) hat nur Einer philosophische Bedeutung, **Jakobi.*** Die drei Philosophen sind daher der nächste Gegenstand unserer **Betrachtung.*** Wir schicken der genaueren Entwickelung eine kurze vorläufige Charakteristik ihres Verhältnisses zur Kantschen **Philosophie** voraus.*

Why is "S" bold-faced? h. who stepped forward
S. writers e. illustrative
E. execution A. application
e. received L. scientific system s. even
V. defenders, supporters V. perfecter
b. mindful (to what?) Note Rule 7.
a. which was accepted
f. more solid U. foundation **t. partly (to what?)**
b. remove bem. which were noticed
f. more consistently d. carry through
herv. outstanding (what?) F. progress
e. which was epoch making
What does "ein" go with?
G. opponents
E. one B. importance
G. subject B. consideration
g. more exact E. development **v. tentative**
V. relation v. to preface to

Kant hatte* den **Dogmatismus** kritisch vernichtet, seine Kritik der reinen Vernunft hatte zum Resultate die theoretische Unbeweisbarkeit der drei **Vernunftideen,** Gott, Freiheit und **Unsterblichkeit.*** Zwar hatte* Kant die* vom Standpunkt des theoretischen **Wissens** aus abgewiesenen Ideen in praktischem Interesse wieder eingeführt, als Postulate der praktischen **Vernunft;** aber als **Postulate,** als nur praktische **Voraussetzungen,** gewähren sie keine theoretische **Gewissheit** und bleiben* dem **Zweifel** ausgesetzt. Um* diese Ungewissheit, diese Verzweifelung am Wissen, welche* das Ende des Kantschen **Philosophierens** zu sein schien, niederzuschlagen, stellte ein jüngerer Zeitgenosse Kants, Jakobi, dem Standpunkt des Kritizismus als Antithese den Standpunkt der **Glaubensphilosophie** gegenüber.[2]

v. destroyed
V. reason U. indemonstrability
U. immortality Z. to be sure
d. the (what?) W. knowledge
a. g. which were rejected **For use of "aus"** see App. 21, a. e. introduced V. reason
V. suppositions g. afford
G. certainty b. remain (See Rule 6.)
a. exposed U. in order (to what?)
V. despair
n. beat down, quell
What goes with "stellte"? Z. contemporary
S. stand point
G. religious philosophy g. contrast, place opposite to, match

Spinoza

Baruch Spinoza wurde* in Amsterdam den 24. Nov. 1632 geboren. Seine Eltern, Juden aus portugiesischem Geschlecht, waren wohlhabende Kaufleute,* die* ihm eine gelehrte **Erziehung** geben liessen. Er studierte mit vielem Fleiss die **Bibel.*** Bald vertauschte er jedoch das Studium der Theologie mit dem der Physik und der Werke des **Cartesius**;* gleichzeitig trennte er sich vom **Judentum**, **mit dem er* frühzeitig innerlich gebrochen hatte, auch äusserlich, ohne[7] jedoch förmlich zum Christentum überzugehen.**

Indicate the rule where the * appears. Numbers are gradually being left out except on difficult sentences K. merchants E. education F. diligence v. exchanged j. however d. d. that of t. separated f. at an early time i. inwardly
o. without (Note call for "zu".)

Um* den Verfolgungen der Juden, die* ihn excommunicirt hatten und[8] ihm sogar nach dem Leben trachteten, zu entgehen, verliess er Amsterdam und begab sich nach Rynsburg bei Leyden; zuletzt siedelte er sich nach dem Haag über,* wo er, einzig mit wissenschaftlichen Arbeiten beschäftigt,[11] in grösster Eingezogenheit lebte. Seinen Unterhalt erwarb er sich mit dem Schleifen optischer Gläser,* welche seine Freunde* verkauften. Der Kurfürst von der Pfalz, Carl Ludwig, liess* ihm, unter dem Versprechen völliger Lehrfreiheit, eine Professur der Philosophie, in Heidelberg antragen: Spinoza schlug sie aus.* Von Natur schwächlich, lange Jahre an der Schwindsucht kränkelnd,[11] starb Spinoza, erst 44 Jahre alt, den 21. Febr. 1677. In seinem Leben spiegelte sich überall die wolkenlose Klarheit und erhabene Ruhe des vollendeten Weisen.* Nüchtern, mit Wenigem zufrieden, Herr seiner Leidenschaften, nie unmässig traurig oder fröhlich, mild und wohlwollend, ein bewundernswerter Charakter,* hat* er die Lehren seiner Philosophie auch im Leben getreulich befolgt. Sein Hauptwerk, die Ethik, erschien in seinem Todesjahre.* Wahrscheinlich wollte er sie noch bei Lebzeiten selbst herausgeben, aber das gehässige Gerücht, dass er* ein Atheist sei, hat* ihn wohl davon abgehalten. Sein vertrautester Freund, Ludwig Meyer, ein Arzt, besorgte die Herausgabe,* seinem Willen gemäss, nach seinem Tode.*

V. persecutions What does "um" call for? die? und? s. even t. try
e. escape v. left b. s. betake oneself, go
z. finally What does "über" go with?
b. while occupied (why while?) E. solitude
U. sustenance S. grinding
v. sold V. promise

v. complete L. academic freedom
a. offer, propose
s. a. declined s. weak
k. (while) ailing s. reflected
e. sublime v. complete, perfect
W. wise man N. temperate z. satisfied
L. passions u. immoderately
w. charitable b. admirable
L. teachings g. faithfully
b. followed H. main work w. probably
L. during life g. odious, hateful G. rumor
a. detained v. most trusted
b. took care of H. publication
gem. according to (App. 15, 3, b)

Das spinozistische System ruht auf drei Grundbegriffen, aus deren Fassung sich alles Übrige* mit mathematischer Notwendigkeit ergibt. Diese Begriffe sind der Begriff der Substanz,* der des Attributs, und der des Modus. Spinoza geht aus vom cartesianischen Begriff der Substanz.* Bei diesem Begriff der Substanz kann* jedoch nach Spinoza nur eine einzige Substanz existieren. Nach Spinoza ist die absolute Substanz vielmehr die reale Ursache aller und jeder Existenz.* Diese eine Substanz nennt Spinoza Gott. Spinoza erklärt ausdrücklich, dass er von Gott eine ganze andere Vorstellung habe, als die Christen; er behauptet entschieden, dass alles Dasein, auch das materielle, unmittelbar der Natur Gottes als der Einen Substanz entstamme. Man muss* dabei, wie[8] sich von selbst versteht, die christliche Gottesidee, die Vorstellung einer geistigen Einzelpersönlichkeit[9] bei Seite lassen.

r. rests, depends
G. basic concepts F. style, frame, formulation
N. necessity s. e. results
B. concept d. d. that of
g. proceeds B. idea

n. according to
v. moreover U. cause e. one
a. emphatically V. idea
b. maintain e. decidedly
D. existence u. directly
e. originates from
s. v. is understood
g. intellectual, spiritual
l. b. S. leave aside, disregard

Leibnitz

Gottfried Leibnitz ist* 1646 in Leipzig geboren, wo sein Vater Professor war. Im Jahr 1661 bezog er, nachdem er* die Jurisprudenz zu seinem Berufsfach erwählt, die Universität, 1663 verteidigte er zur Erlangung der philosophischen Doktorwürde seine Dissertation de principio individui (ein[3] für die Richtung seines spätern Philosophierens charakteristisches Thema), darauf ging er nach Jena, später nach Altdorf, wo er* Doktor der Rechte wurde. Eine* ihm in Altdorf angebotene Professur der Jurisprudenz schlug er aus.* Sein weiteres Leben ist ein unstetes, vielgeschäftiges Wanderleben, meist an Höfen, wo er* als gewandter Hofmann zu den verschiedenartigsten, auch diplomatischen Geschäften verwandt wurde. Im Jahr 1672 ging er nach Paris zunächst mit dem Auftrag,[7] Ludwig XIV. zur Eroberung Ägyptens zu bereden und* damit die gefährlichen Kriegsgelüste des Königs von Deutschland abzuwenden, dann nach London, von dort als Rat und Bibliothekar des gelehrten katholischen Herzogs Johann Friedrich nach Hannover, in welcher Stadt er* die meiste Zeit seines spätern Lebens zubrachte, freilich mit zahlreichen Unterbrechungen durch Reisen nach Wien, Berlin usw.

Signals are given where the * appears.
Underline all nouns that should be in bold-face
type. State why certain rules are involved.
e. chosen v. defended
E. obtaining D. doctor's degree
e. a (what?)
R. direction c. which was characteristic
d. thereupon
w. became (App. 7, 3, b) e. a (what?)
a. which was offered (Why which?)
a. declined u. irregular g. busy H. courts
g. versatile v. most different kind
G. affairs v. used, employed
z. for the time being A. commission (to what?)
b. persuade u. and (to what?)
g. dangerous K. war desires
a. avert, turn away from g. scholarly H. duke
S. city z. spent
f. to be sure z. numerous U. interruptions

In besonders nahem Verhältnis stand er zur preussischen Königin Sophie Charlotte, einer geistreichen Frau, die* um sich einen Kreis der bedeutendsten Gelehrten jener Zeit versammelte, und für welche Leibnitz seine* auf ihr Anrathen unternommene Theodicee zunächst bestimmt hatte. Sein Vorschlag zur Errichtung einer Akademie in Berlin trat[9] im Jahr 1700 ins Leben; er wurde der erste Präsident derselben. Auch in Dresden und Wien machte er, obwohl erfolglos, Vorschläge zur Errichtung von Akademien.

n. near, close V. relation
g. brilliant, ingenious K. circle
G. scholars v. assembled
u. which was undertaken
b. determined V. proposal E. erection
w. became (App. 7, 3, b)
o. although e. without success
V. suggestions

Leibnitz war nächst Aristoteles der genialste Polyhistor, der* je gelebt. Er verband die höchste, durchdringendste Kraft des Geistes mit der reichsten, ausgebreitetsten Gelehrsamkeit. Deutschland hat besondere Ursache,[7] auf ihn stolz zu sein, da er* nach Jakob Böhme der erste bedeutende Philosoph ist, der* den Deutschen angehört: mit ihm ist* die Philosophie in Deutschland einheimisch geworden.

n. next to
v. combined d. most penetrating G. mind
a. most wide spread G. scholarship
U. reason, cause (to what?) s. proud
da since (See App. 25,2.)
a. belongs
e. native

Leider liess ihn teils die Vielseitigkeit seiner Bestrebungen und literarischen Unternehmungen, teils seine wandernde Lebensart[4] zu keiner zusammenhängenden Darstellung seiner Philosophie kommen. Er hat* seine Ansichten meist nur in kleinen Gelegenheitsschriften und in Briefen entwickelt, grösstenteils in französischer Sprache.

l. unfortunately (Rearrange the "Ihn".)
V. versatility
U. enterprises L. type of life
z. coherent D. presentation
A. views G. occasional writings
e. developed g. for the most part

Die Grundeigentümlichkeit der Leibnitzschen Lehre ist der Unterschied vom Spinozismus. Spinoza hatte* die Eine und allgemeine Substanz zum einzigen Positiven gemacht. Auch Leibnitz legt[9] seiner Philosophie den Substanzbegriff zu Grund, aber er definiert ihn anders, als tätige Kraft. Dass die tätige Kraft* das Wesen der Substanz* ausmacht, ist ein Satz, auf den Leibnitz* immer wieder zurückkommt, und mit welchem die übrigen Lehrsätze seiner Philosophie im engsten Zusammenhange stehen.

G. basic peculiarity
L. theory U. distinction a. general
l. lays – as a basis Note Rule 9.
s. concept of substance
a. differently K. power, force
W. nature, essence a. makes up
S. theory, axiom, proposition a. d. to which
ü. other L. axioms
e. closest Z. connection

LITERATUR

Umfang und Aufgabe der Literaturwissenschaft†

Literatur ist dem Wortlaute nach die Gesamtheit der[3] durch die **Sprache** ausgedrückten und schriftlich aufgezeichneten **Geisteserzeugnisse.**[1] Demnach hätte[6] die Literaturgeschichte im weitesten Sinne die Entwicklung des menschlichen **Geistes,** soweit diese[4] in Denkmälern sprachlicher **Form** schriftlich niedergelegt ist, darzustellen. Ausgeschlossen bleiben indessen gewöhnlich solche **Werke,**[1] die[5] im Dienste einer **Fachwissenschaft** geschrieben sind, während anderseits auch manche[4], die[5] ursprünglich nicht aufgeschrieben, sondern nur mündlich überliefert waren, z. B. das Volkslied, in der **Literaturgeschichte** berücksichtigt werden. Im Mittelpunkte der Betrachtung steht die **Poesie,**[1] in der[5] sich das Gemüts- und **Geistesleben** am reinsten widerspiegelt. Doch gehören nebenbei auch Werke der Wissenschaft von allgemeinerem **Charakter,**[1] namentlich der Geschichte, Philosophie und **Beredsamkeit,**[1] in ihren **Bereich,**[1] wenn sie[4] bedeutend auf die allgemeine **Geistesbildung** eingewirkt haben und[8] die Gediegenheit des Inhalts mit geistiger Durchdringung und künstlerischer **Form** verbinden.

n. according to (App. 15, 3, d, f) G. totality
S. language a. which were **expressed**
a. which were recorded G. intellectual **productions**
i.w.S. in the broadest sense E. development
D. monuments
d. to present n. laid down s. in writing
A. excluded g. ordinarily W. works
D. service F. special science
an. on the other hand u. originally
Note that waren goes also with "aufge."
b. considered (App. 7, 5, a)
M. center B. consideration
Gem. inner life G. intellectual life
w. reflected g. belong
W. science a. more general n. especially
B. eloquence B. realm b. significantly
G. intellectual development e. influenced
G. soundness D. penetration k. artistic
v. combine

Hauptaufgaben der Literaturgeschichte sind:[7] 1. die wichtigeren Einzelwerke der Literatur, vorzüglich der Dichtkunst, nach Inhalt und Form, nach Entstehung und **Wirkung** zu kennzeichnen, 2.[7] die geschichtlichen Zusammenhänge, in denen diese Einzelerscheinungen des Geisteslebens[4] zueinander und zur ganzen **Zeitbewegung** stehen, aufzuweisen, 3.[7] die äusseren Lebensumstände der Schriftsteller, insofern sie[4] für ihre Werke von **Bedeutung** sind, darzulegen.

H. main tasks s. are (to what?)
w. more important E. individual works
D. poetic art I. content E. origin
W. effect k. mark, characterize
Z. connections E. individual phenomena
Z. progress of the time a. to show a. outer
L. life conditions B. importance d. to present

Poesie und Prosa

Die Poesie entspringt dem inneren **Drange,**[7] einer Empfindung einen[3] über die alltägliche **Rede** erhobenen **Ausdruck** zu verleihen. Einbildungskraft und Gefühl sind die dabei vorzüglich wirkenden **Kräfte,**[1] die[5] durch Vorgänge im Natur- und **Menschenleben**[9] in Tätigkeit versetzt werden. Lange vor Erfindung der Schrift hat[6] es Poesie gegeben; das gesprochene oder gesungene,[3] durch die Kraft des **Gedächtnisses** bewahrte Wort war ursprünglich das einzige **Mittel,**[1] durch das Dichtungen[4] von einem Geschlecht zum **anderen** fortgepflanzt wurden. Der Form nach unterscheidet sich die Poesie von der gewöhnlichen Redeweise durch den **Rhythmus,**[1] d. h. eine taktmässige Bewegung der **Sprache,**[1] die[5] durch einen geregelten Wechsel zwischen betonten und unbetonten **Silben** hervorgebracht wird. Die Entwicklung rhythmischer Poesie geht der der unrhythmischen überall voraus.[2] Erst der höher gebildete Mensch lernte[6] auch die Prosa, d. h. die[3] durch keinen **Rhythmus** gebundene **Rede,** der Poesie dienstbar machen, so dass dann Dichtungen in gebundener und ungebundener Rede (poetischer und prosaischer **Form**) unterschieden werden.

e. originates from D. urge (to what?)
E. feeling Why Rule 3? a. every day R. speech
e. which is raised A. expression
v. to lend E. (power of) imagination w. active
i. T. in activity v. set
E. invention S. writing h.e.g. **there has been**
(App. 10, 2, j) Why Rule 3? G. memory
b. which was preserved u. originally
M. means d. d. by which D. poetic products
f. transmitted d.F.n. according to form (App. 15, 3, f) u. distinguishes t. rhythmical
B. movement g. regulated W. exchange
b. stressed E. development
v. precedes d.d. that of ü. everywhere
g. developed l. d. m. learned to make serviceable ("lernen" and "lehren" act like modal auxiliaries in Rule 6 occasionally) R. speech
u. w. are distinguished (App. 7, 5, a)

Da die Literatur[4] der vollkommenste Ausdruck des menschlichen **Geisteslebens** ist, so zeigt sich das geistige Gepräge eines Volkes,[1] seine **Eigenart,**[1] die[5] es von andern **Völkern** unterscheidet, am deutlichsten in seiner **Literatur.**[1] Dabei ist jedoch zu beachten, dass kein Kulturvolk[4] sich der geistigen Einwirkung andrer, zunächst seiner Nachbarn, namentlich wenn diese höher entwickelt sind, entziehen kann.

v. most perfect A. expression
G. intellectual life z. s. is shown
g. intellectual G. stamp E. peculiarity
u. distinguishes a. d. most clearly
z. b. to be observed (App. 12, 1, abc)
g. intellectual E. effect, influence
N. neighbors n. especially
e. withdraw

†Gotthold Ludwig Klee, **Grundzüge der deutschen Literaturgeschichte**

Alfred Lord Tennyson

Wenn man[4] einst in späteren Jahrzehnten und Jahrhunderten **auf das** Zeitalter der Königin Viktoria von Grossbritannien und **Irland** zurückblickt, wird[6] man erkennen müssen, dass es[4] in literarischer und künstlicher Beziehung ein Zeitalter der **Blüte** war. Künste, die[5] sonst unter dem trüben Himmel des **Landes** nicht gedeihen schienen, wie die Malerei und die **Musik**, entwickelten sich in ungeahnter **Weise**,[1] bewiesen ihre Unabhängigkeit von bloss klimatischen **Einflüssen**[1] und erzielten selbst im Ausland höchste **Anerkennnung**.[1]

e. once s. later J. decades
Z. age
z. glances back e.m. have to recognize
k. artistic B. respect
B. bloom, flourish t. dismal
g. thrive M. painting
e.s. were developed (App. 11, 4, b)
U. independence b. merely
E. influences e. achieved A. recognition

Die Kunstgewerbe nahmen einen grossartigen **Aufschwung**, **der Geschmack** wurde ein **edlerer**,[1] der Luxus, den keuschen Geboten der **Schönheit** sich **unterwerfend**,[11] weniger aufdringlich. **Vor allem aber** entwickelte sich auf dem Gebiete der Dichtkunst **und der Literatur** im allgemeinen eine **Blüte**,[1] die[5] mit den früheren Glanzzeiten englischen Schrifttums einen vorteilhaften **Vergleich** auszuhalten imstande ist.

K. art industries g. magnificent
A. upswing, growth G. taste
s. u. while subjecting itself
a. obtrusive v.a. above all
D. poetic-art i.a. in general
f. earlier S. literature v. advantageous
V. comparison i. able What rules are used to take out verbs?

Namen wie Carlyle, Tennyson, Browning gehen Hand in Hand mit den Namen Darwins, Tyndalls und Huxleys auf dem Gebiete der **Wissenschaft**,[1] und an sie schloss sich eine lange Recht zusammen genannt werden, weil ein wunderbarer Zug **Philosophen**[1], die,[5] wenn sie[4] auch nicht jenen Sternen erster **Grösse** beizuzählen sind, doch dazu beitrugen,[7] das Licht über immer weitere Schichten des **Volkes** auszubreiten, und[8] immer grössere Kreise desselben seinem veredelnden **Einfluss** zu unterwerfen.

G. field W. science s.s. was joined
b. significant D. poets (Note the inserted clause.)
w.au. even if b. to be numbered (App. 12, 1)
b. contributed there to Note Rule 7.
i. g. ever greater K. circles
u. to subject (What calls for this verb?)

Drei der oben genannten, Carlyle, Tennyson und Browning ragen um Hauptes Länge unter den berühmten Männern des viktorischen **Zeitalters** hervor.[2] Sie dürfen[6] auch deshalb mit Recht zusammen genannt werden, weil ein wunderbarer Zug der **Übereinstimmung**[4] durch sie hindurchgeht. Derselbe Hass **gegen das Unwahre**[1], allen leeren **Dogmatismus**,[1] dieselbe Sympathie mit dem gedrückten **Stande**,[1] derselbe prophetische Ton vieler ihrer Predigten wider die modernen **Zeitsünden**,[1] dieselbe tiefe Religiosität erfüllt sie alle,[1] und diese Gesinnung kleidet sich in das gleiche Prachtgewand vollkommenster **Sprachbeherrschung**.[1] Sie alle haben[6] unvergängliche **Saat** gesät, doch werden[6] wir nicht irre gehen, wenn wir[4] den grössten Einfluss auf alle Schichten der englisch redenden Menschheit demjenigen unter den **Dreien** zuschreiben, der[5] der gottbegnadete **Dichter** war: Alfred Tennyson.

g. named What goes with ragen?
H. L. by a head's length
Z. age d. therefore
z. together w. wonderful
Ü. agreement h. pervades H. hate
U. untruth l. empty
g. oppressed S. class
P. sermons w. against t. deep
e. fills G. sentiment, feeling
g. same P. cloak v. most perfect
u. imperishable S. seed w. shall (App. 7, 4)
E. influence S. levels r. speaking d. to that one (App. 14, 2) z. ascribe D. poet

Wie sehr seine Schöpfungen[4] schon in Fleisch und Blut **der Nation** übergegangen sind, beweisen die vielen Zitate und **Sprüche**,[1] an denen das Volk[4] sich erbaut und erfreut von der Schule aufwärts bis ins späteste **Alter**.[1] Auch in Deutschland hat[6] Tennyson **Anerkennung** gefunden. Seine Dichtungen wurden[6] mehrfach in **Auswahl** übersetzt, freilich ohne Berücksichtigung der später erschienenen **Gedichtssammlungen**.[1] "Enoch Arden", die reizende **Schifferidylle**,[1] ist[6] sogar von acht oder neun Übersetzern der deutschen **Lesewelt** dargeboten worden; ja selbst die grossen Schwierigkeiten der beiden Hauptwerke Tennysons des Gedichtcyklus "In Memoriam" und der "Idylls of the King" hielten berufene Männer nicht von dem **Versuche**[7] ab,[2] sie zu überwinden, so dass uns nun von der "Freundesklage" in der Übersetzung von **Waldmüller** bereits die fünfte Auflage vorliegt, während die "Königsidyllen"[4] in dem deutschen Gewande von Feldmann einen **bewundernden**, wenn auch kleineren **Leserkreis** gefunden hat.

S. creations F. flesh
ü. gone over b. prove
S. proverbs, sayings a. d. on which
erb. edify erf. rejoice s. latest
A. recognition D. poetry
ü. translated A. selection F. indeed, to be sure
B. consideration e. appearing
r. charming s. even i.d.w. has been offered
(App. 7, 5, c) s. even (App. 13, 2)
S. difficulties H. main-works Note Rule 2 and 7.
a. hinder b. famous, competent
ü. overcome
Ü translation b. already
v. exists w. while
b. admirable w. a. even though
l. reading-circle What rules have you used on the page?

Th. A. Fischer, **Tennyson, Leben und Werke**

Dennoch kann[6] man mit **Recht** sagen, dass Tennyson[4] in seinem gesamten poetischen Schaffen nur wenig, in seinem **Leben** und Persönlichkeit fast gar nicht in **Deutschland** bekannt ist. Der Grund dieser letztgenannten Tatsache lag bisher in den[3] nur höchst sporadisch zu uns gedrungenen Nachrichten über das Leben eines **Dichters,** der[5] die **Einsamkeit** liebte.

D. still m. R. with justice
g. total S. work
L. life f. almost g.n. not at all
b. known G. reason l. last-named
b. hitherto g. which have come
N. reports D. poet E. solitude

Während wir[4] es hier mit einem[3] selbst von den Berufensten kaum je ganz zu überwindenden **Übelstande** zu tun haben, ist[6] der andere Grund unzureichenden Verständnisses durch die Veröffentlichung des lange erwarteten zweibändigen Lebens des Dichters von seinem Sohne, dem jetzigen Lord **Tennyson** gänzlich und glücklich beseitigt. Vieles in dem Buche, das die Engländer[4] mit grosser Breite zu behandeln pflegen, wie die **Familienverwandtschaften,** religiöse Ansichten, können[6] für uns Deutsche nur von geringerem **Interesse** sein. Uns genügt die Person des **Dichters.**[1]

W. while Why Rule 3? B. most competent
z. ü. which is to be overcome (App. 12, 2)
Ü. drawback u. insufficient
V. understanding V. publication
e. expected z. two volume S. son
g. totally g. happily b. removed
d. d. which the English b. treat
p. are accustomed F. family relations
g. lesser
g. suffices, satisfies

Wir werden[6] daher vieles aus dem **Buche** als unbrauchbar beiseite lassen, und[8] uns mit Zuhilfenahme auch anderer Quellen mit denjenigen **Zügen** begnügen, die[5] uns zur Zeichnung der physischen wie geistigen Physiognomie **Tennysons** notwendig erscheinen. Vor allem aber werden[6] wir versuchen,[7] der poetischen Bedeutung des Dichters in seinem Verhältnis zur Vergangenheit, in seinen Beziehungen zur Jetztzeit, in allen seinen charakteristischen **Eigenschaften** gerecht zu werden.

w. shall (App. 7, 4) a. u. as unusable
b. aside Z. aid
Q. sources b. be content Z. features
n. necessary g. intellectual
v. a. above all v. try (to what?)
B. importance V. relation
V. past B. relations J. present
E. attributes g. z w. to do justice

Alfred Tennyson wurde[6] als der vierte Spross einer zahlreichen Familie von zwölf Kindern im Pastorate zu Sommersby, einem Dorfe in der Grafschaft Lincoln, am 6. August **1809** geboren. Wer[5] die charakteristischen Eigenschaften der **Landschaft** kennt, wird[6] keine **Mühe**[7] haben, sie in vielen Schilderungen des **Dichters** wiederzuerkennen. Träge,[3] mit **Wasserrosen** bedeckte Gräben durchziehen das **Moorland,** dessen Lieblingsbäume Pappeln und Ulmen bilden; hier wuchs der Knabe heran[2] und zeigte schon früh neben einem leicht erregbaren Temperament, und tiefem Gefühl, eine grosse Liebe zur **Natur.**[1] Ihr hing er an[2], in allen ihren Erscheinungen, im perlenden Tau des **Morgens,**[1] in Blumen, Quellen und Farnkräutern und in allem **Lebendigen.**[1]

w. – g. was born (App. 7, 5, b)
z. twelve
G. county
w. whoever E. qualities
M. trouble S. description
w. to recognize t. lazy, slow
b. which are covered
d. pass through h. grew up
n. along with e. excitable
G. feeling L. love I. to it
E. manifestations T. dew
F. ferns L. that lives

So legte er schon als Kind den Grund zu jener genauen Kenntnis der Naturgeschichte und jener erstaunlichen Kunst der Beobachtung und **Naturbeschreibung,**[1] die[5] ihn später als **Dichter** auszeichnete. Neben der Natur war es hauptsächlich seines Vaters reiche **Bibliothek**[1] die[5] den lernbegierigen und wissensdurstigen **Knaben** anzog. Dort fand und studierte er neben Shakespeare vor allem **Milton,** Homer, Bunyan und viele andere aus der langen Reihe der **Unsterblichen.**[1]

G. basis
K. knowledge e. astonishing
B. observation N. nature-description
a. distinguished h. chiefly
l. desirous of learning
w. thirsty-for-knowledge a. attracted
v. a. above all
R. list U. immortals

Früh offenbarte sich gleichfalls seine grosse, poetische **Begabung,**[1] wie denn die ganze Familie[4] Sinn und Talent für **Dichtkunst** besass. In seinem achten Lebensjahre füllte er zwei Schiefertafeln mit fünffüssigen **Jamben,**[1] in seinem zehnten oder elften schrieb er ein langes Gedicht in dem **Versmass,**[1] welches Pope[4] bei seiner Übersetzung der **Ilias** gebrauchte. Als er[4] zwölf **Jahre** alt war, verfertigte er ein ebenso langes Epos nach dem Muster der Scottschen **Gedichte:**[1] Marmion, Lady of the Lake, usw. verbrannte es jedoch, nachdem er[4] zum ersten mal **Shelly** gelesen hatte. Einige Jahre später floss sogar ein Drama aus seiner **Feder.**[1]

o.s. was revealed (App. 11, 4, b)
B. talent
D. poetic art b. possessed
S. slate tablets J. iambic
G. poem
V. verse-meter Ü. translation
g. used v. made, wrote
M. pattern G. poem
v. burned
e. some J. years
s. even F. pen

Nur wenige Jahre hatte[6] Tennyson die Schule zu Louth, einem benachbarten Städtchen, wo seine Grossmutter lebte, besucht. So sehr er[4] sich danach gesehnt hatte,[7] in eine **Schule** zu kommen, um so schmerzlicher wurde[6] er jetzt enttäuscht. Der Lehrer war ein leidenschaftlicher,[3] bei jeder Gelegenheit zur **Rute** greifender Mann; seine Mitschüler zeigten, wie so oft, kein Verständnis für den feinfühlenden Knaben. So waren denn des Dich-

w. a few
b. neighbouring S. town
b. attended (What calls for this verb?)
g. hatte had longed (to what?)
u.s. the more painful e. disappointed
l. passionate, vehement
g. who grasps for (Why who?)

ters Erinnerungen an diese Schule die trübsten.[1] Den kalten Morgen, an dem er[4] einst auf den steinernen Stufen des **Schulhauses** gesessen und geweint hatte, weil ihn ein grober Flegel[1] ohne andere **Gründe** prügelte, als um[7] dem neuen Ankömmling seine **Autorität** zu beweisen, vergass er bis zu seinem Lebensende nicht.[1] "Wie hasste ich diese Schule," schrieb er später einmal,[1] der einzige Nutzen, den ich[4] von ihr hatte, war die Erinnerung an eine alte,[3] mit Gras und **Unkraut** bewachsene Mauer.

E. memories
t. most gloomy e. once
s. stony S. steps g. sat
g. cried F. bully G. reasons
p. whipped A. arrival b. prove v. forget
h. hated s. wrote
N. use E. memory
b. which was grown over, covered

Es wäre jedoch unrecht,[7] aus dem obigen auf eine durchaus unglückliche Jugend **Tennysons** schliessen zu wollen. Mit inniger, ritterlicher Liebe hing der Dichter an seiner **Mutter,**[1] von ihr, **einer**[3] in ihrer **Jugend** gefeierten Schönheit, ererbte er einen humoristischen **Zug**, der[5] zwar in seinen Gedichten nicht oft, desto mehr aber in der Unterhaltung mit **Freunden** hervortrat, und die schon erwähnte, grosse Liebe zur Natur und allem **Lebendigen.**[1]

w. would be u. incorrect (to what?)
d. altogether u. unhappy
i. close r. chivalrous
g. who was celebrated J. youth
e. inherited Z. trait
G. poems d. so much the
h. stood out e. mentioned
L. living

Auch der tiefe, religiöse Zug rührt wohl von seiner **Mutter** her[2], die[5] jede Gelegenheit[7] wahrnahm, ihres Sohnes **Glauben** zu befestigen. So schreibt sie noch nach Empfang der Königsidyllen an den **Dichter:** "Liebster Ally! Wie innig habe[6] ich seit **Jahren** gebetet, dass unser Erlöser[1] in seiner Gnade Dir von unserem himmlischen Vater den heiligen **Geist** erwirken möge, der[5] Dich antriebe,[7] die Talente, die Gott[1] Dir gegeben hat, zur Einprägung der Gebote seines heiligen Wortes in die Herzen Deiner **Mitmenschen** bei jeder **Gelegenheit** zu benutzen. Mein geliebter Sohn, Worte sind zu schwach,[7] meine **Freude** darüber auszusprechen, dass Du,[4] wie ich sehe, versucht hast,[7] es zu tun. Liebster Alfred. Nichts ist[6] auch nur im entferntesten mit der Liebe **Gottes** zu vergleichen."

Z. trend, trait
h. comes G. opportunity w. observe
b. strengthen G. faith
Empf. receipt i. fervently
g. prayed E. redeemer Gn. grace
G. spirit
e. procure a. might motivate
E. impressing G. commands **bidding**
M. fellow-men
b. use (What calls for this verb?)
a. express v. tried (to what?)
N. nothing
z. v. to be compared (App. 12, 1)

Im Februar des Jahres 1828 immatrikulierten Charles und Alfred **Tennyson** und zwar ohne[7] Fachwissenschaft im Auge zu haben, auf der Universität **Cambridge.**[1] Zur Erklärung dieser Tatsache muss[6] man sich die[3] von den deutschen durchaus abweichenden englischen Universitätsverhältnisse ins **Gedächtnis** zurückrufen. Man bezieht in England nicht die **Hochschule,**[1] um[7] sich sofort einem **Fachstudium** zu widmen, sondern man betreibt in den ersten Jahren die **Gegenstände,**[1] die[5] bei uns etwa in Obersekunda und **Prima** vorgenommen werden, d. h. also vorzugsweise die schwereren lateinischen und griechischen Schriftsteller und höhere **Mathematik.**[1] Daran reihen sich meistens noch Vorlesungen über **Logik,** Metaphysik, und **Geschichte.**[1] Erst nach Beendigung dieses Kurses widmet man sich einer **Berufswissenschaft,**[1] doch geschieht dies in England, wo die Universitätsbildung[1] lediglich zur Erziehung eines **Gentleman** gehört und[5] nur den Wohlhabenden erreichbar ist, von den wenigsten **Studenten.**[1] Die jungen Leute leben in grossen, mehr oder weniger kostspieligen **Colleges** zusammen[2] und sind[6] beständiger Aufsicht auch ausserhalb desselben durch die **"Proctors"** unterworfen.

J. year
z. indeed o. without (calls for zu)
z.h. having (Note—ing.) E. explanation
T. fact d. very
a. which deviates (Why which?)
G. memory z. call back b. register
H. university, college O.n.P. last 3 yrs. of h.s.
w. to devote
b. carries on G. subjects
v. undertaken (App. 7,5a)
v. preferably s. more difficult S. writers
r. s. are arranged, grouped V. lectures
G. history B. finishing w. devotes
B. professional training g. happens
l. solely E. education
g. belongs W. well-to-do e. attainable
k. expensive z. together
b. constant A. supervision
u. subject to

Überall aber ist die Universitätszeit so recht eigentlich die Zeit der Freundschaft und frohen **Lebensgenusses.**[1] Auch Tennyson fand in Cambridge bald einen Kreis genialer junger **Männer,**[1] die[5] das gemeinsame Band der bewundernden Liebe zur Literatur der Vergangenheit und des[3] von deutscher **Philosophie** beeinflussten Enthusiasmus für die Freiheit des **Gedankens** verknüpfte. Viele aus diesem Kreise sind[6] im späteren **Leben** berühmt geworden.

ü. everywhere
e. really L. enjoyment of life
K. circle
g. common b. admirable
V. past
b. which was influenced
v. connected s. later
s. later

PSYCHOLOGIE

Gegenstand, Methode und Problem der Psychologie†

Wissenschaft und Erfahrung — Eine Wissenschaft besteht aus einer grossen Gruppe von **Beobachtungstatsachen,**[1] die[5] zueinander in **Beziehung** gesetzt[8] und unter allgemeine **Gesetze** geordnet sind. Wenn man[4] z. B. ein Lehrbuch der **Physik** aufschlägt, so findet man die Ergebnisse zahlreicher Beobachtungen oder Anleitungen zu **Experimenten,**[1] in denen man[4] selbst **Beobachtungen** wiederholen kann; diese Ergebnisse oder Experimente sind[6] weiterhin nach **Klassenbegriffen** geordnet (wie Mechanik, Wärme und Elektrizität) und veranschaulichen auf diese Weise zusammenfassende Gesetze (wie Newtons Gesetze der Bewegung, Kirchhoffs Gesetz der Strahlung, Ohms Gesetz der Stärke des elektrischen **Stroms.**)[1] Alle wissenschaftlichen **Lehrbücher,** mag[6] es sich um Physik oder Chemie, Biologie oder Psychologie, Philologie oder **National-ökonomie** handeln, weisen dieses gleiche **Schema** auf.[2]

Proceed to the bold-face nouns and take out elements located beyond them. Note Rule 8 E, sent. 1.
B. relation g. arranged
L. text book
E. results z. of numerous
B. observations A. instructions, directions (for)
s. oneself B. observations w. repeat
w. further K. categories
g. arranged v. illustrate
z. comprehensive G. laws
G. laws B. movement G. law
S. radiation S. strength, power
w. scientific u. with h. deal
w. a. manifest, exhibit g. same

Es lohnt sich daher,[7] ehe wir[4] an die eigentliche Darstellung der **Psychologie** gehen, in Kürze einige **Fragen** zu erörtern, welche diese Definition der Wissenschaft nahelegt. Wie entsteht überhaupt die Mannigfaltigkeit der **Wissenschaften?** Wie scheiden sie sich voneinander und wie bestimmen sich ihre **Grenzlinien?**[1] Was verstehen wir darunter, dass die Tatsachen einer Wissenschaft[4] zueinander in **Beziehung** gesetzt sind? Worin besteht das Wesen dieser **Beziehungen?** Was ist überhaupt ein wissenschaftliches **Gesetz?** Warum ist es für die Entwicklung der Wissenschaft von **Bedeutung,**[1] dass Gesetze[4] anerkannt werden? Eine wenn auch kurze Beantwortung dieser Fragen wird[6] uns auch das Verständnis der Aufgaben und Ziele der **Psychologie** erleichtern.

e.l. s. it pays e. real D. presentation
K. brief F. questions Note Rule 7.
n. suggests
W. how e. arises M. variety
s. s. are separated
b. s. are defined, determined
T. facts B. relation W. wherein
W. nature B. relations
ü. really w. scientific G. law
E. development
B. significance a. recognized E. one
B. answering V. understanding
A. tasks Z. goals e. facilitate

Von vornherein leuchtet ein,[2] dass alle Wissenschaften[4] letzten Endes ihren **Gegenstand** gemeinsam haben; sie nehmen alle unter irgendeinem Gesichtspunkte an unserer menschlichen **Erfahrungswelt**[2] teil.[10] Nehmen wir ein Bruchstück aus dieser **Welt** heraus[2]—etwa unsere eigene Erfahrung im Laufe eines einzelnen **Tages**—so haben wir ein hoffnungsloses Durcheinander vor uns. Unser Springbrunnen gehorcht dem dritten Gesetz der **Bewegung,**[1] während unsere Freude,[7] ihn zu besitzen, eine Tatsache der **Psychologie** ist; die Zubereitung unserer Nahrung ist ein Kapitel aus der angewandten **Chemie,**[1] ihre Verfälschung hängt von wirtschaftlichen **Bedingungen** ab.[2] **Endlich** ihr Einfluss auf unsere Gesundheit ist eine Tatsache der **Physiologie;**[1] unsere Sprechweise ist[6] durch phonetische **Gesetze** beherrscht, während der ausgesprochene Satz[4] vielleicht das moralische Empfinden unserer **Zeit** widerspiegelt: mit einem Wort, eine Wissenschaft scheint[6] mit der anderen zu verschmelzen, wie sie der Zufall[4] zusammenführt, ohne **Ordnung** oder **Abgrenzung.**[1]

v. v. from the outset e. is clear
l. E. in final analysis g. in common
i. some G. viewpoint
E. world of experience Note Rule 2, 10.
B. fragment e. perhaps e. own
L. course e. single h. hopeless D. confusion
g. obeys S. fountain
B. motion w. while, F. joy (to what?)
b. possess T. fact Z. preparation
N. nourishment a. applied
V. adulteration w. economic
B. conditions a. depends E. influence
G. health S. manner of speaking, speech
b. controlled w. while S. sentence E. feeling
w. reflects W. science
s. seems v. fuse s. them (object)
Z. chance, accident (subject) z. combines

Wenn man[4] indessen den Blick auf die Welt als **Ganzes** richtet, oder[8] in geschichtlicher Betrachtung eine lange Periode menschlichen **Lebens** prüft, ist der Überblick weniger verwirrend. Das Ganze der Natur scheidet sich dann zuerst in lebende **Objekte,**[1] d. h. solche, die[5] sich durch **Wachstum** ändern, leblose Objekte, d. h. solche, die[5] sich nur durch **Zerstörung** ändern. Die lebenden Objekte zerfallen wieder in solche, deren Wachsen[4] an einer **Stelle** geschieht, die Pflanzen, und andere, die[5] während ihres Wachsens sich von Ort zu **Ort** bewegen, die Tiere. So haben[6] wir einstweilen den Stoff von drei verschiedenen **Wissenschaften** abgegrenzt: **Geologie, Botanik, Zoologie.**[10]

i. meanwhile B. glance
r. directs B. consideration
p. examines Ü. survey, outlook
w. less v. confusing G. whole
s. s. is separated (App. 11, 4, a) W. growth
s. ä. are changed Z. destruction
z. break down, are divided W. growth
S. place P. plants
b. move w. during O. z. O. place to p.
e. for the present s. Substance
a. defined, limited

†E. B. Titchener, **Lehrbuch der Psychologie**

Versetzen wir uns nun in irgendein Stadium der menschlichen **Entwicklung** zurück:[2] wir wählen das soziale Leben der Menschheit vor dem Anbruch der **Kultur.**[1] Der primitive Mensch war[6] durch die **Not** **gezwungen,**[7] sich Waffen herzustellen, Tiere zu seiner **Nahrung** zu erlegen; den eigenen Körper durch Kleidung und **Obdach** zu schützen und nichts Giftiges oder **Verdorbenes** zu essen oder zu trinken. Wenn er[4] sich auf das **Wasser** wagte, musste er seinen Lauf nach den Sternen richten; wenn er sich mit seinesgleichen zusammentat, war sein Gesetzbuch nur die **Stammesehre.**[1] Er träumte und erzählte seine **Träume,**[1] war[10] er freudig, oder zornig, oder erschrocken, so gab er seine Gefühle in Bewegungen und im **Gesichtsausdruck** kund.[2] Zweifelsohne erschien ihm seine tägliche **Erfahrung,**[1] wenn er[4] überhaupt darüber nachdachte, ebenso chaotisch, wie uns vorhin die unsere. Aber dank unserem weiteren Überblick über diese Erfahrung können[6] wir in ihr die Keime mancher **Wissenschaften** sehen; der Mechanik, Zoologie und Physiologie, — der Astronomie, Ethik und **Psychologie.**[1]

[10]See Rule 10 B 3; C 1, 2. Note prefix that goes with the verb. i. any E. development
w. choose M. mankind A. dawn
N. necessity g. forced (to what?)
h. produce (See Rule 8 B, sent. 11 for this sentence.)
e. own K. body K. clothing
O. shelter z. s. to protect G. poisonous
e. eat W. water
w. ventured L. course S. stars
s. his equals z. combined G. law book
S. tribal-honor t. dreamed e. narrated
w. e. if he was z. angry e. frightened
G. feelings B. movements G. facial expression
Z. doubtlessly e. appeared t. daily
v. previously n. thought about it
d. thanks w. broader
U. outlook E. experience K. germs m. various
W. sciences Note Rule 1.

Wir kommen so zu dem **Schluss,**[1] dass die Welt der menschlichen Erfahrung[4] nicht gänzlich verwirrt und ordnungslos ist. Sie zeigt **Einteilungslinien;** in einem gewissen Umfang ordnet sie sich für uns, so dass der Rohstoff oder die Keime,[4] die[5] in den höheren Kulturformen zu einzelnen **Wissenschaften** werden, sich als solche der **Aufmerksamkeit** aufdrängen. Aber wir haben bis jetzt noch nichts als den **Rohstoff.** Wissenschaft entsteht nur dann, wenn jemand[4] nach den Fingerzeigen der Natur mit Überlegung einen bestimmten Forschungsplan durch die ganze **Erfahrung** hindurch verfolgt. Brücken, Häuser, Waffen, Geräte, Werkzeuge wurden hergestellt, lange bevor es[4] eine Wissenschaft der **Mechanik** gab. Die Wissenschaft beginnt, wenn der Mensch[4] das Weltganze in mechanischen **Begriffen** zu deuten beginnt, wenn er[4] es als eine **Riesenmaschine** betrachtet, die[5] genau wie eine künstliche **Maschine** arbeitet. Die Träume, die Zustände der Ekstase, die Ausdrucksbewegungen der Gefühle, sind[6] längst beobachtet worden, bevor es[4] eine wissenschaftliche **Psychologie** gab.

S. conclusion W. world
E. experience g. totally v. confused
o. without order E. division lines
g. certain U. extent o.s.s. is arranged
R. raw-material h. higher
e. individual sciences w. become
s. a. are imposed upon d. A. the attention (dat.)
R. raw material W. science e. arises
j. someone F. tips, hints
Ü. consideration b. certain F. research-plan
E. experience B. bridges v. pursues
W. weapons G. utensils W. tools
e. g. there was M. man W. whole of the world
d. interpret B. concepts
b. considers R. gigantic machine
a. works Z. conditions
A. expression movements G. feelings
w. scientific

Die Wissenschaft beginnt, wenn der Mensch[4] das Weltganze in psychologischen **Begriffen** zu deuten beginnt, wenn er[4] es als etwas **Geistiges** betrachtet, als eine Gruppe von **Erfahrungen,**[1] die[5] psychologischen **Gesetzen** unterworfen sind. Mit einem Wort, jede Wissenschaft nimmt eine bestimmte Stellung unter einem bestimmten **Gesichtspunkte,** und es ist die Aufgabe der Wissenschaft,[7] die Welt so zu beschreiben, wie sie[4] von diesem Standpunkte aus und unter diesem **Gesichtspunkte** erscheint. So ist es die Verschiedenheit der menschlichen **Interessen,**[1] welche[5] auch die Mannigfaltigkeit der **Wissenschaften** nach sich zieht; was sie zusammenhält und[8] ihre Beobachtungen zueinander in Beziehung bringt, ist die Tatsache, dass ihre ganze Arbeit[4] sich unter der Leitung derselben Prinzipien und unter denselben **Gesichtspunkten** vollzieht.

B. concepts
b. considers G. spiritual, intellectual
E. experiences u. subject to
b. certain, definite S. position g. viewpoint
A. task b. describe

e. appears G. viewpoint
V. variety
n. s. z. entails, brings with it
z. combines B. observations
B. relation T. fact
L. guidance
s. v. is accomplished

Wir haben nun einige unserer allgemeinen **Fragen** beantwortet. Die Erfahrung bietet sich, so sahen wir, unter verschiedenen **Gesichtspunkten** dar.[2] Diese Verschiedenheiten sind[6] nur ungefähr angegeben worden, aber doch bestimmt genug, um[7] als **Ausgangspunkt** dienen zu können. Diese verschiedenen Gesichtspunkte nehmen die Aufmerksamkeit verschiedener **Menschen** in Anspruch.[9]

F. questions
b. answered What goes with "bietet"?
v. different G. viewpoints
a. indicated u. approximately
b. definitely A. starting point
v. different n. i. A. engage A. attention
v. different

Die gegenwärtige Lage der Psychologie

(Underline the nouns that should be bold-faced; give reasons for the numbers or the*.)

Die Lehrbücher der Psychologie, die* die Ergebnisse der experimentellen Untersuchungen enthalten, zerfallen in drei Hauptgruppen.* An dem einen Ende stehen Systeme der Psychologie,* in denen die experimentellen Ergebnisse* nur als Veranschaulichungen für allgemeine psychologische Prinzipien erscheinen. An dem anderen Ende stehen Werke,* die* sich der Reihe nach mit den verschiedenen Gebieten der experimentellen Forschung befassen, und* sich dabei begnügen. Zwischen diesen beiden Klassen stehen die Bücher, (zu denen* auch das vorliegende Lehrbuch gerechnet sein will.) die[5] die Notwendigkeit einer experimentellen Kontrolle der Selbstbeobachtung betonen, aber[8] weiterhin die experimentellen Befunde in ein System zu bringen neigen und[8] die Psychologie des Laboratoriums zu der präexperimentellen und nichtexperimentellen in Beziehung zu setzen suchen.

L. texts E. results
U. investigations e. contain z. break down
d. e. the one E. results
V. illustrations a. general
e. appear
d. R. n. in succession v. different
G. fields F. study b. are concerned (App. 11, 4, a)
z. between g. counted v. present
N. necessity
S. self-observation b. stress w. further Note how "und" calls for the verb. n. tend Note Rule 8 again. B. relation s. seek

Alle drei Arten haben ihre Vorzüge und ihre Nachteile.[1] Der Psychologe, dessen systematisches Denken* fest umrissen ist, schreibt unter vereinheitlichenden Gesichtspunkten;* sein Werk wird[6] logisch zusammenhängend und wohl geordnet sein; und das Suchen nach Beispielen innerhalb der Beobachtungstatsachen wird[6] immer Probleme darbieten, **die* zu lösen** das Interesse des **Lesers** fesselt. Anderseits wird[6] er die Gefahr laufen,[7] die Tatsachen unter sein System zu zwingen, und[8] solche ganz zu vernachlässigen, an deren Hartnäckigkeit sein Klassifikationsbemühen scheitert. Der Psychologe, der* sich freiwillig auf eine Darstellung der bisher ausgeführten experimentellen Untersuchungen beschränkt, hat den grossen Vorteil auf seiner Seite*, dass er* niemals über die Beobachtung hinauszugehen braucht; sein Werk gibt uns das sichere Material, aus dem[5] eines Tages eine Wissenschaft erbaut werden kann; aber er ist insofern im Nachteil, als es[4] ihm an Gesichtspunkten mangelt, an einer richtigen Perspektive, und als er* nicht imstande ist,[7] die Ansichten derjenigen, denen das Laboratorium[4] noch fremd oder sogar zuwider ist, durch neue experimentelle Untersuchungen zu prüfen und zu würdigen.

A. types V. advantages N. disadvantages
D. thinking u. outlined
v. unifying G. viewpoints
z. coherent w. g. s. is probably arranged
S. search n. for B. examples i. within
d. offer d. z. l. which to solve
f. captivates a. on the other hand
G. l. run the risk (of what?) z. force
v. neglect a. d. H. on whose obstinacy
K. classification-efforts s. fails
f. voluntarily D. presentation
a. carried out U. investigations
s. b. limits himself V. advantage
h. go out b. needs B. observation
S. sure W. science e. built
N. disadvantage G. viewpoints
r. correct
i. able (to what?) A. views d. of those (app. 14, 2) denen to whom
f. strange z. offensive, odious
z. w. to appreciate

Der Psychologe, der einen mittleren Standpunkt einnimmt, hat den Vorteil der Gesichtspunkte und den der Tatsachen.* Seine Schwierigkeit liegt darin,[7] die experimentellen Ergebnisse—Ergebnisse von den verschiedensten Graden der Zuverlässigkeit, die[5] unter weit verschiedenen Gesichtspunkten erlangt worden sind, und[8] oft der Vollständigkeit entbehren—mit seinen psychologischen Prinzipien zu verbindenund[8] sie mit dem in Einklang zu bringen, was[5] in der traditionellen und Reflexions-Psychologie nach seiner Meinung beständig ist; und seine Gefahr ist die Gefahr einer vorzeitigen Systematisierung.*

e. occupies V. advantage d. d. that of
T. facts S. difficulty d. in the fact (to what?) App. 23, 3 E. results
Z. reliability v. different
e. acquired
e. lack, miss, want V. completeness
v. combine E. harmony m. d. with that
w. which
b. stable n. s. M. according to his opinion
G. danger v. premature

Solange die Menschen* nach ihrem Temperament verschieden sind, so lange wird[6] es Werke von diesen verschiedenen Arten geben. Alle tragen an ihrem Teile zu einer Weiterentwicklung der Psychologie bei;* denn es steht ausser Frage, dass die Psychologie der Zukunft* eine experimentelle Psychologie sein wird.

n. according to
w.e.g. there will be
T. part
b. contribute (beitragen)
F. question Z. future

Die James–Langesche Theorie der Affekte

Die eben umrissene Theorie der Affekte hat* viele Kontroversen hervorgerufen. Einige Psychologen begrüssten sie als eine grosse psychologische Entdeckung,* andere, und zwar die einsichtigsten, wünschten[7] sie einer Kritik zu unterwerfen,[8] ihre Behauptungen zu prüfen,[8] ihre Beweise abzuwägen,[8] die Einwürfe zu untersuchen. Darüber kann* kein Zweifel bestehen, dass sie[4] einen tiefen Einfluss auf die gegenwärtige Psychologie ausgeübt hat, obgleich auch nach der Meinung des Verfassers nicht zweifelhaft sein kann, dass ihre ursprüngliche Formulierung* sowohl einseitig wie übertrieben war.

e. just u. outlined A. emotions
h. evoke, produce E. some b. greeted
E. discovery
z. what is more e. most prudent
w. wished (to what?) and to what?
and to what? Note Rule 8. B. assertions
D. about that Z. doubt b. exist
E. influence g. present a. exerted
o. although n. according to M. opinion
z. doubtful u. original
e. one sided ü. exaggerated

Ein naheliegender Einwand ist, z. B. , dass die körperlichen Veränderungen,[4] auf die sich James[4] bezieht, bei sehr verschiedenen Affekten, dieselben sein können. Es gibt Tränen der Wut,* ebenso wie Tränen der Trauer;* die Gesten der Furcht und der Drohung können* dieselben sein, wie die des Zornes*; wir können* ebensoschnell laufen, um[7] einen Freund einzuholen, wie wir[4] von dem Bären davonlaufen; wir können[6] vor Wut oder Rührung ebenso zittern, wie vor Schreck*. Dieser Einwurf ist entscheidend für die früheren Behauptungen von James.* Gegenüber diesem und anderen kritischen Einwürfen hat[6] James eine Revision seiner Theorie vorgenommen, deren Abweichung von der ursprünglichen Fassung[4] zwar sehr verschieden eingeschätzt wird, die[5] aber doch dem Verfasser das definitive Aufgeben eines[3] jetzt unhaltbar gewordenen Standpunktes zu bedeuten scheint.

n. obvious, near lying E. objection
V. changes s. b. refers
d. the same v. different
e. g. there are T. tears W. rage Trauer sorrow
F. fear D. threat
d. d. those of Z. anger e. overtake
z. tremble R. being touched
S. fright E. objection e. decisive
f. earlier B. assertions
E. objections
v. undertaken A. deviation
e. appreciated, evaluated
V. writer A. abandonment
u. untenable g. which has become
s. seems

Hier sind* zwei Hauptpunkte zu nennen. Erstens lässt James einen Gefühlscharakter der Wahrnehmung zu,[2] die[5] den Affekt einleitet. Er spricht von einer Lust oder Unlust,* die* unmittelbar den sinnlichen Qualitäten der Wahrnehmung anzuhaften scheint und die* mit ihnen im Bewusstsein verschmolzen wird; und während er* bei sich selbst findet, dass diese Gefühlsbetonung[4] "eine sehr sanfte, sozusagen nur platonische Erregung darstellt," sagt er doch, "dass der primäre Gefühlston[4] in seiner Klarheit (oder wie wir sagen würden, in seiner Intensität) bei verschiedenen Menschen enorm variieren kann." Es ist daher nicht der Gefühlston des Affektes*, der[5] aus den reflektorisch erregten Organempfindungen stammt, sondern vielmehr sein spezifischer Affektcharakter, mit dem er[4] von unserem **Bewusstsein**[9] Besitz ergreift. Zweitens erklärt James, dass die Wahrnehmung,[4] die[5] den Affekt einleitet, nicht die nackte Wahrnehmung von einem Objekte ist, sondern die Auffassung einer Gesamtsituation.*

H. main points E. first(ly)
G. affective character W. perception
e. initiates L. pleasantness
u. immediately s. sensible
a. inhere i. them B. consciousness
v. fused w. while s. s. himself
G. emotional stress s. gentle
E. excitement d. represents
G. affective tone
v. different M. people d. therefore
G. feeling-tone
e. excited G. organ sensations
v. rather A. emotional-character
B. e. takes possession of (Note Rule 9.)
W. perception A. emotion
n. bare A. apprehension

Die James-Langesche Theorie verdankt ohne Zweifel einen grossen Teil ihrer Beliebtheit unter den Psychologen englischer Zunge der Art,* wie sie* vorgetragen wurde. Die Darstellungen der Affekte in den Lehrbüchern der Psychologie waren* zu akademisch und konventionell geworden, und James führte uns auf den echten rauhen Boden der Erfahrung zurück.[2] Trotzdem wäre es ganz unrichtig[7]— und überdies ein[3] für James und **Lange** entbehrliches Kompliment—die Theorie als etwas absolut **neues** hinzustellen. Die Betonung der organischen Grundlagen des **Affektes** ist in Wirklichkeit ebenso alt wie die systematische Psychologie überhaupt.

v. owes Z. doubt
T. part B. popularity
Z. tongue d. A. to the manner, way
v. presented D. presentations, accounts
w. g. had become What goes with "führte"?
e. genuine B. ground
E. experience T. nevertheless
w. e. it would be u. incorrect (to what?)
e. which is unnecessary Note that you cannot go back past **neues** as this expects a noun.
W. reality ü. in general, (itself)

Die Willenshandlung

In den Kindestagen des Reaktionsversuches wurde* wenig von seiner systematischen Bedeutung innerhalb der Psychologie gesprochen. Der Versuch erwies sich als ein nützliches Mittel für die Messung der Dauer gewisser psychischer Vorgänge;* aber er blieb ein Mittel, kein Zweck.*

K. early days R. reaction-experiment
B. significance i. within
V. experiment e. s. showed itself
Me. measurement D. duration g. of certain
V. processes M. means Z. aim

Da er* sichtlich eine Folge von Wahrnehmungen oder Vorstellungen einschloss — da ja die Wahrnehmung der eigenen Bewegung* auf die des Reizes oder auf eine[3] mit der Wahrnehmung des Reizes assoziierte Vorstellung folgte—, konnte[6] er in Zusammenhang mit der Assoziation betrachtet werden. Unter diesen Voraussetzungen lenkte sich die Aufmerksamkeit der Psychologen auf die Zeitwerte, nicht auf die Vorbereitung und den Inhalt des Reaktionsvorganges.* Hierin liegt die geschichtliche Rechtfertigung dafür, dass in diesem Kapitel der Reaktionsversuch* ohne eine psychologische Interpretation als eines der klassischen Experimente der experimentellen **Psychologie** eingeführt wurde. Wir haben* aber nicht die Reaktionszeiten, sondern die Reaktion **selbst** erörtert. Und nun erhebt sich die Frage:* Was ist die Reaktion in ihrem psychologischen Gehalt?*

D. since (App. 25, 2) s. obviously
V. ideas e. included d. since
B. movement d. d. that of R. stimulus
a. which was associated (why which?)
b. considered Z. connection
V. suppositions l. s. was guided
Z. time values V. preparation
I. content R. reaction process
g. historical R. justification
R. reaction experiment o. without
e. d. one of the e. introduced
s. itself
e. s. is raised (App. 11, 4a)
G. content
s.n.a however close

So nahe auch die Antwort liegt, ist[6] sie doch erst Anfang der neunziger Jahre des vergangenen Jahrhunderts gegeben worden und hat* noch immer viele Vorurteile zu überwinden. Die Reaktion ist eine Willenshandlung, sie gehört zu derselben Gruppe von Tatsachen*, wie der Reflexvorgang*, die willkürliche Handlung,* die Instinkthandlung.* Sie ist eine Willenshandlung,* die* im Falle der einfachen Reaktion, auf ihr einfachstes Schema zurückgeführt ist; und sie ist eine künstliche Willenshandlung,* die[5] unter experimentellen Bedingungen der **Untersuchung** unterzogen wird. Aber sie ist eine echte Willenshandlung,* und die Bewusstseinsvorgänge,* die wir* bei ihr zu schildern haben, sind Willensvorgänge.*

A. answer i. g. w. has been given (App. 7, 5, c)
v. past J. century V. prejudices
ü. to overcome W. will-action
g. belongs T. facts
w. voluntary
i. F. in case e. simple
z. traced back to
k. artificial
B. conditions d. U. to investigation
u. w. is subjected to
B. consciousness-processes s. describe

Im allgemeinsten Sinne ist eine Willenshandlung eine organische Bewegung,* in einem weniger allgemeinen ist sie die Bewegung eines lokomotorischen Organismus;* innerhalb der Psychologie verstehen wir darunter besonders menschliche Bewegungen,* die* in irgendeiner Art und irgendeinem Grade[9] im Bewusstsein repräsentiert sind. Die Ausdrücke "irgendeine Art, und irgendein Grad" sind* absichtlich hinzugesetzt; denn das Bewusstsein des Wollens ist äusserst schwankend und veränderlich; nirgendwo vielleicht verdankt die Psychologie der Physiologie mehr denn hier den Zusammenhang und die Kontinuität ihrer Beschreibungen.*

a. most general S. sense
B. movement w. less
Note the signal the noun gives you.
i. within v. understand b. especially
B. movements i. some one A. manner
B. consciousness
A. expressions i. any
a. intentionally h. added d. for
ä. extremely s. fluctuating v. variable
n. nowhere v. perhaps v. owes Z. relation
B. descriptions

[10]Versuchen[7] wir aber trotzdem auf Grund der vorangegangenen Analysen die typischen Bestandteile des Willensvorganges festzustellen, so finden wir etwa die folgenden; eine vorangehende Phase,* in der[5] kinästhetische Elemente und die Vorstellung des Zweckes oder Ergebnisses vorherrschen; eine mittlere Phase, in der ein Objekt[4] in seiner Beziehung auf die Endvorstellung, oder im Sinne dieser Vorstellung, aufgefasst wird; und eine Endphase, in der sich die Wahrnehmung des erreichten Zieles[4] von dem kinästhetischen Hintergrunde der[3] durch die wirkliche **Bewegung** erregten **Empfindungen** abhebt. Jede dieser Phasen kann[6] durch ein besonderes **Gefühl** ausgezeichnet sein, das[5] in seiner Qualität zwischen Lust und Unlust wechselt, und[8] mit irgendwelchen reproduktiven oder **Empfindungsbestandteilen** verbunden ist.

Note Rule 10. V. try (Why if?) What is the rest of the verb? B. components
f. to determine e. perhaps
f. following v. preceding
V. idea Z. purpose
E. result v. dominate m. medium
B. relation E. end-idea
S. sense a. comprehended
W. perception e. attained
H. background Note Rule 3.
e. which are excited (Why which?)
a. contrasts ausg. marked G. feeling
w. changes L. pleasure
i. some E. sensation-components
v. combined (Note how "und" calls for this verb.)

Einleitende Betrachtungen über die Verschiedenartigkeit des Naturgenusses†

Wenn ich es unternehme,[7] nach langer Abwesenheit aus dem deutschen Vaterlande, in freien Unterhaltungen über die Natur die allgemeinen physischen Erscheinungen auf unserem Erdkörper und das Zusammenwirken der Kräfte im **Weltall** zu entwickeln, so finde ich mich mit einer zwiefachen **Besorgniss** erfüllt. Einesteils ist der **Gegenstand,** den ich zu behandeln habe, so unermesslich und die[3] mir vorgeschriebene Zeit so beschränkt, dass ich fürchten muss,[7] in eine encyclopädische **Oberflächlichkeit** zu verfallen oder, nach Allgemeinheit strebend,[11] durch Kürze zu ermüden. Andernteils[6] hat eine vielbewegte Lebensweise mich wenig an öffentliche **Vorträge** gewöhnt; und in der Befangenheit meines Gemüts wird[6] es mir nicht immer gelingen,[7] mich mit der Bestimmtheit und **Klarheit** auszudrücken, welche die Grösse und die Mannigfaltigkeit des Gegenstandes[4] erheischen. Die Natur aber ist das Reich der **Freiheit;** und um[7] lebendig die Anschauungen und **Gefühle** zu schildern, welche ein reiner Natursinn gewährt, sollte[6] auch die Rede stets sich mit der Würde und **Freiheit** bewegen, welche nur hohe Meisterschaft[4] ihr zu geben vermag.

u. undertake n. after A. absence
U. chats
a. general E. phenomena E. globe
Z. working together K. forces e. develop
z. twofold B. fear, concern
G. object b. treat u. immeasurable
v. which is prescribed b. limited f. fear
O. superficiality f. fall into
s. while striving e. fatigue
A. on the other hand g. accustomed, familiarized
V. lectures B. embarrassment
G. mind, soul g. succeed B. definiteness
a. express M. variety, diversity
e. demand R. realm
F. freedom l. vividly A. views
s. describe g. affords
R. discussion b. move
M. mastery i. to it v. is able

Wer[5] die Resultate der Naturforschung nicht in ihrem Verhältniss zu einzelnen Stufen der Bildung oder zu den individuellen Bedürfnissen des geselligen Lebens, sondern in ihrer grossen Beziehung auf die gesammte **Menschheit** betrachtet, dem bietet sich, als die erfreuliche Frucht dieser Forschung, der **Gewinn** dar,[7] durch Einsicht in den Zusammenhang der Erscheinungen den Genuss der **Natur** vermehrt und veredelt zu sehen. Eine solche Veredlung ist aber das Werk der **Beobachtung,** der Intelligenz und der **Zeit,** in welcher alle Richtungen der Geisteskräfte sich reflektieren. Wie seit Jahrtausenden das Menschengeschlecht dahin gearbeitet hat,[7] in dem ewig wiederkehrenden Wechsel der Weltgestaltungen das Beharrliche des **Gesetzes** aufzufinden und[8] so allmählig durch die Macht der Intelligenz den weiten **Erdkreis** zu erobern, lehrt die Geschichte den, welcher[5] den uralten Stamm unseres Wissens durch die tiefen Schichten der Vorzeit bis zu seinen **Wurzeln** zu verfolgen weiss. Diese Vorzeit befragen, heisst dem geheimnisvollen Gange der **Ideen** nachspüren, auf welchem dasselbe Bild,[4] das[5] früh dem inneren Sinne als ein harmonisch geordnetes Ganze, Kosmos, vorschwebte, sich zuletzt wie das Ergebnis langer, mühevoll gesammelter **Erfahrungen** darstellt.

wer he who, whoever V. relation
S. stages B. education, development
B. needs g. social Bez. relation
g. total b. considers dem to him b.s.dar is
offered Fr. fruit G. profit, gain
E. insight E. phenomena G. enjoyment
v. enhanced vere. ennoble, enriched ·V. refinement
B. observation
R. directions G. intellectual forces w. as s. for
M. human race d. to that point
e. eternally w. recurring W. change W. world
formations B. persistence a. gradually M. power
E. sphere, globe e. conquer
d. that one u. primeval S. strata
W. roots w.v. knows how to follow
b. to question h.n. means to trace g. mysterious
d. the same (App. 14, 1) f. early
S. sense g. arranged G. whole
v. hover before, be in one's mind E. result
g. collected E. experiences

In diesen beiden Epochen der Weltansicht, dem ersten Erwachen des Bewusstseins der Völker und dem endlichen, gleichzeitigen Anbau aller Zweige der Kultur, spiegeln sich zwei Arten des **Genusses** ab.[2] Den einen erregt, in dem offenen kindlichen Sinne des **Menschen,** der Eintritt in die freie Natur und das dunkle Gefühl des **Einklangs,** welcher[5] in dem ewigen Wechsel ihres stillen **Treibens** herrscht.

b. two, both W. world-view E. awakening
B. consciousness A. cultivation g. simultaneous
s. are reflected Z. branches
G. enjoyment D. e. is not the subject.
E. entrance What is the subject here?
E. harmony W. change e. eternal
T. work, activity h. prevails

† Alexander von Humboldt, **Kosmos**

Der andere Genuss gehört der vollendeteren Bildung des Geschlechts und dem Reflex dieser Bildung auf das **Individuum an:**[2] er entspringt aus der Einsicht in die Ordnung des Weltalls und in das Zusammenwirken der physischen **Kräfte.**[1] So wie der Mensch[4] sich nun **Organe** schafft, um[7] die **Natur** zu befragen und[8] den engen Raum seines flüchtigen **Daseins** zu überschreiten, wie er nicht mehr bloss beobachtet, sondern[8] Erscheinungen unter bestimmten **Bedingungen** hervorzurufen weiss, wie endlich die Philosophie der Natur,[4] ihrem alten dichterischen Gewande entzogen,[11] den ernsten Charakter einer denkenden Betrachtung des **Beobachteten** annimmt.	G. enjoyment v. more complete B. education development G.race a. belong e. arises E. understanding, insight O. order K. forces M. man s s. creates (for himself) b. question e. narrow f. fleeting, hasty ü. overstep b. observes b. merely b. certain h. to produce B. conditions w. knows how to call (call forth) entz. while divested of d. poetic G. cloak e. serious B. consideration a. assumes, accepts B. Rule 3 C 2, B c (p. 19)
Die Natur ist für die denkende Betrachtung Einheit in der **Vielheit,** Verbindung des Mannigfachen in Form und **Mischung,** Inbegriff der Naturdinge und Naturkräfte, als ein lebendiges **Ganze.**[1] Das wichtigste Resultat des sinnigen physischen Forschens ist daher dieses:[7] in der Mannigfaltigkeit die **Einheit** zu erkennen,[8] von dem Individuellen **alles zu** umfassen, was die Entdeckungen der letzteren Zeitalter[4] uns darbieten,[8] die Einzelheiten prüfend zu sondern und[8] doch nicht ihrer Masse zu unterliegen, der erhabenen Bestimmung des **Menschen** eingedenk,[7] den Geist der **Natur** zu ergreifen, welcher[5] unter der Decke der **Erscheinung** verhüllt liegt. Auf diesem Wege reicht unser Bestreben über die enge Grenze der **Sinnenwelt** hinaus,[2] und es kann uns gelingen, die Natur begreifend,[11] den rohen Stoff empirischer Anschauung gleichsam durch **Ideen** zu beherrschen.	d. thinking V. multiplicity M.diversity, variety M. mixture I. inclusion, sum total l. living s. thoughtful F. study dieses (to what?) e. recognize Note Rule 8 B. E. discoveries Z. agesd. offer p. testingly s. separate u. be subject to, succumb to e. sublime e. mindful of e. comprehend D. cover E. phenomenon v. veiled, concealed in B. endeavor e. narrow G. limit h. extend g. succeed b. while comprehending r. raw A. view, perception g. as it were b. control, master
Ein anderer **Naturgenuss,**[1] ebenfalls nur das Gefühl ansprechend,[11] ist der, welchen wir[4] nicht dem blossen Eintritt in das Freie (wie wir tief bedeutsam in unserer Sprache sagen) sondern dem individuellen Charakter einer Gegend, gleichsam der physiognomischen Gestaltung der Oberfläche unseres **Planeten** verdanken. Eindrücke solcher Art sind lebendiger, bestimmter,[1] und[8] deshalb für besondere **Gemütszustände** geeignet.	e. likewise a. (while) appealing to, addressing E. entrance b. significantly G. region g. as it were G. formation O. surface v. owe to E. impressions l. more alive b. more definite b. appropriate G. mental, soul conditions
Naturgemälde, nach leitenden Ideen an einander gereiht,[11] sind nicht allein dazu bestimmt, unseren **Geist** angenehm zu beschäftigen; ihre Reihenfolge kann[6] auch die Graduation der **Natureindrücke** bezeichnen, deren allmählig gesteigerten Intensität wir[4] aus der einförmigen Leere pflanzenloser Ebenen bis zu der üppigen Blütenfülle der heissen **Zone gefolgt sind.**	n. l. according to guiding g. when arranged b. determined b. to concern, occupy R. sequence b. designate a. gradually e. uniform L. emptiness ü. luxuriant
Es ist ein besonderer Zweck dieser Unterhaltungen über die **Natur,**[7] einen Teil der Irrtümer, die aus roher Empirie entsprungen sind und[8] vorzugsweise in den höheren **Volksklassen** fortleben, zu berichtigen und so den Genuss der Natur durch tiefere Einsicht in ihr inneren **Wesen** zu vermehren. Das Bedürfnis eines solchen veredelten Genusses wird[6] allgemein gefühlt; denn ein eigener Charakter unseres Zeitalters spricht sich in dem Bestreben aller gebildeten **Stände aus,**[2] das Leben durch einen grösseren Reichtum von **Ideen** zu verschönern.	Z. purpose U. chats I. errors e. arisen v. preferably f. continue to live b. to correct t. deeper W. nature, being v. increase B. need v. ennobled g. felt e. individual, peculiar B. striving, endeavor g. educated a. expresses R. wealth v. beautify B. considerations

Begrenzung und wissenschaftliche Behandlung einer physischen Weltbeschreibung

In den allgemeinen **Betrachtungen**, mit denen ich[4] die Prolegomenen zur Weltanschauung eröffnet, wurde entwickelt und durch **Beispiele** zu erläutern gesucht, wie der Naturgenuss,[4] verschiedenartig in seinen inneren Quellen, durch klare Einsicht in den Zusammenhang der Erscheinungen und in die Harmonie der belebenden Kräfte erhöht werden könne. Es wird jetzt mein **Bestreben** sein,[7] den Geist und die leitende Idee der nachfolgenden wissenschaftlichen **Untersuchungen** spezieller zu erörtern,[8] das **Fremdartige** sorgfältig zu scheiden,[8] Begriff und den Inhalt der Lehre vom **Kosmos**, wie ich[4] dieselbe aufgefasst und[8] nach vieljährigen Studien unter mancherlei **Zonen** bearbeitet, in übersichtlicher Kürze anzugeben. Möge[6] ich mir dabei der **Hoffnung** schmeicheln dürfen, dass eine solche Erörterung den unvorsichtigen Titel meines **Werkes** rechtfertigen und ihn von dem Vorwurfe der **Anmassung** befreien werde. Die Prolegomenen umfassen in vier Abteilungen nach der einleitenden Betrachtung über die Ergründung der **Weltgesetze:**[1]

1) den Begriff und die Begrenzung der physischen Weltbeschreibung, als einer eigenen und abgesonderten **Disciplin;**[1]

2) den objektiven **Inhalt**, die reale, empirische Anischt des Natur-Ganzen in der wissenschaftlichen Form eines Natur-**Gemäldes;**[1]

3.) den Reflex der Natur auf die Einbildungskraft und das **Gefühl**,[1] als Anregungsmittel zum Naturstudium durch begeisterte Schilderungen ferner Himmelsfrische und naturbeschreibende **Poesie** (ein Zweig der modernen Literatur), durch veredelte Landschaft-Malerei, durch Anbau und kontrastierende Gruppierung exotischer **Pflanzenformen;**[1]

4.) Die Geschichte der **Weltanschauung**, d. h. der allmählichen Entwickelung und Erweiterung des Begriffs vom **Kosmos**, als einem Natur-**Ganzen**.[1]

Je höher der Gesichtspunkt gestellt ist, aus welchem[5] in diesem Werke die **Naturerscheinungen** betrachtet werden, desto bestimmter muss[6] die zu begründende **Wissenschaft** umgrenzt und von allen verwandten **Disziplinen** geschieden werden. Physische Weltbeschreibung ist Betrachtung alles **Geschaffenen**, alles Seienden im Raume (der Natur-Dinge und Natur-Kräfte als eines gleichzeitig bestehenden Natur-**Ganzen**.[1] Sie zerfällt für den **Menschen**, den Bewohner der **Erde**, in zwei Hauptteilungen, den tellurischen und siderischen (uranologischen) **Teil**.[1] Um[7] die wissenschaftliche Selbstständigkeit der physischen **Weltbeschreibung** festzustellen und ihr Verhältniss zu anderen Gebieten, zur eigentlichen Physik oder Naturlehre, zur Naturgeschichte oder speziellen Naturbeschreibung oder **Erdbeschreibung** zu schildern, wollen[6] wir zunächst bei dem tellurischen (irdischen) Teile der physischen **Weltbeschreibung** verweilen. So wenig als die Geschichte der Philosophie[4] in einer rohen Aneinanderreihung verschiedenartiger philosophischer **Meinungen** besteht, eben so wenig ist der tellurische Teil der Weltbeschreibung ein enzyclopädisches Aggregat der oben genannten **Naturwissenschaften**.[1] Die Grenzverwirrungen zwischen so innigst verwandten Disciplinen sind um so grösser,[1] als seit Jahrhunderten man[4] sich gewöhnt hat,[7] Gruppen von Erfahrungskenntnissen mit **Namen** zu bezeichnen, die[5] bald zu eng, bald zu weit für das **Bezeichnete** sind, ja im klassischen Altertum, in den Sprachen, denen man[4] sie entlehnte, eine ganz andere Bedeutung als die hatten, welche wir[4] ihnen jetzt beilegen. Die Namen einzelner **Naturwissenschaften**, der Anthropologie, Physiologie, Naturlehre, Geographie sind entstanden und allgemein gebräuchlich geworden, bevor man[4] zu einer klaren Einsicht über die Verschiedenartigkeit der Objekte und ihre möglichst strenge Begrenzung, d. i. über den Einteilungsgrund selbst, gelangt war. In der Sprache einer der gebildetsten Nationen Europas ist[6] sogar, nach einer tief eingewurzelten Sitte, Physik kaum von der **Arzneikunde** zu trennen, während technische Chemie, Geologie und Astronomie,[4] ganz empirisch behandelt,[8] zu den philosophischen Arbeiten einer[3] mit Recht weltberühmten **Akademie** gezählt werden.

Note absence of auxiliary, so common with many sentences of Humboldt's. P. introd. remarks
N. nature enjoyment v. different
Q. sources E. insight
E. phenomena
K. forces e. enhanced B. endeavor (to what?)
l. leading, guiding
e. to discuss F. foreign-like
(8-B) s. carefully I. content
a. comprehend. Note absence of aux.
ü. clear, distinct K. brevity
a. indicate s. flatter
E. discussion u. inconsiderate, unwise
r. justify (borrow "werden") V. reproof A. presumption P. preliminary observations u. embrace
A. divisions e. introductory E. exploration
Begre. limitation
e. individual a. separated
I. content A. view
N. nature-portrait

R. reflection E. (power of) imagination
A. means of stimulation b. enthusiastic
S. descriptions
Z. branch v. ennobled
A. cultivation
P. plant-forms

W. world view, philosophy a. gradual
Er. broadening B. concept

j.h. the higher (App. 26)
b. considered d. goes with "je" the—the
u. encircled, bound
v. related g. separated
G. created (See Rule 3 C 2, Bc) R. space

z. breaks down b. existing B. inhabitant
H. main-divisions
s. starry What does "um" call for?
f. to establish
V. condition, relation G. regions e. real

E. earth description z.s. to depict
v. linger, tarry upon a subject

A. grouping-together v. of different type
M. opinions
W. world descriptions
G. border confusions i. intimately v. related
um – so (App. 26) all the greater
s. g. h. has been accustomed b. designate
b. b. now now B. 3 C 2, Bc (p. 19)
S. languages
e. borrowed a. d. h. as those had
i. to them b. add, give e. individual
e. arisen g. g. become customary

E. insight, V. Differentness, variety s. strict
B. demarcation, boundary E. division-reason
g. most educated s. even einge. rooted S. custom

z.t. to be separated (App. 12, 1)
g. quite b. treated (borrow "werden", Rule 8) supply "und" after "behandelt".

Die physische **Weltbeschreibung**, indem sie[4] die Welt "als Gegenstand des äusseren Sinnes" umfasst, bedarf allerdings der allgemeinen Physik und der Naturgeschichte als **Hülfswissenschaften**; aber die Betrachtung der körperlichen Dinge unter der Gestalt eines,[3] durch innere **Kräfte** bewegten und belebten Naturganzen hat als abgesonderte Wissenschaft einen ganz eigentümlichen **Charakter.**[1] Die Physik verweilt bei den allgemeinen Eigenschaften der **Materie,**[1] sie ist eine Abstraction von den Kraftäusserungen der **Stoffe**;[1] und schon da, wo sie[4] zuerst begründet wurde, in den acht Büchern der physischen Vorträge des **Aristoteles,** sind alle Erscheinungen der Natur als bewegende Lebenstätigkeit einer allgemeinen **Weltkraft** geschildert. Der tellurische Teil der physischen Weltbeschreibung, dem[5] ich[4] gern die alte ausdrucksvolle Benennung physischer **Erdbeschreibung** lasse, lehrt die Verteilung des Magnetismus auf unserem Planeten nach Verhältnissen der Intensität und der **Richtung,** nicht die Gesetze magnetischer Anziehung und Abstossung oder die Mittel,[7] mächtige electro-magnetische **Wirkungen** bald vorübergehend, bald bleibend hervorzurufen. Die physische Erdbeschreibung schildert in grossen Zügen die Gliederung der Kontinente und die Verteilung ihrer Massen in beiden **Hemisphären,** eine Verteilung, welche[5] auf die Verschiedenheit der Klimate und die wichtigsten meteorologischen Prozesse des **Luftkreises** einwirkt; sie fasst den herrschenden Charakter der tellurischen **Gebirgszüge** auf,[2] wie sie, in gleichlaufenden oder sich rostförmig durchschneidenden Reihen erhoben, verschiedenen Zeitepochen und Bildungs-**Systemen** angehören, sie untersucht die mittlere Höhe der Kontinente über der jetzigen Meeresfläche oder die Lage des Schwerpunktes ihres **Volums,** das Verhältniss der höchsten Gipfel grosser Ketten zu ihrem **Rücken,** zur Meeresnähe oder zur mineralogischen Natur der **Gebigsarten.**[1]

i. in that, by -ing G. object ä outer
u. embraces b. needs a. of course
H. helping-sciences, auxiliary sciences
G. form
What does "eines" call for? be. u. b. which is animated and moved a. separate e. peculiar
v. lingers E. attributes, properties
K. manifestations of force of
S. matter b. established
V. lectures
E. phenomena b. moving L. life activity
g. depicted W. world force
d. i. to which I a. expressive B. designation
V. distribution
V. conditions, relations, proportions
R. direction G. laws A. attraction
A. repulsion M. means (to what?)
v. transitorily b. permanently, constantly h. produce Z. outlines G. structure, organization
b. both
Vert. distribution V. difference
w. most important L. atmosphere
e. influences h. prevailing
G. mountain ranges a. comprehends g. parallel
d. intersecting R. series e. elevated
a. belong u. investigates
M. sea level L. location
V. relation, condition G. summit
R. ridges, backs, saddles M. nearness of the sea
G. mountain types

Spezielle Länderbeschreibungen sind allerdings das brauchbarste Material zu einer allgemeinen physischen **Geographie**;[1] aber die sorgfältigste Aneinanderreihung dieser Länderbeschreibungen würde[6] eben so wenig das charakteristische Bild des tellurischen **Naturganzen** liefern, als die blosse Aneinanderreihung aller einzelnen Floren des Erdkreises[4] eine Geographie der **Pflanzen** liefern würde.

L. land-descriptions a. of course b. most usable
s. most careful A. grouping together
descriptions
l. furnish b. mere e. single
E. sphere of the earth

Anregungsmittel zum Naturstudium

Reflexe der Aussenwelt auf die Einbildungskraft: Dichterische Naturbeschreibung

Wir treten aus dem Kreise der Objekte in den Kreis der **Empfindungen.**[1] Die Hauptresultate der **Beobachtung,** wie sie,[4] von der Phantasie entblösst,[11] der reinen Objektivität wissenschaftlicher **Naturbeschreibung** angehören, sind,[6] eng an einander gereiht,[11] in dem ersten Buch dieses Werkes, unter der Form eines **Naturgemäldes,** aufgestellt worden. Jetzt betrachten wir den Reflex des[3] durch die äusseren **Sinne** empfangenen Bildes auf das Gefühl und die dichterisch gestimmte **Einbildungskraft.** Es eröffnet sich uns eine **Welt.**[1] Wir durchforschen sie, nicht um[7] in diesem Buche von der **Natur** zu ergründen,—wie es[4] von der Philosophie der **Kunst** gefordert wird,—was in der Möglichkeit ästhetischer Wirkungen dem Wesen der Gemütskräfte und den mannigfaltigen Richtungen geistiger **Tätigkeit** zukommt; sondern vielmehr um[7] die Quelle lebendiger Anschauung, als Mittel zur Erhöhung eines reinen **Naturgefühls,** zu schildern, um[7] den Ursachen nachzuspüren, welche,[5] besonders in der neueren Zeit, durch Belebung der Einbildungskraft so mächtig auf die Liebe zum Naturstudium und auf den Hang zu fernen **Reisen** gewirkt haben.

K. circle
E. feelings, sensations B. observation
e. divested
N. nature-description a. belong e. closely
g. as arranged N. portrait of nature
a. set up b. consider
a. outer, external e. which is received G. feeling
g. attuned E. imagination(force) e.e.s is revealed
d. study, examine
e. ascertain, investigate g. demanded
M. possibility W. effects
W. nature, essence m. varied R. directions
G. emotional force v. rather Q. source l. lively, active M. means E. enhancing, increasing
z.s. to describe U. causes n. trace, sense
n. more recent B. animation m. powerfully
H. inclination
R. journeys

Die Anregungsmittel sind, wie wir[4] schon früher bemerkt haben von dreierlei **Art:** ästhetische Behandlung von **Naturscenen,** in belebten Schilderungen der Tier- und **Pflanzenwelt,** ein sehr moderner Zweig der **Literatur;**[1] Landschaftmalerei, besonders insofern sie[4] angefangen hat,[7] die Physiognomik der **Gewächse aufzufassen;** mehr verbreitete Kultur von Tropengewächsen und kontrastirende Zusammenstellung exotischer **Formen.**[1] Jedes der hier bezeichneten Anregungsmittel könnte[6] schon seiner historischen Beziehungen wegen der Gegenstand vielumfassender **Erörterung** werden; aber nach dem Geiste und dem Zweck meiner Schrift scheint es geeigneter[7] nur wenige leitende **Ideen** zu entwickeln, daran zu erinnern, wie die Naturwelt[4] in verschiedenen Zeitepochen und bei verschiedenen Volksstämmen so ganz anders auf die Gedanken- und **Empfindungswelt** eingewirkt hat, wie in einem Zustande allgemeiner Kultur das ernste Wissen und die zarteren Anregungen der Phantasie[4] sich gegenseitig zu durchdringen streben. Um[7] die Natur in ihrer ganzen erhabenen **Grösse** zu schildern, darf[6] man nicht bei den äusseren **Erscheinungen** allein verweilen; die Natur muss[9] auch dargestellt werden, wie sie[4] sich im Inneren des Menschen abspiegelt, wie sie[4] durch diesen Reflex bald das Nebelland physischer Mythen mit anmutigen **Gestalten** füllt, bald den edlen Keim darstellender **Kunsttätigkeit** entfaltet.

A. means of stimulation b. noted
d. of threefold type B. treatment
b. animated, brightened
Z. branch
a. begun G. plants, growths a. comprehend
v. more extended
Z. grouping, arranging b. designated
B. relations
w. because of (App. 15, 3) v. comprehensive
E. discussion Z. purpose g. more appropriate
l. leading, guiding er. remind
v. different
V. (folk)-tribes g.a. quite differently
e. acted, influenced Z. condition
e. serious z. more delicate A. excitations, stimulations d. penetrate
e. sublime s. depict
v. linger, stay
d. presented s.a. is reflected
N. fog-land
a. graceful, pleasant G. forms e. noble
e. displays, unfolds, develops

Indem wir[4] uns hier auf die einfache Betrachtung der Anregungsmittel zum wissenschaftlichen **Naturstudium** beschränken, erinnern wir zuerst an die mehrfach sich wiederholende **Erfahrung,** dass oft sinnliche Eindrüke und zufällig scheinende Umstände[4] in jungen Gemütern die ganze Richtung eines **Menschenlebens** bestimmen. Kindliche Freude an der Form von Ländern und eingeschlossenen **Meeren,**[1] wie sie[4] auf **Karten** dargestellt sind, der Hang nach dem Blick der südlichen **Sternbilder,** dessen unser Himmelsgewölbe entbehrt, Abbildungen von Palmen in einer Bilderbibel können[6] den frühesten Trieb nach Reisen in ferne Länder in die

I. while e. simple B. consideration A. stimulants, means of excitation b. limit
e. remind w. repeating E. experience
z. accidentally U. circumstances
G. minds R. direction b. determine
F. joy e. enclosed
K. maps d. presented H. inclination, penchant
B. Anblick, sight H. firmament
e. lacks T. inclination
f. distant

Seele pflanzen.[10] Wäre es mir erlaubt eigene **Erinnerungen** anzurufen, mich selbst zu befragen, was[5] einer unvertilgbaren Sehnsucht nach der **Tropengegend**[9] den ersten Anstoss gab, so müsste ich nennen: Georg Forsters Schilderungen der **Südsee-Inseln;** Gemälde von **Hodges,** die Ganges-Ufer[11] darstellend, im Hause von Warren-Hastings zu **London;** einen kolossalen Drachenbaum in einem alten Turme des botanischen Gartens bei **Berlin.** Die Gegenstände, welche wir[4] hier beispielsweise aufzählen, gehörten den drei Klassen von **Anregungsmitteln** an,[2] die wir früher bezeichneten: Der Naturbeschreibung, wie sie[4] einer begeisterten Anschauung des **Erdenlebens** entquillt, der darstellenden Kunst als **Landschaftmalerei,** und der unmittelbaren objektiven Betrachtung charakteristischer **Naturformen.**[1] Diese Anregungsmittel üben aber ihre Macht nur da aus,[2] wo der Zustand moderner Kultur und ein eigentümicher Gang der Geistesentwicklung[4] unter Begünstigung ursprüngler Anlagen die Gemüter für Natureindrücke empfänglicher gemacht hat.

f. distant
S. soul, spirit p. plant
e. permitted e. my own E. memories
b. question u. ineradicable
A. impetus Note rule 9
S. descriptions
G. paintings d. representing
T. tower G. objects
a. enumerate
a. belonged b. designated
b. enthusiastic
E. life on earth e. issue from, flow forth
u. immediate, direct
ausü. exert Z. condition e. peculiar
G. intellectual development B. favoring
A. inclinations, gifts G. minds N. nature-impressions e. more receptive

Naturgefühl nach Verschiedenheit der Zeiten und der Völkerstämme

Es ist[6] oftmals ausgesprochen worden, dass die Freude an der Natur, wenn auch dem Altertum nicht fremd, doch in ihm als Ausdruck des Gefühls sparsamer und minder lebhaft gewesen sei, denn in der neueren **Zeit.**

a. expressed
w.a. even though f. foreign
A. expression s. more frugal, saving l. lively, active d. than

Beschreibung der Natur in ihrer gestaltenreichen **Mannigfaltigkeit,** Naturdichtung als ein abgesonderter Zweig der Literatur war[6] den Griechen völlig fremd. Auch die Landschaft erscheint bei ihnen nur als Hintergrund eines **Gemäldes,** vor dem[5] menschliche Gestalten sich bewegen. Leidenschaften in Taten ausbrechend fesselten fast allein den **Sinn.** Ein bewegtes öffentliches Volksleben zog ab von der dumpfen schwärmerischen Versenkung in das stille Treiben der **Natur;** ja den physischen Erscheinungen wurde immer eine Beziehung auf die **Menschheit** beigelegt, sei es in den Verhältnissen der äusseren Gestaltung oder der inneren anregenden **Tatkraft.**[1] Fast nur solche Beziehungen machten die Naturbetrachtung würdig[7] unter der sinnigen Form des **Gleichnisses,** als abgesonderte kleine Gemälde voll objektiver Lebendigkeit in das Gebiet der **Dichtung** gezogen zu werden.

g. form-rich M. variety, diversity
a. separate Z. branch
f. foreign e. appears
H. background G. forms
s.b. move L. passions a. breaking out f. fascinated, bound b. moving, stirring
d. unconscious, naive
T. work, activity
B. relation M. mankind b. attributed V. conditions G. formation a. stimulating
T. energy
w. worthy (of what) s. thoughtful G. parable, simile a. separate
G. area D. poetry g. drawn (What calls for the "zu"-verb?)

Wir haben bisher die **Kontraste** geschildert, die bei Griechen und Römern, in zwei so nahe mit einander verwandten Literaturen, sich nach Verschiedenheit der **Zeitepochen** offenbarten. Aber nicht die Zeit allein, d. h. die **Weltbegebenheiten,** welche[5] Regierungsform, Sitten und religiöse **Anschauungen** unaufhaltsam umwandeln, bringen diese Kontraste in der **Gefühlsweise** hervor;[2] noch auffallender sind die,[5] welche die Stammverschiedenheit der Menschen und ihre geistigen **Anlagen** erzeugen. Wie ganz anders zeigen sich uns Lebendigkeit des Naturgefühls und dichterische Färbung der Naturschilderungen bei den **Hellenen,** den Germanen des **Nordens,** den semitischen **Stämmen,** den Persern und **Indern.** Es ist eine vielfach geäusserte **Meinung,** dass bei den nordischen Völkern die Freude an der Natur, eine alte Sehnsucht nach den anmutigen Gefilden von Italien,[4] hauptsächlich einer langen winterlichen Entbehrung alles **Naturgenusses** zuzuschreiben sei.

b. hitherto g. depicted
n. near, closely v. related
V. difference Z. periods s.o. were revealed
W. world events
S. customs u. incessantly u. change
G. manner of feeling a. more striking
S. family difference, tribal, racial difference
e. produce z.s. are shown
L. liveliness F. color, tint
N. nature-descriptions H. Greeks
S. tribes
g. expressed M. opinion
a. gracious, charming, pleasant
G. open country, fields E. deprivation
z. to be ascribed (App. 12. 1)

ANATOMIE UND PHYSIOLOGIE

GESUNDHEITSPFLEGE†

Viele Krankheiten entstehen durch **Lebewesen,** die[5] dem freien Auge unsichtbar und[8] dem **Menschen** feindlich sind. Ob nun eine Krankheit[4] rasch oder langsam heilt oder[8] zum **Tode führt,** hängt nicht nur von der Stärke der **Krankheitserreger** ab,[2] die[5] den **Körper** befallen haben, sondern auch von der Widerstandsfähigkeit des Körpers.[1] Deshalb muss[6] jeder lernen, wie man[4] seinen **Körper** widerstandsfähig und gesund erhält.

e. arise L. organism
u. invisible (borrow "sind")
f. hostile o. whether
h. heals f. leads
a. depends (Note Rule 2.) b. attacked
W. resistance, resist-ability
d. therefore w. how w. hardy
e. keeps

Der Arzt hilft nicht nur[7] Krankheit zu heilen, sondern[8] auch sich vor ihr zu bewahren. Er vermag[7] viele Krankheiten schon im ersten Beginn, bevor sie[4] offenkundige **Erscheinungen** machen, zu erkennen.[10] Befolgt und versteht man die[3] von der allgemeinen Erfahrung und von der ärztlichen **Wissenschaft** vorgeschriebenen Regeln, so kann[6] man die Entstehung vieler **Krankheiten** verhüten. Oder man vermag eine Krankheit, die[5] nicht vermieden werden konnte, leichter zu verstehen. Jeder sollte[6] daher die **Gesundheitspflege** lernen und befolgen. Dadurch erfüllt er nicht nur eine Pflicht gegen sich selbst, erspart sich **Schmerz**[1] und steigert die Tüchtigkeit seines eigenen Körpers und seines **Geistes,**[1] sondern er dient auch dem **Volke,**[1] denn das Wichtigste sind für ein Volk möglichst viele gesunde und arbeitsstarke, heitere, lang jung bleibende, in **Gesundheit** alt werdende Menschen.

h. helps K. sickness
b. preserve v. is able (to what?)
What does "sie" call for? o. obvious
e. recognize B. if one follows
v. if one understands (Why if?)
v. which are prescribed
E. origin v. prevent
v. is able Note call for "to". v. avoided
v. understand
G. care of health d. thereby
P. duty e. s. saves himself
S. pain s. increases T. efficiency
G. mind d. serves
W. most important g. healthy
a. hardy h. cheerful
w. who become M. people

Viele Krankheiten sind ausserdem ansteckend, so dass ein Kranker[4] die **Gesunden** gefährdet. Es besteht die Gefahr, dass sich ansteckende Krankheiten[4] von dem Krankheitsherd aus in der Nachbarschaft oder gar über ganze **Landstrecken** verbreiten.

a. besides ans. contagious
K. patient g. endangers
b. exists G. danger
v. aus See App. 21, 1.
v. s. are spread (App. 11, 4, a)

Wir haben heute eine so nützliche Gesundheitspflege vor allem deshalb, weil die Wissenschaft[4] den wunderbaren menschlichen Körper in all seinen Teilen und **Verrichtungen** uns schon sehr gut kennen gelehrt hat. Um die **Gesundheitspflege**[9] mit Verständnis zu üben, müssen[6] wir schon in den jungen **Jahren**[9] das Wichtigste davon lernen.

n. useful v.a. chiefly
G. hygiene W. science
w. wonderful m. human T. parts
V. functions g. taught
ü. exercise V. understanding
Note Rule 9 in both cases.

BAU UND LEBEN DES MENSCHLICHEN KÖRPERS

B. structure

Der Körper des Menschen und der Säugetiere ist[6] von der **Haut** umhüllt und besteht aus verschiedenen **Organen,**[1] die wir[4] einzeln kennen lernen wollen. Von diesen Organen ist nur das Blut flüssig. Wenn man[4] ein Organ zerschnitten im **Vergrösserungsapparat** untersucht, so sieht man, dass die einzelnen Bestandteile[4] in lockerem oder festem **Zusammenhang** stehen, wie bei **Geweben.** Man spricht deshalb hier auch von **Gewebe.**[1] Dieses ist[6] bei den verschiedenen **Organen** ganz verschieden gebaut, eins aber ist[6] allen Geweben gemeinsam; sie sind[6] nicht, wie z. B. eine Metallmünze, eine gleichmässige **Masse,**[1] sondern[8] aus kleinsten, verschieden gestalteten **Körperchen** zusammengesetzt. Diese heissen "Zellen" und sind die einfachsten **Grundformen,**[1] aus welchen sich Pflanzen und **Tiere** aufbauen. Wir unterscheiden beim Menschen und beim Tiere Knochenzellen, Leberzellen, **Muskelzellen usw.;**[1] sie sind von ganz verschiedener **Gestalt,**[1] bestehen aber innen aus lebendem Eiweiss,[1] dem Protoplasma, dem Träger des **Lebens.**[1] Wenn der menschliche Körper[4] nichts wäre, als eine grosse Zellenmasse, ähnlich wie die Bienenwabe, so wäre er tot. Es wirken Kräfte in ihm, die[5] die Zellen zu einzelnen **Organen** anordnen.

S. mammals
u. enclosed b. consists
e. individually
f. liquid
z. cut up u. investigates
e. individual B. components
Z. connection G. tissues
v. different
i. g. is common to
M. metal coin
g. shaped
z. composed h. are called
e. simplest
s. a. are built up
What do the nouns tell you to do?
G. form, shape b. consist
l. living E. albumen, protein T. carrier
w. were
ä. similar w. would be
e. w. there operate K. forces

†Fischer, **Anatomie des Menschen**

Der Mensch braucht Nahrung von aussen, wie die Maschine Brennmaterial und Öl,* aber die Nahrung wird* von ihm nicht nur zur Arbeitsleistung verwendet, sondern auch zur Bildung von neuem Gewebe,* so dass er* wächst und* Schädigungen heilen kann. Wir sprachen vorhin von dem Zellenbau der Honigwabe.* Dieses Werk der kleinen Bienen ist ein Wunder an zweckmässigem Baue* und es ist nur möglich durch geschickte Arbeitsteilung im Bienenstaat.* Das Leben der Biene ist geregelt; es gibt Bienen,* die* für die Aufzucht der jungen Bienen sorgen, andere, die* für die Anordnung und Sauberkeit im Stocke aufkommen, indem sie* schädliche Stoffe herauswerfen oder* sie unschädlich machen. Ganz ähnlich ist es im menschlichen Körper;* die verschiedenen Zellen haben ihre bestimmte Aufgabe,* sie sind gleichsam Staatsbürger.* Eine Sorte von Blutzellen sorgt dafür, dass Fremdkörper, die* durch die Haut eingedrungen sind, durch **Eiterung** ausgestossen werden, andere Zellen wandeln die **Nahrung** so um,* dass neues Blut entsteht, wieder andere scheiden die unbrauchbaren Stoffe aus.*

GIVE REASONS FOR THE *. Also indicate what nouns should be boldfaced.
A. work out put v. used B. forming
G. tissue w. grows S. injuries
v. previously Z. cell structure
W. work W. miracle
z. systematic m. possible
A. work division B. bee colony
e. g. there are A. raising
s. care or provide for A. order
S. cleanliness S. hive i. in that, by -ing
h. throw out u. harmless
v. different
b. definite A. task g. as it were
S. type s. provides
F. foreign bodies e. penetrated
a. expelled E. pus What goes with "wandeln"? scheiden? e. arises
u. unusable S. materials

Der Körper wächst durch Vermehrung der Zellen,* dabei teilen sich einzelne Zellen in zwei Teile,* von denen jeder* eine neue Zelle bildet. Ein inniger Zusammenhang besteht zwischen allen Teilen des Körpers,* ein gegenseitiges Anregen und Unterstützen zu dauernder normaler Tätigkeit.* Dabei zu helfen, dass alle Organe des Körpers* harmonisch zusammenarbeiten, durch Gesunderhaltung der einzelnen Teile und durch Schonung der **Kraft***, die* die einzelnen Teile beherrscht und schützt, ist Lebenskunst,* die man* von Jugend üben soll.

V. multiplication
t. s. are divided (App. 11, 4, a)
i. close Z. connection
T. parts g. mutual A. stimulus
U. support d. lasting T. activity
h. help
z. work together G. maintaining health
S. saving, sparing K. strength
b. governs, controls s. protects
ü. exercise

Das Knochengerüst oder Skelett

Die Knochen, die* in ihrer Gesamtheit das Skelett bilden, sind die festen Teile des Körpers.* Sie stützen die weicheren Teile und ermöglichen es, dass der Mensch steht und* kraftvoll seine Glieder gebrauchen kann. Sie bestimmen die Gestalt des Körpers und schützen die inneren Organe gegen äusseren Schäden.* So erfordert beispielsweise die Weichheit und Zartheit des Gehirns den harten Schädel als Schutz.* An diesem Beispiel sehen wir, dass die Gestalt des Knochens von seiner Aufgabe abhängt. Am Kopfe hat der Knochen die schützende Gestalt der Schale,* am Arm und Bein die Gestalt der tragfähigen und beweglichen Röhre.* Die feinere Untersuchung ergibt, dass jeder Knochen* aus Bälkchen und Lamellen, das sind übereinander geschichtete dünne Platten, fest gefügt ist. Diese sind* z. B. an den Röhrenknochen des Beines so angeordnet, dass sie* am besten den Druck der Körperlast ertragen und dass sich die Beinmuskeln* an den Knochen am besten ansetzen können. Unsere Baumeister haben* mit vielem Ausprobieren schliesslich die Form des Balkenwerks und der einzelnen Balken für das Bauen gefunden, welche* beim geringsten Gewicht am besten tragen. Es hat sich gezeigt, dass die tragfähigsten Balken* genau wie die Knochen im Körper gebaut sind.

K. bones G. totality
T. parts s. support
w. softer e. make it possible
g. use g. limbs
b. determine G. shape
a. outer B. harm e. requires
W. softness Z. delicateness G. brain
S. protection G. form
a. depends A. task K. head
s. protecting G. shape B. leg
t. capable of carrying R. tube
e. shows B. beams
g. bedded (what calls for "ist"?)
g. joined together R. tubular bones
a. arranged B. leg
e. bear, carry D. pressure
a. attach B. architects
A. testing s. finally
e. individual
g. with g. least G. weight
e. h. s. g. it has been shown, App. 11, 4, c
g. built

Um jeden Knochen gewahrt man, wenn man* von ihm die Muskeln entfernt, eine sehnige Haut als Überzug,* die Beinhaut.* Sie ist weniger ein schützendes Kleid als eine nährende Hülle für den Knochen,* denn durch sie laufen die kleinen Blutgefässe und Nerven,* die* für Zufuhr und Abfuhr verbrauchter Nahrung sorgen.

u. around g. perceives
e. removes e. sinewy
w. less s. protecting K. cover
l. run
B. blood vessels Z. import
A. export N. nourishment

BLUT, HERZ, KREISLAUF UND DRÜSEN

(For drill purposes, give reasons for the numbers or the *. Indicate why certain nouns are bold-faced.)

Auf der einen Seite der Brusthöhle,* eingebettet zwischen den beiden **Lungenflügeln,*** liegt das Herz, ein faustgrosser, hohler **Muskel.*** Das Herz pumpt das Blut in den Körper und in die **Lungen*** und saugt das zurückfliessende **Blut** wieder an.[2] Die Aufgabe des Blutkreislaufs, so nennt man die **Blutbewegung,*** ist,[7] dem Körper dauernd Ernährungsflüssigkeit und **Sauerstoff** zuzuführen und[8] die[3] im **Gewebe** sich ständig bildenden **Zersetzungsprodukte** wegzuführen.

B. chest cavity e. imbedded
L. pulmonary lobes f. fist sized
Note Rule 1 K. body
What goes with "saugt"? z. back flowing
a. sucks up A. task B. blood-circulation
Note Rule 7 and the call for a "to" verb.
z. to supply "und" to what?
w. carry away Note Rule 3

Das Blut, der wichtigste Stoff des menschlichen **Körpers,*** ist eine rote, klebrige **Flüssigkeit.*** Der Hauptbestandteil ist das Blutwasser, in dem[5] in millionenfacher Zahl die Blutzellen oder **Blutkörperchen** schwimmen. Man unterscheidet rote und weisse **Blutzellen,**[1] erstere überwiegen sehr stark, daher die rote Farbe des **Blutes,**[1] die roten Zellen sind die Träger des **Sauerstoffes,**[1] sie nehmen ihn bei ihrem Lauf durch die Lungen mit ins **Gewebe.*** Die weissen Blutzellen haben die Aufgabe,[7] schädliche Stoffe, die[5] ins Blut dringen, unschädlich zu machen. Man hat[6] sie daher als **Gesundheitspolizei** bezeichnet. Sie umringen den Eindringling, z. B. einen Holzsplitter, der[5] nicht entfernt wird, und grenzen ihn durch einen[3] von ihnen selbst gebildeten Schutzwall vom übrigen **Gewebe** ab.[2] So entsteht der Eiter aus dem **Blut.*** **Ausserhalb** der Gefässe gerinnt das **Blut.*** So kommt es, dass viele Wunden von selbst aufhören zu bluten. Die roten Blutkörperchen bilden eine weiche Masse*, welche* die Wunde verklebt. Die Blutwärme ist etwa 37 **Grad C.***

w. most important S. substance
k. sticky F. liquid H. chief component
Z. number Use the relative to remove the verb if possible. u. distinguishes
ü. predominate
d. therefore Z. cells
T. carriers S. oxygen L. course
m. along G. tissue
A. task (to what?) s. harmful
b. designated G. health-police
u. surround E. invader
e. removed
g. which is formed S. protecting wall
a. bound off e. arises E. pus
A. outside of G. vessels a. cease
w. soft
v. agglutinates B. blood-heat

Ein zweiter wichtiger Lebenssaft ist die **Lymphe.*** Sie enthält die **Nährstoffe,*** die der Darm[4] aus der Nahrung bildet, und auch die unbrauchbaren und die[3] im **Körper** nicht verbrauchten **Stoffe.** Die Lymphe, eine milchähnliche Flüssigkeit, fliesst in einem eigenen Gefässsystem zu den grossen **Blutadern** zurück.[2] Sie durchfliesst Drüsen, welche[5] Lymphdrüsen heissen. Die **Lymphdrüsen** halten **Giftstoffe,*** die* im Körper beim **Stoffwechsel** entstehen, zurück[2] und zerstören sie. Die Lymphkörperchen gelangen zum Teil in das **Blut** und sind ein Teil der weissen **Blutkörperchen,*** welche* die Keime **(Bakterien)** bekämpfen, die[5] bei verschiedenen Krankheiten besonders bei Blut-Eiterkrankheiten, von aussen in den **Körper** eindringen. Bei dieser Arbeit schwellen oft die **Drüsen** an.[2]

e. contains N. nourishment-materials
L. life-fluid
e. contains N. nourishment-material
u. unusable
v. which are not consumed M. milk like
e. own G. vessel system
Note rule 2 z. flows back
L. lymph glands G. poison materials
e. arise S. metabolism z. destroy
bei in connection with g. come z. T. in part
K. germs, bacteria E. blood-pus-diseases
b. combat v. different K. diseases
e. penetrate
a. swell up

Um[7] den Blutkreislauf zu verstehen, betrachten wir zunächst den Bau seines **Kanalsystems*.** Die Blutgefässe des Körpers sind: Herz, Puls- und Blutadern und **Haargefässe.***

B. circulation of blood u. understand
b. consider B. structure
H. capillary vessel

Das Herz ist[6] von einer weissen Haut, dem Herzbeutel, eingeschlossen. Der innere hohle Raum des Herzens ist* durch eine Längs- und durch eine Querscheidewand in vier **Herzräume** abgeteilt, von denen die zwei oberen[4] Vorkammer oder Vorhof, die zwei unteren **Herzkammern** heissen. Demnach unterscheidet man eine rechte und eine linke **Herzkammer.*** Von der Vor- zur Herzkammer führt je eine **Öffnung,*** welche[5] durch dünne, aber starke häutige Klappen (Ventile) so verschlossen wird, dass das Blut[4] wohl von der Vor- in die Herzkammer, aber nicht wieder zurückfliessen kann.

w. white H. membrane He. Pericardium
e. enclosed h. hollow
L. longitudinal Q. septum
H. heart cavities o. upper V. auricle
H. ventricle d. accordingly
u. distinguishes r. right
V. auricle H. ventricle
v. closed so that . . .
z. flow back

Die Adern. Das Blut ist in ständiger **Bewegung.*** Ohne unser Zutun zieht sich nämlich das **Herz** regelmässig zusammen[2] und zwar bei Kindern in einer Minute etwa hundertmal, bei Erwachsenen etwa siebzigmal.[1] Durch jede Zusammenziehung wird[6] vom Herzen aus eine Blutwelle in die **Adern** getrieben. Diese Adern nennt man Puls- oder **Schlagadern** (Arterien.)

A. veins, arteries s. constant B. movement
O. without Z. (conscious) doing, action z. is contracted (App. 11, 4a)
z. indeed
E. adults Z. contraction
v. H. aus. from the heart (App 21, a, b, c)

(Supply the numbers where they have been intentionally omitted. Underline all nouns that should be bold-faced.)

Die Adern bilden häutige Röhrchen von verschiedener **Dicke.** Die meisten Pulsadern liegen, um[7] geschützt zu sein, tief im Innern des Fleisches, ihre Verletzung kann den Tod **durch Verbluten**[9] zur Folge haben. Die[3] durch den Körper rollende Blutwelle kann man an einigen Stellen, wo die Adern[4] der **Oberfläche** näher liegen, als **Puls** fühlen, wie z. B. hinter dem **Handgelenk.***

g. protected
F. flesh V. injury
z. F. h. lead to, result in
Why Rule 3? What does "kann" call for?
Adern? Why is "Puls" bold-faced? H. wrist

Die Pulsadern verzweigen sich und bilden endlich so feine Äderchen, dass sie mit blossem **Auge** nicht mehr bemerkt werden können: das sind die Haargefässe. Diese liegen als dichtes Netz in allen Geweben und um die Zellen und versorgen alle Körperteile mit Blut und Nahrung.

v. s. are branched (App. 11, 4a)
Note Rule 1 and the rules that help to remove the verbs. H. capillaries
d. thick G. tissues v. supply
N. nourishment

Wie sich die Adern verzweigt haben, so sammeln sie sich auch wieder.[2] Die Haargefässe vereinigen sich zu dünnen Äderchen, diese laufen zusammen und bilden immer weitere Röhren; das sind die Blutadern (Venen). Diese ziehen zum Teil dicht unter der Haut hin,[2] und sind[6] dann als dunkelblaue **Streifen** sichtbar. Die Verletzung einer Blutader ist nicht so gefährlich, weil hier das Blut leicht gestillt werden kann. Durch die Blutadern wird das Blut wieder zum **Herzen** zurückgeleitet und hat so seinen Kreislauf vollendet. Das Blut geht von den Herzkammern aus, kehrt in die Vorkammern zurück und gelangt durch die Öffnungen der Querscheidewand in die **Herzkammern.**

s. v. h. have been branched
w. collect v. s. are combined
i. w. wider and wider
R. tubes What goes with "ziehen"?
d. closely h. extend s. s. are visible
V. injury
g. dangerous What does "das Blut" call for?
"wird"? "hat"? What do the nouns then tell you to do?
a. proceeds from What does "aus" go with?
"zurück"? O. openings H. ventricles

DER GROSSE UND DER KLEINE KREISLAUF.

Man unterscheidet den grossen und den kleinen Blutkreislauf, oder den Körperkreislauf und den Lungenkreislauf. Der grosse Kreislauf beginnt in der linken Herzkammer. Durch die Zusammenziehung des Herzens wird* ihr Inhalt, das frische, hellrote Blut, in die Körperschlagader getrieben und[8] weiter durch die verschiedenen Pulsadern und Haargefässe im ganzen Körper verteilt. Durch die dünnen Wandungen der Haargefässe hindurch nimmt nun jeder Körperteil aus dem Blut die Stoffe, deren er bedarf, besonders den Sauerstoff, und gibt dagegen andere[3] für ihn unbrauchbar gewordene Stoffe zurück,[2] besonders Kohlensäure. Das Blut, das in den Blutadern wieder zum Herzen zurückkehrt, ist sehr verändert; es hat seine hellrote Farbe verloren und[8] eine tiefdunkle angenommen. So kommt es in die rechte Vorkammer zurück.[2] Diese Änderung der Blutfarbe ist die Folge jenes Lebensvorganges, der[5] den Stoffwechsel der Tiere auszeichnet, im Gegensatz zum Stoffwechsel der **Pflanzen**. Die Kohlensäure ist nämlich verbrannter Kohlenstoff, d. h. Kohlenstoff, der[5] sich mit Sauerstoff vereinigt hat, denn das ist der Vorgang bei jeder Verbrennung. Alle lebenden Zellen verbrennen also die[3] ihnen zugeführten Nährstoffe, dadurch entsteht, wie in einer Maschine, Wärme und ein Vorrat von Kraft.*

u. distinguishes B. circulation
K. body circulation L. pulmonary
l. left H. ventricle
Z. contraction w. g. is driven App. 7, 5, a
h. bright red What does "und" call for? g. entire
W. walls
durch-hindurch (App. 21, j) through and through
b. needs S. oxygen
z. gives back Why Rule 3?
What does "das" call for?
z. returns v. changes
a. taken on
V. auricle z. comes back
F. result L. life process S. metabolism
a. distinguishes G. contrast
v. consumed K. carbon dioxide
S. v. h. has been combined (App. 11, 4, c)
V. combustion
v. burn up N. food materials
Why Rule 3? V. supply
K. strength

Durch das Ventil der Scheidewand tritt das Blut nun in die rechte Herzkammer, wo der kleine Blutkreislauf seinen Anfang nimmt. Durch die Herztätigkeit wird es von hier aus durch die Lungenschlagader in die **Lungen** getrieben. Hier scheidet es durch die dünnen Wandungen der Haargefässe hindurch die Kohlensäure aus* und nimmt dafür Sauerstoff auf.* Dadurch wird es wieder erneuert und wird wieder hellrot. Das erfrischte Blut fliesst dann nach der linken Vorkammer, von wo aus es durch das Ventil in die linke Herzkammer tritt und seinen **Kreislauf** aufs neue beginnt.

S. septum
H. ventricle B. blood circulation
A. beginning H. heart activity
w. e. g. it is driven (App. 7, 5, a)
What goes with "scheidet"?
nimmt? D. thereby
e. renewed w. becomes
V. auricle
l. left
a. n. anew

DAS MENSCHLICHE AUGE†

BAU DES AUGES. Der Augapfel besteht, physikalisch betrachtet,[11] aus einer fast kugelförmigen,[3] von vorn nach hinten etwas zusammengedrückten **Kammer,**[1] die[5] mit einem[3] als **Objektiv** dienenden System von brechenden **Substanzen** ausgerüstet ist. Er ist[6] durch sechs Muskeln in der Augenhöhle wie in einem Kugelgelenk nach allen **Richtungen** drehbar.

A. eye ball **b. consists**
b. when considered (Why when?)
n. h. toward the back, rear z. compressed
K. chamber d. which serves
a. equipped M. muscles
A. eye socket K. joint socket R. directions
d. rotatable

Die äussere Hülle des Augapfels ist die weisse **Lederhaut** (Sclerotica), die[5] sehr fest und derb ist und[8] das Auge vor **Verletzungen** schützt. Die Lederhaut ist in ihrem vorderen Teile durchsichtig und heisst hier **Hornhaut**[1] (Cornea). Im Innern ist[6] die Lederhaut mit der dunkel gefärbten **Aderhaut,** (Choroidea), ausgekleidet, die[5] gleichzeitig die[3] das **Auge** ernährenden Blutgefässe und die[3] das Augeninnere vor zerstreutem **Licht** schützende dunkle **Pigmentschicht** enthält.

a. outer H. shell
w. white f. solid d. compact, firm
s. protects V. injuries
v. anterior T. part d. transparent
h. is called I. inside
d. darkly g. colored
a. lined g. at the same time e. which
nourish (Why which?) B. blood vessels
s. which protects e. contains

Die Aderhaut geht in ihrem vorderen Teile in **die**[3] mit einem **Loch** versehene Regenbogenhaut **(Iris)** über.[2] An die Aderhaut schliesst sich nach innen die rosa gefärbte Netzhaut **(Retina)** an[2], die[5] aus den Verzweigungen und Endigungen des **Sehnerven** besteht. Abb. 996 zeigt in einem stark vergrösserten Schnitt den sehr verwickelten, geschichteten Bau der **Netzhaut.**[1] Die[3] durch die **Pfeile** gekennzeichnete Seite ist[6] dem **Licht** zugewandt. Als eigentlich lichtempfindlicher Teil wird[6] die Schicht **Sch** angesehen, die[5] aus einer sehr grossen Anzahl von Stäbchen St und **Zäpfchen Z** zusammengesetzt ist, die[5] merkwürdigerweise vom **Lichte** abgewandt sind.

What goes with "geht"?
Why Rule 3? v. which is provided
s. s. is attached
What does "an" go with? V. branchings
S. optic nerves b. consists of
v. magnified, enlarged S. section v. complicated
g. bedded, layered B. structure
g. which is marked P. arrows z. turned
e. really l. light sensitive T. part
A. number
S. rods Z. cones z. composed
m. strangely a. turned away from

Die[3] der **Pupille** gerade gegenüberliegende Stelle der Netzhaut enthält die grösste Zahl der **Zäpfchen,**[1] sie ist die Stelle der Netzhaut mit dem grössten **Auflösungsvermögen.** Sie wird[6] **Netzhautgrube** genannt. Ihre Umgebung heisst wegen ihrer Farbe gelber **Fleck.** Dort, wo der Sehnerv[4] in das **Augeninnere** eintritt, befinden sich keine **Nervenden.**[1] Diese Stelle ist[6] für **Licht** unempfindlich, sie wird[6] blinder **Fleck** genannt. Der blinde Fleck liegt vom gelben Fleck aus an der[3] der **Nase** zugekehrten Seite.

g. which lies opposite
e. contains Z. number
A. resolving power
g. called (App. 7, 5, a)
U. surrounding w. because of
S. optic nerve e. enters b. s. are found
u. insensitive F. spot
g. yellow vom – aus See App. 21, 1.
z. turn to, face toward

Vom Vorhandensein des blinden Fleckes kann[6] man sich überzeugen, wenn man[4] das Kreuz von Abb. 997 mit dem rechten **Auge** fixiert, während man[4] die ganze Abbildung etwa 20 cm vom **Auge** hält. Der kreisförmige Fleck verschwindet dann, weil sein Bild[4] auf den blinden **Fleck** fällt. Dass wir[4] gewöhnlich vom Vorhandensein des blinden **Fleckes** nicht gestört werden, beruht vorwiegend darauf, dass wir[4] alle Dinge gleichzeitig mit beiden **Augen** betrachten.

V. existence F. spot
ü. convince K. cross
r. right w. while
A. picture, figure k. circular
v. disappears
g. ordinarily V. presence
g. disturbed b. depends, rests **v. predominately**
g. simultaneously
b. observe

Hinter der Iris liegt die **Kristallinse,**[1] ein durchsichtiger, hornartiger **Körper,**[1] dessen Brechungsverhältnis[4] von aussen nach innen zunimmt.[10] Führt man zur leichteren Übersicht einen mittleren **Wert** ein[2] (Totalindex), so ist dieser **1,4085.** Die Kristallinse teilt den Innenraum des Auges in zwei ungleich grosse **Räume:**[1] Die vordere Augenkammer vA zwischen Kristallinse und Hornhaut ist[6] mit einer farblosen Flüssigkeit (dem Kammerwasser) gefüllt, deren Brechungsverhältnis[4] mit dem des **Wassers**

H. behind
d. transparent d. whose B. refractive index
z. increase Why Rule 10?
What does "ein" go with? Ü. review
t. divides
u. unequal R. spaces
v. anterior A. eye chamber K. aqueous humor
What does "ist" call for? f. colorless
g. filled B. refractive index

†E. Grimsehl, **Lehrbuch der Physik,** R. Tomaschek, ed.

übereinstimmt; der Raum zwischen Kristallinse und **Netzhaut enthält einen gallertartigen** durchsichtigen **Stoff** (Glaskörper), **Brechungszahl der des Wassers fast gleich.** Die Verbindungslinie **der Mitte der Pupille oder des** Hornhautscheitels **mit der Mitte der Netzhautgrube heisst die Augenachse;**[1] sie steht auf allen[3] **die brechenden Substanzen des Auges begrenzenden** Flächen **senkrecht.**

ü. agrees R. space
N. retina e. contains g. jelly like
B. refractive index d. d. that of
V. connecting line
H. apex, vertex of the cornea N. pit of the retina
What does "allen" call for?
b. which border s. perpendicular

Das Auge als optisches System

[10] Treten Lichtstrahlen in das **Auge** ein,[2] so werden[6] sie **an den drei brechenden Flächen:** Hornhaut, Vorderfläche der **Kristallinse** und Hinterfläche der **Kristallinse gebrochen.** In einem **rechtsichtigen** (emmetropen) Auge im Ruhezustand werden[6] die[3] **parallel** mit der **Augenachse** eintretenden Strahlen zur **Netzhautgrube** konvergent gemacht; diese ist demnach der Brennpunkt für das[3] die **Lichtstrahlen** brechende System. Das Auge **sieht im Ruhezustand sehr weit** entfernte Dinge scharf.

Why Rule 10? L. light rays What does "ein" go with? b. refracting F. surfaces
H. posterior surface g. broken
R. resting state
w. g. are made (App. 7, 5, a) e. (which enter) (Why which?)
d. accordingly B. focal point b. which breaks
e. removed
s. sharply

Empfindlichkeit des Auges

E. sensitivity

Die lichtempfindliche Netzhaut des Auges dient als Auffangeschirm für die[3] von dem optischen **System** entworfenen Bilder. Nicht alle Teile der Netzhaut sind[6] in gleicher **Weise befähigt,**[7] einerseits geringe Lichtreize zum **Bewusstsein** zu **bringen,**[8] andererseits an einem betrachteten Ding feinere **Einzelheiten zu** erkennen. Beide Arten von Empfindungen sind[6] in **ihrer** grössten Leistungsfähigkeit an verschiedene Teile der **Netzhaut** gebunden.

l. light sensitive N. retina
A. collecting screen
e. which are sketched
b. enabled (to what?) g. small
B. consciousness a. on the other hand
e. recognize b. considered
E. sensations L. efficiency
v. different T. parts N. retina

Die Fähigkeit,[7] möglichst viele Einzelheiten an einem betrachteten **Ding** zu erkennen, ist in anderer Ausdrucksweise das **Vermögen,**[7] zwei optisch verschiedene, nahe beieinander stehende **punktförmig** kleine **Dinge** noch als getrennt zu erkennen. Das **Mass** dieser Fähigkeit nennt man Sehschärfe.[1]

F. ability (to what?) E. details
b. observed
V. ability o. optically
p. punctiform
g. separate e. recognize M. measurement
S. acuteness of vision

[10]**Wird beim** Sehen nur ein Zäpfchen **erregt,** so haben wir **die Empfindung** eines leuchtenden **Punktes.**[1] Ist[10] daher das Ding **so klein oder so weit entfernt,** dass sein Bild auf der Netzhaut[4] **nicht gleichzeitig auf mehrere Zäpfchen** fällt, so können[6] wir **keine** Einzelheiten des **Dinges** erkennen, das Auflösungsvermögen **ist überschritten.** Die Grösse des Netzhautbildes eines leuchtenden Dinges hängt von seiner Grösse und seiner **Entfernung ab.**[2] **In der Netzhautgrube** stehen die Zäpfchen am dichtesten; **hier beträgt** ihr Abstand nur etwa 0,004 mm.[1] Ein Netzhautbild **von dieser Grösse kommt zustande,**[2] wenn durch den Knotenpunkt **des Auges** zwei Strahlen eintreten, die[5] einen Winkel von 1' einschliessen, die[5] also auch unter diesem **Winkel**[9] in das Auge eintreten. Das tun beispielsweise zwei **Lichtstrahlen,**[1] die[5] von zwei 0,2 mm voneinander entfernten **Punkten** ausgehen, welche[5] vom **Auge 1 m** entfernt sind.[10] Sind zwei Punkte in der Entfernung von 1 m mehr als **0,3 mm** voneinander entfernt, so fällt ihr **Bild auf zwei verschiedene Zäpfchen;**[1] sie werden[6] daher getrennt **wahrgenommen.** Es ist hingegen noch möglich,[7] die **Verschiebung zweier gerader Linien gegeneinander bei günstiger Beschaffenheit derselben** zu bemerken, wenn sie etwa 10″ beträgt. **Die Sehschärfe ist in der Netzhautgrube bei weitem am grössten; von ihr aus nach dem Rande der Netzhaut zu** nimmt sie schnell **ab.**[2]

Why Rule 10? Z. cone e. excited
l. lighted What do you do when the verb is first?
e. removed
g. simultaneous m. several
E. details
A. resolving power ü. exceeded
What goes with "hängt"?
v. on E. distance
a. d. closest together b. amounts
A. distance N. retina image
z. comes about K. point of junction
S. rays e. enter in W. angle
e. include, enclose Note Rule 9; try to pick up a noun whenever possible.
a. go out, proceed from e. which are removed from one another Why Rule 10?
E. distance
v. different Z. cones
w. perceived h. on the other hand
V. displacement g. one against the other
g. favorable B. composition, nature, disposition
S. acuteness of vision
v. – aus App. 21, 1, n-d. R. d. N. zu (also App. 21, 1 and 2) a. decreases

Linsenkrümmung

Die stärkste Brechung erfahren die Lichtstrahlen beim Eintritt in die **Hornhaut.**[1] Die[3] durch die **Kristallinse** hervorgerufene Ablenkung ist nur gering. Die Kristallinse hat vorwiegend die Aufgabe eines korrigierenden Organes.[1] An ihr greift ein ringförmiger **Muskel,** der Ziliarmuskel, an,[2] durch dessen Tätigkeit ihre Krümmung[4] vergrössert werden kann.

s. strongest B. refraction
What is the subject? How can you tell?
h. which is called forth, evoked
v. predominately A. task
What goes with "greift"?
a. touches, attacks d. d. through whose T. activity
v. enlarged (w. k. App. 7, 6)

Der mittlere Krümmungsradius der vorderen Linsenfläche eines normalen jugendlichen Auges schwankt zwischen 10,4 mm bei nicht zusammengezogenem **Ziliarmuskel**[1] und etwa 5,7 mm bei voller **Entspannung.**[1] Bei grösserer Krümmung der Kristallinse werden[6] die **Strahlen** stärker abgelenkt; parallele Strahlen werden[6] dann also schon vor der **Netzhaut** vereinigt, während Strahlen,[4] die[5] divergent in das **Auge** eintreten, auf der **Netzhaut** vereinigt werden können. Das Auge besitzt infolgedessen die **Fähigkeit,**[7] auch von Dingen, die[5] im Endlichen liegen, deutliche, reelle Bilder auf der **Netzhaut** zu erzeugen.

m. mean K. curvature radius
s. varies
bei in the case of z. contracted
E. relaxation
K. curvature w. a. are deflected
S. rays
v. combined What does "Strahlen" call for? "die"? CONSTANTLY OBSERVE THE RULES THAT "PULL" THE VERBS OUT.
E. finite, ultimate d. clear
B. pictures e. produce

Anpassung

A. adaptation

Die Fähigkeit des Auges,[7] seine Brennweiten der Entfernung der beobachteten **Objekte** anzupassen, heisst Anpassungsvermögen oder Akkommodation des **Auges.**[1]

F. ability (to what?) B. focal distance
E. distance b. observed a. adapt
A. adaptability

Die Änderung der Brennweite der Linse beim Akkommodationsvorgang beruht aber nicht allein auf der Änderung der **Krümmung,** besonders der vorderen **Fläche.**[1] Vielmehr spielt dabei auch noch nach Gullstrands Untersuchungen der eigenartige Bau der Kristallinse eine **Rolle.**[1] Der Körper der Linse ist nämlich nicht homogen, sondern besteht aus einer grossen Anzahl kleinster **Häutchen,**[1] die[5] wie Schalen einer **Zwiebel** übereinanderliegen und[8] in der **Linsenkapsel** zusammengehalten werden. Die Brechungszahl dieser Häutchen nimmt von aussen nach innen zu.[2] Beim Akkommodationsvorgang verschieben sich die Häutchen gegenseitig.

Ä. change
b. depends a. alone Ä change
K. curvature v. anterior F. surface
n. according to U. investigations
e. peculiar B. structure
b. consists
A. number H. membranes
S. scales, shell, skin Z. onion
z. held together B. refracting index
z. increases
v. s. are displaced g. mutually

Fernpunkt

F. distant point

Ein rechtsichtiges Auge vereinigt **Strahlen,**[1] die[5] aus dem **Unendlichen** kommen, auf der Netzhaut, wenn das Auge[4] nicht akkommodiert; es erzeugt von unendlich fernen Dingen scharfe Bilder auf der **Netzhaut.**[1] Der Fernpunkt eines normalen **Auges,** d. i. der am weitesten entfernte **Punkt,** den ein Auge[4] noch scharf sehen kann, liegt also im **Unendlichen.**[1] Ein rechtsichtiges Auge ohne Anpassung ist[6] immer auf den **Fernpunkt** eingestellt.

v. combines S. rays
N. retina
e. produces D. things
s. sharp F. distance point
e. removed
U. infinite
A. adaptation
e. focused

Nahpunkt

N. near point

Ein jugendliches, rechtsichtiges Auge vermag[6] die **Kristallinse** so umzuformen, dass es[4] noch von Dingen, die[5] 10 cm vor dem **Auge** liegen, scharfe Bilder auf der Netzhaut erzeugt. Der nächste Punkt, auf den das Auge[4] noch einstellen kann, wird[6] der Nahpunkt genannt. Bei der Akkommodation auf sehr nahe Entfernungen wird[6] der **Ziliarmuskel** angestrengt; man empfindet das als Schmerzgefühl im **Auge.**[1] Infolge der Gewohnheit des **Auges,**[7] sich der Entfernung von 20 bis 30 cm (der Entfernung des Buches beim Lesen und Schreiben) anzupassen, empfinden wir die Anstrengung des Ziliarmuskels bei dieser Entfernung nicht. Die Entfernung von 25 cm wird[6] deutliche **Sehweite** genannt.

v. is able (to what?)
u. transform What does "es" call for? "die"?
e. adjust, focus
N. near point
E. distances
a. strained S. pain feeling
I. on account of, due to G. habit
E. distance L. reading
a. adapt e. sense A. strain
E. distance
d. clear S. seeing distance

Das menschliche Gehörorgan

(Indicate the rules for the *. Also show why certain nouns are in bold-face type)

Das menschliche Gehörorgan besteht aus der **Ohrmuschel,*** dem Gehörgang, dem Trommelfell, den Gehörknöchelchen (Hammer, Amboss, und Steigbügel), dem Vorhof mit den drei halbkreisförmigen Kanälen (Bogengängen), der Schnecke und der Eustachischen Röhre (**Ohrtrompete**).*

G. auditory organ b. consists O. external ear
T. tympanic membrane G. auditory ossicles
A. anvil S. stirrup
h. semi-circular
S. cochlea, spiral R. tube

Ein[3] durch die Ohrmuschel und den Gehörgang in das **Ohr** eindringender Ton bringt das Trommelfell in **Schwingungen,** die* durch die Gehörknöchelchen auf das ovale Fenster des **Vorhofes** übertragen werden. Das* aus Hof, Bogengängen und **Schnecke** zusammengesetzte Labyrinth ist* mit **Flüssigkeit** gefüllt, die* ebenfalls in **Schwingungen** versetzt wird. Die Schnecke ist* durch eine Scheidewand in zwei getrennte, übereinanderliegende Hohlräume: die Paukentreppe und die **Vorhofstreppe,** geteilt. Diese Scheidewand besteht aus einem knöchernen,[3] von der Achse der **Schnecke** ausgehenden Teil, an den[5] sich ein häutiger Teil nach **aussen** anschliesst. Die Scheidewand ist der eigentlich tonempfindende **Teil.*** Der häutige Teil der Scheidewand und eine Reihe äusserst feiner Härchen (das Cortische Organ) kommen durch die Schwingungen der* das **Innere** ausfüllenden Flüssigkeit ebenfalls in **Schwingungen.*** Die einzelnen Fasern des Cortischen Organes und der häutigen Scheidewand sind verschieden dick und lang (die Zahl der Fasern beläuft sich auf etwa 5000)* und daher für Schwingungen verschiedener Tonhöhe resonanzfähig. An die Basis der einzelnen Fasern schliessen sich die einzelnen Nervenenden der **Gehörnerven** an.* Wenn nun ein Ton von bestimmter Tonhöhe[4] das **Ohr** trifft, so bringt er, nachdem er* durch die Gehörknochelchen und das Gehörwasser auf die häutige **Scheidewand** übertragen worden ist, eine ganz bestimmte Faser des Cortischen Organes wahrscheinlich durch Wirbelbildungen in der umgebenden Flüssigkeit in **Schwingungen.*** Die* an diese schwingende **Faser** sich anschliessende Nervenfaser leitet den Reiz zum **Gehirn.*** (Resonanztheorie des Hörens.)

Why Rule 3? G. auditory channel
e. which penetrates
S. vibrations V. vestibule ü. transmitted
What does "das" call for? "ist"?
F. liquid e. likewise
Schw. septum
g. separate H. cavities P. scala tympani
S. septum k. bone like (what?)
a. which goes out a. d. to which
h. membranous e. really t. tone sensitive
R. series ä. extremely
S. vibrations a. which fills
e. single F. fibres e. likewise
S. septum
v. differently Z. number b. amounts to
d. hence T. pitch
s. s. a. are attached Note Rule 2.
b. definite t. strikes Note inserted clause.
n. after
ü. transferred b. definite
w. probably W. whirl formation (vortex)
u. surrounding S. vibrations
s. a. which attaches F. fibre G. brain

Die Bogengänge stehen in drei[3] aufeinander senkrechten Ebenen. Man nimmt an,[2] dass wir* durch ihre Mitwirkung die **Fähigkeit**[7] erlangen, uns im Raume (oben, vorn, seitlich) zu orientieren und[8] uns im **Gleichgewicht** zu halten.

B. semi-circular canals d. three
s. which are perpendicular (Why which?)
e. acquire F. ability (to what?)
G. balance

Der Umfang des Gehöres ist[6] bezüglich Frequenz und Stärke der Töne aus der **Abb. 661** ersichtlich. Die obere Hörgrenze ist* für die einzelnen **Menschen** verschieden. Sie nimmt mit dem **Alter** ab[2]: mit 20 Jahren ist die obere Hörgrenze 19 000, mit 35 15 000, mit 47 Jahren etwa 13 000 Hz. **(Hertz).** So vermögen[7] ältere Leute z. B. das Zirpen der Grille, den Pfiff der **Fledermaus** nicht mehr zu vernehmen. Hunde hören bis 38 000 Hz.

U. scope b. with reference to
S. strength e. visible, apparent
H. auditory limit
v. different a. decreases
v. are able
G. cricket F. bat
v. perceive

Geübte Musiker besitzen andererseits auch eine ausserordentliche Empfindlichkeit für den Unterschied zweier **Töne;*** es genügt schon, dass zwei Töne im Tonbereich mittlerer Tonhöhe* sich um Bruchteile einer **Vollschwingung** unterscheiden, um[7] als von verschiedener **Tonhöhe** erkannt zu werden. Im ganzen dürfte[6] das Ohr nach Höhe oder Stärke oder beiden zugleich etwa 300 tausend **Töne** unterscheiden.

g. expert b. possess
a. extraordinary E. sensitivity
U. distinction g. suffices T. tone range
B. fractions V. complete vibration
s. u. are distinguished
e. recognized i. g. on the whole
S. strength b. both
u. distinguish

GESCHLECHTSVERERBUNG- UND BESTIMMUNG

Das Wesen der Sexualität†

(Numbers of rules appear in the first few pages of this section. Later an * appears where certain rules are involved. In very difficult sentences the numbers may still appear. In the last pages of the section, both the numbers and the * gradually disappear.)

Die Mehrzahl der biologischen **Geschlechtsprobleme,**[1] und nur von biologischen Problemen ist in diesem Buche die **Rede,**[1] ergibt sich aus der Tatsache des Vorhandenseins zweier verschiedener Geschlechter im Reich der Lebewesen.[1] Die Fragestellungen und ihre **Lösungen,**[1] die[5] von einer **Tatsache** ausgehen, bildeten stets eines der anziehendsten Kapitel der Wissenschaft vom **Leben;**[1] heute gehören sie auch zu den erfolgreichsten, sowohl in bezug auf die Fülle des **Tatsachenmaterials,** als auch die Tiefe des Eindringens in der Richtung auf kausales und physiologisches **Verständnis.**[1] Wir werden[6] ihrer Darstellung daher den grössten Teil der folgenden **Ausführungen** zu widmen haben. Aber sie stellen nicht das gesamte **Geschlechtsproblem** dar.[2] Die Voraussetzung für die Unterscheidung von Geschlechtern ist das Vorhandensein einer geschlechtlichen **Fortpflanzung.**[1] Und diese stellt bekanntlich eines der Grundprobleme der **Biologie** dar,[2] dessen vollständige Lösung[4] den Schleier von einem grossen Teil des Geheimnisses des **Lebens** lüften würde. Dieser Augenblick ist[6] noch nicht gekommen; aber das Material, das[5] in unzähligen Versuchen und **Beobachtungen** zusammengetragen ist, lässt[6] bei richtiger Betrachtung wohl schon die **Richtung** erkennen, in der die Lösung[4] einmal liegen mag.

(Give reasons for the numbers.)
M. Majority G. sex problem
R. the discussion T. fact V. presence
z. two G. sexes L. living beings
F. question(ing) L. solutions
a. emanate b. formed a. most attractive
W. science g. belong
e. most successful i. b. a. in regard to
T. fact material E. penetration V. understanding
R. direction V. understanding
D. presentation w. shall (App. 7, 4)
z. w. to devote A. statements
d. present g. total V. supposition, assumption
U. distinction G. sexes V. presence
g. sexual F. reproduction
b. as one knows e. one
d. represents v. complete S. veil
G. mystery l. raise A. moment n. n. not yet
u. countless V. experiments z. compiled
l. permits B. consideration
e. recognize l. lie

Es ist nicht so lange her, dass man[4] ganze Gruppen von **Lebewesen** für so einfach organisiert hielt, dass sie[4] sich dauernd und in alle Ewigkeit fort durch **Zweiteilung** zu vermehren vermögen. Mit wachsender Kenntnis hat[6] sich die Zahl solcher **Lebewesen** mehr und mehr verringert und heute können wir sagen, dass im **Tierreich** – und im folgenden beschränken wir uns auf das **Tierreich** – es[4] wohl kein sicheres Beispiel einer **Form** gibt, die[5] sich dauernd ungeschlechtlich vermehren kann. In der Regel ist ein Befruchtungsvorgang bei allen tierischen Organismen eine Vereinigung männlicher und weiblicher **Elemente.**[1]

g. entire
L. organisms, living beings h. considered (work back to the noun, then rearrange these words)
v. are able
v. decreased h. s. verr. See App. 11, 4, d.
T. animal kingdom
b. limit e. g. there is (App. 10, 3, c)
s. sure d. constantly u. asexually
i. d. R. as a rule
B. fertilization process V. combination
m. male w. female

Die Sexualität muss[6] daher zunächst unabhängig von der **Befruchtung** betrachtet werden; sie stellt einen elementaren Prozess für sich dar,[2] zu dem[5] die Befruchtung als eine Teilerscheinung hinzukommt. Das Hauptproblem lautet also: Warum bedarf der tierische **Organismus,** auch der allereinfachste, regelmässig wiederkehrender geschlechtlicher Vorgänge,[1] um[7] unbegrenzt in seinen **Nachkommen** fortbestehen zu können? Oder anders ausgedrückt: die Vermehrung und Fortpflanzung ist zweifellos eine Form des Wachstums über die Grenzen des **Individuums** hinaus, wobei jedes folgende[4] mit jedem **vorhergehenden** stofflich kontinuierlich ist. Warum ist[6] ein dauerndes Wachstum unmöglich, es sei denn, dass ein eingeschalteter Geschlechtsvorgang[4] den **Prozess** wieder von neuem beginnen lässt?

z. first of all u. independent
b. considered What goes with "stellt"?
f. s. by itself zu dem, to which
H. comes in T. separate phenomenon
l. reads b. need
a. very simplest r. regularly
w. recurring u. without limit
f. continue to exist a. expressed
F. propagation z. doubtless
ü – h. over and beyond (App. 21, h, g)
folg. following (one) v. preceding
one (Note absence of the noun.)
e. s. d. unless e. interposed, connected
G. sexual process v. n. anew

Diese Fragen zeigen ohne weiteres, dass die Wurzeln des Sexualitätsproblems zusammenlaufen mit den Problemen von Alter, Tod und **Unsterblichkeit.**[1] Sie alle haben[6] reichliche Berücksichtigung in den Forschungen der neueren **Biologie** gefunden, und wir brauchen[7] nur die Namen Bütschli, Hertwig und **Weismann** zu nennen. Aber wir wollen[6] nicht die zahlreichen mehr oder

o. w. without more ado W. roots
z. merge
U. immortality r. rich, plentiful
B. consideration F. studies
b. need (to what?)
w. want to
z. numerous m. order m. more or less

†Richard Goldschmidt, **Mechanismus und Physiologie der Geschlechtsbestimmung**

minder formalistischen Theorien erörtern, die[5] in alter, neuer und neuster Zeit aufgestellt wurden, sondern[8] uns die Haupttatsachen in einer Form vorführen, die[5] uns erkennen lässt, in welcher Richtung die Lösung[4] zu suchen ist.

e. discuss a. formalistic
H. main facts v. present
e. recognize l. lets R. direction
z. s. i. is to be sought (App. 12, 1)

Die elementaren Tatsachenkomplexe

Wenn wir[4] von den Problemen sprechen, die[5] sich aus der Tatsache der Zweigeschlechtigkeit der Tiere ergeben, so meinen wir damit nur die Sexualprobleme im engeren Sinne,[1] die[5] allgemein als die Frage der Vererbung und Bestimmung des Geschlechts zusammengefasst werden können. Da die zweigeschlechtliche Fortpflanzung[4] aufs tiefste in Bau, Physiologie und Lebensweise der **Tiere** einschneidet, so ist die Biologie der tierischen Fortpflanzung wohl das umfangreichste Gebiet der gesamten **Biologie**, aus dem[5] auch nur die **Hauptdaten** hier anzuführen uns fern liegt. Wir setzen seine **Hauptzüge** als bekannt voraus,[2] und erwähnen nur solche Tatsachen, die[5] für unser engeres **Problem** notwendig sind. Dieses engere Problem haben[6] wir als Vererbung und Bestimmung des **Geschlechts** bezeichnet. Die elementare Tatsache ist, dass, abgesehen von den[3] besonders zu besprechenden Ausnahmen und Besonderheiten, die[3] bei oberflächlicher **Betrachtung** gleich verlaufende **Befruchtung identisch erscheinender Eier** zwei Arten von Organismen in ungefähr gleicher Zahl den **Ursprung** gibt, männlichen und weiblichen, die[5] oft in jedem Teil ihres **Körpers** so verschieden sind, dass man[4] sie aus Unkenntnis zu verschiedenen Arten oder **Gattungen** rechnen könnte. Die Regelmässigkeit und scheinbare Unverrückbarkeit dieses Vorgangs muss[6] auf einem elementaren **Vererbungsmechanismus** beruhen. Und so ist das erste Problem der Zweigeschlechtigkeit die Frage nach dem **Mechanismus**, der[5] die regelmässige Sonderung zweier **Geschlechter** bedingt. Dieses Grundproblem der Geschlechtsvererbung ist[6] heute, wie wir[4] sehen werden, bereits vollständing gelöst.

s. e. result
Z. bi-sexuality T. animals
e. narrower S. sense
V. transmission, inheritance B. determination
G. sex z. grouped together d. since
F. propagation a. t. in the deepest way
e. cuts in L. way of life
w. indeed u. the most comprehensive
G. field g. all a. d. from which
a. to introduce, mention H. main data
v. presuppose H. main features
n. necessary e. narrower, more immediate
V. inheritance, transmission B. determination
G. sex b. designated
a. apart from z. b. which are to be discussed (App. 12, 2) o. superficial
v. which proceeds (Be sure to pick up all of the subject here.) u. about
j. each T. part
v. different U. ignorance A. species G. genera
R. regularity s. apparent U. immovability
V. hereditary process
b. depend, rest Z. bisexuality
n. about r. regular
b. causes, stipulates S. separation
G. sex inheritance v. completely g. solved

Der Mechanismus der normalen Geschlechtsvererbung

Jedermann weiss heute, dass es[4] Mendel in den 60er Jahren des vorigen **Jahrhunderts**[7] gelungen ist, den Mechanismus aufzudecken, durch den[5] bestimmte Erbeigenschaften in gesetzmässiger Weise auf die **Nachkommen** übertragen werden, Gesetze, die[5] zahlenmässig formuliert werden können. Da nun die Vererbung des Geschlechts[4] ein Vorgang ist, bei dem,[5] wie im Mendel-Versuch, bestimmte Klassen von Individuen—nämlich die beiden Geschlechter—in bestimmten Zahlenverhältnissen—nämlich in gleicher Zahl—auftreten, so lag der Gedanke einer Anwendung dieser Gesetze auf das Geschlechtsproblem nicht fern.[2] Und Mendel selbst verfehlte nicht[7] ihn anzudeuten, und das in einer Zeit, in der[5] noch nichts von den zellulären Vorgängen der Befruchtung, der Reifung der Geschlechtszellen und den **Chromosomen** bekannt war. Bald nach der Wiederentdeckung der Mendelschen Gesetze im Jahre 1900 wurde[6] diese Idee zunächst von Strassburger und **Castle** wieder aufgenommen und[8] dann vor allem von G. Smith, Bateson und **Corvens** durchgeführt und bewiesen. Da zu ihrem Verständnis die Kenntnis der Mendelschen Gesetze[4] eine Voraussetzung ist, so seien[6] deren so oft dargestellte Grundprinzipien für den **Nichtbiologen** kurz rekapituliert.

w. knows
e. g. ist (has) succeeded in –ing
a. to disclose b. certain g. regular
E. hereditary qualities ü. transmitted
N. offspring z. numerically
V. process b. d. in which
b. certain n. namely
Z. numerical relationships
a. appear (What calls for this verb?)
f. lie distant (l. n. f. was obvious)
v. did not fail a. indicate
d. i. e. Z. and that in a time
R. maturation G. sex cells
b. known W. rediscovery
z. first of all
a. resumed, taken up u. and (what?)
d. carried through b. proved
d. since V. understanding
V. prerequisite (App. 28, 1, b)
k. briefly

DIE MENDELSCHEN GESETZE

Mendels Ausgangspunkt war die **Überzeugung,**[1] dass ein Gesetz der Vererbung[4] nur gefunden werden könne, wenn eine einzelne, rein erbliche Eigenschaft einer Rasse[4] durch Bastardierung mit der entsprechenden, aber typisch verschiedenen einer anderen Rasse verbunden (X) und dann das Verhalten dieses Paares von Erbeigenschaften[4] im Bastard und seiner **Nachkommenschaft** verfolgt wird. Mendel benutzte zu seinen Versuchen verschiedene Erbsenrassen; wir nehmen aber aus gleich ersichtlichen Gründen einen[3] später von Corvens studierten Fall [9]als Ausgangspunkt.

A. starting point ü. conviction
G. law V. heredity
e. hereditary E. property R. race, strain
B. hybridization e. corresponding
Let the X stand for the aux. "wird" which goes with the subject.
v. followed b. used V. experiments
E. types of peas e. visible, apparent
G. reasons s. which was studied
A. starting point

Es gibt zwei Rassen der Wunderblume Mirabilis **Jalapa,** die[5] sich in einer **Erbeigenschaft** unterscheiden. Die eine blüht rot, die andere weiss.[10] Werden sie miteinander gekreuzt, so wird[6] ein hellrotblühender Bastard in der ersten Bastard-generation (F_1 Generation genannt) erhalten. Die beiden Eigenschaften haben[6] sich also im Bastard zu etwas mittlerem gemischt. Die Nachkommen dieses **Bastards,** die[5] durch Selbstbestäubung oder Wechselbestäubung zweier **Geschwisterbastardpflanzen** gewonnen werden, sind nun nicht etwa wieder hellrot, sondern bestehen aus weissen, roten und hellroten, und zwar genau im Zahlenverhältnis von 1/4 weisse: 2/4 hellrote: 1/4 rote.[10] Werden diese F_2 Pflanzen nun wieder ebenso durch Selbstbestäubung vermehrt, so zeigt es sich, dass die weissen nur rein weisse **Nachkommenschaft** erzeugen, die[5] ihrerseits auch wieder nur **weisse** hervorbringt, also[8] für weiss rein züchtet, dass ebenso die roten F_2 Pflanzen[4] für rot rein züchten, während die hellroten sich nun wieder genau so verhalten wie ihre hellroten F_1 Eltern, nämlich[8] wieder in drei Typen in gleicher Weise spalten. Durch Spaltung werden[6] also in der zweiten Bastardgeneration die elterlichen Typen rein erhalten. Mendel fand nun den einfachen Schlüssel zu diesen **Tatsachen,**[1] eine Lösung, auf der[5] sich seitdem eine ganze **Wissenschaft** aufgebaut hat. Wenn zwei gleichartige Eltern ihnen gleiche Nachkommenschaft[9] erzeugen, so beruht es darauf, dass ihre Geschlechtszellen oder Gameten[4] bei der Befruchtung die gleichen **Erbfaktoren** mitbringen.

e. g. there are M. J. four o'clocks
s. u. are distinguished (App. 11, 4, a)
Why Rule 10? g. crossed
w. is (App. 7, 5, a) B. hybrid
e. obtained E. qualities
h. s. g. have been mixed
N. offspring S. self pollination
W. inter-pollination G. brother sister hybrid plants b. consist
z. what is more g. exactly
Z. numerical proportion
w. again Why rule 10?
e. z. s. it is shown
N. descendants, progeny e. produce i. in turn
z. breeds
w. while
v. s. behave (Note that the verb is in front of "wie".) n. namely (often calls for a verb)
e. obtained r. pure
e. simple S. key T. facts
a. d. on which s. since then
a. h. has been built (App. 11, 4, c)
e. produce gleiche which are like them (Why which?)
m. bring along

Bei einer rotblühenden Pflanze enthält z. B. sowohl jeder männliche Gamet wie jeder weibliche den Rotfaktor A, die Nachkommenschaft ist also immer wieder AA. Das gleiche gilt natürlich für eine rein weissblühende **Pflanze,**[1] deren Gameten[4] alle den Weissfaktor a enthalten, so dass die Befruchtung[4] immer die Pflanze aa ergibt. Bei der Bastardierung sind[6] die Eltern in dem Punkt verschieden, dass der eine[4] einen Faktor für rot, A, der andere einen für weiss, a, enthält. Bei der Befruchtung kommen diese beiden zusammen,[2] der Bastard heisst damit Aa. Wenn nun in der Nachkommenschaft dieses Bastards wieder die rein roten und rein weissen Typen auftreten, die[5] rein weiterzüchten, so ist dies nur möglich, wenn sowohl die männlichen wie die weiblichen Gameten des Bastards[4] zum Teil A und zum Teil a enthalten, somit[8] sich zu AA und aa vereinigen können. Das heisst mit anderen Worten: im Bastard mischen sich die Erbfaktoren nicht, sondern bleiben rein, und werden rein, so wie sie[4] in den Bastard kamen, auf dessen Gameten wieder überliefert. Dies ist das erste Mendelsche Grundgesetz,[1] das Gesetz von der Reinheit der **Gameten,** das[5] seitdem tausendfach bestätigt wurde.

e. contains
m. male w. female
N. offspring
g. is true w. white blooming
d. G. whose gamets
B. fertilization e. yields
v. different
d. s. the one
z. come together
h. is called
As long as there is no "call" for the verb, stay in line.
s. as well
e. contain
s. therefore, hence v. k. can be combined (App. 11, 4)
b. remain u. w. and are transmitted pure
G. basic law R. purity
b. verified

GESCHLECHT ALS MENDELNDE EIGENSCHAFT

(Numbers of the rules will now gradually disappear. An * will appear where certain rules are involved.)

Es ist klar, dass wir* auf Grund der Mendelschen Regeln das Resultat einer jeden Bastardbefruchtung und einer jeden[3] mit solchen Bastarden oder ihrer Nachkommenschaft ausführbaren **Befruchtung** voraus berechnen können. Die wichtigste Kombination, die* sich nun ausführen lässt, ist die Rückkreuzung eines Bastards mit einem seiner Eltern.[10] Nehmen wir die hellrote Bastardwunderblume der rot- und weissblühenden elterlichen Rasse, so führen wir eine Mendelsche Rückkreuzung aus.* Wir wissen, dass der hellrote Bastard Aa* reine Gameten für A und für a bildet. Bei der Rückkreuzung können* sich daher ebensoviele mütterliche Gameten A mit väterlichen a vereinigen, als mütterliche a ebenfalls mit a. Das Resultat der Rückkreuzung ist daher 1 Aa: 1aa. Aa und aa aber waren ja die hellroten und weissen Elternpflanzen dieses Versuchs.* Wir sehen somit, dass eine Rückkreuzung* in diesem Fall zu gleichen Teilen die Typen der[3] zur Rückkreuzung verwandten Formen wiedergibt.

A. * will appear where certain rules are involved.
G. basis R. rules B. hybrid fertilization
N. offspring WHAT NOUNS SHOULD BE BOLD-FACED? a. executable B. fertilization
b. compute v. in advance s. l. can be (Rule 6)
R. back crossing Why Rule 10?
h. light red w. white blooming R. race
a. carry out
w. know B. hybrid
k. s. v. can be combined
d. hence V. paternal
e. likewise Underline the nouns that should appear in bold-face type.
E. parent plants
V. experiment s. therefore
F. case Why Rule 3?
v. which are used w. reproduces

Was ist aber das Resultat einer Rückkreuzung,* wenn der Bastard* nicht intermediär ist, sondern[8] dominant erscheint, wie in dem obigen Beispiel der Wildenten. Der Bastard gleicht daher nun wieder Aa, A ist dominant über a und der Bastard gleicht daher äusserlich dem seiner Eltern,* der* A lieferte.[10] Kreuzen wir nun diesen Bastard zurück,[2] mit demjenigen seiner Eltern, der* das dominante Merkmal besitzt, also in Symbolen Aa×AA, dann erhalten wir nach dem gleichen Vorgang wie in dem letzten Beispiel als Nachkommen 1AA: 1aA. Da nun A dominant ist, so erscheint die gesamte Nachkommenschaft äusserlich dem einen der Bastardeltern gleich,[1] obwohl die Hälfte* (aA) Bastardbeschaffenheit besitzt. *Führen wir nun aber die entsprechende Rückkreuzung so aus,[2] dass der Bastard mit der* das rezessive **Merkmal** enthaltenden Rasse rückgekreuzt wird, so ist das Resultat anders. Die Formel lautet jetzt Aa aa und dies gibt natürlich als Nachkommenschaft 1Aa: 1aa.* Dies zeigt uns, dass wenn wir* den Bastard mit seinen rezessiven Eltern rückkreuzen, wir* wieder zu gleichen Teilen die beiden Typen erhalten, die* zur Rückkreuzung dienten, genau wie bei der Mirabilisrückkreuzung.*

w. what
s. but (Note Rule 8.)
e. appears o. above
g. is like, resembles
ä. externally d. to that one
l. furnished Note Rule 2.
d. that one (App. 14,2)
b. possesses e. obtain
g. same V. process B. example
D. since
g. total ä. outwardly d. to that
o. altho B. hybrid nature
What does a "verb first" construction tell you to do? What does "der" call for?
e. which contains (Why which?)
a. differently l. reads N. offspring
E. parents
g. similar T. parts
e. obtain d. served g. exactly

Es ist nun ohne weiteres ersichtlich, dass dieses Resultat* eine grosse Ähnlichkeit mit dem Vorgang der normalen Geschlechtsvererbung zeigt. In beiden Fällen zeigen die Eltern eine typische Verschiedenheit,* und die Nachkommen zeigen in gleicher Zahl die gleiche Differenz.* Wenn daher Männlichkeit und Weiblichkeit* nach dem Typus mendelnder Faktoren vererbt würden, so könnte* die Geschlechtsvererbung als eine Rückkreuzung aufgefasst werden, wobei ein Geschlecht* immer die Faktoren für beide Geschlechter enthält; ein Bastardgeschlecht ist rein mit Dominanz des einen, das andere aber ist rein in bezug auf die Geschlechtsfaktoren.*

o. w. without further ado
A. similarity V. process
G. sex inheritance F. cases
V. difference
g. like Z. number
M. masculinity
v. inherited G. sexual heredity
a. comprehended w. whereby
e. contains
r. pure
i. b. a. in regard to

Wir müssen* nun hier die übliche Terminologie erwähnen, die wir* auch im **folgenden** immer benutzen werden: Der Bastardcharakter wird* stets als heterozygot (d.h. durch Vereinigung verschiedenartiger Geschlechtszellen zustandegekommen[11]) und die reine Form als homozygot (Vereinigung gleicher Geschlechtszellen) bezeichnet.

ü. customary
e. mention b. use
w. shall, will (App. 7,4) s. always
V. combination v. varied type
z. having come about Note Rule 11.
b. designated

Die zellulare Seite des Geschlechtsproblems

(Give reasons for the * and also indicate what nouns should be bold-faced)

Der Mendelsche Erbmechanismus arbeitet mit Vorgängen in den Geschlechtszellen,* ohne[7] bestimmte Ideen zu erfordern, wo und wie in ihnen die Verteilung der Faktoren erfolgt. Es wäre* Mendel auch gar nicht möglich[7] gewesen, irgendwelche Ideen aufzustellen, da zu seiner Zeit noch nicht einmal die Grundlagen* gelegt waren, auf denen er* hätte bauen können. Erst in den Dekaden nach 1875 wurde* die feinere Geschichte der Geschlechtszellen enthüllt. Als dann im Jahre 1900 Mendels Gesetze* der Vergessenheit entrissen wurden, dauerte es auch nicht lange, bis die entscheidenden Schritte* getan wurden,[7] sie mit der[3] inzwischen bekannt gewordenen Geschichte der Geschlechtszellen[9] in Beziehung zu setzen. Und dabei fand denn auch der Mechanismus der Geschlechtsverteilung seine zelluläre Aufhellung.* Ihn zu verstehen, ist* natürlich die Kenntnis der Hauptzüge der Lebensgeschichte der Geschlechtszellen notwendig, oder richtiger gesagt, ihres interessantesten Bestandteiles,* der Chromosomen,* die* wiederum für den Nichtbiologen kurz rekapituliert ist.

E. hereditary mechanism V. processes
G. sex cells o. without
e. requiring (why -ing?) Wie, how
e. takes place e. w. g. it would have been (App. 28, 2) i. any a. to set up
e. even G. basis
h. b. k. could have built
G. history G. sex cells e. disclosed
V. oblivion e. removed from
d. lasted, required e. decisive
s. steps g. done (to what?)
g. which had become known Note Rule 9.
B. relation
G. sex distribution A. explanation
l. z. v. to understand it K. knowledge
H. main features L. life history
n. necessary
B. constituent part w. again
Underline all nouns that should be your "pivot" nouns.

Die Chromosomen in Reifung und Befruchtung und als Träger der Mendelschen Faktoren

Was[5] dem Forscher, der[5] die Lebenserscheinungen der Zelle studiert, immer wieder als das Merkwürdigste entgegentritt, ist die Fähigkeit der Zelle,[7] sich durch Teilung zu vermehren und* diese Teilung auf eine höchst eigentümliche Art durchzuführen. Die Teilung besteht darin, dass die beiden Hauptbestandteile der Zelle, der Zelleib oder das Protoplasma und der Zellkern* halbiert werden und so zwei Tochterzellen entstehen, die* ausser in der zunächst geringeren Grösse genau der Mutterzelle gleichen. Nun verläuft aber in der überwältigenden Mehrzahl der tierischen und pflanzlichen Zellen der Teilungsprozess nicht als eine einfache Halbierung,* sondern in der komplizierten Weise, die Fig. 18* darstellt, dem Vorgang der Karyokinese. Die Teilung wird* dadurch eingeleitet, dass neben dem Kern sich im Umkreis eines Körperchens, des Zentrosoms, eine Strahlenfigur* bildet, die* durch die Teilung des Zentrosoms, sich bald verdoppelt und* in ihren beiden Hälften auseinanderweichend zwei gegenüberliegende Pole der Zelle einnimmt. Inzwischen haben* im Innern des Kerns komplizierte Umlagerungen seiner wichtigsten Substanz stattgefunden, die man* wegen ihrer Neigung,[7] gewisse Farbstoffe festzuhalten, Chromatin nennt, und die* damit enden, dass sich eine bestimmte Anzahl,* sagen wir vier, festere Schleifen ausbilden, die vielgenannten Chromosomen. Nun lösen sich die Kerne auf*, und die Chromosmen ordnen sich in einer Reihe im Äquator der zweipoligen Strahlenfigur an.* Dann wird* ein jedes Chromosom der Länge nach gespalten, so dass jetzt zwei Spalthälften* einander gegenüberliegen; und diese beginnen sich zu trennen und[8] nach den beiden Zellpolen auseinander zu wandern, bis sie* nahe bei den Zentrosomen angelangt sind. Jetzt aber verläuft der ganze Prozess wieder rückwärts; die Chromosomen verlieren ihre individuelle Abgrenzung,* es bildet sich aus ihnen ein neuer Kern,* die Strahlung erlischt und es sind* zwei Zellen von gleicher Art wie die Ausgangszellen gebildet.

W. what F. scientist
i. w. again and again M. most remarkable
F. ability v. reproduce
d. carry through h. highly e. peculiar
b. consists H. main components
Z. cell body
Z. cell nucleous h. divided
e. arise z. first of all
g. exactly g. resemble v. proceeds
ü. predominant M. majority
T. division process e. simple
W. manner d. presents
K. karyokinesis (same as mitosis)
n. along with U. circumference
S. b. is formed S. ray figure
v. is doubled u. and (what?)
b. two a. separating e. occupies I. meanwhile
K. nucleous U. rearrangements
s. taken place N. tendency
f. retain, hold fast n. calls
b. certain A. number S. bands, loops
a. are dissolved (App. 11, 4, a)
What does "an" go with?
g. split d. L. n. in length (See App. 15, 3, e.)
S. split halves e. j. each
t. separate u. and to what?
a. apart
a. come, arrived v. proceeds
r. in reverse v. lose
A. boundary, demarcation
e. extinguish g. same
A. starting cells

Im Vordergrund dieses Prozesses stehen nun sichtlich die Chromosomen und auf sie konzentriert sich denn das Interesse der Zellforschung seit ihrer Entwickelung in immer steigendem Masse.* Denn ihr Verhalten bei der Befruchtung führte zu der Überzeugung,* dass sie* die Träger von Substanzen sind, die* auf das engste mit den Vererbungsprozessen verbunden sein müssen. Und um* es gleich vorauszunehmen, so können* wir heute mit Sicherheit sagen, dass sie* die Träger der Mendelschen Faktoren sind. Die Umrisse der Grundtatsachen,* die* zu diesem Schluss führten, sind aber die folgenden:

V. foreground
s. obviously k. s. has been concentrated
(See App. 11, 4, a.) Z. cell study
E. developmnet s. increasing
V. behaviour B. fertilization Ü. conviction
T. carriers a. d. e. in the closest way
v. anticipate it g. right away
S. certainty T. carriers
U. outlines G. basic facts
S. conclusion f. the following

Bei der Befruchtung dringt eine männliche Samenzelle in die weibliche Eizelle ein.* Beide Zellen, die sogenannten Gameten, bestehen trotz verschiedener äusserer Form aus den typischen Bestandteilen der Zelle,* Kern und Protoplasma.* Nun zeigen viele Samenzellen die Form eines langen Fadens,* dessen besonders gestaltetes Vorderende, der Kopf*, den Kern darstellt, wie seine Entstehung lehrt, das übrige aber, Mittelstück und Schwanz,* dem Protoplasma entspricht. In vielen Fällen wird* nun beobachtet, dass bei der Befruchtung nur der Kopf* in die Eizelle dringt (und ganz entsprechend bei den höheren Pflanzen nur der Kern des Pollenschlauchs) der Schwanz* aber abgeworfen wird. Innerhalb des Eiprotoplasmas nimmt dann der Kopf die Gestalt eines gewöhnlichen Kerns an* und verschmilzt mit dem Kern der Eizelle.* Da bei der Befruchtung die Eigenschaften beider Eltern* auf die Nachkommen übertragen werden, so müssen* diese Eigenschaften in irgend einer Weise in den Kernen der Gameten enthalten sein.

What goes with "dringt"?
S. sperm cell w. female e. penetrate
b. consist t. in spite of
ä. outer B. components
K. nucleus (Underline all nouns which show that Rule 1 is involved.) F. string
g. formed V. front end K. head
d. represents E. origination ü. rest
S. tail e. corresponds b. observed F. cases
E. ovum cell
e. correspondingly h. in the case of
P. pollen tube a. thrown off
I. within What goes with "nimmt"?
G. shape g. ordinary v. fuses
D. since (App. 25, 2)
E. properties b. both N. offspring
w. ü. are carried over (App. 7, 5, a)
e. contained

Im Kern dürfen* wir also mit Recht die Träger der Vererbung suchen. Wo sie* dort liegen, zeigt ein weiter eindringendes Studium der Befruchtung.* Wir sagten, dass bei ihr die Kerne der Gameten[4] verschmelzen. Oft ist[6] dies aber nicht ganz wörtlich zu nehmen, vielmehr bleiben[6] die Kerne zunächst nebeneinander liegen. Die weitere Entwickelung zum Organismus,* die* nach der Befruchtung einsetzt, besteht nun in einer unübersehbaren Folge von Zellteilungen,* deren erste* bald nach der Befruchtung eintritt. Da kann es dann sein, dass die Zellteilungsfigur sich bildet, ohne dass die beiden Kerne* miteinander verschmolzen sind, und da tritt das gleiche ein,[2] wie bei jeder anderen Zellteilung, die Chromosomen bilden sich aus.[2] Aber nun bilden sie sich in jedem Kern getrennt aus,[2] in dem nebenstehend abgebildeten Beispiel je zwei in jedem Kern.* Die fertige Zellteilungsfigur enthält also eine Anzahl,* hier vier Chromosomen,* von denen die Hälfte von der Eizelle, die Hälfte von der Samenzelle stammt. Bei der nun folgenden Teilung werden* alle der Länge nach gespalten und[8] auf die Tochterzellen verteilt. Es erhält somit jede Tochterzelle zur Hälfte väterliche und zur anderen Hälfte mütterliche Chromosomen* und ebenso geht es bei jeder weiteren Zellteilung.* Nun werden[6] bei der Befruchtung die Eigenschaften beider Eltern auf die Nachkommen vererbt.

R. justice, right
V. heredity l. lie e. penetrating
b. in the case of v. fuse
g. entirely w. literally z. n. to be taken
(App. 12, 1) b. l. remain lying w. further
e. sets in, starts b. consists
F. sequence, series Z. cell divisions
e. starts d. then (App. 25, 1)
s. bi. is formed b. two
V. fuse d. then (App. 25, 1) e. occurs
K. nucleus g. separately n. adjacent, standing near
f. finished
A. number
H. half S. sperm cell
d. L. in length (App. 15, 3, e)
v. distributed e. e. j. T. See App. 10, 1, c.
v. paternal
b. with, in the case of Z. cell division
E. properties N. offspring
v. handed down, devolved

Das, was die Zellen der Nachkommen* in gleicher Weise von beiden Eltern besitzen, sind aber nur die Chromosomen, und somit müssen wir schliessen, dass auch in den Chromosomen die betreffenden Eigenschaften* lokalisiert sind.

d. w. that which g. like
b. possess
s. conclude
b. concerned E. qualities

Wir haben* nun bisher keinen besonderen Wert auf die Zahl der Chromosomen gelegt. Und doch ist diese nicht etwa gleichgültig. Es zeigt sich vielmehr, dass sie* bei allen Tier- und Pflanzenarten eine typische, konstante ist. Eine Tomate zeigt in ihren sich teilenden Zellen 24, ein Mensch in allen Zellen 24.* Kurzum, jede Art von Lebewesen besitzt eine* für sie charakteristische Chromosomenzahl in den Kernen ihrer Zellen.* Nun haben wir gehört, dass bei der Befruchtung zwei solche Kerne* sich miteinander vereinigen.[10] Hätten sie auch die typische Zahl, so wäre[6] nach der Befruchtung in der Zelle die doppelte Anzahl vorhanden. Alle Zellen der Nachkommenschaft,* also auch ihre Geschlechtszellen,* bergen jetzt die doppelte Chromosomenzahl,* und wenn sie* sich wieder bei der Befruchtung vereinigen, so bekäme die Enkelgeneration bereits die vierfache Zahl,* und so fort.[10] Soll das nicht eintreten, und tatsächlich ist ja die Chromosomenzahl eine konstante, so kann* es nur auf einem Wege erreicht werden; es muss* eine Einrichtung bestehen, die bewirkt, dass in den Geschlechtszellen vor ihrer Vereinigung die Chromosomenzahl* auf die Hälfte herabgesetzt wird. Nur so kann* nach der Befruchtung immer noch die Normalzahl bewahrt bleiben. Tatsächlich findet sich eine solche Einrichtung, bestehend in einer besondern Teilung,* die eine jede Geschlechtszelle[4] durchmachen muss, bevor sie* befruchtungsfähig wird, der Reduktionsteilung, deren besonderer Mechanismus so verläuft, dass durch sie die Hälfte der Chromosomen* aus der Zelle entfernt wird. Eine jede befruchtungsfähige Geschlechtszelle enthält also nur die Hälfte der normalen Chromosomenzahl.*

W. value
Z. number d. still
g. immaterial e. z. s. it is shown
b. with k. constant (one) (Note absence of noun.)
M. human

L. organism c. which is characteristic
(why which?) B. fertilization
v. are combined (Why are?) Why Rule 10?
w. would be (See App. 28, 2e.)
v. present
b. conceal, harbor d. double

b. would get (Note App. 28, 2, 3.)
b. already v. four-fold Why Rule 10?
e. enter in t. actually
e. attained W. way E. contrivance b. exist
b. causes V. union
h. reduced H. half
i. always b. preserved f. si. is found
E. arrangement b. consist
T. division d. pass through
b. capable of fertilization
d. whose v. proceeds d. s. thru it
e. removed b. fertilizable
e. contains

Nun fragt es sich, ob nicht bei der Entfernung der halben Chromosomenzahl die Erbmasse[4] eine Beeinträchtigung erfährt. Wir hörten, dass eine jede befruchtungsbedürftige Geschlechtszelle, Ei oder Samenzelle tierischer oder pflanzlicher Natur (im Pflanzenreich sind[6] vielfach die hier behandelten Prozessse durch den eigenartigen Generationswechsel nicht direkt mit der Geschlechtszellenbildung verknüpft, was[5] aber keine prinzipielle Anderung bedingt), bevor sie* befruchtungsfähig wird) eine zweimalige Teilung erfährt. Diese Reifeteilungen sind es, die* auf das engste mit der Halbierung der Chromosomenzahl zusammenhängen, und auf sie muss* sich daher die Aufmerksamkeit konzentrieren, wenn obige Frage* beantwortet werden soll.

f. s. is asked E. removal
B. impairment
e. undergoes b. fertilization-needy, wanting
E. ovum S. sperm cell
P. plant kingdom
b. treated e. peculiar
G. sex cell formation
v. connected b. stipulates
b. capable of fecundation
R. maturation divisions
z. (hang together) depend, are connected
m. s. k. must be concentrated (See also App. 11, 4.) s. is to

Nun zeigt es sich, dass aber bereits im Beginn dieser Teilungen in der mitotischen Figur nur die Hälfte der[3] der Art zukommenden Chromotinelemente sichtbar war: die Elemente unterschieden sich allerdings deutlich von gewöhnlichen Chromosomen durch den Aufbau aus mehreren Teilstücken.* Man nennt sie wegen einer besonders typisch auftretenden Vierteilung Tetraden.* Ihre Entstehung muss* somit erst klar sein, ehe ihre Verteilung bei den Reifeteilungen verstanden werden kann.

b. already
T. divisions
z. which belongs to s. visible
a. of course g. ordinary
A. structure T. fragments
n. calls w. because a. appearing
E. origin
e. before V. distribution

VERERBUNG VON SEKUNDÄREN GESCHLECHTSCHARAKTEREN

(Pivot nouns are bold-faced on this page; indicate what rules remove elements on the right side of these nouns.)

Unter den Einzelfragen des **Sexualproblems,** deren **Besprechung** wir uns zuwenden, schliesst sich dem vorhergehenden am nächsten das Problem der Vererbung der sekundären **Geschlechtscharaktere** an. Wir haben mancherlei über sie erfahren, müssen sie nun aber im **Zusammenhang** betrachten.

B. discussion z. turn to What goes with "schliessen"? v. preceding
V. inheritance
e. learned m. many things
b. consider Z. connection, context

Es scheint angebracht, uns zunächst einmal darüber klar zu werden, was dies Problem bedeutet.[10] Erinnern wir uns einmal an die Tatsachen der geschlechtsbegrenzten **Vererbung.** Da hatten wir **Eigenschaften** kennen gelernt, die in bestimmter Beziehung zum **Geschlecht** vererbt wurden. Die Analyse hatte uns dann gezeigt, was das bedeutete; es bedeutete das Vorhandensein gewöhnlicher mendelnder **Merkmale,** die durch ihre Lage im X-Chromosom mit in den Mechanismus der **Geschlechtsverteilung** hineingezwungen werden. Sie hatten also mit dem **Geschlecht** selbst ebensowenig zu tun, wie ein Passagier in einem Zug mit der Dampfspannung, die die **Lokomotive** treibt.[10] Vergleichen wir damit nun aber die sekundären **Geschlechtscharaktere.** Die Tatsachen der Intersexualität haben uns gezeigt, dass ein jedes Individuum imstande ist, die Charaktere eines jeden **Geschlechts** zur Entwickelung zu bringen: was sich entwickelt, wird ausschliesslich durch die Wirkung der lokalisierten oder nichtlokalisierten (Insekten und Wirbeltiere) Hormone der definitiven **Gestaltung** bestimmt. Die Erbanlagen sind somit für beide **Geschlechter** völlig identisch.

a. appropriate (to what?) z. first
z. w. become b. means E. w. let us remind
e. first g. sex limited
d. then (App. 25, 1) k. to know
d. which (Why which?) B. relation
g. shown d. that b. means
V. existence g. usual
M. characteristics m. conjointly
h. forced in G. sex distribution
s. itself If in doubt, indicate the number of the rules which "pull" the verbs from the end position.
D. steam power
V. w. let us compare (Note the absence of the "so".) T. facts i. in a position (to what?)
Why do you pick up "Entwickelung" with the verb?
s. e. is developed a. exclusively
W. vertebrates
G. form, formation E. hereditary tendencies
v. completely

Aber gewisse Differenzierungs- und Wachstumsvorgänge sind so beschaffen, dass sie durch die Einwirkung spezifischer Hormone in die eine oder andere **Richtung** gedrängt werden können. Dies aber ist nichts Besonderes sondern eine **Tatsache,** die für jeden morphogenetischen **Prozess** gilt. Denn wir wissen z. B. dass das Fehlen der Schilddrüsenhormone einen missgestalteten, verzwergten **Kretin** hervorrufen kann, der sicher von der Venus von **Milo** quantitativ nicht weniger verschieden ist, als vielfach die beiden **Geschlechter.** Wir wissen, dass die Bienen imstande sind, durch chemische Veränderungen im Futterbrei, die wir auch als hormonisch bezeichnen können, aus der gleichen Larve eine Arbeiterin oder Königin mit all ihren morphologischen und physiologischen **Differenzen** heranzuziehen.

g. certain W. growth processes
b. constituted What does "sie" call for?
R. direction
g. crowded b. special T. fact
g. holds F. absence, lack
S. thyroid gland hormone m. misshaped
verz. stunted K. cretin
What calls for "ist"? How far back do you then go? v. frequently
i. able (to what?) V. changes
b. designate g. same
h. bring into play, attract
What calls for the "zu" verb? Did you "flag" it?

Wenn also theoretisch eine jede morphologische oder physiologische Eigenschaft eines Tieres unter dem Einfluss der Geschlechtshormone in männlichen und weiblichen **Typus** ausdifferenziert werden kann, so besagt das nicht, dass es entsprechend viele sekundäre **Geschlechtscharaktere** gibt, deren Vererbung zu studieren ist, sondern dass die ererbten Eigenschaften mit zwei Sorten von Hormonen zwei verschiedene **Reaktionen** eingehen können. Ein sekündärer Geschlechtscharakter ist also ein **Charakter,** der in seiner Morpho- oder Physiogenese von den spezifischen männlichen und weiblichen **Hormonen** verschieden beeinflusst werden kann. (Tandler hat dies vor allem stets hervorgehoben). Es folgt daraus, dass für den normalen Geschlechtsmorphismus ein Problem der Vererbung der sekundären Geschlechtscharaktere nicht existiert; ihre identische Grundlage ist die Gesamtheit der Erbcharaktere und ihre Divergenz ist das Produkt der spezifischen **Hormonenreaktion.** Es gibt ein Erbproblem somit nur für die **Hormonenproduktion** und dessen Lösung ist uns bereits bekannt.

a. therefore
E. quality, attribute T. animal
E. influence
b. claims, states
e. correspondingly e. g. there are
z. s. i. is to be studied (App. 12. 1)
v. different
e. enter in G. sex character
a. hence
w. female
v. differently b. influenced
h. emphasized d. therefrom
V. heredity
G. basis G. totality
E. heredity problem s. therefore
d. its (App. 22, 4)

Nun gibt es natürlich **Erbprobleme,** die sich auf **Körpereigenschaften** beziehen, die imstande sind, mit den **Geschlechtshormonen** zu reagieren und[8] daher als sekundäre **Geschlechtscharaktere** unterschieden werden. In einem solchen Falle handelt es sich darum, die **Frage** zu unterscheiden, wie die betreffenden Eigenschaften vererbt werden, von der **Frage,** wie das Endresultat nach der **Hormonenwirkung** aussieht. Solche Probleme sind nun gegeben, wenn Formen mit verschiedenen sekundären **Charakteren** gekreuzt werden, oder wenn bei einer sexuell dimorphen Form Mutationen auftreten, die nur sichtbar werden können, wenn die eine der Hormonenwirkungen einsetzt, also unisexueller Polymorphismus vorliegt. Von derartigen Erscheinungen werden wir im folgenden zu sprechen haben. Als die einfachsten Fälle bieten sich da zunächst wieder die **Objekte** dar, bei denen keine innersekretorische Funktion der Geschlechtsdrüsen vorliegt, also die **Insekten.** Und zwar betrachten wir zuerst normale **Vererbungsfälle,** denen sich später als wichtige Ergänzung der **Gynandromorphismus** anschliessen wird.

E. hereditary problems
s. b. relate (to) K. physical qualities
Note Rule 8. u. w. are distinguished
h. e. s. (it deals with) the problem is
b. concerned E. qualities
w. how n. after
a. appears Observe constantly what rules are used to "pull" the verbs out from the end position.

e. sets in a. appear s. visible
v. exists d. such
w. h. we will (App. 7, 4)
F. cases d. are offered
b. d. in which G. sex glands
z. what is more b. consider
V. heredity cases d. to which
E. supplement a. attached
What calls for this verb?
V. experiments

VERSUCHE MIT NORMALER VERERBUNG

Formen ohne Innersekretion der Geschlechtsdrüsen

In dieser Gruppe trennen wir wieder zwei äusserlich verschiedene aber innerlich eng zusammengehörige **Gruppen,** nämlich Kreuzungen von Formen mit differenten Geschlechtscharakteren und die Erscheinung des unisexuellen **Polymorphismus.**

t. separate w. again ä. externally
v. different e. closely z. connected
K. crossings
E. phenomena
What do the nouns tell you to do?

Vererbung differenter Sexualcharaktere bei Kreuzung

Die[3] im vorhergehenden vorgetragenen Anschauungen über das Wesen der sekundären Geschlechtscharaktere lassen erwarten, dass bei Kreuzung von **Formen,** die sich in bezug auf sekundäre **Geschlechtsmerkmale** unterscheiden, irgendeine Form Mendelscher Vererbung gefunden wird, die sich nur dadurch von gewöhnlichen **Fällen** unterscheidet, dass die Mendelschen Kombinationen nur in dem einen **Geschlecht** sichtbar werden können, also geschlechtskontrolliert sind. Wir können z. B. so einen Versuch an den **Schwammspinnerrassen** durchführen, von denen bei der Betrachtung der zygotischen **Intersexualität** die Rede war. So unterscheiden sich die Männchen der Rassen Hokkaido, Schneidemühl, Aamori sehr deutlich in dem sichtbarsten sekundären **Geschlechtscharakter,** der **Flügelfärbung.** Erstere sind sehr hell, die Schneidemühlmännchen mehr graubraun und die Aaomorimännchen tief schwarzbraun. Die Kreuzungen zeigen nun, dass diese Eigenschaft mendelistisch vererbt wird, selbstverständlich nur innerhalb des männlichen **Geschlechts.** Die Weibchen aber vererben die betreffenden Charaktere genau wie die **Männchen,** sie können sie bloss selbst nicht zeigen, weil die weiblichen Hormone überhaupt keine **Flügelfärbung** zustande kommen lassen. Die Richtigkeit dieses Satzes lässt sich nun hier direkt zeigen: wenn bei geeigneter Kreuzung solche Weibchen intersexuell werden, dann zeigen sie genau den Typus der **Flügelfärbung,** wie er den Männchen der betreffenden **Kreuzung** zukommt. Wenn aber unter den Männchen der betreffenden Kombination eine Spaltung in Typen der **Flügelfärbung** eintritt, so finden wir genau die gleiche Spaltung bei den intersexuellen **Weibchen.**

What rules do you use to "remove" verbs from the end position?
d. the Why Rule 3? vorg. which was presented
W. nature i. b. a. in regard to
s. u. are distinguished i. any
d. thereby g. ordinary
S. w. become visible (App. 7, 3)
g. sex-controlled
S. gypsy moth d. carry out
v. d. of which (Note how this removes the verb.)
R. the discussion (What permits you to pick up this noun?) F. wing coloring E. the former

s. dark brown
E. attribute
s. of coursee i. within
v. treatment g. precisely
b. merely s. themselves
w. female
z. about (let develop)
l. s. z. can be shown
g. exactly
F. wing coloration
z. belongs b. concerned
S. splitting
g. same

PARTHENOGENESE UND GESCHLECHT—Goldschmidt

Zu den bekanntesten Erscheinungen der Sexualität gehören die Beziehungen zwischen Parthenogenese und Geschlecht, die bei manchen Tiergruppen den auffallendsten und meist diskutierten Teil ihrer Biologie bilden. Eine jede Lösung des Geschlechtsproblems sollte daher auch eine genügende Erklärung jener Erscheinungen liefern, ja[8] teilweise an ihnen ihren Prüfstein finden. Tatsächlich lassen die Erscheinungen sich vollständig in unsere vorher gewonnenen Erkenntnisse einordnen, wie[8] im folgenden ausgeführt ist:

b. best known E. phenomena
g. belong B. relations
G. sex (Why is "die" a relative?)
m. most discussed b. form
L. solution G. sex problem d. hence
g. satisfactory E. explanation
Why Rule 8? t. partially T. actually
s. l. can be v. completely
g. gained E. knowledge e. classified
Why Rule 8? a. stated

Parthenogenese und der Mechanismus der Geschlechtsverteilung

Wir wissen, dass der normale Mechanismus der Geschlechtsverteilung in dem Chromosomenmechanismus gegeben ist, der das quantitative Verhältnis der Geschlechtsenzyme regelt. Wenn daher im Zusammenhang mit der Parthenogenese eine besondere Verteilung der Geschlechter erfolgt, so ist dies erklärt, wenn ein entsprechender Chromosomenmechanismus sich nachweisen lässt. Wenn wir nun auf unseren früheren Erörterungen über diesen Mechanismus und seine Bedeutung fussen, so sind die Erwartungen folgende: Wir hatten stets zwischen zwei Typen unterscheiden müssen, dem mit weiblicher und dem mit männlicher Heterozygotie. Für den ersteren Fall war die Formel (F) Mm= ♀(F), (F)MM=♂; auf die Geschlechtschromosomen übertragen,[11] bedeutete es, dass die Anwesenheit von einem X-Chromosom die quantitativen Verhältnisse zugunsten der Weiblichkeit regulierte, die von 2 X-Chromosomen aber zugunsten der Männlichkeit. Umgekehrt bedingten bei männlicher Heterozygotie mit den Formeln (M)Ff= ♂und, (M)FF ♀, ein X-Chromosom männliche, zwei X-Chromosomen weibliche Entwicklung. Daraus folgt, dass, wenn Parthenogenese zur Entwicklung nur eines bestimmten Geschlechts führt, ein Mechanismus dafür sorgen muss, dass die richtige Kombination der X-Chromosomen erzielt wird. Das Vorhandensein normaler oder reduzierter Chromosomenzahl im parthenogenetischen Ei hat daher nur soweit Bedeutung, als es auch das Vorhandensein von 1 oder 2 X-Chromosomen betrifft. Es ist gut, sich darüber völlig klar zu sein, da sonst eine heillose Verwirrung entstände, angesichts der Tatsache, dass es parthenogenetische Eier gibt, die ohne Reduktion nur Weibchen liefern, solche, die mit Reduktion nur Männchen liefern usw. Betrachten wir nun von diesem Gesichtspunkt aus die hauptsächlichsten Tatsachen.

Focus your attention on the rules that aid to remove the verb from the end position. Your object is to get back to the pivot noun. V. ratio
r. regulates Z. connection
V. distribution e. takes place
e. explained e. corresponding
s. n. l. can be detected
E. discussions B. importance
E. expectations
u. distinguish d. that (App. 22, 1, c, 2)
d. that (App. 22, 1, c, 2) e. former
G. sex chromosoms
ü. when transferred (Why when?)
A. presence V. conditions z. in favor of
W. femininity
U. conversely b. caused H. heterozygosis
m. male
w. female E. development d. from that
b. certain
d. for that s. provide, care for
e. achieved, obtained V. presence
Underline the pivot nouns.
E. ovum B. importance
b. concerns
g. good (to what?) v. completely
da, since (App. 25, 2) a. in view of
e. g. there are (App. 10, 2, c)
l. furnish What calls for this verb?
B. let us consider (Why "let"?) See Rule 10.
H. chief T. facts

Parthenogenese als Mittel zur normalen Verteilung der Geschlechter

Die Hymenopteren, und unter ihnen vor allem die Biene, bilden das klassische Beispiel einer Anteilnahme der Parthenogenese am Mechanismus der Produktion beider Geschlechter. Die allgemein bekannte Grundtatsache ist, dass parthenogenetisch sich entwickelnde Bieneneier normalerweise nur Männchen, die Drohnen, liefern, befruchtete Eier dagegen Weibchen, die Arbeiterinnen und Königinnen. Die biologischen Tatsachen wie die Vererbungsexperimente haben ihre Richtigkeit erwiesen und die Zellforschung hat den Mechanismus vollständig aufgedeckt, durch den das Resultat erreicht wird.

v. a. above all
B. example A. interest, participation
b. both What do the nouns on the breaks tell you to do? b. known
B. bee eggs
l. furnish b. fertilized
d. on the other hand
T. facts V. hereditary
e. proved B. correctness Z. cell study
a. disclosed d. d. by which
e. achieved

(On this page the pivot nouns are again bold-faced. Indicate what rules are now used to remove the elements on the right side of these nouns.)

Die biologische Grundtatsache ist bekanntlich die, dass unbefruchtete oder alte Königinnen, deren Samenvorrat im **Receptaculum** erschöpft ist, drohnenbrütig sind, also[8] nur **Männchen** produzieren. Von Vererbungsexperimenten liegt nur ein einwandfrei durchgeführtes vor, das von **Newel.** Die Schwierigkeiten des Experiments bestehen natürlich darin, dass die Begattung der Königin auf dem Hochzeitsflug, also unkontrolliert, erfolgt. Ein Experiment ist also nur einwandfrei, wenn ausgeschlossen werden kann, dass andere **Drohnen,** als die beabsichtigten, zur **Begattung** kommen können, und lässt sich nur in völlig isolierter **Umgebung** durchführen. Newel konnte dies in **Texas** ausführen. Er kreuzte die gelben italienischen Bienen mit den grauen **Kärtnern.** Die Kreuzung italienische Königin + Kärtner Drohnen gab lauter gelbe F_1 **Tiere.** Gelb ist also dominant über grau im heterozygoten **Weibchen.** Die Drohnen mussten natürlich alle gelb sein, wenn parthenogenetisch erzeugt. Die reziproke Kreuzung Kärtner Königin + Italiener Drohnen ergab gelbe Arbeiterinnen und graue **Drohnen,** was ebenfalls der **Erwartung** entspricht.

d. that, this
e. exhausted d. laying only drone eggs
V. heredity experiments
v. exists d. executed (one)
S. difficulties b. consist
b. mating H. nuptial flight
e. takes place e. perfect
a. excluded, made impossible
a. then b. intended (ones)
s. l. can be v. fully U. environment
B. mating
k. crossed g. yellow
K. crossing
l. nothing but
W. female
m. had to
e. produced
A. workers
e. likewise e. corresponds What calls for this verb?

Der Mechanismus dieser Form der Geschlechtsdifferenzierung ist nun vor allem durch die Arbeiten von Petrunkewitsch, **Meves** ebenfalls bekannt. Die normale Chromosomenzahl der Bienenkönigin beträgt **32.** Ein Geschlechtschromosom ist dabei morphologisch nicht von den übrigen unterscheidbar. In jedem Ei findet die **Reifeteilung** statt und die Chromosomenzahl wird auf **16** reduziert. Wird das Ei nun befruchtet, so entwickelt es sich zu einem **Weibchen.** Wenn wir eines der elterlichen Chromosomen als **X-Chromosom** betrachten, so enthält ein solches Ei zwei **X-Chromosomen.** Wird das Ei aber nicht befruchtet, so entwickelt es sich zu einem **Männchen.**

v. a. above all
b. known
b. amounts to G. sex chromosom
d. thereby, in this case
u. distinguishable R. maturation division
What does "statt" go with?
Why should there be a "10" over wird? e. parent
b. consider e. contains
Why should there be a "10" over wird in this line?

Alle Samenzellen sind also einerlei **Art,** nämlich mit 16 Chromosomen und damit ist der **Zyklus** geschlossen. Es ist ohne weiteres klar, dass die Tatsachen völlig in den Rahmen des **uns** schon bekannten Mechanismus fallen und dass die Besonderheit nur die ist, dass die Biene zur Herstellung des Sexualverhältnisses nicht den sonst eingeschlagenen Weg der **Heterogametie** benutzt, sondern genau den gleichen Effekt in bezug auf die quantitative Kombination der Geschlechtsenzyme durch Verwendung der Parthenogenese bei Homogametie beider **Geschlechter** erzielt. Vom Standpunkt der Geschlechtsvererbungstheorie ist dies übrigens von weitgehender allgemeiner **Bedeutung.**

S. sperm cells.
n. namely d. with that
o. w. directly T. facts
v. completely R. structure b. which is known
(Why which?) n. d. only this
H. production S. sexual condition
s. otherwise e. adopted
What does "sondern" call for?
G. sex enzymes V. use
b. both
e. achieved What calls for this verb?
ü. moreover w. far going B. importance

Wollten wir nun den Fall der Biene einer mendelistischen **Symbolik** einordnen, so kämen wir in grösste **Schwierigkeiten.** Beide Geschlechter sind homogametisch, produzieren also nur eine Sorte von **Keimzellen:** aber für das Mendelschema brauchen wir eine **Heterogametie.** Anderseits ist das Männchen heterozygot, da es nur einen **Geschlechtsfaktor** hat; aber trotzdem produziert es nur einerlei **Gameten.**

Why a "10" over wollten?
e. classify k. would come (See App. 28, 2, e and discussion.)
S. type b. need, use
A. on the other hand
d. since (App. 25, 2) t. nevertheless
e. one type

Die Hereinbeziehung der Parthenogenese in den Mechanismus aber ermöglicht der Mutterbiene sozusagen die Kontrolle des **Geschlechts.** Dass diese tatsächlich ausgeübt wird und dass in der sogenannten Spermapumpe die anatomischen Vorausbedingungen dafür gegeben sind, ist allgemein bekannt.

H. inclusion
e. makes possible for
t. actually a. exerted
V. conditions d. for it
i. a. in general b. known

DIE GESCHLECHTSBESTIMMUNG BEIM MENSCHEN

(An * appears where certain rules are involved; if in doubt indicate the rules.)

Es besteht kein sachlicher Grund,* die Geschlechtsbestimmung beim Menschen getrennt von der im übrigen Tierreich zu behandeln. Es ist* nur aus sentimentalen Erwägungen gerechtfertigt, sowie auf Grund der Tatsache, dass die Verhältnisse beim Menschen* nicht oder kaum experimentell studiert werden können und* deshalb ihre Erklärung durch Vergleich mit den anderen Säugetieren finden müssen. Dazu kommt, dass das vielfach unwissenschaftliche Interesse, dass die Frage* in Beziehung auf den Menschen gefunden hat, zu den absurdesten Ideen geführt hat, die* heute noch alljährlich produziert werden, weshalb die spezielle Einordnung der Verhältnisse beim Menschen in das übrige Tatsachenmaterial nützlich erscheint. Wir wollen* es in der gleichen Reihenfolge tun, in der jenes Material* präsentiert wurde.

b. exists s. material G. basis (to what?)
G. sex determination
E. considerations
g. justified T. fact
V. conditions How far back do you go here when you pick up the verb?
S. mammals d. in addition
u. not scientific B. relation
Do not forget that "Interesse" is the subject to one of your verbs.
w. wherefore E. integration
ü. remaining n. useful
t. show R. sequence i.d. in which

Der Mechanismus der Geschlechtsverteilung

Die Aufklärung des Chromosomenmechanismus der Geschlechtsverteilung beim Menschen hat* sich als ziemlich schwierig erwiesen, da das Material,* wie auch bei einigen anderen Tiergruppen, z. B. den Vögeln, nicht günstig zu sein scheint. Die älteren Angaben,* die* die Möglichkeit von Geschlechtschromosomen nicht berücksichtigten, lauteten auf eine diploide Zahl von 24 Chromosomen beim Menschen.* Guyer, der* dann die Spermatogenese mit Rücksicht auf Geschlechtschromosomen untersuchte, fand nur 22 Chromosomen und glaubt, dass die Reifeteilungen* zwei Sorten von Spermatiden erzeugen, solche mit 10 und solche mit 12 Chromosomen.* Dem wurde* dann von Gutherz widersprochen, wie auch von allen weiteren Beobachtern.* Montgomery fand wieder 24 als Normalzahl, von denen zwei* ein XY-Paar sind. Bei den Reifeteilungen werden* diese nun in manchen Fällen so verteilt, wie es das Digametieschema[4] erfordert, und die Hälfte der Spermien enthalten 11+ X, die andere Hälfte 11+Y.* In sehr vielen Fällen ist aber die Verteilung eine andere, so dass schliesslich nicht weniger als 4—6 Arten von Spermatozoen* gebildet werden. Von dieser Darstellung weicht nun wieder vollständig die von Winiwarter ab.* Er findet als Normalzahl der Spermatogonien 47 und in den Reifeteilungen werden* zwei Sorten von Spermien gebildet, solche mit 23 und solche mit 24 Chromosomen.* Da er* ferner im Ovarium eines Foetus 48 Chromosomen findet, so hätten wir typische männliche Heterogametie mit 47 Chromosmen als männlicher, 48 als weiblicher Zahl.*

A. explanation
G. sex distribution z. rather
e. shown e. some
V. birds g. favorable
A. data M. possibility
b. considered l. pointed
M. man
R. regard
u. investigated
g. believe R. maturation division
e. produce d. that
w. contradicted
B. observers
v. d. of which (why?)
F. cases v. distributed
e. requires (it) H. half
a. other
V. distribution s. finally
w. less
D. presentation v. completely
a. deviated d. v. that of
w. are (App. 7, 5, a)
d. since (App. 25, 2)
h. would have (App. 28, 3)
Z. number

Diese ausserordentliche Differenz in den Befunden von Guyer und Montgomery einerseits, Winiwarter anderseits hat* man so zu erklären gesucht, dass erstere* Negermaterial untersuchten, letzterer Europäer, und[8] darauf hingewiesen, dass im Tier- wie im Pflanzenreich Fälle* bekannt sind, in denen nahe verwandte Rassen* sich durch Chromosomenzahlen in dem Verhältnis n: 2n unterscheiden. Man vergass dabei allerdings, dass auch Fleming und Duesberg* beim Europäer 24 als Normalzahl gefunden hatten. Die letzte Untersuchung vom Wieman ist* nun sowohl an Material von Negern wie von Weissen ausgeführt, und er findet als Normalzahl stets 24. Unter diesen ist ein XY-Paar, das* sich, wie auch sonst, durch besonderes Verhalten während der Spermatogenese auszeichnet. In der zweiten Spermatozytenteilung soll* es dann getrennt werden, und das Resultat wären weibchenbestimmende Spermien mit 11+X und männchenbestimmende mit 11+Y Chromosomen.*

a. extraordinary B. findings
e. on the one hand
e. explain
u. investigated h. pointed d. to the fact
F. cases
n. near v. related
V. ratio u. are distinguished
all. of course
U. investigation
a. carried out
N. normal number
s. otherwise V. behaviour
a. marks, designates, characterizes
g. separated
w. would be w. female determining

GESCHLECHTSBEGRENZTE VERERBUNG

(An * appears only with difficult sentences. Underline the nouns that should be bold-faced)

Wir haben gesehen, wie die Verbindung zwischen Chromosomenforschung und Mendelscher Faktorenlehre in bezug auf das Geschlecht durch die Tatsachen der geschlechtsbegrenzten Vererbung hergestellt wurde. **Auch beim Menschen sind eine ganze Reihe von geschlechtbegrenzt vererbten Charakteren bekannt, deren Analyse vollständig mit der Annahme der männlichen Heterogametie übereinstimmt. Die bekanntesten Fälle sind die der Haemophilie (Bluterkrankheit) und der Farbenblindheit. Es gehören dahin ferner die Nachtblindheit (Hemeralopie), erbliche Muskelatrophie, und sogar gewisse Anlagen, wie die Wanderlust. Die genetische Erforschung dieser Verhältnisse ist natürlich beim Menschen viel schwieriger, da sie ausschliesslich auf statistischem Material beruht, in dem vor allem die Kombination Bruder und Schwester völlig fehlt.**

w. how V. combination
C. Chromosom study F. factor theory
i. b. a. in regard to T. facts
g. sex limited V. inheritance
h. produced R. series
What calls for "bekannt"? d. whose
A. assumption ü. agrees
b. best known F. cases d. d. those of
F. color blindness E. there (App. 10, 1, d)
d. thereto f. further N. night-blindness
e. hereditary s. even g. certain
E. study V. conditions
s. more difficult d. since
a. exclusively b. depends i. d. in which (why?)
f. is lacking

Eine Schwierigkeit ist ferner dadurch gegeben, dass vielfach Krankheiten und Abnormitäten, die identisch erscheinen, verschiedenartig vererbt werden. So gibt es eine geschlechtsbegrenzte Hypospadie und eine direkt dominant vererbte; geschlechtsbegrenzte Farbenblindheit und vielleicht mehrere andere Typen. Allerdings ist das nicht ohne Analogie im Tierreich: so gibt es bei Insekten dominant vererbten Melanismus und geschlechtsbegrenzt vererbten. Aber bei dem Stammbaummaterial vom Menschen bedeutet es eine grössere Schwierigkeit. Immerhin gibt es genügend Fälle, die völlig klar sind.

S. difficulty d. by the fact
What calls for "werden"? "erscheinen"?
v. inherited g. e. there is
g. sex limited
v. inherited one
v. perhaps m. several a. of course
T. animal kingdom
M. excessive pigmentation
S. ancestral material
b. means S. difficulty i. at any rate
g. sufficiently v. fully

Als Beispiel diene die Bluterkrankheit, also die erbliche Abnormität des unstillbaren Blutens von Wunden. Die Krankheit tritt nur im männlichen Geschlecht auf und überspringt in der Vererbung eine Generation. Heiratet ein kranker Mann eine gesunde Frau, so sind alle Kinder gesund. Auch die Nachkommen der Söhne bleiben gesund. Dagegen sind die Hälfte der Söhne der scheinbar gesunden Töchter wieder krank. Die nur bei den Männern manifeste Krankheit wird also nur durch scheinbar gesunde Frauen übertragen. In Fig. 108 ist der berühmte Stammbaum der Bluterfamilie Mampel wiedergegeben, die kranken Individuen schwarz, und ein Blick darauf zeigt, wie die Vererbung hier arbeitet.

B. example d. let serve (App. 28, 1)
u. unstoppable B. bleeding W. wounds
What does "auf" go with? m. male
ü. skips Why Rule 10 here? H. marries
g. healthy How does the "so" help you?
N. offspring
D. on the other hand H. half s. apparently
T. daughters What does "die" call for? Why do you say "which is manifested"?
ü. carried over w. reproduced
B. glance V. heredity
a. works

Wir haben früher ausführlich erörtert, wie die geschlechtsbegrenzte Vererbung völlig erklärt wird, durch die Annahme, dass der Faktor für die betreffenden Charaktere im X-Chromosom enthalten ist. Wie zu erwarten, trifft dies auch für den Menschen zu, wie nochmals an Wilsons Schema Fig. 109 erläutert sei. **Es ist dabei angenommen, dass das heterogametische männliche Geschlecht nur ein X Chromosom besitzt, das homogametische weibliche deren zwei. Falls es richtig ist, dass ersteres X und Y enthält, so muss an Stelle des Strichs, der kein X bedeutet, ein Y gesetzt werden. Wir können nun das den Krankheitsfaktor tragende X Chromosom in Kürze das kranke X-Chromosom nennen. Der Krankheitsfaktor ist aber recessiv. Da das X-Chromosom des Mannes keinen Partner hat, so muss natürlich ein Mann mit einem kranken X Chromosom auch immer manifest krank sein.**

e. discussed a. extensively
g. sex limited V. heredity
A. assumption b. concerned
e. contained e. expect What goes with "trifft"?
n. once more
e. illustrated a. assumed
m. male
b. possesses d. of them
F. in case e. contains
S. place S. dash
What does "das" call for?
t. which carries K. brevity d. since
n. call
What does "muss" call for? Then how far back do you go?

BAKTERIOLOGIE UND CHEMIE

CHEMIE DER BAKTERIENZELLE†

Die chemische Erforschung des Bakterienleibes bietet dem **Untersucher** die allergrössten **Schwierigkeiten,**[1] da nicht nur die **Gewinnung** des nötigen Materials[4] für genaue quantitative **Analysen durchaus** nicht leicht, sondern auch die Reinigung desselben **von den anhaftenden** Nährbodenbestandteilen[4] ohne Verluste an **Zellenbestandteilen** sozusagen unmöglich ist. Ausserdem ist[6] die **Zusammensetzung** der Bakterien von ihrem Alter und ihrem **momentanen Entwicklungszustand** abhängig. Deshalb ist[6] es für **die exakte chemische Erforschung** äusserst notwendig,[7] möglichst **gleichaltrige Individuen** zur Analyse heranzuziehen. Dieser **Forderung** können[6] aber die makrochemischen **Methoden** nur **wenig gerecht werden.** Selbst die[3] zwischen den Makro- und **Mikromethoden** liegenden Arbeitsweisen leiden teilweise unter der **gleichen** Schwierigkeit.[1] Man erhält immer nur Durchschnitts**werte,**[1] **die**[5] aber hinsichtlich des Wassergehaltes, der Trocken**substanz** und der Elementarzusammensetzung der ganzen **Zellen**[9] einen wertvollen Eindruck gewähren.

E. study B. bacteria body
U. investigator a. very greatest
d. since G. obtaining n. necessary
d. at all Note the call for "ist."
l. easy s. but R. purifying
a. adhering N. food constituents V. loss
Z. cell constituents u. impossible
A. besides Z. composition
Al. age E. developmental state a. dependent
d. therefore E. study
ä. extremely n. necessary (to what?)
h. to draw on, take F. requirement
g. w. satisfy Note position of subject
S. even See App. 13-2a
l. which lie (Why which?) A. work methods
S. difficulty e. obtains D. average values
h. with regard to W. water content
E. elementary composition
g. entire cell Note use of Rule 9.
g. afford E. impression

WASSERGEHALT DER BAKTERIENZELLE

Der Bakterienleib ist ausserordentlich wasserreich.[1] Das **Wasser spielt ja auch** als Lösungsmittel für die Bau— und Betriebsstoffe **der Zelle die allergrösste Rolle.**[1] Die Bakterien **sind**[6] **überhaupt für das Leben im Wasser** oder zumindest in sehr **wasserreichen Substraten** besonders angepasst, was[5] sich natur**gemäss auch** in einem grösseren Wasserreichtum des Zytoplasmas **und der Zellwand** widerspiegeln muss. Der Wassergehalt der **einzelnen Bakterienarten zeigt** gewöhnlich nur geringe **Unterschiede,** wie[8] aus den wenigen älteren und neueren **Bestimmungen zu entnehmen ist.** In der folgenden Tabelle ist[6] darüber eine **Reihe von Daten zusammengestellt.**

B. bacteria body a. extraordinarily
w. rich in water L. solvent
Ba. nutrient Be. fuel a. very greatest
ü. on the whole
z. at least a. adapted What calls for this word?
n. naturally See App. 16,1.
W. wealth of water
Z. cell wall w. reflect
z. shows g. ordinarily
g. slight U. differences w. as See discussion of Rule 8, c.
B. determinations z. e. is to be derived See App. 12, 1.
z. compiled

Schon aus dieser Zusammenstellung ist ersichtlich, dass der Wassergehalt der Bakterien[4] ein sehr hoher ist. Im allgemeinen fällt er mit zunehmendem Alter der **Kultur.**[1] Aber auch bei einer und derselben Art schwankt derselbe bei Anwendung verschiedener Kulturbedingungen.[1]

Z. table, compilation
e. visible, apparent W. water content
h. high one i. a. in general
z. increasing A. age
s. vary A. application v. different
K. culture conditions

Über den Wassergehalt von Sporen liegen nur wenige **Bestimmungen vor.**[2] Drymont hat[6] denselben von Milzbrandsporen mit 85,4% festgestellt. Diese Angabe dürfte[6] kaum der Wirklichkeit entsprechen, da die[3] in den zerfallenen und stark verquollenen Resten des **Sporangiums** eingebetteten Sporen gewiss nicht allein zur **Bestimmung** gekommen und gerade die Nebenbestandteile[4] ganz besonders wasserreich sind. Nach den Bestimmungen des spezifischen **Gewichtes,**[1] die Almquist[4] mit den **Heubazillensporen machte,** ist[6] ein sehr viel geringerer Wassergehalt der **Dauerformen** anzunehmen.

W. water content
B. determinations, provisions v. exist
f. established M. anthrax spores
A. statement, estimate e. correspond
z. decomposed v. swollen, warped
e. which are imbedded Why which?
B. determination Note abs. of auxiliary.
N. secondary components n. according to
G. weight
H. hay bacillus
g. slight D. permanent forms
a. to be assumed See App. 12,1.

†F. Fuhrmann, Einführung in die Grundlagen der technischen Mykologie

TROCKENSUBSTANZ DER BAKTERIENZELLE

Die Trockensubstanz setzt sich aus einem organischen und anorganischen oder mineralischen **Anteile** zusammen.[2] Sowohl das Mengenverhältnis als auch die Zusammensetzung beider Anteile weisen bei den verschiedenen Bakterien **Unterschiede** auf.[2] Die gesamte Trockensubstanz, also organischer und mineralischer Teil,[1] ist[6] ebenfalls sowohl bei den einzelnen Bakterienarten als auch bei einer und derselben **Art** verschieden. Im letzteren Falle gehen die Unterschiede in erster Linie auf die Zusammensetzung des verwendeten **Nährbodens** zurück.[2] Anderseits verursachen Verschiedenheiten die Züchtungsdauer also das Alter der[3] zur **Untersuchung** verwendeten Kulturen und die **Züchtungstemperatur.**[1]

s. s. z. is composed (See App. 11, 4a, b.)
A. part
M. quantity ratio Z. composition
b. both v. different
U. differences g. total
T. part e. likewise
e. individual B. bacteria-type i.l.F. in the latter case
v. different See Rule 6 E 1, 2, 6.
U. differences
v. used N. substratum A. otherwise
v. cause Note that subject follows the verb
Z. culture period (This is the subject!)
Z. culture temperature v. which were used

Cramer stellte diesbezügliche Untersuchungen mit dem Bazillus prodigiosus, einer weitverbreiteten kurzen **Stäbchenbakterie an.**[2] Bei gleicher Temperatur und Züchtungsdauer erhält man verschiedene Werte für die Trockensubstanz bei Verwendung verschiedener **Nährsubstrate,** wie beispielsweise gelben Rüben und **Kartoffeln.** Das Mengenverhältnis zwischen organischen und anorganischen Anteilen in der Trockensubstanz wird[6] durch dieselben **Umstände** ebenfalls wesentlich beeinflusst.

d. related thereto
U. investigations w. widespread
S. rod bacteria Note Rule 2.
Z. culture period v. different
W. values V. use, application
N. foods b. for example g. R. carrots
K. potatoes M. quantity ratio
A. portions w. is (See App. 7, 5, a.)
U. circumstances w. essentially

Aus den Untersuchungen von Cramer ist[6] zu entnehmen, dass die Zucht dieser Bakterienart auf der gelben Rübe[4] die Menge der Trockensubstanz fast auf die **Hälfte** herunterdrückt, gegenüber der[3] bei der Züchtung auf **Kartoffeln** erhaltenen Menge.[10] Vergleicht man den Wassergehalt beider Nährsubtrate, so findet man für die Kartoffel einen solchen von 75% im **Mittel,** für die gelbe Rübe einen solchen von 87% im **Mittel.**[1] Es liegt der **Gedanke** nahe,[2-7] mit einer gewissen Berechtigung den **Schluss** zu ziehen, dass diese Bakterien[4] und vielleicht die Bakterien überhaupt bei vermehrtem Wassergehalt des Nährsubstrates eine Verminderung ihrer **Trockensubstanz** erfahren. Weiter ist ersichtlich, dass eine erhöhte Züchtungstemperatur[4] ebenfalls zu einer Zunahme der **Trockensubstanz** führt, während eine verlängerte Züchtungsdauer dieselbe herabsetzt.

b. influenced
e. to be derived (See App. 12, 1.) g. R. carrots
H. half h. reduced g. opposite
e. which is obtained (Why which?)
V. if one compares (Why if?)
M. average
g. yellow
n. l. it suggests itself (to what?)
Note use of "es". See App. 10, 1, a-e.
ü. in general v. increased
V. diminution, reduction
e. undergo e. apparent
e. increased Z. culture temperature
Z. increase w. while v. increased
h. reduces

Die mineralische Trockensubstanz

Die mineralische Trockensubstanz oder der Aschegehalt der Bakterien ist verschieden bei verschiedenen **Arten**[1] und schwankt bei den Kulturen einer und derselben **Art.** Der Aschegehalt ist häuptsächlich abhängig von demjenigen des **Nährsubstrates,**[1] wie folgende[3] aus Krauses **Mikrobiologie** entnommene Zahlen[4] nach den Untersuchungen Cramers an **Choleravibrionen** es dartun. Man sieht sofort, dass mit steigendem Aschegehalt des Nährsubstrates auch ein Ansteigen des Aschegehaltes der[3] darin wachsenden Bakterien sich einstellt. Die Zunahme der Asche erfolgt bei diesem Beispiel fast streng gesetzmässig mit derjenigen der Asche des **Nährbodens.**[1]

A. ash content v. different
s. vary The number for rule 1 will be gradually left off. h. mainly
a. dependent on d. that
f. following (Rule 3)
U. investigations
d. show s. immediately s. rising
A. increase A. ash content
w. which grow e. sets in
Z. increase e. take place B. example
g. uniformly N. nutrient base

Im allgemeinen ist der Aschegehalt der Bakterientrockensubstanz keine konstante **Grösse.**[1] So finden wir nach den Angaben von Hammerschlag für Tuberkulosebakterien einen Aschegehalt von 8%.[1] Cramer gibt für Choleravibrionen einen Aschegehalt von 8-30% der **Trockensubstanz** an.[2]

A. ash content
G. size, magnitude
A. estimates, statements
What goes with "gibt"?
T. dry substance

ENZYME (FERMENTE)

Unter Enzymen oder Fermenten verstehen wir eine[3] von einer lebenden **Zelle** gebildete **Substanz,** die,[5] ohne[7] in das Endprodukt der Reaktion **selbst** einzutreten, die Geschwindigkeit **derselben** vergrössert oder[8] gegebenenfalls verkleinert. Dabei vollzieht sich diese Wirkung ohne irgendwelchen Einfluss von seiten der Lebensvorgänge der Zelle selbst.[1] Damit sind[6] die Enzyme in die Kategorie der **Katalysatoren** eingereiht oder[8] vielleicht denselben untergeordnet.

v. understand, mean
g. which is formed (Why which?)
o. without (See Rule 7 C, 1, 2.)
G. velocity v. enlarges g. in a given case
v. diminishes v. s. is accomplished
(See App. 11, 4, a.)
Z. cell s. itself (See App. 13, 1a.)
e. classified v. perhaps
u. subordinated

Kein Enzym wurde[6] bisher als chemisches **Individuum** rein dargestellt oder gewonnen. Aus allen ihren Wirkungen und ihrem Auftreten ist[6] aber der **Schluss** berechtigt, dass sie[4] kolloidale **Natur** besitzen. In dieser Hinsicht haben sie gemeinsame Eigenschaften mit **Eiweisskörpern,**[1] ohne[7] selbst solche zu sein. Je reiner sie[4] in der **Tat** hergestellt werden, um so mehr verlieren sie die Eigenschaften echter **Eiweisskörper** und geben dann auch keine Eiweissreaktionen mehr.[1]

w. was (See App. 7, 5, b.)
d. produced g. obtained
W. effect A. appearance
b. justified S. conclusion b. possess
H. respect g. common E. properties
E. protein bodies o. See Rule 7, c, 1.
je-umso (App. 26, 2,a) h. produced
v. lose E. attributes e. genuine
k. m. no more

Mit Ausnahme der echten Lipasen sind alle Enzyme in Wasser sehr leicht löslich und leicht löslich in verdünnten **Salzlösungen.**[1] Es handelt sich hier um Scheinlösungen eines **Emulsionskolloides.** Die Enzyme werden[6] durch starken Alkohol, wenn auch nicht quantitativ, gefällt. Auch Ammonsulfat fällt in gesättigter Lösung die **Enzyme.**[1] Feine Niederschläge und Eiweissfällungen reissen die **Enzyme** ebenfalls mit.[2]

A. exception L. enzyme prec. fats
l. soluble le. easily
v. dilute S. salt solutions Note Rule 1.
h. s. um it deals with S. false sol.
w. are (App. 7, 5, a) w. a. even if
g. precipitated f. precipitates
ges. saturated N. precipitates
E. protein precipitations m. carry along

Die Enzyme werden[6] bei der **Dialyse** teils zurückgehalten, teils gehen sie durch die **Membranen** hindurch.[2] Von grossem Einfluss auf die Durchlässigkeit ist die Membran.[1] In dieser Hinsicht verhalten sich die Enzyme aber sehr verschieden.[1]

t. partly w. are (See App. 7, 5, a.)
What goes with "gehen"?
E. influence D. permeability
H. respect v. behave
v. differently

Alle Enzyme besitzen in hohem Grade die Fähigkeit,[7] sich an feste **Körper** zu binden oder zu adsorbieren. Hier ist[6] nun eine Adsorption auf mechanischem **Wege** anzunehmen und eine solche infolge eines bestimmten elektrischen **Ladungssinnes.** Vielfach werden[6] beide Ursachen zusammenwirken, wie beispielsweise bei der Adsorption der Enzyme an **Kohleteilchen.**[1] Die Beeinflussung der Adsorption durch den elektrischen Ladungszustand sehen wir sehr schön, wenn wir[4] als Adsorbens Kaolin und **Tonerde** verwenden. An dem anodisch wandernden Kaolin werden[6] nur Basen, an der kathodisch wandernden Tonerde nur **Säuren** gebunden. Das Enzym 'Invertase' wird[6] nun nur von der **Tonerde** gebunden, einerlei, welche Reaktion das Lösungsmittel aufweist, vom Kaolin aber niemals.[1] Es besitzt dieses Enzym also einen ausgesprochenen **Säurecharakter.**[1] Anders liegt die Sache bei den meisten anderen Enzymen,[1] die[5] bei dieser Prüfung einen amphoteren **Charakter** aufweisen, wie die **Eiweisskörper.** Bei ihnen wechselt die Adsorption mit der Reaktion des **Lösungsmittels.**[1]

b. possess G. degree
F. ability (to what?) f. solid
i. a. is to be assumed (App. 12, 1, a, b, c)
i. as result of b. certain L. charging sense
w. will (See App. 7, 4, 2.) b. for example
K. carbon particles B. influence
L. charge state
T. clay earth, aluminum oxide w. is (App. 7, 5, a)
v. use w. are (App. 7, 5, a)

e. immaterial L. solvent
a. shows n. never E. b. d. See App. 10, 1, a, b;
This Enz. possesses
S. matter b. in the case of
P. test a. show
b. i. in them, in the case of them (See App. 18.)
L. solvent

Entsprechend der Definition der Enzyme haben wir ihre **Wirkung** als katalytisch anzusehen. Die Gesetze, nach denen diese erfolgt, decken sich auch mit jenen, die wir[4] von den **Katalysatoren** kennen. Allen katalytischen Vorgängen ist[6] die **Eigentümlichkeit** gemeinsam, dass spontan verlaufende Reaktionen[4] durch Zutun eines Katalysators in ihrer **Geschwindigkeit** eine Änderung[9] erfahren.

E. corresponding to
W. effect a. regard G. laws
n. d. according to which d. s. coincide
k. know a. to all
V. processes g. common E. peculiarity
v. proceeding Z. aid, help
A. change (Note Rule 9.)
e. undergo

Es wird[6] also die **Reaktionsgeschwindigkeit** geändert, entweder beschleunigt oder verzögert. Bei den Enzymen tritt die Beschleunigung oder positive **Katalyse**[9] in den Vordergrund. Weder das Enzym noch der Katalysator sind[6] dabei an eines der entstehenden **Endprodukte** gebunden.

e. there (See App. 10, 1a, c.) R. r-speed
e. either b. accelerated v. retarded
t. i. d. V. steps into the foreground
B. acceleration W. n. neither, nor
e. arising Note Rule 6.

Die Enzyme vermögen[6] ebensowenig eine **Reaktion** auszulösen wie die **Katalysatoren.** Sie ändern, wie schon gesagt, nur die Reaktionsgeschwindigkeit von[3] in **Gang** befindlichen Reaktionen, die[5] ohne ihr Zutun in vielen Fällen in fast unmessbar langer Zeit[9] einen **Endzustand** erreichen würden. Niemals führen Enzyme einer Reaktion **Energie zu.**[2]

v. are able (to what?) Note verb before "wie".
a. induce See Rule 7, F, 1, 2. ä. change
Note Rule 3. "von in" cannot be consecutive.
b. which are found
F. cases u. immeasurably E. end state
e. reach n. never
z. supply, furnish

Nach van Hoff können[6] aber nur solche **Vorgänge** freiwillig eintreten, bei denen **Arbeit**[4] **geleistet wird.** Auch nur sie können[6] deshalb enzymatisch bzw. katalytisch beschleunigt werden. Im allgemeinen wird[6] bei allen exothermisch verlaufenden **Prozessen** Arbeit[9] geleistet, doch wurden[6] auch endothermisch verlaufende **Vorgänge** bekannt, die[5] sich unter Leistung von **Arbeit** abspielen. Allgemein begünstigen hohe Temperaturen das freiwillige Eintreten von endotherm verlaufenden **Vorgängen,**[1] niedrige Temperaturen dasjenige von exothermen **Vorgängen.**[1] Damit hängt die endgültige **Gleichgewichtseinstellung** zusammen.[2]

N. according to V. processes
f. voluntarily e. occur, enter in g. performed
b. or, respectively d. therefore
w. is (See App, 7, 5, a.)
v. proceeding A. work (Note Rule 9.)
w. became (App. 7, 3, b)
b. known s. a. take place L. perfomance
a. generally g. favor
E. beginning V. reaction Note Rule 1
n. low d. that (See App. 14, 2.)
D. with that e. ultimate G. equilibrium adjustment z. is associated, hangs together

Bei allen Reaktionen,[1] die[5] ohne **Wärmeänderungen** verlaufen, erfolgt die Einstellung des Gleichgewichtszustandes nach dem Gesetze von Guldberg und **Waage,**[1] ist also allein abhängig von der relativen Konzentration der einzelnen Teilverbindungen des reagierenden **Gemisches.**[1] Dabei ist es ohne **Belang,** bei welcher Temperatur die Reaktion[4] vor sich geht, denn diese kann[6] nur auf die **Geschwindigkeit** einwirken.

W. heat changes
v. occur, proceed e. takes place
n. according to G. law
a. alone abh. dependent
T. partial compounds G. mixture
B. importance
v. s. g. goes on
G. velocity e. act, influence

Sobald es[4] sich aber um Vorgänge mit **Wärmeumsetzungen** handelt, wird[6] die Temperatur, bei der[5] die **Umsetzungen** erfolgen, einen wesentlichen Einfluss auf den **Endzustand** ausüben. Bei gewöhnlicher Temperatur exotherm verlaufende **Vorgänge,**[1] die[5] keinen **Gleichgewichtszustand** erkennen lassen, können[6] bei sehr hohen Temperaturen entgegengesetzte endotherme **Reaktionen** eingehen, so dass auf diese Weise ebenfalls ein Gleichgewichts**zustand**[4] hergestellt wird, der[5] bei niederer Temperatur aber wegen des unmessbar langsamen Verlaufes der entgegengesetzten **Reaktion** nicht merklich vorhanden ist. Dieselben müssen[6] dennoch katalytisch beschleunigt werden können.

e. h. s. um it deals with W. heat changes
w. will See App. 7, 4, 1.
U. transformations e. take place
a. exert g. usual
G. state of equilibrium
e. recognize l. let
e. enter in
a. d. w. in this way e. likewise
h. brought about, produced Note Rule 5.
w. because of u. immeasurably l. slow
e. opposite m. noticeably v. present
b. accelerated How far do you go back in this line?

Es ist demnach eine theoretische **Forderung,**[1] dass die enzymatisch beschleunigten Reaktionen[4] auch umkehrbar oder reversibel sind. In der Tat erfüllen die Enzyme diese **Forderung,**[1] wie[8] aus mehreren **Untersuchungen** hervorgeht. Mit Hilfe der Enzyme können[6] also auch Synthesen ausgeführt werden, was[5] für die Wirkung der[3] ausschliesslich in der **Zelle** tätigen Enzyme beim **Aufbau der Leibessubstanz**[9] von der grössten Bedeutung ist.

d. accordingly F. requirement
b. accelerated
e. fulfill
Note how "wie" calls for the verb.
h. follows H. aid k. can be carried out (See App. 7, 6, a, b.) W. effect
a. exclusively t. which are active
A. synthesis L. body substance
B. important Note Rule 9.

PHYSIOLOGIE DER BAKTERIENERNÄHRUNG

Das Leben und Wachstum besteht auch in der einfachsten Form in einem ständigen Zerfall und Aufbau der lebendigen **Substanz,**[1] des eigentlichen Trägers des **Lebens.**[1] Dieser ständige Stoffaustausch kann[6] aber nur dann stattfinden, wenn diejenigen Verbindungen, aus denen[5] sich das Zytoplasma, bzw. die ganze **Zelle** aufbaut, in genügender und auch passender Form zur Verfügung[9] stehen. Die[3] in der **Nahrung** dargereichten Nahrungsstoffe allein können[6] wohl den Verbrauch an lebender Substanz in chemischem **Sinne** decken; sie könnten[6] aber gleichzeitig auch die[3] zum **Leben** notwendige Energie kaum in genügender Menge der **Zelle** zuführen. Deshalb ist man gewohnt,[7] den gesamten Stoffwechsel des Organismus in einen Baustoffwechsel und **Betriebsstoffwechsel** zu scheiden.

L. life W. growth b. consists
e. simplest s. constant Z. decay
A. building up l. living e. real
S. metabolism s. a. is built (App. 11, 4, a)
s. occur d. those V. compounds
g. sufficient p. suitable
z. V. at disposal N. food d. which are given
N. food materials V. consumption
S. sense d. take care of
g. at same time n. which is needed
k. scarcely g. sufficient d. Z. to the cell
g. accustomed (to what?) g. total
S. metabolism B. nutrient exchange
B. fuel exchange s. separate

Alle Stoffwechselvorgänge sind[6] auf das innigste mit der Bildung und der Tätigkeit der Enzyme in und ausserhalb der **Zelle** verknüpft. Wie[8] schon mitgeteilt, sind[6] alle Enzyme als **Zellprodukte** aufzufassen. Sie werden[6] vom lebenden **Protoplasma** zwar gebildet, äussern ihre Wirkung aber unabhängig von den lebenden **Zellen.** Sowohl die Menge eines Enzymes als auch die Bildung desselben überhaupt ist[6] aber von einer Reihe äusserer **Bedingungen** abhängig. So werden[6] die eiweissspaltenden, proteolytischen **Enzyme** dann am besten ausgebildet, wenn den Bakterien im allgemeinen komplizierte eiweissartige Körper[4] im Kultursubstrat in genügender **Menge** zur Verfügung stehen. Es findet dabei eine gewisse **Anpassung** statt.[2]

S. metabolic processes a. d. i. very closely
B. formation T. activity
a. outside of v. tied w. as
m. reported s. a. are to be interpreted (See App. 12, 1, a, b.) w. are (App. 7, 5, a)
ä. manifest w. effect u. independently
M. quantity
ü. in general i. a. See Rule 6, E, 7.
B. conditions w. are (App. 7, 5, a)
e. protein splitting
a. formed d. B. to the B. (Note the case.)
e. protein like
g. sufficient M. amount z. V. at disposal, available
E. there See App. 10, 1, a, b. c.

Die Bildung von Proteasen erfährt aber eine starke **Einschränkung**[1] oder kann[6] gänzlich unterdrückt werden, wenn gleichzeitig eine grosse Menge vergärbarer Kohlehydrate der Bakterienart zur Verfügung steht. Viele Substanzen haben die Eigenschaft,[7] nur die Bildung eines oder mehrerer **Enzyme** zu hemmen, ohne[7] das Wachstum und die Vermehrung der **Bakterien** zu beeinträchtigen. Folgendes Beispiel soll[6] dies näher beleuchten.

e. undergoes
s. strong E. limitation
u. suppressed g. at the same time
v. fermentable E. quality (to what?)
B. formation h. inhibit
o. without (See Rule 7, c, 1.)
b. impair f. following B. example
b. clear up n. closer

Es entwickelt sich Bacillus prodigiosus in Nährbouillon mit einem Zusatz von 0,5% Morphium, Strychnin oder Antipyrin noch gut.[1] Proteasen konnten[6] aber nur in den Kulturen mit Morphium nachgewiesen werden. Bacillus pyocyaneus wächst mit den genannten Zusätzen oder mit beigegebenem Chinin gut,[1] vermag[6] aber sein protolytisches Enzym sowohl bei Morphium- als auch Strychnin- und **Antipyrinzusatz** zu produzieren, und wird[6] darin nur vom **Chinin** gehindert. Der Vibrio der asiatischen Cholera gedeiht in Bouillon mit einem Zusatz von 0,5% Morphium oder **Antipyrin,**[1] erzeugt seine Protease aber nur in dem morphinhaltigen **Nährsubstrat.**[1] Durch länger dauernde Zucht einer Bakterienart unter ungünstigen äusseren Bedingungen wird[6] ebenfalls eine Verminderung der Proteasenbildung herbeigeführt. So beobachtete man ein Zurückgehen der Fähigkeit zur Gelatineverflüssigung beim Vibrio **Cholerae.**[1]

e. there e. s. is developed (See App. 10, 1, abc.)
k. n. w. See App. 7, 6, a, b.
n. detected
w. be w. grows g. named
Z. additions b. added v. is able (to what?)
g. hindered
g. thrives
Z. addition e. produces
N. nourishing substratum
d. lasting Z. culture
u. unfavorable ä. outer B. conditions
V. reduction h. brought about
b. observed Z. recession F. ability
G. gelatine liquification b. in the case of

PHYSIKALISCHE EINFLÜSSE AUF DAS BAKTERIENWACHSTUM

Der günstig zusammengesetzte Nährboden an sich verbürgt noch keineswegs ein optimales Wachstum der **Bakterien.**[1] Dazu sind[6] auch die entsprechenden physikalischen Zustände der **Umgebung** notwendig, durch die[5] in vielen Fällen eine günstige oder ungünstige Beeinflussung der Vermehrung und des Ablaufes aller **Lebensvorgänge** erfolgt.

g. favorably z. composed N. nutrient base
v. guarantees k. in no way
D. thereto, to that purpose
Z. conditions U. environment
F. cases g. favorable B. influence
V. reproduction A. course L. life process
e. ensue, take place, result

Thermische Einwirkungen

Von grösster Bedeutung für den normalen Ablauf des Bakterienlebens ist die[3] in den **Kulturen** herrschende Temperatur.[1] Auch hier können[6] wir drei **Kardinalpunkte** festlegen: das Temperaturoptimum, bei welchem[5] die maximale Vermehrung erfolgt; **das Temperaturminimum;** das ist die niederste Temperatur,[1] bei **der**[5] eben noch eine äusserst langsame **Vermehrung** erfolgt und endlich das Temperaturmaximum, jene Höchsttemperatur,[1] die[5] gerade noch ein Wachstum zulässt.

B. importance A. course
h. which prevails (why which?)
f. establish
b. w. at which
V. reproduction
n. lowest a. extremely
l. slow
H. highest temperature g. barely
z. admits W. growth

Für die einzelnen Bakterienarten liegen die Kardinalpunkte ausserordentlich verschieden.[1] Unter Zugrundelegung des Temperaturoptimums können[6] wir trotzdem mit Fischer die Bakterien in drei grosse Gruppen einteilen: 1. Das Optimum liegt bei Zimmer-oder Sommertemperatur (20-30°): alle[3] bei uns im **Freien** lebenden proto- und metatrophen Bakterien. 2. Das Optimum liegt bei Brüttemperatur (Bluttemperatur der Megathermen) Hierher gehören im allgemeinen die tierpathogenen **Bakterienarten.** 3. Das Optimum liegt bei der Koagulations-temperatur mancher **Eiweisskörper:** die sonderbare Gruppe der thermophilen **Bakterien.**[1]

e. individual
a. extraordinarily v. different
Z. establishment t. nevertheless
e. divide Z. room
l. which live (Why which?) F. open
bei uns in our country

h. hereto g. belong **i. a. in general**
m. of some E. protein bodies

Diese Gruppen sind[6] durch eine Reihe von **Zwischengliedern** verbunden, so dass natürlich eine strenge Sonderung[4] unmöglich erscheint. Ausserdem müssen[6] wir in Betracht ziehen, dass es Bakterien gibt, die[5] ihr Optimum allerdings bei sehr hoher Temperatur, etwa 50° haben, die[5] sich aber auch bei niedrigeren **Temperaturen** gut vermehren. Sie können[6] wir mit Schillinger als thermotolerant bezeichnen zum Unterschied von den Orthothermophilen, die[5] auch ein sehr hochliegendes **Minimum** aufweisen.

R. series Z. intermediate members
s. strict S. separation
u. impossible e. appears a. besides
z. draw e. g. there are
Note Rule 5 in this paragraph.
n. low v. reproduce S. them (See App. 9, 1, b, e.) b. designate
u. distinction
a. show

Über den Einfluss extremer Temperaturen wurden[6] **Untersuchungen** angestellt, die[5] im allgemeinen zu dem **Ergebnis** führten, dass die Lebensfähigkeit[4] durch hohe **Temperaturen** schnell erlischt, während sehr niedrige Temperaturen[4] verhältnismässig gut selbst durch längere **Zeit** ertragen werden, ohne dass die Lebensfähigkeit[4] geschädigt wird.

E. influence w. were (App. 7, 5, b)
a. made i. a in general
f. lead l. viability
e. expire w. while
v. relatively (App. 16, 1) s. even
e. endure
g. impair, harm

Gegen sehr niedrige Temperaturen,[1] sog. inframinimale Temperaturen sind die meisten Bakterien und Sporen äusserst widerstandsfähig.[1] Dabei ist es einerlei, ob sie[4] psychrophil oder psychotolerant sind. So haben[6] Versuche mit Micrococcus **phyogenes** ergeben, dass derselbe[4] selbst nach einer wochenlangen Aufbewahrung im zugeschmolzenen Rohr bei einer Temperatur von **–80°C** noch entwicklungsfähig war. Man kann[6] Bakterien und deren Sporen selbst 20 Stunden bei Temperaturen von –172 bis **190°** aufbewahren, ohne[7] sie zu töten oder[8] auch nur in der **Entwicklungsfähigkeit** zu schädigen. Nach Macfadyet sollen[6] Milchbakterien einen einwöchentlichen Aufenthalt in flüssiger **Luft** schadlos überdauern. Selbst eine zehnstündige Abkühlung in **flüssigem Wasserstoff,** also bei–252°C, konnte[6] diese Mikroorganismen nicht vernichten.

sog. so called (sogenannt)
m. most You may go straight ahead on some **adj.** See page 1, type 4
V. experiments e. shown
s. even (App. 13, 2, a, d, e) z. sealed
R. tube e. capable of development
d. their (App. 24, 4, b, e)
a. store preserve
t. killing (Why –ing?) What does "oder" call for?
s. impairing
s. without harm A. stay
ü survive S. even (App. 13,2,a)
H. hydrogen a. hence
v. destroy

Ein Absinken der Temperatur unter das Temperaturminimum der betreffenden Bakterienart führt zuerst zu einer sehr beträchtlichen Verlangsamung der **Teilungen.** Weiter fallende Temperaturen führen dann zum Ausfall verschiedener die Lebensvorgänge begleitender **Erscheinungen,** wie zum Beispiel des Leuchtens bei **Photobakterien.** Schliesslich herrscht nur mehr eine Art latenten Lebens in der **Zelle.** Die Reaktionsgeschwindigkeiten beim Stoffumsatz werden immer kleiner[1] und nähern sich bei der Temperatur des flüssigen Wasserstoffes schon sehr dem **Nullwert.** Damit ist[6] ein vollständiger Stillstand im Ablauf der **Lebensvorgänge** erreicht, der[5] allmählich wieder in die normale Zelltätigkeit durch **Wärmezufuhr** übergeleitet werden kann, sofern durch Eiskrystallbildungen in der Zelle nicht eine mechanische Schädigung[4] eingetreten ist.

A. drop u. below
b. concerned f. leads Note Rule 1.
b. considerable V. retardation
T. divisions w. further
A. dropping away v. of different (what?)
What does the "er" tell you to do?
S. finally h. prevails
R. reaction speed, velocity
S. metabolism w. become
n. approach b. in the case of
W. hydrogen N. zero value v. complete
S. pause A. course W. heat supply
e. reached a. gradually Z. cell activity

Im allgemeinen sind[6] die Bakterien gegen supramaximale Temperaturen, die[5] also über dem **Maximum** liegen, wesentlich empfindlicher. Diese Empfindlichkeit ist[6] aber bei den einzelnen **Arten** sehr verschieden. Ausserdem besteht ein grosser Unterschied zwischen der Resistenz der vegetativen Bakterienformen und der Widerstandsfähigkeit der **Sporen.**

S. harm e. entered in
s. e. are more sensitive (Rule 6 E, 1, 2, 3)
l. lie w. essentially E. sensitivity
v. different A. besides b. exists
U. difference
W. resistance

Im Wasser genügt im allgemeinen eine halbstündige Erwärmung auf **70° C,** um[7] alle vegetativen **Bakterienzellen** zu vernichten, wenn wir[4] von den wenigen thermophilen **Bakterien** absehen, die[5] sich bei Temperaturen gegen **70° C** noch vermehren. Viel widerstandsfähiger sind die Sporen der **Bakterien.** Man muss[6] viel höhere **Temperaturen** anwenden. So hat[6] Blau für eine Reihe von Sporen die Tötungszeit bei Anwendung von 100° in **Wasser** ermittelt.

g. suffice h. half hour
E. heating What does "um" call for?
v. destroy
a. disregard, look away from
v. reproduce w. more resistant (Watch -er or comparative forms) a. use
R. series T. time of death A. use
e. ascertained

Wirkungen des Lichtes

Gegen Lichtwirkungen im allgemeinen verhalten sich die Bakterien sehr verschieden.[1] Dabei spielt noch die Qualität der Lichtstrahlen eine sehr wesentliche **Rolle.** Auch hier kann[6] allgemein gesagt werden, dass die schädliche Wirkung[4] mit der Abnahme der Wellenlänge des **Lichtes** steigt.

L. light effects v. behave
v. differently d. in this case
L. light rays w. essential
k. g. w. (App. 7, 6, 1, 2)
s. harmful A. decrease W. wave length
s. rises

Sonnenlicht

Das direkte Sonnenlicht enthält neben den sichtbaren Strahlen noch reichlich ultraviolette **Strahlen.** Es wirkt sicherlich auf das Bakterienwachstum hemmend,[1] bzw. bei genügend langer Einwirkungsdauer auch bakterientötend.[1] Bei allen Wirkungen darf[6] aber nicht vergessen werden, dass der Nährboden selbst[4] durch die Lichtwirkungen in seiner **Zusammensetzung** Veränderungen[9] erleiden kann, die[5] dann indirekt sich auf das **Bakterienwachstum** auswirken. Daher muss[6] zwischen den Lichtwirkungen auf die Zelle selbst und die[3] durch das **Licht** verursachten **Nährbodenänderungen** unterschieden werden. So konnte[6] Dieudonne zeigen, dass auf einer[3] dem **Sonnenlicht** ausgesetzten sterilen Agarplatte Wasserstoffsuperoxyd entsteht, welches[5] für das Bakterienwachstum sehr schädlich wirkt. Anderseits sollen[6] die bakteriziden Wirkungen des Sonnenlichtes nach Miramond ihre Ursache darin haben, dass die zu erhebliche Speicherung von Lichtenergie in den Zellen zu

e. contains n. along with S. sunlight
s. visible S. rays r. abundantly, richly
S. rays s. sicher, surely
h. inhibitingly g. sufficient
E. period of effect b. in the case of
d. v. w. must not be forgotten (App. 7, 6, 1)
L. light effects Z. composition
V. changes (Note Rule 9.) e. undergo
a. effect d. hence
m. u. w. must be distinguished (App. 7, 6, 1)
v. which are caused (Why which?) z. show
a. which is exposed
e. arises
s. harmful a. on the other hand
s. h. are said to have U. cause
z. e. too considerable, great S. storage

einem heftigen hydrolytischen **Abbau** des Eiweisses und damit verbundenen Zerfall der lebenden **Substanz** führt.

Dem Licht gegenüber nehmen die Purpurbakterien eine **Ausnahmestellung** ein,[2] indem sie[4] dasselbe im **Stoffwechsel** offenbar verwerten. Nach Molisch soll[6] es sich dabei um eine neue Art von **Photosynthese** handeln, bei der[5] organische Substanz im **Lichte** assimiliert wird. Für diese Bakterien ist die Lichtbestrahlung also günstig, wenn sie[4] auch nicht notwendig ist, da Purpurbakterien[4] auch im **Finstern** wachsen.

h. violent, enormous
A. decomposition E. protein
v. connected Z. disintegration
g. opposite to (App. 15, 3, c)
e. occupy i. in that
v. utilize o. obviously n. according to
s. it is supposed to h. deal L. light
L. light radiation
g. favorable w. a. even if (App. 19)
F. darkness w. grow

Wirkung der ultravioletten Strahlen

Besonders bakterizid erweisen sich die kurzwelligen **Strahlen.** Bei allen diesen Versuchen ist[6] nur zu beachten, dass Glas[4] gerade die wirksamsten, ganz kurzen **Wellen** vollständig absorbiert. Für solche Experimente sind[6] daher nur Gefässe aus durchsichtigem Quarz oder mindestens **Uviolglas** brauchbar, um[7] einwandfreie **Ergebnisse** zu erhalten.

e. s. are shown (App. 11, 4, a)
S. rays V. experiments
z. b. to be observed g. just v. completely
G. vessels d. transparent
s. b. are usable (Rule 6 E)
e. obtain E. results

Als Lichtquelle für die Untersuchung der Wirkung kurzwelliger Strahlen kommen in erster Linie die Quecksilberdampflampe im Quarzgefäss und die elektrische Bogenlampe mit eisenimprägnierter Kohle oder Eisenstäben als **Elektroden**[9] in Frage. Dadurch ist es möglich,[7] Wellenlängen bis herunter zu 300mi mi anzuwenden.

U. investigation
W. effect k. short waved
Q. mercury vapor lamp
B. arc lamp K. carbon E. iron rods
Note how "in Frage" goes with the verb.
Review Rule 9. a. use

Für Untersuchungen der Wirkung sehr kurzwelliger Strahlen auf einzelne Zellen ist[6] das elektrische **Funkenlicht** besonders geeignet, das,[5] mit Quarzprismen spektral zerlegt,[11] die Anwendung eines eng begrenzten ultravioletten **Strahlenbezirkes** gestattet. Mit dem[3] mit **Quarzoptik** ausgestatteten Mikroskop kann[6] man mit einer Hilfsbeleuchtung an beweglichen Bakterien, z. B. dem Bacillus prodigiosus, bei Anwendung von Cadmiumelektroden bei einer Wellenlänge **L=275 mi mi** beobachten, dass zu Beginn der Bestrahlung die Bewegung lebhafter wird. Schon nach wenigen Minuten stellen die Bakterien die **Bewegung** ein.[2]

S. rays e. individual Z. cells
F. spark light g. suited
z. when analyzed (Why when?) A. use
S. ray area g. permits Why a "3"? Why Rule 11? a. which is equipped
H. emergency light b. movable
A. use
b. observe
B. radiation l. more active
B. movement
e. stop

Wirkung der Radiumstrahlen

Die[3] von radioaktiven **Substanzen** ausgehenden Strahlungen setzen sich aus A-, B- und G- **Strahlen** zusammen,[2] die[5] in ihrer **Natur** wesentlich verschieden sind. Die A- und B-Strahlen sind fliegende materielle **Teilchen,** während die G-Strahlen sehr kurze **Ätherwellen** vorstellen, die[5] den **Röntgenstrahlen** gleichen,[8] nur von noch kürzerer **Wellenlänge** sind. Die Untersuchungen über die Wirkung dieser Strahlungen auf das Bakterienwachstum, bzw. über die bakteriziden Eigenschaften derselben, hat zu sehr auseinandergehenden **Befunden** geführt.

a. which go out, emanate
S. rays z. are composed
w. essentially
w. while
v. represent g. are alike
Note how "nur" is calling for the verb.
bzw. or
E. attributes a. divergent
B. findings What takes the verb out?

Wirkung der Röntgenstrahlen

Über die Wirkung der Röntgenstrahlen auf Bakterien gehen die Meinungen stark auseinander.[2] Während die einen[4] ihnen für Mikroorganismen besonders deletäre **Eigenschaften** zusprechen, wollen[6] die anderen höchstens sehr geringe **Schädigungen** wahrgenommen haben. Übrigens stehen eingehende und erschöpfende **Versuche** darüber noch aus.[2]

M. opinions a. go apart, separate
W. while d. e. the ones
z. assign E. attributes d. a. the others
w. claim to have perceived
Note the use of wollen in this tense.
e. thorough e. exhaustive
a. are missing

MYKOLOGIE DES WASSERS

(Note: an Asterisk will appear where a certain rule is involved; indicate the rule.)

Aus der Erkenntnis heraus, dass in vielen Fällen von schweren Epidemien das Wasser* der Verbreiter derselben war, hat* man der Mykologie des Wassers schon lange die entsprechende **Aufmerksamkeit** zugewendet. Im allgemeinen unterscheidet man praktisch zwischen **Trinkwasser,*** Nutzwasser und Abwasser von gewerblichen und industriellen Betrieben und **Anlagen.*** Es liegt in der Natur der Wassergewinnung, dass häufig eine gegenseitige Beeinflussung dieser Wassergruppen* in äusserst unerwünschter Art eintritt. Wenn auch das* aus dem Erdinnern in den **Quellen** austretende Wasser ausserordentlich arm an **Organismen** ist, so ändert sich dieses Bild doch sofort in den* von diesen Quellen gespeisten Brunnen und **Wasserläufen.** Diese sind* ständigen natürlichen **Verunreinigungen** ausgesetzt. In die Flussläufe werden* ja auch die Abwässer der* an denselben gelegenen **Anlagen** eingeleitet. Dazu kommen noch die menschlichen und tierischen **Exkremente,*** abgesehen von den Leichen und Abfallstoffen der* im Fluss **selbst** lebenden Tiere und **Pflanzen.***

a. h. (App. 21, 1, 1) E. knowledge, realization
F. cases V. distributor
d. of the same (App. 14, 1)
e. suitable, adequate A. attention
z. turned (What calls for this verb?)
u. distinguishes N. use water A. waste water
g. commercial B. operations
A. plants (factory) W. obtaining of water
h. frequently g. mutual
ä. extremely u. undesirable
e. enters in w. a. even though
a. which escapes (Why which?) a. unusually
a. s. is changed (App. 11, 4, a)
d. the (what?) g. which are fed
W. water streams s. constant
V. contaminations a. exposed to
w. are (App. 7, 5, a) g. which are situated
e. introduced m. human
t. animal a. apart from
A. waste products Why an "*" here?
l. which live (Why which?) P. plants

Mykologie des Trinkwassers

Der erwachsene Mensch gibt in seinen Ausscheidungen, also im gesamten Stoffwechsel im Durchschnitt täglich zwei bis drei Liter **Wasser ab.*** Diese Menge muss* auch täglich wieder ersetzt werden. Dies geschieht einerseits durch die **Nahrung,*** welche* immer sehr wasserreich ist, und anderseits durch unmittelbare Aufnahme als Trinkwasser.* Man war* von altersher bestrebt,* ein reines und wohlschmeckendes Trinkwasser für den **Menschen** zu beschaffen. Man hat* auch im Altertum keine **Mühe** und **Kosten** gescheut,[7] einwandfreies Trinkwasser selbst durch lange **Zuführungen** dem Haushalte der **Menschen** zugänglich zu machen. Diese Reinheit des Wassers muss* man aber nicht nur **für Trinkzwecke,** sondern auch für alle häuslichen **Gebrauchszwecke fordern, wie Reinigung der Ess-und Trinkgeschirre, Badezwecke usw.**

e. grown What goes with "gibt"?
g. total S. metabolism D. average
What does "ab" go with?
M. quantity e. replaced
e. on the one hand N. food
u. immediate A. absorption Note Rule 1.
a. from olden times
b. endeavoring (to what?) w. good tasting
b. procure, create A. antiquity
g. spared M. effort (to what?)
Z. conduits H. household
z. accessible R. purity
T. drinking purposes
h. domestic G. use purposes
f. demand T. drinking utensils
B. bathing purposes

Der Nahrungsmittelchemiker fordert vom Trinkwasser und dem* für menschliche **Gebrauchszwecke** bestimmten Wasser, dass es* klar, geruch-und geschmacklos, farblos, gleichmässig kühl temperiert, angenehm schmeckend und erfrischend sei. Ausserdem darf* es keine **Bestandteile** enthalten, welche* irgendwie gesundheitsschädlich wirken.

N. food chemist, dietician
d. the (what?) b. which is designed, intended
Why which? g. odorless g. tasteless
g. uniformly a. pleasantly
e. refreshing A. besides d. must
B. ingredients g. harmful to health
w. act i. in any way

Dementsprechend muss* seine chemische und biologische **Zusammensetzung** sein. Uns interessiert in erster Linie letztere. Der Gehalt an Mikroorganismen wird* nun wesentlich von der Herkunft des Wassers und seiner Aufsammlung vor dem **Konsum** beeinflusst. Zur Trinkwasser– und der häuslichen Gebrauchswasserversorgung werden herangezogen: 1. das* aus dem Erdinnern, aus der **Tiefe** künstlich gewonnene Grundwasser, 2. Tiefenwasser, das* freiwillig die Erdoberfläche in Form der **Quellen** erreicht, also Quellwasser und endlich 3. das* auf der **Erdoberfläche** fliessende oder stehende Wasser, das man* als Oberflächenwasser bezeichnet.

D. corresponding to that
Z. composition i. e. L. primarily
G. content
w. is (why?) (App. 7, 5, a) w. essentially
A. collection, accumulation
h. domestic G. use-water-supply
d. the (what?)
g. which is gained
E. earth surface
e. reaches Q. well water
f. which flows (Why which?)
b. designates O. surface water

Das Quell— und Grundwasser ist im allgemeinen biologisch nicht verunreinigt und kann* bei entsprechender **Tiefe** als steril bezeichnet werden. Eine Reinigung des Grundwassers von etwa vorhandenen Organismen ist daher nicht notwendig.* Sofern es* sich nach seiner chemischen Zusammensetzung überhaupt zum **Trinkwasser** eignet, kann* es höchstens durch einen zu grossen Gehalt an kohlensäurem, und humussaurem **Eisenoxydul** verunreinigt sein. Dies gibt dem Wasser einen tintenartigen bitterlichen **Geschmack,*** der es weniger genussfähig macht. Ausserdem kann* das Grundwasser einen geringen Gehalt an Schwefelwasserstoff aufweisen, der* es übelriechend macht. Infolge Zutrittes von Luftsauerstoff findet eine rasche **Enteisenung** statt,* da die oben genannten Eisenverbindungen* als **Eisenoxydhydrat** ausgeschieden werden. Beim Stehen verliert sich auch der Schwefelwasserstoffgeruch alsbald.* Für Grossbetriebe hat* die Technik auch besondere, sehr wirksame **Enteisenungsverfahren** erfunden und herausgebildet, auf die* hier nicht weiter eingegangen werden soll.

G. ground water i. a. in general
v. contaminated e. suitable
T. depth b. designated w. be (App. 7, 6, a)
v. existing
n. necessary s. in as far as
Z. composition ü. at all, in general
e. adapts z. g. too large G. content
What does "kann" call for?
t. ink like G. taste g. enjoyable
A. besides a. show g. slight
ü. nauseating I. due to Z. access
What does "statt" go with? E. iron compounds
a. separated S. standing v. s. is lost
G. big or large scale
T. industry (has what?)
E. de-ironizing processes e. invented
a. d. upon which LET THE RELATIVE TAKE OUT THE VERB IF POSSIBLE

Wenn dagegen Oberflächenwasser jeglicher Art* zur **Trinkwasserversorgung** dienen soll, dann muss* eine sicher funktionierende Reinigung **desselben** vorgenommen werden. Jedes Oberflächenwasser enthält neben Schwebestoffen organischer und unorganischer Natur noch reichlich **Mikroorganismen.** Selbst im reinsten Flusswasser, dem[5] verunreinigende **Zuflüsse** vollkommen fehlen, ist die Zahl der nachweisbaren Bakterien eine recht beträchtliche.[1] Die Anwesenheit dieser normalen Wasserbewohner bedeutet aber keineswegs eine schädliche Verunreinigung. Erst die* in den Fluss von den **Siedlungen** kommenden Zuflüsse und Kanäle führen neben reichlichen Bakterienmassen auch eine erhebliche Menge toter organischer **Substanz** zu,[2] wodurch die Flora und Fauna des Wassers* wesentliche **Änderungen** erfährt. Die Keimzahl wird* in der **Volumseinheit** mächtig ansteigen und auch die Qualität der Mikroben wird* dadurch geändert werden. Die* von den verschiedenen **Abwässern** stammenden löslichen organischen Verbindungen geben eben einen selbst in grosser Verdünnung noch brauchbaren **Nährboden** ab. Von einschneidender Bedeutung übrigens sind die* mit den Abwässern in den **Fluss** gelangenden pathogenen Mikroben; dieselben vermehren sich zwar in dem* für sie jedenfalls schlechten Nährboden nicht, doch bleiben sie lange entwicklungs— und infektionsfähig, also virulent. Es sei* hier auf die[3] mit Sicherheit nachgewiesene Verbreitung von Cholera durch das Wasser selbst grosser **Flüsse** hingewiesen. Der Choleraerreger, der* sich in den Defäkationen Cholerakranker in ungeheurer **Anzahl** findet, erhält sich in dem organisch verunreinigten Flusswasser lange Zeit virulent.*

d. on the other hand j. any
T. drinking water supply s. is to
v. undertaken (see App. 7, 6, a, b)
O. surface water e. contains
S. suspended materials
S. even (App. 13, 2a) r. purest
F. river water v. contaminating
f. are absent n. detectable
b. considerable (one) A. presence
W. water inhabitants b. means
s. harmful E. only d. the (what?)
S. settlements k. which come Why which?
What goes with "führen"? M. quantity z. supply
w. essential Ä. changes
K. germ count m. enormously a. increase
w. g. w. will be changed (App. 7, 5, e)
s. which come
What goes with "geben"? HAVE YOU FLAGGED THE PREFIXES BEFORE YOU BEGAN THE PARAGRAPH? e. incisive
ü. moreover
g. which come
What does "dem" call for?
j. at any rate s. which is poor
e. capable of development
es s. h. let be referred (App. 28, 1e)
n. which is detected
s. even C. cholera exciter, bacillus
s. f. is found (App. 11, 4, a) u. vast
A. number e. s. is preserved (App. 11, 4, a)

Jedenfalls muss[6] jedes Oberflächenwasser, das[5] dem menschlichen Genuss oder **Gebrauch** zugeführt wird, einerseits von den pathogenen Mikroben befreit

J. at any rate What verb does "6" call for? "5"?
G. enjoyment Gebr. use
b. liberated (add "werden") See Rule 8 E—absence of the auxiliary verb.

und[8] andererseits möglichst frei von toter organischer Substanz gemacht werden. Für diese Wasserreinigung kommt[9] die Filtration desselben in erster Linie in Frage. Dabei ahmt man möglichst jene Vorgänge nach,[2] die* sich in der Natur beim Einsinken des Meteorwassers in den Boden abspielen, so dass ein[3] dem Grundwasser annähernd ähnliches Produkt zustande kommt. Als Filtermaterial wird* vorwiegend Sand benützt, der* von oben nach unten im Filter an Korngrösse zunimmt und* schliesslich in Schichten von walnuss— bis kopfgrossen Steinen übergeht. Im wesentlichen sind* die Sandfilter gleich aufgebaut. Sie bestehen aus offenen oder gedeckten rechteckigen Bassins, die* im Erdboden versenkt und[8] von unten nach oben bis etwas über ein Drittel der Höhe mit Schichten von groben Steinen, Kies und Sand als **Filterkörper** angefüllt sind.

Underline the nouns which should be in bold-faced type. d. of the same (App. 14, 1) Note Rule 9.
n. copies n. as much as possible
s. a. take place B. soil, floor e. a (what?)
ä. which is similar a. approximately
v. predominantly b. used K. grain size
s. finally S. layers, beds d. walnut
Note how "und" picks up the verb—Rule 8.
a. built up b. consist of g. covered
E. earth, soil v. submerged
u. and (what?) e. somewhat
S. layers K. gravel Note Rule 8-E.
a. filled

Die Wasserzuführungsöffnung befindet sich oberhalb der letzten Filterschicht in der Mitte einer schmalen Wand. Das Wasser wird* nach Durchrieselung der Filterschichten in einem Sammelkanal durch zahlreiche Nebenkanäle gesammelt und* von dort als Reinwasser dem Filterbrunnen zugeführt. Das Reinwasserzuführungsrohr leitet das Wasser in das sogenannte Aufstandsrohr in der Höhe der Sandschichtoberfläche.* Das* im Filterbrunnen einfliessende Reinwasser gelangt dann durch eine besondere Rohrleitung zum Reinwassersammelbecken, von wo es* den Verbrauchern zugeführt wird.

w. water supply opening b. s. is found
o. above M. middle
s. narrow D. trickling through
S. collection channel, canal z. numerous
u. and (what?)
z. supplied R. pure-water-supply-tube
s. so called
H. level S. sand layer surface d. the
e. which flows in (why which?)
R. pipe conduit R. pure water basin
z. supplied V. consumers

Im allgemeinen äussern die Sandfilter ihre Wirkung in dreifacher Weise.* Sie fungieren als mechanische Reiniger, indem sie* alle Schwebeteilchen von Dimensionen, die* grösser als die Porenweite sind, zurückhalten. Die kleinsten Teilchen,* wie Tonpartikeln*, Bakterien usw. werden* rein mechanisch jedoch nicht zurückgehalten. Das Filter hat erst eine biologische Wirkung,* die darin besteht,[7] Mikroorganismen möglichst vollständig zurückzuhalten.

ä express W. effect d. threefold
R. purifier i. in that S. suspended particles
z. hold back What calls for this verb?
for sind? w. are (App. 7, 5, a) j. however
z. held back
b. consists d. there in (App. 23, 3, d)
v. completely

Die Reifung des Filters kommt dadurch zustande,[2] dass sich die sog. Filterhaut bildet. Darunter versteht man eine dünne,[3] sich auf dem Filter aus den Schwebestoffen ansammelnde Decke. Die Schwebestoffe des Oberflächenwassers bestehen zum grossen Teil aus organischen Substanzen, wie lebende und tote pflanzliche und tierische Organismen.* Dementsprechend ist die Filterhaut für die weitere Entwicklung von anspruchsloseren Fäulnisbakterien ein sehr geeigneter Nährboden.* Man beobachtet daher in der Filterhaut zuerst ein starkes Ansteigen der Bakterienzahl gegenüber jener des Rohwassers.* Von der Filterhaut wandern die beweglichen Bakterienarten aktiv in die tieferen Filterschichten ein,[2] unbewegliche werden* passiv vom Wasserstrom hineingespült. Ein grosser Teil setzt sich an den Körnern des Filters **fest*** und trägt so zur Verkleinerung der Filterporen bei.* Es kommt so allmählich zu einer Verschleimung des Sandes.* In diesem Zustande wird* das Filter als "reif" bezeichnet.

Why Rule 2? s. b. is formed d. by that
v. understands d. thin (what?)
S. suspended substances a. which is collected
b. consist z. g. T. in large part
l. living
t. animal D. correspondingly
E. development a. unpretending
F. putrefactive g. appropriate
b. observes d. therefore A. increase
g. opposite to j. that (App. 14, 3)
b. movable
e. immigrate u. immovable w. are
(App. 7, 5, a) h. washed in
What does "fest" go with? "bei"?
V. diminishment
a. gradually V. gelatinization
Z. condition
b. designated

MORPHOLOGIE DER VEGETATIVEN BAKTERIENZELLE

The object is now to leave out as many numbers of the rules as possible. Wherever an asterisk appears, indicate the rule involved. Also underline the nouns that should be in bold-faced type. Numbers and cross references to the rules of the Appendix will be given on difficult sentences.

Die Bakterien treten uns in der freien Natur und in der Laboratoriumskultur meist in mannigfacher äusserer Form entgegen.* Selbst eine* unter schärfster Kontrolle von einer einzigen Zelle aus angelegte Reinkultur zeigt schon nach wenigen Tagen eine gewisse Vielförmigkeit der Gestalt der betreffenden Bakterienart, die* so weit gehen kann, dass Zweifel* an der Reinheit der Kultur auftauchen. Diese Vielgestaltigkeit der Zellen hat ihre Ursache vornehmlich im verschiedenen Entwicklungszustand der Zellen* und in Veränderungen des Nährsubstrates beim Wachstum der Bakterien.* Die Formen der vegetativen Bakterienzellen,* also jener, die* sich normal durch Querspaltung teilen und* auch als Oidien bezeichnet werden, lassen sich* trotzdem auf einige wenige Grundtypen zurückführen: die Kugel, den Zylinder und die Schraube.*

t. meet What goes with "treten"?
m. mostly m. varied a. outer
S. even (App. 13, 2, a, e) s. sharpest
e. single von-aus (App. 21, 1, a, b)
g. certain V. polymorphism G. form
b. concerned
Z. doubt a. arise R. purity
V. polymorphism U. cause v. especially
v. different E. developmental state
V. changes N. nourishing substratum
Note Rule 1.
j. those (App. 14, 3) Q. cross division
b. designated w. are (App. 7, 5, a)
z. trace back K. sphere
S. spiral

Kugelbakterien (Kokken)

Unter normalen Ernährungsbedingungen besitzen zahlreiche Bakterien eine reine oder sehr annähernde Kugelgestalt,* welche* besonders an den eben freigewordenen Teilungsprodukten,* den jungen Tochterzellen, sehr gut zu beobachten ist. Bei ihnen kann* natürlich von einer Mannigfaltigkeit oder Veränderung der Gestalt nicht gesprochen werden, wenn man* davon absieht, dass bei allen Vertretern dieser Bakteriengruppe unmittelbar vor und ganz besonders nach der Teilung eine Abweichung von der Kugelform* festzustellen ist. Die Tochterzellen nehmen aber, sobald sie* frei werden, in kürzester Zeit die Kugelgestalt wieder rein an.* Man ist* überhaupt nur dann berechtigt,[7] eine Bakterienart in die Gruppe der Kugelbakterien einzureihen, wenn sie* bei guter Vermehrung also in allen ausnutzbaren Nährsubstraten und bei günstigen Temperaturverhältnissen kurz nach der Teilung die Kugelform annimmt, sofern die Teilungsprodukte* frei werden und* als einzelne Zellen weitervegetieren. [10]Treten im Verlaufe der Entwicklung einer Kugelbakterienkultur gewisse,[3] später noch genau zu beschreibende Wuchsverbände auf, in denen die Zellen* nach der Teilung festgehalten werden, dann können* Abflachungen der Kugelgestalten an den Berührungsstellen auftreten, die* die reine Kugelform beeinträchtigen. Ein gutes Beispiel für diese Erscheinung geben uns diejenigen Kugelbakterienarten,* welche* die Neigung[7] besitzen, nach der Teilung noch längere Zeit vereint zu bleiben, zusammengehalten von einer gemeinsamen Kapsel.* Solche Kugelbakterien bezeichnet man auch als Doppelkugelbakterien oder Diplokokken.*

E. nutritional conditions b. have
a. approximate K. spherical form
T. division products
b. i. is to be observed (App. 12, 1, a, b)
M. variety V. change
k. g. w. can be spoken (App. 7, 6, b)
V. representatives u. directly A. deviation
f. i. is to be established (App. 12, 1, a)
w. become (App. 7, 3, a)
K. spherical form ü. in general
b. justified (to what?)
e. to classify V. reproduction
a. utilizable N. nutrient base
g. favorable T. temperature conditions
K. spherical form u. and (what?) e. individual
Why rule 10? V. course
g. certain (what?) z. b. to be described
See App. 12, b on use of z. beschreibend
A. leveling off B. contact-places a. appear
b. impair Is "ein gutes Beispiel" the subject?
d. those (App. 14, b)
N. tendency (to what?) b. possess
v. united z. held together
g. common b. designates

Stäbchenbakterien

Mannigfach ist die Form derjenigen Bakterienarten,* die* einen zylindrischen Zellleib besitzen. Man bezeichnet sie kurzweg als Stäbchenbakterien.* Bei ihnen ist* eine grössere Abwechselung in der äusseren Gestalt schon dadurch bedingt, dass bei den verschiedenen Arten die Dicke und Länge variiert.

S. rod bacteria
M. varied d. those (App. 14, b) Z. cell body
b. labels k. simply B. with
g. larger A. alteration
b. conditioned, caused d. by the fact
D. thickness L. length

(Boldfacing of nouns is omitted on this page. Underline the nouns that should be bold-faced.)

Wir finden Arten,* deren Vertreter* sehr dick und kurz aussehen. Anderseits gibt es Stäbchenbakterien von zartem und schlankem Aussehen. Diese beiden Extreme sind* von allen erdenklichen Übergangsformen verbunden. Die Formverschiedenheiten werden* dann noch dadurch bedeutend bereichert, dass die Zellenden* sehr verschieden gestaltet sind. Wir finden Stäbchenbakterien mit halbkugeligen Enden,* wie eines* in der Figur 5 im optischen Längschnitt abgebildet ist. Die Ausbauchung der Enden kann* immer geringer werden und* schliesslich ganz aufhören, so dass die Stäbchenbakterien wie abgehackt erscheinen. In b, c und d der Figur 5 sind* einzelne Formen der Zellenden wiedergegeben, die* natürlich durch alle erdenklichen Übergangsformen verbunden sind.

V. representatives d. whose
A. on the other hand S. rod bacteria
z. delicate s. slender A. appearance
e. conceivable Ü. transition-forms
F. form differences w. are (App. 7, 5, a)
d. by the fact b. enriched
g. fashioned h. semi-spherical
a. pictured L. longitudinal-section
A. swelling i. g. less and less
a. finally u. and (what?) a. cease
e. appear w. a. as chopped off
e. individual w. reproduced e. conceivable
Ü. transition forms

Die Ausbauchung der Bakterienenden nimmt aber auch bei vielen Arten eine mehr spitze Form an,* wie es* in e der Figur 5 dargestellt ist. Es sind* aber auch zahlreiche Stäbchenbakterienarten bekannt geworden, deren ausgebauchtes, meistens ziemlich spitz auslaufendes Ende* nicht in der Zellachse liegt, wie es h und i der Figur 5 dartut, wobei die strichpunktierte Linie* die Achse markiert.[10] Werden nach der Teilung die Zellen frei und[10] kommen als Einzelzellen zur Beobachtung, so bemerkt man meistens an ihnen gleichgestaltete Zellenden,* wie es g der Figur 5 zeigt. . . . In weitaus den meisten Fällen zeigen Stäbchenbakterien nur Wuchsgestalten,* die* den zylindrischen Charakter wahren. Dies gilt vornehmlich für die reproduzierbaren Formen,* das heisst, für diejenigen Wuchsgestalten,* die* bei ihrer Teilung wieder der Mutterzelle gleich geformte Tochterzellen liefern.

A. bulging n. takes (what goes with this verb?
H. have you "flagged" the line?
d. presented e. s. g. there have become (App. 10, 2. g)
z. numerous b. known
g. become (App. 7, 3, c) m. mostly s. a. tapering
d. shows w. whereby s. dotted
Say "if" for the verb; proceed word for word till you get the subject, then drop back for the verb.
B. observation g. equally formed
w. by far F. cases
W. growth forms d. which (why?)
w. preserve v. especially
d. h. i. e. d. those (App. 14, 2)
b. in the case of
l. furnish g. like, identical

SCHRAUBENBAKTERIEN (Spirillen)

Wie schon der Name aussagt, besitzen die hierher gehörigen Bakterienarten einen regelmässig schraubig gekrümmten Vegetationskörper,* dessen Form* mitunter einem Schraubenumgang entspricht. Figur 8 zeigt uns das Photogramm von Modellen zweier Schraubenbakterien.* Oben gewahren wir ein Spirillum,* dessen Zelle* die Krümmung eines vollständigen Schraubenumganges aufweist, während das untere Spirillum* nur einem Bruchteil eines Umganges entspricht. Die äussere Gestalt erscheint dem Beschauer bei ein und demselben Schraubenbakterium verschieden.

a. states b. possess
g. belonging r. regularly
s. spirally g. bent m. at times
e. corresponds S. spiral loop, circuit
z. shows z. of two
O. up above g. perceive
K. curvature v. complete
a. shows w. while
B. fragment U. loop, coil e. corresponds
G. form B. spectator
v. different

Die Gruppe der Schraubenbakterien weist ebenfalls einen grossen Formenreichtum auf,* der* auf Verschiedenheiten der Zelldicke und der Höhe der Schraubenwindungen zurückzuführen ist. Daneben ist auch von Bedeutung der Durchmesser der Schraubenumgänge.* Die Zellenden weisen keine so zahlreichen Formen auf,* wie man* sie bei den Stäbchenbakterien zu sehen gewohnt ist.

What goes with "weist"?
e. likewise F. richness in form
V. differences Z. zell thickness
S. spiral-coils z. i. is to be traced back
(See App. 12, 1, a.) z. numerous
a. show
g. accustomed

LEUCHTEN DER BAKTERIEN

Eine grosse Anzahl von Bakterienarten vermag[6] unter geeigneten Züchtungsbedingungen und in der freien Natur [9]Licht zu entwickeln. In einfachster Weise kann* man sich auf folgende Weise leuchtendes Bakterienmaterial verschaffen.

A. number v. is able (to what?)
g. appropriate Z. culture-conditions
e. develop (Why do you pick up "Licht"?)
l. luminescent v. procure

Wir legen ein Stück frischen Seefisches, wie es* auf jedem Fischmarkt jetzt leicht erhältlich ist, samt der Haut, aber ohne Eingeweide, in eine Schale und übergiessen dasselbe mit so viel einer 3 proz. Chlornatriumlösung, dass das Fischstück* noch ungefähr einen halben Zentimeter aus der Flüssigkeit hervorragt. Die Schale bedecken wir mit einer lose aufgelegten Glasplatte, um* der Luft einigermassen den Zutritt zu ermöglichen. Dann stellen wir die ganze Versuchsanordnung in einen kühlen Raum mit 4-6° C ins Dunkle, zumindest geschützt vor einer direkten Sonnenbestrahlung. Schon nach etwa 12-16 Stunden leuchten die Ränder des Seefisches im Dunkeln prachtvoll in einem grünlichen Licht. Die Lichtwirkung geht von Bakterien aus*, die* sich besonders an der Oberfläche der Salzlösung[9] am Fischstück ansiedeln.

l. put What nouns should be bold-faced?
e. obtainable s. together with
E. viscera S. dish ü. pour over
Where necessary, give reasons for the * and for the numbers on some sentences. h. projects
b. cover l. loosely a. applied, put on
e. to some degree Z. access e. make possible
V. experimental arrangement
z. at least g. protected
S. sun ray
l. glow R. edges D. darkness
L. light effect p. brilliantly
What does "aus" go with? b. especially
a. lodge, settle

Die verschiedenen leuchtenden Bakterienarten vereint man in der physiologischen Gruppe der "Leuchtbakterien" oder "Photobakterien", unter denen wir* Kugel-, Stäbchen- und Schraubenbakterien vertreten finden. Sie sind fast ausschliesslich Meeresbakterien. Alle Leuchtbakterien leuchten nur unter gewissen Bedingungen. Im allgemeinen verlangen sie dazu in dem Nährsubstrat eine gewisse Menge von Salzen neben den notwendigen Nährstoffen und freien Luftsauerstoff; letzterer genügt in minimalen Quantitäten. Für alle Leuchtbakterien genügt zum Wachstum und zum Leuchten ein Kochsalzgehalt der Nährlösung von 2,5%. Er kann* aber auch höher sein und* bei einigen Arten ohne Schaden auf annähernd 6% steigen.

v. different
v. combines L. illuminating bacteria
u. d. under which, among which, Rule 5
K. spherical S. rod S. spiral
f. almost a. exclusively
L. photo bacteria l. glow g. certain
v. demand d. for that N. nutrient base
M. quantity n. along with n. necessary
N. nutritional materials g. suffices
W. growth K. saline content
h. higher (hoch)
u. and (what?) S. harm a. approximately
s. rise

Für die Leuchtbakterien scheinen* übrigens sowohl als Lichtnährmittel als auch als Nährmittel für das Wachstum im allgemeinen die Extraktivstoffe des Fleisches zu wirken. Für eine[3] sich immer auf Nordseefischen einstellende Leuchtbakterienart kommen dabei nur jene Substanzen[9] in Frage, die* in einer Fleischabkochung nach Ausfällung mit Alkohol bei einem Gehalt von 80-85% des Fällungsmittels noch in Lösung bleiben. Es kann* hier nicht auf diese Einzelheiten eingegangen werden, es soll* damit aber gezeigt werden, dass die Leuchtbakterien* äusserst genügsam sind.

s. seem (to what?) Note the call for "zu".
N. means of nourishment
i. a. in general
z. w. to effect, act Why a "3" here?
einst. which sets in, starts
i. F. kom. to come into question Rule 9
F. meat decoction
F. precipitate
e. gone into, discussed E. details
s. g. w. and also k. e. w. See App. 7, 6, a, b.
g. undemanding

Einige brauchen zum Leuchten neben Stickstoffquellen noch besondere Kohlenstoffquellen, von denen diejenigen* wahrscheinlich die brauchbarsten sind, die* nur wenig vergoren werden und* daher wenig Säure liefern.

E. some b. need S. nitrogen sources
K. carbon sources
b. most useful
v. fermented S. acid
l. furnish

Eine[3] für den Leuchtprozess günstige Aufschliessung des Nährbodens bewirken häufig gleichzeitig vorhandene, nicht leuchtende Bakterien, die[5] sich in Rohkulturen von Photobakterien immer als Begleitbakterien einstellen.

g. which is favorable, why which?
A. breakdown N. nutrient base
v. existing
B. accompanying bacteria e. set in, are present

PHYSIOLOGIE UND BIOLOGIE DER HEFE

Wie die Bakterien, brauchen auch die Hefen zur Entwicklung und zur Entfaltung der verschiedenartigsten Lebensäusserungen eine Nahrung. Dieselbe setzt sich aus anorganischen und organischen Verbindungen zusammen,* die* .wieder eine Reihe von unbedingt notwendigen Elementen in ganz bestimmter Bindung enthalten müssen. Die* zum Aufbau der Leibessubstanz unerlässlichen Elemente sind Stickstoff, Sauerstoff, Wasserstoff, Kohlenstoff, Kalium, Magnesium, Schwefel und Phosphor.

Give reasons for the * and indicate what nouns should be bold-faced.
L. expressions of life N. food
Z. is composed V. compounds
R. series u. unconditionally
b. definite B. bond A. building up
u. which are indispensable (Why which?)
S. nitrogen S. oxygen K. carbon
S. sulphur

Dieselben werden* teils als organische Verbindungen, wie Kohlehydrate und Abkömmlinge oder Bruchstücke der Eiweisskörper, von den Hefen unmittelbar oder nach voraufgehender Spaltung aufgenommen und assimiliert, teils in Form von Salzen mit anorganischen und organischen Säuren, wobei als Lösungsmittel immer das Wasser* reichlich zugegen sein muss.

What does "w" call for?
K. carbohydrates A. derivatives
E. albumen bodies u. immediately
v. advanced, preceding S. splitting
w. a. u. a. are absorbed (App. 7, 5, a)
S. acids L. solvent
r. abundantly z. present

Dabei muss* aber immer berücksichtigt werden, dass die Verhältnisse* hinsichtlich der Ernährung ganz anders geartet sind, wenn von der Hefe eine ganz bestimmte Leistung[4] verlangt wird, wie zum Beispiel die grösstmögliche Alkoholbildung oder die maximale Vermehrung, wie sie* bei der Presshefeerzeugung angestrebt wird.

b. considered m. b. w. (App. 7, 6, a, b)
V. conditions h. with regard
a. differently g. of quite different type
L. achievement v. demanded
V. reproduction
a. striven for P. press-yeast-production

Anorganische Nahrungsstoffe

N. foods

Wie schon gesagt, gehört Kalium zu den lebenswichtigen und unerlässlichen Baustoffen. Dasselbe kann* durch Natrium, Kalzium und Lithium keinesfalls ersetzt werden. Allerdings genügen schon sehr geringe Mengen von Kalium, um* das Hefewachstum zu ermöglichen. Grössere Gaben wirken als Gift, unterdrücken und verzögern nicht nur das Wachstum und die Vermehrung, sondern wirken auch ungünstig auf die Gärtätigkeit. Am besten eignen sich für die Kaliumzufuhr das Chlorid und Phosphat.*

g. belongs L. vital
u. indispensable B. building substances
k. in no case e. replaced
A. of course g. satisfy g. slight
e. to make possible H. yeast growth
u. suppress v. retard
W. growth w. act
u. unfavorably G. fermenting-activity
K. supply of potassium

Das Magnesium, besonders im Magnesiumsulfat, ist* zum Wachstum ebenfalls unumgänglich notwendig. Es übt auch nach neueren Untersuchungen einen wesentlichen Einfluss auf die Farbstoffbildung der Hefen aus* und lenkt dieselbe in ganz bestimmte Bahnen. Es kann* durch Kalzium nicht vertreten werden, obwohl letzteres* als Phosphat oder Chlorid das Wachstum der Hefe und auch ihre Gärtätigkeit in hervorragendem Masse fördert.

u. unavoidably n. necessary
ü. exerts n. according to
w. essential E. influence F. dye formation
g. quite b. certain
v. replaced, represented o. although
W. growth G. fermenting activity
f. promotes h. outstanding

Schwefel und Phosphor haben* wir ebenfalls als unerlässliche Baustoffe kennen gelernt. Dieselben stehen[9] den Hefen in den oben angeführten Salzen bereits in genügender Menge[9] zur Verfügung. Jedenfalls werden[6] dieselben aber auch aus organischen Verbindungen bezogen, wie es* beim Wachstum der Hefe in Bierwürze geschieht.

e. likewise
u. indispensable B. building substances s. zur
V. are available
Note Rule 9. j. in any case
b. obtained V. compounds
g. occurs B. (beer) wort

Ob auch Eisen[4] ein[3] zur Hefeentwicklung unbedingt notwendiger Bestandteil der Hefennahrung ist, kann* noch keineswegs mit Sicherheit erklärt werden. Auffallend ist jedenfalls, dass man* das Nukleoproteid der Hefe eisenhaltig fand, so dass an die Möglichkeit gedacht werden muss, dass Eisen[4] ein wichtiger Bestandteil der Hefenukleinsäure ist. Durch Eisen wird* auch das Wachstum der Hefe gefördert und[8] besonders die Teilungsgeschwindigkeit derselben wesentlich erhöht, so dass durch Eisen-

H. yeast development Why Rule 3?
n. necessary B. constituent
s. surety e. explained A. striking, noticeable
j. at any rate
e. as iron containing M. possibility
g. thought w. important (App. 7, 6, a, b)
W. growth
g. advanced T. division, splitting velocity
w. essentially e. raised

gaben die Hefeernte* entschieden bedeutend vergrössert wird. Dies gilt besonders für die Darreichung des Eisens in Form von Ferrosulphat,* aber weniger für diejenige in Form des Chlorides.*

Give reasons for the * e. decisively
v. increased D. administration g. is true
E. iron w. less
d. that (App. 14, 2)

So wie den Bakterien muss* auch der Hefe eine ausreichende Menge von Wasser[9] zur Verfügung stehen, und die meisten Nahrungsstoffe müssen* darin gelöst dargereicht werden. Das beste Wachstum und die grösste Hefeernte erhält man dementsprechend auch bei der Zucht derselben in Nährlösungen.*

d. B. to the bacteria d. H. to the yeast
a. sufficient z. V. at disposal
N. foods g. dissolved
W. growth H. yeast production
e. obtains d. correspondingly Z. culture,
N. nourishing-solutions

Organische Nahrungsstoffe

N. foods

Der Stickstoffbedarf der Hefe kann* nun in verschiedener Weise gedeckt werden; jedenfalls muss* aber gebundener Stickstoff gegeben werden. In bezug auf die Art der assimilierbaren Stickstoffverbindungen erweisen sich die obergärigen Hefen am wählerischsten, während die untergärigen Hefen* in dieser Hinsicht leichter zu befriedigen sind. Im allgemeinen sind die Amide die[3] den Hefen zuträglichsten und von ihnen am besten und leichtester assimilierbaren Stickstoffverbindungen. Dies gilt besonders für die Kulturhefen,* also Bier- Wein- und Presshefen.* Peptone werden* fast ebensogut verarbeitet, nachdem sie* vorher von den Hefen in Amide gespalten worden sind. Nitrate können* im allgemeinen den Hefen nicht als Stickstoffquellen dienen.

S. nitrogen need v. different
g. taken care of j. at any rate
I. b. auf in respect to
S. nitrogen compounds e. s. are shown
o. H. top yeast w. most particular
w. while u.H. bottom fermenting
l. more easily z. b. to be satisfied
z. which are most beneficial
See for this sentence Rule 3 C 1, s.5.
g. is valid K. culture yeast
w. are (App. 7, 5, a)
v. processed n. after
g. split
S. source of nitrogen

Übrigens herrscht ein inniger Zusammenhang zwischen der Ausnützbarkeit einer Stickstoffquelle und den[3] gleichzeitig zur Verfügung stehenden Kohlenstoffquellen. Es können* durch Variierung der letzteren erhebliche Änderungen in der Art der brauchbaren Stickstoffverbindungen herbeigeführt werden, wie die darauf angestellten Versuche ergaben.

ü. moreover i. close Z. connection
A. utilizability
a. which stand (Why which?) z. V. at disposal
e. k. h. w. there (App. 10, 1, d)
e. considerable Ä. changes
h. brought about
a. made V. experiments e. showed

In bezug auf besondere Kohlenstoffquellen erweisen sich die einzelnen Hefespezies als mehr oder weniger wählerisch. Peptone und Asparagin sind Nahrungsmittel für die Hefe, deren Stickstoff- und Kohlenstoffbedarf sie[4] gleichzeitig zu decken vermögen.

b. special K. carbon sources
e. s. are shown (App. 11, 4, a)
w. particular N. means-of-nourishment, food
S. nitrogen need
v. are able z. to take care of

Die Quantität der notwendigen Kohlenstoff- und Stickstoffverbindungen ist sehr gering. Wir pflegen[7] bei allen unseren Züchtungsversuchen von Hefen im Laboratorium viel zu hohe Konzentrationen besonders der Kohlenstoffnahrung zu verwenden, sofern wir* eben nur Wachstum und Vermehrung zu erreichen wünschen. Anders sind die Verhältnisse, wenn gleichzeitig eine kräftige Vergärung von Zuckern zu Alkohol und Kohlensäure herbeigeführt werden soll, wie es* in der Praxis der Wein- und Bierherstellung und Brennerei geschieht.

n. necessary
g. slight p. are accustomed (to what?)
Z. culture-experiments z. too
v. use s. as far as
W. growth V. reproduction e. attain
V. conditions g. at the same time
V. fermentaion h. brought about
s. is supposed to w. be (App. 7, 6, a)
g. happens B. beer-production Br. distilling

Man hat* nun verschiedene Zucker und Glyzerin in Bezug auf ihre Brauchbarkeit als Kohlenstoffquellen für einzelne Hefearten untersucht; die spätere kleine Tabelle soll* in diese Verhältnisse[9] einen Einblick gewähren.

v. different
B. usefulness
e. single u. investigated s. later
s. is to E. insight g. afford

Die chemische Reaktion des Nährbodens ist ebenfalls von grosser Bedeutung für das Hefewachstum. Die meisten Spaltpilze bevorzugen eine leicht alkalische Reaktion des Nährsubstrates. Sehr geringe Mengen freier H-Ionen werden* von ihnen ebenfalls vertragen, wenn auch dadurch meist bald eine Verzögerung des Wachstums[1] herbeigeführt wird.

N. nutrient-base
e. likewise B. importance
S. split fungi b. prefer
N. nourishing substratum
v. endure, tolerate w. a. even though
V. retardation h. brought about

ENTKEIMUNG DURCH CHEMISCHE MITTEL

Die Entkeimung durch chemische Mittel kann* entweder eine vollständige Abtötung aller[3] in oder auf dem betreffenden **Substrat** befindlichen Mikroorganismen erzielen oder nur eine Vernichtung aller krankheiterregenden Mikroben; im letzteren Falle sprechen wir von chemischer Desinfektion.[10] Reichen die chemischen Mittel nur dazu[7] hin,[2] eine Hemmung in der Entwicklung von **Bakterien** herbeizuführen, so sprechen wir von Antisepsis. Eine und dieselbe chemische Verbindung kann* entsprechend ihrer Konzentration, der herrschenden Temperatur und der Einwirkungsdauer sowohl zur völligen Entkeimung als auch zur Desinfektion und Antisepsis dienen. Eine grosse Anzahl organischer und anorganischer Verbindungen hat die Eigenschaft,[7] schon in sehr grosser Verdünnung schädigend und schliesslich tötend auf Bakterien einzuwirken. Man fasst diese Mittel als Antiseptika kurz zusammen,[2] wobei man* für die Praxis von denselben noch einige weitere Eigenschaften, bzw. die möglichste Entkeimungskraft fordert. Von dem Antiseptikum verlangt man im allgemeinen, dass es* in möglichst kurzer Zeit und in grosser Verdünnung auch die widerstandsfähigsten Sporen tötet und* dabei keine Nebenwirkung äussert, die* dessen Gebrauch im täglichen Leben beeinträchtigt.

Underline all nouns that should be bold faced. Give reasons for the *. In some instances this asterisk is intentionally left out.
e. gain, obtain V. destruction
k. sickness-exciting F. case
Why Rule 10? 2? Note how the "da"-word calls for "zu". See App. 23, 3.
h. to bring about V. compound
e. corresponding h. prevailing
E. duration of effect v. complete
E. disinfection d. serve A. number
E. attribute (to what?)
s. harmful V. dilution t. deadening
e. to act What goes with "fasst"?
z. combine w. in which case What does "man" call for? e. some w. further f. requires
v. demands m. as possible
w. most resistant
t. kills What does "und" call for?
ä. manifests d. its (App. 22, 4)
b. impairs, damages

Es soll[6] also für Kleinlebewesen besonders giftig, für den höheren Organismus in den verwendeten Dosen aber möglichst ungiftig sein. Ausserdem soll[6] es auf die[3] mit ihm in Berührung kommenden Geräte nicht schädigend wirken. So ist[6] z. B. ein an sich vorzügliches Desinfektionsmittel im Gärungsbetrieb unbrauchbar, wenn es* Rohrleitungen, u. dgl. stark angreift.

s. is supposed to K. microorganisms
g. poisonous v. used
A. besides
G. utensils k. which come (Why which?)
Ber. contact s. harmful v. excellent
G. fermentation business, operation u. unusable
a. attacks, corrodes R. pipe systems

Zur Beurteilung eines Antiseptikums ist* daher eine Reihe von Versuchen notwendig, die* hinsichtlich der bakteriziden Kraft desselben in zweierlei Richtung unternommen werden. Vor allem ist der "Hemmungswert" zu ermitteln, der eigentlich eine reine Konzentrationsangabe ist, bei der[5] ausser der Art der probierten Mikroorganismen die Temperatur und die Menge der vorhandenen Bakteriennährstoffe zu berücksichtigen ist. Dann ist* der "Tötungswert" zu bestimmen, der* durch die Zeit der Abtötung einer bestimmten Bakterienart bei einer bestimmten Konzentration und Temperatur definiert ist.

B. judgement, evaluation
R. series V. experiments n. necessary
h. with regard to K. strength z. two fold
u. undertaken v. a. above all
z. e. to be ascertained e. really
b. d. in the case of which (Let the relative take out the verb when possible.)
v. existing z. b. to be considered
i. z. b. to be determined (App. 12, 1)
A. killing off b. certain

Die Vergleichung von verschiedenen Desinfektionsmitteln ist nur dann möglich, wenn unter peinlicher Einhaltung gleichgearteter äusserer Verhältnisse eine Wertbestimmung der Desinfektionskraft[4] vorgenommen wird. Dazu sind heute ziemlich exakte Methoden[9] in Verwendung, auf die[5] hier nicht im einzelnen eingegangen werden kann. Im wesentlichen muss dabei verlangt werden, dass ein genau bekanntes[3] und für diese **Versuche** auch geeignetes Testmaterial von Bakterien verwendet wird. Die Temperaturen, bei denen[5] die Einwirkung der zu untersuchenden Substanz in genau bekannter Konzentration erfolgt, müssen konstant eingehalten bleiben. Ausserdem müssen die Versuche möglichst so gemacht werden, dass alle Keime des Testmaterials[4] den Schädigungen gleich ausgesetzt werden und[8] sich daher unter gleichen Bedingungen befinden.

V. comparison v. different
m. possible
p. painstaking E. maintenance
W. value determination v. undertaken
d. for that purpose z. rather
a. d. to which (How far backward do you go when you pick up this verb "kann"?)
b. known (what?) V. experiments
g. which is appropriate v. used
b. d. in the case of which E. effect
z. u. to be investigated (App. 12, 2)
e. kept A. besides
m. as much as possible
S. damages a. exposed
s. b. be found g. similar B. condition

Die Testobjekte müssen* dem Desinfektionsmittel so ausgesetzt sein, dass die Einwirkung* eine gleichmässige und vollkommene ist. Wie schon angedeutet, muss* nach dem Versuch das Desinfektionsmittel so vollkommen und so rasch als möglich entfernt werden. Dabei ist* ganz besonders darauf zu achten, dass durch chemische Massnahmen nicht etwa neue Verbindungen entstehen, die* an sich ebenfalls zumindest entwicklungshemmende Eigenschaften aufweisen. Ein Beispiel dafür ist das Formaldehyd, das man* durch Ammoniak in Hexamethylentetramin überführen kann. Es verläuft diese Reaktion verhältnismässig langsam und liefert im Hexamethylentetramin eine Substanz, die* an sich entwicklungshemmende Eigenschaften besitzt.

a. exposed E. effect
Note absence of the noun. a. indicated
n. after v. completely
r. rapidly e. removed
i. z. a. is to be regarded (App. 12, 1)
M. measures, precautions e. perhaps
a. s. in themselves z. at least
a. show entw. development-inhibiting
ü. convert e. v. d. this reaction proceeds (App. 10, 1, d, e) l. furnishes
E. qualities
b. possess

In den meisten Fällen genügt bei der Verwendung von Kulturaufschwemmungen die mechanische Trennung der Keime von der Flüssigkeit durch Zentrifugieren oder Fällung, worauf man* neuerlich mit Wasser versetzt, wieder ausschleudert und[8] dies einigemal wiederholt. Diese Art der nachherigen Reinigung genügt ganz besonders bei den Phenolen, da ja in geringer Menge Phenole ohne jede Schädigung von den Bakterien vertragen werden. In vielen Fällen wird[6] schon die* durch Eintragen kleinerer Suspensionsmengen in das **Nährmittel** hervorgerufene Verdünnung vollkommen ausreichen.

F. cases g. suffices V. use
K. culture-depositing T. separation
F. liquid
F. precipitation n. anew v. mixes
a. centrifuges w. repeats
n. subsequent R. cleansing
g. slight M. quantity
S. harm v. tolerated (App. 7, 5, a)
F. cases w. will (App. 7, 4)
h. which is produced
V. dilution a. reach, suffice

Grössere Schwierigkeit macht die Entfernung von Metallsalzen, wie Silbernitrat, Kupfersulfat und Quecksilberchlorid. Um* hier eine rasche Entgiftung zu erreichen, ist es notwendig,[7] die Metalle chemisch unlöslich zu binden, wozu man* Sulfide und Schwefelwasserstoff anwendet. Aber diese Gegengifte sind selbst schon ausgesprochene Zellgifte. In diesen Fällen ist* mit möglichst äquivalenten Mengen zu arbeiten und* überdies Soda beizugeben, um* sofort eine Überführung der frei werdenden Säure in ein Neutralsalz zu ermöglichen. Die Wirkung der Desinfektionsmittel auf die Zelle kann* sich nun verschieden äussern und wird* durch äussere Umstände wesentlich beeinflusst.

S. difficulty What is the subject?
E. removal
What does "um" call for? E. detoxification
e. reach n. necessary w. for which purpose
a. uses G. antidotes s. themselves
a. pronounced Z. cell poisons
m. as much as possible i. z. a. is to be worked (App. 12, 1)
e. make possible U. conversion W. effect
ä. manifest ä. outer U. conditions
b. influenced

Entkeimung durch Licht

E. removal of germs, degermination

Über die wachstumhemmende Wirkung des Lichtes gegenüber Mikroorganismen gehen die Anschauungen weit auseinander.[2] Dazu trug wohl auch viel die angewendete Untersuchungstechnik bei.* Das Sonnenlicht wird* sowohl in seiner Intensität als auch in seiner Zusammensetzung im kurzwelligen Teil von atmosphärischen Verhältnissen und dem * durch Staub und Rauch geschaffenen Dunst wesentlich beeinflusst. Dabei sind diese Einflüsse meist vollkommen unkontrollierbar und wechseln ständig. Überdies ist die Wirkung der* im Sonnenlicht und überhaupt in jeder **Lichtquelle** vorhandenen Strahlen der verschiedenen Wellenlänge sehr ungleich. Wie[8] schon auf Seite 152 auseinandergesetzt, sind die kurzwelligen Strahlen die wirksamsten. Zur Entkeimung kommen auch nur diese in Frage. Das ultraviolette Licht besitzt jedenfalls eine stark keimtötende Kraft, die[5] sich einerseits den Nährboden derart chemisch zu verändern vermag, dass eine Schädigung der Bakterien* eintreten kann.

w. growth-inhibiting W. effect
g. as opposed A. views What goes with "gehen"?
d. in addition a. used
b. contributed What goes with "wird"?
Z. composition
k. short waved V. conditions
g. which is created (Why Rule 3?)
D. haze, vapor w. essentially b. influenced
v. perfectly w. change s. constantly
Ü. moreover S. sunlight
v. which are present S. rays
W. wave length w. as (what?)
a. discussed w. effective (ones)
F. question
j. at any rate k. germ-killing
e. on the one hand N. nutrient base
v. is able S. injury
e. occur

ENTKEIMUNG UND KONSERVIERUNG

Certain rules are involved where the * appears; indicate the rules.
In difficult sentences numbers will still appear.

Unter Entkeimung und Sterilisation im strengsten Sinne des Wortes versteht man die Freimachung eines Gegenstandes oder irgendeines Substrates von jeglicher Art von Organismen.* Man benützt dazu entweder physikalische oder chemische Eingriffe oder endlich beide miteinander.[1] Die Untersuchungsergebnisse über die Sterilisation sind sowohl für technische Betriebe als auch für die Medizin von grösster Tragweite.* Den eigentlichen Entkeimungsmethoden schliessen sich jene Verfahren an,* die* nicht eine völlige Abtötung jeglicher Organismen in und auf dem betreffenden Stoff[9] zum Ziele haben, sondern nur die Hemmung jeglicher Weiterentwicklung der bereits vorhandenen lebenden Mikroorganismen. Endlich hat* sich die Entkeimungslehre auch mit jenen Massnahmen zu beschäftigen, die* das Hinzutreten von lebenden Mikroorganismen zu bereits entkeimten Stoffen verhindern. Wir wissen bereits, dass die organischen Verbindungen,[4] wie sie[4] in den verschiedenen Nahrungs- und Genussmitteln vorliegen, in erster Linie durch kleine Lebewesen in kürzester Zeit in Fäulnis oder Gärung übergehen und[8] so verdorben werden. Die Entkeimungslehre zeigt uns nun jene Mittel und Wege auf,[2] die* uns in den Stand setzen, Nahrungs- und Genussmittel zu machen. Die* für die Volksernährung so wichtige Konserventechnik fusst auf den* durch die Entkeimungsversuche gewonnenen Erkenntnissen und Erfahrungen.

E. removal of germs, degermination
v. understands F. liberation
G. subject, object i. any j. every
b. utilizes e. either E. operations, methods
U. investigation-results s. as well
B. business
T. significance e. real d. to the
a. are attached V. processes
A. killing off. destruction j. any
z. Z. h. to have as a goal B. inhibit
W. further development v. existing
E. theory of germination
z. b. to be concerned H. accession
v. prevent b. already V. compounds
N. food G. condiments
v. exist L. mikroorganisms
F. putrefaction G. fermentation
v. spoiled
M. means a. shows S. position (to what?)
V. national diet
f. is based, bases d. the (what?)
g. which are gained Erk. knowledge
Erf. experience, experiments

Die Physikalische Entkeimung

Für die Entkeimung kommen[9] als physikalische Mittel in erster Linie die Wärme, die mechanische Trennung der Organismen vom Substrat durch Filtration und endlich das **Licht** in Frage.

What goes with "kommen"?
M. means T. separation
e. finally Review rule 9

Entkeimung durch Wärme

Wir haben* bereits gehört, dass eine Entwicklung von Bakterien* nur innerhalb verhältnismässig enger Temperaturgrenzen möglich ist. Wenn wir* die Temperatur über das "Maximum" erhöhen, so werden* nach längerer oder kürzerer Zeit die Mikroben vernichtet. Wir haben also in der Hitze ein ausgezeichnetes Sterilisationsmittel. Dieselbe kann* als trockene Wärme oder als feuchte Wärme angewendet werden. Da für letztere alle Mikroorganismen* empfindlicher sind, wird* man letztere Form der Sterilisation bevorzugen. In letzter Linie wird[6] für die Wahl der trockenen oder feuchten Hitze die Beschaffenheit des Substrates, das[5] sterilisiert werden soll, ausschlaggebend sein.

E. development
v. relatively e. narrow
m. possible
e. increase n. after
v. destroyed
a. excellent
a. used t. try f. moist
d. since
e. more sensitive
b. prefer i. l. L. in final analysis
f. moist B. nature

Bei der trockenen Sterilisation in der Wärme werden* die Substrate in Luft von 150-160° ein bis zwei Stunden erhitzt. Dies geschieht in besonderen Schränken, den "Heissluftsterilisatoren." Die Sterilisation durch feuchte Wärme wird* entweder mit strömendem Dampf von der Temperatur des* bei gewöhnlichem **Luftdruck** siedenden Wassers oder mit erhitztem Wasserdampf durchgeführt. Im strömenden Dampf von der Temperatur des* bei gewöhnlichem **Luftdruck** siedenden Wassers werden* alle vegetativen Bakterienzellen sicher in einer Viertelstunde vernichtet, nicht aber die Sporen, von denen ja bekanntlich einige[1] sogar vielstündiges Kochen vertragen.

a. decisive b. in the case of
w. are (App. 7, 5, a)
e. heated g. takes place S. cabinets
d. by
s. flowing D. steam
s. which boils g. ordinary
e. heated d. carried through
g. ordinary L. air pressure s. which boils
v. destroyed
b. as one knows s. even
v. endure

BOTANIK

GEGENSEITIGE BEZIEHUNGEN ZWISCHEN PFLANZEN UND TIEREN†

ALLGEMEINES. Die gegenseitigen Beziehungen zwischen Pflanzen und **Tieren,**[1] in erster Linie das Verhältnis zwischen Blumen und Tieren (Blütenbiologie) ist ein scheinbar gut bearbeitetes Gebiet der **Ökologie.**[1] Die umfangreiche Literatur aber zeigt, wie oberflächlich viele Beobachtungen sind und wie sie[4] die Tendenz haben,[7] irgendwie eine zweckmässige **"Anpassung"** aufzudecken. Wie **fruchtbar** demgegenüber die experimentelle Forschung[4] auf diesem **Gebiete** sein kann, zeigen die schönen Untersuchungen **Knolls.**[1] Sie können[6] als Beispiel für eine exakte und kritische Bearbeitung blütenbiologischer **Probleme** dienen.

g. mutual B. relations
P. plants T. animals V. condition
B. floral-biology Note Rule 1.
s. apparently b. worked up G. field
o. superficial B. observations
T. tendency (to what?) i. any
z. appropriate A. adaptation a. disclose
f. fruitful (opposite-to-that) F. study
G. field s. fine U. investigations
B. example B. treatment d. serve

Geographische Verbreitung der Bestäubungsvorrichtungen

Durch die Untersuchungen Sprengels und Darwins,[5] welchen solche von Fr. und H. Müller und vielen anderen **Forschern** ergänzend hinzutraten, ist[6] endgültig der **Nachweis** geliefert worden, dass viele Blüten[4] zu ihrer Bestäubung der Mitwirkung gewisser Tiere, zumal Insekten, seltener **Vögel** bedürfen und[8] **diesem** Umstande viele ihrer **Eigentümlichkeiten** verdanken.

V. distribution B. pollination devices
w. to which Note Rule 5.
F. scientists
e. supplementarily h. come in
B. flowers B. pollination M. cooperation
g. of certain (Why of?) b. need
v. owe U. circumstance E. peculiarities

Zahlreiche Blüten werden[6] von den mannigfachsten **Besuchern** ausgebeutet und bestäubt, indem ihr Pollen und Nektar[4] jedem frei oder doch leicht zugänglich zur **Verfügung** steht. Andere Blüten sind[6] in mehr oder weniger hohem Grade an bestimmte **Sippen** "angepasst", sei es, dass ihre Lockmittel[4] charakteristische **Liebhabereien** voraussetzen, sei es, dass der Zugang zum Nektar[4] nur beim Besitze gewisser Körperformen oder gewisser **Fähigkeiten** möglich ist.[10] Sind "Anpassungen" der letzteren Art an Tiersippen beschränkter **Verbreitung** gebunden, so ist[6] ihr Vorhandensein oder Fehlen für die Vegetation bestimmter **Gebiete** charakteristisch.

Z. numerous m. most varied
a. exploited b. pollinated i. in that, by
z. accessible z. V. at disposal
G. degree
b. certain S. tribes L lures
v. presuppose
Z. access B. possession g. certain
F. abilities m. possible S. if - are (Why?)
A. adaptations T. animal-groups
V. presence F. absence b. of certain

Ornithophile Blüten

Pflanzengeographische Bedeutung hat die Bestäubung der Blüten durch **Vögel,**[1] die Ornithophilie,[1] weil blütenbesuchende Vögel[4] auf bestimmte **Gebiete** beschränkt sind. Die Vogelblumenforschung der neueren Zeit hat gezeigt, dass die Vogelblumen[4] nicht mehr als ein **Ausnahmefall** zu betrachten sind, sondern als ein Faktor, mit dem[5] die Blütenökologie, besonders die der Tropen und **Subtropen** zu rechnen hat.

B. importance B. pollination
V. birds b. flower-visiting
b. limited G. regions
V. bird-flower-study
z. b. to be considerd A. exceptional-case
b. especially d. d. that of
z. r. to figure

Die Ornithophilie ist eine **Erscheinung,**[1] die[5] hauptsächlich, aber nicht ausschliesslich auf die **Tropen** beschränkt ist, wie es[4] fälschlich angenommen wurde. Auf der südlichen Hemisphäre reicht sie über die ganze temperierte Zone bis zur südlichen Baumgrenze in **Feuerland.**[1] Nach Werth (1915) machen[9] die ornithophilen Erscheinungen in der Alten Welt bei den grossen nordafrikanischen, west- und innerasiatischen Wüsten- und **Steppengürteln** Halt. Die nördliche Verbreitungsgrenze der ornithophilen Pflanzen oder Tropen Afrikas und Asiens läuft ungefähr mit der nördlichen Verbreitungsgrenze der **Nektariniden** zusammen.[2] Letztere läuft von den Senegambien nach Abessinien, Palästina, Siam bis zu den **Philippinen.**[1] Dass die nördliche Verbreitungsgrenze der ornithophilen Pflanzen[4] mit der der **Nektariniden** ungefähr zusammenfällt, sehen wir an Karten von Musa, Loranthus, Bombax und vielleicht auch von **Rhododendron.**[1] Das einzige Gebiet, in dem[5] sich die Nektariniden weit über den 30, Breitengrad (hinaus) vorschieben, ist Palästina, wo Loranthus Acasiae[4] als **Vogelblume** gefunden wird und[8] dem Auftreten des[3] zu den **Nektariniden** gehörenden **Chinnyris osae** entspricht. Sichere Angaben über das Vorkommen ornithophiler Pflanzen in Europa fehlen.

E. phenomenon h. chiefly
a. exclusively b. limited
a. assumed f. falsely
g. entire
B. tree-limit N. according to
Note Rule 9. b. with
W. waste- und steppe-bands H. halt
(Note how this noun goes with verb.)
V. distribution-limit u. about
z. coincides
l. runs
n. northern
P. plants d. d. that of
u. approximately K. charts
v. perhaps e. only G. region
ü. h. over and beyond (App. 21, 1g)
v. pushed
A. appearance d. of the (what?)
g. which belong e. corresponds
A. data V. occurrence

†A. F. W. Schimper, **Pflanzengeographie auf physiologischer Grundlage**

DAS LICHT

Nach dem Wasser ist das Licht der mächtigste äussere Faktor für die Gestalt der **Pflanze.**[1] Während die Wärme,[4] die[5] die pflanzliche Maschine in **Bewegung** setzt und[8] während der ganzen Dauer ihrer Entwicklung und Tätigkeit in erster **Linie** reguliert, deren **Gestaltung** nicht wesentlich beeinflusst, ist[6] das Licht beim Aufbau des Pflanzenkörpers in hervorragendem **Masse** architektonisch beteiligt. Aber auch für die Ernährung ist das Licht von fundamentaler **Bedeutung,** weil es[4] für die **Kohlensäureassimilation** unentbehrlich ist. Mit gewissen Ausnahmen brauchen alle Pflanzer Licht für ihre **Existenz.**[1]

N. next to m. most powerful ä. outer
G. shaping, form W. while
p. plant B. movement w. during
g. entire D. duration E. development
d. its (See App. 22, 4) G. formation
A. building up P. plant body
h. outstanding M. degree b. involved
E. nourishment B. importance
u. indispensable
A. exceptions b. need
Give reasons for the numbers.

Die grosse ökologische Bedeutung des Lichtes zeigt sich z. B. in seinem Einfluss auf die räumliche Verteilung der **Pflanzen.**[1] Die Epiphyten und Lianen verdanken ihre räumliche Verteilung dem Drange nach **Licht.**[1]

ö. biological B. importance
z. s. is shown (App. 11, 4a) E. influence
V. distribution v. owe
r. spatial V. distribution D. urge

Die ungleiche Intensität der Beleuchtung in den verschiedenen klimatischen Zonen und die zunehmende Dauer der Beleuchtung vom Äquator zu den Polen verfehlen nicht,[7] der **Vegetation**[9] ihren Stempel aufzudrücken. Weit grösser bleibt allerdings die Bedeutung des Lichtes für die pflanzliche **Topographie,**[1] da für die Charakterisierung der einzelnen Formationen eines Gebietes die grossen Unterschiede der Beleuchtung[4] wichtig sind.

u. unequal B. illumination
v. different z. increasing
D. duration B. illumination
v. do not fail (to what?)
a. imprint (upon)
e. individual
G. region U. differences
B. illumination

Das Lichtklima der Erde

ALLGEMEINES: Bekanntlich besteht das Sonnenlicht aus Strahlen verschiedener **Wellenlänge,**[1] die[5] sichtbar werden, wenn das Licht[4] durch ein **Quarzprisma** gebrochen und[8] in ein **Spektrum** zerlegt wird. Die Wirkungen dieser Strahlen sind verschieden: die kurzwelligen, blauvioletten sind wirkungsvoll für die Photomorphosen und die tropistischen Bewegungen, die Strahlen mittlerer Wellenlänge, grün, gelb und rot, sind von fundamentaler Bedeutung für die Ernährung (Kohlensäureassimilation)[1], während die langwelligen, ultraroten,[4] die Wärmestrahlen sind. Diese drei Spektralbezirke werden[6] auch nach ihrer chemischen (blauviolett), Licht- (grünrot) und **Wärmewirkung** (ultrarot) geschieden, doch kann[6] diese Sonderung der Wirkung nach nicht scharf sein.

B. as is known b. consists
S. rays W. wave length s. visible
Note Rule 8 E, and sentence 1. Observe how you borrow "wird" for the participle "gebrochen"
v. different
B. movements
S. rays m. middle
B. importance E. nourishment
w. while
W. heat rays S. spectral-regions
w. g. are separated (App 7, 5, a)
W. heat effect S. separation
W. effect

LICHTMESSUNG. Die Messung der Gesamtstrahlung der Sonne hat für die Pflanzengeographie eine grosse **Bedeutung.**[1]

L. light measurement G. total radiation

Die[3] mittels **Kompensationspyrheliometer** gemessenen Werte der Strahlungsenergie der Sonne sind[6] je nach dem Orte, den Jahres- und **Tageszeiten** verschieden. Aus den Beobachtungen amerikanischer Forscher ging zuerst hervor,[2] dass die Intensität der Gesamtstrahlung[4] mit der Höhe über dem **Meeresspiegel** zunimmt, weil der Strahlungsverlust[4] durch Absorption der Atmosphäre geringer wird. Bei mittlerer Sonnenhöhe gehen auf höchsten Berggipfeln etwa 1/5, auf bewohnten Höhen etwa 1/4—1/3, in der Ebene mehr als 1/2 der einfallenden **Sonnenstrahlen** verloren. Die Zunahme der Intensität der Sonnenstrahlen mit der Höhe geht aus Fig. 21 hervor,[2] welche[5] die Verhältnisse auf Java graphisch darstellt.

m. by means of
g. which are measured (why which?)
j. n. according to O. place
B. observations F. scientist
G. total-radiation
M. sea-level z. increases R. radiation-loss
g. w. becomes less (App. 7, 3)
h. highest B. mountain-peaks
b. inhabited H. hills
e. incident v. lost (go-lost) Note the idiom.
Z. increase
V. conditions
d. represents

Langdauernde Messungen der Strahlungsenergie an einem bestimmten Orte der Erde geben eine Vorstellung von dem Strahlungsklima dieses **Ortes.**[1] Diese Strahlungsenergie wird,[6] da etwa 80 Proz. der gesamten Energiemenge der

L. long-lasting M. measurements
b. certain V. idea
S. radiation-climate
g. total What rules did you use on the page?

Sonnenstrahlen[4] von den ultraroten **Strahlen** erzeugt werden, in **Kalorien** ausgedrückt. Die Messung der mittleren täglichen Wärmesumme für verschiedene Orte hat gezeigt, dass, je höher die geographische **Breite**, desto geringer die jährliche Strahlungssumme ist. Die Jahreszeiten dagegen verhalten sich anders, da im Sommer im Norden, z. B. in Stolkholm, die Strahlungssumme[4] genau so gross ist wie südlicher, in Washington.[1] Der niedrigere Stand der Sonne im Norden wird[6] durch die längeren Tage im **Sommer** ausgeglichen. Im nördlichen kommen also Pflanzen mit kurzer **Vegetationsperiode** besser fort[2].

S. sun-rays S. rays e. produced
a. expressed M. measurement
t. daily v. different
j. d. the higher – the less (App. 26, 2)
J. seasons d. on the other hand
v. s. behave a. differently
g. exactly Note the verb before "wie."
s. more southerly n. lower
a. balanced
P. plants
f. thrive

Es ist eine bekannte Tatsache, dass die Pflanzen[4] verschieden lichtbedürftig sind. Die Lichtintensität, die[5] für ein normales **Gedeihen** unerlässlich ist, schwankt für jede Pflanze innerhalb gewisser **Grenzen.**[1] Unter dem minimalen Wert ist eine Existenz nicht mehr möglich.

T. fact
l. in need of light
u. indispensable s. varies
l. in need of light
i. within g. certain
W. value m. possible

Einfluss von Lichtintensität und -qualität auf die Kohlensäureassimilation

E. influence

Die **Wirkungen** des Lichtes auf die Pflanze sind je nach der Intensität desselben und je nach der einzelnen physiologischen Funktion fördernd, schaffend oder zerstörend.[1] Das Ergrünen der Pflanzen ist[6] mit einzelnen Ausnahmen an die Anwesenheit von **Licht** gebunden, und nur mit Hilfe von Licht ist[6] die Kohlensäureassimilation durch das **Chlorophyll** möglich. Es wirkt also das Licht in hohem Masse schaffend.

W. effects P. plant
j. n. according to (App. 26, 1)
f. promoting, helpful s. creating-ive
z. destructive E. turning green
E. exceptions A. presence H. aid
m. possible Review Rule 6 E.
s. creative

Die Kohlensäureassimilation ist[6] von Quantität und Qualität des **Lichtes** abhängig, und da beide[4] auf der Erde, wie wir[4] gesehen haben, sehr wechselnd sind, so muss[6] die Pflanze je nach dem Standort die Assimilation in Einklang zum **Licht** bringen, um[7] überhaupt existenz- und konkurrenzfähig zu sein.

v. on
a. dependent (Note Rule 6.)
w. changeable
S. habitat
E. harmony e. capable of existence
Note Rule 7.

Es soll[6] nun hier die Assimilation in bezug auf **Licht** nur so weit besprochen werden, als sie[4] ökologisch und pflanzengeographisch von **Bedeutung** ist. Die Geschwindigkeit, womit[5] die **Assimilation** sich vollzieht, ist[6] von gleichzeitiger Anwesenheit und Intensität verschiedener **Faktoren** abhängig. Die wichtigsten sind: 1. Lichtintensität und -qualität,[1] 2. Gehalt der Atmostphäre an Kohlensäure,[1] 3. Höhe der Temperatur, 4. Chlorophyllgehalt.[1] Die Assimilationskurve ist[6] von all diesen Faktoren und **Faktorenkombinationen** abhängig, abgesehen von den inneren **Faktoren,**[1] die[5] grösstenteils noch unbekannt sind. Alle diese inneren und äusseren Faktoren wirken direkt oder indirekt.[1] So übt die Erhöhung der Kohlensäurezufuhr gleichzeitig Förderung der Assimilation, aber auch Hemmung durch **Spaltöffnungsschluss** usw. aus.[2]

E. there (See App. 10, la, b, c.) i. b. a. in reference b. w. be discussed (App. 7, 6)
G. velocity
s. v. is accomplished
g. simultaneous A. presence
a. dependent w. most important
G. content of
H. height of
Note Rule 6 E.
a. dependent a. apart from
g. for the most part ä. outer
E. increase
g. simultaneously F. furthering
H. hindering S. stomate-closure

Die exakte Forschung über das Verhältnis von Licht und Assimilation hat nicht allein für die Physiologie,[1] sondern auch für die Ökologie grosse Bedeutung.[1]

F. study V. relation, condition
a. alone
O. ecology B. importance

Die Betrachtung des Verlaufs der Assimilationskurve bei verschiedenen Lichtstärken[1] und bei konstantem Kohlensäuregehalt[1] und konstanter Temperatur zeigt, dass die Assimilation[4] bei schwachen Lichtintensitäten fast proportional der **Lichtstärke** ansteigt, um[7] langsam schwächer zu werden und[8] zuletzt annähernd konstante Grösse zu erreichen.

B. consideration V. course
v. different L. light-intensities
K. carbon-dioxide-content
s. weak f. almost
a. increases L. light-strength
s. weaker a. approximately
e. reach What calls for the "zu"?

LICHT UND WACHSTUM DER PFLANZE

(Give reasons for the numbers or the *. Underline the nouns that should be bold-faced.)

Dass das Licht* für die Pflanzengestaltung einen der wichtigsten Faktoren darstellt, geht schon daraus hervor,[2] dass die Pflanze,* je nach der Intensität des Lichtes,* in dessen Genusse sie[4] steht, eine verschiedene **Gestalt** annimmt. Nicht nur die Lichtintensität,* sondern auch die tägliche Dauer der Belichtung ist* für die Entwicklung der **Pflanze** massgebend. Blütenbildung und Fruchtreife,* sowie die Entwicklung von vegetativen Organen,* sind* von der Belichtungszeit sehr abhängig. Der Einfluss der Tageslänge auf den Zuwachs der Blatt- und Wurzelmasse geht u. a. deutlich aus den Untersuchungen Johannsons hervor.[2] Seine bisherigen Versuche berechtigen zu der Schlussfolgerung,[1] dass die Wurzelentwicklung* bei Zunahme der Tageslänge bis zu 12 Stunden stets mehr befördert wird. Wie die **Wurzeln*** auf noch längere Tage reagieren, muss* dahingestellt bleiben. Diese Gesetzmässigkeit gilt im allgemeinen auch für die Blattmasse.* Wie[8] aus den Kurven in **Fig. 25** ersichtlich ist, ruft eine Verlängerung über 12 Stunden hinaus keine wesentliche Vergrösserung der **Blattentwicklung** hervor.* Es zeigt sich auch, dass die oberirdischen Organe[4] im Verhältnis zu den Wurzeln bedeutend unempfindlicher gegen die Variationen in der Belichtungszeit sind; die Kurven der Blattentwicklung steigen nicht so steil wie die der Wurzelentwicklung.[1]

P. plant-formation
d. represents w. most important
h. goes-forth j. n. according to
i. d. G. in whose enjoyment G. form
t. daily
D. duration B. light exposure E. development
m. decisive B. flower-formation
F. maturity, ripening of fruit
a. dependent (what calls for this word?)
Z. growth E. leaf-mass u. a. among other things U. investigations
b. previous V. experiments b. justify
S. deduction W. root-development
b. promoted W. roots
l. longer m. d. b. remain uncertain
G. uniformity g. is true
Note Rule 8 e. visible ü.h. over and beyond (App. 21, 1g)
w. essential V. magnification B. leaf-development z. s. is shown (App. 11, 4a)
V. relation u. more insensitive
B. light-exposure
s. rise s. steep d. d. that of
W. root-development

Die[3] im **Dunkeln** entwickelten Sprosse weichen von normalen in mannigfacher **Weise** ab[2] und werden[6] als vergeilt oder etioliert bezeichnet. Sie entbehren des Chlorophylls und sind daher weiss oder gelblich.[1] Ihre Achsenteile sind weit länger als unter normalen Bedingungen.* Ihre Blätter hingegen—mit Ausnahme derjenigen der Gräser und einiger anderen Monocotylen*—sind sehr klein und meist verkrümmt.

e. which are developed (See page 20:F-4.)
m. manifold a. deviate v. etiolated
e. lack
g. yellowish
B. leaves h. on the other hand B. conditions
A. exception e. some
v. curved, bent

Durch Dunkelheit etiolierte Pflanzen kommen in der Natur nur selten vor;* man sieht sie zuweilen in Höhlen.* So fand Schimper in der bekannten Guacharrohöhle bei Caripe in Venezuela den Boden stellenweise von einer dichten, bis halbmeterhohen etiolierten **Vegetation** bedeckt, die[5] aus dem Kot der Guacharrovögel, der einzigen Bewohner der **Höhle**, hervorgegangen war.

D. darkness
v. occur z. at times H. caves
b. famous
B. soil s. in places
d. thick b. covered-found covered
K. excrement
B. inhabitants H. cave

Da Etiolelementserscheinungen* nicht allein im Dunkeln,* sondern auch bei jeder Herabsetzung des Lichtes wahrgenommen werden, spielen diese Erscheinungen in der Natur eine sehr grosse Rolle.* Die Etiolelementserscheinungen sind die sichtbaren Folgen der Wirkung des Lichtes,* entweder auf die Wachstumsgeschwindigkeit oder auf die Gestaltung der Pflanze.*

a. alone
D. darkness H. reduction
w. perceived E. phenomena
g. great
s. visible F. results W. effect
W. growth-speed G. formation

Auf dem hemmenden Einfluss des Lichtes auf das Längenwachstum des Stengels beruht zum Teil der rosettenförmige Wuchs vieler Alpenpflanzen,* die[5] in Gegenden wachsen, wo sie[4] der intensiven Bestrahlung ausgesetzt sind.

h. inhibiting E. influence
L. length-growth s. stalk, stem
W. growth A. Alp-plants G. regions
B. radiation a. exposed

Das Flächenwachstum der Blätter ist im Dunkeln sehr gering,* doch erreicht es bereits bei sehr mässiger Lichtintensität sein Optimum.* Zunahme der Beleuchtung wirkt retardierend, schliesslich hemmend. Darum besitzen bei manchen Pflanzen,* wie z. B. bei der Buche, die[3] im Innern der **Krone** befindlichen Schattenblätter eine grössere Spreite als die Sonnenblätter.*

F. surface growth B. leaves
g. slight e. reaches m. moderate
Z. increase B. illumination
s. finally b. possess b. in case of
B. beech
b. which are found (why which?)
S. leaf blade S. sun-leaves

DER WIND UND DIE PFLANZENWELT

(Give reasons for the numbers and the *; tell why certain nouns are bold-faced.)

Der Wind beeinflusst die Pflanzenwelt in verschiedener **Hinsicht,*** Luftströmungen wirken auf die **Transpiration** ein;[2] sie gleichen die CO_2 Konzentrationsunterschiede in der **Luft** aus[2] und wirken, wenn sie[4] andauernd und stark sind, modifizierend auf die **Pflanzenform.*** Wind ist häufig der Samen- und Pollenverbreiter auf kleinere oder grössere **Strecken.***

b. influences P. plant world
H. respect L. air-currents e. have an effect
K. concentration-differences a. equalize
a. permanent, lasting
h. frequently
S. seed P. pollen-distributor
S. distances

Der Wind wirkt als Überbringer von Trockenheit oder **Feuchtigkeit,*** sowie von Kälte oder Wärme modifizierend auf die Physiognomie der **Vegetation.*** Bekannt ist der günstige Einfluss der **Föhnwinde,*** jener warmen Fallwinde der **Alpentäler.*** Der grosse Einfluss dieser Winde wird* dadurch illustriert, dass an Hauptföhnstrassen der nördlichen Abhänge der Alpen viele südliche Arten wachsen, die[5] geradezu als **"Föhnpflanzen"** bezeichnet werden. Der Föhn beschleunigt durch seine Wärme die **Schneeschmelze*** und damit den Eintritt des **Frühlings.*** Durch seine wüstenartige Trockenheit kann[5] er aber auch viel **Schaden** bringen. Auch in der Arktis ist[6] ein **Föhn** bekannt, der[5] an Wärme und Trockenheit dem **Alpenföhn** nicht nachsteht. Rikli notierte zur Zeit seines Sommeraufenthaltes in Godhavn auf der Insel Disko in Nordgrönland während des Föhns Temperaturen von 16-20° C.[1] Die bevorzugte Lage der Küstengebiete Nordwestgrönlands dürfte[6] nach ihm, wenigstens zum Teil, auf den[3] zuweilen wochenlang herrschenden grönländischen **Föhn** zurückzuführen sein.

Ü. transmitter T. dryness
F. moisture K. cold
m. modifyingly B. known
g. favorable E. influence
A. Alp-valleys E. influence
d. by the fact that n. northern
A. slopes s. southerly A. types
b. designated b. accelerates
W. heat S. melting of snow
E. beginning F. spring w. desert like
S. harm, damage
b. known
n. n. not inferior
S. summer-sojourn
N. north Greenland w. during
b. preferred L. location
w. at least z. T. in part
h. which prevailed (why which?)
z. trace back

Sehr trockene, heisse Winde kommen im Sommer aus dem Wüstengebiete **Nordafrikas.*** Ein solcher trockener Wind ist der Scirocco,* der[5] bis nach **Südeuropa** kommt und[8] durch seine grosse Trockenheit sehr grossen Schaden an den dortigen Oliven- und **Traubenkulturen** anrichtet.

t. dry h. hot
W. waste-region, desert
Why rule 5? rule 8?
S. harm
d. local T. grape vineyards a. cause

Durch seine austrocknende Wirkung übt der Wind vielfach einen pflanzenpathologischen **Einfluss aus.***

a. desiccating, parching h. hot.
a. exerts v. frequently What does 'aus' go with?
p. plant disease

Wind und Pflanzenwuchs

Landschaften mit beinahe konstant stark bewegter Luft— wie flache Küsten und **Inseln,*** die[5] den ersten Anprall des **Seewindes** erhalten, oder hochgelegene freie Stellen der Gebirge— sind[6] im allgemeinen durch abnormen Baumwuchs, wenn solcher überhaupt vorhanden, charakterisiert, während die niedrige Vegetation[4] einen Einfluss des **Windes** nur wenig oder gar nicht zeigt. Der Unterschied zwischen baum- und niedrigem strauch-krautartigem Wuchs in bezug auf die Windwirkungen ist[6] durch die Zunahme der Luftbewegung mit steigender Entfernung vom **Boden** bedingt.

L. landscapes b. nearly
b. moving L. air f. flat
e. get, obtain A. impact
S. places G. mountains
v. (sind) are present
w. while, whereas n. low
g. n. not at all U. difference
b. tree n. low s. bush k. weed-like
i. b. in regard to W. wind effects
Z. increase L. air-movement s. rising

Auf Grund der Messungen ist es begreiflich, dass nur wenig über dem Boden sich erhebende Gewächse die Wirkungen der **Winde** weit weniger spüren als hochwachsende, also in erster Linie die **Bäume.***

M. measurements b. conceivable
s. e. elevating G. growths
W. effects s. sense (Note the position of the verb before "als".) B. tree

Da Winde,[4] die[5] über das Meer kommen, stärker sind als die auf dem Lande, haben[6] die Pflanzen an den Meeresküsten im allgemeinen mehr unter dem Wind zu leiden als die im Innern.* Die Windformen an den Pflanzen sehen wir deshalb am häufigsten in der Nähe der Küsten.* Die direkte Beeinflussung des Pflanzenwuchses durch die Winde zeigt sich meist nur da in augenfälliger **Weise,*** wo letztere[4] konstant und in bedeutender **Stärke** wehen.

D. since
a. than (Why is the verb here?)
z. l. to suffer (note position of the verb)
d. therefore
a. h. most frequently N. nearness
B. influencing P. plant growth
a. noticeable W. way
w. blow b. significant S. force

(If drill is necessary, cite the reasons for the * and the bold-faced nouns on this page.)

Es ist an solchen Standorten eine gewöhnliche Erscheinung,* dass Stämme und Äste der Bäume* durch die herrschenden Winde von ihrer normalen **Wachstumsrichtung** abgelenkt werden und* der Windrichtung folgen. Die Windformen der Bäume können dazu dienen,[7] die Richtung der vorherrschenden **Winde** zu bestimmen. Da das Wachstum der Äste[4] durch den vorherrschenden **Wind** einseitig gehemmt ist, wachsen die Zweige nach der entgegengesetzten **Richtung,*** aus welcher der Wind kommt.	S. habitat g. ordinary S. trunks A. branches h. prevailing W. growth-direction a. deflected f. follow d. d. serve to (App. 23, 3) b. determine d. since (App. 25, 2) e. unilaterally g. checked Z. branches e. opposite R. diiection
In der Arktis und Antarktis,* sowie in den Alpen,* aber auch auf ozeanischen Inseln wird der Baum durch den starken Wind zum Strauch,* der* sich dann nicht selten dem Boden anlegt. Dass hier der Wind* grösstenteils die Ursache dieser **Form** ist, geht daraus hervor,[2] dass an Stellen, wo Windschutz* vorhanden ist, die Bäume* sich wieder normal erheben. Wenn auch nicht zu leugnen ist, dass der Wind* in mancher Beziehung für die Physiognomie der Pflanzen eine grosse **Rolle** spielt, muss* doch vor Übertreibungen in dieser Hinsicht, die* leider nicht so selten sind, gewarnt werden. Es sind* viele Formen als sogenannte "anemophile" geschildert worden, von denen es* noch lange nicht feststeht, welche Rolle der Wind* für die Entstehung dieser **Formen** spielt. Wir verfügen noch über zu wenig experimentelle Arbeit in dieser Beziehung.*	s. as well as w. becomes (App. 7, 3, a) S. bush s. a. is attached (App. 11, 4a) g. for the most part U. cause h. goes forth from the fact W. wind-protection v. present s. e. are raised up z. l. to be denied B. respect P. plants Ü. exaggeration H. respect l. unfortunately e. s. there have been (App. 7, 5, c) n. l. n. not by a long ways E. origin v. have at our disposal, control over A. work B. respect
Schimper schildert anschaulich den Einfluss der regelmässig wehenden Stürme auf die Pflanzenwelt in der Antarktis.* Er vergleicht die waldlosen, subantarktischen Inseln mit Gebieten,* die* durch Wassermangel [9]Wüstencharakter tragen und bezeichnet diese Inseln als "Windwüste",* die* nur an geschützten Stellen ein Pflanzenkleid von etwas üppigerem Aussehen trägt.	s. describes a. clearly r. regularly w. blowing v. compares w. forest-less G. regions W. lack of water W. waste-like character b. marks W. wind-deserts g. protected u. more luxuriant A. appearance
Es ist nicht statthaft,[7] die Baumlosigkeit einer Meeresküste oder einer Insel stets nur auf die starken **Winde** allein zurückzuführen. Es gibt viele Beispiele dafür, dass der Wind[4] Baumwuchs, wenn auch nur in Form von Gebüschen und Baumkrüppeln, an Küsten oder auf **Inseln** zulässt, solange die klimatischen Bedingungen* für Baumwuchs günstig sind.	s. permissible (to what?) B. tree-less-ness s. always z. to trace back e. g. there are What is the verb for "Wind"? G. bushes B. deformed trees z. admits B. conditions g. favorable

Der Wind als Bestäubungsvermittler

B. pollination mediator

Die Flora offener, windiger Landschaften zeigt nicht minder als in den vegetativen auch in den reproduktiven Funktionen den Einfluss der **Luftbewegungen.*** "Anpassungen" an Bestäubung durch Wind sind an offenen Standorten, wo die Luft[4] bewegt zu sein pflegt, weit häufiger als im windstillen Innern der Wälder.* Die Hauptmasse — wenn auch nicht der **Artenzahl** nach — der Grasflur- und Sumpfgewächse sind Windblütler,* wie Gräser. Auch hohe Bäume sind* in vielen Fällen auf **Windbestäubung** angewiesen. Hingegen sind die Sträucher und Kräuter des Waldes im gemässigten Klima **Insektenblütler,*** während im relativ insektenarmen tropischen Regenwald Apogamie und Selbstbestäubung* vielfach beobachtet wird.	L. landscapes m. less E. influence L. air-movements B. pollination pf. is accustomed to wenn a. even though n. according to type (See App. 15,3,c,d and f.) i. v. F. in many cases s. a. are dependent h. on the other hand g. temperate w. while R. rain-forest S. self-pollination b. observed

DAS WASSER ALS PFLANZENGEOGRAPHISCHER FAKTOR

(Many of the numbers and the * are omitted intentionally on this page.)

Die Rolle des Wassers im Leben der Pflanze ist von fundamentaler Bedeutung. Ist doch die Grundsubstanz des pflanzlichen Körpers, das Plasma, eine kolloidale Lösung, bei der das Wasser als Dispersionsmittel fungiert. Nur dann, wenn die Pflanze über eine bestimmte Menge **Wasser** verfügt, kann sie existieren.

B. importance I. d. See Rule 10 D, 1, 2.
K. body L. solution
What calls for the verb? f. functions
b. certain M. quantity v. disposes
What nouns should be bold faced?

Die ausserordentliche Bedeutung des Wassers kommt in der geographischen **Verbreitung**[9] zum Ausdruck. In Gebieten, in welchen die Aufrechterhaltung der Wasserbilanz—auf die es[4] in erster Linie ankommt — durch äussere **Gründe** erschwert ist, können nur solche Pflanzen dauernd Fuss fassen, deren Organisation die Überwindung dieser Schwierigkeiten ermöglicht.

a. extraordinary B. meaning, significance
k. z. A. comes to expression V. distribution
A. maintenance G. regions
a. depends What calls for "ist"? for "fassen"?
ermöglicht? d. permanently
U. overcoming S. difficulties
e. makes possible

Durch seine grosse geographische Bedeutung wird dem Wasser unter den Faktoren, die am Standort auf die Pflanze einwirken, der erste Platz eingeräumt, deshalb wird das Wasser hier in erster Linie berücksichtigt.

B. significance What does "wird" call for?
"die"? the second "wird"?
e. effect e. conceded d. therefore
b. considered

Auf keinem Gebiete der Ökologie haben sich unsere Anschauungen in den letzten Jahren so verändert, wie gerade auf dem der "Anpassungen" der Pflanzen an die Wasserverhältnisse.

G. field Ö. ecology h. s. v. have been changed
(App. 11, 4c) g. specifically
A. adaptations W. water conditions
What nouns should be bold faced?

Die beiden ersten Auflagen dieses Werkes zeigen uns, wie die damaligen Anschauungen waren. Sie standen vorwiegend im Banne der Morphologie. Der Besitz transpirationsfördernder oder einschränkender Merkmale galt als ausschlaggebend für die Unterbringung einer Pflanze zu den Hygrophyten oder Xerophyten.

A. editions z. show
d. then A. views
v. predominantly B. spell B. possession
t. promoting e. limiting M. factors
a. decisive U. sheltering, putting

Die experimentelle Ökologie, die besonders auf dem Gebiete des Wasserhaushaltes der Pflanzen in Beziehung zum Standort wichtige Arbeiten geliefert hat, lehrt aber, dass andere Merkmale entscheidend sind für die Unterbringung einer Pflanze in eine der obengenannten Gruppen, dass also die Anschauung der damaligen "teleologischen" Ökologie[4] nicht mehr aufrecht gehalten werden kann. Das physiologische Experiment ist unumgänglich, wenn entschieden werden soll, zu welchem ökologischen Typus eine Pflanze gehört. Die experimentelle Ökologie steckt aber in den Anfängen, so dass es noch nicht möglich ist,[7] einen allseitig befriedigenden Überblick über die "Anpassungen" der Pflanzen an das Wasser zu geben.

Why should a "5" be on "die"?
W. water-house-hold B. relation
S. habitat w. important A. works
M. factors e. decisive
U. placement o. above named
A. view d. then, at that time
How far do you go back in this line?
u. unavoidable
e. decided (supply "es") g. belongs
s. remains, stays A. beginnings
m. possible (to what?) b. satisfactory
Ü. survey A. adaptations g. give

Aufnahme und Abgabe des Wassers durch die Pflanze sind von äusseren und inneren Faktoren abhängig. Die ersteren, wozu Boden- und Luftfeuchtigkeit gerechnet werden müssen, sind in der Natur sehr ungleichmässig verteilt und haben, entsprechend der Anpassungsfähigkeit der Pflanzen, ungleiche Vorrichtungen zur Regelung des Wasserhaushaltes hervorgerufen. Diese Vorrichtungen sind die veränderlichen Innenfaktoren (Saugkraft der Wurzel und Transpirationsvermögen), sowie die Struktur der Gewächse; beide entscheiden über Aufnahme und Abgabe des Wassers, über die Wasserbilanz. Die Wasserbilanz ist von grosser pflanzengeographischer Bedeutung.[10] Sind die Standortbedingungen derart, dass die Pflanze nicht imstande ist, ein dauerndes Defizit an Wasser zu beseitigen, d. h.[10] ist die Transpiration dauernd grösser als die Absorption, so wird die Pflanze den Standort nicht behaupten können.

A. taking up A. giving off
ä. outer a. dependent Note Rule 6.
w. to which L. air moisture g. counted
u. irregularly v. distributed
e. corresponding A. adaptability
u. unequal V. contrivances R. regulation
h. produced (What calls for this verb?)
S. suction force W. roots
G. plant e. decide
W. water balance What nouns would you put in bold-faced type? Note Rule 10 which occurs twice in this sentence.
i. able (to what?)
b. remove d. h. that is Note that you can say "if" twice in the same sentence.
b. claim, maintain

Die Pflanze ist bestrebt,[7] die Wasserbilanz aufrechtzuerhalten; sie kann dies durch verschiedene Kombinationen physiologischer, morphologischer und anatomischer **Einrichtungen.**

Trotzdem wir noch keinen endgültigen Überblick über die verschiedenen Möglichkeiten zur Aufrechterhaltung der Wasserbilanz in der Natur haben, ist es doch wünschenswert,[7] die Pflanzen in Bezug auf ihren Wasserhaushalt in ökologische **Gruppen** einzuteilen. Eine solche Einteilung kann[6] aber augenblicklich nur als vorläufig betrachtet werden.

B. endeavoring (to what?)
a. e. keep upright, maintain
Note the absence of a verb with kann.
T. even though e. ultimate Ü. survey
M. possibilities A. maintenance
w. desirable (to what)
i. B. a. in regard to
e. to divide E. division How far back do you go when you pick up the verb?
v. tentative (as tentative)
E. attributes

Die morphologischen und anatomischen Eigenschaften zur Aufrechterhaltung der Wasserbilanz

Pflanzen, welche über hohe osmotische Werte verfügen, sind imstande, an trockenen Standorten zu leben. Die Tatsache aber, dass die meisten Xerophyten ausserdem noch xeromorphe Strukturen besitzen, die auf eine Herabsetzung der Transpiration abzielen, beweist, dass auch sie eine grosse Rolle für die Aufrechterhaltung der Wasserbilanz spielen.

W. values v. control
i. able (to what?) t. dry T. fact
X. xerophytes, drought plants
H. reduction a. aim
b. proves What calls for "leben"? besitzen? abzielen? spielen?

Den Gipfel der Xerophytie haben solche Pflanzen erreicht, die sowohl über physiologische als auch über morphologische und anatomische Eigenschaften zur Aufrechterhaltung der **Wasserbilanz** verfügen.

G. peak (Is this the subject?) e. reached
What does "die" call for?
E. qualities A. maintenance
v. control over

Xeromorphe Strukturen dienen entweder als "Schutzmittel" gegen starke Wasserverluste oder gleichzeitig auch zur Speicherung von Wasser für Zeiten der Not. Bezüglich der Beurteilung, ob die[3] als "Schutzmittel" gegen übermässige Transpiration beschriebenen strukturellen Merkmale auch wirklich die Transpiration wirksam herabsetzen, ist Vorsicht geboten. Es sind[6] verschiedene derartige **"Schutzmittel"** beschrieben worden, die einer kritischen Beurteilung nicht stets standhalten können. Eingehende experimentelle Studien sind noch nötig, um[7] Klarheit über den direkten Zusammenhang von xeromorphen Strukturen und **Transpiration** zu bekommen. So ist auch über die ökologische Bedeutung der schleimigen Zellinhalte und der sogenannten verschleimten Membranen der Epidermis für die Transpiration noch nichts **Sicheres** bekannt.

d. serve e. either S. protective-agents
W. water losses g. simultaneous
S. storage N. need b. with regard to
B. judgement Why Rule 3?
s. M. structural factors b. which are described
V. caution g. indicated
e. s. b. w. there have been described (App. 7, 5, c)
s. hold up to n. necessary K. clarity

b. get Why Rule 6 here? Z. connection
B. importance Z. cell content
v. slimy, sticky
n. S. nothing sure, definite What calls for "bekannt"?

Die Verkleinerung der einzelnen Blätter wird häufig als ein "Schutzmittel" gegen zu hohen Wasserverlust angeführt. Wie vorsichtig man aber bei der Beurteilung hiervon sein muss, zeigen die Versuche Stockers an Pflanzen mit erikoiden Blättern. Die Verkleinerung des Einzelblattes geht bei diesen mit einer starken Vermehrung der Anzahl der Blättchen einher,[2] was[5] eine unvermeidliche Vergrösserung der Gesamtoberfläche und der Transpiration bedeutet.

B. leaves
a. cited S. protective agent
w. cautious B. judgement
V. experiments P. plants
V. diminution E. single leaf
e. accompany A. number
u. unavoidable V. enlargement
G. total surface b. signifies

Das Wasser und die Pflanzenverbreitung

P. plant distribution

Für die Verbreitung von Sporen und Samen spielt das fliessende Wasser eine hervorragende Rolle, so z. B. bei allen echten Wasserpflanzen. Die Sporen der meisten Algen und vieler Pilze werden durch **Wasser** verbreitet. Die Pflanzenarten der Gewässer und ihrer Ufer besitzen häufig im Bau ihrer Früchte oder Samen Vorrichtungen, durch welche[5] ein längeres Schwimmen und dadurch die Verbreitung durch Wasserströmungen ermöglicht werden. In vielen Fällen besitzen solche Früchte oder Samen besondere Schwimmorgane, selten in der Form einer[3] von wasserdichter **Wand** umgebenen Schwimmblase, weit häufiger in derjenigen eines[3] als dicke **Hülle** ausgebildeten Schwimmgewebes, dessen **Zellen** lufthaltig sind.

S. seeds
f. flowing h. prominent
e. genuine
v. distributed
U. banks b. possess h. frequently
V. contrivances
W. water currents e. made possible
F. cases F. fruits
s. seldom Why Rule 3?
u. which is surrounded d. that (App. 14, 2)
S. swim-tissue
l. air-containing

ALLGEMEINE EIGENTÜMLICHKEITEN DES TROPENKLIMAS

Die jährliche Regenmenge schwankt in den Tropengürteln ausserordentlich.* An einigen Punkten sind[6] mittlere Jahresmengen von 10 m und im Gebirge sogar von 12 m, in Wüsten von 5—10 mm (in Chile Iquique mit 5 mm, Antofagasta mit 6 mm, im ehemaligen Deutsch-Südwestafrika Walfischbai mit **10 mm)** festgestellt worden. Sie ist im allgemeinen am grössten im Äquatorialgürtel* und nimmt in nördlicher Richtung schneller ab als in südlicher. Die Wüstengebiete innerhalb der Wendekreise gehören, mit wenigen Ausnahmen, den **Grenzgürteln** an[2] und stellen nur die tropische Fortsetzung der ausgedehnten subtropischen **Wüsten** dar.[2]

j. annual R. amount of rain s. varies
a. extraordinarily e. some
G. mountains s. even
W. deserts
e. former
f. established (what calls for this verb?)
Ä. equatorial-belt
Note position of "ab" before "als".
i. within g. belong w. few
E. exceptions G. border belts
d. present F. continuation

Mindestens ebenso wichtig wie die Menge der Niederschläge ist für das Pflanzenleben ihre zeitliche Verteilung.* Das Jahr zerfällt im grössten Teil der Tropenzone in Perioden mit verschieden hohen Niederschlagsmengen.*

M. at least w. important M. amount
N. precipitation P. plant life
V. distribution z. breaks down
N. amounts of precipitation

Die wichtigsten Typen der jährlichen Perioden von Regen- und Trockenzeiten in niederen **Breiten,*** in denen die Regen und nicht die Wärme* die Jahreszeiten bilden, seien[6] hier nach Hann-Süring etwas genauer erörtert. In der tropischen Zone können* zwei Haupttypen der Regenverteilung über das **Jahr** verzeichnet werden, nämlich: die doppelte Regenzeit der Äquatorialzone und die einfache Regenzeit.*

w. most important
T. dry seasons B. latitudes
b. form
e. discussed g. more exactly m. detailed
H. main types
v. marked
R. rain period e. simple

Die doppelte Regenzeit der Äquatorialzone.* Ende März und Ende September steht die Sonne im Zenith am Äquator,* die Regenzeiten treten bald darauf ein,[2] nämlich im April und im November,* wobei die zweite Regenzeit sich mehr verspätet als die erste. Im Juli, nach dem tiefsten Sonnenstand,* tritt die grosse Trockenzeit, im Januar die kleine Trockenzeit ein.[2] Die grosse Regenzeit herrscht vom Februar bis Mai, die kleinere im November und Dezember.* Hierbei muss[6] berücksichtigt werden, dass grosse Verschiedenheiten bestehen und dass die doppelten Regenzeiten[4] keinen zusammenhängenden äquatorialen Gürtel um die ganze **Erde** bilden; in den Monsungebieten, wie im Indischen Ozean, Nordaustralien und in Westindien, fehlen sie.

d. double
s. stands
e. enter in, appear d. thereupon
Note the position of "verspätet" before **als.**
t. lowest
What goes with "tritt"? T. dry period
h. prevails
H. in this connection
b. considered V. differences b. exist
z. connected G. belt g. entire
M. m-regions
f. are absent

Die einfache tropische Regenzeit herrscht ausserhalb der äquatorialen Zone bis zu und noch etwas über die Wendekreise hinaus; wo sie* typisch auftritt, dauert die Regenzeit etwa 4, die Trockenzeit 8 Monate.* Während der Regenzeit der südlichen Hemisphäre herrscht in der nördlichen Erdhälfte die Trockenzeit* und umgekehrt. Zu der einfachen Regenzeit können* die Monsun- und **Passatregen** gerechnet werden.

e. simple a. outside of
e. somewhat
Note the use of "über—hinaus," over and beyond
W. during (could also mean while, but not here)
u. conversely
e. simple
g. counted

MONSUNREGEN. Die Erwärmung grosser Landoberflächen in den Tropen und den[3] daran unmittelbar grenzenden Gebieten im Sommer der betreffenden Erdhälfte, ist die Ursache andauernder Seewinde,* die[5] über dem erwärmten Lande aufsteigen und[8] Regen bringen. Die periodisch wehenden Winde werden[6] Monsune genannt und die[3] durch sie verursachten Niederschläge Monsunregen. Die Monsune folgen wie die beiden vorhin genannten Regenzeiten auch dem Zenithstande der Sonne* und verursachen keine grössere Abänderung der sogenannten tropischen Regen.* Im äquatorialen Gebiet aber stören sie das Auftreten doppelter Regenzeiten,* die* dann zu einer einzigen verschmelzen. Die übrige Zeit des Jahres ist es viel trockener als unter gleichen Breiten ausserhalb des Monsungebietes.* Die Monsunregen der nördlichen Hemisphäre treten von Juni bis **September** ein.[2]

E. heating
u. immediately, directly
g. which borders G. regions
b. concerned U. cause a. enduring, steady
a. rise w. blowing
v. which are caused N. precipitation, rains
b. two v. previously
A. change
s. co called
s. disturb, destroy A. appearance
v. fuse, blend ü. remaining
B. latitudes
e. enter in, occur

GEOLOGIE

DIE BEDINGUNGEN DES LEBENS†

Die Erdoberfläche ist gegenwärtig der Schauplatz von zwei verschiedenen Arten der Veränderung der **Materie,**[1] die man[4] als anorganische und organische **Bewegungen** nur schwer scharf von einander trennen kann. Die Veränderungen und Bewegungen der unbelebten Natur werden[6] durch mehrere **Ursachen** veranlasst. Die Abkühlung der Erde bewirkt **Dislokationen,** Erdbeben und vulkanische **Erscheinungen,**[1] die Anziehung der Sonne und Mond verändert die Gestalt der **Hydrosphäre** und dadurch auch die Massenverteilung an den **Küsten,**[1] und die leuchtenden und wärmenden Strahlen der Sonne leiten den Kreislauf des **Wassers** ein[2] und üben durch Luftströmungen, Stürme und Meeresströmungen eine umgestaltende Wirkung auf die **Erdoberfläche** aus.[2]

E. earth surface g. at present
S. scene v. different V. change
B. movements (Why shift on "man"? **how far back do you then go?**) t. separate
u. inanimate w.v. are caused (App. 7, 5, a)
U. causes b. causes
Abk. cooling off E. earth quakes
A. attraction v. changes G. form
What do the bold face nouns tell you to do?
l. luminous w. warming S. rays
e. introduce K. circulation
L. air currents M. sea currents
u. transforming W. effect a. exert

Die Bewegungen der **Materie,**[1] welche man[4] als organische bezeichnet, sind scheinbar ganz anderer Art wie die anorganischen **Veränderungen,**[1] und doch hat[6] die Naturforschung die Kluft zwischen der belebten und unbelebten **Natur** mehrfach überbrückt. Die synthetische Darstellung organischer **Stoffwechselprodukte,**[1] der experimentelle **Nachweis,**[1] dass auch die scheinbar spontanen Bewegungen niederer Organismen[4] durch mechanische **Ursachen** notwendig bedingt sind, und andere Gründe sprechen dafür, dass die organische Welt, mit ihren eigenartigen Lebenserscheinungen,[4] nur durch die Art der Bewegung von der unbelebten **Natur** verschieden ist.

B. movements
b. designates s. apparently
w. than V. changes
N. nature study K. cleft, gap
ü. bridged over D. production
S. metabolic products
N. proof s. apparently
n. lower U. causes
n. necessarily b. conditioned, caused **d. for the fact**
e. peculiar L. life phenomena
v. different u. inanimate

Wenn wir[4] die Bedingungen dieser organischen Bewegung, wie wir[4] sie in der **Gegenwart** beobachten können, mit jenen **Zuständen** vergleichen, welche[5] in früheren Entwicklungsphasen der **Erde** geherrscht haben müssen, so drängt sich unabweisbar der **Gedanke** auf,[2] dass das organische Leben[4] auf der Erde einmal einen **Anfang** gehabt haben muss. Es kann[6] nicht unsere **Aufgabe** sein,[7] hier das Problem der Entstehung des Lebens **selbst** zu behandeln, denn dieses gehört nicht in den Kreis geologischer **Betrachtungen,**[1] wohl aber scheint es uns wichtig,[7] diejenigen empirischen **Grenzwerte** festzustellen, innerhalb deren heute organisches Leben[4] möglich ist, denn auf diese Weise nur können[6] wir **Anhaltspunkte** dafür gewinnen, unter welchen Bedingungen und in welcher Erdperiode organisches Leben[4] möglich war.

What does the first 'wir' call for? the second?
b. observe G. at present, v. compare
E. evolutionary phases g. prevailed
a. rises u. unavoidably
What does 'Leben' call for? kann?
A. task (Note the call for "zu".) E. origin
s. itself g. belongs
K. sphere B. considerations
w. important to what?
f. establish i. d. within which
A. clues Why shift on "können"?
g. gain B. conditions
m. possible E. geologic period

Man pflegt[7] die organischen Körper in Pflanzen und **Tiere** einzuteilen. Aber sowohl vom morphologischen wie vom physiologischen Standpunkt ist es unmöglich,[7] diese beiden **Gruppen** scharf von einander zu trennen. Wenn wir[4] den histologischen Bau zur Grundlage unserer **Einteilung** machen, so finden wir an der Wurzel des Pflanzenreiches wie des Tierstammes einzellige **Formen,**[1] deren Merkmale[4] so wenig **Unterschiede** erkennen lassen, dass man[4] die einzelligen Pflanzen mit den einzelligen Tieren zu einem besonderen **"Protistenreich"** vereinigt hat.[10] Legen wir aber physiologische Charaktere unserer **Betrachtung** zugrunde,[2] so müssen[6] wir, wenn wir[4] konsequent sein wollten, die schmarotzenden Pilze zu den **Tieren** rechnen, und[8] die chlorphyllhaltigen **Aktinien**[9] als Pflanzen bezeichnen.

p. is accustomed (to what?)
e. to divide T. animals S. as well
u. impossible (to what?) Have you flagged the "zu"-verbs? t. separate
B. structure E. classification
W. root P. plant kingdom
e. single cell M. characteristics
l. let e. recognize NOTE THE CALLS THAT ARE MADE FOR VERB FORMS.
P. realm of the Protista Why Rule 10?
z. to lay as a basis B. consideration
What does "müssen" call for? "wir"?
P. fungi (Note how "und" calls for the verb.)
b. designate A. actinia

Indem wir[4] uns dieser **Schwierigkeiten** voll bewusst bleiben, können[6] wir aber immerhin die Mehrzahl der Tiere von den typischen Vertretern des **Pflanzenreiches** leicht unterscheiden, denn die Pflanzen sind allein imstande,[7] zu assimilieren,

I. while S. difficulties
b. conscious i. at any rate
M. majority V. representatives
u. distinguish i. able

†Johannes Walther, **Einleitung in die Geologie als historische Wissenschaft**

d. h. [8]unter dem Einfluss des Lichtes in ihrem Chlorophyll organische Materie aus Kohlensäure und **Wasser** zu bilden, während alle Tiere[4] organische **Substanzen** verbrauchen und[8] dem anorganischen **Reiche** wieder zuführen.

E. influence L. light why rule 8?
K. carbon dioxide
w. while T. animals
v. consume (Note Rule 8.)
z. supply

Wenn wir[4] unter Fäulnis die Zersetzung stickstoffhaltiger Verbindungen, unter Verwesung den Zerfall von **Kohlenstoffverbindungen** verstehen, so werden[6] durch diese beiden Vorgänge beständig organische **Stoffe** zerstört und die Masse der lebenden organischen Substanz auf der Erde wird[6] ununterbrochen vermindert. Und wenn wir[4] nicht nur die Fäulnis und Verwesung in der **Gegenwart** [9]ins Auge fassen, sondern bedenken, dass jede Versteinerung, jedes Stück Kohle, jeder **Kalkstein,**[4] der[5] im Laufe der geologischen **Vergangenheit** gebildet worden ist, nur Zeugen prähistorischer Verminderung der belebten **Substanz** sind, so können wir ermessen, welche Masse organischer Materie[4] im Laufe der **Erdgeschichte** zerstört worden ist.

F. putrefaction Z. decomposition
V. compounds V. decay Z. decomposition
v. understand w.z. are destroyed (See App. 7,5,a.)
b. constantly l. living
u. uninterruptedly v. diminished
G. at the present time
i.A. f. keep in mind b. remember
V. fossil S. piece Note that these are subjects—to what verb?
Z. witnesses V. diminishment e. estimate
L. course z.w.i. has been destroyed (App. 7, 5, c)

Die Physiologie des Tierkörpers zeigt uns, dass bei den chemischen organischen Umsetzungen im Protoplasma der Tiere ebenfalls beständig organische Verbindungen[4] zerstört werden, dass also durch die blosse Existenz einer Fauna die Summe der belebten Materie[4] vermindert wird. Das Tier lebt, wächst und pflanzt sich fort,[2] indem es[4] Pflanzen verzehrt oder[8] von dem Fleisch von **Pflanzenfressern** lebt. Der[3] bei der **Atmung** aufgenommene Sauerstoff dient nur dazu,[7] diese Zerstörung der **organischen Substanz** zu beschleunigen. Das Tierreich lebt auf Kosten des **Pflanzenreichs,**[1] und kein Tier ausser den chlorophyllhaltigen Formen ist imstande,[7] unorganische Kohlenstoff-Verbindungen durch seine Lebenstätigkeit in den Kreislauf des **Lebens** aufzunehmen. Aus diesem Grunde müssen[6] wir annehmen, dass das organische Leben[4] auch auf der Erde mit solchen **Formen** begonnen habe, welche[5] physiologisch zum **Pflanzenreich** gehörten. Ja, wir könnten[6] die Pflanzen als eine Bedingung des **Lebens** bezeichnen, auf jeden Fall aber müssen[6] wir zuerst die Bedingungen des Assimilationsprozess der **Pflanzen** besprechen, ehe wir[4] die Bedingungen tierischen **Lebens** weiter behandeln können.

T. animal body b. in the case of U. decomposition
e. likewise V. compounds
T. animals
v. reduced a. hence b. mere
w. grows f. reproduces i. in that, by –ing
v. consume (Why Rule 8?)
a. which is absorbed S. oxygen
d. there to (to what? See App. 23, 3)
b. accelerate K. expense a. except

i. in a position, able (to what?)
L. life activity K. cycle
aufz. to take up, absorb anneh. assume G. reason
What does "Leben" call for?
"welche"? g. belonged
k. might B. condition
a. j. F. at any rate
b. discuss
e. before b. treat

Wenn die Summe der belebten Materie auf der Erde[4] nicht beständig abnimmt, wenn nicht die Pflanzen und Tiere[4] endgiltig aussterben, wenn die Erdoberfläche[4] sich nicht ihres organischen **Lebens** entkleidet, so ist der einzige Grund hierfür der Assimilationsprozess der **Pflanzen.**[1] Die[3] mit einem grünen, braunen, roten, gelben Farbstoff, dem **Chromophyll,** versehenen Pflanzenteile haben die Fähigkeit,[7] unter dem Einfluss des Lichtes aus Kohlensäure und Wasser organische **Substanzen** zu erzeugen. Man kann[6] grüne Pflanzen in ausgeglühtem Sand und in **Wasser** erziehen, welches[5] keine Spur organischer **Körper** enthält, wenn diesem Nährboden die[3] ausser Kohlenstoff, Wasserstoff und Sauerstoff für den vegetablischen **Organismus** unentbehrlichen Elemente in anorganischer **Verbindung** zugesetzt werden. Andererseits gewinnt eine[3] in kohlensäurefreier **Atmosphäre** kultivierte Pflanze keinen Kohlenstoff und verliert an diesem **Element.**

W. if b. living
b. constantly
e. ultimately a. die out
e. denudes
e. only h. for this
Why Rule 3? Why is "F" not the right noun?
v. which are provided
F. ability e. to produce
e. grow a. heated
S. trace d. N. to this base
What does "die" call for?
u. which are indispensable
z. w. are added
k. which is cultivated
K. carbon v. loses

(An * is placed where certain rules are involved. Indicate the rules in each case.) Also account for the bold face nouns.

So bedarf also die Pflanze: Wasser, Licht, **Kohlensäure,*** und Chromophyll, damit sie* assimilieren kann; und somit sind diese vier Faktoren die notwendige Voraussetzung des organischen **Lebens.***

d. so that
s. consequently n. necessary
V. (pre)requisites

Das Wasser existierte nicht immer als flüssiges Element auf der **Erde.*** Wenn wir in diejenigen Phasen der **Erdgeschichte** zurückgehen, wo die Erde* noch ein sehr heisser **Himmelskörper** war, so finden wir kein Wasser auf der **Erdoberfläche;*** denn alles Wasser schwebte in Dampfform in der **Atmosphäre.*** In diesem Stadium der Dinge musste der Siedepunkt des Wassers von dem hohen Druck des **Wasserdampfes** abhängig sein, welcher* damals den grössten Teil der **Atmosphäre** bildete. In dem Mass, als sich die **Erde** abkühlte, wurde* ein Teil des Wasserdampfes nach dem anderen **Teil** kondensiert, und zwar bei einer **Temperatur,*** welche* dem jedesmaligen Siedepunkt des **Wassers** entsprach. Der Siedpunkt des Wassers hatte sein **Maximum,*** als die Kondensation des Wasserdampfes begann, und das erste flüssige Wasser* auf der **Erdrinde** erschien; seitdem sank der Siedepunkt im Verlauf der Erdbildung mehr und mehr, bis die Erde* sich soweit abkühlte, dass der jetzige Siedepunkt von 100°* erreicht wurde.

n. i. not always f. liquid
What calls for "zurückgehen"?
E. geology, history of the earth
h. hot H. planet
E. earth surface s. was suspended
S. boiling point
D. pressure a. dependent
d. then b. formed M. degree, measure a. cooled off W. water vapor
w. k. was condensed (App. 7, 5, b)
j. prevailing S. boiling point
e. corresponded W. water vapor
e. appeared E. earth crust
s. since then V. course E. earth formation
s. so far j. present e. reached (App. 7, 5, b)

Wir können* hier die Temperatur des **Wassers** noch ausser acht lassen; jedenfalls war organisches Leben erst dann möglich, als flüssiges Wasser* sich auf der **Erdrinde** kondensiert hatte.

Note constantly the rules that call for verbs.
a. a. l. leave out of consideration m. possible
s. k. h. had been condensed (App. 11, 4, d)

Als zweite Voraussetzung der Assimilation lernten wir das **Licht** kennen. Eine Pflanze kann* zwar im **Dunklen** so lange gedeihen und* sogar wachsen, als sie* von assimilierten **Reservestoffen** zu zehren vermag, aber ohne Einwirkung des Lichtes ist die chlorophyllhaltige Pflanze nicht fähig,[7] **Kohlensäure** zu ersetzen und[8] organische **Substanz** neu zu bilden, d. h. zu assimilieren.

V. supposition
l. k. learned to know
g. thrive D. darkness s. even
v. is able z. consume
E. effect
f. capable (to what?) und what?
b. form

Die Intensität der Belichtung hat bei verschiedenen Pflanzen ein verschiedenes **Optimum,*** und so wie es[4] für jede Lebensäusserung der Pflanzen eine obere **Temperaturgrenze** gibt, die[5] ohne **Schädigung** nicht überschritten werden darf, so gibt es auch eine obere Grenze der **Belichtung,*** bei welcher das Chlorphyllkorn* nicht mehr assimiliern kann. Manche **Pflanzen,*** besonders gewisse **Meeresalgen** gedeihen im Halbdunkel besser als im vollen **Sonnenlicht,*** aber ohne Sonne vermag keine einzige[4] zu assimilieren. Da nun die **Lichtstrahlen**[4] beim Eindringen in eine Wassersäule eine fortdauernde Schwächung ihrer **Intensität** erleiden, so muss* mit zunehmender **Meerestiefe**[9] die Assimiliation immer geringer werden.

B. exposure to light
v. different
e. g. there is L. life manifestation
T. temperature limit ü. exceeded
G. limit Why Rule 4? 5?
b. w. at which
g. certain M. sea algae
g. thrive H. semi darkness
v. is able k. e. no single one
E. penetration W. water column
f. continuous S. weakening e. suffer
i. g. less and less w. become (See App. 7, 3.)

Bei Ville France hat[6] man durch Versenken lichtempfindlicher **Platten** in sehr reinem Wasser bei sonnigem Wetter und zur **Mittagszeit** 400m als die grösste **Tiefe** beobachtet, bis zu der chemisch wirksame Lichtstrahlen[4] eindringen. Die **Wasserschichten** von 0-300 m werden[6] jeden **Tag** so lange erleuchtet, als die Sonne am **Himmel** steht, dagegen dringt das Licht nur 8 Stunden lang bis in eine Tiefe von **350 m.**[1]

V. submerging
l. light sensitive r. clean
M. noon b. observed w. effective
L. light rays e. penetrate
w. e. are illuminated (App. 7, 5, a)
d. on the other hand

Die[3] im Genfer **See** angestellten Versuche ergaben, dass im Winter chemisch wirksame Strahlen* bis **250 m** eindringen, während im Sommer durch die Trübung der einmündenden Flüsse die Lichtdurchlässigkeit des Wassers* so vermindert wird, dass chemisch wirksame Strahlen[4] nur bis **45 m** nachgewiesen werden konnten.

a. which were made V. experiments
e. demonstrated w. effective
e. penetrate w. w. while T. turbidity
e. discharging L. light permeability
v. diminished n. detected

URSPRUNG UND FRÜHSTER ZUSTAND DER ERDE

Die Erde hat denselben Ursprung wie die übrigen Planeten unseres Sonnensystems und die Sonne selbst.[1] Ursprünglich bildeten alle diese Körper einen einzigen, gewaltigen **Gasball.**[1] Von diesen haben[6] sich einer nach dem anderen die **Planeten** losgelöst, während die übrigbleibende Hauptmasse[4] sich zum Centralkörper des ganzen Systems, der Sonne, gestaltete.

U. origin ü. remaining, other
S. solar system s. itself
e. single g. mighty, powerful
Observe constantly the bold-face noun.
l. detached w. while ü. remaining
g. entire g. s. was formed

Dies ist in wenigen Worten die Ansicht von der Entwickelung unseres Planetensystems,[1] die[5] als die Kant-La Place **Theorie** bekannt ist. Zu Gunsten derselben lassen sich[6] eine ganze Reihe astronomischer und physikalischer **Tatsachen** anführen, wie die übereinstimmende Bewegungsrichtung und das nahezu vollständige Zusammenfallen der Bahnebenen aller **Planeten,**[1] ferner der Ring des Saturn und die allmähliche Dichtezunahme der Planeten in der Richtung nach der **Sonne,** wie auch bei jedem einzelnen von der Oberfläche nach innen. Andere noch wichtigere Beweise verdanken wir der spektralanalytischen Erforschung unserer Sonne und anderer noch fernerer **Himmelskörper.**[1] Dieselbe hat ergeben, dass 1. gewisse unter ihnen, (die sogenannten Nebelflecken,[4]) gewaltige,[3] ausschliesslich aus glühenden **Gasen** bestehende Massen sind, dass 2. andere, die sogenannten Sonnen,[4] zu denen auch unsere Sonne gehört, **Körper** darstellen, bei denen es[4] infolge lange fortgesetzten Wärmeverlustes und der damit zusammenhängenden Verdichtung ihrer Masse zur Bildung eines flüssigen **Kernes** gekommen ist, welche[5] somit aus einem inneren glühendflüssigen Teil und einer äusseren **Gashülle** bestehen, während endlich 3. eine letzte Art von Weltkörpern solche sind, die[5] infolge noch weiterer Abkühlung von der Oberfläche aus in **Erstarrung** übergegangen sind und[8] damit ihr früheres Leuchtvermögen eingebüsst haben. Zu dieser letzten Art von Körpern gehören unsere **Erde,**[7] sämtliche Planeten und Monde wie gewisse dunkle Sterne anderer Sonnensysteme.[1]

w. few A. view
E. development
b. known G. favor l. s. can be
R. series T. facts
a. cited ü. conforming B. movement-direction
n. nearly v. complete
Z. coincidence a. gradual
D. density-increase R. direction
j. e. every single O. surface n. additional
w. more important v. we owe
E. exploration
H. celestial bodies e. shown
g. certain g. tremendous (Why Rule 3?)
a. exclusively b. which consist
s. so-called
g. belongs d. represent i. owing to
f. continued W. heat loss
V. condensation f. liquid
g. glowing-liquid
a. outer G. gas-shell, covering
i. due to
A. cooling O. surface E. solidification
f. earlier L. illuminating-ability g. belong
s. all M. moons g. certain
S. stars

Wir wissen also jetzt, dass von allen Hauptzuständen, welche die La Place Theorie[4] für die Entwicklung sämtlicher **Himmelskörper** annimmt, nämlich 1. dem ursprünglichen Gasball, 2. dem Gasball mit schmelzflüssigen Kern und 3. dem erstarrten Weltkörper, Beispiele[4] noch jetzt nebeneinander vorhanden sind, und dieser Umstand verleiht der genannten Theorie eine so hohe **Wahrscheinlichkeit,**[1] dass wir[4] dieselbe als gesichert ansehen dürfen.

H. main stages
E. development, evolution
s. all a. assumes s. molten
e. solidified B. examples
n. side by side U. circumstance v. lends
W. probability
a. g. as assured

Wenn wir[4] demgemäss den angegebenen Entwickelungsgang als den aller Weltkörper betrachten und[8] infolgedessen auch für unsere **Erde** annehmen, dass dieselbe[4] in einer sehr weit zurückliegenden Zeit eine schmelzflüssige leuchtende **Kugel** darstellte, welche[5] sich später von der Oberfläche aus mit einer festen **Erstarrungskruste** bekleidete, so steht diese Annahme nicht nur in vollstem Einklang mit alten,[3] aus rein geologischen **Tatsachen** abgeleiteten Schlüssen, sondern ebenso mit den Ergebnissen der neuesten, astronomischphysikalischen **Forschung.**[1]

d. accordingly a. stated
b. consider i. consequently
z. remote dieselbe the same ann. assume
l. luminous d. represented O. surface
b. clothed, covered
A. assumptions E. harmony Why Rule 3?
a. which are derived S. conclusions
E. results F. research

Die Annahme einer ehemaligen Erstarrungskruste ist nach obigen Ausführungen eine durchaus notwendige.[1] Diese Annahme kann[6] aber auch aus dem **Grunde** nicht umgangen werden, weil sowohl die ältesten Sedimente[4] eine Unterlage voraussetzten, auf der sie[4] sich ablagerten, als auch die ältesten Eruptivgesteine etwas, was sie durchbrachen.

A. assumption e. former
A. statements d. altogether
u. circumvented
U. foundation, basis v. presupposed
a. deposited

Man darf[6] auch nicht vergessen, dass die ersten Sedimente,[1] einerlei ob sie[4] chemischer oder mechanischer **Natur** waren, mit Notwendigkeit ein älteres, bereits vorhandenes **Gesteinsmaterial** voraussetzen, aus dessen chemischer oder mechanischer Zerstörung **sie**[4] hervorgingen.

v. forget
e. immaterial
N. necessity v. existing
v. presuppose a. d. from whose
h. proceeded Z. destruction

Wenn somit die Annahme einer Erstarrungsdecke,[4] obwohl dieselbe[4] unbegreiflicherweise zeitweilig als blosses Phantasiebild betrachtet worden ist, eine unumgängliche **Notwendigkeit** ist, so ist es doch eine andere Frage, ob irgendwo Gesteine[4] vorhanden sind, die[5] sich mit mehr oder weniger Wahrscheinlichkeit als Reste **derselben** deuten lassen.[10] Ist eine solche Deutung überhaupt für irgend ein **Gestein** zulässig, so für kein anderes mit gleichem Rechte wie für den **Gneiss**,[1] welcher[5] mit erstaunlicher Gleichartigkeit als die tiefste bekannte Gesteinsbildung über den ganzen **Erdenrund** verbreitet ist. Aber auch wenn man[4] diese **Anschauung** nicht teilen will, immer wird[6] man zugeben müssen, dass wenn wir[4] uns ein Bild von der Zusammensetzung jener ältesten Gesteinsbildung unserer **Erde** machen wollen, wir[4] uns dieselbe mehr oder weniger gneissähnlich vorstellen müssen. Denn einmal darf[6] man wohl annehmen, dass die Erstarrungskruste[4] stofflich nicht wesentlich verschieden gewesen ist, von dem ältesten[3] sie durchbrechenden Eruptivgestein, und dies ist der[3] von dem Gneiss nur **in der Struktur** abweichende Granit.

A. assumption
u. incomprehensibly z. at times
b. considered u. unavoidable
N. necessity
F. question i. anywhere v. present
s. l. can be W. probability
Why Rule 10? D. interpretation
z. admissible
g. same e. astonishing
G. similarity b. known s. w. even if
v. distributed
A. view t. share z. concede B. picture
Z. composition G. rock formation
d. the same (App. 14, 1)
v. m. must imagine a. assume
w. essentially v. different
d. which broke through
a. which deviates

Dann aber hat[6] man ganz richtig bemerkt, dass wir[4] ein[3] ungefähr der ursprünglichen **Erstarrungsdecke** ähnliches Gebilde erhalten würden, wenn wir[4] alle Gesteine der **Rinde** zusammenschmelzen könnten. Dass wir[4] aber in diesem Falle ein saures **Silikat** erhalten würden, steht bei der ausserordentlichen Verbreitung des **Quarzes** ausser Frage.[9] Da indessen die Eruptivgesteine[4] in späterer geologischer Zeit aus immer grösseren **Tiefen** emporgestiegen sind, in welchen wahrscheinlich basischere Gemenge[4] als an der Oberfläche angesammelt sind, so würde ein solches Einschmelzungs-**Produkt** wahrscheinlich basischer ausfallen, als die ursprüngliche **Erstarrungskruste.**

D. a. then too b. noted
u. approximately
ä. which is similar
z. fuse together
e. obtain F. case
Note Rule 9. V. distribution
a. F. beyond question i. however
e. risen w. probably
G. admixtures a. accumulated
w. probably
a. result, turn out u. original

Über den Zustand der Erde unmittelbar nach Bildung der Erstarrungsrinde können[6] nur **Andeutungen** gegeben werden. Mit der stetigen fortschreitenden Abkühlung musste[6] eine stetige Zusammenziehung des Erdkörpers und damit eine sich immer wiederholende Berstung und Zerstückelung der zuerst gebildeten **Erstarrungsdecke** Hand in Hand[9] gehen. Aus diesen Rissen und Spalten drang dann in ungeheuren Massen das glutflüssige **Innere** hervor,[2] um[7] nach seiner Erstarrung wie ein Kitt die zerstückelten **Rindenteile** wieder zu vereinigen.

Z. condition u. immediately
A. hints, suggestions
s. constant f. progressing
Z. contraction E. globe
w. repeating B. bursting
Z. dismemberment E. solidified covering
Note Rule 9.
u. vast What does "hervor" go with?
h. pressed-forward n. after K. cement
R. crust-parts v. combine

Es ist klar, dass in jenen frühesten Zeiten bei der ungeheuren,[3] selbst in der **Atmosphäre** herrschenden Temperatur noch **kein Wasser**[4] vorhanden gewesen sein kann, dass also jene so entlegene Periode der Erdgeschichte[4] eine anhydrische war. **Erst als die Temperatur**[4] infolge fortgesetzten **Wärmeverlustes** erheblich gesunken war, konnte[6] sich eine Wasserhülle um den festen **Kern** bilden. Aber auch dieses Urmeer muss,[6] da es[4] unter dem **Druck** einer sehr viel dickeren als die heutige **Atmosphäre** stand, **einer** Atmosphäre, welcher noch die gesamte Menge der Kohlen-

f. earliest
u. enormous Why Rule 3? h. which prevailed
(Why which?) e. remote E. geology
E. only a. when i. due to
W. heat loss e. considerable
W. water-covering
What does "muss" call for? es?
h. present
w. to which g. total M. amount, quantity

säure und wahrscheinlich auch vieler anderer **Körper** angehörte, eine sehr hohe,[3] den Siedepunkt des Wassers bei gewöhnlichem **Druck** weit übersteigende **Temperatur** besessen haben, so dass es[4] noch nicht die[3] für die Entwickelung von **Organismen** nötigen Bedingungen bot. Das Erscheinen von Lebewesen war[6] vielmehr erst in einer noch späteren,[3] einem weiteren bedeutenden Fortschritte in der Abkühlung des **Erdkörpers** entsprechenden **Phase** möglich.

w. probably a. belonged
h. high (what?) s. boiling D. pressure
ü. which exceeds b. possessed
E. development n. which were necessary
E. appearance L. organisms What does "war" call for? späteren?
F. progress A. cooling off
e. which corresponds m. possible

FORMATIONSKUNDE Allgemeine Vorbemerkungen

Die Formationskunde ist nur ein Teil der ausgedehnten Wissenschaft der **Geologie,**[1] d. h. der Lehre von der stofflichen und zwar besonders mineralischen **Zusammensetzung,**[1] dem Bau und der Bildungsgeschichte des **Erdkörpers.**[1]

F. science of formation T. part
a. extensive L. theory
z. to be sure Z. composition
B. structure E. globe

Wie in anderen Wissenschaften, so kann* man auch in der Geologie mehrere verschiedene **Zweige** unterscheiden; so die physische Geologie, welche[5] sich mit der Gestalt und Grösse, den Dichtigkeits- und Wärmeverhältnissen, den allgemeinen Reliefformen der Erdoberfläche und anderen ähnlichen **Gegenständen** beschäftigt, ferner die dynamische oder mechanische Geologie, welche[5] die geologischen Wirkungen des Vulkanismus, des **Wassers** usw. behandelt, die tektonische Geologie oder Geotektonik, welche[5] uns mit den **Lagerungsformen** der[3] die Erdrinde zusammensetzenden **Gesteine** bekannt macht, die petrographische Geologie oder Petrographie,[1] welche[5] uns die chemische und mineralische Zusammensetzung, sowie die Art des Vorkommens und die Verbreitung der verschiedenen **Gesteinstypen** kennen lehrt, und endlich die Formationskunde.[1] Diese hat die Aufgabe,[7] die Zusammensetzung, Verbreitung und organischen Einschlüsse der geologischen Formationen, d. h. der Gesteinsbildungen, welche[5] in den verschiedenen[3] auf einander folgenden grossen Zeitabschnitten der Erdgeschichte entstanden sind, zu erforschen, und gibt uns damit eine Art Entwickelungsgeschichte des **Erdballs** und der[3] ihn bewohnenden Tier-und Pflanzenwelt von den ältesten Zeiten an bis auf die Gegenwart. Als wesentlich gleichbedeutend mit der Bezeichnung Formationslehre werden[6] auch die Ausdrücke Stratigraphie und historische **Geologie** gebraucht.

a. other
u. distinguish v. different
G. form G. size
D. density and heat conditions
E. earth surface ä. similar
G. objects b. is concerned
W. effects b. treats
L. relief-forms
z. which compose b. known, familiar
Why Rule 3?
Z. composition V. occurrence
V. distribution v. different
e. finally
V. distribution E. inclusions
G. rock formations
v. different (what?) f. which follow
Z. periods of time e. arisen
z. e. to study (What calls for this verb?)
b. which inhabit
G. present w. essentially
g. identical B. designation A. **expressions**
g. used

[10]Überblickt man nun die Gesamtheit der[3] die feste **Erdrinde** bildenden Gesteine, so findet man, dass sie[4] sich in zwei **Hauptklassen** trennen lassen: 1. Eruptivgesteine, welche[5] nach der Art der heutigen Laven in heissflüssigem Zustande aus dem Innern der **Erde** emporgestiegen sind und[8] durch Erstarrung in den festen **Zustand** übergegangen sind und 2. Sedimentgesteine, welche[5] entweder Ablagerungen fester,[3] vom **Wasser** mechanisch mitgeführter Teile oder Abscheidungen aus mineralischen **Lösungen** darstellen.

ü. if one surveys
b. which form
s. l. can be t. separate
n. d. A. according to the type
e. arisen u. and (what?)
Z. state ü. gone over
A. deposits f. of solid (what?)
m. which are carried along
L. solutions d. represent

Die Sedimentgesteine unterscheiden sich von den Eruptivgesteinen namentlich durch zwei **Eigenschaften,**[1] nämlich ihre Schichtung und ihre Versteinerungsführung.[1] Die Schichtung kommt zwar nicht allen, aber doch den allermeisten Sediment- oder Schicht-**Gesteinen** zu.[2] Man versteht darunter die Eigenschaft, dass sich die ganze Gesteinsmasse[4] in parallele, platten- oder tafelförmige **Körper** (Schichten) teilt. Jede Schicht ist[6] von der über- und unterliegenden durch eine **Schichtfuge** getrennt und[8] als Ergebnis eines ununterbrochenen sedimentären **Vorganges** zu betrachten, während jede Schichtfuge[4] einen wenn auch noch kurzen Stillstand, eine Pause in der **Sedimentation** andeutet.

u. s. are distinguished
n. especially E. properties
S. bedding V. fossil-bearing
What goes with kommt?
z. belongs v. understand
G. rock mass t. tablet-form
S. bed g. separated E. result
V. process b. to be considered (App. 12 1)
a. indicates

[10]Besitzt eine Anzahl übereinanderliegender Schichten eine ähnliche Beschaffenheit und Bildungsweise, so bezeichnet man dieselben als Schichtenfolge, Schichtenreihe,[1] Schichtenkomplex

B. if a number possesses (Why if?)
ä. similar B. nature b. denotes
S. bed-series, sequence

oder Schichtensystem.[1] Was die Versteinerungen betrifft, so kommen sie auch nicht allen, aber doch der grossen Mehrzahl der **Sedimentgesteine zu.*** Sie stellen im Gestein eingebettete, mehr oder weniger mineralisierte Reste der Tiere und **Pflanzen dar,*** welche* zur Zeit der Bildung der betreffenden Schichten gelebt haben.

Indicate the rule involved where the * appears.
M. majority What goes with "stellen"?
e. imbedded
R. remnants d. represent
b. concerned What calls for "haben"?

Unsere ganze geologische Zeitrechnung beruht nun ausschliesslich auf den Sedimentgesteinen,* da nur sie* infolge ihrer Schichtung und **Versteinerungsführung** die Möglichkeit[7] bieten, ihre Bildungszeit gleichmässig auf weite Erstreckung,* ja über die ganze **Erde** zu verfolgen. Die Eruptivgesteine lassen sich[6] zu diesem **Zwecke** nicht verwerten, weil sie[4] keine Merkmale besitzen, die* einen sicheren Schluss auf ihr **Alter** zulassen. Ihr Alter lässt sich[6] nur nach dem Alter der **Sedimentgesteine** bestimmen.

g. entire Z. calendar
a. exclusively d. since
i. owing to S. bedding
M. possibility (to what?) b. offer
E. extent, distance v. follow
l. s. can be Z. purpose
v. utilized b. possess M. characteristics
z. admit s. sure S. conclusion a. as to
l. s. can be
b. determined

Inbetreff der Schichtung ist[6] bereits hervorgehoben worden, dass jede einzelne Schicht* als Vertreter eines besonderen, wenn auch verhältnismässig sehr kurzen geologischen **Zeitabschnittes** anzusehen ist. Da aber jede Schichtenreihe[4] aus zahlreichen,[3] gleich den Blättern eines **Buches** übereinanderliegenden **Schichten** zusammengesetzt ist, und ebenso jede Formation aus einer Mehrzahl übereinanderliegender Schichtenreihen,* so erhalten wir dadurch die Möglichkeit,[7] das Alter jeder Schicht im Verhältnis zu einer anderen Schicht derselben Reihe, und ebenso das Alter einer jeden Schichtenreihe im Verhältnis zu einer anderen **Schichtenreihe** zu ermitteln. Dabei gilt als die wichtigste **Regel,** dass unter normalen Umständen, d. h. bei ungestörter oder wenig gestörter Lagerung der Schichten, jede höher liegende Schicht[4] jünger ist als die tiefere. Nach diesem Hauptgrundsatze der Lagerunglehre hat* man seit alter Zeit, noch ehe es[4] eine geologische Wissenschaft gab, das Ältere von dem jüngeren oder, wie unsere alten Bergleute sich ausdrückten, das Liegende vom **Hangenden** getrennt.

I. regarding S. bedding b. already
h. emphasized V. representative
w. a. even though v. relatively
Z. period of time a. i. is to be regarded
(App. 12, 1) g. like B. leaves
ü. which lie over one another
z. composed M. majority
e. obtain S. bed series
M. possibility (to what?)
V. relation, proportion d. of the same
A. age z. e. to ascertain
g. holds w. most important
U. conditions u. undisturbed
L. deposition l. lying
t. lower N. according to
L. deposition-theory e. before
e. g. there was
j. more recent B. miners
a. expressed g. separated

Hinsichtlich der gegenseitigen Lagerung zweier Schichtenreihen hat[6] man zwischen concordanter oder gleichförmiger und discordanter oder ungleichförmiger **Lagerung** zu unterscheiden. Im ersten gewöhnlichen Falle besitzen beide Schichtenreihen eine gleiche Lagerung.* Man darf dann annehmen, dass zwischen der Ablagerung des älteren und des jüngeren Gliedes keine grössere zeitliche Unterbrechung[4] stattgefunden hat. Bei ungleichförmiger Lagerung dagegen besitzen beide Gesteinsfolgen ihre besondere,[3] von derjenigen der **anderen** abweichende Lagerung, und in diesem Falle muss[6] zwischen der Bildung des älteren und des jüngeren Gliedes eine gewisse **Zeit** verflossen sein, während welcher das ältere Glied aus seiner ursprünglichen horizontalen **Lage** herausgerückt und unter **Umständen** gefaltet worden ist.

H. with regard to g. mutual L. deposition
S. bed series g. uniform
z. u. to distinguish g. usual
F. case b. possess g. similar
d. may, must a. assume
A. deposition G. member
z. time, temporal U. interruption
s. occurred u. ununiform
G. rock series. Why Rule 3?
a. which deviates F. case
B. formation
g. certain v. elapsed
w. w. during which
Borrow "ist"; see Rule 8, E, 1.

Eine besondere Art der Lagerung, die* bei ihrer **Wichtigkeit** hier nicht unerwähnt bleiben darf, ist die übergreifende oder transgredierende Art.* Transitionen weisen stets darauf hin,[2] dass nach Ablagerung des älteren Schichtensystems eine Überflutung der Ränder des Ablagerungsbeckens eintrat, infolge welcher die jüngere Schichtenreihe über einem grösseren Gebiete als die ältere **Schichtenreihe** abgelagert wurde.

L. deposition b. in view of
u. unmentioned b. remain
ü. overlapping
h. refer d. to the fact
S. bed system Ü. overflooding R. edges
A. deposit basin i. w. due to which
G. area, field
a. deposited

(Numbers may appear or an * Give reasons for such. Indicate what nouns should be bold-faced.)

Es kann* nicht zweifelhaft sein, dass ebenso wie heutzutage schon in der geologischen Vorzeit der Charakter der Tier- und Pflanzenwelt[4] durch geographische Unterschiede beeinflusst worden ist. Dazu kamen dann noch allerhand andere örtliche Verschiedenheiten.* Die Landtiere waren stets andere als die Wassertiere und unter diesen wiederum die Meerestiere andere als die Süsswasserbewohner.* Endlich mussten sich auch zu allen Zeiten, wie heute, die Einflüsse der verschiedenen Höhenlage,* der Feuchtigkeit,* des **Bodens** geltend machen. Alle diese Umstände mussten zusammenwirken, um[7] seit den ältesten Zeiten allerlei regionale Verschiedenheiten der[3] unsere Erde während einer bestimmten **Epoche** bevölkernden Tier- und Pflanzenwelt hervorzubringen.

z. doubtful e. even so
h. now days V. early time
T. animal U. differences
b. influenced D. to that a. all kinds of.
ö. local L. land animals
a. different w. again
M. sea animals S. fresh water inhabitants
Z. times E. influences
H. altitude F. moisture B. soil
m. g. assert themselves U. conditions
a. all kinds of V. differences
Why rule 3? b. which inhabit
h. to bring forth What calls for this verb?

Nichtsdestoweniger ist es ein[3] durch hundertfältige Erfahrungen bestätigter, sich alle **Tage** aufs neue bewährender Satz, dass abgesehen von allen örtlichen Unterschieden die allgemeine Reihenfolge der Faunen und Floren der verschiedenen geologischen Perioden auf der ganzen Erde[1] die nämliche gewesen ist. So ist nicht nur die Aufeinanderfolge der verschiedenen grossen paläozoischen Faunen vom Cambrium an bis zum Perm an den entlegensten Punkten des Erdrundes die gleiche;[1] nein, auch die verschiedenen Ammonitenfaunen der Juraformation,* welche[5] doch nur verhältnismässig kurzen geologischen **Zeitabschnitten** entsprechen, wiederholen sich in geradezu staunenswerter Übereinstimmung in den verschiedensten Teilen Europas ebenso wie in Indien und Südamerika.*

N. nevertheless Why Rule 3? See Rule 3 C 1, sent. 4. What does " –er" on "bestätigter" tell you? R. series v. different
g. entire n. same
A. sequence, series
e. most remote
P. points
v. different
v. relatively Z. time-periods, eras
e. correspond to w. repeat
Ü. agreement T. parts

Die Altersbestimmung der Schichten mittelst ihrer Versteinerungen wird[6] aber nicht nur dann ausführbar sein, wenn es[4] sich um Ablagerungen einer und derselben **Gegend** handelt, sondern auch dann wenn dieselben[1] weit von einander getrennt sind, wenn also z. B. europäische[1] mit amerikanischen Schichten verglichen werden sollen. Auch in diesem Falle nämlich wird man annehmen dürfen, dass

1. gleichzeitige Ablagerungen[4] auch mehr oder weniger ähnliche Faunen und **Floren** einschliessen und dass

2. mit der Jugend einer Fauna und Flora im Allgemeinen auch ihre Ähnlichkeit[4] mit den jetzt lebenden Faunen und Floren zunimmt.

A. age determination S. beds
m. by means of V. fossils
A. deposits G. region
e.h.s.u. it deals with, we are concerned with
g. separate
S. beds
v. compared s. are to be F. case
a. assume
g. simultaneous A. deposits
ä. similar e. include

J. recency A. general
A. similarity
z. increases (zunehmen)

Die[3] durch örtliche Abweichungen der **Lebensbedingungen** verursachten Verschiedenheiten im Charakter der organischen Reste gleichalteriger Schichten werden[6] als paläontologische **Facies** bezeichnet. So findet sich nicht selten sogar in einer und derselben Gegend neben einer Ammoniten- oder überhaupt Cephalopodenfacies eine gleichalterige Brachiopoden-, Korallen- oder sonstige Facies.[1]

Why rule 3? ö. local A. deviations
v. which are caused V. differences
g. of similar aged beds
b. designated f. si. is found
G. region n. along with Why Rule 3 in this paragraph? 6? 1?
s. other

Die Unterschiede in der Gesteinsbeschaffenheit der verschiedenen Formationen und Formationsabteilungen geben nur sehr geringe Anhaltspunkte für die Altersbestimmung der Schichten.* Es gab allerdings eine Zeit, wo man glaubte, dass sich während eines jeden grösseren geologischen Zeitabschnittes ganz bestimmte,[3] für die betreffende **Epoche** auszeichnende Gesteine gebildet hätten und aus dieser Zeit stammen die Ausdrücke Kreideformation, Oolith-Grauwacken- Kohlengebirge.* Diese Anschauung hat[6] sich indessen als irrtümlich erwiesen. Man weiss jetzt dass z. B. Oolithgesteine und Steinkohlen in allen verschiedensten **Formationen** vorkommen. Umgekehrt können[6] aber gleichalterige Ablagerungen in verschiedenen Gegenden durch ganz abweichende **Gesteine** vertreten sein; so in einer Gegend durch Sandsteine und Konglomerate, in einer anderen durch Schiefer, in einer dritten durch Kalkgesteine.*

U. differences G. nature of the rock
F. formation-divisions
g. slight A. clues A. l. age determination
e. g. there was
w. during Z. period Why Rule 3 now?
a. which are characteristic
betr. concerned s. come
A. expressions A. view
h.s.e. has been shown (App. 11, 4, c)
ind. meanwhile
v. occur U. conversely
A. deposits G. regions
a. deviating G. rocks v. represent
What do the nouns tell you to do?
S. shales K. limestone

GEOLOGIE†

Geologie, wörtlich übersetzt,[11] heisst Wissenschaft oder Lehre von der **Erde.** Wenn aber der Geologe[4] von Erde spricht, so versteht er darunter vor allem die feste **Erdrinde.**[1] Allerdings gehören zu letzterer untrennbar auch die Wasser- und **Lufthülle,**[1] von denen[5] die erstere die grössten Vertiefungen der **Kruste** ausfüllt, die letztere[4] den Erdball in einer Dicke von mehreren hundert **Kilometern** umgiebt, und ausserdem noch die Tier- und **Pflanzenwelt,**[1] welche[5] die Erdoberfläche seit undenklichen **Zeiten** bevölkert; allein das organische **Reich,**[1] die Atmosphäre und die Hydrosphäre, haben für den Geologen nur insofern **Interesse,**[1] als sie[4] eine Einwirkung auf die **Erdrinde** ausüben. Diese Lithosphäre bleibt immer der Hauptgegenstand der geologischen **Forschung.**[1] Da nun aber die feste Rinde[1] aus Gesteinen besteht, so lässt sich[6] noch genauer aussprechen, dass sie es sind, welche die Geologie[4] in erster **Linie** zu erforschen hat.

ü. when translated literally W. science
E. earth W. when
v. understands d. by that v. a. above all,
g. belong u. inseparably
e. former V. depths, indentations
a. makes up, fills up E. globe
u. surrounds a. besides
P. plant world E. earth surface
b. populates a. but i. insofar
a. exercise
H. main subject F. study
d. since (App. 25, 2) G. rocks
s. l. s. a. can be expressed
e. study i. e. L. primarily

Die Geologie bleibt[6] aber nicht bei der Erforschung der Gesteinsbildungen der **Kruste** stehen; sie geht noch weiter und lehrt[6] uns auch die Entwicklungsgeschichte unseres **Planeten** kennen. Dass dies[4] möglich ist, dass wir[4] durch das Studium der Gesteine auch zu einer Bildungsgeschichte der **Erde** gelangen, hängt damit zusammen, dass, ehe der Erdkörper[4] seine heutige Gestalt und **Beschaffenheit** erhielt, er[4] eine ganze Reihe von **Entwickelungszuständen** zu durchlaufen hatte, die[5] im Einzelnen in physikalischer, klimatischer und biologischer **Beziehung** sehr verschieden waren. Diese verschiedenen Entwickelungsphasen und örtlich wechselnden Bildungszustände spiegeln sich nun in den Gesteinen der **Kruste** ab,[2] die,[5] im Laufe ungemessener **Zeiträume** entstanden,[11] ihre verschiedene Beschaffenheit eben jenen verschiedenartigen **Bildungsumständen** verdanken. Die Gesteine spielen mithin für den Geologen eine ähnliche **Rolle,**[1] wie für den Geschichtsforscher geschriebene **Urkunden** und für den Erforscher vorgeschichtlicher Zeitalter Baureste, Waffen, **Werkzeuge usw;**[1] sie sind für ihn das Mittel zur Konstruction der Geschichte der **Erde.**[1]

E. study
G. rock formations
l. teaches (acts like a modal verb)
k. know m. possible
G. rocks B. developmental history
e. before E. earth (body)
G. form B. nature e. obtained
E. evolutionary conditions d. pass through
B. respect
v. different E. development ph.
ö. locally w. changing
G. rocks a. are reflected
e. having arisen (Rule 11)
v. owe B. formation circumstances
m. therefore ä. similar
G. historian g. written U. records
E. student v. of prehistoric ages
We. tools M. means
G. history E. earth

Ein paar Beispiele mögen erläutern, welche weitreichende Schlüsse[4] sich aus der Beschaffenheit der **Gesteine** ableiten lassen.

B. examples e. illustrate

Die Geschichte ist aber nichts anderes als ein Stück der allgemeinen **Erdgeschichte.**[1] Wir brauchen[7] nur jene **Einzelberichte** zu vereinigen, um[7] eine Geschichte der gesamten **Erde** zu erhalten. Dabei ist es wichtig, dass sich diese Geschichte[4] nicht blos auf den leblosen Teil des **Erdkörpers** bezieht, sondern[8] sich auch auf seinen organischen **Teil** erstreckt. Dies hängt damit zusammen,[2] dass ein grosser **Teil der Gesteine**[4] ausser den mineralischen Bestandteilen noch Reste der Pflanzen und **Tiere** enthält, die[5] zur Zeit ihrer Ablagerung lebten. Das Studium dieser Reste, der Versteinerungen, die genaue Verfolgung der grossen **Unterschiede,** die sie[4] in den verschiedenen übereinanderfolgenden Gesteinsablagerungen zeigen, macht uns auch mit dem Entwickelungsgange des organischen Lebens unserer Erde bekannt.[1]

s. a. l. can be derived
a. general b. need (to what?)
E. individual reports
e. obtain g. total w. important
b. merely l. inanimate s. b. refers
s. but (what?) s. its
e. s. extends itself
G. rocks a. outside of B. components
R. residue, remnants e. contains
A. deposition V. fossils
g. exact V. pursuit U. differences
v. different G. rock deposits ü. consecutive
E. evolutionary course
b. familiar

[10]Untersuchen wir jetzt, wie sich der umfangreiche Stoff der Geologie[4] gliedern lässt. Nachdem wir[4] uns zunächst einen Überblick über die **Eigenschaften** verschafft haben, die[5] der Erde als Ganzem, als **Weltkörper** zukommen, werden[6] wir zuerst mit dem Studium der Erdkruste uns zu beschäftigen und[8] ihre Gestalt, ihre stoffliche Zusammensetzung und **Architektonik** kennen zu lernen haben. Sodann werden[6] wir fragen müssen, auf welche Weise die verschiedenen Gesteinsbildungen der Kruste[4] entstanden sind.

U. w. let us investigate (See Rule 10 B, 2 and C 1.)
s. g. l. can be analyzed v. procured Ü. survey
E. qualities z. belong G. whole
b. concern. Borrow "haben" Rule 8 E 7.
s. material Z. composition
f. ask W. manner
v. different G. rock formations

†Emanuel Kayser, **Abriss der Geologie**

Diese Frage wird[6] nicht auf spekulativem **Wege** beantwortet werden können, sondern dadurch, dass wir untersuchen, durch welche Kräfte gegenwärtig Gesteine entstehen. Denn noch heute schreitet die **Gesteinsbildung** ununterbrochen fort,[2] und die[3] dabei wirksamen Kräfte sind dieselben wie in der geologischen **Vorzeit.**[1] Es wird[6] mit anderen Worten eine weitere Aufgabe der Geologie sein,[7] die noch jetzt tätigen geologischen **Vorgänge** zu erforschen. Erst wenn die Forschung[1] nach beiden bezeichneten Richtungen einen gewissen **Abschluss** erreicht hat, wird es möglich[7] sein, mit Aussicht auf Erfolg die letzte Aufgabe der Geologie, die Konstruktion der Entwickelungsgeschichte der **Erde,** in Angriff zu nehmen.

w. will (App. 7, 4) b. answered
k. be able d. by the fact
K. forces g. at present e. arise
f. progresses u. uninterruptedly
w. which are effective
V. early time w. further
A. task (to what?) t. active
v. processes e. study E. only
b. designated R. directions A. conclusion
e. reached mö. possible
E. success A. task
E. development-history i.A. z. n. to attack

Die Aufgabe der Geologie ist nach diesen Ausführungen eine dreifache, ähnlich wie die aller nicht rein beschreibenden **Naturwissenschaften.**[1] Wie sich die Anthropologie, die Zoologie und Botanik,[4] zuerst mit dem Studium des[3] ihnen unterbreiteten **Stoffes zu beschäftigen haben,** dann mit der Erforschung der[3] auf die allgemeinen chemischen und physikalischen **Gesetze** zurückführenden Vorgänge der betreffenden Körper und zuletzt, als höchste **Aufgabe,**[1] mit ihrer Entwicklungsgeschichte, so auch die **Geologie.**[1] In der Anthropologie und den biologischen Wissenschaften überhaupt bezeichnet man diese drei Teile bekanntlich als Systematik oder Anatomie, Physiologie und **Entwickelungsgeschichte.**[1]

A. statements
ä. similarly d. a. that of all
N. natural sciences
z. first (Why Rule 3? 4?)
u. which was submitted to them
E. study a. general
G. laws z. which are traced back
h. highest A. task
What does rule 1 tell you to do?
W. sciences ü. in general
b. designates b. as one knows
How many rules are you using on the **page?**

In der Geologie entspricht 1. der Anatomie die Lehre von der **Gestaltung,**[1] Zusammensetzung und vom Bau des **Erdkörpers.**[1] Wir bezeichnen diesen Teil als die physiographische **Geologie.**[1] 2. der Physiologie entspricht die Lehre von den[3] sich auf der **Erde** abspielenden geologischen Vorgängen. Dieser Teil wird[6] mit einem[3] durch J. Dana in die **Wissenschaft** eingeführten Ausdruck als dynamische **Geologie** bezeichnet. Der Entwickelungsgeschichte endlich entspricht 3. die historische **Geologie,** die[5] uns die Bildungsgeschichte der Erde von ihren Anfängen bis auf die **Gegenwart** kennen lehrt. Innerhalb dieses letzten Teiles lassen[6] sich wieder unterscheiden: a) die stratigraphische Geologie oder **Formationskunde,**[1] die Lehre von der Verbreitung, Ausbildungsweise und dem organischen Inhalt der verschiedenen geologischen **Formationen,**[1] und b) die Geogenie, die Lehre von den[3] auf die Bildung der Erde bezüglichen **Theorien.**[1]

e. corresponds to
L. theory G. formation Z. composition
E. globe T. part
d. P. to physiology e. corresponds
a. s. which take place
V. processes Why Rule 3 here?
e. which was introduced why which?
b. designated e. finally D. to the
B. formation history
A. beginnings
G. present time I. within
s. l. can be u. distinguished
V. distribution
A. manner-of-formation I. content
v. different Why Rule 3 now?
b. which pertain to

[10]Spricht man nun von allgemeiner **Geologie,** so versteht man darunter namentlich die physiographische und die dynamische Geologie im Gegensatz zur historischen Geologie und insbesondere zur **Formationskunde,**[1] von welchen die allgemeine Geologie[4] nur die allgemeinsten **Endresultate** verwertet.[10] Betrachten wir jetzt etwas eingehender den Inhalt der beiden Hauptabteilungen der allgemeinen **Geologie.**

S. m. if one speaks
d. by that n. particularly
Geg. contrast
i. especially
a. most general
v. utilizes B. w. let us consider
See Rule 10 b. H. main divisions

Physiographische Geologie.

Es wird[6] zuerst die Erde als kosmischer **Körper** [9]ins **Auge** zu fassen, und[8] ihre Stellung im Weltraume sowie ihre Beziehungen zu den[3] sie umgebenden **Himmelskörpern** zu betrachten sein. Daran wird[6] sich zweckmässig **sogleich** die Besprechung der Ansichten über den Ursprung unseres Planetensystems und damit der Erde **selbst** knüpfen. Darauf soll folgen die Betrachtung der allgemeinen Gestalt und Grösse, der Dichte, der Wärmeerscheinungen—und zwar sowohl die äusseren als die inneren—sowie der magnetischen Erscheinungen der **Erde,**[1] soweit alle diese Dinge[4]

z. at first Note Rules 9, 8.
S. position W. universe
B. relations u. which surround
b. consider z. appropriately
B. discussion A. views
w. s. k. will be joined s. itself
(App. 13, 2, f) B. consideration
G. size D. density W. heat phenomena
a. outer D. things

für die Geologie von **Wichtigkeit** sind. Da dieser Abschnitt der Physiographie[1] hauptsächlich **Gegenstände** behandelt, die[5] der Astronomie und der **Geophysik** entlehnt sind, so kann[6] er als der astronomisch-**geophysikalische** bezeichnet werden.

W. importance D. since (App. 25, 2) A. section h. chiefly **G. subjects b. treats** e. borrowed, derived, gathered Note the absence of noun. e. it b. designated w. be (App. 7, 6)

Nachdem wir[4] so die Eigenschaften der Erde als **Weltkörper** kennen gelernt, werden[6] zunächst ihre Hauptglieder, nämlich die beiden flüssigen Hüllen, die Atmosphäre und die Hydrosphäre, und dann die feste Erdkugel selbst einer allgemeinen **Betrachtung** zu unterziehen sein. Da dieser Abschnitt[1] Gegenstände behandelt, mit denen sich[5] auch die **Geographie** beschäftigt, so bezeichnen wir ihn als den geographischen.[1]

N. after E. properties W. world body w. will b. two H. shells, coverings E. earth sphere e. to a a. general B. consideration d. since (app. 25-2) G. objects s. b. is concerned b. designate

Ein letzter Abschnitt der physiographischen Geologie wird[6] naturgemäss der Betrachtung der **Erdrinde** gewidmet sein, womit wir[4] spezifisch geologischen **Boden** betreten. Es wird[6] hier zuerst ein Überblick über die chemische und mineralische Zusammensetzung und die Hauptstrukturverhältnisse der Gesteine, dann eine kurze Übersicht über die wichtigsten **Gesteinstypen** zu geben sein. Daran wird[6] sich eine Besprechung der Absonderungs- und weiter der Lagerungsformen der Gesteine knüpfen. Den Schluss dieses Abschnitts endlich soll[6] ein Abriss der Lehre vom Schichtenbau oder der **Tektonik** bilden. Nach seinem Inhalt kann[6] dieser Teil der Physiographie als der petrographisch- **tektonische** bezeichnet werden.

A. section w. will (App. 7, 4) B. consideration g. devoted w. with which b. enter upon Ü. survey w. will Z. composition H. chief-structure-conditions G. rocks Ü. survey G. rock types D. to that w. will (App. 7, 4) L. deposition-forms s. k. be tied, joined D.S. the conclusion (What is the subject here?) S. bed structure b. form I. content A noun is expected after "tektonische". Observe this point carefully.

Dynamische Geologie

Die Gesamtheit der[3] auf der **Erde** stattfindenden geologischen Vorgänge lässt sich naturgemäss in zwei grosse **Gruppen** bringen, nämlich 1. endogene, die[5] durch **Kräfte** hervorgerufen werden, die[5] ihren Sitz und Ausgangspunkt im Erdkörper **selbst** haben, und 2. exogene die[5] ihren Ursprung ausserhalb der Erde, auf fremden Himmelskörpern, namentlich auf der Sonne und dem **Monde** haben. Unter den Kräften der letzten Art steht allen anderen an Bedeutung weit voran die[3] von der **Sonne** ausgestrahlte Wärme. Sie ist es, die[5] ebensowohl den Kreislauf des Wassers auf der Erde, wie die Bewegungen der Atmosphäre und des Meeres und das organische Leben, und damit eine Reihe der wichtigsten Hülfsmittel zur fortwährenden Umgestaltung der **Erdoberfläche** hervorbringt. Die Quelle der endogenen Vorgänge dagegen ist,[6] wie[8] später gezeigt werden soll, in der[3] durch die gesamte geologische **Zeit** hindurch erfolgten und noch jetzt fortdauernden Abkühlung des **Erdballs** zu suchen. Diese ist der Hauptgrund für die **Gebirgsbildung**,[1] die Erdbeben, die Hebungen und Senkungen der **Kruste** und noch andere verwandte **Erscheinungen**.[1]

G. totality s. which take place (why which?) V. processes n. naturally s. l. can be h. called forth S. seat, location A. starting point E. globe a. outside of f. foreign n. especially K. forces voranstehen stand ahead B. importance a. which is radiated S. i. e. it is that e. just as well K. circulation B. movements L. life d. with it R. series H. aids f. continuous U. transformation E. earth surface V. processes d. on the other hand Why Rule 3? g. total e. which took place f. which lasted E. globe H. main reason G. mountain formation E. earthquakes K. crust v. related E. phenomena

Exogene Vorgänge

Dieselben können[6] in der allgemein üblichen **Weise** eingeteilt werden in 1. solche der Atmosphäre, 2. solche des Wassers und 3. solche der **Organismen**.[1] Am wichtigsten und am mannigfaltigsten sind die Wirkungen des **Wassers**,[1] schon weil letzteres[1] in doppelter **Gestalt**,[1] als Wasser und als Eis, wirksam ist.

D. the same (App. 14, 1) ü. customary e. divided s.d. such of W. water w. most important W. effects G. form l. latter w. effective

Endogene Vorgänge

Diese lassen sich einteilen in 1. die vulkanische Ausbruchstätigkeit und die[3] damit zusammenhängenden Erscheinungen und 2. die verschiedenartigen Bewegungsvorgänge der Erdkruste und deren **Begleiterscheinungen**:[1] Gebirgsbildung, Niveauschwankungen, Erdbeben und mechanische **Gesteinsumformung**.[1]

V. processes e. divided s. l. can be A. eruptive-activity z. associated v. different-type B. movement processes d. their B. accompanying-phenomena G. mountain formation E. earthquake G. rock-transformation

Ausser den genannten Gegenständen hat[6] sich aber die dynamische Geologie noch mit der wichtigen Frage nach der Entstehungsart der verschiedenen,[3] die **Kruste** zusammensetzenden **Gesteine** zu beschäftigen. An vielen Stellen wird[6] sich Gelegenheit[7] bieten, auf die Bildungsweise dieses oder jenes **Gesteins** einzugehen; ausserdem soll[6] am Schluss der Besprechung der exogenen sowie der endogenen Vorgänge ein zusammenfassendes Kapitel über die[3] aus diesen hervorgegangenen **Gesteine**[9] Platz finden.

A. outside of g. (above-)mentioned
w. important n. about
E. type-of-origination v. different (Why Rule 3?)
z. b. to concern z. which compose
G. opportunity e. to enter in
a. besides S. conclusion
B. discussion V. processes
z. comprehensive h. which proceed
P. room, place (Why Rule 9? 3?)

Es leuchtet ein,[2] dass das Studium der heutigen geologischen Vorgänge[4] von der allergrössten **Bedeutung** ist, insofern sie[4] uns den Schlüssel zum Vorhandensein der geologischen Vorgänge der **Vergangenheit** bieten. Es ist freilich noch nicht lange her, dass diese Einsicht[4] sich allgemein **Bahn** gebrochen hat; früher hielt man die jetzt wirkenden Kräfte zur Erklärung der älteren geologischen Erscheinungen nicht für ausreichend.[1] Erst in neuerer Zeit hat[6] sich die Theorie, dass die gegenwärtigen geologischen Kräfte[4] zur Erklärung aller geologischen **Tatsachen** genügen, überall **Eingang** verschafft.

e. is clear h. present
a. very greatest (Why Rule 2? 4?)
S. key V. presence
V. past b. offer
f. to be sure l. h. long ago E. idea
B. path, way h. considered
w. effective E. explanation
E. phenomena a. adequate E. only
g. present K. forces
g. suffice T. facts
v. procured E. acceptance, entry

ANSICHTEN ÜBER DIE ENTSTEHUNG DES SONNENSYSTEMS A. views E. origin

Wir haben oben gesehen, dass alle Planeten[4] eine übereinstimmende Umlaufsrichtung um die **Sonne** haben, dass in gleicher Richtung die Monde[4] sich um ihre Planeten, ja endlich auch die Sonne und alle Planeten um ihre eigenen **Axen** bewegen. Dazu kommt weiter, dass die Bahnen aller Planeten[4] in übereinstimmender Weise wenig excentrische **Ellipsen** sind und dass alle[4] mit einander und mit dem Äquator des **Centralkörpers** nahezu zusammenfallen. Diese auffällige Übereinstimmung brachte zwei ausgezeichnete Geister des vorigen **Jahrhunderts**,[1] den Philosophen Kant und den Astronomen La Place zu der **Überzeugung**,[1] dass alle Körper unseres Planetensystems[4] eine gemeinsame und gleiche **Entstehung** besässen. Nach der "Kant-LaPlaceschen Theorie" haben[6] dieselben ursprünglich einen einzigen, riesigen,[3] weit über die jetzige **Neptunbahn** hinausreichenden glühenden **Gasball** gebildet.[10] Erhielt dieser, vielleicht durch Anziehung seitens anderer Körper im Weltenraum, eine Bewegung um seine Axe so musste[6] dieselbe mit fortschreitender Verdichtung seiner **Masse** allmählich immer schneller werden, und es musste[6] sich (ganz wie bei dem bekannten Plateausschen Versuche, wo man[4] eine Ölkugel in Alkoholwasser immer schneller um ihre Achse, rotieren lässt) mit wachsender Centrifugalkraft eine äquatoriale Anschwellung und zugleich eine polare **Abplattung** bilden, die[5] schliesslich zur Loslösung eines **Ringes** führte. Bei der geringsten Ungleichmässigkeit musste[6] der Ring zerreissen, worauf dessen Stücke,[4] unter Fortsetzung ihrer Kreisbewegung, einander allmählich anzogen und[8] sich zu einem Planeten ballten.

ü. like, corresponding, agreeing
U. circulation-direction
g. like M. moons
i. their e. own
b. move B. paths
ü. corresponding Note Rule 4 in this paragraph.
z. coincide, fall together n. nearly
a. striking extraordinary Ü. agreement
a. excellent, renowned G. minds
Ü. conviction
g. common
E. origin b. possess N. according to
u. originally r. gigantic (Why Rule 3? 6?)
j. present h. which extends
g. glowing E. if this obtained
A. attraction s. on the part of
B. movement f. progressive
V. condensation a. gradually
s. w. become faster (App. 7, 3)
b. known V. experiment Ö. oil-bulb
i. s. faster and faster
w. increasing C. -force
A. swelling z. at the same time
L. detach, severance
g. slightest U. irregularity z. break up.
d. its F. continuation
K. circle-movement a. gradually anz. attract

Die Lostrennung eines Ringes wiederholte sich mit fortschreitender Verdichtung des Hauptkörpers noch öfter,[1] und in allen **Fällen**,[1] mit einziger Ausnahme von demjenigen, der[5] zur

L. detachment w. s. was repeated
f. progressive V. condensation H. main body
ö. more often A. exception

Bildung der **Asteroiden** führte, ging aus der Zerstörung des Ringes ein einheitlicher Planet hervor.[2] Erst als die Abkühlung des Hauptballs[4] soweit gediehen war, dass die Centrifugalkraft[4] die **Schwerkraft** nicht mehr zu überwinden vermochte, war[6] der Gegensatz zwischen Centralkörper und peripherischen **Körpern** für immer festgestellt.

B. formation f. led
Z. destruction e. uniform h. proceeded
E. only A. cooling H. main ball
S. gravity
v. was able ü. overcome G. contrast
f. established

Die Planeten hatten[6] aber inzwischen ihrerseits eine ähnliche Entwickelung wie der **Hauptkörper** durchgemacht, d. h.[8] Ringe abgesondert, die[5] zur Entstehung von Nebenkörpern oder **Trabanten** führten. Nur in einem **Falle**, nämlich bei Bildung des **Saturn**, erfolgte die Ringbildung so regelmässig, dass derselbe[4] erhalten blieb, gleichsam als ob die Natur[4] uns an einem Beispiele hätte vor Augen führen wollen, wie die Bildung der Trabanten und Planeten[4] vor sich gegangen sei.

i. meanwhile i. in turn
ä. similar E. development H. main bodies
a. separated E. origin
f. led F. case n. namely
e. took place r. r. regularly
e. preserved g. as it were, as if
B. example h. u. v. a. f. w. had wanted to lead before our eyes w. how
v. s. g. had gone on

Nach obigen Anschauungen sollen[6] also Sonne, Planeten und Monde einen gemeinsamen Ursprung und einen und denselben allgemeinen **Entwickelungsgang** besitzen: alle sollen[6] durch allmählichen Zerfall eines sich mehr und mehr verdichtenden **Gasballes** entstanden sein.

o. above A. views
g. common U. origin
a. general E. development-course
a. gradual Z. disintegration
v. condensing e. s. have arisen

[10]Ist die Theorie richtig, so müssen[6] sich alle Planeten und Trabanten in gleicher Richtung um die Sonne und um ihre **Axen** drehen und ihre Bahnen müssen[6] mit der Äquatorialebene der **Sonne** zusammenfallen. Wie wir[4] gesehen haben, ist dies der **Fall.** Eine weitere Stütze bilden die Dichtigkeitsverhältnisse der **Planeten.**[10] Ist sie nämlich begründet, so müssen[6] die äusseren Planeten, weil sie[4] zu einer Zeit entstanden, als die Verdichtung des Hauptballs[4] noch nicht weit gediehen war, weniger dicht sein als die inneren **Planeten,** die[5] erst später entstanden. Auch dieses trifft zu.[2] Auch der Umstand, dass die Dichte des Mondes erheblich geringer ist als diejenige der Erde, entspricht durchaus den Voraussetzungen der **Theorie,** da der Mond[4] sich von der Erde zu einer **Zeit** ablöste, als diese noch weniger verdichtet war als heute.

Why 'if' here?
T. satellite R. direction
d. turn, rotate B. paths
z. coincide
F. case S. support D. density-conditions
g. justified ä. outer
e. arose V. condensation
g. developed Note "sein" in front of "als"–a break.
s. later z. applies U. circumstance
Why is "ist" here? d. that one (App. 14, 2)
V. suppositions
a. released itself, detach
v. condensed Note "war" before "als".

Weitaus ihre stärkste Stütze aber hat[6] die Kant-Laplace'sche Theorie durch die Anwendung der Spektralanalyse auf die Erforschung der fernen **Himmelskörper** erhalten.

w. by far S. support a. however
A. use E. study f. distant
e. obtained

Wir haben[6] die Frage nach Zustand und Entstehung der Körper unseres **Sonnensystems** ausführlicher besprochen, als es[4] sonst in Lehrbüchern der **Geologie** zu geschehen pflegt. Allein diese Frage ist untrennbar verknüpft mit derjenigen nach dem Ursprung der Erde selbst;[1] und da die Antwort,[4] die uns die Geologie[4] auf diese Frage gibt, bis jetzt nicht völlig ausreichend und einwandfrei ist, so erschien es umso mehr geboten,[7] uns etwas genauer mit den bewunderungswürdigen **Aufschlüssen** bekannt zu machen, die uns die Astrophysik[4] über die Beschaffenheit der **Gestirne** geliefert hat. Wir haben[6] so eine feste Grundlage für unsere weiteren Untersuchungen über die Beschaffenheit des **Erdinnern** gelegt.[10] Führen uns diese zur Annahme eines hochtemperirten Erdkerns, so werden wir uns erinnern, dass dies Ergebnis[4] mit den Anschauungen der neuesten physikalisch-astronomischen **Forschungen**[9] in vollstem Einklang steht.

Z. condition E. origin
b. discussed a. in more detail
L. texts g. happen s. otherwise A. but
p. is accustomed u. inseparably
v. connected U. origin
A. answer What does this subject call for?
"Geologie"? a. adequate
e. appeared u. m. all the more
b. familiar b. admirable A. disclosures
B. nature G. stars
g. furnished What does 7 call for? 4? 6?
U. investigations B. nature
g. put, laid A. assumption F. u. d. if this leads us
E. earth core e. remember
E. result A. views
F. studies i. v. E. in fullest harmony

METEORITEN

(In some places an asterisk will appear where certain rules are involved. Indicate the rules if more drill is needed. Also underline nouns which should be bold-faced.)

Ausser den Planeten gibt es noch andere,[3] gleichfalls unserem **Sonnensystem** angehörige Körper, nämlich die Kometen und die Meteoriten.* Die ersteren können* wir umso eher übergehen, als sie[4] keine vollwertigen Bürger unseres Sonnensystems und[8] überdies noch wenig erforscht sind. Dagegen sind die Meteoriten schon deshalb von grösstem Interesse,* weil sie[4] der einzige[3] aus dem **Weltenraum** stammende Stoff sind, der[5] in unsere Hände kommt und den wir[4] ebenso untersuchen können, wie jedes irdische Gestein.*

a. which belong, why which?
u.e. all the sooner (App. 26, 2.)
ü. moreover e. studied D. on the other hand
d. therefore g. greatest e. only (what?)
s. which comes u. investigate

What rules are you using to 'pull the verbs out'? Review Rule 3.
i. earthly G. rock

Allgemeine Erscheinungsweise

Mit den Meteoriten sind aufs engste verwandt die Sternschnuppen oder Leuchtkugeln.* Beide stammen von kleinsten,[3] die Sonne umkreisenden Körpern her,[2] von deren Vorhandensein wir[4] keine Ahnung haben würden, wenn sie[4] nicht zeitweise in ihrem Laufe, die Erdbahn kreuzend,[11] der Erde so nahe kämen, dass sie[4] von dieser angezogen und[8] zum Herabfallen gebracht würden. Alle diese Körper dringen mit planetarischer, übrigens je nach ihrer Bewegungsrichtung verschiedener Geschwindigkeit in die **Atmosphäre** ein.[2] Da mit diesem Eindringen eine starke Reibung und Erhitzung[4] verbunden ist, so werden[6] die meisten schon in den oberen Regionen der Atmosphäre unter glänzender Feuererscheinung aufgelöst. Nur die widerstandsfähigsten gelangen bis auf die **Erde** hinab.* Infolge der starken Erhitzung während des Fluges durch die Luft pflegen[7] die Meteoriten mit einer dunkeln, glänzenden **Schmelzkruste** bekleidet zu sein. Häufig nimmt man auf derselben kleine flache **Vertiefungen** wahr,[2] die[5] wie von **Fingereindrücken** herrührend aussehen. Daubree hat* experimentell nachgewiesen, dass diese sogenannten Näpfchen[4] durch den Druck der comprimirten Luft gegen das fliegende **Meteor** entstehen.

a. e. in the closest way v. related
S. falling stars. B. both
u. which circle h. originate from
V. presence A. idea
z. occasionally L. course k. while crossing
a. attracted What goes with "dringen"? ü. moreover j. n. each according to
B. movement-direction v. of different
G. velocity E. penetration
R. friction E. heating
w. a. are dissolved (App. 7, 5, a)
w. most resistant
h. come down I. inconsequence of
F. flight p. are accustomed
b. lined, clothed g. shiny What goes with "nimmt"? d. the same (App. 14, 1) F. finger imprints wie-her as coming from
N. cups D. pressure
f. flying e. arise What rules are calling for the verbs? prefixes?

Hinter diesem letzteren bildet sich ein stark luftverdünnter **Raum,** in den die Luft* mit donnerartigem Schall einströmt. Häufig zieht das Meteor beim Fluge hinter sich einen langen **Schweif** her.* Derselbe besteht offenbar aus Meteorstaub und erhält sich oft als ein dunkles Wölkchen noch lange nach dem Herabfallen des Meteoriten.* Der schliessliche Fall des letzteren ist nur die Folge des stets sich mehrenden[3] und endlich die Eigenbewegung des **Meteors** aufhebenden **Luftwiderstandes.***

l. air-rare, air thin R. space
e. flows in S. sound F. flight
S. tail h. draw with, draw forth
o. obviously M. meteor-dust
W. cloud H. descent
F. fall s. final
F. result m. increasing Why rule 3?
L. air resistance a. which cancels

Über die äussere Form der Meteoriten ist zu bemerken, dass dieselben[4] stets die Gestalt zufälliger Bruchstücke mit scharfen Ecken und **Kanten** haben und[8] sich dadurch als Trümmer oder Splitter grösserer **Körper** zu erkennen geben. Auch ihre Grösse ist meist gering. Steine von 5 Kilo Gewicht sind schon eine Seltenheit,* wenn auch weit grössere* niedergefallen sind. Die schwersten bekannten wiegen einige hundert Kilogramm.* Nicht selten, wie bei dem bekannten Fall von Pultusk,* fallen mit einem Male mehrere Tausend kleinere Steine.* In manchen Fällen gelangt sogar nur eine feine, staubförmige Masse,* die[5] überwiegend aus magnetischem Eisenoxyd zu bestehen pflegt, auf die **Erde** herab[2] und dann spricht man von Staubmeteoriten.*

i. z. b. is to be noted (App. 12, 1.)
d. the same, they (App. 14,1) G. form
B. fragments E. corners K. sides
T. ruins S. fragments
e. recognize G. size g. slight
G. weight S. rarity, scarcity w. a. even if
n. s. have fallen b. known
w. weigh s. scarce
m. e. m. with one time, at once
g. comes s. even
s. dust-like ü. predominately
b. p. is accustomed to consist
herabgelangen come down

HÄUFIGKEIT DER METEORITEN

(If need arises, give reasons for the * and indicate what nouns should be bold-faced.)

Im Unterschiede von den Sternschnuppen,* die* häufig und oft in grossen **Massen** fallen, gehören Meteoritenfälle zu den selteneren Ereignissen.* Bedenkt[10] man aber, dass die allermeisten[4] ins Meer, in Wüsten oder in unbewohnte **Gegenden** fallen, dass die Hälfte[4] in der **Nacht** fällt und dass überhaupt ein Zusammentreffen verschiedener günstiger Umstände[4] erforderlich ist, damit ein Meteoritenfall* beobachtet wird, so gelangt man zu dem Schluss, dass wahrscheinlich kein Tag vergeht, ohne dass an verschiedenen Punkten der Erde Meteoriten* niederfallen. Man **hat*** denn auch schon wiederholt hervorgehoben, dass der Zuwachs an **Masse,**[4] den die Erde* auf diesem Wege im Laufe der geologischen **Zeiten** erfahren hat, nicht zu unterschätzen und[8] vielleicht sogar von Einfluss auf ihre Drehungsgeschwindigkeit gewesen **ist.** In der Tat sind[6] bei Tiefseeuntersuchungen vom Meeresgrunde wiederholt mit einer Magnetitrinde umgebene Kügelchen von metallischem **Eisen** heraufgebracht worden, die[5] nur von Meteoriten herrühren können und[8] den Beweis liefern, dass auch kosmische Materie* an der **Sedimentbildung** Anteil[9] hat.

U. distinction S. shooting stars
h. frequently g. belong
s. more rare B. m. if one remembers
(Why if?) M. sea W. desert G. regions
H. half N. night
ü. in general Z. meeting-together
e. necessary d. so that b. observed
g. comes S. conclusion w. probably
v. passes v. different
n. fall
w. repeatedly h. stressed Z. increase
W. way L. course
e. undergone n. zu. u. is not to be underestimated Note Rule 8. D. rotation-velocity
i. d. T. indeed T. deep-sea-investigations
M. bottom-of-the-sea u. which are surrounded
E. iron h. come B. proof
A. part, share

Sehr merkwürdig sind die periodischen Meteoriten oder Sternschnuppenfälle.* Die Hauptsächlichsten erfolgen am 10. August und 14. November.* Zu ihrer Erklärung muss man annehmen, dass geschlossene **Meteoritenringe** vorhanden sind, die[5] sich nach den Kepplerschen Gesetzen um die **Sonne** bewegen und[8] die Erdbahn in der Nähe des Perihels schneiden. Der Augustfall ist alle Jahre gleich stark, der Novemberfall alle 33 Jahre am **stärksten.*** Bei letzterem muss* daher eine Stelle des Ringes, die* nach je 33 Jahren zum Perihel zurückkehrt, besonders dicht sein, womit zugleich die Umlaufszeit dieses Ringes gegeben ist.

m. remarkable
S. shooting-star-falls H. chief
e. take place E. explanation
a. assume v. exist, are present
b. move G. laws What does "die" call for? "und"?
s. cut, intersect
P. point nearest to the sun
a. s. strongest b. l. in the case of the latter
S. place z. returns d. dense
w. whereby, by which U. circulation-time

Chemische und mineralische Zusammensetzung

Z. composition

Die Hauptrolle für die Zusammensetzung der Meteoriten spielt bekanntlich das metallische Eisen.* Dasselbe ist* durch einen kleinen **Nickelgehalt** ausgezeichnet und zeigt beim Anätzen die sogenannten Widman Figuren,* die* von einer schaligen Zusammensetzung nach der Octaederfläche, bzw. einem Wechsel nickelarmer und nickelreicher **Lagen** herrühren. Auf diese Rolle des Eisens hat[6] Daubree seine **Einteilung** der **Meteoriten in die** beiden Hauptgruppen der Siderite (eisenhaltige Steine) und Asiderite (der eisenfreien) gegründet. Nach der Menge des Eisens teilt er die erstgenannte Gruppe weiter in Holosiderite, Syssiderite und Sporadosiderite (Steine, die* ganz, solche die grösstenteils, und solche, die nur zum kleinern Teil aus **Eisen** bestehen.)

H. main role
b. as one knows d. the same (App. 14, 1)
N. nickle content a. distinguished
A. etching, begin to erode
s. shell-like O. octahedral surface
W. change h. come from
E. classification
b. two H. main groups e. iron-containing
e. iron free
N. according to M. quantity
w. further
g. for the most part g. entirely
b. consist

Neben dem Eisen **nehmen**[9] folgende Stoffe an der Zusammensetzung der Meteoriten[9] Teil: Schreibersit (Phosphornickeleisen), Graphit, Diamant und amorphe Kohle;[1] Troilit (Einfach-Schwefeleisen) Magnetkies, Magnetit, Chromit und Tridymit; ferner von Silicaten: Olivin, Bronzit u. a.*

N. along with Note Rule 9. f. following
T. part (take part) What do the nouns tell you to do?
f. further

Struktur der Meteoriten

Die Struktur der Meteoriten ist[6] derjenigen der irdischen **Eruptivgesteine** ähnlich. Sie ist häufig deutlich krystallinisch-körnig oder auch durch einzelne,[3] in grösseren **Krystallen** auftretende Gemengteile porphyrisch. Daneben kommen aber auch **klastische** Strukturen vor.[2]

i. ä. is similar Note Rule 6. d. to that (App. 14, 2) h. frequently
e. individual
a. which appear G. admixtures
v. occur

(The * and the numbers are gradually omitted. Indicate what rule aids to remove elements beyond the bold-faced nouns.)

Bei den Chondriten treten, wie schon erwähnt, in einer erdig-pulverigen oder dichten Grundmasse kleine **Kügelchen** auf. Nach Tschermak zeigen diese* häufig aus **Olivin** bestehenden Körperchen das Verhalten von Erstarrungsprodukten. Er betrachtet sie deshalb als erstarrte Tropfen eines eruptiven Magmas, während er das umschliessende Gestein mit unseren vulkanischen **Tuffen** vergleicht. Von Interesse ist weiter die* vom englischen Mikroskopiker Sorby an einigen **Meteoriten** beobachtete Fluidalstruktur, ähnlich wie solche bei irdischen,[3] aus heissem **Fluss** erstarrten **Gesteinen** vorkommt. Endlich verdient[7] auch das Auftreten innerer Gleitflächen, die unseren irdischen Harnischen und **Reibungsspiegeln** vergleichbar sind, erwähnt zu werden.

e. earth-powder d. dense
K. balls h. frequently What does "diese" call for?
b. considers e. solidified T. drops
w. while u. enclosing
v. compares What does "er" call for? "die"?
b. which was observed
ä. similarly
e. which were solidified
v. deserves (to what?) A. appearance
What does "die" call for? Why?
v. comparable e. mentioned

Ursprung der Meteoriten U. origin

Es wurde oben hervorgehoben, dass alle Meteoriten die Gestalt von Trümmern oder **Splittern** haben.[10] Denkt man sich diese Splitter mit Daubree wieder zu kosmischen **Körpern** vereinigt, so liegt die **Annahme** nahe, dass die leichten, eisenarmen und kieselsäurereichen Steine von der Oberfläche dieser **Körper** herstammen, wo das Eisen zum grössten Teil der **Oxydation** unterlag und[8] mit der Kieselsäure zu **Verbindungen** zusammentrat; die schweren, eisenreichen Steine dagegen aus deren Innerem, wo das Eisen vor der **Oxydation** geschützt blieb. Man würde so **Himmelskörper** erhalten, die ähnlich gebaut waren, wie unsere Erde, deren Inneres[4] aus weit schwereren, als die oberflächlichen Massen—wie man[6] gewöhnlich annimmt, ebenfalls aus grossen Eisenmassen besteht. Zusammensetzung und Gefüge der Meteoriten sprechen für die Annahme, dass die Himmelskörper,[4] deren Reste[4] die **Meteoriten** sind, **Erstarrungsgebilde** waren, während kein Merkmal[4] auf eine sedimentäre **Entstehung** hinweist. Dass auf jenen Körpern oftmals heftige Bewegungsvorgänge,[4] ähnlich den[3] auf der Erde zu beobachtenden, sich abgespielt haben müssen, beweisen die nicht seltenen Breccienstrukturen und Reibungsspiegel der Meteoriten. Auf Grund des Umstandes, dass den Meteorsteinen alle schlackigen und lavaartigen Gebilde völlig fehlen, nimmt **Tschermak** an, dass die vulkanische Tätigkeit der meteoritischen Himmelskörper überwiegend explosiver Art und durch plötzliche heftige **Gasausbrüche** bedingt gewesen ist. Als ein Anhaltspunkt für diese Annahme könnte[6] der[3] durch Graham im Meteoriten von **Lenarte** nachgewiesene freie Wasserstoff, sowie die grossartigen Wasserstofferuptionen der Sonne und anderer **Gestirne** betrachtet werden. Tschermak glaubt auch, dass die Zertrümmerung der Meteoritenweltkörper nicht durch Zusammenstoss, sondern durch vulkanische **Tätigkeit** erfolgt sei. Waren[10] die planetarischen Körper von geringer **Grösse**, so genügte ihre Schwerkraft nicht, um[7] die ausgeworfenen Stücke sämtlich wieder zur **Oberfläche** zurückzuführen.

h. stressed
G. form **S. debris** S. fragments
d. v. imagines combined Why if?
A. assumption
l. light k. rich in silicic acid
h. come from O. surface
u. was subject K. silicic acid
V. compounds z. merged s. heavy
d. on the other hand
g. protected e. obtain
ä. similarly E. earth d. whose
See the chapter on Inserted Elements.
g. generally a. assumes e. likewise
Z. composition G. structure
See chapter on Inserted Elements.
E. solidification-structure
h. points to E. origin
h. violent B. movement processes
b. to the ones which are to be observed
R. frictional surfaces
U. circumstance
s. slag like G. formations f. are lacking
T. activity
ü. predominately
b. caused G. gas eruptions A. clue
What does "kö." call for? "der"?
n. which was detected W. hydrogen
g. imposing
G. stars, planets b. considered
Z. dismemberment Z. impact
T. activity e. taken place
W. if the p. bodies were
g. did not suffice a. discharged
s. totally z. to lead or bring back

Wie dem auch sei, das Studium der Meteoriten hat sehr wesentlich zur Erweiterung und Vertiefung unserer Einsicht in die Beschaffenheit und Vorgänge auf den Körpern unseres **Planetensystems** beigetragen. Das Ergebnis, dass die ausserirdischen Glieder desselben zum grossen Teil aus denselben **Mineralien** aufgebaut sind, wie unsere Erde, und dass sich wahrscheinlich auch auf ihnen vulkanische Vorgänge ähnlicher Art, wie auf der Erde, abgespielt haben, ist als eine sehr bedeutsame **Errungenschaft** anzusehen.

w. d. a. s. be that as it may
What does "hat" call for? w. essentially
E. understanding B. nature V. process
b. contributed E. result
G. members z. g. T. in large part
a. built up
w. probably V. processes
ä. of similar type s. a. have taken place
E. achievement a. to be regarded (App. 12, 1)

GESTALT UND GRÖSSE DER ERDE

Es war schon ein Lehrsatz der Pythagoräischen Schule, dass die Erde **Kugelgestalt** besitze; indessen hat erst Aristoteles ihre **Kugelform** überzeugend bewiesen. Heute bedient man sich zur Ermittelung der Erdgestalt besonders der **Gradmessungen,** die auf dem **Prinzip** beruhen, dass man die Dimensionen einer **Kugel** berechnen kann, wenn man ein Bogenstück eines ihrer grössten Kreise sowohl nach seiner Amplitude als nach seiner **Länge** kennt. Die ältesten Gradmessungen wurden von Picard und Cassini in den Jahren 1670-1718 in **Frankreich** ausgeführt und führten zu dem Ergebnis, dass die Erde keine vollkommene **Kugel** sei, sondern[8] die Form eines Ellipsoides mit längerer Rotations- und kürzerer **Aequatorialaxe** habe. Dieses Ergebnis stand aber im Widerspruch mit den Ansichten von Newton,[5] der,[11] ausgehend von der Voraussetzung eines ehemaligen flüssigen Zustandes der Erde (in welchem Falle die[3] durch die **Axenrotation** hervorgerufene Centrifugalkraft eine **Polarabplattung** bewirkt haben musste), behauptete, dass die Erdgestalt einem Ellipsoide mit längerer Äequatorial- und kürzerer **Polaraxe** entspreche. Zur Schlichtung dieses Streites sandte die Pariser Akademie in den Jahren 1735—1744 zwei Expeditionen, die eine nach Peru, die andere nach **Lappland** aus.[2] Ihr Ergebnis war, dass die Ansicht von Newton als richtig anerkannt und die Polarabplattung der Erde ausser **Zweifel** gestellt wurde. Seit jener Zeit sind zahlreiche **Gradmessungen** ausgeführt worden, von denen die[3] in den Jahren 1816—1851 von **Struve** geleitete, die[5] den ungeheueren Bogen zwischen Hammerfest und **Bessarabien** mass, als die **genaueste** gilt.

L. principle
K. spherical form b. possessed
ü. convincingly b. proved
b. makes use E. determination
G. measurement of degrees b. rest
b. compute B. curved piece
K. circles n. according to
L. length ä. oldest **What rules are you using to "remove" the verbs?**
a. carried out E. result
v. perfect K. sphere s. but
(what?) Note Rule 8. k. shorter
E. result W. opposition
A. views a. while proceeding from (Why while?)
Review Rule 11. V. supposition
i. w. F. in which case
h. which was called forth (Why which?)
b. maintained **What calls for this verb?**
E. corresponds S. settlement
S. dispute s. sent
d. e. the one
What does "aus" go with? A. view
a. r. as correct e. recognized
P. flattening at the poles
z. numerous a. executed
Supply "one" after g. The one which was conducted by Struve u. enormous
g. is valid, as the most exact

Die neueren Gradmessungen haben nur verhältnismässig geringe Korrekturen der[3] von den französischen **Expeditionen** erhaltenen **Werte** herbeigeführt. Der Mittelwert aus den zehn zuverlässigsten Gradmessungen beträgt nach Bessel 1/299, woraus sich in runden Zahlen berechnet: Länge der Erdaxe=1713 geogr. Meilen; Länge des Aequatorialdurchmessers=1719 geogr. Meilen. Auch Helmert hält 1/299 für den[3] der **Wahrheit** am nächsten kommenden Wert, während der französische Astronom Faye denselben zu 1/292, der Amerikaner Clarke zu **1/295** berechnet.

n. more recent
v. relatively
e. which were obtained h. produced
z. most reliable b. amounts to
b. s. is computed
L. length
h. holds, considers W. truth
k. which comes a. n. closest Why Rule 3?

Ausser den Gradmessungen benutzt man zur Bestimmung der Erdgestalt noch Pendelbeobachtungen. Die Verwendbarkeit des Pendels zu diesem Zweck beruht darauf, dass die Schwingungen desselben eine Wirkung der **Schwerkraft** sind und[8] daher schneller oder langsamer werden müssen, je nachdem die Intensität der **Schwere zu-** oder abnimmt.[10] Besitzt nun die Erde Abplattung, so kann die Schwere nicht überall auf der **Erdoberfläche** gleich sein. Denn alle Aequatorialpunkte werden dann weiter vom **Mittelpunkte** der Erde entfernt sein und daher schwächer angezogen werden, als die[3] mehr nach den **Polen zu** gelegenen Punkte. Aus diesem Grunde also wird[6] die Grösse der Anziehung vom Aequator nach **den Polen zu** beständig zunehmen müssen. Ein Pendel, welches für den Aequator **Sekunden** schlägt, wird in höheren **Breiten** schneller gehen; man wird es verlängern müssen, wenn es auch hier noch **Sekunden** schlagen soll. Durch zahlreiche **Versuche** ist nun in der Tat die stetige Zunahme des Sekundenpendels nach den **Polen zu** nachgewiesen worden.

b. computed
A. outside of b. uses
B. determination **E. form of the earth**
V. use Z. purpose b. rests
S. effect Schwer. gravity
s. faster j. n. according as
zunimmt increases Why if here?
S. gravity E. earth surface
M. center
e. removed a. attracted
n. d. P. z. toward the poles (Note the extra "zu".)
A. attraction b. constantly z. increase
w. g. will go (App. 7, 4)
v. lengthen
s. is to s. strike z. numerous
V. experiments s. constant Z. increase
n. demonstrated

CHEMIE

SCHMELZPUNKTSBESTIMMUNG†

ALLGEMEINE BEMERKUNGEN.

Die Art, wie im Laboratorium fast ausschliesslich Schmelzpunktsbestimmungen[4] ausgeführt werden, ist gewiss nicht die genaueste, aber für die Zwecke des Chemikers vollkommen ausreichend.

A. manner w. how, in which a. exclusively
S. melting point determinations
g. certainly g. most exact Z. purposes
v. completely a. adequate

Als Schmelzpunkt ist[6] jene Temperatur anzusehen, bei der die Substanz[4] nach der **Meniscusbildung** vollkommen klar und durchsichtig erscheint. Bei vollkommen reiner Substanz pflegt[7] das "Schmelzintervall" innerhalb eines oder höchstens zweier **Grade** zu liegen.

a. to be regarded (App. 12, 1) b. d. at which
d. transparent v. perfectly
p. is accustomed i. within
h. at most

Es wird[6] daher bei einer reinen Substanz unscharfes **Schmelzen** nur dann eintreten, wenn sie[4] sich beim Erwärmen unterhalb des **Schmelzpunktes** zersetzt und[8] daher beim Schmelzpunkt ein Gemisch der ursprünglichen Substanz mit deren **Zersetzungsprodukt** bildet.

e.w.-eint. there will enter in
u. unsharp S. melting
u. below S. melting point
d. hence G. mixture u. original
Z. decomposition product b. forms

Besondere Bedeutung hat das sorgfältige Trocknen für die Untersuchung krystallwasserhaltiger und hygroskopischer **Substanzen.**[1] Es genügen bereits einige zehntel Prozent **Feuchtigkeit,**[1] um[7] den Schmelzpunkt der wasserfreien Oxalsäure um **80-90°** herabzudrücken. Erst nach längerem Verweilen im Schwefelsäurevakuum verliert die[3] aus konzentrierter Essigsäure krystallisierte Oxalsäure ihre letzten Feuchtigkeitsspuren und schmilzt dann bei **189°.**[1]

What is the subject here? s. careful
T. drying
g. suffice b. already
F. moisture u.—h. in order to suppress um by
h reduce e. only
V. stay v. loses
k. which is crystallized (Why which?)
F. moisture traces s. melts

Aber auch Umlagerungen gröberer Art können[6] beim Schmelzpunkt oder vor Erreichung **desselben** eintreten und[8] zum Wiedererstarren der **Probe** führen, die[5] dann bei höherer Temperatur zum zweiten **Male** flüssig wird. Gleiches kann[6] durch Abgabe von Krystallwasser **(Natriumacetat)** bedingt sein.

U. rearrangement g. of rougher A. type
E. attainment e. enter in, occur
f. fluid
G. the same A. giving off
b. caused

Man nennt den Schmelzpunkt konstant, wenn er[4] sich durch weitere Reinigung der Substanz, (Umkrystallisieren, Lösen und Wiederausfällen, Regeneration aus **Derivaten usw.)** nicht mehr verändern lässt. Man prüft auf Konstanz des **Schmelzpunktes,**[1] indem man[4] eine Probe der auskrystallisierten Substanz und eine Probe, die[5] durch weiteres Einengen der **Mutterlauge** erhalten wurde, vergleicht: beide Proben müssen[6] sich bei der gleichen **Temperatur** verflüssigen. Meist ist es von Vorteil,[7] beim Reinigen durch wiederholtes **Umkrystallisieren**[9] das Lösungsmittel zu wechseln. Beim Umkrystallisieren aus Alkoholen kann[6] partielle **Veresterung** eintreten. Auch wenn die Möglichkeit der Bildung von physikalisch Isomeren[4] gegeben ist, haben gewisse Substanzen, je nach der Darstellungsart und dem Lösungsmittel oft innerhalb 10 und mehr Grade differierende **Schmelzpunkte.**[1]

n. names, calls
R. purification, refining
W. reprecipitation
s. l. can be
i. in that, by —ing
What does "man" call for? die?
e. obtained
v. compares
v. liquify
V. advantage w. repeated
L. solvent w. change
e. enter in
M. possibility B. formation g. certain
j. n. according to
G. degrees

†Hans J. L. Meyer, **Analyse und Konstitutionsermittlung organischer Verbindungen**

BESTIMMUNG DES SIEDEPUNKTS

Zur Siedepunktsbestimmung wendet man gewöhnlich die Methode der Destillation an[2] und bezeichnet als Siedepunkt die Temperatur,[1] bei der[5] das Thermometer während nahezu der ganzen Operation konstant bleibt.

S. boiling-point-determination g. generally
a. uses b. designates
S. boiling point b. d. at which
w. during g. entire

Es ist hierbei zu beachten, dass zwar die Thermometerkugel[4] fast augenblicklich die Temperatur des Dampfes annimmt, dass es[4] aber geraume Zeit braucht, bis der Quecksilberfaden,[4] der[5] durch eine dicke Glasschicht bedeckt ist, sich ins Wärmegleichgewicht stellt. Ausserdem rinnt die[3] zuerst an den oberen Teilen des Siedekolbens kondensierte Flüssigkeit am Thermometer herunter[2] und kühlt die Kugel ab.[2]

z. b. to be observed (App. 12, 1) z. indeed
a. momentarily
a. assumes b. needs
Note 4 and 5. G. glass layer
b. covered W. heat-balance a. besides
What goes with "rinnt"? "die"? T. parts
k. which is condensed (Why which?) h. runs down a. cools off

Anderseits wird[6] eine wenn auch oft geringfügige Veränderung der Substanz während des andauernden Siedens (durch Zersetzung, Polymerisation usw.) unvermeidlich sein, ebenso wie sich Überhitzen des Dampfs[4] am Schluss der Operation kaum vermeiden lässt. Dadurch wird[6] die Destillationstemperatur schliesslich über den eigentlichen Siedepunkt steigen.

a. on the other hand w. a. even though
g. slight V. change w. during
Z. decomposition u. unavoidable
Ü. superheating D. vapor
S. close s. lassen can be (See Rule 6.)
v. avoided w.-s. will rise (App. 7, 4)
e. real S. boiling point

Es ist daher im allgemeinen besser,[7] die Flüssigkeit in einem[3] mit angeschmolzenem Rückflusskühler versehenen Kölbchen bis zum Konstantwerden der Temperatur im ruhigen Sieden zu erhalten. Das Thermometer muss[6] selbstverständlich ganz im Dampf sein. Das Kühlerende kann[6] zum Schutz gegen Feuchtigkeit mit einem Absorptionsröhrchen versehen werden.

d. therefore i. a. in general
f. liquid a. which is sealed-in R. reflux condenser v. which is provided (why which?)
z. e. to keep
s. self-evidently
S. protection F. moisture k. v. w. can be provided (App. 7, 6)

Zur Vermeidung von Überhitzung dient eine[3] mit entsprechender kreisförmiger Durchlochung versehene Asbestplatte, auf der[5] das Kölbchen ruht, oder elektrische Anheizung innerhalb des Kolbens.[1]

V. avoidance Ü. overheating
e. proper k. circular D. perforation
r. rests
A. heating i. within K. flask

Zur Verhinderung des stossweisen Siedens bringt man in das Kölbchen einige Platinschnitzel, Granaten, Porzellanschrott od. dgl.[1] Geeignet für diesen Zweck sind auch die Magnesia-Siedestäbchen.[1]

V. hindering, prevention s. intermittent, sporadic
K. flask, piston
P. porcellan scrap G. suited

[10]Soll zur Charakterisierung (Identifizierung) eines Stoffes dessen Siedepunkt[4] bei gleichbleibender Zusammensetzung bestimmt werden, so bringt man den Kühler in die aufrechte Stellung, so dass er[4] als Rückflusskühler wirkt, und senkt das Thermometer so weit herab,[2] dass sich das Quecksilbergefäss mindestens 5 mm unterhalb der Flüssigkeitsoberfläche befindet. Wenn durch die Siedepunktsbestimmung der Reinheitsgrad einer Flüssigkeit[4] festgestellt werden soll, wird[6] der Kühler nach unten gedreht.

d. its (App. 22, 4) g. constant
Z. composition b. determined K. condenser
a. upright S. position
w. acts What goes with "senkt"?
Q. mercury vessel m. at least
u. below s. b. is found f. liquid surface
S. boiling point determination
s. is to w. be f. established (App. 7, 6)
g. rotate, turn

SIEDEPUNKTSBESTIMMUNG KLEINER SUBSTANZMENGEN

Ein Kölbchen K von 100 ccm Kapazität ist[6] mit einer geeigneten Badflüssigkeit beschickt. In seinem Hals befindet sich ein Stopfen mit engem Seitenkanal und einer Öffnung in der Mitte,[1] durch die[5] ein dünnwandiges Probierglas E (15—20 cm lang, 5—7 mm breit) geht. Das untere, geschlossene Ende dieses Probierglases taucht in die Badflüssigkeit.[1] Über dem Hals des Kölbchens ist in der Eprouvette eine Öffnung von 2mm Durchmesser. Man bringt in die Eprouvette 0,5—1,5 ccm der Flüs-

How many rules are you using in each paragraph?
g. appropriate, suitable b. loaded H. neck
f. s. is found (App. 11, 4a)
O. opening d. d. by which Note Rule 5.
P. test tube
g. closed
t. dips
D. diameter

sigkeit und befestigt darüber ein Thermometer.[1] Das Quecksilber bleibt bei einem bestimmten Punkt einige Zeit konstant—dieser ist der gesuchte Siedepunkt.[1]

b. fastens d. over-it
b. certain e. some
g. desired

BESTIMMUNG DES NORMALEN SIEDEPUNKTS

B. determination

Da der Siedepunkt[4] vom Druck in hohem **Masse** abhängig ist, hat[6] man mit der Bestimmung **stets** eine Ablesung des Barometerstandes zu verbinden, falls man es nicht vorzieht,[7] den Druck im Siedeapparat auf 760 mm zu reduzieren.

d. since (App. 25, 2) a. dependent v. on
s. always A. reading
v. combine v. prefers (to what?)
D. pressure S. boiling apparatus

Korrektur für den herausragenden Faden.

h. projecting F. thread

Falls man[4] nicht unter Verwendung entsprechend abgekürzter **Thermometer** zu arbeiten imstande ist, so dass der gesamte Quecksilberfaden[4] sich im Dampf befindet, muss[6] man den Siedepunkt je nach der Länge des herausragenden Teils und nach der herrschenden Lufttemperatur korrigieren, was[5] genauer als durch Formeln nach den Fluchtlinientafeln von Berl, Kullman geschieht.

F. in case V. use c. corresponding
i. able
g. total s. b. is found (App. 11, 4a)
j. n. according to L. length
h. projecting T. part h. prevailing
L. air temperature g. more exactly
g. takes place F. nomagraphs

In vielen Fällen hilft man sich einfach nach Baeyers Vorschlag so, dass man[4] in demselben Apparat unter Benutzung desselben Thermometers bei gleichem Barometerstand eine Flüssigkeit von ähnlichem, aber genau bekanntem **Siedepunkt** destilliert und[8] die entsprechende Korrektur errechnet.

F. cases e. simply
V. suggestion d. the same (App. 14, 1)
u. by B. use g. the same
F. liquid a. similar
g. takes place F. nomagraphs
e. computes

Bestimmung der Dampftension

Der Siedepunkt einer Substanz gibt die Temperatur an,[2] bei der ihr Dampfdruck[4] die Grösse des herrschenden Atmosphärendrucks erreicht. Man kann[6] daher auch den Siedepunkt bestimmen, indem man[4] die Temperatur misst, bei der die Dampftension der untersuchten Substanz[4] dem Barometerstand entspricht.

Zu diesem Zweck sind[6] Methoden von Schleiermacher, **Haselt usw.** angegeben worden.

What goes with "gibt"?
a. indicates b. d. at which D. vapor-pressure
h. prevailing e. reaches i. in that, by —ing
b. d. at which (This rel. may not always call for the verb.) e. corresponds
Z. purpose
a. indicated (App. 7, 5, c)

Methode von Schleiermacher

Diese Methode dürfte[6] von den angegebenen die **bequemste** sein. Sie kann[6] namentlich auch zur Siedepunktsbestimmung sehr geringer (auch fester) Substanzmengen[9] Verwendung finden und gestattet[7] ausserdem die verwendete Substanz wiederzugewinnen.

See Rule 6 C, 1, 2, 4 on this sentence.
b. most convenient n. especially
g. less
V. use; note Rule 9. g. permits (to what?)
w. recover

Die Substanz befindet sich im geschlossenen Schenkel eines **U-Rohrs.**[1] der[5] mit Quecksilber gefüllt ist. Der offene Schenkel bleibt bis auf seinen untersten,[3] ebenfalls mit **Quecksilber** gefüllten Teil leer und nimmt das Thermometer auf.[2] Um[7] das Rohr herzustellen und luftfrei mit der Substanz und Quecksilber zu füllen, zieht man ein zirka 50cm langes, 6-8 mm weites Biegerohr, das[5] rein und trocken sein muss, an einem Ende zu einer etwa 1-2 mm weiten Capillare **aus.**[2] Die Capillare wird[6] da, wo sie[4] an das weitere Rohr grenzt, nochmals zu einer haarfeinen, etwa 5cm langen **Capillare** ausgezogen und[8] das weitere Ende bis auf ein kurzes Stück abgeschnitten. Das Rohr wird[6] nun zu einem U gebogen, so dass der offene Schenkel[4] etwa doppelt so lang ist als der geschlossene, letzterer[4] also zirka 15 cm lang wird. Hierzu lässt[6] man das Rohr vor der Flamme an der bezeichneten Stelle auf ungefähr halbe Weite einsinken und biegt um.[2] Die Schenkel sollen[6] dann parallel stehen.

g. closed
Q. mercury
o. open S. arm u. lowest (what?)
g. which is filled
What does "um" call for?
f. fill z. draws out Note Rule 2.
B. bent tube
t. dry
e. about
b. bounds
a. drawn out
k. short
a. cut off w. g. is bent (App. 7, 5, a)
l. the latter R. tube
b. designated S. place u. about
What does "um" go with? s. are supposed

(An * is placed where a number of a rule should be. Try to see what rule is involved.)

Nun wird* das Rohr gefüllt, indem man* die Substanz in den offenen Schenkel bringt und* durch die Biegung in den **geschlossenen** überführt. Hierauf lässt* man in den offenen Schenkel (am bequemsten aus einer **Hahnburette)** Quecksilber[9] einfliessen, bis es[4] auf beiden Seiten etwa 2 cm unter dem geschlossenen **Ende** steht.[10] Ist die Substanz flüssig, so hat* sie sich von selbst über dem Quecksilber gesammelt, sonst bringt man sie leicht durch vorsichtiges Erhitzen und Schmelzen nach oben.[1] Etwa im offenen Rohr zurückgebliebene Teile schaden keineswegs.[1] Nunmehr bringt man die Substanz im geschlossenen Schenkel zum schwachen Sieden* und erreicht dadurch, dass Luft,* die* in ihr oder an der Rohrwand absorbiert ist, durch die feine Capillare entweicht. Dann lässt* man vorsichtig soviel Quecksilber zufliessen, dass das obere Ende des geschlossenen Schenkels* bis in die weitere Capillare hinein mit der flüssig erhaltenen **Substanz** erfüllt ist, und schmilzt die feine Capillare in der Mitte ab. Bei richtiger Ausführung bleibt in der Spitze nur eine minimale Gasblase zurück,[2] die* auf die Genauigkeit der **Bestimmung*** ohne Einfluss ist und* vorteilhaft wirkt. Endlich entleert man den offenen Schenkel bis zur Biegung von Quecksilber,* indem man* das U-Rohr, den geschlossenen Schenkel nach abwärts, bis zur Horizontalen neigt.

g. filled i. in that, by — ing,
b. bending
g. closed (one)
a. b. most convenientlv Note Rule 9.
e. flow in S. sides
g. closed I. if—is
v. s. of itself, spontaneously
s. otherwise l. easily v. careful
E. heating S. melting
e. perchance, perhaps s. harm (See Rule 3F, 4, page 20.)
s. weak, slight
e. attains L. air What is the verb?
What calls for "ist"?
e. escapes v. carefully
z. flow in g. closed
f. liquid
e. kept What goes with "schmilzt"?
M. middle a. melts down b. in the case of, with
A. execution
O. E. without influence G. accuracy
v. advantageous e. empties
i. in that, by —ing
a. downward
n. leans, inclines

Nachdem so das Rohr* zum Versuch fertiggestellt ist, bringt man es in das Heizrohr eines V. Meyerschen Dampfdichteapparats,* das* mit einer passend gewählten Flüssigkeit beschickt ist. Das U-Rohr wird* möglichst vertikal und frei schwebend aufgehängt, dass es* sich mit seinem unteren Ende zirka 5 cm oberhalb des Bodens des Gefässes und mit seiner capillaren Spitze zirka 5 cm unterhalb des Flüssigkeitsspiegels befindet. Das offene Ende ragt aus der Heizflüssigkeit heraus.*

N. after f. readied V. experiment
H. heating tube
D. vapor-density-apparatus p. suitably
b. loaded m. as much as possible
a. suspended (s. floating)
u. below B. bottom
G. vessel
u. below
h. projects out H. heating liquid

Man erwärmt, und sobald sich eine Dampfblase* gebildet hat, reguliert man die Heizung so, dass das Quecksilber* im geschlossenen Schenkel möglichst langsam sinkt. In dem Augenblick, wo die Quecksilberkuppen* in beiden Schenkeln gleiche Höhe haben, gibt das Thermometer die Siedetemperatur für den herrschenden Barometerstand an.* Den "normalen" Siedepunkt findet man, indem man* das Quecksilber im offenen Schenkel um ebenso viele Millimeter über das Niveau treibt, als der Barometerstand* unter 760 mm liegt. Es genügt hierbei eine Schätzung nach dem Augenmass. Auf den Flüssigkeitstropfen braucht[7] man nicht Rücksicht zu nehmen.

D. vapor or steam bubble
H. heating
l. slowly
A. moment b. both
H. height What goes with "gibt"?
h. prevailing
i. in that, by —ing S. arm
o. open N. level
g. suffices S. estimation
F. liquid drop b. needs
R. regard n. to take

Genauer erhält man die Siedetemperatur,[1] wenn man[4] die Quecksilberkuppen durch abwechselndes geringes Steigern oder Erniedrigen der Temperatur bald in der einen und bald in der anderen **Richtung** bewegt und[8] jedesmal das Thermometer abliest, sobald die richtige Einstellung* erreicht ist. Man nimmt dann den Mittelwert der Bestimmungen. Bedingung für die Anwendbarkeit der Methode ist, dass die Substanz[4] vollkommen rein und unveränderlich ist, nicht über 300° siedet und[8] von Quecksilber nicht angegriffen wird. Man reicht in jedem Fall mit 0,1 g aus.[2]

g. more exactly e. obtains
Q. mercury-tip a. alternating S. increase
E. lowering b. bald – bald now – now
b. moves j. each time
a. reads off r. correct E. adjustment
e. reached
B. condition A. applicability
r. clean u. invariable
s. boils
a. attacked, reacted with
a. manages

BESTIMMUNG DES SCHWEFELS

(Underline the nouns that should be bold-faced. Also give reasons for the position of the *.)

Qualitativer Nachweis des Schwefels. Ausser den* auch zur quantitativen Schwefelbestimmung dienenden Methoden sind* folgende qualitative Proben angegeben worden:

N. detection, proof S. sulphur a. aside from
d. which serve
a. indicated f. following

Reaktion von Vohl

Eine geringe Menge Substanz wird* in einem unten zugeschmolzenen Glasröhrchen (wie bei der Lassaigneschen Stickstoffprobe) mit einem Stückchen von Petroleum sorgfältig befreiten Natrium erhitzt.

g. slight M. quantity u. underneath
z. sealed in
S. piece s. carefully
What calls for "erhitzt"?

Das entstandene Schwefelnatrium wird* nach dem Lösen in Wasser durch die[3] auf Zusatz von **Nitroprussidnatrium** entstehende rotviolette Färbung, durch Schwärzung von Silberblech oder, nach Zusatz einer Auflösung von Bleizucker in Natronlauge, durch die Bildung von Schwefelblei nachgewiesen.

e. developed What does "wird" call for? "die"?
Z. addition
e. which arises (Why which?) F. coloring
Z. addition A. solution
Bl. lead acetate B. formation
S. lead sulphide n. detected

An Stelle des Natriums kann* man nach Schonn auch Magnesiumpulver verwenden. Manchmal muss* Kalium benutzt werden. Marsch empfiehlt Zinkstaub.*

S. place
v. use (What calls for this verb?) m. often
m. b. w. must be used (App. 7. 6)
emp. recommends Z. zinc dust

Mikrochemische Reaktion von Emich

Die Substanz wird* mit Chlorkalciumlösung befeuchtet und* mit Bromdampf oxydiert, worauf[5] in vielen Fällen die characteristischen Gipskrystalle sichtbar werden. Zum Nachweis von Schwefelwasserstoff und somit auch von Schwefel in organischen Verbindungen empfiehlt E. Fischer die Methylenblaureaktion.*

b. moistened
B. bromine vapor w. whereupon Try to use the relative form to remove the verb.
N. detection S. hydrogen sulphide
S. sulphur e. recommends
What rules are you using?

Quantitative Bestimmung des Schwefels

Alle Methoden zur Schwefelbestimmung basieren auf seiner Oxydation zu Schwefelsäure,* die* entweder gewichtsanalytisch oder titrimetrisch bestimmt wird.

S. sulphur-determination
S. sulphuric-acid e. either
g. by weight analysis b. determined

Methoden des Schmelzens oder Erhitzens mit oxydierenden Zusätzen. Methode von Asboth. Dieses Verfahren besteht in der Anwendung von der Hohnel-Kassnerschen Methode, d. h. der Benutzung von Natriumsuperoxyd zur Aufschliessung schwefelhaltiger Substanzen,* auf organische Verbindungen.*

S. melting
Z. additions V. procedure
b. consists in A. use
d. h. that is B. use
A. decomposition, hydrolysis
V. compounds

0,15—0,2 g Substanz werden* in einem ungefähr 17 cm langen und 2,7 cm weiten Wägeröhrchen mit 8 g calcinierter Soda und 5 g Natriumperoxyd gut durchgemischt,[8] in einen Nickeltiegel von zirka 80 ccm Inhalt gebracht und[8] noch zweimal mit je 1 g Soda nachgespült. Man bringt zunächst in einen Trokkenschrank* und erhitzt dann mit einem kräftigen Brenner* oder im elektrischen Ofen auf 320—360° und schliesslich über offener Flamme*, bis die Schmelze* dünnflüssig geworden ist. Der Tiegel wird* nur so weit erkalten gelassen, dass er* nicht mehr glüht und* hierauf in eine[3] mit destilliertem Wasser gefüllte Porcellanschale von ungefähr 22 cm Durchmesser gestellt. Nach dem Auslaugen wird* in ein Becherglas von 1 L Inhalt filtriert,[8] dieses mit einem durchlochten Uhrglas bedeckt, in dessen Öffnung[5] ein kleiner Trichter steckt, durch den man[4] verdünnte Salzsäure einfliessen lässt. Das Ende der Kohlendioxydentwickelung wird* durch vorsichtiges Erwärmen auf dem Wasserbad bewirkt. Man dampft dann zur Trockene, raucht mit Salzsäure ab,* nimmt mit Wasser auf* und entfernt die* aus der Porcellanschale stammende Kieselsäure.

u. about What does werden call for?
W. weighing-tube
d. mixed Note that a new verb may be called for without "und," "aber".
n. rinsed, washed z. first of all
T. incubator
k. strong B. burner O. oven
o. open
S. fusion, melting T. crucible
g. let, allowed
g. which is filled (Why which?)
What calls for "gestellt"?
A. leaching out
Once in a while a verb may be called for in Rule 8 without an "und", etc.
v. dilute v. careful
b. brought about d. evaporates
a. vaporized
s. which comes

KRYSTALLISIEREN UND UMKRYSTALLISIEREN

[10]Hat man eine Substanz durch Erhitzen in Lösung gebracht, so gelingt es manchmal nicht mehr oder nur unvollständig[7] sie wieder zum Auskrystallisieren zu bringen, wenn sie[4] auch in der Kälte in dem Lösungsmittel genügend schwer löslich war. Diese Erscheinung kann* verschiedene Gründe haben: 1. kann* die Substanz mit dem **Lösungsmittel** reagiert und[8] ein leichter lösliches Produkt gebildet haben; 2. kann* das Lösungsmittel, wenn auch nur partiell, mit dem Gelösten ein Derivat gebildet haben, das für die Substanz grosses Lösungsvermögen besitzt (Veresterung hochmolekularer Fettsäuren beim Umkrystallisieren aus Alkoholen); 3. kann die[3] zur Lösung erforderliche allzu hohe Temperatur zersetzend auf die Substanz gewirkt haben. Endlich kann* 4. bei der Benutzung von Gemischen zweier oder mehrerer Lösungsmittel teilweise Verflüchtigung eines der Bestandteile erfolgt sein. Im letzteren Fall ist* das Umkrystallisieren unter Zuhilfenahme eines Rückflusskühlers vorzunehmen.

E. heating L. solution
g. succeeds u. incompletely (to what?)
w.-a. even though L. solvent
E. phenomenon v. different
G. reasons, basis
Borrow a "haben" for "reagiert".
L. solvent G. dissolved (material)
L. solving power
F. fatty acids
e. which is necessary
z. decomposing g. acted
B. use G. mixtures
t. partially V. volatilization
B. components l. latter
Z. aid R. reflux-condenser
v. to be undertaken

Bemerkenswert ist das Verhalten des Tetrasalicylids zu einigen Lösungsmitteln, wie Chloroform, Aethylenbromid, Pyridin, Benzoesäureäthylester. Es löst sich leicht in diesen Lösungsmitteln auf*, besonders beim Erwärmen.* Beim Erkalten krystallisiert es mit dem Lösungsmittel als Doppelverbindung aus,* die* beim Erwärmen wieder zerlegt wird. Analog verhält sich das β-Kretosid und ähnlich Pepton bei Gegenwart von Wasser.*

B. remarkable V. behaviour
e. some L. solvents
What do the nouns tell you to do? the prefixes?
L. solvent
E. heating
z. decomposed v. s. behaves
ä. similarly G. presence

[10]Sind* Gemische von Substanzen durch Krystallisation zu trennen, so wird[6] man häufig das Lösungsmittel wechseln.[10]* Zeigen zwei Substanzen im gleichen Lösungsmittel merklich verschiedene Krystallisationsgeschwindigkeit, so kann[6] man sie gelegentlich auch vermittels dieser Eigenschaft voneinander scheiden. Weiteres über die Trennung von Gemischen und über untrennbare Gemenge siehe S. 310.* Von grosser Wichtigkeit ist natürlich die Anwendung tunlichst gereinigter Lösungsmittel.*

What do you do when verb is first?
s. z. t. are to be separated. App. 12, 1
z. If two sub. show g. the same
m. noticeably v. different K. c-velocity
g. occasionally v. by means of
E. characteristic s. separate
T. separation G. mixtures u. inseparable
G. admixtures W. importance
A. use t. as far as possible

Auswahl des Lösungsmittels
Wasser

A. selection

Im allgemeinen genügt die Verwendung des gewöhnlichen destillierten Wassers,* das man,[4] wenn nötig, kurz vor Gebrauch durch Auskochen luftfrei macht.

i.a. in general g. suffices V. use
g. ordinary n. necessary
G. use

Man arbeite auch stets in Gefässen aus resistentem Glas; evtl. ist es sogar notwendig,[7] zur Vermeidung der Aufnahme von Aschenbestandteilen, im Platintiegel umzukrystalliseren. Siehe hierzu noch S. 34.

man arbeite let one work (App. 28, 1a)
n. necessary V. avoidance
A. Absorptions A. ash-ingredients
u. recrystallization

Zum Umkrystallisieren der α-Phenylpyridintricarbonsäure ist[6] keines der organischen Lösungsmittel geeignet. Aus Wasser erhält man gut ausgebildete Krystalle, aber nur nach längerem Stehenlassen der heiss gesättigten Lösung in luftdicht verschlossenen Gefässen.* Bei Luftzutritt und der Möglichkeit von Wasserverdunstung scheidet sich stets ein dichter Filz feiner farbloser Nadeln aus,* die* viel weniger leicht auf konstanten Schmelzpunkt zu bringen sind.

i.g. is appropriate L. solvents
e. obtains a. developed
n. only
g. saturated L. solution l. air tight
G. vessels L. access of air M. possibility
W. water evaporation s. always
f. colorless N. needles
S. melting point

Manche Stoffe, die* aus Wasser gut krystallisieren, vertragen das Kochen nicht. Hierher gehören viele Ester, die Tryhalogenverbindungen der Brenztraubensäure, Aloin, die Diazbenzolsulfosäuren, Benzoylaminooxybuttersäure, usw.*

S. substances
v. endure g. belong

LÖSLICHKEITSBESTIMMUNG

Bestimmung der Löslichkeit fester Substanzen in Flüssigkeiten

For drill answer all questions.

Unter Löslichkeit eines festen Körpers sei das Maximum der Gewichtsmenge verstanden, das ohne Übersättigung unter bestimmten Verhältnissen durch die Gewichtseinheit der Flüssigkeit in Lösung erhalten bleiben kann.

s. v. let be understood, meant (App. 28,1)
What does "sei" call for? "das"?
b. certain V. conditions G. weight unit Why pick up "Lösung"?

Die Löslichkeit ist in erster Linie von der Temperatur abhängig; jeder Temperatur entspricht eine bestimmte Löslichkeitszahl.

L. solubility What does "ist" call for?
What is the subject in this last part of the sentence?

Im allgemeinen ändert sich die Löslichkeit nicht proportional der Temperatur; meist wächst sie mit einer Erhöhung derselben, doch ist auch der umgekehrte Fall (namentlich bei organischen Calcium- und Zinksalzen) nicht allzu selten.

ä.s. is changed (App. 11, 4a), does not change
w. grows
E. increase Note Rule 1.
n. a. not all too

Löslichkeitsbestimmung bei Zimmertemperatur

Die Substanz bzw. die miteinander zu vergleichenden Substanzen werden in einem 50-60 ccm fassenden Reagensglas in dem heissen Lösungsmittel gelöst, hierauf die Reagensröhren in ein geräumiges Becherglas mit kaltem Wasser gestellt und nun mit scharfkantigen Glasstäben so lange kräftig umgerührt, bis der Röhreninhalt die Temperatur des umgebenden Wassers angenommen hat. Nach zweistündigem ruhigen Stehen notiert man die Temperatur, rührt nochmals sehr heftig um, filtriert dann sofort die für die Bestimmung erforderliche Menge durch trockene Faltenfilter in mit den Deckeln gewogene Tiegel und wägt die Flüssigkeit und dann den Abdampfrückstand bzw. bestimmt auf beliebige Art—z.B. durch Titration—die Menge der Substanz.

bzw. or z. v. to be compared (App. 12, 2)
w.g. are dissolved
(App. 7, 5, a) What calls for "gelöst"? "gestellt"?
g. spacious
s. sharp edged u. stirred
R. tube content —calls for what?
z. two hour r. quiet
um. stirs Note Rule 2.
e. which is necessary (Why which?)
g. which are weighed (Why which?)
b. determines Note Rule 1.
b. desirable

Natürlich muss man so viel zur Bestimmung verwenden, dass beim Erkalten ein Teil wieder ausfällt, evtl. wird Übersättigung durch Impfen mit einem Krystallstäubchen verhindert. Setzt sich die ungelöste Substanz gut ab, so kann auch einfach ein bestimmter Teil der Lösung herauspipettiert werden, wozu am besten die Landolt- oder Ostwaltsche Pipette dient.

v. use
E. cooling a. precipitates
Ü. over saturation I. inoculation, seeding
w. v. is hindered (App. 7, 5a)
b. certain
h. w. (App. 7, 6) w. to which

Oft sind geringe Übersättigungen nur sehr schwer zu beheben; man muss daher für genaue Bestimmungen einen anderen, etwas umständlicheren Weg einschlagen. Man beschickt in solchen Fällen gläserne Flaschen mit dem Lösungsmittel und überschüssiger feingepulverter Substanz und lässt sie im Thermostaten mehrere Stunden bis 2 oder 3 Tage rotieren.

s. z. b. are to be eliminated (App. 12, 1)
g. exact B. determinations
u. more troublesome, involved e. adopt
b. charges, loads
ü. excess
l. r. lets them rotate, circulate

Die Schnelligkeit der Lösung ist bei gleicher Temperatur ausser von dem Charakter der Substanz namentlich von der Form ihrer Verteilung abhängig; man verwendet daher durch Pulverisieren oder Ausfällen möglichst feinkörnig erhaltene Proben.

S. rapidity What does "ist" call for?

v. uses
A. precipitation
e. obtained

Einen einfachen und praktischen Apparat zur Beschleunigung der Lösung hat Hopkins beschrieben. Ein Glaszylinder mit doppelt durchbohrtem Stopfen trägt ein 6mm weites Glasrohr, das oben einen Schlauch mit Quetschhahn besitzt und unten in ein Y-Rohr ausläuft. Der dritte Arm des letzteren ist an seinem Ende, wie die Abbildung zeigt, zurückgebogen. Durch die zweite Bohrung des Stopfens führt ein kurzes mit der Pumpe kommunizierendes Rohr. Saugt man an, so reisst der Luftstrom gesättigte Lösung nach oben und neues Lösungsmittel kommt mit den am Boden des Gefässes liegenden Substanzen[9] in Berührung.

What is the subject here?
B. acceleration
S. cork, stopper
G. glass tube What calls for "besitzt"?
"ausläuft"? "zurückgebogen"?
A. figure
B. hole
What calls for "Rohr"?
g. saturated
What goes with "kommt"? "der"?
l. which lie G. vessel

GESETZ DER KONSTANTEN UND MULTIPLEN PROPORTIONEN †

Zu einer viel schärferen Unterscheidung zwischen physikalischem Gemisch und chemischer Verbindung hat[6] die quantitative Untersuchung der **Anteile** geführt, mit welchen die verschiedenen Elemente[4] in jenen zugegen sind. Die Zusammensetzung eines physikalischen Gemisches können[6] wir in weiten **Grenzen** variieren; diejenige aber einer chemischen Verbindung erweist sich als konstant, auf welchem Wege sie[1] auch bereitet wird.

U. distinction
G. mixture
U. investigation A. parts, portions
z. present
Z. composition
w. wide G. limits d. that (App. 14, 2)
e. s. is shown
b. prepared

Für die Mengenverhältnisse, mit welchen die einzelnen Elemente[4] in Verbindungen von konstanter **Zusammensetzung** enthalten sind, hat[6] John Dalton (1808) ein ungemein einfaches und überraschendes **Gesetz** aufgefunden, welches man[4] das Gesetz der konstanten und multiplen **Proportionen** nennt. Dasselbe besagt, dass man[4] für jedes Element eine gewisse **Zahl** ermitteln kann, die wir[4] als "**Verbindungsgewicht**" bezeichnen wollen, und welche[5] dafür massgebend ist, in welchem Mengenverhältnis das Element[4] in die verschiedensten **Verbindungen** eingeht. Die Mengen der verschiedenen Elemente in der Verbindung stehen entweder direkt im Verhältnis der **Verbindungsgewichte** oder aber im Verhältnis einfacher Multipla derselben.

M. quantity ratios
V. compounds
e. contained
e. simple ü. surprising G. law
D. the same (App. 14, 1)
e. ascertain g. certain
b. designate V. combination weight
m. decisive M. quantity ratio
v. most different e. enters in
M. quantities
V. ratio
e. simple
d. of the same (App. 14, 1)

Dieser Satz bildet das Grundgesetz der chemischen **Forschung**; wie unzählige Analysen und insbesondere die[3] auf die verschiedenste Weise mit denkbar grösster **Sorgfalt** ausgeführten Bestimmungen der Verbindungsgewichte von Elementen beweisen, gilt der Satz bei denjenigen Vereinigungen von **Elementen**, die[5] ihrem ganzen Charakter nach als chemische **Verbindungen** sich darstellen, mit praktisch absoluter **Genauigkeit**.[1]

S. principle G. basic law
F. research, study u. countless
d. conceivably
S. care a. which were carried out
b. prove g. holds S. law
Note nach. (See App. 15, 3, d.)
d. present
G. accuracy

Obwohl es[4] durchaus angängig erscheint,[7] auf Grund obiger[3] die Umsetzungen des Stoffes und der **Energie** betreffender Erfahrungssätze ein chemisches **Lehrgebäude** zu errichten, in welches sich die Ergebnisse der Erfahrung[4] übersichtlich einordnen lassen, so hat[6] man zu diesen Erfahrungssätzen eine Hypothese über die Konstitution der stofflichen **Aggregate** zugezogen, welche,[5] obwohl schon im Altertum aufgestellt, doch erst Anfang vorigen Jahrhunderts von Dalton und Wollaston als eine[3] der tieferen und anschaulicheren Erfassung der chemischen Vorgänge nützliche(x) erwiesen wurde und[8] seitdem in der Entwicklung der Chemie und Physik das leitende **Prinzip** geblieben ist. Im Sinne dieser Hypothese erfüllt ein stoffliches **Aggregat** den[3] von ihm eingenommenen Gesamtraum nicht kontinuierlich in allen seinen **Punkten**, sondern es setzt sich zusammen aus zwar sehr kleinen, aber endlichen **Massenteilchen**,[1] die[5] mehr oder weniger weit voneinander entfernt sind und[8] die Moleküle des **Stoffes** genannt werden.

O. although d. absolutely a. feasible
(to what?) o. above (what?)
E. empirical theorems b. which concern
Erg. results Erf. experience
s. l. can be
What does "hat" call for?
z. taken in s. material
a. set up A. antiquity A. beginning
Why Rule 3? Let X stand for the missing noun. (See Rule 3 C 2, 1.)
n. which was useful to e. proved
What does "und" call for?
S. sense e. fills, fills up
e. which is assumed, occupied
P. points
s. s. z. is composed e. removed.
What does "die" call for? "und"?

Dass uns die Lücken[4] zwischen den einzelnen **Molekülen** entgehen und[8] ebensowenig wie diese selber unmittelbarer **Erkenntnis** zugänglich sind, vielmehr die Materie[4] den Raum stetig zu erfüllen scheint, erklärt sich natürlich aus der Kleinheit der **Moleküle**.

L. gaps, holes e. escape us
What does "und" call for?
e. just as little
z. accessible v. moreover
e. fill up e. s. is explained
K. minuteness

†W. Nernst, Theoretische Chemie

TABELLE DER ELEMENTE

Da man[4] von den stöchiometrischen Verbindungsverhältnissen nur zu den relativen, nicht zu den absoluten **Atomgewichten** gelangen kann, so handelt es sich um die Wahl einer Einheit derselben. Von Dalton wurde[6] das Atomgewicht des Wasserstoffs als das kleinste unter allen **Elementen** hierzu gewählt; da aber gerade die genaue Feststellung der relativen Verbindungsgewichte bezüglich des **Wasserstoffs**[9] experimentelle Schwierigkeiten bietet, und ausserdem die meisten Verbindungsgewichte der Elemente[4] aus **Sauerstoffverbindungen** bestimmt wurden, so legte Berzilius das Atomgewicht des **Sauerstoffs** zugrunde, welches er[4] gleich **100** setzte, um[7] kein Atomgewicht kleiner als **Eins** werden zu lassen.

Da since V. combination ratios
NOTE THE RULES THAT CALL FOR VERBS.
g. come, arrive e. h. s. u. the problem concerns
W. choice E. unit d. of the same
w.g. was chosen (App. 7, 5, b) W. hydrogen
d. since g. exact F. determination
b. with regard to
b. offers S. difficulties
a. besides
b. determined S. oxygen compounds
z. take as a basis
g. equal to A. atomic weight
w. become l. let

Neuerdings ist[6] man aus mancherlei Gründen wieder zur Daltonschen **Einheit** zurückgekehrt; allein der Uebelstand, dass das Verhältnis,[4] in welchem Wasserstoff und Sauerstoff[4] sich zu **Wasser** vereinigen, noch nicht mit hinreichender **Genauigkeit** sich feststellen liess, besteht nach wie vor, und es müsste[6] nach jeder neuen Bestimmung dieses Verhältnisses eine Umrechnung sämtlicher **Atomgewichte** erfolgen. Wie unzweckmässig es ist,[7] mit **Atomgewichten** zu operieren, die[5] "Kurswert" besitzen, liegt auf der **Hand.** Dass gerade das Verbindungsgewicht des Wasserstoffs[4] einer scharfen **Bestimmung**[9] so grosse Schwierigkeiten bietet, erklärt sich aus dem **Umstande,**[1] dass dieses Gas[4] so ungemein schwierig genügend rein sich erhalten lässt.

n. recently m. various G. reasons
z. returned a. but U . drawback
V. ratio, proportion
s. v. are combined s.f.l. could be determined
h. sufficient
n. w. v. after as before e. there
U. recalculation s. all
e. result, take place u. inexpedient K. "Wall St. value" b. possess
a. d. H. liegen is clear
g. S. great difficulties (Note Rule 9.)
s. e. n. can be obtained

Es ist[6] daher von verschiedenen Seiten neuerdings ein vermittelnder **Vorschlag** gemacht worden, dessen allgemeine Annahme[4] gegenwärtig erfolgt ist. Das Verhältnis der Atomgewichte des Wasserstoffs und Sauerstoffs ist nahe **1:16,** wenn man[4] daher als Normale des Atomgewichts den **Sauerstoff** annimmt, dieses aber nicht gleich 1, sondern O=16,000 setzt, so wird das Atomgewicht des Wasserstoffs nicht genau, aber sehr nahe gleich 1 und mit dem Vorteil der Daltonschen Einheit diejenige der Berzeliusschen Wahl vereinigt; man ist[6] so der **Notwendigkeit** überhoben, nach jeder genaueren Bestimmung der Zusammensetzung des Wassers eine Änderung der Atomgewichte aller übrigen **Elemente** vornehmen zu müssen. In der vorhergehenden Tabelle sind[6] neben den Namen der alphabetisch geordneten Elemente ihre chemischen Zeichen und ihre **Atomgewichte** aufgeführt, wie sie[4] von der internationalen **Atomgewichtskommission** zusammengestellt wurden.

d. therefore v. different
e. i. g. w. there has been made
e. taken place g. at the present time
S. oxygen
n. near to a. assumes
s. but What does it call for?
g. exact g. equal
V. advantage d. that (one) W. selection
ü relieved N. necessity (to what?)
A. change v. undertake
v. preceding
g. arranged Z. signs
a. presented z. compiled
w. were (App. 7, 5, b)

Klassifizierung der Naturvorgänge.

N. natural processes

Bekanntlich teilt man die Veränderungen in der Natur seit langem in physikalische und **chemische** ein;[2] bei den ersteren spielt in der Regel die Zusammensetzung der Materie eine mehr sekundäre oder wenigstens untergeordnete **Rolle,**[1] während bei den letzteren gerade auf die rein stofflichen Veränderungen das Hauptgewicht[4] gelegt wird. Vom Standpunkte der Molekulartheorie erblickt man in den physikalischen Prozessen Vorgänge, bei denen die Moleküle[4] als solche intakt bleiben, während die chemischen Prozesse die Zusammensetzung der Moleküle verändern.

B. as is known What goes with "teilt"?
s. l. for a long time Note that "chemische" expects a noun; how can you tell?
w. at least u. subordinate
w. while g. exactly, directly
V. changes H. stress
S. stand point
e. sees V. processes
a. s. as such (Note the absence of noun.)
Z. composition
v. change

PHOTOCHEMIE

Wirkungen des Lichtes. Wenn Ätherschwingungen[4] ein beliebiges materielles **System** passieren, so sind sie imstande,[7] zwei wesentlich verschiedene **Wirkungen** hervorzurufen: einerseits erhöhen sie die Temperatur des **Systems,**[1] indem ihre Energie[4] sich teilweise in **Wärme** umsetzt; andererseits erzeugen sie Veränderungen chemischer **Natur.**[1] Die erste Erscheinung haben[6] wir bereits **S.391** als Lichtabsorption[9] kennen gelernt; die Besprechung der zweiten wird[6] den Gegenstand dieses **Kapitels** bilden.

W. effects A. ether vibrations
b. arbitrary
i. able w. essentially v. different
h. call forth e. on the one hand
e. increase i. since t. partially
u. is changed a. on the other hand
erz. produce E. phenomena Why is it permitted to pick up the noun?
B. discussion w. will (why?) G. object

Während die gewöhnliche Lichtabsorption[4] eine ganz allgemeine **Erscheinung** ist, indem jeder Stoff,[4] freilich in einer[3] mit seiner Natur und der Wellenlänge des **Lichtes** sehr veränderlichen Weise, die Energie der Aetherschwingungen teilweise und bei hinreichender Dicke der durchstrahlten **Schicht**[9] sogar vollständig in Wärme umzusetzen vermag, beobachtet man die sogenannten "chemischen Wirkungen des Lichtes" nur in **Ausnahmefällen,**[1] indem nur relativ selten Belichtung[4] einen Einfluss auf die Reaktionsgeschwindigkeit eines[3] in chemischer **Ruhe** befindlichen **Systemes** auszuüben vermag; freilich ist[6] dadurch keineswegs ausgeschlossen, dass auch die photochemische Wirkung[4] allgemein ist und[8] nur häufig einen zu geringen **Betrag** besitzt, um[7] unter den untersuchten **Bedingungen** merklich zu werden.

w. while g. ordinary
a. general i. since S. material
f. to be sure What does "einer" call for?
v. which is very changeable
h. sufficient D. thickness
S. layer, v. completely
u. to transform b. observe
W. effects A. exceptional cases
B. exposure, illumination E. influence
R. reaction speed e. of a (what?)
b. which is found a. exert v. is able
a. made impossible
a. general u and (what?) h. frequently
g. slight B. amount b. possesses
m. noticeable B. conditions

Die chemischen Wirkungen des **Sonnenlichtes,**[1] wie sie[4] sich **z. B.** im Bleichprozess, in der Bildung der grünen Farbe der **Pflanzen,** in seinem zerstörenden Einfluss auf gewisse **Malerfarben** zeigen, sind[6] seit dem **Altertum** bekannt; doch erst die neuere **Forschung** hat[6] uns die Lichtempfindlichkeit zahlloser **Verbindungen** kennen gelehrt und[8] zur **Überzeugung** geführt, dass man[4] es hier mit einer sehr merkwürdigen Wechselwirkung zwischen den Aetherschwingungen und den chemischen **Kräften** zu tun hat, welche[5] das höchste Interesse verdient. Die Aufzählung und **Beschreibung** der einzelnen hierhergehörigen Erscheinungen würde[6] zu viel **Raum**[9] in Anspruch nehmen, und es sei[6] hierüber auf eine Anzahl **Monographien** verwiesen, die[5] besonders in neuerer **Zeit** veröffentlicht worden sind. Es sei[6] nur betont, dass sowohl Gase, **z. B. Chlorknallgas,** als auch Flüssigkeiten, wie z. B. Chlorwasser, **welches**[5] unter dem Einflusse des **Lichtes**[9] Sauerstoff entwickelt, **als auch feste Körper,** wie weisser **Phosphor,** der[5] im Lichte in **roten sich verwandelt,** oder Zinnober, der[5] im **Lichte** schwarz wird, **auf Aetherschwingungen** reagieren können; dass ferner der photchemische Prozess[4] sowohl in der Bildung, wie es[4] beim **Chlorknallgas**[9] der Fall ist, als auch im Zerfall einer **Verbindung** bestehen **kann,** wofür die Zersetzung des Phosphorwasserstoffs unter Ausscheidung von Phosphor ein Beispiel bildet; auch kennt man **Isomerisationen** im **Licht,** wie den Übergang von o-Nitrobenzaldehyd in o-Nitrosobensoesäure. Ferner hat[6] in neuerer Zeit **Trautz** nachgewiesen, dass bisweilen das Licht[4] verzögernd wirkt und dass bei der gleichen Reaktion die eine Lichtart (z. B. **violettes Licht)**[4] verzögernd, die andere, z. B. rotes Licht, beschleunigend wirkt.

What rules are you using to pull the verbs out?
B. bleaching process
F. color z. destroying
g. certain z. show
b. known A. antiquity
F. study L. light sensitivity
V. compound g. taught u. and What?
Ü. conviction What does "man" call for?
welche? W. interrelation
K. forces h. highest
A. enumeration B. description
e. individual h. pertinent z. too
i. A. n. take into claim, demand
e. s. v. let there be referred (App. 28, 1e)
v. published e.s.b. let it be emphasized (App. 28, 1, e) F. liquids
Why pick up "Sauerstoff"? e. develops
w. white v. transforms w. becomes s. black
s. both F. case Note Rule 9.
Z. disintegration b. exist, consist
Z. decomposition
A. separation B. example Ü. transition
What do the nouns on the breaks tell you to do?
n. demonstrated b. at times
v. hesitatingly, retardingly L. type of light
b. acceleratingly
w. acts

VERWANDELBARKEIT DES STOFFES

(An asterisk * will appear on some sentences. Indicate the rule involved in each case.)

Die Eigenschaften eines Stoffes ändern sich mit den äusseren **Umständen,*** unter denen wir* ihn untersuchen, doch entspricht im allgemeinen einer kleinen Änderung der äusseren Bedingungen, insbesondere des Druckes und der Temperatur, auch nur eine kleine Änderung der physikalischen Eigenschaften des Stoffes.[10] Bringen wir hingegen verschiedene Stoffe, z. B. Zucker und Wasser, Schwefel und **Eisen** zusammen,[2] so geht häufig auch unter konstant erhaltenen äusseren Bedingungen eine tiefgehende Veränderung der Eigenschaften der **Stoffe** vor sich,[2] die[5] zur Bildung von im Vergleich zu den ursprünglichen in vieler Hinsicht ganz verschiedenen **Stoffen** führt. Es vermag[6] also dieselbe Materie unter gleichen äusseren Bedingungen ganz verschiedene äussere **Eigenschaften** anzunehmen; die Materie ist ineinander verwandelbar.

E. qualities S. substance
ä. outer U. conditions u. investigate
e. corresponds A. change
D. pressure The subject here follows the verb "ent". What is it?
E. attributes B.w. If we bring (and what goes with "bringen"? Z. sugar
S. sulphur What goes with "geht"?
e. maintained B. conditions t. radical
v. s. g. goes on; what does "von" call for? (See Rule 3D, 2,3,4 on this sentence.)
B. formation V. comparison
v. different
v. is able ("vermag" may be used with either Rule 6 or 7.) ä. outer
a. to take on v. convertible

Nach unseren bisherigen Erfahrungen aber ist[6] die Verwandelbarkeit der Materie an gewisse **Bedingungen** geknüpft. Das Gesetz von der Unzerstörbarkeit des Stoffes liefert die erste **Beschränkung,*** nämlich, dass es* sich jedenfalls nur um Ueberführbarkeit gleicher Gewichtsmengen von Stoffen verschiedener **Eigenschaften** handeln kann; die weitere[3] nach dieser Richtung hin aufgespeicherte Erfahrung — das Resultat vieler mühevollen Arbeiten des chemischen **Laboratoriums,*** von den Versuchen,* welche die Alchemisten anstellten, um[7] unedle Metalle in **Gold** zu verwandeln, bis zu den bewunderungswürdigen Synthesen unserer heutigen **Organiker*** — brachte die weitere **Erkenntnis,*** dass im allgemeinen selbst gleiche Gewichte stofflich verschiedener Materie* ineinander nicht überführbar sind.

n. according to b. previous, up to now
V. convertibility g. certain
g. linked G. law U. indestructability
l. furnishes B. limitation
j. in any case Ü. transmissibility
G. weight amounts
h. k. can deal Why Rule 3? a. which is stored up. E. experience
m. laborious
V. experiments a. made What does "um" call for? b. admirable
h. present day
E. knowledge
s. even s. materially ü. convertible

Einfache und zusammengesetzte Stoffe

Unzählige Versuche, welche* darauf hinzielten,[7] einerseits zusammengesetzte Stoffe in **einfachere** zu zerlegen — chemische Analyse—, anderseits durch Zusammenbringen verschiedener Stoffe einen **neuen** zu erzeugen — chemische Synthese –, haben* zu der **Überzeugung** geführt, dass man* bei der Zerlegung der[3] in der **Natur** vorkommenden Stoffe stets zu einer Anzahl weiter nicht zerlegbarer, der sogenannten Grundstoffe oder **Elemente**, gelangt, deren man[4] bisher etwa **90** aufzählte. An diesen Grundstoffen scheiterte bis jetzt jeder Versuch einer weiteren willkürlichen **Zerlegung;*** aus diesen Grundstoffen aber lassen[6] sich durch geeignete Operationen die[3] uns bekannten **Stoffe** sämtlich synthetisch herstellen. Ineinander überführbar sind demgemäss nur diejenigen **Stoffe***, welche* die gleichen Elemente und zwar von jedem einzelnen die gleiche **Gewichtsmenge** enthalten.

U. countless V. attempts h. aimed (to what?)
z. decompose z. composite
Note that "einfachere" expects a noun.
Z. consolidation e. produce
Ü. conviction
What does "man" call for? "der"?
v. which occur (Why which?) s. always
zer. of decomposable g. comes
a. enumerated b. up to now
s. failed V. attempt w. arbitrary
Z. analysis
s. l. can be (See Rule 6.) g. suitable
b. which are known s. totally
d. accordingly d. those (App. 14, 2)
What does "welche" call for? g. same
z. to be sure G. weight quantity

Unzerstörbarkeit der Energie

indestructability

Viele fruchtlose **Bemühungen,**[7] ein Perpetuum mobile, d. h. eine **Maschine** zu erfinden, die[5] fortwährend und ins Unbegrenzte von sich aus äussere **Arbeit** zu leisten vermag, haben[6] schliesslich zu der **Überzeugung** geführt, dass eine solche unmöglich, und der Gedanke, welcher[5] der Konstruktion einer **solchen** zugrunde liegt, im Widerspruch mit einem **Naturgesetze** sei.

f. fruitless B. efforts (to what?)
e. invent f. constantly
U. unlimited v. s. a. of itself
z. l. v. is able to perform
u. impossible (What verb is understood here?)
z. l. lies at the base W. contradiction

MASS DER ENERGIE

(Indicate the reasons for the *. Also underline nouns that should be bold-faced.)

Da wir* gerade mit Energiegrössen viel zu operieren haben werden, so dürften[6] einige besondere Bemerkungen über die hier zu benutzenden **Masse**[9] am Platze sein. Zunächst liefert das absolute Massystem als Einheit der Arbeit diejenige, die[5] geleistet wird, wenn der Angriffspunkt der Kraft Eins[4] um einen Zentimeter verschoben wird. Die Kraft eins, genannt Dyne, ist nun aber im obigen System diejenige,[1] die* der Masse 1g in einer Sekunde die Beschleunigung **Eins** erteilt, sie ist übrigens nahe gleich dem Gewicht eines Milligrams.* Die so bestimmte Arbeitseinheit heisst Erg und sie ist natürlich gleich der lebendigen Kraft $(m/2-v^2)$ von zwei Gramm, die* eine Geschwindigkeit von 1cm pro Sekunde besitzen.

d. since App. 25, 2 What does 'wir' call for?
dürften? B. remarks
z. b. to be used (App. 12, 2)
Z. first of all. l. furnishes E. unit
d. that one (App. 14, 2) g. performed
A. attacking point v. shifted
o. above d. that one
e. gives, grants B. acceleration
G. weight b. determined A. work unit
h. is called g. equal l. living
K. power G. velocity
b. possess

Die Arbeitseinheit ist nun häufig unbequem klein und es sind[6] seit langem die[3] schon den jeweiligen **Zwecken** angepassten anderen **Energieeinheiten**[9] im Gebrauch. In der Technik verwendet man in der Regel das "Meterkilogramm", d. h. die Arbeit,* die* beim Heben eines Kilogramms um einen **Meter** geleistet wird, wobei also als Einheit der Länge das Meter und als Einheit der Kraft das Gewicht eines Kilogramms dient.

u. inconveniently e. s. i. G. there are in use Note Rule 9.
j. actual, existing
a. which are adapted (Why which?)
v. uses i. d. R. as a rule
H. lifting u. by
g. performed w. in which case
Repeat the verb with both subjects.
d. serves

Da nun aber Arbeit* auch geleistet wird, wenn eine Volumvermehrung* gegen einen **Druck** erfolgt oder eine Elektrizitätsmenge* eine elektromotorische **Gegenkraft** überwindet, so liegt als Einheit der Arbeit in solchen Fällen das Produkt von Druck- und Volumeneinheit oder von Elektrizitäts- und **Spannungseinheit** nahe.[2] Hält[10] man sich konsequent, wie[8] bei wissenschaftlichen **Rechnungen** üblich, an das absolute cgs-System, so gelangt man natürlich stets zur gleichen Arbeitseinheit;* wenn man[4] es aber, wie auch wir[4] aus Gründen der Anschaulichkeit es bisweilen tun werden, vorzieht,[7] der jeweiligen konventionellen **Masse** sich zu bedienen, so wird[6] natürlich die Wahl der Arbeitseinheit in verschiedenen **Fällen** verschieden ausfallen.

d. since (why?) A. work
V. volume increase D. pressure
E. quantity of electricity ü. overcomes
E. unit
V. volume unit
S. voltage unit What does "nahe" go with?
Why Rule 10? w.ü. as common
R. calculations g. comes
g. same A. work unit What does "man" call for?
wir? G. reasons A. clearness
v. prefers (to what?) z. b. to make use of
w. will (App. 7, 4)
a. result

Die Einheit der Wärme ist* prinzipiell durch das Gesetz von der Erhaltung der Energie natürlich ohne weiteres als **diejenige** gegeben, welche* der **Arbeitseinheit** äquivalent ist. Aber auch hier erspart man sich aus praktischen Rücksichten häufig die Umrechnung* und benutzt eine besondere Wärmeeinheit,* die mit den Messungsmethoden in enger Beziehung steht; als solche werden[6] wir die Grammkalorie (cal) verwenden, d. h. die Wärmemenge, die* erforderlich ist, um[7] die[3] am **Luftthermometer** gemessene Temperatur eines Gramms Wasser um 1° zu steigern. Da aber die spezifische Wärme des Wassers[4] mit der **Temperatur** nicht unbeträchtlich sich ändert, so bedarf es eines Zusatzes zu obiger **Definition,*** nämlich der Angabe der Temperatur,* bei welcher das Wasser* erwärmt wird. Nun werden* weitaus die meisten kalorimetrischen Messungen, insbesondere fast alle thermochemischen Untersuchungen, in der Weise angestellt, dass man* die Temperatursteigerung misst, welche Wasser[4] von Zimmertemperatur infolge der hinzugeführten Wärme erfährt, so dass es[4] für unsere **Zwecke** am meisten sich empfiehlt, diejenige **Wärmemenge**[9] als Einheit zu wählen, die[5] einem Gramm Wasser von 15° hinzugeführt werden muss, um[7] seine Temperatur um 1° Celsius zu erhöhen.

What does "ist" call for?
G. law E. preservation
o. w. directly d. that one
e. saves
R. regards h. frequently U. recalculation
W. heat unit
e. close B. relation w. shall (why?)
v. use W. heat amount e. necessary
What does "um" call for? "die"? g. which is measured (Why which?) d. since
W. water
u. inconsiderably b. needs Z. supplement
A. indication
e. heated w. are (why?)
i. especially
U. investigations W. manner
a. made (What does this verb go with?)
i. due to h. added
e. undergoes Z. purposes
e. recommends W. heat quantity
z. w. to choose
e. increase

CHEMISCHES GLEICHGEWICHT IN SALZLÖSUNGEN

(An * is inserted where certain rules are involved. Indicate the rules. Questions on the right side of the page are for drill only.)

Reaktionsfähigkeit der Ionen. In den vorhergehenden Kapiteln haben* wir die allgemeine **Theorie** kennen gelernt, die* uns über das chemische Gleichgewicht in beliebigen Systemen bezüglich seiner Abhängigkeit vom Mengenverhältnis der reagierenden **Bestandteile** unterrichtet. Wir haben* uns jedoch bisher noch nicht mit dem **Falle** beschäftigt, dass die freien Ionen* an der **Reaktion** teilnehmen, d. h. noch nicht mit den wässerigen Lösungen der **Elektrolyte*** oder, kurz gesagt, den **Salzlösungen.*** Teils der Übersichtlichkeit halber, teils um[7] den **Nachweis** zu führen, dass die Hypothese der elektrolytischen Dissoziation* unabweisbar hinzugezogen werden muss, wenn man* das Gesetz der Massenwirkung auch auf die **Salzlösungen** übertragen will, habe* ich der Behandlung der letzteren ein besonderes **Kapitel** gewidmet.

a. general k. to know, become acquainted with
G. equilibrium b. arbitrary, optional
b. with regards to A. dependence v. on
B. constituents u. instructed
b. hitherto F. case b. concerned
t. take part What calls for this verb? for "beschäftigt"? w. aqueous
S. salt solutions T. partly
h. on account of (App. 15, 1, 3, g (2))
f. lead
u. imperatively h. taken in
G. law M. mass action ü. transfer
B. treatment
g. devoted

Vom Standpunkte der Hypothese der elektrolytischen Dissoziation erledigt sich die ganze Frage durch den einfachen **Schluss***, dass die freien Ionen* genau wie jede andere Molekülgattung proportional ihrer Konzentration (aktiven Masse) an einer **Reaktion** sich beteiligen müssen. Ohne[7] irgend eine neue **Hypothese** einzuführen, sind* wir nun in den **Stand** gesetzt,[7] das chemische Gleichgewicht zwischen elektrolytisch leitenden Stoffen in genau derselben einfachen **Weise** zu behandeln wie die Reaktionen zwischen lauter elektrisch neutralen **Molekülgattungen.*** Und so enthalten denn die nachfolgenden Abschnitte eigentlich nichts prinzipiell **Neues;*** aber sie werden* uns weitere überraschende Anwendungen des Guldberg-Waageschen **Gesetzes** bringen. Das Verdienst,[7] diesen Gesichtspunkt in gewissen speziellen **Fällen zuerst zur Geltung gebracht zu haben, gebührt Arrhenius.**[1]

S. standpoint
e. s. is settled g. entire
e. simple S. conclusion g. exactly
M. type of molecule
b. take part
What does "ohne" call for? e. introducing (Why –ing?) S. position (to what?) Note that the verb falls right in front of "wie" (a break).
l. nothing but, purely
e. contain n. subsequent A. chapters
e. really
w. b. will bring (App. 7, 4)
Anw. applications V. credit (to what?)
G. view point g. certain
Why do you pick up "Geltung"? g. is due

Elektrolytische Dissoziation und **chemische Natur.** Es entsteht nun die **Frage**, wie die Grösse der elektrolytischen Dissoziation[4] von der Natur des betreffenden **Elektrolyten** abhängt, eine Frage, die[5] um so wichtiger ist, als die Reaktionsfähigkeit* in ausgesprochenster Weise von jener **Grösse** abhängt. Im folgenden seien[6] daher einige der wichtigsten bisher erkannten Regeln auf diesem **Gebiete** zusammengestellt, deren Kenntnis[4] uns den Überblick über das chemische Gleichgewicht in **Salzlösungen** ausserordentlich erleichtern wird.

e. there (App. 10, 1)
e. arises F. question w. how
b. concerned
a. depends u. s. all the more
a. most pronounced
W. way a. depends s. let be (App. 28, 1,b,e,)
w. most important
z. compiled d. whose K. knowledge
Ü. survey a. extraordinarily e. facilitate
w. will (Why?) (App. 7, 4)

1. Die Salze der Alkalien, des Ammoniums, des **Thalium** und Silbers mit einbasischen Säuren sind in verdünnten Lösungen bei äquivalenten Konzentrationen gleich stark[1] und[8] zwar, wie die[3] S. 417 mitgeteilten, (x) auf **Chlorkalium** bezüglichen Zahlen beweisen, sehr weitgehend dissoziiert.

e. monobasic S. acids v. dilute
g. equally u. (what?) Let X stand for the noun "Zahlen" (See Rule 3, C 1, diagram, discussion and sentence 3.)

2. Hingegen findet man bei den einbasischen Säuren und einsäurigen Basen die allergrössten Unterschiede; Stoffe wie **Essigsäure,**[1] Ammoniak, usw. sind in ein Zehntel normaler Lösung **nur zu wenigen Prozenten,**[1] andere wie Salzsäure, Kali usw. **ebensostark** dissoziiert wie die oben aufgezählten **Salze.**[1]

H. on the other hand
eins. monoacidic U. differences
S. materials E. acetic acid
L. solution What do the nouns on the breaks tell you to do?
a. enumerated

3. Elektrolyte, wie Zinksulfat, Kupfersulfat usw.* die* ebenfalls durch Dissoziation sich in zwei Ionen, jedoch von doppelter elektrischer **Ladung**, spalten, sind* bedeutend weniger (Zink- und Kupfersulfat bei der Konzentration 1 Mol pro Liter z. B. nur zu ca. 25%) dissoziiert.

K. copper sulfate
e. likewise s. sp. are split
j. however L. charge
b. significantly w. less
What does "sind" call for?
ca. about

4. Komplizierter liegen die Verhältnisse bei denjenigen Elektrolyten,* die* in mehr als zwei **Ionen** sich spalten; nach dem, was man* bisher darüber weiss, findet hier im allgemeinen eine stufenweise Dissoziation statt;[2] so zerfällt Schwefelsäure nicht direkt in die SO_4 - Gruppe mit doppelter negativer elektrischer **Ladung*** und die beiden Wasserstoffionen mit je einer einfachen positiven **Ladung,*** sondern der Zerfall verläuft nach den beiden **Reaktionsgleichungen:*** I. $H_2SO_4=HSO_4+H$; II. $HSO_4—SO_4+H$, und ähnlich dürfte es bei Stoffen wie $BaCl_2$, K_2CO_3 der **Fall** sein. Im allgemeinen gilt aber auch hier der **Satz:*** Analog zusammengesetzte Salze sind* in äquivalenten **Lösungen** gleich stark elektrolytisch dissoziiert. Allein dieser Satz ist keine Regel von ausnahmsloser **Gültigkeit;*** so sind[6] zwar die Chloride des Calciums, Strontinums, Bariums, Magnesiums, **Kupfers nahe gleich, die analog** konstituierten Chloride des Kadmiums und des Quecksilbers jedoch viel weniger stark (wahrscheinlich übrigens infolge sekundärer Komplexsalzbildung) in die **Ionen** gespalten.

k. more complicated V. conditions
d. those (App. 14, 2) What does "die" call for?
"man"? w. knows
What goes with "findet"? s. stepwise
s. takes place z. decomposes
What does the Noun "L" tell you to do?
j. each e. simple
v. proceeds n. according to
b. two R. reaction equations
ä. similarly d. might S. materials
F. case i. a. In general g. holds
S. theorem z. composed
What does "sind" call for?
A. but S. theorem R. rule
G. validity z. to be sure n. nearly g. equal
Q. mercury w. probably
ü. moreover i. due to g. split

Von der Dissoziation kann[6] man von vornherein mit grosser **Wahrscheinlichkeit** annehmen, dass sie* der[3] bisher für alle[3] aus zwei einwertigen **Ionen** kombinierten **Neutralsalze** als gültig befundenen **Regel** gehorchen, also[8] z. B. der des Chlorkaliums gleich sein wird. Für Bleichlorid hat[6] v. Ende diesen **Satz** experimentell bestätigt gefunden.

v. from the outset
a assume What does "sie" call for? "der"? "alle"?
k. which are combined
b. which are found a. g. as valid (Why which in these two cases?) What does "also" call for? "hat"?
b. true, corroborated

5. Viele mehrbasische Säuren leiten in einem weiten Konzentrationsintervall ebenso wie einbasische, d. h. es ist[6] auf sie die[3] S. 580 für binäre **Elektrolyte** abgeleitete Gleichung der Dissoziationsisotherme anwendbar; erst bei grossen Verdünnungen **beginnen**[7] sie auch das zweite, dritte **Wasserstoffion** abzuspalten. Der Umstand, dass es[4] zur Abspaltung weiterer Wasserstoffionen immer grösserer **Verdünnungen** bedarf, deutet darauf hin,[2] dass der Säurerest[4] die weiteren Quanta negativer **Elektrizität** immer schwieriger aufnimmt.

m. multibasic S. acids
w. wide
d. h. that is e.i. a. there is applicable (App. 10, 1) abg. which is derived g. large
V. dilutions
a. split off U. circumstance
A. splitting off w. of further
b. needs h. points d. thereto
S. acid residue
a. absorbs s. with more and more difficulty

6. Mit der Temperatur ändert sich die elektrolytische Dissoziation verhältnismässig sehr wenig,[1] und zwar nimmt sie mit steigender Temperatur langsam bald ab,[2] bald zu[2] — im Gegensatze zur gewöhnlichen, die[5] mit der Temperatur fast stets rapide anwächst.

s. s. is changed (App. 11, 4)
v. relatively
z. indeed abnehmen decrease; zun. increase
G. contrast g. usual
a. increases

Man kann[6] die obigen Regeln, wie Ostwald[4] gezeigt hat, sehr gut zur Ermittelung der Basizität der **Säuren** verwenden; da mit jener Grösse der Dissoziationszustand, z. B. des Natriumsalzes der betreffenden Säure,[4] in ausgesprochener **Weise** sich ändert, so verschafft die einfache Untersuchung des Leitungsvermögens in seiner Abhängigkeit von der Konzentration Aufklärung über jenen **Punkt.*** Natürlich kann* die gleiche Frage durch Messung der **Gefrierpunktserniedrigung** entschieden werden.

o. above R. rules
g. shown E. ascertainment
v. use d. since
b. concerned
a. pronounced v. provided
e. simple U. investigation L. conductivity
A. dependence v. on
A. enlightenment M. measurement
e. decided G. freezing point reduction

BESCHLEUNIGUNG CHEMISCHER REAKTIONEN
durch Temperatursteigerung

(Give reasons for each * and underline all nouns that should be in bold-faced type.)

Während wir* in den beiden vorhergehenden Kapiteln den Einfluss der Temperatur auf das chemische Gleichgewicht zu formulieren gesucht haben, wenden wir uns nun wiederum der chemischen Kinetik zu.* In dem letzten Kapitel des vorigen Buches lernten wir die Gleichungen kennen, die* den Verlauf von[3] bei konstanter Temperatur sich abspielenden Reaktionen zu berechnen gestatten, und daher muss* der Einfluss der Temperatur in den Zahlenwerten der Geschwindigkeitskoeffizienten[9] zum Ausdruck kommen.

W. while b. both v. preceding
E. influence G. equilibrium
g. sought What goes with "wenden"?
w. again z. turn to l. last
K. chapter v. preceding G. equations
V. course
a. which take place b. compute
ges. to permit Z. numerical values
A. to expression

Rein empirisch hat* sich folgendes Resultat ergeben: alle messenden Versuche haben gelehrt, dass die Geschwindigkeit,[4] mit welcher ein chemisches System[4] seinem Gleichgewichtszustande zustrebt, mit wachsender Temperatur ausserordentlich ansteigt; es scheint[7] dies eine allgemeine Erscheinung zu sein, deren Wichtigkeit für den Verlauf der chemischen Umsetzung und deren Bedeutung für die Existenz der sogenannten "stürmischen Reaktionen" (Explosionen)* alsbald einleuchten wird.

e. resulted, demonstrated
V. experiments
G. velocity Why does this word not call for "zustrebt"? w. increasing
a. extraordinary a. rises
E. phenomenon W. importance
U. change B. importance
s. violent
e. will become apparent

Als Beispiel für jenen Satz seien* einige[3] für die Geschwindigkeit, mit welcher unter sonst gleichbleibenden Umständen Rohrzucker[4] bei den daneben stehenden Temperaturen t invertiert wird, erhaltene Zahlen angeführt.

B. example S. theorem s. let be (App. 28, 1) g. identical
U. circumstances R. cane sugar
e. which are obtained

t	Inversionskoeffizient
25°	9,67
40	73,4
45	139
50	268
55	491

Eine Temperaturerhöhung von nur etwa 30° genügt bereits, um* die Reaktionsgeschwindigkeit auf das Fünfzigfache zu vergrössern, und ähnlich rapide ist ihr Anwachsen in vielen anderen bisher untersuchten Fällen.*

T. temperature increase
g. suffices R. reaction speed
ä. similarly
An. increase u. investigated F. cases

Vom Standpunkte der Molekulartheorie kann* man allerdings sich leicht davon Rechenschaft geben, dass in homogenen, gasförmigen oder flüssigen Systemen die Stoffe* in um so schnellere Wechselwirkung treten, je höher die Temperatur steigt, weil mit der Temperatur die Lebhaftigkeit der Wärmebewegung und somit auch die Zahl der Zusammenstösse der reagierenden Substanzen zunimmt; allein wenn man bedenkt, dass die Geschwindigkeit der Molekularbewegung* in Gasen und aller Wahrscheinlichkeit nach auch in Flüssigkeiten der Quadratwurzel aus der absoluten Temperatur proportional ist, also* bei Zimmertemperatur nur um etwa 1/6% pro Grad ansteigt, so stösst man offenbar auf eine gewisse Schwierigkeit. Wenn man* aber die Annahme einführt, dass nur diejenigen Moleküle reagieren, deren Geschwindigkeit* einen extrem hohen Mittelwert übersteigt, so wird* der gewaltige Temperatureinfluss auch kinetisch verständlich.

S. standpoint
a. of course R. g. give an account
g. gaseous S. materials
u.s. in all the more rapid
W. interrelation j. h. the higher L. vividness
W. heat movement s. consequently
Z. impacts z. increases
b. considers
a.W. n. according to all probability
F. liquids d. Q. to the square root
What does "also" call for?
s. strikes o. obviously
g. certain S. difficulty
d. those (App. 14, 2) deren whose
ü. exceeds M. medium value
w. becomes (Why?) (App. 7, 3 a)
v. understandable

[10]Betrachten wir bei gleicher Temperatur verschiedene Systeme, so finden wir die denkbar grössten Abstufungen der Reaktionsgeschwindigkeit;* während z. B. bei der Neutralisation einer Basis durch eine Säure die Vereinigung der reagierenden Bestandteile* so schnell vor sich geht, dass die Reaktionsgeschwindigkeit sich bisher jeder Schätzung entzog, so wirken auf der anderen Seite Wasserstoff und Sauerstoff bei gewöhnlicher Temperatur so ausserordentlich träge aufeinander ein,[2] dass aus diesem Grunde eine Messung[4] zur Unmöglichkeit wird.

B. if we consider
d. conceivably A. gradations
R. reaction velocity
S. acid V. union B. constituents
b. hitherto
e. escaped S. estimate
What goes with "wirken"?
a. extraordinarily t. inert
M. measurement U. impossibility

PHYSIK

AUFGABE DER PHYSIK†

Physik bedeutete ursprünglich die Wissenschaft von der **Natur.**[1] Seitdem man[4] gelernt hatte,[7] in der Natur zwischen Belebtem und **Unbelebtem** zu unterscheiden, ist[6] Physik in weitestem Sinne die Wissenschaft von der unbelebten **Natur** geworden. Die Erforschung derselben, die systematische Zusammensetzung der **Erscheinungen,** die Aufdeckung der Zusammenhänge und die Zurückführung der komplizierten Vorgänge auf einfache Gesetzmässigkeiten ist ihre **Aufgabe.**[1] Die Physik geht prinzipiell quantitativ vor,[2] Gegenstand ihrer Forschung sind nur Dinge und **Vorgänge,**[1] die[5] sich messen lassen. Einige Teile der Physik haben[6] sich zu besonderen **Wissenschaften** entwickelt, wie z. B. die **Chemie,** welche[5] die Physik der Atomgruppierungen ist, oder die **Astronomie,**[1] welche[5] die physikalischen Vorgänge, soweit sie[4] in kosmischen **Dimensionen** verlaufen, behandelt. Die Abzweigung solcher Teile ist[6] meist dadurch begründet, dass sich in ihnen besondere,[3] für den betreffenden **Sonderzweck** besonders geeignete Methoden entwickeln.

b. signified u. originally W. science
S. since g. learned (to what?)
B. animate u. distinguish
w. broadest S. sense u. inanimate
g. become E. study
Z. composition E. phenomena
A. disclosure Z. grouping Z. reduction
V. processes G. principles
A task v. proceeds p. in principle
G. object F. study V. processes
s. m. l. can be (See rule 6) E. some
h. s. e. have been developed (App. 11, 4, c)
Note the rules that are "removing" the verbs from the end position.
s. in as far as v. proceed b. treats
A. branching off b. justified
b. special (what?) b. concerned
S. special purpose g. which are suited

Man kann[6] bei der Erforschung einer physikalischen Tatsache drei **Stufen** unterscheiden. Zunächst handelt es sich meist darum,[7] die Erscheinung hervorzubringen, da sehr viele Erscheinungen[4] in reiner Form oder in merklichem Ausmasse nicht oder nur selten in der **Natur** vorkommen. Weiterhin muss[6] die Erscheinung beobachtet werden. Die dritte Stufe ist es,[7] den Vorgang zu verstehen. Es muss[6] genau festgestellt werden, welche Bedingungen[4] für sein **Zustandekommen** wesentlich sind und welcher quantitative Zusammenhang[4] unter den Bedingungen vorhanden sein muss, um[7] die Erscheinung in einer gewissen quantitativen **Form** auftreten zu lassen. Wir verstehen eine **Erscheinung,** wenn wir[4] sämtliche Bedingungen, die[5] zu ihrem **Zustandekommen** notwendig sind, quantitativ kennen. Wir haben[6] sie dann auf ihre einfacheren **Bestandteile** zurückgeführt. Wenn wir[4] eine **Erscheinung** verstanden haben, dann können[6] wir sie jederzeit quantitativ wieder hervorbringen, und wir können[6] die **Anfangsbedingungen** so wählen, dass der zukünftige Verlauf[4] ein gewollter wird. Das heisst, wir können[6] den zukünftigen Verlauf einer verstandenen **Erscheinung** voraussagen. Dies ist der hervorragende praktische **Wert,** den die Physik[4] besitzt

E. study
T. fact S. stages u. distinguish
e.h. s. it deals with (App. 23, 3)
r. pure m. noticeable
A. degree, amount s. seldom v. occur
W. furthermore b. observed
S. stage v. understand V. process
f. established B. conditions
Z. formation w. essential
Z. connection v. present
What does "um" call for? g. certain
a. appear v. understand
s. all R. conditions
n. necessary Z. occurrence k. know
e. simpler B. components
z. reduced v. understood
h. produce j. at any time
w. choose A. initial conditions
x. future V. course g. intended (one)
z. future v. understood
v. predict h. outstanding
W. value

Die Zurückführung der Erscheinungen der unbelebten Welt führt nun auf gewisse einfachere **Bestandteile,**[1] die[5] selbst sich nicht mehr auf **einfachere** zurückführen lassen. Es sind dies einesteils fundamentale **Begriffe,**[1] die[5] gegeben sind in der Struktur unseres erkennenden **Geistes** oder aber in der Art unserer **Naturbetrachtung,** die[5] ja durch unsere jahrtausendelangen Erfahrungen und auch durch mancherlei **Zufälligkeiten** geworden ist. Zu den ersteren gehören etwa die Begriffe Raum und **Zeit,** zu den anderen etwa die Begriffe Kraft, Masse, **Temperatur.** Andernteils sind es gewisse **Zusammenhänge,**[1] die wir[4] nicht in einfachere **Bestandteile** zerlegen können. Solche Zusammenhänge nennt man **Prinzipien.** Aus diesen einfachen Bestandteilen setzt sich nun das Bild des Physikers von der ihn umgebenden **Wirklichkeit** zusammen.[2]

Z. reduction u. inanimate
W. world g. certain B. components
s. l. can be e. simpler (ones) Note absence of the noun. E. s. these are B. concepts
e. recognizing, detecting G. mind
N. nature observation What does "die" call for?
E. experiences
m. many kinds Z. chances, accidents
g. belong e. perhaps B. concepts
K. power A. on the other hand
s. e. there are Z. contexts
z. separate
e. simple What goes with "setzt"?
u. which surround (Why which?)
W. reality z. is composed

†E. Grimsehl, **Lehrbuch der Physik,** R. Tomaschek, ed.

Aus diesen[3] von ihm ausgesonderten (X) und ihm als menschlichen **Geist** gegebenen Elementen stellt er gewisse Bilder der physikalischen **Vorgänge** auf.[2] Die historische Betrachtung der Entwicklung der Physik zeigt, dass je nach der menschlichen Eigenart des betreffenden Erforschers zwei besondere Richtungen[4] bei der Aufstellung solcher **Bilder** feststellbar sind. Einerseits können[6] sie sich ganz darin erschöpfen,[7] quantitative Beziehungen zwischen beobachtbaren **Grössen** zu sein. Sie sind in diesem Falle vollkommen darstellbar in Gestalt mathematischer **Formeln.**[1] Diese Art wurde[6] von Kirchhoff die mathematische Beschreibung der **Natur** genannt, und es ist der Weg, den er und viele andere grosse Forscher, wie Helmholz u. a.[4], bevorzugt haben. Daneben gibt es aber eine grosse Zahl anderer und mindestens ebenso erfolgreicher **Geister,**[1] die[5] eine zweite Art der Darstellung bei ihren **Entdeckungen** bevorzugen. Es ist die,[7] sich die Vorgänge bildlich im Geiste als Bewegungen, dynamische Zustände, vorzustellen. Diese Art der Bilder gestattet[7] nicht nur das mathematische Denkvermögen, sondern auch die geometrische und dynamische **Vorstellung** zu verwerten. So gelangte Faraday zu seinen Entdeckungen, auf denen[5] das ganze Gebäude unserer heutigen **Elektrizitätslehre** ruht, dadurch, dass er[4] sich anschauliche Bilder über die elektrischen und magnetischen **Kräfte** machte.

(See Rule 3 C, 1 diagram and disc. on this sentence.) Let X stand for the missing noun.
a. which are separated
g. and which are given B. observation
j. n. according to E. peculiarity
E. scientist R. directions A. setting up
f. determinable E. on the one hand
e. exhaust themselves d. therein (to what?)
(App. 23, 3) b. observable
d. presentable G. form
w. g. was named (App. 7, 5,b)
B. description W. way Be sure to take all of the subject. F. scientists
b. preferred D. along with that
m. at least e. successful G. minds
D. presentation b. in the case of
b. prefer d. this (to what?)
v. imagine, represent B. movements
g. permits (to what?)
D. thinking capacity
V. representation v. utilize g. arrived at
E. discoveries a. d. upon which G. edifice

Auch bei der Übersetzung des Bildes Faradays in die Darstellung erster Art durch Maxwell haben[6] mechanische Modelle eine grosse **Rolle** gespielt. Besonders beim Vordringen in unbekannte **Gebiete**, wo es[4] sich um probeweise gemachte Bilder handelt, sind[6] solche Bilder dynamischer Art stets von ausserordentlichem **Wert** gewesen. Man nennt solche probeweise Bilder dann Arbeitshypothesen oder schlechthin **Hypothesen.**[10] Ist ein Bild als richtig erkannt worden, so bildet die Gesamtheit der[3] sich aus diesem Bilde logisch ergebenden(X), vor allem auch quantitativen Folgerungen eine Theorie.

Ü. translation B. picture, form, image
D. presentation R. role
B. especially b. in the case of
V. penetration u. unknown G. fields
e. h. s. u. it deals with
a. extraordinary W. value
p. test wise A. working hypothesis
s. simply Why Rule 10? What does "ist" call for? G. totality
e. which result v. a. above all
q. which are quantitative
(See Rule 3 C, 1, 3 for the X.)

Ein gutes Beispiel für die gleichzeitige Anwendung der zwei Arten von Bildern gibt die **Wärmetheorie.**[1] Während die **Thermodynamik,**[4] nur mit beobachtbaren Grössen arbeitend,[11] ein vollendetes Beispiel der Bilder erster Art ist, gibt die mechanische Wärmelehre unter dem Bild der Bewegung der Moleküle ein ebenso vollendetes und ebenso quantitativ durchgebildetes Bild der zweiten **Art.**[1] Eine Vergleichung der beiden Beschreibungsarten wird[6] jeden die Vor- und Nachteile dieser **Darstellungsmethoden** erkennen lassen, je nach dem **Zweck**, zu dem er[4] sie verwenden will, und je nach seiner **Veranlagung**. Hierbei ist[6] nicht zu leugnen, dass die eigentlichen Grenzen der Theorie und die Bedeutung vieler Begriffe erst durch die anschauliche **Betrachtungsweise** klar geworden sind. Das Bild, das wir uns heutzutage vom Standpunkt der Bilder zweiter Art von der physikalischen **Wirklichkeit** machen, weist einige Grundzüge auf,[2] die[5] im folgenden kurz dargelegt werden sollen.

A. use What is the subject here, Be. or W.?
W. while b. observable G. quantities
a. while working (Why while?)
W. heat theory
B. movement v. complete d. well formed
V. comparison b. two B. types of description
V. advantages D. methods of presentation
j. each n. according to
Z. purpose v. use V. inclination
i. n. z. l. is not to be denied (App. 12, 1)
B. concepts a. clear h. now days
S. stand point
W. reality What goes with "weist"?
What does "die" call for? Then how far back do you go? s. are to
d. presented

MATERIE UND ÄTHER

(for the sake of drill, give reasons for the rules indicated on this page)

Wenn wir[4] die Erscheinungen, die[5] uns umgeben, genauer untersuchen, so erkennen wir, dass sie[4] teils an greifbare, wie wir sagen, materielle **Körper** geknüpft sind, wie etwa Bewegung, Wärme, **Schall,**[1] teils von solchen unabhängig sind, wie gewisse Erscheinungen der **Elektrizität**[1] und des **Lichtes.**[1] Alle greifbaren Körper lassen sich[6] aus etwa 100 Grundstoffen, den sogenannten chemischen Elementen, aufbauen, und alles, was[5] aus diesen **Grundstoffen** besteht, wollen[6] wir **Materie** nennen.

E. phenomena u. surround
u. investigate g. more closely
g. connected gr. tangible
B. movement S. sound u. independent
g. certain
L. light g. tangible l. s. can be
a. built up s. so called
b. consists G. basic elements
n. call

Ausserdem muss[6] es aber, wie die Erforschung der Naturerscheinungen[4] gezeigt hat, noch eine **Grundsubstanz** geben, die[5] nicht die Eigenschaften der **Materie** hat, und die[5] vor allem der Träger der elektromagnetischen **Erscheinungen** ist. Es ist der **Äther.** Die[3] uns umgebende Welt ist also aufgebaut aus Materie und **Äther.**[1] Beide sind Qualitäten verschiedener Art und gehorchen eigenen **Gesetzen.**[1] Die historische Entwicklung der menschlichen Erfahrung hat[6] es mit sich gebracht, dass die Kenntnis der Materie und das[3] auf Grund dieser stets betätigten **Kenntnis** entwickelte Gefühl für materielle Erscheinungen viel weiter, ja fast ausschliesslich sich entwickelt hat. Und daher war man verleitet,[7] die Erfahrungen und Begriffe, die[5] an der Materie gewonnen und gebildet waren, auf die Bilder vom **Äther** zu **übertragen.** Es hat[6] sich aber gezeigt, dass der Äther[4] auf diese Weise nicht begreifbar, nicht widerspruchsfrei abbildbar ist. Um[7] ihn zu verstehen, sind[6] ganz andere **Begriffsbildungen** notwendig, **die**[5] mit den[3] an der Materie gewonnenen [9]keine Ähnlichkeit **haben.** Nur immer mehr und mehr ausgebreitete Erfahrung **kann**[6] hier allmählich zum Aufbau richtiger, d. h. widerspruchsfreier **Bilder** führen. Wir stehen heute erst ganz im Anfang dieser **Entwicklung,** und die Erforschung dieses ungeheueren Gebietes ist die lohnende Aufgabe und das glänzende Ziel der zukünftigen **Physik.**[1]

A. besides E. study
N. natural phenomena G. basic substance
m. e. g. there must be (App. 10, 2, e)
v. a. above all T. carrier
u. which surrounds (Why which?)
b. both v. different
g. obey e. peculiar, individual
E. development m. human Er. experience
K. knowledge G. f. feeling for
e. which is developed (Why which?)
E. phenomena j. indeed
s. e. has developed v. tempted, misled (to?)
B. concepts
ü. transfer
e. h. s. g. it has been shown (App. 11, 4, c)
b. comprehensible
v. understand n. necessary
Ä. similiarity g. (ones) which were gained
a. spread out
a. gradually A. building up
w. uncontradictable f. lead
A. beginning Er. exploration
u. enormous G. field l. profitable
g. brilliant Z. goal z. future

Wir werden[6] so zu einem Dualismus in unserem Weltbilde der unbelebten **Natur** geführt. Und doch führt die immer mehr fortschreitende Erforschung der Äthereigenschaften zu der **Erkenntnis,**[1] dass im Grunde wahrscheinlich nur eine Ursubstanz[4] das unbelebte **Weltall** aufbaut, nämlich der **Äther.**[1] Die Materie wäre aber danach nur geformter **Äther,**[1] ähnlich wie etwa **Wolken,**[1] **die**[5] doch etwas ganz **Reales** sind, nur geformtes **Wasser** sind, ja sogar nur ein geformter Vorgang in einem **Wasserdampfstrom,** oder wie Wirbelringe in der **Luft,** die[5] ein ganz bestimmtes und bemerkwertes **Verhalten** zeigen, nur geformte Luft sind . . . .

w. g. are led (App. 7, 5,a)
W. world picture u. inanimate
f. progressive E. study
Ä. ether qualities E. knowledge
w. probably U. original substances
w. would be d. according to that
ä. similar e. perhaps et. something
j. indeed sog. even
V. process W. steam stream
W. whorl rings b. definite
b. remarkable V. behaviour

Einteilung des Gegenstandes der Physik hat sich zunächst vollzogen nach den Einwirkungen der Aussenwelt auf unsere **Sinnesorgane.**[1] Die genaue Durchführung der Erscheinungen hat[6] aber Beziehungen entdeckt und[8] Zurückführungen erlaubt, die[5] gänzlich ausserhalb dieser **Zusammengehörigkeit** stehen. So ist[6] heutzutage eine so spezifische Grundempfindung wie die Wärme auf eine reine **Bewegungserscheinung** zurückgeführt. Das gleiche gilt vom **Schall,** der[5] ebenso vollkommen verschiedene **Grundempfindungen** darstellt. In beiden Fällen handelt es sich nur um verschiedene Arten der Bewegung ein und derselben **Grundsubstanz, der Materie.**

E. division G. object, subject
v. accomplished E. effects
g. exact D. carrying through
B. relations e. permitted
g. entirely a. outside of
h. now days G. basic feeling, sensation
z. reduced to
g. same S. sound v. perfectly
G. basic sensations F. cases
A. types e. u. d. of one and the same
G. basic substance

DIE FORMARTEN DER KÖRPER

Schon eine kurze Betrachtung unserer Umgebung lehrt **uns,**[1] dass die Körper unserer Umwelt[4] in drei **Gruppen** geschieden werden können, die festen, flüssigen und gasförmigen. Man nennt diese drei Zustände **Formarten** oder Aggregatzustände der **Körper.**[1] Die Formarten bezeichnen die **Weise,**[1] in der die Körper[4] den **Raum** erfüllen. Wir wissen auch, dass ein und derselbe Stoff, z. B. Wasser,[4] unter gewissen Bedingungen von einer Formart in die **andere** übergehen kann, z. B. beim Gefrieren aus der flüssigen Form in die feste, beim Schmelzen aus der festen in die flüssige, beim Sieden aus der flüssigen in die gasförmige und beim Kondensieren aus der gasförmigen in die flüssige **Formart.**[1] Es zeigt sich, dass alle Materie, die wir[4] kennen, in einer dieser drei **Formarten** uns entgegentritt, wobei es[4] nur in manchen Fällen unter **Umständen** Schwierigkeiten[9] geben kann, zu entscheiden, welche Formart[4] in einem gegebenen Fall vorliegt.

B. consideration U. environment
U. environment, surroundings
g. divided f. solid fl. liquid
g. gaseous Z. conditions
F. form types b. designate
W. manner e. fill R. space
w. know S. material
g. certain B. conditions
ü. go over G. freezing
f. liquid S. melting
Si. boiling
g. gaseous beim—in the case of
s. zeigt, is shown (App. 11, 4, a)
k. know e. meets w. in which case
e. g. k. there can be S. difficulties
(See App. 10, 2, e for "es kann geben".)
e. decide v. exists g. given E. division

Man kann zur ersten Einteilung etwa folgende **Kennzeichen** benutzen: Ein fester Körper hat eine bestimmte **Gestalt** und demgemäss auch einen bestimmten **Rauminhalt.**[1] Ein flüssiger Körper hat keine bestimmte **Gestalt,** dagegen einen bestimmten **Rauminhalt.**[1] Er füllt daher ein **Gefäss,**[1] in welchem er[4] enthalten ist, nur bis zu diesem **Rauminhalt** aus.[2]

e. perhaps K. characteristics
G. form d. accordingly R. space content
f. liquid d. on the other hand
f. fills G. vessel
e. contained
What does the "aus" go with?

Ein Gas hat weder eine bestimmte **Gestalt,**[1] noch einen bestimmten **Rauminhalt**[1] und füllt daher jeden ihm zur Verfügung stehenden **Raum** aus.[2]

w. — n. neither nor
What goes with "füllt"?
V. disposal s. which stands

Es tritt nun natürlich die Frage auf,[2] womit es[4] zusammenhängt, d. h. welche Vorgänge[4] in den einzelnen **Körpern** der Erscheinung zugrunde liegen, dass ein Stoff bald flüssig, bald fest, bald gasförmig sein kann. Um[7] diese **Frage** beantworten zu können, müssen wir nun noch tiefer in den Aufbau der materiellen **Körper** vordringen.

a. appears (On use of "es" see App. 10-1, a, c.)
z. is associated
l. z. lie at the base of Note how you pick up the noun. b. now
b. answer
A. structure v. penetrate

Teilbarkeit MOLEKULARTHEORIE DER MATERIE

Eine wesentliche Eigenschaft der **Materie,**[1] aus welcher[5] die[3] uns umgebenden **Körper** bestehen, ist ihre **Teilbarkeit.**[1] Man kann[6] beispielsweise einen Golddraht mit einer Zange in zwei **Teile** teilen.[10] Untersuchen wir beide Stücke genau, d. h.[10] bestimmen wir die[3] für sie charakteristischen Eigenschaften, wie Farbe, Elastizität, **Biegsamkeit,**[1] Dichte und andere, so finden wir, **dass** diese,[4] abgesehen von der Länge, dieselben sind, und auch dieselben wie die des ursprünglichen **Drahtes.**[1] Die Materie des Drahtes ist teilbar, ohne[7] ihre wesentlichen **Eigenschaften** einzubüssen. Man kann[6] nun jedes **Stück** weiter zerlegen, ohne dass dabei das Gold[4] seine **Eigenschaften** ändert. Man kann[6] schliesslich das Gold durch Hämmern zu Häuten von ausserordentlicher **Dünnheit** ausschlagen, wie es die Goldschläger[1] tun, so dass 1 Kubikmillimeter eine dünne Haut von etwa 10000 Quadratmillimeter **Fläche** bildet. Bei einer solchen Zerteilung bleibt,[6] wie man festgestellt hat, der **Rauminhalt** ungeändert, die Dicke der Metallhaut beträgt also 0,0001 mm.[1] Die oben bestimmten physikalischen Eigenschaften sind[6] hierbei noch nicht wesentlich geändert, so das man[1] schliessen kann, dass ein Würfelchen von 0,0001 mm Kantenlänge[1] noch dieselben Eigenschaften hat wie der ursprüngliche **Draht.**

T. divisibility
w. essential E. attribute
b. consist u. which surround us (why which?)
b. for example
t. divide U. if we investigate Why Rule 10?
c. which are characteristic (Why which?)
a. apart from L. length
d. d. those of u. original
D. wire What does "ohne" call for?
w. essential e. losing
z. analyze
ä. changes s. finally
H. hammering H. sheets
a. beat out
b. forms
Z. dismemberment, analysis
u. unchanged (Note Rule 6.) b. amounts
b. determined E. attributes
n. n. not yet
s. conclude W. die
K. side length Why is "hat" in this position?
u. original D. wire

Die heutigen Hilfsmittel **haben jedoch** gezeigt, dass man[4] schliesslich an eine Grenze der Teilbarkeit der **Materie** kommt. Einige dieser Versuche werden[6] noch in diesem **Abschnitt** besprochen werden. **Man stösst schliesslich auf Teilchen,** die[5] einzeln nicht mehr dasselbe Verhalten zeigen wie der ursprüngliche **Körper,** durch dessen Teilung sie[4] erhalten wurden. Man kann[6] die Materie etwa mit einem **Sandsteinfelsen** vergleichen, der[5] als Ganzes ein wesentlich anderes physikalisches Verhalten zeigt als ein einzelnes der ungeheuer vielen **Sandkörner,** aus denen er[4] aufgebaut ist. Die Materie hat also eine Art körniger **Struktur,** d. h. alle Körper sind[6] aus sehr kleinen Körperelementen von selbständiger **Existenz** zusammengesetzt, die[5] in Gestalt und **Grösse** unveränderlich und[8] durch kleine **Zwischenräume** voneinander getrennt sind. Diese Körperelemente werden[6] **Moleküle** genannt. Die Grösse der **Moleküle** hat[6] sich auf verschiedenen **Wegen** bestimmen lassen, und sie ist[6] für die verschiedenen Stoffe als verschieden gross gefunden worden. Für die chemisch einfacheren Stoffe hat[6] sich eine mittlere lineare Ausdehnung derselben von etwa **10^{-7} cm** ergeben.

h. present H. aids g. shown
s. finally G. limit T. divisibility
E. some w. will (why?)
A. section s. strikes, thrusts
T. particles V. behaviour (Why is "zeigen" in this position?) u. original
e. perhaps
v. compare w. essentially
(Why is "zeigt" in this position?)
u. vastly a. constructed
k. granular
K. body elements
s. independent z. composed G. form
u. invariable (Note that you must borrow "sind" for this adjective.)
g. separated G. size, magnitude
b. defined i. g. w. has been found
a. v. as different
e. simpler m. mean, average
A. dimension s. e. resulted

Wenn es[4] auch infolge dieser Kleinheit der **Moleküle** nicht möglich ist,[7] sie unmittelbar zu sehen, so ist[6] es doch möglich gewesen,[7] mit Hilfe der[3] dem Licht verwandten Röntgenstrahlen die räumliche Lage der Moleküle in vielen Körpern, insbesondere **Kristallen,** nachzuweisen. Die Einzelheiten können[6] erst später behandelt werden. Die Beschaffenheit der Materie, also die Gesamtheit der **Eigenschaften,** etwa eines Stückes Golddraht muss[6] demnach durch zwei **Umstände** bestimmt sein: erstens durch die Beschaffenheit der Moleküle und zweitens durch die Struktur des **Körpers,** d. h. die **Art,** wie die Moleküle in dem betreffenden **Körper** angeordnet sind. Die Aufgabe der Forschung ist es,[7] festzustellen, inwiefern die Eigenschaften der Körper[4] von einem dieser beiden **Faktoren** abhängen, und[8] ferner umgekehrt aus den Eigenschaften der **Körper,** wie wir[4] sie im groben beobachten können, auf die Eigenschaften der **Moleküle,** die[5] viel zu klein sind, als dass wir[4] sie je einzeln fassen oder beobachten könnten, zu schliessen.

w.—a. even though i. due to
m. possible (to what?) u. directly
Note Rule 7. v. which are related
R. X-rays r. spatial L. position
n. to show, prove
E. details b. treated
B. nature G. totality
e. perhaps G. gold wire
U. conditions, circumstances
z. secondly
A. manner w. how
a. arranged b. concerned
F. research, study f. establish
E. attributes
a. depend u. and (to what?)
i. g. approximately
z. k. too small
f. comprehend b. observe
s. conclude (What calls for this verb?)

Dieser Weg ist natürlich ausserordentlich schwierig. Man geht meist so vor,[2] dass man[4] zunächst versucht,[7] den Molekülen probeweise gewisse **Eigenschaften** zuzuschreiben, die[5] den Beobachtungen nach ihnen zukommen könnten, dass man[4] sich also ein vorläufiges Bild der Eigenschaften und **Vorgänge** macht. Wenn nun die[3] aus diesem **Bilde** logisch sich ergebenden Konsequenzen[4] mit den tatsächlichen **Erscheinungen** übereinstimmen, so kann man aus dieser Bestätigung umgekehrt auf die Richtigkeit des **Bildes** schliessen, und zwar mit um so grösserer Sicherheit, je grösser der Kreis der Erfahrungen ist, der[5] mit den logischen Konsequenzen des **Bildes** übereinstimmt. Man hat[6] auf diese Weise heutzutage ein ziemlich weitgehendes Bild vom Aufbau der Materie und den Eigenschaften der **Moleküle** entwickelt, und im folgenden sollen[6] schrittweise die einzelnen Züge **desselben** entwickelt werden, wenn auch die vollkommene Darstellung[4] erst in **Bd. II** gegeben werden kann.

a. extraordinarily
s. difficult v. proceeds z. first of all
v. attempts (to what?)
z. belong n. according to
v. tentative
V. processes e. which result
t. actual
ü. agree
B. verification u. conversely
s. conclude u. s. g. so much the greater
j. g. the greater (App. 26, 2)
ü. agrees What does "hat" call for?
w. extensive
A. building up
e. developed s. are to s. step wise
ei. individual Z. features
v. perfect D. presentation

ELASTIZITÄT UND FESTIGKEIT

DEHNUNG UND PRESSUNG

Wenn eine Kraft auf einen Körper einwirkt, wenn wir z. B. mit der Hand gegen einen auf dem Tisch liegenden Körper drücken, so tritt an der Stelle, wo der Druck ausgeübt wird, eine Formveränderung (Deformation) des Körpers ein, die allerdings in vielen Fällen so gering ist, dass sie der oberflächlichen Beobachtung entgeht. Hört die deformierende Kraft auf, zu wirken, so kann der Körper nachher entweder seine ursprüngliche Gestalt wieder vollständig annehmen, oder er kann die veränderte Gestalt beibehalten. Im ersten Fall nennen wir den Körper elastisch, im zweiten unelastisch.

e. acts K. force
What does "wir" call for? einen?
d. press What goes with "tritt"?
ausg. exerted
a. of course (What calls for "ist"?)
o. superficial e. escapes
What does "auf" go with? What do you do when the verb is first? u. original
G. form a. take on b. retain
Note the rules that are taking out the verbs and prefixes.

ELASTIZITÄT DER DEHNUNG Um die Formveränderung, die ein Körper unter dem Einfluss einer Kraft erfährt, zu messen, hängen wir einen Draht unverrückbar auf und belasten ihn am unteren Ende. Hierbei wird er verlängert und nimmt (wenn die Verlängerung eine gewisse, noch näher zu bestimmende Grösse nicht überschreitet) nach Aufhören der Belastung seine ursprüngliche Länge wieder an. Bei zwei Drähten derselben Art, von denen der erste doppelt so lang ist wie der zweite, beträgt die Verlängerung durch dieselbe Kraft beim ersten doppelt so viel wie beim zweiten. Allgemein gilt:

D. extension What does "um" call for? "ein Körper"? What does "auf" go with?
u. immovable b. burden
v. elongated What goes with "nimmt"?
g. certain z. b. to be determined
(App. 12, 2) A. cessation
What does "an" go with? D. wires
Note the position of "ist".
b. amounts V. lengthening
A. generally g. holds true

Die Verlängerung ist bei gleicher Belastung der ursprünglichen Länge proportional.

g. equal B. weight
What calls for "proportional"?

Hängen wir zwei Drähte derselben Art und gleicher Länge nebeneinander auf und belasten sie beide zusammen durch ein Gewichtstück, so ist die Verlängerung, welche beide Drähte gleichzeitig erfahren, halb so gross wie die Verlängerung eines einzelnen Drahtes durch dieselbe Belastung. Statt zweier gleichartiger Drähte können wir auch einen Draht verwenden, dessen Querschnitt doppelt so gross ist wie der des ursprünglich benutzten Drahtes. Allgemein ergibt sich:

What do you do if the verb is first?
What does "auf" go with?
G. (piece of) weight
e. undergo g. at the same time
e. single B. weight
S. instead of g. equal type
v. use Note that "ist" is in front of "wie".
d. d. that of
e. results

Die Verlängerung ist dem Querschnitt des Drahtes bei gleicher Belastung umgekehrt proportional.

Q. cross section
u. inversely What calls for "pro."?

Um die Verlängerung zweier Drähte aus verschiedenen Stoffen miteinander zu vergleichen, wählen wir die Drähte von gleicher Länge (1 m) und gleichem Querschnitt (1 mm^2). Es ergibt sich, dass für sonst gleiche Drähte aus verschiedenen Stoffen die Verlängerung durch dieselbe Kraft P verschieden ist.

What does "um" call for?
v. compare w. choose
g. equal
s. otherwise
K. power What is the subject here?

ELASTIZITÄTSGRENZE Wenn man die Belastung des Drahtes allmählich vergrössert, so wird von einer bestimmten Belastung an (Proportionalitätsgrenze) die Verlängerung des Drahtes nicht mehr der Belastung proportional. Vergrössert man die Belastung weiter, so kommt man schliesslich zu einer Belastung, nach deren Wegnahme der Draht seine ursprüngliche Länge nicht wieder annimmt. Die Elastizitätsgrenze des Drahtes ist überschritten. Die Elastizitätsgrenze ist für verschiedene Körper sehr verschieden. Die Elastizitätsgrenze wird bestimmt durch die in kg ausgedrückte Belastung, bei welcher der Draht seine ursprüngliche Form nach Aufhören der Belastung nicht wieder annimmt. In Tabelle IV ist die Elastizitätsgrenze für die wichtigsten Körper verzeichnet.

E. elasticity limit B. burden
a. gradually What calls for "verg."?
for "proportional"? And if the verb is first, what procedure do you follow?
s. finally
n. d. W. after the removal of which
a. assumes
ü. exceeded
v. different
a. which is expressed (Why which?)
A. cessation What calls for "annimmt"?
w. again
v. mark, register, record

PRAKTISCHE ANWENDUNG DER ELEKTROLYSE

(Underline the nouns that should appear in bold face type. Indicate the reason for the *.)

Wenngleich die ersten Anwendungen der Elektrolyse* schon auf Davy zurückgehen, der* 1807 die Alkalien durch den elektrischen Strom zerlegte und* das Kalium und Natrium in metallischem Zustand herstellte, und wenngleich schon Jakobi 1838 lehrte,[7] metallische Nachbildungen metallischer Gegenstände auf elektrolytischem Wege herzustellen und* unedle Metalle mit Überzügen von Edelmetallen zu versehen, so konnte* sich doch die Elektrochemie zu einem ausgedehnten Zweig der Technik und Industrie erst entwickeln, als man gelernt hatte,* elektrische Ströme von beliebiger Spannung und beliebiger Stromstärke mit Hilfe dynamoelektrischer Maschinen herzustellen.	W. even though A. applications z. go back S. current z. analyzed u. and what h. produced l. taught (to what?) G. objects v. provide Ü. coating a. extended Z. branch e. develop g. learned (to what?) S. voltage, pressure h. produce
Im folgenden soll* eine kurze Übersicht über die wichtigsten* in der Technik angewandten Prozesse angegeben werden.	f. following Ü. survey a. which are used (Why which?) a. indicated
ELEKTROLYSE DER METALLSALZE. Eines der* in grösstem Massstab technisch betriebenen Anwendungsgebiete ist die Elektrolyse der Metallsalze. Einerseits benutzt man diese Methode, um* die Metalle elektrolytisch zu gewinnen oder* elektrolytisch zu reinigen, andererseits dazu, um* Gebrauchs- oder Schmuckgegenstände mit Metallüberzügen zu versehen oder* plastische metallische Nachbildungen von Gegenständen herzustellen.	M. amount, degree b. which are carried on, operated E. on the one hand b. uses g. obtain r. refine a. on the other hand v. provide N. copy, imitation, reproductions
Elektrolytische Gewinnung von Metallen.[10] Verwendet man eine unlösliche Anode und eine Metallsalzlösung als Elektrolyten, so kann* man an der Kathode unter Umständen das reine Metall abscheiden.	G. manufacture Why Rule 10? u. insoluble u. U. under circumstances a. precipitate
So werden* sehr grosse Mengen von Kupfer (1936 etwa 180 000 t im Jahr) aus $CuSO_4$ haltigen Elektrolyten abgeschieden, wobei Anoden* aus einer Legierung von Cu mit Si, Fe und anderen Metallen benutzt werden.	w. a. are precipitated (App. 7, 5, a) h. containing L. alloy b. used
Auch Zink wird* in ähnlicher Weise in grossen Mengen gewonnen (1936 etwa 520 000 t.) Als Anodenmaterial verwendet man Platten aus MnO_2.	ä. similar M. quantities v. uses
Elektrolytische Reinigung von Metallen. Das Prinzip besteht darin, dass Anoden* aus dem noch unreinen Metall unter Anwendung eines Salzes desselben Metalles als Elektrolyten durch den elektrischen Strom[9] in Lösung gebracht werden und an der Kathode das reine Metall[4] abgeschieden wird. Die wichtigste Anwendung findet diese Methode zur elektrischen Kupferraffination. Man verwendet gegossene Anoden von einem Kupfergehalt von etwa 98 – 99%.	R. refining b. consists u. by A. use i. L. in solution (Why Rule 9?) g. brought a. precipitate w. most important v. uses K. copper content e.about
Das* an der Kathode auf feinen Blechen aus reinstem **Kupfer** sich abscheidende Metall zeigt einen sehr grossen Reinheitsgrad bis zu 99,99% Kupfer. Allerdings is für die modernen Zwecke der Elektrotechnik ein solcher Reinheitsgrad durchaus erforderlich, da Verunreinigungen* schon in geringster Menge die elektrische Leitfähigkeit des Kupfers ausserordentlich beeinflussen können. So soll* schon ein Gehalt von wenigen tausendstel Prozent Arsen genügen, um* das Kupfer für elektrische Leitungen unbrauchbar zu machen.	B. sheets s. a. which precipitates Why which? A. of course Z. purposes d. altogether e. necessary (What calls for this word?) V. impurities b. influence a. extraordinarily s. is said G. content g. suffice L. (conduction) lines u. unusable
Die* auf diese Weise raffinierten Mengen sind ausserordentlich gross; allein die Jahresproduktion der Kupferraffinerien in den Vereinigten Staaten betrug 1936 etwa 800 000 t Elektrolytkupfer. Das bedeutet, dass allein in USA ein dauernder Strom von 100 Mill. Ampere verwendet wird.	M. quantities a. but, alone, only V. S. USA b. amounted b. means d. constant S. current v. used

OXYDATIONS-UND REDUKTIONSPROZESSE

(Insert the number of the rules involved on this page. Underline the nouns that should appear in bold-faced type)

Man kann* die Elektrolyse mit grösstem Vorteil zur Ausführung von Oxydationen (an der Anode) oder von Reduktionen (an der Kathode) benutzen, da diese Prozesse hierbei keine Verunreinigung der Lösungen mit sich bringen, wie es durch chemische Reduktions- oder Oxydationsmittel[9] der Fall ist.

A. execution
b. use
h. hereby V. impurification L. solutions
What does "es" call for?
Why pick up this noun?

Oxydationsvorgänge, die in grösstem Masstab ausgeführt werden, sind die Gewinnung von Ferrizyankalium aus Ferrozyan-kalium gemäss der Gleichung $Fe(CN)_6'''' \rightarrow Fe(CN)_6''' + \ominus$. Auch $KMnO_4$ wird in Deutschland fast ausschliesslich elektrolytisch **durch Oxydation von Manganatlösung dargestellt. Weitere Anwendungsgebiete sind die Darstellung von Persulfaten, Wasserstoffsuperoxyd und Perchloraten, ferner von organischen Stoffen wie Jodoform.**

O. oxydation processes M. amount, extent
What calls for "werden"?
g. according to G. equation
Some numbers on this page deal with chemical compounds. a. exclusively
d. prepared A. fields of application
D. preparation
f. further S. materials

Elektrolyse des Wassers

Da Wasserstoff und Sauerstoff aus anderen Quellen in genügender Menge zur Verfügung stehen, hat die Elektrolyse des Wassers, die entweder in schwefelsauerer Lösung in Bleigefässen mit Bleielektroden oder in alkalischer chloridfreier Lösung mit Eisenelektroden vorgenommen wird, vorläufig keine Bedeutung erlangt.

W. hydrogen S. oxygen Q. sources
g. sufficient M. quantity
v. undertaken v. for the time being e. acquired

Elektrolyse geschmolzener Salze

Diese wird hauptsächlich zur Gewinnung der Alkali- und Erdalkalimetalle, des Magnesiums, Aluminiums, und Berylliums **benutzt. Die Darstellung von metallischem Natrium erfolgt meist durch Elektrolyse geschmolzenen Natriumhydroxyds bei Temperaturen bis zu 330° in eisernen Kästen mit Kathoden aus Eisen und Anoden aus Nickel. Die Ausbeute wird besonders durch das** anodisch sich abscheidende Wasser beeinträchtigt, lässt sich aber **durch neuere Konstruktionen weitgehend verbessern. Auch durch direkte Elektrolyse von NaCl hat man Natrium herzustellen versucht; doch muss man, da die Schmelztemperatur des NaCl in der Nähe der Siedetemperatur des Natriums liegt, als Elektrolyten ein Gemisch von Fluoriden und Chloriden des Natriums und Kaliums verwenden, wodurch man den Schmelzpunkt des Elektrolyten von 800° auf etwa 600° herabdrücken kann.**

g. melted
h. chiefly G. manufacture
What does "wird" call for?
b. used D. preparation
e. takes place g. melted
e. iron K. boxes
A. yield w. is (why?) b. impaired
l. s. can be
v. improved
v. attempted h. to produce
What does "muss" call for? "Schmelz"?
l. lies
G. mixture
v. use w. whereby S. melting point
h. reduce

Die Gewinnung des metallischen Kalziums durch Elektrolyse von geschmolzenem $CaCl_2$ ist dadurch erschwert, dass sich Ca bei hoher Temperatur mit $CaCl_2$ zu CaCl verbindet.

K. calcium
g. melted e. complicated
s. v. is combined

Die Gewinnung des Magnesiums erfolgt durch Elektrolyse des Karnallits ($KCl \cdot MgCl_2 \cdot 6H_2O$), der vor reinem $MgCl_2$ den Vor**teil grösserer Wasserfreiheit und niedrigeren Schmelzpunktes hat. Das verbrauchte $MgCl_2$ wird neuerdings in der Form ersetzt, dass man das sich anodisch entwickelnde Chlor auf MgO in** Anwesenheit von CO einwirken lässt, wobei sich $MgCl_2$ und CO_2 bilden. **Hierdurch ist die sehr erwünschte Möglichkeit gegeben, als Ausgangsmaterial Magnesit zu benutzen.**

e. takes place
V. advantage
n. lower S. melting point
e. replaced n. recently
e. developing
l. lets e. act, operate
e. desirable
M. possibility

Der wichtigste hierher gehörige Prozess ist die Gewinnung des Aluminiums. Das Ausgangsmaterial ist eine Lösung von Al_2O_3 in Kryolith Na_3AlF_6. Zur Erniedrigung der Schmelztemperatur werden weitere Zusätze, z. B. CaF_2, benutzt.

b. use w. most important g. which belongs
A. starting material
E. reduction
Z. additions

DAS GRAVITATIONSGESETZ

An einem Punkt der Erdoberfläche haben alle Körper dieselbe **Fallbeschleunigung.**[1] Wir schliessen daraus auf eine[3] nach dem **Erdmittelpunkt** gerichtete **Kraft,**[1] die Schwerkraft, die[5] den Massen der **Körper** proportional ist. Auf Grund dieser Überlegung wurde[6] im vorangehenden das Gewicht als **Kraftmass** benutzt. Diese Kraft wirkt aber nicht nur zwischen der Erde und den[3] auf ihrer **Oberfläche** befindlichen **Körpern,** sondern sie ist eine **Kraft,** die[5] zwischen allen Massen an jedem Ort und zu jeder **Zeit** wirksam ist. Es sollen[6] im folgenden die Gesetzmässigkeiten, die[5] das Wirken dieser **Kraft** bestimmen, behandelt werden.

E. earth surface K. bodies
F. falling acceleration s. conclude
g. which is directed K. force
G. basis
Ü. consideration v. foregoing
b. used K. power w. acts
b. which are found (Why which?)
j. any O. place
w. effective e. s. there are to
G. uniformities, laws b. determine
b. treated w. be (App. 7, 6, 3)

1. Jeder Planet bewegt sich in einer elliptischen **Bahn,**[1] in deren einem Brennpunkt die Sonne steht.

b. moves B. path, orbit
B. focal point S. sun

2. Der[3] von der Sonne zum **Planeten** gezogene Leitstrahl überstreicht in gleichen Zeiten gleiche **Flächen.**[1]

L. radius vector g. which is drawn (Why which?)
ü. passes over

3. Die **Quadrate** der Umlaufszeiten zweier Planeten verhalten sich wie die Kuben der grossen Halbachsen ihrer **Bahnen.**[1]

Q. squares U. periodic motions
v. behave **What do the nouns tell you to do?**

Die Keplerschen Gesetze geben die Bewegungen der Planeten nicht mit aller Strenge wieder.[2] Die Abweichungen lassen sich[6] jedoch auf den Einfluss der Anziehung der einzelnen Planeten untereinander zurückführen. Nur beim Merkur überschreitet die Abweichung die vorauszusehenden Störungen, und zwar besteht sie darin, dass die grosse Achse der Umlaufsellipse[4] sich in ihrer Ebene um etwa 43″ im **Jahrhundert** stärker dreht, als man berechnet.

G. laws B. movements
S. strictness w. reproduce
Ab. deviations s. l. can be
An. attraction z. traced back
ü. exceeds S. disturbances
b. consists
d. rotates s. more strongly
b. calculates

Newton führte nun in Kenntnis dieser Gesetze die **folgende Überlegung** durch:[2] Wenn die Planetenbewegungen (insbesondere auch die des Mondes) **Zentralbewegungen** sind, dann muss[6] eine Kraft da sein, die, nach dem Mittelpunkt dieser Zentralbewegung gerichtet,[11] den Mond in seine (annähernde) Kreisbahn zwingt. Sollte[6] das nicht vielleicht dieselbe Kraft sein, die[5] auch einen fallenden Apfel in der Richtung zum Mittelpunkt der **Erde** zieht? Dies war der grosse **Gedanke,** der[5] eine einheitliche Auffassung der ganzen Erscheinungen, sowohl im Himmelsraum als auch auf der **Erde** ermöglichte und der[5] es gestattete,[7] aus den[3] auf der **Erde** gewonnenen Erfahrungen auf das Verhalten der **Himmelskörper** zu schliessen. Nun ist aber die[3] auf den **Mond** wirkende Radialbeschleunigung nur $\frac{1}{3600}$ der Fallbeschleunigung auf der Erdoberfläche. Es ist aber die Entfernung des Mondes 60mal grösser vom **Erdmittelpunkt,**[1] als die Entfernung einer[3] an der **Erdoberfläche** befindlichen **Masse.** Da $\frac{1}{3600} = \frac{1}{60^2}$ ist, so führt also ein Vergleich der Fallbeschleunigung des Mondes und der Grösse der Fallbeschleunigung einer Masse auf der Erdoberfläche zum **Ergebnis,**[1] dass offenbar, wie Newton schloss, die Anziehungskraft der Erde[4] dem Quadrat der **Entfernung** umgekehrt proportional ist, wie es die Keplerschen Gesetze[4] erfordern. Daraus folgt wieder die Erkenntnis, dass das Gewicht eines Körpers[4] von seiner Entfernung vom **Erdmittelpunkt** abhängen muss.

K. knowledge G. laws
Ü. consideration d. carried thru
d. d. that of
d. there M. center
g. when directed (Why when?)
K. circular orbit z. forces
A. apple R. direction
G. thought
e. uniform A. conception
H. universe e. made possible
g. permitted (to what?)
gew. which were gained (Why which?)
w. which acts

F. acceleration due to gravity E. earth surface
E. distance E. earth center point
a. than einer what?

b. which is found (Why which?)
V. comparison G. size
E. result o. obviously s. concluded
A. attraction force Q. square
e. require
D. from that E. knowledge
G. weights a. depend

GRÖSSE UND RICHTUNG DER SCHWERKRAFT AUF DER ERDOBERFLÄCHE

Die[3] auf einen Körper auf der **Erdoberfläche** wirkende anziehende Kraft ist[6], wie[8] schon früher ausgeführt, von der geographischen **Lage** abhängig, was[5] seine Ursache einerseits in der **Zentrifugalkraft** hat, andererseits in der verschiedenen Entfernung der Körper vom Erdmittelpunkt infolge der[3] an den **Polen** abgeplatteten Gestalt der Erde. Aber auch Sonne und Mond beeinflussen das Gewicht der Körper auf der **Erdoberfläche**; ihr Einfluss ist[6] auch gemessen worden. Die verschiedene Dichte einzelner Erdschichten oder die Umgebung eines **Ortes**, z. B. das Vorhandensein von Bergen in der Nähe, beeinflusst ebenfalls Grösse und Richtung der **Schwerkraft.** So zeigt das Lot etwa am Fusse eines isoliert stehenden Berges eine durchaus messbare Abweichung von der Vertikalen (Richtung nach dem **Erdmittelpunkt**).[1] Wenn die Masse des ablenkenden Berges[4] bekannt ist, so kann[6] man sogar aus der beobachteten Ablenkung die Masse bzw. die Dichte der **Erde** bestimmen (zuerst ausgeführt von **Maskelyne 1775** am Berge Shehallien in **Schottland**).[1]

E. surface of the earth
w. which acts a. attracting K. force
a. stated a. dependent w. which
U. cause e. on the one hand
v. different E. distance
E. earth center point i. as a result of
a. which is flattened G. form
G. weight E. influence
g. measured D. density e. of single
E. layers of the earth U. surrounding
V. presence B. mountains N. neighborhood
e. likewise R. direction S. gravity
L. plumb F. foot
d. very m. measurable A. deviation
R. direction
a. deflecting s. even
b. observed A. deflection bzw. or
b. determine a. carried out

Zur Bestimmung der Grösse der Schwerebeschleunigung benutzt man **Pendelmessungen**,[1] die[5] sich heute mit einer **Genauigkeit** durchführen lassen, die[5] etwa 0,002 **cm/s** entspricht.

B. determination G. size, magnitude
S. gravity, weight acceleration
d. carried through s. l. can be
e. corresponds

Die Drehwaage

D. torsion balance

Ausserordentlich genaue Messungen der räumlichen Änderungen des Betrages und der Richtung der Schwerkraft lassen sich[6] mit der Drehwaage von **Eötvös** gewinnen. (Schwerevariometer)

A. extraordinary g. accurate
r. space A. changes B. amount
S. gravity l. s. can be
g. gained

In ihrer einfachsten Form besteht die Drehwaage aus einem sehr leichten **Hohlstab**, der[5] an einem möglichst dünnen **Draht** aufgehängt ist und[8] an den Enden in gleicher Höhe zwei kleine **Gewichte** trägt. Bei der zweiten Ausführungsart sind[6] die Belastungsgewichte in verschiedener **Höhe** angebracht. Die Balkenlänge beträgt etwa 25—40 cm, die Einzelmassen haben 15—20 g, der Höhenunterschied ist **50—60 cm.** Als Aufhängedrähte verwendet man solche aus Platin-Iridium von einigen hundertsteln Millimetern **Durchmesser.** Die Wirkung der Drehwaage ist folgende: Der Waagebalken befindet sich in **Ruhe** und der Aufhängedraht ist drillungsfrei, wenn die Schwerkraft[4] auf beide Massen in gleicher Grösse und gleicher **Richtung** wirkt. (Dies ist der Fall im homogenen **Felde**, wo die Kraftlinien[4] unter sich parallel sind.)[10] Ist aber das Schwerefeld gestört, das Feld also inhomogen, so erfahren die einzelnen Teile der Waage eine[3] von Punkt zu Punkt in bezug auf Richtung und **Grösse** verschiedene Schwere. Es werden[6] also an den beiden Gewichten der Drehwaage ungleiche **Kräfte** angreifen, die[5] nicht vertikal sind, sondern[8] auch eine horizontale **Komponente** haben, wie es[4] in Abb. **192** dargestellt ist.[10] Ist B das Balkenende, so greift an demselben die Kraft **BS** an.[2] Die vertikale Komponente derselben wird[6] vom **Aufhängedraht** aufgenommen, die horizontale bewirkt eine Drehung des **Waagebalkens.** Dieser Drehung entgegen wirkt die Drillung des **Fadens**; es resultiert eine Ablenkung, die[5] mit Hilfe eines **Spiegels** abgelesen wird. Man kann[6] die Richtung der **Schwerkraft** festlegen.

e. simplest b. consists
l. light H. hollow rod
a. suspended d. thin D. wire
g. equal H. level G. weights
A. model B. loading weights
a. attached, applied
E. individual masses H. difference in height
v. uses e. some
D. diameter W. effect
b. f. is found R. rest
A. suspension wire F. case
g. same R. direction
K. lines of power Why Rule 10 here?
g. disturbed e. undergo
e. single Why Rule 3?
v. which is different
S. weight, gravity e. w. there will
a. attack, act u. unequal K. forces
s. but (What does this word call for?)
d. presented Why Rule 10?
What does "an" go with?
A. suspension wire
a. taken up b. causes
e. contrary to D. rotation, Dri. twist
A. deflection
a. read S. mirror
f. establish S. gravity

LÄNGENMESSUNG

Längeneinheit: Um[7] die Messungsergebnisse, also die Masszahlen der Längenmessung, auch dann vergleichen zu können, wenn die Messungen[4] von verschiedenen **Personen** ausgeführt worden sind, ist man übereingekommen,[7] allerorts dieselbe **Längeneinheit** zugrunde zu legen. Als solche dient die Länge des **Urmeters,**[1] eines[3] im Bureau der Masse und Gewichte im Pavillon de Breteuil bei **Paris** aufbewahrten Stabes aus einer Legierung von 90% Iridium von der[3] in **Abb. 1** abgekürzt gezeichneten **Form.** Auf dem Grunde der Rinne sind[6] je drei feine **Striche** eingerissen. Der Abstand der mittleren derselben ist bei der Temperatur 0° C. "ein Meter" (1 m).

L. length unit M. measurement results
M. measuring numbers v. compare
M. measurements v. different
a. carried out ü. agreed (to what?)
a. everywhere z. z. l. to take as a basis
U. original, standard meter
G. weights
a. which is kept (Why which?) L. alloy
b. which is designated
G. base, bottom S. lines
e. carved in A. distance

Das Meter wird[6] nach dem Dezimalsystem in 10 Dezimeter (dm), 100 Zentimeter (cm), 1000 **Millimeter** (mm) eingeteilt. Dort, wo noch kleinere Masseinheiten[4] erwünscht sind, nimmt man wieder Dezimalteile des Millimeters als **Masseinheit.**[1] Der tausendste Teil eines Millimeters heisst **Mikron,** es wird[6] mit μ bezeichnet, der millionte Teil eines Millimeters ist ein Millimikron ($m\mu$). Für grössere Längen verwendet man als Masseinheit das Kilometer[1] (1 km=1000 m)

WATCH THE BOLD-FACED NOUN. THEN OBSERVE THE RULES THAT REMOVE VERBS FOUND ON THE RIGHT SIDE OF THESE NOUNS. e. divided
e. desirable
M. measuring unit
h. is called
b. designated
g. larger
v. uses

Eine[3] von der französischen Nationalversammlung **1791** eingesetzte Kommission beschloss,[7] den vierzigmillionten Teil des[3] durch die Pariser Sternwarte gehenden **Meridians**[9] als Längeneinheit zu wählen. Zu dem Zwecke wurde[6] eine Messung des[3] zwischen Dunkirchen und Monjuich bei **Barcelona** liegenden Bogens dieses Meridians mit den damals besten **Hilfsmitteln** ausgeführt. Spätere, noch genauere **Messungen,** die[5] von **Bessel** ausgewertet wurden, ergaben, dass die Länge des Erdquadranten, nach dem festgesetzten **Meter** gemessen,[11] 10000856 m beträgt, dass also das[3] von der französischen **Kommission** festgesetzte Meter[4] um 0,0856 mm zu kurz ist. Man hat[6] trotzdem die Länge des[3] von der französischen **Kommission** angenommenen **Meterstabes**[9] als **Längeneinheit** beibehalten, da es[4] ganz unmöglich ist und[8] zwecklos wäre,[7] nach jeder genaueren Erdmessung wieder eine andere **Längeneinheit** einzuführen.

What does "eine" call for?
e. which was appointed b. resolved (to what?)
g. which goes
w. choose Why do you pick up "L"?
z. between
l. which lies B. d. M. arch of this meridian
(Be sure to take all of your subject.) a. utilized
e. showed
g. when measured (Why when?)
b. amounts f. which was established
Note that "Meter" is after all your subject which calls for "ist".
b. retained u. impossible
z. without purpose (to what?)
E. earth measurement e. introduce

Alle[3] im **Gebrauch** befindlichen Meterstäbe sind[6] mittelbar mit dem **Urmeter** verglichen worden. Um[7] dieses zu ermöglichen, hat[6] man eine Anzahl von Stäben aus demselben **Stoff** und von derselben Form wie das Urmeter und von möglichst genau gleicher Länge mit den vollkommensten **Hilfsmitteln** hergestellt und[8] ihre Längenabweichung durch wiederholtes, sorgfältiges Vergleichen mit dem **Urmeter** ausgemessen. Dann sind[6] die Kopien an die einzelnen **Staaten** verteilt worden. Sie dienen in diesen Staaten als Normale der **Längeneinheit.**[1] Das[3] bei der Verteilung an **Deutschland** gekommene Normalmeter führt die Nummer 18 und wird[6] in Charlottenburg aufbewahrt. Die möglichst sorgfältig hergestellten Kopien der Normalen sind[6] an die **Eichämter** verteilt worden, deren Aufgabe es ist,[7] die Länge der Gebrauchmassstäbe durch direktes oder indirektes Vergleichen mit den[3] ihnen amtlich **gelieferten Normalen** zu prüfen.

b. which are found G. use
s. v. w. have been compared (App. 7, 5, c
e. make possible A. number
S. material
g. same v. most perfect
H. aids h. produced ("und" what?)
w. repeated s. careful V. comparison
a. measured e. individual
v. distributed
V. distribution
g. which came (note "which") f. bears
a. stored
s. carefully h. produced
E. bureau of weights and measures
A. task (to what?)
V. comparison g. which are furnished
HAVE YOU FLAGGED THE "zu"-VERBS?

Für technische Zwecke hat[6] man sich auf eine Normaltemperatur von 20° C zur Ausführung aller **Messungen** geeinigt. Demnach ist ein technischer Meterstab bei 20° genau so lang wie das Urmeter bei 0°, während etwa ein Stahlmeter[4] bei dieser Temperatur um 0,223 mm kürzer wäre.

Z. purposes
A. carrying out M. measurements
g. agreed on D. accordingly
g. exactly w. while
S. steel meter w. would be

VOLUMENBESTIMMUNG FESTER KÖRPER

[10]Ist Berechnung nicht möglich, so misst man den Rauminhalt eines **Körpers**, indem man[4] ihn in **Wasser** eintaucht und[8] das Volumen der verdrängten Wassermenge mittels einer der angegebenen **Methoden** misst.

B. computation m. possible m. measures
i. by —ing e. immerse
u. and (what?) v. displaced m. by means of
a. indicated

Man kann[6] auch den festen Körper unmittelbar in ein[3] teilweise mit **Wasser** gefülltes **Massgefäss** tauchen und beobachten, um wieviel das Wasser steigt. Die scheinbare Volumenzunahme des Wassers ist gleich dem Volumen des eingetauchten **Körpers.**[1]

u. directly Why Rule 3?
t. partly g. which is filled
b. observe u. by s. apparent
V. increase in volume g. equal
e. submerged

Endlich kann[6] man mittels eines Pyknometers das Volumen eines[3] in das **Pyknometer** gebrachten Körpers (z. B. Sand) messen, indem man[4] bestimmt, wieviel Wasser[4] weniger zur Füllung ausreicht, als wenn das ganze Pyknometer[4] ohne den **Körper**[9] mit Wasser gefüllt wird.

e. finally
g. which is brought
m. measure b. determines
a. suffices
Why Rule 9? g. filled

Die Zeit

Der Zeitbegriff entspringt aus der **Erfahrungstatsache**[1], dass jeder Vorgang[4] aus einer Aufeinanderfolge von **Ereignissen** besteht.

OBSERVE THE BOLD-FACED NOUNS AND THE RULES USED TO REMOVE ELEMENTS ON THE RIGHT SIDE OF THESE NOUNS.
Z. time concept V. process A. sequence
E. events b. consists

Wir nennen zwei Zeiten gleich, wenn in ihnen vollkommen gleiche Vorgänge stattfinden.

g. equal, identical
v. completely s. occur

Wenn z. B. der Sand[4] aus dem oberen Gefässe einer Sanduhr in das untere **Gefäss** abläuft, so erfordert das eine gewisse **Zeit.**[10] Erfolgt dann das Ablaufen des Sandes[4] bei umgekehrter Sanduhr aus dem oberen Gefäss in das untere unter genau gleichen **Bedingungen,**[1] so schliessen wir, dass zu beiden Vorgängen die gleiche Zeit[4] erforderlich ist.

G. vessel
a. flows off e. requires d. that
g. certain (Why Rule 10?) u. inverted
o. upper
g. exactly g. similar B. conditions
z. b. at or for both V. processes

Die Einheit der physikalischen Zeitbestimmung wird[6] von der Umdrehung der Erde gegenüber dem **Sternenraum** abgeleitet. Die Gleichförmigkeit der Erddrehung ist[6] weit über das **Mass** der[3] bisher von der **Messung** erreichten **Genauigkeit** vorhanden. Die fundamentale Zeiteinheit ist der **Sterntag,** die Zeit einer Umdrehung der Erde gegenüber dem **Fixsternraum,** die[5] durch Beobachtung zweier aufeinanderfolgender Kulminationen eines beliebigen **Fixsterns** gewonnen wird.

E. unit Z. time determination
w. a. is derived (App. 7, 5, a) g. as opposed to
G. uniformity
w. ü. far beyond e. which is reached
v. present Z. time unit
S. sidereal day U. rotation, revolution
B. observation a. successive
b. arbitrary, optional g. gained

Während eines **Jahres,** also während eines einmaligen Umlaufes der Erde um die Sonne (tropisches **Jahr**), dreht sich die Erde 366,24224 (abgerundet 366 1/4 mal) um ihre **Achse.** Das erkennen wir an der Stellung der Fixsterne zur **Erde.**[1] Da sich während dieser Zeit die Erde[4] einmal um die **Sonne** dreht, so erfolgt die scheinbare Drehung der Erde im Vergleiche zur Stellung der Sonne nur **365 1/4** mal.[1] Wir nennen den 365 1/4ten Teil des tropischen Sonnenjahres einen mittleren **Sonnentag.**[1] Der wahre Sonnentag, d. h. die Zeit zwischen zwei aufeinanderfolgenden Kulminationen der **Sonne,** hat nicht zu allen Zeiten des Jahres dieselbe **Länge,** ist[6] daher nicht zur **Zeitberechnung** geeignet.

w. during
U. rotation, revolution
a. in round numbers
d. that e. recognize S. position
d. since
d. rotates s. apparent
D. rotation V. comparison n. name
w. true S. sun day
a. successive Z. time
L. length Z. time computation
g. appropriate

Zur Zeitmessung ist[6] jeder **Vorgang** geeignet, der[5] sich in regelmässiger Folge in immer derselben **Weise** wiederholt. Vorwiegend werden[6] die Pendelschwingungen und die elastische **Schwingungen**[9] zur Zeitmessungen benutzt, da diese,[4] wie[8] später eingehend dargelegt werden wird, in immer gleichen **Zeiten** erfolgen, wenn die Schwingungsweite[4] genügend gleichmässig gehalten wird.

Z. time measurement g. suited
r. regular F. sequence W. way
w. repeats V. predominately
b. used Z. time measurements
w. as (Note Rule 8.) d. presented
g. equal e. takes place
g. sufficiently g. uniform g. kept

WARMEÜBERTRAGUNG

(Observe all "3" constructions. Give reasons for bold-faced nouns on this page.)

Die Ausbreitung der Wärme von einem Orte zum anderen geschieht auf dreierlei **Weise,**[1] durch Konvektion, Leitung und **Strahlung.**[1]

A. spreading, dispersion O. place
g. happens d. three fold W. way
L. conduction S. radiation

Konvektion. Bei der Konvektion bewegt sich der[3] die **Wärme** tragende Körper selbst von einem Ort zum anderen. Die Fortpflanzung der Wärme geschieht in flüssigen und gasförmigen Körpern vorwiegend in dieser **Weise,**[1] also durch gleichzeitigen Transport von **Materie.**[1] Man erkennt dies bei **Wasser,** das[5] in einem **Gefäss** von unten erwärmt wird, daran, dass kleine schwebende Körperchen, z. B. Sägespäne oder Bernsteinstückchen,[4] an der[3] von einer kleinen **Flamme** erwärmten **Stelle**[9] in die Höhe steigen, und[8] dann an den **Wandungen** nach unten sinken und[8] nun so einen dauernden **Kreislauf** beschreiben.

b. in the case of b. is moved
t. which carries
F. transmission, convection
g. gaseous v. predominately
g. simultaneous
e. recognizes G. vessel
e. heated s. suspended
S. chips of saw dust B. pieces of amber
e. which is heated
n. u. to the bottom Note Rule 8.
b. describe K. cycle

Wenn man[4] ein rechteckig gebogenes **Glasrohr** [9]mit Wasser füllt und[8] dann an einer **Ecke** erwärmt, so steigt das erwärmte, also spezifisch leichtere Wasser hier in die Höhe und sinkt im anderen **Schenkel** wieder nach unten.[2] Das erkennt man gut, wenn man[4] während der Erwärmung in die obere Öffnung einen Tropfen Farblösung oder eine Spur eines festen Farbstoffs (z. B. **Methylviolett)** bringt, und[8] nun den Verlauf des **Farbstreifens** verfolgt.[10] Nimmt man die erwärmende Flamme von der bisher erwärmten **Stelle** fort[2] und setzt sie unter den anderen **Schenkel,** so kehrt der Wasserstrom seine **Richtung** um.[2]

r. rectangular g. bent G. glass tube
Why pick up "m. W."? e. heats
l. lighter
H. top What goes with "sinkt"?
g. well
E. heating Ö. opening T. drop
S. trace F. dye material
u. and (what?) V. course
Why Rule 10? e. heated
f. take away S. place
S. leg, pillar W. water current
u. reverses R. direction

Die[3] unter dem Einfluss der **Erwärmung** entstehenden Luftströmungen in einem Zimmer kann[6] man durch hinein geblasenen **Tabaksrauch** sichtbar machen. Dieser steigt in der Nähe des Ofens in die **Höhe** und sinkt beim **Fenster** wieder herunter.[2] Eine[3] an die Türspalte eines erwärmten **Zimmers** gehaltene brennende Kerze zeigt die Strömung der erwärmten **Luft** an.[2] Die[3] in ruhiger **Luft** brennenden Flammen züngeln nach oben, weil die[3] die **Flammen** umgebende Luft und die Verbrennungsgase wärmer und leichter sind als die übrige **Luft** und[8] daher nach oben steigen. Der Zug in den Lampengläsern und im Schornstein ist ein[3] ebenfalls durch Erwärmung erzeugter Luftstrom, der[5] gleichzeitig die **Wärme** fortführt.

e. which arise E. influence
h. blown in
s. visible
N. neighborhood O. stove
h. sinks down Why Rule 3?
g. which is held b. burning K. candle
a. indicates b. which burn
z. flash u. which surrounds
Note the position of "sind". (Verbs may be found in front of "als" and "wie".)
Z. draft S. chimneys
erz. which is produced
g. simultaneously

Eine grosse Rolle spielt die Wärmekonvektion bei den Winden und bei den **Meeresströmungen.**[1] Die Ostwinde bringen uns im Sommer die Wärme aus den heissen Teilen **Russlands;**[1] sie halten im Winter den Wärmestrom von **Westen** zurück,[2] während die[3] vom **Osten** kommende Luft dann kalt ist. Der Golfstrom bringt uns mit dem Wasser die Wärme aus den tropischen **Gebieten** und erhöht dadurch die mittlere Jahrestemperatur in West- und **Mitteleuropa,**[1] die[5] um annähernd 10° höher ist als die mittlere Jahrestemperatur der **Gegenden,** die[5] im Osten von Nordamerika und Asien auf demselben **Breitegrad** liegen.

What is the subject here?
b. in the case of M. sea currents
h. hot
T. parts What goes with halten?
z. hold back k. which comes
G. gulf stream
G. regions e. increases
m. mean
Note the position of "ist". Why is it here?
G. regions O. east
B. degree of latitude

Die Konvektion ist[6] infolge des Vorhandenseins von Temperaturunterschieden im Innern des Körpers stets mit einer **Wärmeleitung** verbunden, doch ist diese für Flüssigkeiten und Gase nur gering und kann[6] neben der Konvektion bei grösseren **Raumausdehnungen** vernächlässigt werden.

i. as a consequence of V. existence
T. temperature differences I. inside
W. heat conduction (What calls for "verbunden"?)
g. slight n. along with
v. neglected R. space dimensions

WÄRMELEITUNG

Bei der Wärmeleitung geht die Wärme von wärmeren zu kälteren Stellen eines **Körpers** über,[2] während die Teile des Körpers[4] selbst gegeneinander in **Ruhe** bleiben. Es erfolgt also kein Transport der **Materie,** sondern nur ein Energietransport durch die Stosswirkung der schneller bewegten Moleküle des heisseren **Teiles.** Die Wärmeleitung ist[6] also an **Materie** gebunden. Ein[3] mit dem einen Ende in eine **Flamme** gehaltener Nagel wird nach wenigen Minuten auch am anderen Ende so warm, dass man[1] ihn nicht mehr mit den **Fingern** halten kann, ohne[7] sich zu verbrennen.

W. heat conduction W. heat
S. places w. while
e. there
e. takes place
S. collision or shock effect
b. moving T. part
Why Rule 3?
g. which is held w. becomes (why?)
a. other
v. burning (why—ing?)

Wenn man[1] nach der Anordnung von Abb. 653 das eine Ende des Metallstabes von etwa 50cm Länge und 1cm Querschnitt durch eine[3] darunter gesetzte **Flamme** erwärmt, so zeigen bald die[3] in gleichen Abständen in den **Stab** eingesetzten Thermometer Temperaturerhöhungen an,[2] die[5] um so grösser sind, je näher die Thermometer[4] dem erwärmten **Ende** liegen. Die Wärme pflanzt sich von dem erwärmten Ende aus nach dem freien Ende zu durch **Leitung** fort.[2] Nach einiger Zeit wird der Stand in den Thermometern stetig; die beigezeichnete Kurve zeigt den Stand der verschiedenen **Thermometer** an.[2]

A. arrangement, pattern
M. metal rod Q. cross section
g. which is placed d. under it
What goes with "zeigen"? e. which are put
u. s. so much the je. the (See App. 26,1,2,5.)
e. heated
f. is transmitted
L. conduction e. some
s. constant, steady b. drawn-in, here added
a. indicates v. different

Man kann[6] sich den Verlauf der **Wärmeleitung** so vorstellen, dass immer je zwei unmittelbar benachbarte Stabelemente[4] ihre **Temperatur** ausgleichen und dass dieser Ausgleich[4] dauernd erfolgt. Hieraus würde[6] nun folgen, dass nach einiger Zeit der ganze Stab[4] dieselbe Temperatur, nämlich die des unmittelbar erhitzten **Endes** annehmen würde. Nun wird[6] aber gleichzeitig dem Stab durch die umgebende Luft an der Oberfläche dauernd **Wärme** entführt. Der Stab wird[6] also an den nicht erhitzten **Stellen** dauernd abgekühlt, und zwar um so stärker, je grösser die Temperaturdifferenz des betreffenden Stabteiles und der Umgebung ist. Daraus folgt, dass die Temperatur des Stabes an einer bestimmten **Stelle** bedingt ist durch die Wärmezufuhr von der wärmeren Seite des **Stabes** her und durch die Wärmeabgabe nach der kälteren Seite des **Stabes** hin und in die Umgebung des **Stabes.** Der stationäre Zustand ist[6] dann eingetreten, wenn an jeder Stelle des Stabes die Wärmezufuhr[6] gleich der **Wärmeabgabe** ist.

V. course
v. imagine b. neighboring
a. equalize, balance
e. takes place d. constantly
g. entire S. rod
d. d. that of e. heated a. assume
g. simultaneously u. surrounding
e. carried away
w. a. is cooled off (App. 7, 5, a)
u. s. je. the stronger, the larger
b. concerned U. environment
Note position of the verb.
W. heat supply
v,—her (See App. 21,1,f.)
n,—hin (See App. 21,1,i.) U. vicinity
Z. state e. occurred
Wärmea. heat delivery, output

Bei dem beschriebenen Versuch kommen zwei von einander verschiedene **Faktoren**[9] in Frage, nämlich erstens die Leitung der Wärme innerhalb des **Stabes** (die innere Wärmeleitung), und die Wärmeabgabe an die **Umgebung,** die[5] durch Konvektion oder **Wärmeübergang** erfolgt.

b. described V. experiment
F. k. come into question
i. within
W. heat output U. environment
e. takes place

Die (innere) Wärmeleitung ist[6] allein von der Natur der **Substanz** abhängig, ist also eine spezifische Eigenschaft der **Stoffe.** Um[7] ihren Begriff festzusetzen, denkt man sich zwei grosse Gefässe durch eine grosse, 1 cm dicke Platte der zu untersuchenden **Substanz** getrennt und[8] mit einer Flüssigkeit von 1 Grad **Temperaturdifferenz** gefüllt. Es geht dann in jeder Sekunde durch jedes Quadratzentimeter der trennenden,[3] die **Wärme** leitenden Platte eine gewisse **Wärmemenge** hindurch.[2]

i. a. is dependent Note Rule 6.
a. therefore
E. quality f. to establish B. concept
d.—g. one imagines – separated
z. u. to be investigated (App. 12, 2)
F. liquid g. filled
What goes with "geht"?
t. separating l. which conducts
g. certain W. amount of heat

Die[3] in **Grammkalorien** bestimmte Wärmemenge, die[5] in einer Sekunde durch den Querschnitt von 1 cm^2 einer 1 cm dicken **Platte** hindurchgeht, wenn auf beiden Seiten eine Temperaturdifferenz von 1° C herrscht, heisst die Wärmeleitzahl λ (**spezifisches** Wärmeleitungsvermögen des **Körpers.**[1])

b. which is defined
Q. cross section
h. passes through
herrscht prevails

RELATIVBEWEGUNGEN UND KOORDINATENSYSTEME

(An * will be placed where a certain rule is involved. Indicate the rule and the reason for it. Underline all nouns that should be in bold-face type.)

Wenn ein Körper gegen einen anderen Körper seinen Ort verändert, so sagen wir: er bewegt sich in bezug auf den zweiten Körper.* Wir lassen hierbei ausser Betracht,* ob dieser zweite Körper* sich selbst etwa gegen einen dritten Körper bewegt.

l. leave h. in this connection a. out of B. consideration o. whether
z. second e. perhaps b. moves

Wir beziehen also die Bewegung stets auf einen* für die betreffende **Betrachtung** als ruhend angenommenen Körper und erkennen und messen sie als die Veränderung des Betrages und der Richtung des Abstandes von diesem **Körper.*** Die* als ruhend betrachtete Umgebung des bewegten Körpers, auf welche man* die Bewegung bezieht, nennt man das Bezugsystem und definiert es allgemein durch Punkte,* Linien, oder Flächen,* die* als unverrückbar gelten. Kleinere Bewegungen auf der Erdoberfläche bezieht man meist auf einen Punkt derselben, ohne Rücksicht darauf, dass die Erdoberfläche* selbst in Bewegung ist. Für grösser ausgedehnte Bewegungen bilden der Äquator, Nullmeridian und der Meeresspiegel ein geeignetes Bezugssystem.* Die Bewegungen der Himmelskörper werden* in der Astronomie auf gewisse Punkte bzw. durch solche festgelegte Koordinatensysteme unseres Planeten- oder Fixsternsystems bezogen, obwohl ersteres* gegen letzteres und dieses gegenüber anderen Milchstrassensystemen ihrerseits Bewegung zeigen.

b. refer
a. which is assumed a. r. as resting
e. recognize m. measure V. change
B. amount R. direction A. distance
b. which is considered (Why which?)
b. bases B. movement
B. reference system a. generally
u. immovable g. are valid, considered
B. movements E. earth surface
d. of the same R. regard
s. itself a. extended
M. sea level
g. appropriate H. celestial body
w. are (App. 7, 5, a) g. certain
bzw. or f. fixed
b. bases o. although e. former
i. in turn
z. show

Jede Bewegung ist also eine Relativbewegung,* nämlich erfolgend relativ zu einem* als ruhend angenommenen Bezugssystem. Eine absolute Bewegung,* ohne Bezugnahme auf etwas anderes als unbewegt angenommenes, als Bewegung "an sich" ist ein Begriff ohne Sinn.*

B. movement
e. taking place a. which is assumed
B. reference
u. immovable a. assumed
B. concept S. meaning

Wohl aber gibt es für viele physikalischen Vorgänge gewisse Bezugssysteme,* welche* insofern eine gewisse Sonderstellung einnehmen, als sie* nicht materielle Körper als Bezugspunkte benutzen. Man betrachtet z. B. den Weltäther als solches Bezugssystem* und nennt Bewegungen, die* relativ zu diesem System erfolgen — in diesem beschränkten Sinne — absolute Bewegungen.*

g. e. there are
g. certain S. special place
e. occupy
b. use b. considers
n. calls
e. take place b. limited
What rules are removing the verbs?

Wenn die Wege,[4] die die einzelnen Punkte eines Körpers* relativ zu dem Bezugsystem zurücklegen, einander parallel und kongruent sind, so heisst die Bewegung eine fortschreitende Bewegung oder Translation.* Wenn bei der Bewegung eines Körpers eine gerade Linie* unverändert dieselbe Lage beibehält, während die anderen Punkte des Körpers* konzentrische Kreise um diese Achse herum beschreiben, so heisst diese Bewegung eine Drehbewegung oder Rotation.*

P. points
z. cover What calls for "zurücklegen"? "sind"?
h. is called
f. progressive
g. straight u. unchanged
L. position b. retains
K. circles b. describe
D. rotating movement

Wenn während der Bewegung eines Körpers die Achse selbst* auf einem bestimmten Wege fortschreitet, so führt der Körper gleichzeitig eine fortschreitende Bewegung und eine **Drehbewegung** aus.* Beispiel: Die Bewegung eines rollenden Rades.*

w. during
f. progresses b. certain
What goes with "führt"?
D. rotating movement
R. wheel

Gleichförmige und ungleichförmige Bewegung Geschwindigkeit

G. uniform Ges. velocity

Die Bewegung eines Körpers ist vollständig bestimmt, wenn der Ort jedes seiner Punkte* in jedem Zeitpunkt bestimmt ist. Führt[10] der Körper nur eine fortschreitende Bewegung aus*, so genügt es,* den Ort eines einzelnen Punktes des Körpers in jedem **Zeitpunkt** zu bestimmen. Der Weg eines Körpers wird* seine Bahn genannt, wenn man* nur auf die Form des Weges[9] Rücksicht nimmt.* Ist die Bahn des Körpers vorgeschrieben, so ist* der Ort des Körpers in der Bahn durch seine Entfernung von einem gegebenen festen Punkt bestimmt.

v. completely b. defined
Z. point of (in) time Why Rule 10 here?
What does "aus" go with?
gen. it suffices (to what?)
B. path, orbit
R. regard What do you do when the verb is first?
E. distance f. fixed

DIE ÄNDERUNG DER FORMARTEN

(Observe carefully the *, for certain rules are involved at these points. Indicate the nouns that should be bold-faced.)

Im allgemeinen wird* ein fester Körper durch Wärmezufuhr bei einer bestimmten Temperatur flüssig (Schmelzpunkt) und ein flüssiger Körper bei einer bestimmten höheren Temperatur (Siedepunkt) gasförmig; es kann* aber auch der Fall eintreten, dass ein fester Körper* unmittelbar in den Gaszustand übergeht (Sublimation). Umgekehrt wird* ein gasförmiger Körper durch Wärmeentziehung bei einer bestimmten Temperatur im allgemeinen flüssig (Verflüssigungspunkt), ein flüssiger Körper durch Abkühlung fest (Erstarrungspunkt). Der Schmelzpunkt und der Erstarrungspunkt*, ebenso der Siedepunkt und der Verflüssigungspunkt sind* bei einem reinen Stoff, d. h. einem solchen, welcher* nur aus einer Sorte von Molekülen besteht, identisch.

W. heat supply
b. certain f. liquid
g. gaseous e. k. d. eintreten (See App.10,1,b.)
u. directly
G. gaseous state U. conversely
Note that "wird" can take a pred. adjective.
See Rule 6.
A. cooling off
E. solidification point
S. boiling point V. liquification point r. pure
b. consists

In den festen Körpern zeigen die Moleküle keine fortschreitende Bewegung,* sondern man muss* sich vorstellen, dass die Moleküle oder Atome* um eine mittlere Gleichgewichtslage schwingen. In dieser Lage halten sie sich gegenseitig durch anziehende und abstossende Molekularkräfte fest im Gleichgewicht.* Bei Wärmezufuhr wird* die Energie der Schwingungen grösser, es wächst also die Schwingungsweite.* Die Moleküle brauchen mehr Platz,* und der erwärmte Körper dehnt sich aus.* Eine genauere Darstellung siehe in Bd. II, 2.* Wird der Schmelzpunkt erreicht, so bricht ziemlich plötzlich das Raumgitter zusammen,* die Bewegung wird teilweise zu einer fortschreitenden, die Moleküle können* ihren Platz verlassen.

z. show
f. progressive B. movement
v. imagine
G. equilibrium position
g. mutually a. attracting a. repelling
G. in balance
S. vibrations e. w. a. d. (See App. 10,1,b.)
b. need P. room
e. heated a. expands g. more exact
D. presentation Why "if" here? R. lattice
z. collapses p. suddenly
t. partly f. progressive one
v. leave

Bei Flüssigkeiten sind die Moleküle in wälzender und fortschreitender Bewegung,* die* aber nicht so gross ist, dass die Moleküle* ihre gegenseitige Anziehung überwinden. Zwar können* die Moleküle der Flüssigkeiten schon bei Einwirkung geringer Kräfte ihre gegenseitigen Stellungen vertauschen; aber infolge der dichten Lagerung und der häufigen Zusammenstösse entfernen sie sich bei der Wärmebewegung nur wenig und langsam von ihrem Platz.* Die Annahme einer fortschreitenden Bewegung wird* durch die Erscheinung der Diffusion gefordert; denn auch Flüssigkeiten diffundieren, allerdings im Vergleich zu Gasen ausserordentlich langsam, durcheinander.[2] Die Diffusion,* wenn auch erst nach Jahren erkennbar, ist[6] übrigens auch für einige feste Körper nachgewiesen worden, z. B. von Gold in Blei. Daraus geht hervor,[2] dass auch bei festen Körpern ein äusserst kleiner Bruchteil der Moleküle* sich in fortschreitender Bewegung befindet. Es ist das der Teil der Moleküle,* die* durch einen zufällig sehr starken Stoss von ihrer Gleichgewichtslage losgerissen wurden. Näheres über den Bau der Flüssigkeiten und festen Körper siehe Bd. II, 2.*

F. liquids
w. rolling What does "die" call for? "Moleküle"?
g. mutual A. attraction Z. to be sure
ü. overcome
E. effect, application
v. exchange i. due to
h. frequent Z. impacts e. remove
l. slowly
A. assumption f. progressive
g. required E. phenomenon
a. of course V. comparison
a. extraordinarily Note Rule 2.
w. a. even though e. recognizable
ü. moreover n. detected
d. from that h. follows
f. solid ä. extremely B. fraction
s. b. is found, is
e. i. d. (See App. 10,1b.)
z. accidentally S. thrust
l. torn loose N. more details
s. see B. volume

Ferner zwingt die Verdunstung der Flüssigkeiten (und auch vieler fester Körper) zur Annahme einer fortschreitenden Bewegung.* Wenn die* in unmittelbarer Nähe der **Oberfläche** sich bewegenden Moleküle einmal durch eine starke Geschwindigkeitsschwankung aus dem Anziehungsbereich der Nachbarmoleküle herauskommen, also[8] die Oberfläche durchbrechen, so entweichen sie als Gasmoleküle in den* über der **Flüssigkeit**

z. compels V. evaporation
A. assumption
B. movement What does "die" call for?
N. vicinity b. which move
G. variation of velocity
N. neighboring molecules
d. penetrate e. escape

(Give reasons for the * and tell also why certain nouns are bold-faced.)

befindlichen Raum.[10] Denken wir uns den freien Raum über der **Flüssigkeit** geschlossen, so wird* dieser Raum allmählich mit immer mehr **Gasmolekülen** gefüllt, die* nun gegen die Wandungen des Gefässes und auf einander stossen und[8] so teilweise wieder in die Flüssigkeit zurückgetrieben und[8] dort festgehalten werden. Nach einiger Zeit stellt sich ein **Gleichgewichtszustand** ein,* indem die Zahl der* in die **Flüssigkeit** zurückgetriebenen Moleküle[4] ebenso gross wird wie die Zahl der* aus ihr heraustretenden Moleküle. Dann ist* der Sättigungszustand erreicht. Bei Wärmezufuhr, also bei Temperaturerhöhung wird* die Geschwindigkeit der Moleküle in der **Flüssigkeit**, entsprechend auch der Anteil der[3] eine gewisse **Geschwindigkeit** überschreitenden **Moleküle** grösser. Die Zahl der entweichenden Moleküle wird grösser, die Verdunstung wird stärker. *Ist endlich die Geschwindigkeit der Moleküle durch **Warmezufuhr** so weit gesteigert worden, dass die Moleküle* sogar den ganzen Druck der* über der Flüssigkeit lastenden **Luft** überwinden, so siedet die **Flüssigkeit.***

F. liquid b. which is found
Why Rule 10? D.—g. if we imagine closed
a. gradually i. m. more and more
g. against W. walls
G. vessel s. thrust u. and (what?)
z. driven back f. held fast
e. some What goes with "stellt"?
G. state of equilibrium i. since
z. which are driven back (Why which?)
Note position of "wird". h. which emerge
e. reached S. state of saturation
G. velocity e. correspondingly
A. part, portion ü. which exceed
What calls for "grösser"? e. escaping
V. evaporation
What do you do when the verb is first?
i. g. w. has been increased (App. 7, 5, c)
g. entire D. pressure
l. which burdens, weighs s. boils

Wenn eine Flüssigkeit* in einem vollkommen reinen Gefäss an einem erschütterungsfreien **Ort** abgekühlt wird, so kann* die Flüssigkeit oft weit unter den normalen **Erstarrungspunkt** abgekühlt werden, ohne dass sie fest wird (Unterkühlung).* In einem reinen Glasgefäss kann* man reines Wasser bei vorsichtiger Abkühlung bis auf —10°C und tiefer abkühlen. Wenn man* dann das Wasser z. B. durch einen kurzen Schlag mit einem harten Gegenstand gegen das **Gefäss** erschüttert, so tritt plötzliche **Erstarrung** ein, wobei das eingetauchte Thermometer* bis auf 0°C (normaler **Erstarrungspunkt**) steigt.

v. completely
e. shock, vibration free O. place
w. far
E. solidification point a. cooled off
G. glass vessel
v. careful A. cooling
t. lower
k. short S. blow G. object
e. shakes, vibrates p. sudden
e. enters in eing. submerged
s. rises

Eine* der **Unterkühlung** ähnliche Erscheinung zeigen die Lösungen einiger **Salze.*** So lösen sich z. B. in 100g Wasser bei 33°C annähernd 50 g **Natriumsulfat,*** bei 15° C nur etwa 13 g desselben **Salzes**. Wenn eine* bei **33° C** gesättigte Lösung[4] erschütterungsfrei abgekühlt wird, so bleiben die überschüssigen 37 g Salz in Lösung (**Übersättigung**).* Wenn man* die abgekühlte **Lösung** aber erschüttert, oder wenn man* ein Körnchen festen Salzes in die übersättigte **Lösung** fallen lässt, so kristallisiert das überschüssige Salz unter gleichzeitiger **Temperaturerhöhung** aus.* Auch das Natriumthiosulfat verhält sich ähnlich, indem es* sich bei 48°C in seinem **Kristallwasser** auflöst, aber[8] beim erschütterungsfreien Abkühlen auch bei **Zimmertemperatur** flüssig bleibt.

U. super cooling, undercooling
ä. which is similar (Why which?)
a. approximately
e. about
g. which is saturated e. free of vibration
ü. excess
Ü. supersaturation K. granule
l. allows
g. simultaneous
What does "aus" go with?
v. behaves ä, similar i. while
a. but (what?) Note Rule 8.
A. cooling f. liquid

Wenn man* reines Wasser in einem reinen **Gefäss** vorsichtig erwärmt, so kann* man es auf mehrere Grade über den normalen **Siedepunkt** (100°C) erwärmen, ohne dass es* zu sieden beginnt. Auch hier pflegt* bei einer kurzen Erschütterung das Sieden meist mit grosser (oft explosionsartiger) **Heftigkeit** einzusetzen, wobei das Thermometer* auf **100° C** sinkt.

r. clean
v. carefully m. several
S. boiling point e. heat
p. is accustomed (to what?)
E. shock
H. violence e. set in, start
w. in which case

Gase können* noch bei einer **Temperatur** gasförmig bleiben, die* unter ihrem normalen Siedepunkt (**Kondensationspunkt**) liegt. Durch hineingeblasene feine Staub- oder Rauchteilchen erreicht man dann eine plötzliche **Kondensation.***

b. remain S. boiling point
h. blown in
S. dust R. smoke particles e. attains
p. sudden

TRÄGHEIT UND GEWICHT DER MOLEKÜLE

Wir müssen[6] den einzelnen Molekülen Trägheit (Masse) und **Gewicht** zuschreiben. Denn die Erfahrung zeigt, dass beim Zerteilen eines Körpers in beliebig viele Stücke die Summe der Massen und auch der Gewichte der einzelnen Stücke gleich sind der Masse und dem Gewicht des ursprünglichen **Körpers.**[1] Dies Gesetz erweist sich selbst bei feinster **Zerteilung,**[1] aber auch bei Änderung der **Formart,** z. B. beim Schmelzen oder **Verdampfen,** als gültig. Masse und Gewicht eines Körpers sind also die Summe der Massen bzw. Gewichte seiner **Moleküle.**[1]

e. individual, single T. inertia
G. weight z. ascribe E. experience
Z. dismemberment b. arbitrarily
S. pieces
g. equal u. original
G. law e. s. demonstrates itself
A. change
S. melting V. evaporation
a. g. as valid (goes with the verb)
G. weights

Atome

Die Moleküle — für einen gegebenen reinen Stoff von gleicher Grösse und **Beschaffenheit** — sind selbst wieder komplizierte **Gebilde,** die man[1] allerdings bei gewissen vereinfachten Betrachtungen als starre elastische **Kugeln** ansehen kann.

g. given r. pure S. substance
g. like B. nature, composition
G. forms, structures a. of course
v. simplified B. considerations
a. look upon

Die chemischen Erfahrungen haben[6] nun gelehrt, dass alle Moleküle der bekannten Stoffe sich aus etwa 90 **Elementarbestandteilen** zusammensetzen lassen. Man nennt diese Elementarbestandteile die **Atome.** Die Moleküle der einzelnen Stoffe unterscheiden sich dadurch voneinander, dass sie[4] aus verschiedenen Atomsorten sowie aus einer verschiedenen Zahl von **Atomen** bestehen und dass diese Atome[4] ferner in verschiedener **Anordnung**[9] die Moleküle aufbauen können. Solche Stoffe, deren Moleküle[4] nur aus einer **Atomsorte** bestehen, nennt man Elemente.[1] Man hat[6] bis jetzt etwa 90 Atomsorten gefunden. Jede Atomsorte wird[6] mit einem Symbol (z. B. H = Wasserstoff, O = Sauerstoff, S = **Schwefel)** bezeichnet. Die Moleküle werden bezeichnet durch die Symbole der **Atomsorten,**[1] aus denen sie[4] zusammengesetzt worden sind, wobei die Zahl der betreffenden Atome im Molekül[4] als **Index** hinzugesetzt wird. So bezeichnet H_2O ein Molekül, das[5] aus zwei Atomen Wasserstoff und einem Atom **Sauerstoff** zusammengesetzt ist; es ist das das Molekül des **Wassers.** H_2 bezeichnet ein **Molekül,** das[5] aus zwei **Wasserstoffatomen** besteht; es ist das das Molekül des gewöhnlichen **Wasserstoffgases.**[1] Den Atomen kommt ebenso wie den Molekülen, die sich ja aus den Atomen aufbauen, Masse und **Gewicht** zu.[2] Man ist[6] zu der **Erkenntnis** gekommen, dass alle Atome einer Sorte[4] zwar chemisch vollständig gleich sind, dass sie[4] aber unter Umständen in Exemplaren etwas verschiedener **Masse** auftreten können. Man nennt solche chemisch gleichen Atome von etwas verschiedener Masse **Isotope.**[1]

E. experience(s)
b. known s. las. can be e. about
z. composed
e. individual
u. s. are distinguished (App. 11, 4, a)
v. different
b. consist f. further
a. build up, synthesize Why Rule 9?
b. consist
A. types of atoms
What goes with "wird"? What does "wird" mean when used with a participle? an infinitive?
b. designated
z. composed w. in which case
b. concerned h. added
b. designates
S. oxygen
e. i. d. d. that is the (App. 10, 1, b)
W. hydrogen atoms e. i. d. (App. 10, 1, b)
g. ordinary d. A. to the atoms
What goes with "kommt"?
s. a. are built up z. belongs
Erk. knowledge v. completely
U. circumstances
v. different a. appear
e. somewhat

Grenzen des Molekularbegriffes

G. limits

Der[3] in obigem abgeleitete Molekularbegriff bietet bei der Betrachtung der gasförmigen und flüssigen Körper keine **Schwierigkeiten.**[1] Anders ist es bei den kristallisierten festen **Körpern.**[1] Es hat sich gezeigt, dass in diesen unter Umständen die Atome[4] eine viel grössere **Selbständigkeit** haben und dass sie[4] oft nicht in kleineren Gruppen zu **Molekülen** zusammengeschlossen sind. Da jedoch die relative Zahl der Atome[4] auch in diesen **Anordnungen** dieselbe ist wie im flüssigen oder gasförmigen **Zustand** (z. B. für Kochsalz NaCl je ein Atom Na auf ein Atom Cl beträgt), kann[6] man auch in diesem Fall eine **Molekularformel aufschreiben,** als ob auch der feste Stoff[4] aus solchen **Molekülen aufgebaut** wäre.

a. which is derived b. offers
B. consideration
S. difficulties A. different
h. s. g. has been shown (App. 11, 4, c)
S. independence
G. groups
z. merged, combined j. however
A. arrangements Note position of "ist".
Z. state
b. amounts to
a. write down a. o. as if, though
a. w. were built up

WÄRMELEHRE

THERMOMETER. Die Temperatur. Die meisten Körper **erfahren** durch **Wärmezufuhr** eine **Volumenvergrösserung**,* durch **Wärmeentziehung** eine Volumenverminderung.* Ist* die Wärmeentziehung ebenso gross wie die Wärmezufuhr, die* **vorher** das Volumen eines Körpers **vergrössert** hatte, so nimmt der Körper wieder sein **ursprüngliches** Volumen an.* Das Volumen eines festen oder **flüssigen** Körpers ist konstant, wenn der **Wärmezustand*** (Temperatur) **unverändert** bleibt. **Daher** kann* das Volumen eines Körpers als **Erkennungszeichen** für einen **bestimmten** **Wärmezustand** **benutzt werden**. Auch das Volumen eines Gases **eignet sich** hierzu, wenn es* unter unverändertem **Druck** steht.

e. undergo
W. added heat V. volume increase
W. heat abstraction Why Rule 10 here?
v. previously
v. enlarged What goes with nimmt?
u. original
fl. liquid W. condition of heat
u. unchanged d. hence
E. recognition sign b. certain
b. w. be used (See App. 7, 6.)
e s. is suitable D. pressure

Eine **Vorrichtung**, bei der* die **Volumenveränderung** eines Körpers als **Mass** für den Wärmezustand verwendet wird, **heisst** Thermometer.*

V. contrivance V. volume change
M. measurement
h. is called

Wenn ein Glas**gefäss** mit **eng auslaufendem** Glasrohr mit einer Flüssigkeit so weit gefüllt wird, dass noch ein Teil der Flüssigkeit in das Rohr **hineinragt**, so steigt die Flüssigkeit im Glasrohr **in die Höhe**,* wenn das Gefäss* mit der Flüssigkeit langsam erwärmt wird. **Hieraus** folgt, dass die Volumenvergrösserung (**Ausdehnung**) der Flüssigkeit* grösser ist als die des Glases. Bei derselben Temperatur hat die Flüssigkeit einen ganz **bestimmten** Stand im **Glasrohr**.* **Daher** kann* der Stand der Flüssigkeit im Glasrohr als Erkennungszeichen für eine bestimmte Temperatur **verwandt** werden. Von allen Flüssigkeiten **hat*** sich das Quecksilber als die am meisten **geeignete** Flüssigkeit für **Temperaturmessungen** erwiesen.

G. vessel e. narrowly a. tapering
h. projects in
i. d. H. up
h. herefrom
A. expansion
Note position of "ist".
b. certain G. glass tube
d. therefore
v. used
h. s. e. has been shown (App. 11, 4, c)
g. appropriate
T. temperature measurements

Quecksilberthermometer. Das Quecksilberthermometer ist ein **enges** Glasrohr von **überall gleichem** **Querschnitt**,* das* an einem Ende zu einem erweiterten Gefäss **aufgeblasen** (X) und so weit mit **Quecksilber** gefüllt ist, dass das Quecksilber* das Thermometergefäss und einen **Teil** des Thermometerrohres **anfüllt**. Der[3] vom Quecksilber nicht **eingenommene** Raum des geschlossenen Rohres ist gewöhnlich **luftleer**.

Q. mercury thermometer
e. narrow ü. everywhere g. equal
A. diameter Let the X stand for the auxiliary verb. a. inflated Gef. vessel
T. part a. fills up
What does "der" call for?
e. which is occupied l. void of air

[10]**Taucht** man das Quecksilberthermometer in **schmelzendes** Eis, so nimmt der Quecksilberspiegel einen **bestimmten** Stand an,* den er* bei jeder **Wiederholung** desselben **Versuches** wieder annimmt. **Desgleichen** zeigt es einen anderen, aber **stets** wieder denselben Stand, wenn es* in die **Dämpfe** des **siedenden** Wassers gehalten wird. Die Temperaturen des schmelzenden **Eises** und des siedenden Wassers (bei **Atmosphärendruck**) sind also **beständig**. Die **beiden** Punkte des Quecksilberthermometers, die* durch diese beiden Temperaturen bestimmt sind, heissen Fundamentalpunkte (Eispunkt und **Siedepunkt**) des Thermometers.* Der **Abstand** der Fundamentalpunkte heisst der Fundamentalabstand.* Es wird[6] (unter der Voraussetzung, dass der Querschnitt des Rohres, das Kaliber[4], überall **gleich** ist) in 100 gleiche Teile geteilt, wodurch das[3] **zwischen** den Fundamentalpunkten **liegende** Volumen des Rohres auch in 100 gleiche Teile geteilt wird. Jeder* durch die Teilung **gebildete** Abschnitt heisst ein **Grad**.* Man **bezeichnet** den Eispunkt mit 0° Celsius (C) und den Siedepunkt mit 100° C.* (**Infolge** dieser **Einteilung** des Thermometers ist es **selbstverständlich**, dass das Eis* bei 0° schmilzt, dass das Wasser* bei 100° **siedet**.)

Why Rule 10? T. dips
s. melting What goes with "nimmt"?
b. certain W. repetition
V. experiment D. likewise
s. always
D. vapors s. boiling
E. ice
A. atmospheric pressure b. constant
b. two
What calls for "sind"?
S. boiling point
A. distance
What does "wird" call for? "Kaliber"?
g. equal
Why Rule 3? z. between
l. which lies
g. which is formed (Why which?)
G. degree b. designates I. due to
E. classification
s. self-evident
s. boils

RAUMMESSUNG

(Give reasons for the * and also for all bold-faced nouns. Underline other nouns that should be bold-faced.)

Die Grösse des* von einem **Körper** eingenommenen Raumes **heisst** sein Rauminhalt oder sein Volumen.* Das Volumen eines Körpers von regelmässiger Form, z. B. eines Würfels, einer **Kugel**, eines Zylinders, kann* berechnet werden, wenn die Länge **der*** die **Form** bestimmenden Strecken bekannt ist. Es kann* **also** die Volumenbestimmung auf die Ausmessung einer **Länge** **zurückgeführt** werden.

e. which is occupied
R. space h. is called R. space content, volume
r. regular
W. cube K. sphere b. computed
b. which determines
S. lines, distances b. known **E. k. a. d.**
V. z. w. See App. 10, 1, b: start with **therefore** the volume determination, etc.

Zur Bestimmung des Volumens eines Körpers von unregelmässiger Form, z. B. eines beliebigen Steines,* muss* man andere **Wege** einschlagen.

u. irregular S. rock
e. take, adopt, follow

Volumenbestimmung einer Flüssigkeit

Am einfachsten gestaltet sich die Bestimmung des Rauminhaltes einer **Flüssigkeitsmenge,** da diese* leicht ohne Volumenveränderung in eine beliebige **Form** gebracht werden kann.

V. volume determination
a. e. most simply g. s. is formed
d. since
l. easily b. arbitrary
What calls for "kann"?

Die Mensur oder der Masszylinder besteht aus einem meist zylindrischen Glasgefäss,* an dessen Wandungen Teilstriche und Zahlen angebracht sind. Diese geben das Volumen der* in dem **Massgefässe** befindlichen **Flüssigkeitsmenge** an, wenn das Gefäss bis zur betreffenden Marke gefüllt ist.

b. consists of
G. glass vessel W. walls
T. graduation marks
b. which are found (Why which?)
What does "an" go with? b. concerned

Pipetten sind aus Glas hergestellte, meist längliche Gefässe,* die* unten in eine Spitze mit enger Öffnung, oben in ein **Rohr** auslaufen. Eine* am oberen **Glasrohr** angebrachte **Marke** gibt an, bis zu welcher Höhe die Pipette* mit Flüssigkeit **gefüllt** werden muss, damit sie* nach dem Ausfliessen das angegebene Volumen hat. Man füllt die Pipette, indem man* sie mit **der** Spitze in ein Gefäss mit **Flüssigkeit** eintaucht und* dann am oberen **Glasrohr** saugt, bis die Flüssigkeit* etwas über die **Marke** **gestiegen** ist, worauf man* das Glasrohr oben mit dem **Finger** **verschliesst.** Es bleibt die Flüssigkeit auch dann noch in der Pipette,* wenn sie* aus dem **Gefäss** herausgenommen wird. Durch **Lüften** des Fingers kann* man die Flüssigkeit so weit ablaufen lassen, dass sie* gerade bis zur **Marke** reicht.

h. produced m. mostly l. elongated
What does "die" call for? S. point
a. run out, taper a. which is attached
H. height
g. w. m. must be filled (App. 7, 6)
i. by —ing
What does "man" call for? "und"?
s. sucks up
g. risen e. somewhat w. whereupon
v. seals, closes E. b. die F. (See App. 10, 1b.)
h. taken out L. raising
l. let a. run off
r. reaches

Mit Teilstrichpipetten kann* man beliebig abgemessene Volumenmengen der **Flüssigkeit** ablaufen lassen.

a. measured off
V. volume quantities

Büretten sind* ähnlich wie die Messpipetten eingeteilt; sie **sind*** aber am unteren Ende durch einen Hahn oder eine Schlauchklemme verschlossen. Man kann* auch hier beliebige Volumenteile der Flüssigkeit durch Öffnen des Hahnes ausfliessen lassen.

ä. similarly e. divided
What does "sind" call for? H. pet cock
S. tube clamp v. closed
O. opening a. flow out

Massflaschen, Pyknometer, sind Glasfläschen mit eingeschliffenem Stöpsel von genau bestimmbarem Rauminhalt.* Der Stöpsel ist* oft mit einer feinen Bohrung versehen, die* es ermöglicht,[7] ihn auf die* bis zum **Rand** gefüllte **Flasche** aufzusetzen. Die überschüssige Flüssigkeit kann* durch die Bohrung **des Stöpsels** austreten und[8] durch Abwischen mit einem Tuch oder mit **Fliesspapier** entfernt werden. Vielfach ist* das Massfläschchen mit einem **Thermometer** versehen.

M. measuring bottles e. ground in
S. stopper, plug b. determinable
v. provided B. hole
e. makes it possible (to what?)
a. mount g. which is filled
a. escape, come out and—what?
Abw. wiping off T. cloth F. blotting paper
v. provided

Einstellung auf den Meniskus.* Die Oberfläche von Flüssigkeiten ist,* vor allem in engen Rohren, merklich gekrümmt; siehe **Abb. 26.** Man stellt Teilungen so ein,* dass der Teilungsstrich* die Tangente an die Meniskurve bildet.

E. adjustment, setting O. surface
m. noticeably
g. curved What does "ein" go with?
T. graduation mark

MATHEMATIK

GESCHICHTE DER GEOMETRIE†

Die Geschichte einer jeden Wissenschaft ist der Spiegel **ihres** innersten **Lebens**,[1] von ihrem Ursprunge an bis auf den jeweiligen Zeitpunkt ihres **Bestandes**.[1] Sie soll[6] in geordneter, organischer Entwickelung einen Gesamtbegriff des Gebäudes der **Wissenschaft** darstellen,[11] anfangend bei dem **Fundament** und fortfahrend bis zur letzten Stufe seiner **Vollendung**.[1] Dabei soll[6] **sie nicht versäumen**,[7] die verschiedenen Arbeiter an diesem Werk an ihrem rechten Ort und zu ihrer rechten Zeit mit dem Ganzen in gehörige **Verbindung** zu bringen und[8] ihnen jene **Stelle** zuzuweisen, die[5] ihnen als Begründer und Entwickeler der **Wissenschaft** gebührt. So nur ist die Geschichte die Biographie der Wissenschaft selbst.[1] Gleichwie der Geschichte der Menschheit, ihren Taten, Sitten und Institutionen der hohe Einfluss[4] auf die Bildung des **Menschengeschlechts** nicht abgesprochen werden kann, so hat auch die Geschichte jeder Wissenschaft in ihrer engen Sphäre die gleiche Berechtigung und ihre grossen **Vorteile**.[1]

G. history W. science
S. mirror L. life U. origin
j. actual Z. point of time B. existence
g. orderly E. development G. total concept
d. present a. while beginning
f. while continuing S. step
d. in this case v. neglect (to what?)
O. place Z. time
G. totality g. due, proper V. connection
z. assign, allot B. founder
g. is due G. history
s. itself (App. 13,1) d. G. to history
T. deeds S. customs E. influence
a. denied M. human race
W. science
B. justification V. advantages

Das jetzt lebende Geschlecht betrachtet sich als den Erben eines reichen, wissenschaftlichen **Gutes**,[1] und es muss[6] ihm daran **gelegen sein**, zu erfahren, auf welche Weise dieses Gut[4] erhalten worden ist, und durch welche Mittel es bewahrt und vermehrt und[8] unseren späten Nachkommen überliefert werden kann. Seit der Entstehung dieses Geschlechts hat[6] es, im Aufsuchen der **Wahrheit**,[1] vorwärts gestrebt, und jetzt, wo wir[4] eine gebietende Stellung erreicht haben, auf der[5] uns das helle Licht des **Tages** umstrahlt, jetzt müssen[6] wir nur mit innigem Danke auf die **Wege** hinblicken, welche wir[4] seit **Jahrtausenden** zurückgelegt haben, zurück auf die grosse **Pilgrimschaft**,[1] die unsere ersten Väter[4] in **dämmernden** Zwielicht mitten unter den Wilden der **Urwelt** begannen, und die[5] Jahrhunderte durch unter unzähligen **Hindernissen** nur sehr langsam vorrückte, bis sie[4] endlich auf mehr offenen und lichten Pfaden uns in weitere und fruchtbarere **Gegenden** geführt hat.

l. living G. race b. considers
G. good, product, estate e. m. i. d.
g. s. it must be important to it (to what?)
erh. obtained
bew. preserved v. enhanced ü. hand down
N. offspring E. origin
g. strive g. commanding S. place
e. attained u. beams upon
i. sincere, fervent h. look toward
z. covered z. back
d. fading Z. twilight
U. primeval world
u. countless H. obstacles
v. moved forward P. paths
w. broader f. more fertile G. region

Gerade die Mathematik ist es, die[5] sich von allen Wissenschaften am besten zur geschichtlichen **Darstellung** eignet; denn **so dunkel auch** ihre ersten Anfänge[4] bei den verschiedenen **Völkern des Altertums** sind, und so schwer es ist,[7] ihrem Ursprung und ihrer ersten Entwickelung bestimmte **Grenzen** zu geben, so **lässt**[6] sich doch ihr weiterer Verlauf mit einer Wahrheit und Sicherheit darstellen, wie dies[4] bei keiner andern **Wissenschaft der Fall** ist. Dieser Umstand liegt in dem Wesen der Mathematik selbst.[1] Sie ist die Wissenschaft der strengen Wahrheit, der unumstösslichen Gesetze in Form und **Natur**.[1] Ihre Schritte sind[6] immer sicher und fest nach vorwärts, niemals nach rückwärts gegangen.

G. exactly
s.e. is adapted D. presentation
s. auch: however A. beginnings
A. antiquity s. difficult (to what?)
E. development
s. l. can be (See Rule 6F 7, 9.)
d. represent d. F. the case
U. circumstance W. nature
s. strict u. irrefutable
Ges. laws
n. never

Aber merkwürdig ist es, dass gerade die Geschichte dieser **Wissenschaft**[4] zu allen Zeiten bis zu Anfang dieses Jahrhunderts am wenigsten gepflegt worden ist. Was[5] bis zur Mitte des 18. **Jahrhunderts** in dieser **Hinsicht** getan wurde, entspricht unseren **Anforderungen** keineswegs. Erstens erstrecken sich die geschichtlichen mathematischen Abhandlungen jener Zeit meistens nur über einzelne Abteilungen der **Mathematik**, bisweilen auch nur über bestimmte **Zeitpunkte**,[1] und zweitens sind diese Werke fast durchschnittlich eine blosse chronologische Aufzählung der Gelehrten und ihrer **Schriften**.[1]

m. noteworthy G. history
A. beginning J. century
a. w. least g. cultivated
g. done (tun) H. respect
e. corresponds A. requirements
A. treatments m. mostly
b. at times b. certain
z. secondly d. average
b. mere A. enumeration

Erst im 19. Jahrhundert scheint[6] die Geschichte der Mathematik die[3] ihr gebührende **Würdigung** zu erfahren, indem mancherlei Schriften[4] zum **Studium derselben** erschienen sind, von denen[5] an dieser **Stelle** nur erwähnt sein mögen: Kästner, Geschichte der Mathematik 1796-1800; Poppe, Geschichte der Mathematik 1828. u. a.

e. not until s. seems (to what?)
g. which belongs (Why which?)
W. appreciation m. many kinds of
e. mentioned

†R. Klimpert, **Lehrbuch der Geschichte der Geometrie . . .** (Kleyers Encyklopädie)

Die Mathematik ist die vornehmste aller **Wissenschaften**,[1] welche die berühmtesten Philosophen des Altertums[4] als einen **Grundpfeiler** der gesamten **Weltweisheit** ansahen. Sie behandelt die Eigenschaften der Grössen und die Gesetze ihrer **Verbindung**.[1] Alle Grössen teilt man in stetige und unstetige ein[2] und rechnet zu ersteren die Raum- und **Zeitgrössen**,[1] bei denen[5] ein allmählicher Übergang von einer Grösse zu einer andern ohne **Unterbrechungen** stattfindet; zu letzteren dagegen die **Zahlengrössen**,[1] weil zwischen einer Zahl und der nächsten ein Zwischenraum von einer Einheit liegt. Derjenige Teil der Mathematik, welcher[5] sich vornehmlich mit **Raumgrössen** beschäftigt, und welcher[5] höchst vielfältig und nützlich in das menschliche **Leben** eingreift, heisst **GEOMETRIE**,[1] und diese ist es besonders, welche[5] in den folgenden **Zeilen** geschichtlich vorgeführt werden soll.

v. foremost W. sciences
b. famous A. antiquity
G. basic pillar g. entire a. look on
E. attributes Ges. laws V. connection
e. divides s. constant
R. space magnitudes b. in which
a. gradual Ü. transition U. interruption
s. occurs d. on the other hand
Z. number-magnitudes Z. interval, space
d. that (App. 14, 2)
v. chiefly s. is concerned
v. varied, n. useful e. interlock, interfere
h. is called s. is to be
v. presented Z. lines

Obgleich die Spuren der Mathematik[4] am weitesten in den Blättern der **Kulturgeschichte** hinaufreichen, so lässt[6] sie sich doch historisch nicht bis auf ihre ersten Anfänge verfolgen, da sich diese Anfänge,[4] der Natur der Sache nach, bis in die Zeiten der allerersten Entwickelung des gesellschaftlichen **Lebens**, bis in das tiefste Dunkel des **Altertums** verlieren. Von dem Augenblick an, wo die Menschen[4] in gesellschaftliche Verbindungen traten und eine bestimmte Tätigkeit entfalten mussten, um[7] sich die nötigen Lebensmittel zu verschaffen, als sie[4] sich **Hütten** bauten und[8] die Oberfläche der Erde in Felder einteilten, von diesem Augenblick an mussten[6] auch schon allerlei Begriffe von **Grössen** entstehen und[8] bis zu einem gewissen Grade ausgebildet werden. So waren[6] schon die ursprünglichsten Zustände der **Völker** geeignet,[7] mathematische und astronomische **Grundbegriffe** zum Bewusstsein[9] zu bringen, und so entwickelten sich durch die Eindrücke der Sinnenwelt auf den menschlichen Geist geometrische Vorstellungen von einfachem **Gehalt**,[1] wie z. B. die der geraden und krummen Linien und **Flächen**,[1] ja selbst die der einfachsten Figuren und Körper mit solch innerer **Notwendigkeit**,[1] dass die Frage[4] nach Zeit und Ort ihrer Entstehung ebenso wenig gestellt werden kann, als die nach Entstehung der **Zahlbegriffe**.[1] Der Wilde besitzt diese Vorstellungen ebenso unmittelbar wie der civilisierte **Mensch**[1] und vielleicht ebenso klar. Ja selbst den Tieren fehlen Anschauungen dieser Art durchaus **nicht**.[1]

O. although S. traces w. farthest
B. leaves h. reach up l. s. can be
(Rule 6F 7, 9) A. beginnings
v. follow d. N. d. S. n. according to the nature of the matter (App. 15, 3 d, f) D. obscurity
s. v. are lost A. moment g. social
V. connections b. definite
T. activity n. necessary L. victuals
z. v. to procure H. huts O. surface
e. divided A. moment
a. all kinds of B. concepts e. arise
a. developed u. most original
Z. conditions g. appropriate
G. basic concepts z. B. to consciousness
e. s. were developed (See App. 11, 4, b.)
Si. external world
Vors. ideas G. content d. d. that of
k. curved s. even (App. 13, 2)
N. necessity F. question
E. origin g. put
d. those Z. number-concepts
V. ideas u. directly
v. perhaps s. even
d. T. to the animals f. are lacking A. views

Die elementaren geometrischen **Gebilde**,[1] die gerade Linie, die Ebene, der rechte **Winkel**[1], der Kreis, das Rechteck und die einfachsten geometrischen Körper, die Kugel, der Cylinder, das Prisma, die Pyramide usw. fanden eine mehr oder minder häufige **Darstellung**[1] und wurden[6] so aus dem Nebel einer unbestimmten Vorstellung in das Licht einer klaren, sinnlichen **Anschauung** versetzt. Die Erfindung des Lineals, der Setzwage und des Zirkels, ohne welche[5] kein **Steinbau** ausgeführt werden konnte, und der häufige Gebrauch dieser Werkzeuge gab[9] schon zu einer abstrakten Vorstellung der Figuren, welche[5] durch sie dargestellt werden sollten, Veranlassung. Durch die häufige Anwendung des Messens wurde[6] der Sinn für **Grössenverhältnisse** geschärft. Ja es mussten[6] auf diesem Wege schon mancherlei **Erfahrungen** gesammelt werden, manche Aufgabe über die Inhaltsbestimmung der[3] zum Bauen verwendeten Körper musste sich aufdrängen.

G. forms
E. plane W. angle K. circle
e. simplest K. sphere
What do the nouns tell you to do?
D. presentation w. were (App. 7, 5, b)
Ne. fog u. indefinite V. concept
v. put, set E. invention L. straight edge
S. level a. carried out St. stone building
h. frequent G. use W. tools
g. gave (what?) V. idea
d. presented V. cause
A. use M. measuring G. size conditions, proportions g. sharpen
g. gathered E. experiences
I. content-determination v. which were used
a. rise, crowd up (in one's mind)

DIE GEOMETRIE DER GRIECHEN

(An * is placed where a certain rule is involved. Indicate the rule. Underline nouns that should be bold-faced.)

Als 560 v. Chr. Aegypten* durch den König Psametich den Griechen geöffnet wurde, da entstand nicht allein ein lebhafter Handelsverkehr zwischen beiden Ländern,* sondern es zogen auch wissbegierige Griechen nach diesem Lande,* um[7] an den dortigen Hochschulen sich soviel **Wissen** anzueignen, als nationale Engherzigkeit[4] gestatten wollte. So wurden[6] den Griechen durch die Aegypter eine Menge von[3] als unzweifelhafte **Wahrheiten** anerkannten Sätzen geboten, Theoreme, welche* dann erst Wert und Geltung gewannen, wenn sie[4] deren Richtigkeit zu beweisen im stande waren. Um[7] aber zu den[3] oft mit grossen **Schwierigkeiten** verbundenen **Beweisen** zu gelangen, waren[6] zunächst scharfe Begriffsbestimmungen und **Grundsätze** nötig; dazu kamen nun noch gewisse Forderungen,* deren Erfüllung[4] als möglich vorausgesetzt wurde. Die Betrachtung eines gegebenen Satzes A musste[6] zunächst dahin führen, dass A[4] nur dann wahr sein kann, wenn B wahr ist; das Gleiche galt nun wieder für den Satz B usw.,* wodurch man* endlich auf Ursätze und Begriffsbestimmungen zurückkam. Es ist klar, dass hierbei im Anfang die Fortschritte* nur sehr langsam sein konnten und dass in derartigen Untersuchungen die Kundgebung einer neuen Zeit lag. Man kann* die Bemühungen der Griechen zur Begründung einer wissenschaftlichen Mathematik als das Streben der Menschheit bezeichnen,[7] aus dem Zeitalter der ungebundenen, regellosen, oft nur instinktartigen **Geistesbewegung** sich loszuwinden und[8] in das des bestimmten, gesetzlichen **Denkens** überzutreten.

g. opened ε arose
l. active H. commerce b. the two
e. z. there moved (App. 10 1, a, d)
What does "um" call for? a. to acquire
E. narrow mindedness g. permit
w. g. were offered (App. 7, 5, b.) M. amount
S. principles a. which were recognized
W. value G. validity
b. prove d. their
n. necessary d. in addition to that
v. which were connected S. difficulties
g. come z. first of all B. definitions
g. certain F. requirements E. fulfillment
v. presupposed B. consideration
d. there to, to that point
G. same g. held true
w. by which U. original principles
B. definitions
A. beginning F. progress
d. such U. investigations K. announcement
B. efforts
B. establishment
S. striving, endeavour b. designate
Note the call for "to". G. intellectual-movement
s. l. to rid themselves
ü. pass over to D. thinking

Die **Mathematik** und später die **Grammatik** waren der **Ausdruck** dieses **Strebens** und neue, früher nicht gekannte **Erzeugnisse**.* Wie überhaupt alles[4] in der Natur nur in allmählichen **Übergängen** erfolgt, so lässt[6] sich auch hier keine **Grenze** ziehen, aber durch die Zusammenfassung aller Tatsachen steht fest,[2] dass erst in Griechenland die Verhältnisse[4] so günstig zusammenwirkten, um[7] diese neue Richtung ins **Dasein** rufen zu können, wofür das ganze geistige und materielle Leben der Griechen[4] den Beweis liefert. Das Streben der Griechen nach Klarheit und Bestimmtheit ergibt sich zunächst daraus, dass sie* alle Sätze der Arithmetik geometrisch auffassten und[8] so alles zur sinnlichen **Anschauung** zu bringen suchten. In dieser Form lernte, nach dem einstimmigen Zeugnis der hauptsächlichsten **Schriftsteller**,* die[5] über das Leben der ersten griechischen **Philosophen** geschrieben haben, Thales von Milet, als dessen **Geburtsjahr** gewöhnlich das Jahr 640 v. Chr. angegeben wird, in schon vorgerücktem Lebensalter in Aegypten eine Reihe elementarer geometrischer **Lehrsätze**,[1] von denen er[4] sofort Gebrauch machte, um[7] für den Hafen seiner Vaterstadt einen einfachen **Distanzmesser** zu konstruieren.

s. later
A. expression S. striving g. known
E. products ü. anyway
e. takes place a. gradual U. transitions
s. l. can be z. drawn Z. compilation, comprising
T. facts Note the prefix.
V conditions z. worked together
R. trend, direction D. existence
g. intellectual B. proof
l. furnish S. endeavour n. for
B. definiteness e. s. is shown
a. comprehended S. theorems
A. view What is the object of "lernte"?
e. unanimous Z. evidence h. chief
L. life g. written
G. birth year g. ordinarily a. indicated
v. advanced R. series
L. axioms s. at once
G. use H. harbor e. simple

Thales, der erste griechische Philosoph und Stifter der ionischen oder physischen Schule lebte anfangs den öffentlichen Geschäften,* verliess aber dann sein Vaterland,* um* bei den ägyptischen Weisen mathematische und astronomische Studien zu machen. Er stiftete nach seiner Rückkehr aus Aegypten die sogenannte ionische Schule* und starb während der Olympischen Spiele,* denen er* als Zuschauer beiwohnte, gegen 550 v. Chr. Die ionische Schule hat nur das Verdienst,[7] den Boden für die mathematischen Studien in der griechischen **Nation** urbar und eben gemacht zu haben.

Note Rule 1. S. organizer, sponsor
a. at the beginning ö. public
G. business, affairs v. left, verlassen (um—what?)
Note Rule 7; constantly review this rule.
s. founded R. return
w. during
b. attended
V. credit (to what?)
B. soil, basis, ground u. arable

DIE PYTHAGORÄISCHE SCHULE

(Both numbers of the rules and * are given on this page. Give reasons for each.)

Pythagoras wurde[6] auf einer Reise, die seine Eltern unternommen hatten, im Jahre 569 v. Chr. in Tyrus geboren, ging 551, im Alter von 18 Jahren, von Samos nach Lesbos zu Pherekydes,[1] einem bedeutenden Lehrer damaliger **Zeit**,[1] dessen Unterricht Pythagoras[4] 2 Jahre lang genoss. 549 wandte er sich nach Milet zu Anaximander und Thales.* In Aegypten verkehrte er mit den Priestern und lernte die Wissenschaft und Sprache der Aegypter,* sowie die dreifache Schrift derselben, nämlich die hieroglyphische und epistolographische und symbolische.[1] Infolge politischer Ereignisse kam Pythagoras 526 als Gefangener nach Babylon,* wo er* sich die Kenntnisse der **Chaldäer** aneignete und auch mit Juden, Brahmanen zusammentraf. 513, in einem Alter von 56 Jahren,* kehrte Pythagoras, mit reichen Kenntnissen versehen,[11] nach der Heimat zurück[2] und begann nach einer 1½ jährigen Rundreise durch Griechenland auf Samos seine Lehrtätigkeit.*

R. journey E. parents
g. born
A. age **What do the pivot nouns tell you to do?**
b. significant L. teacher
U. instruction g. enjoyed w. turned
v. associated
S. language
n. namely
I. due to
E. events G. prisoner
K. knowledge a. acquired
z. came together, met
What goes with "kehrte"? v. supplied with
L. teaching activity

Die mathematischen Leistungen der pythagoräischen Schule hängen aufs innigste mit ihren philosophischen Grundsätzen zusammen.[2] So berichtet uns Proklos in seinem Kommentar zum Euklid:[1] Nach diesen (Thales etc.) gab Pythagoras dem Wissenszweige der Mathematik die Gestalt einer freien Wissenschaft,[1] indem er[4] die Prinzipien derselben von höherem **Gesichtspunkt** aus betrachtete und[8] die Theoreme derselben in materieller und intellektueller **Hinsicht** erforschte. Er ist es auch, der[5] die Theorie des Irrationalen und die Konstruktion der regelmässigen **Körper** erfand. Mit andern Worten: Pythagoras hat[6] zuerst die Geometrie von der steten Rücksicht auf das praktische **Leben** abgelöst und[8] sie zu einer rein theoretischen Erkenntnis, zu einer **Wissenschaft** erhoben und[8] derselben die sogenannte synthetische **Behandlungsweise** zugeeignet.

L. accomplishment a. i. most closely
G. principles
b. reports
W. branch of science G. form
f. free
i. by (viewing) G. viewpoint
u. and (what?)
e. explor(ing), study(ing) H. respect
r. regular
e. invented
z. first s. constant R. regard
u. and (what?) E. cognition
e. raised
z. assigned B. method of treatment

Die Geometrie bestand, ihrer **Entstehung** gemäss, aus einzelnen Sätzen,[1] die[5] unter sich in einen künstlichen **Zusammenhang** gebracht wurden, in der Art, dass jeder folgende Satz[4] den vorhergehenden voraussetzte. Bevor eine solche Reihe[4] vollständig vorhanden war, muss[6] es einzelne **Sätze** gegeben haben, welche, obgleich nicht streng erwiesen, doch als richtig vorausgesetzt wurden, weil dies entweder der Augenschein[4] lehrte oder weil sie[4] sich beim **Erproben** als wahr zeigten; doch wurden[6] zuletzt auch diese Lücken durch strenge **Beweise** ausgefüllt.

g. according to (See App. 15, 3, a, b) Z. connection
A. manner S. principle, theorem
v. presupposed R. series
v. complete e. m. g. h. there must have been (App. 10, 2, e, f, j)
e. either A. appearance
s. z. were shown; proved
a. filled up L. gaps B. proofs

DIE ALEXANDRINISCHE SCHULE

Die reine Mathematik wurde[6] in der aristotelischen Schule nur als **Hilfswissenschaft** betrachtet, daher auch ihre Entwickelung[4] durch dieselbe keinen merklichen **Zuwachs** erfahren hat. Dass Aristoteles[4] in der **Mechanik** übrigens sehr bewandert war, beweisen die zahllosen Stellen seiner Schriften,[1] in denen er[4] mathematische Skizzen[9] zu Hilfe nimmt oder[8] dieselben diskutiert. Über die **Kugelgestalt** des Himmels z. B. äussert er sich folgendermassen: Da die Kreisfläche* die vollkommenste aller **Flächen** ist, weil sie[4] nur von einer in sich geschlossene **Linie** begrenzt ist, so ist auch die **Kugel** der vollkommenste aller Körper,[1] weil sie[4] durch **Drehung** des **Kreises** entsteht. Dem Himmel muss aber notwendig die vollkommenste **Gestalt** zukommen, mithin ist er kugelförmig.

r. pure
b. considered H. ancillary science
E. development e. undergone, experienced
ü. moreover b. versed
b. prove z. countless S. places
z. H. n. takes to or for aid, makes use of
K. spherical-form H. heavens
a. s. expresses himself
b. bounded
K. sphere v. most perfect
e. arises D. turning d. to
z. belong G. form k. spherical

Während bei Platon der Gegensatz der Rechenkunst und der Zahlenlehre, Logistik und Arithmetik,[4] scharf und bestimmt vorhanden war, ist[6] erst bei Aristoteles ein ähnlicher Gegensatz zwischen der Feldmesskunst und der wissenschaftlichen Raumlehre, Geodäsie und **Geometrie** nachweisbar. Aristoteles weiss, dass eine cylindrische Rolle,[4] welche[5] durch eine Ebene parallel oder geneigt

w. while G. contrast R. art of figures
b. definitely
v. present e. only ä. similar
F. surveying
n. demonstrable w. knows
g. inclined

zur Endfläche geschnitten wird, im aufgerollten Zustande das einemal eine gerade Linie, das anderemal eine Kurve zeigt, dass ihm somit der Cylinderschnitt neben dem Kegelschnitt bis zu einem gewissen **Grade** merkwürdig war.

g. cut Z. condition e. one time
g. straight i. to him
K. conic section
g. certain m. worthy of notice

Das weitaus meiste, was[5] uns über die Geometrie vor **Euklides** überliefert ist, stammt aus einer und derselben Quelle,[1] nämlich aus der Geschichte der Geometrie und Astronomie bis auf Aristoteles von Eudemos von **Rhodos**.[1] Da die Blütezeit desselben[4] zwischen 340 und 310 v. Chr. fällt, so steht er Thales und dessen **Nachfolgern** noch nahe genug, um[7] deren Leistungen genau beurteilen zu können. Eudemos hat[6] darin die früheren Leistungen nicht bloss aufgezählt, sondern[8] die Hauptlehrsätze, den Gang und Umfang ihrer Beweise, die allmähliche Verallgemeinerung derselben und das Zusammenfassen mehrerer von ihnen in ein generelles **Theorem** umsichtig und gründlich geschildert. Gleichzeitig wird[6] Theophrastos von Eresos genannt als Verfasser der Geschichte der Geometrie in vier Büchern, der Astronomie in sechs Büchern und der Arithmetik in einem Buche.[1] Besonders aus des Ersteren Werk haben[6] die Schriftsteller geschöpft, die[5] über die astronomischen und mathematischen Entdeckungen der griechischen **Philosophen** geschrieben haben.

w. by far w. (what) that
ü. handed down
n. namely G. history
d. since (App. 25, 2)
z. between
d. his (App. 22, 4, a) d. their (App. 22, 4, b)
L. accomplishments b. judge
a. enumerated b. merely
H. main theorems U. scope B. proofs
a. gradual V. generalization
Z. comprising m. of several
g. described g. at the same time
g. called, named (Note verb before "als".)
V. writer, author
B. especially g. drawn
E. discoveries g. written

Das Werk des Euklides ist[6] wie kein anderes in der Geschichte der griechischen **Mathematik** epochmachend gewesen. Viele versuchten[7] die Elemente der Mathematik von einem andern Gesichtspunkt aus und in anderer **Ordnung** zusammenzustellen, aber keiner hat[6] die euklidische Klarheit und **Übersichtlichkeit** erreicht. Sein Werk war das erste vollständige Lehrbuch des elementaren Teiles dieser Wissenschaft,[1] der[5] dadurch zu einem bestimmten **Abschnitt** gelangt war. Auf Grundlage dieser zusammenhängenden Darstellung der Elemente konnte[6] ein weiterer Ausbau der **Wissenschaft** schneller und sicherer vor sich gehen, und jene **Undeutlichkeit** vermieden werden, die[5] die Beweise der älteren **Geometer** durchweg kennzeichnet. Auch für die Geschichte der Mathematik ist das euklidische Werk ein schätzbarer Beleg,[1] indem es[4] das erste ausführliche Denkmal der mathematischen Kenntnisse der **Griechen** ist, das[5] auf uns gekommen. Mit ihm verschwindet jenes Dunkel, das[5] die tiefere Einsicht in den Entwickelungsprozess der voreuklidischen **Periode** erschwert hat; von nun an können[6] wir die wissenschaftlichen Fortschritte auf diese sichere **Grundlage** zurückführen, wodurch[5] der Zusammenhang der **Sache** deutlicher hervortritt.

What does "ist" call for? w. as
G. history
v. tried (to what?)
G. viewpoint O. arrangement
z. to put together K. clearness
e. reached U. clearly arranged
v. complete T. part
g. reached, come G. basis z. coherent
A. development
v. s. g. go on, proceed U. unclearness
v. avoided B. proofs
k. characterizes, marks s. estimable B. proof
a. extensive D. monument
K. knowledge
v. disappears D. obscurity E. insight
e. made difficult, complicated
F. progress
z. trace back
h. stands out

Ohne Zweifel sind[6] vor Euklides schon gute Elemente der **Geometrie** vorhanden gewesen, die er[4] benutzen konnte. Proklos nennt vier oder fünf frühere Verfasser von Elementen,[1] Euklid aber habe[6] die Entdeckungen seiner Vorgänger vervollkommnet und[8] besonders die noch mangelhaften **Beweise**[9] zur völligen Schärfe gebracht. Pappos bemerkt: Vorzüglich aber dürfte[6] man ihn in bezug auf die Elemente der **Geometrie** bewundern, wegen ihrer Ordnung und Auswahl der[3] für die **Elemente** zubereiteten Theoreme und **Probleme**.[1] Denn er nahm nicht alles auf,[2] was er[4] hätte sagen können, sondern nur das, was[5] sich in der **Reihe** behandeln lässt.

O. without Z. doubt
v. present b. use
V. writers
E. discoveries V. predecessors
m. faulty
B. proofs S. sharpness, acuity, succinctness
V. particularly i. b. a. in respect to
b. admire w. because of
z. which were prepared
a. took up h. s. k. could have said
s. l. can be

Durch Euklid ist[6] der Begriff der Elemente für alle **Zeit** festgestellt worden, und unsere heutigen Lehrbücher der Elementargeometrie behandeln im Wesentlichen denselben Umkreis von Lehren,[1] wie Euklids 13 Bücher;[1] nur dass sie[4] die platonischen Körper, auf welche das Altertum[4] herkömmlich so grossen **Wert** legte, mit weniger **Ausführlichkeit** behandeln.

B. idea i. f. w. (App. 7, 5, c)
f. established
b. treat i. W. essentially
U. circle, scope
h. traditionally
l. laid A. detail

ARCHIMEDES

Bald nach Euklid zeigte sich eine neue Erscheinung,* welche* von jetzt an für immer festgehalten wurde und die* für die praktische Anwendung der Mathematik von der grössten **Wichtigkeit** war: die Einführung der Arithmetik in die **Geometrie.*** Diese Neuerung verdankt man Archimedes.[1] Kein Geometer vor ihm hat* jemals eine Linie durch Zahlen dargestellt oder[8] eine Rechnung zu geometrischen **Zwecken** ausgeführt; dieses war[6] den Feldmessern, überhaupt jenen **Personen** vorbehalten, deren Geschäft es war,[7] die Geometrie auf die gewöhnlichen Verhältnisse des **Lebens** anzuwenden.

B. soon s. s. was shown (App. 11, 4)
f. maintained
A. use W. importance
E. introduction
N. innovation v. owes
j. ever d. presented o. or (what?)
a. carried out Z. purposes
v. reserved d. whose
G. business (to what?) V. conditions a. to use

Archimedes, geb. 287 v. Chr. zu Syrakus, war neben den Alexandrinern unstreitig das grösste mathematische Genie des Altertums,* der eigentliche Schöpfer der Mechanik und der höheren Geometrie.* Er brachte diese Wissenschaften auf den höchsten Punkt der Entwickelung,* den sie* im Altertum erreicht haben und den sie[4] 19 Jahrhunderte lang, bis auf Galilei und Descartes nicht zu übersteigen vermochten. Seine mechanischen und geometrischen Schriften bilden eine einzige fortlaufende Kette von **Erfindungen,**[1] die[5] wohl durch das, was[5] verloren gegangen, noch einen beträchtlichen **Zuwachs** erhalten würden.

n. along with
u. unquestionably g. greatest
e. real S. creator
W. sciences What do the pivot nouns tell you to do? E. development
e. reached J. centuries
v. were able ü. surpass
S. articles, writings f. continuous
E. inventions v. lost
b. considerable Z. increment

Aus dem Leben Archimedes sind[6] nur einzelne hervorragende **Züge** bekannt. Er war Verwandter des Königs **Hiron,*** dessen **Liebe** zu den Wissenschaften[4] ihn in Syrakus festhielt. Sein brennender Eifer für die Wissenschaften hinderte ihn sogar an den notwendigsten Geschäften des täglichen Lebens.* Diener mussten[9] ihn mit Gewalt aus seinem Arbeitskabinet zur **Tafel** reissen. Dieser Zug seines Lebens wird[6] denn auch als die Ursache seines **Todes** angegeben. Archimedes wurde[6] bei der Erstürmung der Stadt Syrakus (212 v. Chr.) von einem[3] in sein **Zimmer** eindringenden römischen Soldaten, während er[4] in mathematische Figuren vertieft auf dem **Boden** sass, niedergestossen. Mehr um diese als um sein Leben besorgt,[11] hatte[6] er jenem das berühmte **Nole turbare circulos meos!** (Verdirb mir meine Kreise nicht) zugerufen. Der[3] über solche **Gleichgültigkeit** erzürnte Krieger machte aber Gebrauch von seiner **Waffe.**[1] Auf Archimedes Grabmal wurde[6] nach seinem Wunsch ein Cylinder mit einer einbeschriebenen **Kugel** gezeichnet, als bescheidener Repräsentant seiner grossen Erfindungen.*

e. single h. outstanding
Z. features V. relative
f. held b. fervent
E. zeal h. prevented
Give reasons for the * or the numbers of the rules.
G. power r. tear, pull Z. feature
U. cause an. indicated
E. storming, siege
e. who penetrated (Why who?)
s. sat n. cast down
b. while worried L. life
j. to the former b. famous
V. ruin K. circles
e. who was angered G. use
W. weapon W. wish
e. inscribed g. marked
b. modest E. inventions

Das fruchtbarste Wirkungsfeld des archimedischen Geistes war die Flächen- und Inhaltsberechnung krummer Linien und Oberflächen.* Seine noch vorhandenen geometrischen Schriften enthalten in systematischer Reihenfolge: die Ausmessung des Kreises,* die des Cylinders und der Kugel,* die Quadratur der Parabel* und die Inhaltsberechnung der Konoiden und Sphäroiden.* Dann folgen zwei Abhandlungen über die Spirallinien und die Schwerpunktsbestimmungen ebener Figuren,* mit Hilfe letzterer er* die Quadratur der **Parabel** bestimmte.

f. most fruitful W. field of work
F. area, surface calculation
v. existing
e. contain R. series
A. measurement K. circle
I. content calculation
f. follow A. treatments
S. gravity point determination
(See compound nouns App. pages 21/22.)

Unter dem, was Archimedes[4] für die Geometrie des **Raumes** leistete, ist zu erwähnen, dass er[4] zu den[3] bereits von **Euklid** erschöpfend behandelten fünf regelmässigen Körpern 13 halbregelmässige **Körper** erfand, welche[5] durch regelmässige Vielecke von mehr als nur einer **Gattung** begrenzt werden. Die Kubierung der Konoide und Sphäroide ist eine der geistreichsten archimedischen **Schöpfungen.***

l. accomplished e. mention
e. exhaustively b. which were treated (Why which?)
r. regular V. polygon b. bounded
g. ingenious S. creations

DAS 17. JAHRHUNDERT

Die Bestrebungen des 17. Jahrhunderts richteten sich in der Geometrie hauptsächlich auf die Inhaltsberechnungen krummer Linien und Oberflächen.* Die Methode, die schon der grosse Archimedes[4] seinen genialen **Untersuchungen** zu Grunde[9] legte, die des Unendlichkleinen, gewann immer mehr an Ausdehnung* und erreichte zuletzt in der Infinitesimalrechnung ihre wissenschaftliche Krone.* Noch ehe das 16. Jahrhundert* zu Ende ging, erhob sich am wissenschaftlichen Himmel Deutschlands ein Gestirn,* dessen Glanz die schwarze Nacht[4], die[5] unser Vaterland in der ersten Hälfte des 17. **Jahrhunderts** bedeckte, nicht zu verdunkeln vermochte: Johann Kepler, ausgerüstet[11] mit wunderbar reicher Geisteskraft,[1] mit einer fast dämonischen Erfindungsgabe,[1] mit einer seltenen Ausdauer in der Arbeit,* verband die kühnsten Gebilde der Phantasie mit dem tiefen geometrischen Blick des Mathematikers.* In ihm lebte das Bewusstsein, dass der Charakter der Naturgesetze[4] mathematisch ist, und die Geometrie war ihm der Schlüssel zu den Geheimnissen der Welt.* Auf der Universität Tübingen durch Michael Mästlein in das kopernikanische System eingeweiht,[11] fasste Kepler die Idee,[7] dieses **System** mathematisch zu begründen; der Schöpfer aller Dinge konnte[6] nur nach den ewigen Wahrheiten[1] und nach der Harmonie, die[5] sich in den geometrischen **Gebilden** ausdrücken, den Bau der **Welt** geordnet haben. Dies zu entdecken, wurde fortan die Aufgabe seines Lebens.[1]

B. efforts r. s. were directed (See App. 11,4,b.)
h. chiefly I. content-calculations
k. curved O. surfaces U. investigations
l. z. G. to take or lay as a basis for
A. expansion e. attained z. finally
w. scientific N. still e. before
e. s. was raised H. sky
G. star, constellation d. whose G. brilliance
H. half
v. obscure
a. equipped
E. gift of invention s. rare
A. perseverance k. most bold, boldest
B. glance, view
B. consciousness
N. natural laws
S. key G. mysteries
Why Rule 11? e. initiated
f. got, received I. idea (to what?)
b. establish S. creator
e. eternal W. truths
s. a. are expressed (Why 'are'?)
g. arranged e. discover
A. task

Nach mehreren erfolglosen Versuchen kam ihm der Gedanke,[7] den Grund der sechs Planetenbahnen um die Sonne in den fünf regulären Körpern der **Geometrie** zu suchen; von jeher hatten[6] diese Körper in den Spekulationen der Pythagoäer,[1] sowie bei den mystischen Philosophen des 15. und 16. Jahrhunderts eine bedeutende **Rolle** gespielt. Dieser kosmologische Traum fand den grössten Beifall der ersten Astronomen der damaligen Zeit und begründete Keplers wissenschaftlichen Ruf.[1] Kein Wunder, dass Kepler* die mathematische Theorie der regulären **Figuren** weiter verfolgte. Sein eminentes mathematisches Talent,* besonders auf dem Gebiet der Geometrie,* tritt hierbei aufs glänzendste zu Tage.* Ausser den regulären Polygonen im gewöhnlichen Sinne zieht er die sogenannten Sternpolygone,* ausser den fünf regularen Körpern auch die dreizehn halbregulären Körper von **Archimedes** in Betracht.[9] Zugleich sann Kepler auf die Bildung neuer Körper,* indem er* Kreis, Ellipse, Parabel, Hyperbel um Durchmesser,* Sehnen, Tangenten und andere **Linien** rotieren liess. So stieg die **Anzahl** der Körper,* zugleich mit den bisher betrachteten, auf 92 und er richtete nun an die Geometer die Aufforderung,*[7] der Inhaltsbestimmung derselben **ihre Aufmerksamkeit**[9] zu widmen.

m. several e. unsuccessful V. attempts
G. thought (to what?) G. basis
P. planet-orbits K. bodies
v. j. from the beginning h. had (what?)
s. as well as
b. significant g. played
T. dream B. approval
d. that b. established
R. reputation
v. followed
b. especially G. field
t. z. T. appeared a. g. most brilliantly
g. ordinary S. sense
a. outside of the
d. thirteen i. B. inconsideration
Note Rule 9. Z. at the same time
D. diameter
l. r. allowed to rotate A. number
z. at the same time b. considered
r. directed A. challenge (to what?)
I. determination of content w. devote

Die alten Geometer bedienten sich zu gewissen Zwecken der Exhaustionsmethode,[1] z. B. Euklid, um* zu beweisen, dass der Flächeninhalt eines Kreises einem **Dreieck** gleich ist, dessen Basis[4] der Umfang und Höhe der Radius ist; noch mehr Archimedes, z. B. bei der Darstellung der Fläche der Parabel und der Berechnung der Konoide.[1]

b. s. made use of g. certain
Z. purposes b. prove
F. area content
U. circumference
D. presentation
B. computation

Die Geometrie bietet uns also unter allen Zweigen der Mathematik das lehrreichste Bild.[1] Wir sehen, wie die Menschen[4] vom Anfang des reinen Denkens an das Einzelne zu fassen suchten und[8] nur dieses mit **Sicherheit** erkennen wollten und konnten.

b. offers
Z. branches l. instructive w. how
D. thinking
Note Rule 8. S. surety e. recognize

VERSCHIEDENE GEBIETE

Erdbeben †

Seitdem in dem ersten Buche dieses Werkes (1845) die allgemeine Darstellung der Erdbeben-Phänomene[4] erschienen ist, hat[6] sich das Dunkel, in welches der Sitz und die Ursachen **derselben** gehüllt sind, wenig vermindert; aber durch die vortrefflichen Arbeiten von Mallet und Hopkins (1847) ist[6] über die Natur der Erschütterung, den Zusammenhang scheinbar verschiedenartiger Wirkungen, und über die Trennung begleitender oder gleichzeitig eintretender physikalischer und chemischer **Processe**[9] einiges Licht verbreitet worden. Mathematische Gedankenentwichlung kann,[6] nach Poissons Vorgang, hier wie überall, wohltätig wirken. Die Analogien zwischen den Schwingungen fester Körper und den Schallwellen der **Luft**,[1] auf welche Thomas Young schon aufmerksam gemacht, sind in den theoretischen Betrachtungen über die Dynamik der **Erdbeben** besonders geeignet,[7] zu einfacheren und befriedigenderen **Ansichten** zu führen.

s. since E. earthquake
D. presentation
D. obscurity S. location U. causes
g. wrapped v. diminished v. excellent

E. shock Z. connection v. of different type
W. effects T. separation b. of accompanying

v. spread G. thought development
w. beneficent w. act, have an effect
S. vibrations S. sound waves
a. g. called attention
B. considerations
g. appropriate (to what?) e. simpler b. more satisfactory A. views

Räumliche Veränderung, Erschütterung, Hebung und Spalten-Erzeugung bezeichnen den wesentlichen Charakter des **Phänomens**.[1] Es ist zu unterscheiden die wirkende Kraft, welche als Impuls[9] die Vibration erregt; und die Beschaffenheit, Fortpflanzung, Verstärkung oder Verminderung der **Erschütterungswelle**.[1] Ich habe in dem Naturgemälde beschrieben, was[5] sich zunächst den **Sinnen** offenbart; was ich Gelegenheit[7] gehabt, so viele Jahre lang selbst zu beobachten auf dem Meere, auf dem Seeboden der **Ebenen**, auf Höhen von acht- bis fünfzehntausend **Fuss**, am Kraterrande entzündeter **Vulkane**, und in Regionen von Granit und Glimmerschiefer, dreihundert geographische Meilen von allen **Feuerausbrüchen** entfernt; in Gegenden, wo die Einwohner in gewissen Epochen die Zahl der Erdstösse nicht mehr als wir[1] in Europa die Zahl der **Regenschauer** zählen; wo Bonpland und ich[1] wegen Unruhe der **Maultiere** absteigen mussten, weil in einem Walde der Boden[4] 15 bis 18 **Minuten** lang ununterbrochen erbebte.

R. spatial V. change H. lifting S.E. fissure production w. essential
(Disregard the "Es".)
e. excites B. nature F. transmission
V. strengthening V. diminution W. shock-wave
z. first of all s.o. is revealed
G. opportunity (to what?)
M. sea E. plains
K. crater edge e. of ignited, active
G. mica-schist
M. miles e. removed
G. regions g. certain E. earth-quakes
z. count
w. because of U. unrest
M. mules B. floor, ground
u. uninterruptedly e. shook

Indem man,[4] wie wir[4] bereits oben angedeutet haben, die Betrachtungen über das, was[5] den Impuls zur Erschütterung gibt, sorgfältig von denen über das Wesen und die Fortpflanzung der **Erschütterungswellen** trennt, so unterscheidet man dadurch zwei Klassen der Probleme von sehr ungleicher **Zugänglichkeit**. Die erstere kann[6] nach dem jetzigen Zustande unseres Wissens zu keinen allgemein befriedigenden **Resultaten** führen, wie bei so vielem, in dem wir[4] bis zu den letzten **Ursachen** aufsteigen wollen.

Eine zweite, unendlich wichtigere Gattung von Erdbeben ist die sehr häufige, welche[5] grosse Ausbrüche von Vulkanen zu begleiten oder ihnen voranzugehen pflegt: sei es, dass die Vulkane,[4] wie unsere europäischen, Lavaströme ergiessen, oder wie Cotopari und Pichiaha[4] nur verschlackte Massen, Asche und **Dämpfe** ausstossen. Für diese Gattung sind[6] vorzugsweise die Vulkane als Sicherheits-Ventile zu betrachten. Die Erdbeben hören **auf**, wenn der grosse **Ausbruch**[4] erfolgt ist.

I. by a. indicated B. considerations
E. shaking, tremor s. carefully
W. nature F. transmission
E. vibration-waves t. separating u. distinguish
Z. accessibility
Z. condition
b. satisfactory
U. causes
G. type, class, kind
h. frequent (one) b. accompany
v. precede p. is accustomed
e. pour forth, discharge
v. slaglike a. discharge
G. type v. preferably
b. to be considered (App. 12 1) a. cease
A. eruption

†Alexander von Humboldt, **Kosmos**

Landschaftmalerei in ihrem Einfluss auf die Belebung des Naturstudiums

Wie eine lebensfrische Naturbeschreibung*, so ist* auch die Landschaftmalerei geeignet,[7] die Liebe zum **Naturstudium** zu erhöhen. Beide zeigen uns die Aussenwelt in ihrer ganzen gestaltenreichen Mannigfaltigkeit*; beide sind fähig,[7] nach dem Grade eines mehr oder minder glücklichen Gelingens in Auffassung der Natur, das Sinnliche und das **Unsinnliche** anzuknüpfen. Das Streben nach einer solchen Verknüpfung bezeichnet das letzte und erhabenste Ziel der darstellenden **Künste.*** Diese Blätter sind[6] durch den wissenschaftlichen Gegenstand, dem sie[4] gewidmet sind, auf eine andere **Ansicht** beschränkt; es kann[6] hier der Landschaftmalerei nur in der **Beziehung** gedacht werden, als sie[4] den physiognomischen Charakter der verschiedenen **Erdräume** anschaulich macht und[8] die Sehnsucht nach fernen **Reisen** vermehrt, und[8] auf eine eben so lehrreiche als anmutige Weise zum Verkehr mit der freien **Natur** anreizt.

l. fresh as life N. nature description
L. landscape painting g. appropriate, apt
e. enhance b. both A. outer world g. form rich
M. variety f. able (to what?) G. degree
Ge. success A. comprehension
S. material U. unphysical S. striving
V. connection b. marks e. most sublime
Z. goal d. descriptive, representational B. pages, sheets G. object g. devoted
A. view b. limited
B. respect, relation g. thought of
v. different a. clear, perceptible
S. longing n. for R. journeys v. increases
l. instructive a. gracious V. association
a. stimulates

In dem Altertum, welches wir[4] vorzugsweise das **klassische** nennen, bei den Griechen und **Römern**, war nach der besonderen Geistesrichtung dieser Völker die Landschaftmalerei eben so wenig als die dichterische Schilderung einer Gegend ein[3] für sich bestehendes Objekt der **Kunst**. Beide wurden* nur als Beiwerk behandelt. Anderen Zwecken untergeordnet,[11] diente die Landschaftmalerei lange nur als Hintergrund historischer Compositionen oder als zufälliges Ornament in **Wandgemälden.** Auf eine ähnliche Weise versinnlichte der epische Dichter durch eine malerische Beschreibung der Landschaft—ich könnte wieder sagen des Hintergrundes, vor dem[5] die handelnden Personen sich bewegen—das Lokal eines geschichtlichen **Vorganges**. Die Kunstgeschichte lehrt, wie allmählig das Beiwerk[4] zur Hauptsache der **Darstellung** wurde; wie die Landschaftmalerei, von der historischen gesondert,[11] als eine eigene **Gattung auftrat**; wie die menschlichen Gestalten[4] bald nur als Staffage einer Berg- und Waldgegend, eines Seestrandes oder einer **Gartenanlage** gedient haben. Die Trennung zweier Gattungen, der Geschichts- und Landschaftmalerei, ist[6] so, den allgemeinen Fortschritt der Kunst auf verschiedenen Bildungsstufen begünstigend,[11] allmählig vorbereitet worden, und man hat mit Recht bemerkt, dass, wenn überhaupt bei den Alten die Malerei[4] der Plastik untergeordnet blieb, insbesondere das Gefühl für die landschaftliche Schönheit,[4] welche der Pinsel[4] wiedergeben soll, kein antikes, sondern ein modernes **Gefühl** ist.

A. antiquity v. preferably
n. call
G. intellectual trend
d. poetic S. description G. region
b. which exists O. objective B. accessory
Z. purposes u. (while) subjected to d. served
z. accidental W. wall painting ä. similar
v. convey clear idea
B. description
h. acting s.b. move
V. event, process K. art history
H. main matter D. presentation
g. while separated
e. specific G. type G. forms, figures
S. figures (in a landscape.) B. mountain S. sea shore g. served T. separation Ga. types, genre
F. progress v. different B. cultural levels
beg. (while) favoring v. prepared
b. noted
ü. at all, in general u. subordinate G. feeling
P. painter's brush w. reproduce
a. ancient

Graphische Andeutung von der Eigentümlichkeit einer Gegend musste[6] sich in den ältesten Gemälden der **Griechen** finden, wenn, um[7] einzelne **Beispiele** anzuführen, nach Herodots Berichte Mandrokles von Samos[4] für den grossen Perserkönig den Übergang des Heeres über den **Bosportus** darstellen liess, oder wenn Polygnot[4] in der Lesche den Übergang von **Troja** malte. Unter den Bildern, die der ältere Philostrat[4] beschreibt, wird sogar eine **Landschaft** erwähnt, in der man[4] den Rauch aus dem Gipfel eines **Vulkans** aufsteigen und Lavaströme sich in das nahe **Meer** ergiessen sah.

a. indication E. peculiarity G. region
G. paintings
e. single B. examples a. cite B. reports
Ü. crossing
d. l. had presented
L. ante-chamber, clubhouse at Delphis
s. even
e. mentioned G. peak
a. rise up (with "sah") e. pour (with "sah")

Die spätere christliche Malerei blieb[6] nach ihrem Kunstcharakter, von Constantin dem Grossen an bis zu dem Anfange des Mittelalters, der echt **römischen** nahe verwandt. Es offenbart uns dieselbe einen Schatz von alten Erinnerungen sowohl in den Miniaturen,[1] welche[5] prachtvolle und wohlerhaltene Manuscripte zieren, wie in den selteneren Mosaiken derselben **Epochen.** Rumohr gedenkt eines Psalmen-Manuscriptes in der Barberina zu **Rom,** wo in einer Miniatur "David die Harfe schlägt, von einem anmutigen Haine umgeben,[11] aus dessen Gezweige Nymphen[4] hervorlauschen. Diese Personification deutet auf die antike Wurzel des ganzen **Bildes.**" Seit der Mitte des sechsten Jahrhunderts, wo Italien[4] verarmt und politisch zerrüttet war, bewahrte vorzugsweise die byzantinische Kunst im östlichen Reiche den Nachklang und die schwer erlöschenden Typen einer besseren Zeit.[1] Solche Denkmäler bilden den Übergang zu den Schöpfungen des späteren **Mittelalters,** nachdem die Liebe zu der Ausschmückung der Manuscripte[4] sich aus dem griechischen Orient nach den Abendländern und dem Norden, in die fränkische Monarchie, unter den Angelsachsen und in die **Niederlande** verbreitet hatte. Es ist daher von nicht geringer Wichtigkeit für die Geschichte der neueren **Kunst,** "dass die berühmten Brüder Hubert und Johann von Eyck[4] dem Wesentlichen nach aus einer Schule der **Miniaturmaler** hervorgegangen sind, welche[5] seit der zweiten Hälfte des 14ten Jahrhunderts in Flandern eine so grosse **Vollkommenheit** erlangt hatte."

s. later M. painting K. art character
A. beginning
e. genuine n.v. closely related o. reveals
(Omit "es".) S. treasure E. memories
p. magnificent w. well preserved z. adorn
s. more rare g. is mindful, refers to

H. harp s. plays a. charming H. grove
u. surrounded h. listen, hearken
d. points W. root
M. middle v. impoverished
z. disrupted b. preserved v. especially
N. echo s. e. die-hard
D. monuments
S. creations
A. embellishment, decoration
A. countries of the west
A. Anglo-Saxons
v. spread W. importance
b. famous
d. W. nach in the main

H. half
V. perfection e. acquired, attained, achieved

Sorgfältige Ausbildung des Landschaftlichen findet sich nämlich zuerst in den historischen Bildern dieser Brüder von **Eyck.**[1] Beide haben Italien nie gesehen; aber der jüngere Bruder Johann genoss den Anblick einer südeuropäischen **Vegetation,** als er[4] im Jahre 1428 die **Gesandschaft** begleitete, welche der Herzog von Burgund Phillipp der Gute[4] wegen seiner Bewerbung um die Tochter König Johanns I. von Portugal nach **Lissabon** schickte. Wir besitzen hier in dem Museum zu Berlin die Flügel des herrlichen **Bildes,** welches die eben genannten Künstler, die eigentlichen Begründer der grossen niederländischen Malerschule,[4] für die Cathedralkirche zu **Gent** angefertigt hatten. Auf den **Flügeln,** welche[5] die heiligen Einsiedler und **Pilger** darstellen, hat[6] Johann von Eyck die Landschaft durch Orangenbäume, Dattelpalmen und **Cypressen** geschmückt, die[5] äusserst naturgetreu über andere dunkele Massen einen ernsten, erhabenen **Charakter** verbreiten. Man fühlt bei dem Anblick des **Bildes,** dass der Maler selbst den Eindruck einer **Vegetation** empfangen hat, die[5] von lauen Lüften umweht ist.

S. careful A. development f.s. is found

B. both (b. nie neither)
g. enjoyed A. view, appearance
G. legation, embassy, b. accompanied H. duke
w. because of B. courting
s. sent
F. wings h. glorious
e. just e. real

a. prepared, made
E. hermits d. represent
g. adorned n. true to nature
e. sublime v. spread
E. impression
e. received l. lukewarm, tepid u. fanned, blow

Bei dem Meisterwerke der Gebrüder Van Eyck stehen wir noch in der ersten Hälfte des 16ten **Jahrhunderts,** als die vervollkommnete Ölmalerei[4] eben erst angefangen hatte,[7] die Malerei in **Tempera** zu verdrängen und[8] doch schon eine hohe technische **Vollendung** erlangt hatte. Das Streben nach einer lebendigen Darstellung der Naturformen war erweckt.

B. with M. master work
v. perfected
Ö. oil painting a. begun
v. displace
V. completion, perfection e. acquired S. striving
n. for l. vivid e. awakened

Allerdings ist[6] die Einsicht in den Zusammenhang der lebendigen Kräfte des Weltalls als die edelste Frucht der menschlichen **Kultur,** als das Streben nach dem höchsten **Gipfel,** welchen die Vervollkommnung und Ausbildung der Intelligenz[4] erreichen kann, zu betrachten; aber das, wovon wir hier **Andeutungen geben,** ist nur ein Teil der Kulturgeschichte selbst.[1] Diese umfasst gleichzeitig, was[5] den Fortschritt der einzelnen Völker nach allen Richtungen erhöhter Geistesbildung und **Sittlichkeit** bezeichnet.

a. of course E. understanding, insight l. living
W. universe e. most noble F. fruit
S. striving n. for, toward G. summit, apex
V. perfection A. improvement, development
e. reach w. of which A. indications
s. itself u. embraces
F. progress e. individual
R. directions e. of increased G. culture
S. morality

Da wir[4] die Geschichte der physischen Weltanschauung als die Geschichte der Erkenntniss eines Naturganzen, gleichsam als die Geschichte des Gedankens von der Einheit in den Erscheinungen und von dem Zusammenwirken der Kräfte im Weltall, definiert haben, so kann[6] die Behandlungsweise dieser Geschichte nur in der Aufzählung **dessen** bestehen, wodurch der Begriff von der Einheit der Erscheinungen[4] sich allmählich ausgebildet hat. Wir unterscheiden in dieser Hinsicht: 1) das selbstständige Streben der Vernunft nach Erkenntniss von **Naturgesetzen,** also eine denkende Betrachtung der **Naturerscheinungen;** 2) die **Weltbegebenheiten,** welche[5] plötzlich den Horizont der **Beobachtung** erweitert haben; 3) die Erfindung neuer Mittel sinnlicher **Wahrnehmung,** gleichsam die Erfindung neuer **Organe,** welche[5] den Menschen mit den irdischen Gegenständen wie mit den fernsten Welträumen in näheren **Verkehr** bringen, welche[5] die **Beobachtung** schärfen und vervielfältigen. Dieser dreifache Gesichtspunkt muss[6] uns leiten, wenn wir[4] die Hauptepochen bestimmen, welche die Geschichte der Lehre vom Kosmos[4] zu durchlaufen hat. Um[7] das Gesagte zu erläutern, wollen[6] wir hier wiederum solche **Beispiele** anführen, welche[5] die Verschiedenheit der **Mittel** charakterisiren, durch welche die Menschheit[4] allmählich zum intellectuellen Besitz von einem grossen Teil der **Welt** gelangt ist: Beispiele von erweiterter **Naturkenntniss,** von grossen Begebenheiten und von der Erfindung neuer **Organe.**

d. since (App. 25—2) W. world conception E. recognition, knowledge g. as it were
G. thought E. unity E. phenomena, appearances
Z. working together K. forces
B. method of treatment
A. enumeration d. of that b. consist B. concept
a. gradually a. developed u. distinguish
H. respect s. independent S. endeavor
N. natural laws d. thinking
N. nature-phenomena W. world-events
p. suddenly e. broadened
E. invention M. means W. perception g. as it were
G. objects f. farthest W. world spaces n. nearer
V. communication s. sharpen v. multiply
G. view point l. guide, direct
b. determine
d. traverse, pass thru G. what has been said (See Rule 3C3.) e. illustrate V. difference a. cite

a. gradually B. possession
g. come e. wider, broadened
B. events Er. invention

Die Kenntniss der **Natur,** als älteste Physik der **Hellenen,** war mehr aus inneren Anschauungen, aus der Tiefe des Gemütes als aus der Wahrnehmung der **Erscheinungen** geschöpft. Die Naturphilosophie der ionischen Physiologen ist[6] auf den Urgrund des Entstehens, auf den Formenwechsel eines einigen **Grundstoffes** gerichtet; in der mathematischen Symbolik der **Pythagoreer,** in ihren Betrachtungen über Zahl und Gestalt offenbart sich dagegen eine Philosophie des Masses und der **Harmonie.** Indem die dorisch-italische Schule[4] überall numerische **Elemente** sucht, hat[6] sie von dieser Seite, durch eine gewisse Vorliebe für die Zahlenverhältnisse, die sie[4] im Raume und in der Zeit erkennt,[8] gleichsam den Grund zur späteren Ausbildung unserer **Erfahrungswissenschaften** gelegt. Die Geschichte der **Weltanschauung,** wie ich sie auffasse, bezeichnet nicht sowohl die oft wiederkehrenden Schwankungen zwischen Wahrheit und **Irrtum,** als die Hauptmomente der allmählichen Annäherungen an die **Wahrheit,** an die richtige Ansicht der irdischen Kräfte und des **Planetensystems.**[1]

K. knowledge H. Greeks
A. views T. depth G. mind, soul
W. perception g. drawn
U. original cause
E. origination F. form-change G. basic substance
g. directed (What calls for this verb?)
B. considerations G. form o.s. is revealed d. on the other hand i. in that, while, by—ing
ü. everywhere
g. certain V. predilection Z. number relations
e. recognizes g. as it were
A. development E. empirical sciences
a. comprehend, view
w. recurring S. variations n. s. not so much
W. truth I. error a. gradual
A. approaches r. correct A. view
i. earthly, terrestial

Grosse Entdeckungen in den Himmelsräumen durch Anwendung des Fernrohrs. Hauptepoche der Sternkunde und Mathematik von Galilei und Kepler bis Newton und Leibnitz. Gesetze der Planetenbewegung und allgemeine Gravitations-Theorie

Indem wir[4] uns bestreben,[7] die am meisten gesonderten Perioden und **Entwickelungsstufen** kosmischer **Anschauung** aufzuzählen, haben[6] wir zuletzt die **Periode** geschildert, in welcher den Kulturvölkern der einen Erdhälfte die andere[4] bekannt geworden ist. Auf das Zeitalter der grössten Entdeckungen im Raume an der Oberfläche unseres Planeten folgt unmittelbar die Besitznahme eines beträchtlichen Teils der Himmelsräume durch das **Fernrohr.**[1] Die Anwendung eines neugeschaffenen **Organes,** eines Werkzeuges von raumdurchdringender Kraft ruft eine neue Welt von **Indeen** hervor.[2] Es beginnt ein glänzendes Zeitalter der Astronomie und **Mathematik;**[1] für die letztere beginnt eine lange Reihe tiefsinniger **Forscher,** die[5] zu dem "alles umgestaltenden" Leonard Euler führt, dessen Geburtsjahr[4] (1707) dem Todesjahr von Jacob **Bernoulli** so nahe liegt.

b. strive g. separated, distinct
E. developmental stages A. view a. to enumerate
g. described den to the
E. hemisphere d.a. the other
Z. age E. discoveries O. surface
u. directly B. occupancy, taking possession
b. considerable F. telescope
A. use n. newly-created W. tool
r. space-penetrating K. force r. calls forth
E. there g. brilliant
R. series
u. transforming d. whose
l. lies

Wenige Namen können genügen, um[7] an die Riesenschritte zu erinnern, welche der menschliche Geist[4] vorzugsweise in Entwickelung mathematischer Gedanken, durch eigene innere Kraft, nicht durch äussere **Begebenheiten** angeregt,[11] im Laufe des siebzehnten **Jahrhunderts** gemacht hat. Die Gesetze des Falles der Körper und der Planetenbewegung werden erkannt. Der Druck der **Luft,** die Fortpflanzung des **Lichts,** seine Brechung und Polarisation werden erforscht. Die mathematische Naturlehre wird geschaffen und[8] auf feste **Grundpfeiler** gestützt. Die Erfindung der Infinitesimal-Rechnung bezeichnet den Schluss des **Jahrhunderts;**[1] und dadurch erstarkt, hat die menschliche Intelligenz sich in den folgenden hundert und fünfzig Jahren mit Glück an die Lösung von **Problemen** wagen können, welche die Störungen der Weltkörper, die Polarisationen und Interferenz der Lichtwellen, die strahlende **Wärme,** die elektro-magnetischen[3] in sich zurückkehrenden **Ströme,** die schwingenden Saiten und **Flächen,** die Capillar-Anziehung enger **Röhren,** und so viele andere Naturerscheinungen[4] darbieten.

g. suffice R. gigantic steps
e. remind v. preferably, especially
G. thoughts
ä. external, outer B. occurrences a. (while) stimulated L. course G. laws
e. recognized D. pressure
F. transmission B. refraction
g. created G. pillars g. supported
b. designates S. close
e. strengthened
L. solution
w. dare, attempt Note the entire subject in this sentence. s. radiating
z. which return, come back
s. vibrating S. strings
e. narrow
d. offer

Die Arbeit in der Gedankenwelt geht nun ununterbrochen und sich gegenseitig unterstützend fort.[2] Keiner der früheren Keime wird erstickt. Es nehmen gleichzeitig zu die Fülle des[3] zu verarbeitenden Materials, die Strenge der Methoden und die Vervollkommnung der **Werkzeuge.**[1] Wir beschränken uns hier, hauptsächlich, **auf** das siebzehnte **Jahrhundert;**[1] das Zeitalter von Kepler, Galilei und Bacon, von Tycho, Descartes und Huygens, von Newton und **Leibnitz.**[1] Die Leistungen dieser Männer sind so allgemein bekannt, dass es[4] nur leiser **Andeutungen** bedarf, um[7] das herauszuheben, wodurch sie[4] in Erweiterung kosmischer **Ansichten** glänzen.

G. thought world un. uninterruptedly
g. mutually u. supporting f. goes on
e. stifled, suppressed zun. increase
z.v. to be worked up V. perfection
W. tools b. limit
Z. age
L. accomplishments
b. known l. slight b. needs
h. emphasize E. broadening
A. views

Wir haben schon früher gezeigt, wie dem **Auge,** dem **Organ** sinnlicher **Weltanschauungen,** durch Erfindung des telescopischen Sehens eine Macht[4] verliehen wurde, deren Grenze noch lange nicht erreicht ist, die[5] aber schon in ihrem ersten schwachen Anfange, bei einer kaum 32 maligen Linear-Vergrösserung der Fernröhre in die[3] bis dahin uneröffneten Tiefen des Weltraums drang. Die genaue Kenntniss vieler **Himmelskörper,** welche[5] zu unserem **Sonnensystem** gehören, die ewigen **Gesetze,** nach denen sie[4] in ihren **Bahnen** kreisen, die vervollkommnete Einsicht in den wahren Weltbau sind das Charakteristische der **Epoche,** die wir[4] hier zu schildern versuchen.

d. Au. to the eye
s. sensory, physical E. invention
v. granted, conferred G. limit, border
e. attained s. weak
k. scarcely F. telescope
b. d. up to that time u. unopened, undisclosed
T. depths K. knowledge
g. belong e. eternal
k. circle v. perfected E. insight W. world-structure s. describe
v. try, attempt

Was diese Epoche[4] hervorgebracht, bestimmt gleichsam die Hauptumrisse von dem grossen Naturbilde des Kosmos;[1] es fügt den neu erkannten Inhalt der Himmelsräume, wenigstens in einer Planetengruppe sinnig geordnet, dem früher durchforschten Inhalt der tellurischen Räume hinzu.[2] Nach allgemeinen Ansichten strebend,[11] begnügen wir uns,[7] hier nur die wichtigsten Objekte der astronomischen Arbeiten des 17ten Jahrhunderts zu nennen. Wir weisen zugleich auf den **Einfluss** hin,[2] welchen diese[4] auf eine **kräftige Anregung zu grossen und unerwarteten mathematischen Entdeckungen wie zu der mehr umfassenden, erhabeneren Anschauung des Weltganzen ausgeübt haben.**

h. brought forth (Note absence of aux.) H. main outlines g. as it were What does "fügt" go with? s. sensibly g. arranged d. studied I. content h. adds a. general A. views s. while striving (Why while?)
b.w. we are content (to what?) h. point, refer
E. influence

k. powerful A. stimulus u. unexpected
E. discoveries u. embracing e. more sublime, lofty a. exerted

Es ist[6] bereits früher erwähnt worden, wie das Zeitalter von Columbus, Gama und Magellan,[4] das der nautischen Unternehmungen, verhängnisvoll mit grossen Ereignissen, mit dem Erwachen religiöser Denkfreiheit, mit der Entwicklung eines edleren Kunstsinnes und der Verarbeitung des copernicanischen **Weltsystems** zusammentraf. Nicolaus Copernicus (in zwei noch vorhandenen Briefen nennt er sich Kopernick) hatte[6] bereits sein 21stes **Lebensjahr** erreicht und beobachtete mit dem Astronomen Albert Brudzewski zu Krakau, als Columbus **Amerika** entdeckte. Kaum ein Jahr nach dem Tode des Entdeckers, nach einem sechsjährigen Aufenthalte in Bologna und Rom, finden wir ihn, wieder in Krakau, mit gänzlicher Umwandlung der astronomischen Weltansicht beschäftigt. Durch die Gunst seines **Oheims, 1510** zum Domherrn in **Frauenburg** ernannt,[11] arbeitete er dort noch 33 Jahre lang an der Vollendung seines Werkes "de Revolutionibus orbium coelestium". Das erste gedruckte Exemplar wurde ihm gebracht, als, an Körper und Geist gelähmt,[11] er[4] sich schon zum Tode bereitete. Er sah es, berührte es auch, aber sein Sinn war[6] nicht mehr auf das Zeitliche gerichtet; er starb nicht, wie Gassendi in dem Leben des **Copernicus** erzählt, wenige Stunden, sondern mehrere Tage nachher, am 24. Mai **1543.**

e. mentioned w. how Z. age
n. nautical U. undertakings
v. fateful E. events E. awakening
e. nobler
K. art-sense V. elaboration, application
v. existing
b. already
e. reached b. was observing
e. discovered K. scarcely

A. stay, sojourn
g. entire U. transformation b. occupied, busy
G. favor
e. appointed
V. completion
g. printed E. copy
g. (while) paralyzed b. prepared
b. touched S. mind
g. directed
e. tells n. afterward

Zwei Jahre früher war[6] aber schon ein wichtiger Teil seiner Lehre durch den Brief eines seiner eifrigsten Schüler und Anhänger, Joachim Rhäticus, an Johann Schoner, Professor zu Nürnberg, durch den **Druck** bekannt geworden. Doch ist[6] es nicht die Verbreitung des copernicanischen **Systems,** die erneuerte Lehre von einer Centralsonne (von der täglichen und jährlichen Bewegung der Erde) gewesen, welche[5] etwas mehr als ein halbes Jahrhundert nach seinem ersten Erscheinen zu den glänzenden Entdeckungen in den **Himmelsräumen** geführt hat, die[5] den Anfang des 17ten Jahrhunderts bezeichnen. Diese Entdeckungen sind[6] die Folge einer zufällig gemachten Erfindung, des **Fernrohrs,** gewesen. Sie haben[6] die Lehre des **Copernicus** vervollkommnet und erweitert. Durch die Resultate der physischen Astronomie (durch das aufgefundene Satelliten-System des Jupiter und die Phasen der Venus) bekräftigt und erweitert, haben die Grundansichten des Copernicus der theoretischen **Astronomie** Wege[9] vorgezeichnet, die[5] zu sicherem **Ziele** führen mussten, ja zur Lösung von Problemen anregten, welche[5] die Vervollkommnung des analytischen **Kalkül** notwendig machten.

What does "war" call for?
e. most zealous A. followers

D. printing D. still, however V. distribution
e. renewed, revived
B. movement

E. appearance g. most splendid
A. beginning
b. designate E. discoveries F. result
z. accidentally F. telescope
v. perfected e. extended

b. affirmed, confirmed
G. basic views
v. sketched, pointed out, marked (Note Rule 9.)
s. sure Z. goal L. solution a. impelled
What does "welche" call for?

Die Deutsche Aufklärung †

Unter dem Einflusse der Leibnitz-Wolffschen Philosophie,* doch ohne direkten wissenschaftlichen Zusammenhang mit ihr,* bildete sich in Deutschland in der zweiten Hälfte des achtzehnten Jahrhunderts eine eklektische Popularphilosophie aus,* deren mannigfaltige Erscheinungen man* unter dem Namen der deutschen Aufklärung zusammenfasst. Sie hat wenig Bedeutung für die Geschichte der Philosophie,* desto mehr für die Geschichte der Kultur;* denn Bildung, geistige Heranziehung von Gebildeten ist es, auf was sie* bezweckt, und gebildete Reflexion, geistreiches Raisonnement ist daher die Form, in der sie* philosophiert. Sie ist das deutsche Gegenbild der französischen Aufklärung.*

E. influence
d. still Z. connection
b. si. was formed (App. 11, 4, b)
J. century What nouns should be bold-faced?
What does "aus" go with? E. phenomena
A. enlightenment z. groups
B. significance G. history
d. so much the more (App. 26, 3, b)
H. attraction G. scholars
b. aims g. clever, ingenious
d. hence i. d. in which
G. counter part A. enlightenment

Das empirische, einzelne Ich als solches gilt den Männern dieser Richtung als das Absolute, als das ausschliesslich Berechtigte;* über ihm vergessen sie alles Andere,* oder vielmehr, alles Andere hat für sie nur in dem Masse Wert,* als es* sich auf das Subjekt bezieht[8], dem Subjekt dient und[8] zu seiner Förderung und innern Befriedigung beiträgt. Daher wird jetzt die Unsterblichkeitsfrage philosophisches Hauptproblem,* in welcher Hinsicht namentlich Mendelssohn,[4] der bedeutendste Mann dieser Richtung,[4] 1739-1786, zu nennen ist; die ewige Fortdauer der einzelnen Seele ist Hauptgegenstand des Interesses;* die objektiven Ideen oder Glaubenwahrheiten,* z. B. die Persönlichkeit Gottes,* werden* keineswegs in Abrede gestellt, aber man interessiert sich im allgemeinen nicht für sie;* dass man* von Gott nichts wissen könne, wird stehender Glaubensartikel.*

e. individual g. is valid, worth
R. direction, trend auss. exclusively
B. justifiable v. forget
A. other, else M. degree W. value b. pertain
d. serves F. advancement
B. satisfaction b. contributes to
U. immortality question H. respect
n. especially b. most important
z. n. ist. Is to be named (App. 12, 1a)
e. individual S. soul H. main object
G. religious truths
k. in no way A. denial
i. a. in general w. know w. becomes (App. 7, 3, a)
G. article of faith

In zweiter Reihe sind es die Moralphilosophie und die Ästhetik, weil beide[4] subjektiveres Interesse gewähren. Im Allgemeinen tritt der Gesichtspunkt des Nützlichen und des Zwecks in den Vordergrund;* der Nutzen wird das eigentliche Kriterium der Wahrheit; was[5] dem Subjekt nicht nützt, wird* auf die Seite geschoben. Im Zusammenhang mit dieser Geistesrichtung steht die vorherrschend teleologische Richtung der Naturbetrachtung und der eudämonistische Charakter der Sittenlehre.* Die Glückseligkeit des Individuums galt als höchstes Prinzip und oberster Zweck.* Selbst die Religion wird* unter diesen Gesichtspunkt gestellt. Reimarus schrieb eine Abhandlung über die "Vorteile" der Religion und suchte zu beweisen, dass die Religion* den irdischen Genuss nicht störe, sondern[8] vielmehr zu seiner Erhöhung beitrage; ebenso Steinbart, der* in mehreren Schriften das Thema durchführte, dass alle Weisheit* nur darin[7] bestehe, Glückseligkeit, d. h. dauerndes Vergnügen zu erlangen, und dass die christliche Religion,[4] fern davon, dies zu verbieten, vielmehr selbst nur Glückseligkeitslehre sei.

R. series s. e. are there
b. both g. afford I. A. in general
N. usefulness Z. purpose V. foreground
e. real W. truth
n. utilizes, avail g. shifted
G. intellectual trend v. predominately
R. trend N. nature consideration
S. ethics G. supreme happiness
g. was valid o. uppermost Z. aim
S. even (App. 13, 2a) G. viewpoint
A. treatise V. advantages
b. prove
G. enjoyment s. but (what?) v. rather
b. contributes m. several E. enhancement
S. articles, papers d. carries through
d. there in (to what?) (App. 23, 3, d)
z. e. to acquire d. therefrom (to what?)
v. forbid v. rather s. itself
G. theory of supreme bliss

Im Übrigen hegte man gegen das Christentum nur gemässigten Respekt;* wo es* eine* dem Subjekt unangenehmere **Autorität**[9] in Anspruch nahm (in einzelnen Dogmen, z. B. dem Dogma der Höllenstraften), lehnte man sich dagegen auf;* überhaupt war man bestrebt,[7] das positive Dogma so weit als möglich in der natürlichen Religion aufgehen zu lassen; Reimarus z. B., der eifrigste Verteidiger des Theismus und der teleologischen Naturbetrachtung, ist zugleich Verfasser der Wolffenbüttler Fragmente.

i. Ü. moreover h. fostered
g. moderate What does "eine" call for?
i.A. n. laid claim to
H. punishment of hell a. rebel against
b. striving (to what?) w. far a. as
m. possible a. let be merged
e. most zealous V. defender
N. nature observation z. at the same time
V. author

† Schwegler, loc. cit.

Aristoteles

Aristoteles hat* ausserordentlich viele Schriften hinterlassen, von denen der kleinere aber ungleich wichtigste Teil* auf uns gekommen ist: jedoch in einer Gestalt, die* manchen Fragen und Bedenken Raum[9] lässt.

a. extraordinarily Indicate the reason for the *. Underline the nouns you would boldface.
w. most important G. form m. to many
B. doubts R. room (Why do you pick up this noun?)

Allgemeiner Charakter und Einteilung der aristotelischen Philosophie.*

A. general E. division

Mit Aristoteles wird[6] die Philosophie, die* in Plato nach Form und Inhalt noch volkstümlich gewesen war, universell, sie verliert ihre hellenische Partikularität*: der platonische Dialog verwandelt sich in trockene Prosa, an die Stelle der Mythen und der poetischen Einkleidung tritt eine feste nüchterne Kunstsprache, das[3] in Plato intuitiv gewesene Denken wird[6] in Aristoteles diskursiv, die unmittelbare Vernunftanschauung des Ersten wird beim Andern Reflexion und Begriff.* Von der platonischen Einheit alles Seins sich abwendend,[11] richtet Aristoteles den Blick mit Vorliebe auf die Mannigfaltigkeit der Erscheinung,* er sucht die Idee nur in ihrer konkreten Verwirklichung* und ergreift daher das Besondere.* Mit gleichem Interesse umfasst er das[3] in der Natur, in der Geschichte und im Innern des Menschen selbst Gegebene. Aber immer geht er am Enzelnen fort,[2] er bedarf immer eines Gegebenen, um* an ihm seine Gedanken zu entwickeln. Immer ist es das Empirische, das Tatsächliche,* was[5] seine Spekulation leitet. Seine ganze Philosophie ist Beschreibung des Gegebenen und nur weil sie* das Empirische in seiner Totalität, seiner Synthese auffasst, weil sie* die Induktion vollständig durchführt, verdient sie den Namen einer Philosophie.* Nur weil er der absolute Empiriker ist, ist Aristoteles der wahrhafte Philosoph.*

w. becomes (App. 7, 3, a)
v. popular g. w. had been (App. 7, 1, d)
v. loses v. s. is transformed
t. dry S. place
E. expression, dress f. solid n. sober
K. technical terminology g. which had been
u. direct V. view of reason
E. former w. becomes
E. unity S. existence a. (while) turning away from r. directs
M. variety E. appearance
V. realization e. comprehends
B. particular g. same u. comprehends
das (—What?) G. history I. interior
G. which is given (See Rule 3 C, 3, 1.)
E. individual G. a 'something' which is given
G. thoughts T. actual
B. description G. that which is given
a. comprehends d. carries through v. deserves
w. true

Aus dem Charakter der aristotelischen Philosophie erklärt sich zuerst ihre enzyclopädische Tendenz,* sofern alles[3] in der Erfahrung Gegebene[4] gleiche Ansprüche auf Berücksichtigung macht. Aristoteles ist daher der Gründer mehrerer,[3] vor ihm unbekannter Disziplinen; er ist nicht bloss der Vater der Logik,* sondern auch der Naturgeschichte, der empirischen Psychologie,* des Naturrechts.*

e. s. is explained (App. 11, 4, a)
G. which was given (See Rule 3, C 2, b.) d. therefore
m. several u. which were unknown
b. merely
N. natural history
N. natural law

Weiter erklärt sich aus der Hinwendung des Aristoteles zum Gegebenen seine vorherrschende Neigung zur Physik;* denn die Natur ist das Unmittelbarste, Tatsächlichste.* Das erste Buch der Metaphysik ist ebenso der erste Versuch einer Geschichte der Philosophie,* wie seine Politik die erste kritische Geschichte der verschiedenen Staatsformen und Verfassungen.* Wie dort durch die Kritik seiner Vorgänger, so legt er hier durch die Kritik der vorliegenden Verfassungen den Grund zu seiner eigenen Theorie:* er will* die letztere überall nur als die Konsequenz des geschichtlich Gegebenen erscheinen lassen.

w. further H. turn towards, devotion
v. predominant N. tendency, love
U. most immediate, direct
T. the most actual, real V. attempt
e. first e. just as much
v. different S. governmental forms
V. constitutions V. predecessors
v. existing
V. constitutions G. basis e. own
l. latter l. let e. appear

Es ist klar, dass hiernach auch die Methode des Aristoteles* eine andere sein musste, als diejenige Platos. Statt synthetisch und dialektisch, wie der letztere, verfährt er vorherrschend analytisch, d. h. je vom Konkreteren rückwärts schreitend,[11] zu dessen letzten Gründen und Bestimmungen.

k. clear
e. a. a different (one)
s. instead of v. proceeds
r. backwards s. progressing

(The * for Rule 1 is now intentionally omitted; underline the nouns that should be bold-faced.)

Aristoteles Methode ist daher die Induktion, d. h. die Ableitung allgemeiner Sätze und Maximen aus einer Summe gegebener Tatsachen und Erscheinungen, seine Darstellung gewöhnliches Raisonnement, ein nüchternes Abwägen von Tatsachen und Erscheinungen. Er verhält sich meist nur als denkender Beobachter. Auf Allgemeinheit und Notwendigkeit seiner Resultate verzichtend,[11] ist er zufrieden,[7] ein approximativ Wahres, möglichste Wahrscheinlichkeit hergestellt zu haben. Er äussert häufig, die Wissenschaft beziehe sich nicht bloss auf das Unveränderliche und Notwendige, sondern auch auf das, was[5] gewöhnlich zu geschehen pflegt: nur das Zufällige falle ausser ihren Bereich. Die Philosophie hat ihm daher den Charakter und den Wert einer Wahrscheinlichkeitsrechnung und seine Darstellungsweise nimmt nicht selten nur die Form des zweifelhaften Überlegens an.* Daher keine Spur von den platonischen Idealen. Daher sein Widerwille gegen dichterischen Schwung und poetische Ausdrucksweisen in der Philosophie.

d. therefore
A. derivation a. general S. theories
T. facts **What do the nouns on the breaks tell you to do?** D. presentation **g. usual**
n. temperate, sober A. weighing
E. phenomena v. behaves
d. thinking B. observer A. generality
N. necessity v. foregoing (Why Rule 11?)
z. satisfied W. truth m. most possible
W. probability What calls for the "zu"?
h. frequently b. s. refers b. merely
U. unchangeable N. necessary
g. ordinarily p. is accustomed
Z. accidental B. realm i. for him
d. therefore W. value
W. probability calculation D. method of presentation **What goes with "nimmt"?**
z. doubtful Ü consideration S. trace
W. repulsion **What does "an" go with?**
S. enthusiasm A. ways of expression
Continue to "flag" lines on which you find prefixes and "zu"-verbs.

Mit dem empirischen Charakter des aristotelischen Philosophirens hängt endlich die zerstückte Art seiner Schriften, der Mangel einer systematischen Einteilung und Anordnung zusammen.* Immer an der Hand des Gegebenen vom Einzelnen zum Einzelnen vorwärts schreitend,[11] fasst er jedes Gebiet für sich und macht es zum Gegenstande einer besonderen Schrift, aber er unterlässt es meistens, die Fäden aufzuzeigen, durch welche die Teile* unter sich zusammenhängen und* zum Ganzen eines Systems sich zusammenschliessen. So erhält er eine Vielheit koordinierter Wissenschaften, von denen jede* ihre unabhängige Begründung hat, aber keine[3] sie zusammenhängende oberste Wissenschaft. Ein leitender und verknüpfender Grundgedanke ist da, alle Schriften verfolgen die Idee eines Ganzen, aber in der Darstellung fehlt so sehr alle systematische Gliederung, jede seiner Schriften ist so sehr eine selbstständige,[3] in sich geschlossene Monographie, dass man* nicht selten über die Frage in Verlegenheit gerät, was Aristoteles selbst für einen Teil der Philosophie gehalten habe oder nicht.

What goes with "hängt"? d. finally
z. dismembered A. way, manner M. lack
E. division A. arrangement **Why an * here?**
a. H. d. by use of
s. (while) progressing Why Rule 11?
G. subject "sich". Rule 1 applies to pronouns!
S. writing, book, treatise u. neglects
(to what?) F. threads T. parts
z. s. are combined u. and (what?)
z. merge e. obtains V. variety W. sciences
u. independent B. foundation (Why Rule 3?)
z. which holds them together (Why which?)
v. connecting G. basic thought
v. follow G. whole D. presentation
f. is missing G. analysis, articulation
sehr much s. independent
g. compact Why Rule 3?
s. seldom V. embarrassment g. (the infinitive is "geraten") falls s. himself (App. 13, 1)
g. considered

Nirgends gibt er ein Schema oder einen Grundriss, selten abschliessende Ergebnisse oder übersichtliche Erörterungen, selbst die verschiedenen Einteilungen der Philosophie, die er* aufstellt, weichen sehr von einander ab.[2] Bald unterscheidet er praktische und theoretische Wissenschaft, bald stellt er neben diese zwei noch eine Wissenschaft von der künstlerischen Hervorbringung, bald spricht er von drei Teilen, Ethik, Physik und Logik; die theoretische Philosophie selbst wieder teilt er bald in Logik und Physik, bald in Theologie, Mathematik und Physik.

N. nowhere **g. e. does he give**
G. outline s. rarely a. conclusive
Ü. clear E. discussions s. even (App. 13, 2)
v. different E. division
aufs. sets up a. deviate b. now
u. distinguishes W. science
b. now s. places n. beside
k. artistic H. production
b. now **What do the nouns tell you to do?**
s. itself (App. 13, 2)
t. divides b.-b. now—now

Logik und Metaphysik

Der Name Metaphysik ist* erst von den aristotelischen Kommentatoren geschaffen worden; Plato hat sie Dialektik genannt und Aristoteles hat dafür die Bezeichnung "erste (Fundamental-) Philosophie, wogegen ihm die Physik* "zweite Philosophie" ist. Das Verhältnis dieser ersten Philosophie zu den andern Wissenschaften bestimmt Aristoteles folgendermassen: Jede Wissenschaft, sagt er, nimmt ein bestimmtes Gebiet, eine besondere Art des Seienden zur Untersuchung heraus,[2] aber keine derselben geht auf den Begriff des Seienden. Es ist* also eine Wissenschaft nötig, welche* dasjenige, was die anderen Wissenschaften* aus der Erfahrung aufnehmen, selbst hinwiederum zum Gegenstand der Untersuchung macht. Dies tut die erste Philosophie, indem sie* sich mit dem Sein als Sein beschäftigt, während die andern* es mit dem bestimmten konkreten Sein zu tun haben. Als diese Wissenschaft des Seins und seiner ersten Gründe ist[6] die Metaphysik, indem sie* die Voraussetzung der andern Disziplinen bildet, erste Philosophie.[10] Würde es nämlich, sagt Aristoteles, nur physische Wesen geben, so wäre die Physik die erste und einzige Philosophie; [10]gibt es aber eine immaterielle und unbewegte Wesenheit, die* der Grund alles Seins ist, so muss es auch eine frühere, und weil sie* früher ist, eine allgemeine Philosophie geben. Dieser erste Grund alles Seins ist nun Gott, deswegen Aristoteles* auch bisweilen die erste Philosophie Theologie nennt.

Why an * here?
g. created w. been (App. 7, 5, c)
g. named d. for it
B. designation w. whereas
V. relation
W. sciences a. other
b. determines f. as follows
b. certain (what does "nimmt" go with?)
S. existence h. singles out
B. concept E.i. there is
What calls for "macht"? for "aufnehmen"?
G. object U. investigation
i. by being b. concerned b. definite
e. first, foremost G. basis
i. is (what?) i. bildet by forming V. prerequisite
w. e. g. if there should be (App. 10, 2, e) Note Rule 10.
w. would be (App. 28, 3, a, d, e)
g. e. if there is
m.e. g. there must be
a. general
d. for which reason b. at times
n. names

DIE LOGIK

Die Hauptaufgabe sowohl des natürlichen logischen Vermögens als auch der Logik als Wissenschaft und Kunst besteht darin[7]: Schlüsse zu bilden und zu beurteilen und[8] durch Schlüsse beweisen zu können. Die Schlüsse aber bestehen aus Sätzen, die Sätze aus Begriffen. Nach diesen natürlichen,[3] in der Sache selbst liegenden Gesichtspunkten hat[6] Aristoteles den Inhalt der logischen und dialektischen Lehre den verschiedenen einzelnen Schriften des Organon zugeteilt. Die erste Schrift im Organon sind die "Kategorieen", eine Schrift welche* die einzelnen Begriffe, die allgemeinen Bestimmungen des Seins abhandelt. Aristoteles zählt zehn solcher Kategorieen auf[2], Einzelsubstanz, Grösse, Beschaffenheit, Verhältnis, Ortsbestimmung, Zeitbestimmung, Lage, Zustand, Tun, Leiden. Die zweite Schrift handelt von der Rede als Ausdruck der Gedanken und handelt die Lehre von den Redeteilen, den Sätzen und Urteilen ab.* Die dritte sind die analytischen Bücher, die zeigen, wie die Schlüsse* auf ihre Prinzipien zurückgeführt und* nach Vordersätzen geordnet werden können.

H. main task V. ability
b. consists d. (there) in (App. 23, 3, d)
b. judge, criticize u. and (what?)
S. conclusions S. principles, theorems
B. concepts n. natural (what?)
l. which lie (Why which?) I. substance
L. theory v. different
z. allotted S. treatise, article
S. treatise, article
B. concepts a. general B. provisions
a. treats What does "zählt" go with?
E. individual substance G. magnitude
B. constitution V. condition O. location-determination Z. state, condition L. passivity
R. speech A. expression h. a. treats
R. parts of speech S. sentences
U. judgements, criticisms S. conclusions
z. traced back (Borrow "werden können".)
k. w. a. can be arranged (App. 7, 6; A, B)
V. prositions

Das Nähere der aristotelischen Logik ist[6] durch die gewöhnlichen formalen Dartstellungen dieser Wissenschaft, für welche Aristoteles[4] das Material fast vollständig geliefert hat, (weswegen Kant sagen konnte, die Logik habe[6] seit Aristoteles keinen Schritt vorwärts und keinen rückwärts getan.) Jederman bekannt. Nur in zwei Punkten ist* die jetzige formale Logik über Aristoteles hinausgeschritten.

N. details What does "ist" call for?
g. usual D. presentations
W. science
g. furnished v. completely w. wherefore
S. step
r. backward g. made b. known (with "ist")
j. present i. has (why?)
h. advanced

Geschichte der physischen Weltanschauung
Hauptmomente der allmählichen Entwickelung des Begriffs vom Kosmos, als einem Naturganzen †

Die Geschichte der physischen Weltanschauung ist die Geschichte der Erkenntniss eines **Naturganzen,** die Darstellung des Strebens der **Menschheit,** das Zusammenwirken der Kräfte in dem Erd- und **Himmelsräume zu** begreifen: sie bezeichnet demnach die Epochen des Fortschritts in der Verallgemeinerung der **Ansichten,** sie ist ein Teil der Geschichte unserer **Gedankenwelt,** in so fern dieser Teil[1] sich auf die Gegenstände sinnlicher Erscheinung, auf die Gestaltung der geballten Materie und die ihr innewohnenden **Kräfte** bezieht.

G. history W. conception of the world
E. knowledge, recognition D. presentation
S. striving Z. working together K. forces
z.b. to understand b. designates d. accordingly
F. progress V. generalization A. views
G. thought world
G. objects s. physical, sensory
G. form g. conglomerate i. which are inherent
s.b. refers A. section

In dem ersten Buche dieses **Werkes,** in dem Abschnitt über die Begrenzung und wissenschaftliche Behandlung einer physischen **Weltbeschreibung,** glaube[7] ich deutlich entwickelt zu haben, wie die einzelnen Naturwissenschaften sich zur Weltbeschreibung, d. h. zur Lehre vom Kosmos **(vom Weltganzen),** verhalten, wie diese Lehre[4] aus jenen Disziplinen nur die Materialien zu ihrer wissenschaftlichen **Begründung** schöpfe. Die Geschichte der Erkenntnis des Weltganzen, zu welcher ich[4] hier die leitenden **Ideen** darlege und welche ich[4] der Kürze wegen bald die Geschichte des Kosmos, bald Geschichte der physischen **Weltanschauung** nenne, darf also nicht verwechselt werden mit der Geschichte der **Naturwissenschaften,** wie sie mehrere unserer vorzüglichen Lehrbücher der Physik oder die der Morphologie der Pflanzen und Tiere[4] liefern.

B. limitation B. treatment
W. world description d. clearly
e. individual
L. theory v. are related
D. subjects
s. draws B. establishment E. recognition, knowledge d. present
w. because of (App. 15, 3) b.– b. now– now
n. call d. must
v. confused
sie (object) it v. excellent
d.d. those of l. furnish
R. account B. significance

Um[7] Rechenschaft von der Bedeutung dessen zu geben, was[5] hier unter den Gesichtpunkt einzelner historischer **Momente** zusammenzustellen ist, scheint es am geeignetsten beispielsweise aufzuführen, was[5] nach dem Zweck dieser **Blätter** behandelt oder ausgeschlossen werden muss. In diese Geschichte des Naturganzen gehören die Entdeckungen des zusammengesetzten **Mikroscops,** des Fernrohrs und der farbigen **Polarisation:** weil sie[4] Mittel[7] verschafft haben das, was[5] allen **Organismen** gemeinsam ist, aufzufinden,[8] in die fernsten Himmelsräume zu dringen und[8] das erborgte, reflektierte Licht von dem selbstleuchtenden **Körper** zu unterscheiden, d. i. zu bestimmen, ob das Sonnenlicht[4] aus einer festen Masse oder aus einer gasförmigen **Umhüllung** ausstrahlte.

e. individual, single z. ist is to be compiled
s. seems a.g. most appropriate b. by way of example Z. purpose a. excluded, left out

g. belong E. discoveries
F. telescope
M. means (to what?)
a. to all (why to?) g. common
f. most distant d. penetrate
e. borrowed (Note Rule 8B.) s. self-illuminating
u. distinguish b. determine
U. covering, envelope

Die Aufzählung der Versuche aber, welche[5] seit Huygens allmählich auf Aragos Entdeckung der farbigen **Polarisation** geleitet haben, werden[6] der Geschichte der **Optik** vorbehalten. Eben so verbleibt der Geschichte der Phytognosie oder Botanik die Entwickelung der **Grundsätze,** nach denen die Masse vielgestalteter Gewächse[4] sich in **Familien** an einander reihen lässt; während die Geographie der Pflanzen,[4] oder die Einsicht in die örtliche und klimatische Verteilung der Vegetation über den ganzen Erdkörper,[4] über die Feste und das algenreiche Becken der Meere,[4] einen wichtigen Abschnitt in der Geschichte der physischen **Weltanschauung** ausmacht. Die denkende Betrachtung dessen, was[5] die Menschen zur Einsicht eines **Naturganzen** geführt hat, ist eben so wenig die ganze Kulturgeschichte der Menschheit als sie,[4] wie wir eben erinnert haben, eine Geschichte der **Naturwissenschaften** genannt werden kann.

A. enumeration V. experiments a. gradually
E. discovery
w. are (why?) d. to the v. reserved
v. remains P. phytology (study of plants)
G. principles v. many-shaped
G. growths, plants
s.r.l. can be classified Note the long subject.
V. distribution E. globe
B. basin
W. world conception
B. consideration d. of that
E. understanding (What calls for "hat"?)
g. whole, entire
e. recalled

†Humboldt, loc. cit.

PRACTICE READINGS

from various fields

Without Numbers, Boldfaced Nouns or Asterisks

KERNSPALTUNG†

Neben den von uns bis jetzt besprochenen Formen der Kernumwandlung und der Kernzertrümmerung gibt es noch eine besondere Form der Kernspaltung, bei der der Atomkern durch Beschuss mit Neutronen in zwei annähernd massengleiche oder doch nicht allzu verschiedene Kerne zerlegt wird. Diese Kernspaltung ist bis jetzt nur bei den schwersten Kernen beobachtet worden und besitzt besondere Bedeutung beim Uran. Auf ihr beruht das Verfahren, die Atomenergie für praktische Zwecke verwendbar zu machen. Die Entdeckung der Kernspaltung hängt eng mit der künstlichen Erzeugung von Elementen höherer Ordnungszahl als 92 zusammen.

1. **Die Transurane.** 1937 hatten Otto Hahn, Lise Meitner und Strassman ein Isotop des Urans mit dem Atomgewicht 239 und der Halbwertzeit 23 Minuten entdeckt. Dieses Element war radioaktiv wie alle schweren Atome jenseits des Wismuts. Es sandte beim Zerfall β-Strahlen aus und wandelte sich dabei in ein Atom der Ordnungszahl 93 um. Dieses aus dem Uranisotop entstandene Element wurde 1940 von Joliot experimentell festgestellt und erhielt den Namen Neptunium. Es war das erste Element jenseits des bis dahin bekannten Endglieds des Periodischen Systems der Elemente, des Urans. Auch das Neptunium ist radioaktiv. Die Halbwertzeit seines Zerfalls ist 2,3 Tage. Es sendet beim Zerfall β-Strahlen aus und wandelt sich dabei in ein Element der Ordnungszahl 94 um. So entsteht ein weiteres Element jenseits des Urans. Dieses neue Element wurde Plutonium genannt. Es hat die Massenzahl 239 und die Ordnungszahl 94. Auch das Plutonium ist radioaktiv. Es strahlt α-Strahlen aus, besitzt aber eine lange Lebensdauer, d. h. eine grosse Zerfallszeit. Sein Umwandlungsprodukt ist das Uranisotop der Massenzahl 235.

2. **Die Entdeckung der Kernspaltung.** Diese Umwandlungen haben nichts mit Kernspaltung zu tun. Sie stehen aber mit ihr insofern in Verbindung, als man im Jahre 1938 beim Beschuss von Uran mit Neutronen einige neugebildete Atomkerne gefunden hatte, die man zunächst für Transurane hielt. Bevor aber diese Elemente chemisch nachgewiesen waren, fanden Otto Hahn und Strassmann, dass es sich bei diesen neu entstandenen Kernen nicht um Transurane, sondern um bekannte Elemente des Periodischen Systems von mittlerer Ordnungszahl handelte. Otto Hahn konnte nachweisen, dass eins der entstandenen Elemente Barium war. Damit war der Beweis erbracht, dass in diesem Falle nicht eine Umwandlung des Kerns in einen im periodischen System benachbarten vorlag, sondern eine Spaltung des Kerns in zwei Teile. Auch der zweite Teil wurde bald darauf festgestellt und als Krypton erkannt. Die Ordnungszahl 56 des Bariums und die Ordnungszahl 36 des Kryptons ergänzten sich zu der Ordnungszahl 92 des beschossenen Urans.

Bei der grossen Kernladung, die die Spaltstücke besitzen, ist es nicht verwunderlich, dass die beiden Massen mit grosser Geschwindigkeit auseinandergetrieben werden. Ihre Energie konnte bald nach der Entdeckung gemessen werden. Man fand sie von der Grössenordnung 170 MeV.

Sehr bemerkenswert ist, dass die Spaltung durch Neutronen eingeleitet wird, deren Geschwindigkeit nicht viel grösser als die Geschwindigkeit von Wasserstoffmolekülen bei der Wärmebewegung ist. Deshalb spricht man von der thermischen Geschwindigkeit der Neutronen.

3. **Spaltung des Urans.** Die Untersuchung der Kernspaltung, die bald nach der Entdeckung überall vorgenommen wurde, ergab, dass beim Uran an der Spaltung vor allem das im reinen Uran enthaltene Isotop 235 beteiligt ist. Zwar ist das Hauptisotop des Urans 238 ebenfalls und zwar durch schnelle Neutronen spaltbar, bei den bei der Gewinnung von Energie aus dem Spaltvorgang auftretenden Geschwindigkeiten ist aber die Spaltung des Kerns 235 bei weitem die wichtigste.

Reines Uran besteht neben Spuren von Uran 234 aus den beiden Isotopen 235 und 238. In ihm findet sich Uran-235 in einem Anteil von 0,7%. Wenn reines Uran von Neutronen bestrahlt wird, reagieren die Kerne folgendermassen: Besitzen die Neutronen eine thermische Geschwindigkeit, so lagern sie sich an die Kerne des Urans-235 an und leiten so ihre Spaltung ein. Da auf 140 Kerne von der Masse 238 nur 1 Kern der Masse 235 kommt, ist die Ausbeute an Reaktionen nicht sehr gross. Besitzen die Neutronen eine grosse Geschwindigkeit, aber keine so grosse, dass der Kern 238 gespalten wird, so verlieren sie, während sie auf den Urankern auftreffen, durch die oben geschilderte Einwirkung der Atome auf die Neutronen allmählich an Geschwindigkeit, ohne dass eine Reaktion stattfindet. Wird aber die Geschwindigkeit dadurch so weit herabgedrückt, dass die Neutronen etwa eine Energie von 25 eV besitzen, so werden sie von den Kernen des Urans-238 eingefangen und, ohne dass eine Spaltung eintritt, festgehalten. Es bildet sich das Uranisotop 239, das radioaktiv ist, β-Strahlen aussendet und in 23 Minuten Halbwertszeit sich in Neptunium umwandelt. Soll daher reines Uran durch Beschuss mit Neutronen zur Kernspaltung veranlasst werden, so kann man eine auf Energiegewinnung gerichtete Wirkung nur von Uran-235 erwarten, wenn man Neutronen mit einer Energie, die nicht grösser als einige eV ist, einschliesst.

Nachdem der Vorgang der Kernspaltung entdeckt war, forschte man eingehend nach der Natur der Spaltstücke. Es zeigte sich, dass Uran 235 in der Regel in zwei Kerne zerfällt, deren Massen sich wie 3:2 verhalten.

DER VERLAUF VON KERNREAKTIONEN

Die Kernreaktionen bei der natürlichen Radioaktivität

Wie wir gesehen haben, sind die Kerne des Atoms eines Elements stabil, wenn das Verhältnis der Neutronen zu den Protonen einen bestimmten Wert hat, der etwa 1 für die leichten und 1,5 für die schwersten Elemente beträgt. Es können für dasselbe Element mehrere stabile Isotope vorkommen, doch ist die Häufigkeit dieser Isotope meist recht verschieden. Darin kann man eine Erklärung dafür sehen, dass das häufigere das stabilere ist. Trotz der grossen Energie, die in einem schweren Atomkern als Bindungsenergie vorhanden ist, ist seine Stabilität nicht entsprechend gross, denn mit der Zahl der Bausteine wächst die Möglichkeit der Zerstörung des bestehenden Gleichgewichts. Dafür spricht z. B., dass natürlich radioaktiv, von einigen Ausnahmen abgesehen, nur die schwersten vorkommenden Elemente (Uran, Actinium und Thorium) sind. Die Kerne der natürlich radioaktiven Elemente sind nicht völlig stabil. Sie besitzen einen Energieüber-

†Karl Hahn, **Physik, ein Lehr- und Handbuch in methodischer Darstellung**

schuss, der aus irgendwelcher Veranlassung heraus dazu führt, dass sich der Kern spontan umwandelt. Es besteht bei ihnen eine relativ grosse Wahrscheinlichkeit, dass einzelne Kernpartikeln die Potentialschwelle um den Kern durchschreiten können.

Die Tatsache, dass bei einer solchen Umwandlung a-Strahlen, aber nicht Protonen oder Neutronen oder andere leichte Kerne ausgesandt werden, können wir so deuten, dass in einem Atomkern der aus 2 Protonen und 2 Neutronen bestehende Heliumkern ein Zwischenbaustein ist. Dieser Heliumkern muss in einem natürlichen α-Strahler locker gebunden sein und ausgestrahlt werden können. Da für denselben Stoff die Reichweite der α-Strahlen dieselbe ist und damit auch die Energie in jedem einzelnen Elementarakt dieselbe Grösse besitzt, können wir schliessen, dass jeder Umwandlungsprozess dieser Art dem anderen gleicht: Die Konfiguration der Protonen und Neutronen oder der Heliumkerne im Atomkern ist so, dass ein bestimmter, schwächer gebundener Heliumkern ausgesandt wird.

Abb. 1282 zeigt die Häufigkeitsverteilung der β-Strahlen in einem kontinuierlichen Geschwindigkeitsspektrum. Horizontal sind die Werte der Energie der Strahlen und vertikal die relative Häufigkeit der Elektronen innerhalb einer bestimmten Strahlung angegeben. Dieser Verlauf der Kurve hat die Theorie vor eine sehr schwierige Frage gestellt. Treten die Elektronen wie die α-Teilchen in allen Atomen unter denselben energetischen Bedingungen aus, was anzunehmen ist, weil nur β-Strahlen ausgesandt werden, so müssten sie dieselbe Geschwindigkeit beim Verlassen des Atoms besitzen. Diese Geschwindigkeit müsste gleich der Geschwindigkeit der Elektronen bei A (Abb. 1282) sein, denn sie entspricht der grössten Geschwindigkeit, die man feststellt. Es müssten also alle Elektronen die Höchstenergie besitzen, es sei denn, dass durch Zusammenstösse in der Atomhülle die β-Strahlen verschieden gehemmt würden. Dann müsste aber die Kurve wesentlich anders verlaufen. So aber ist die Zahl der Elektronen, die einen Höchstwert an Energie besitzen, klein, ebenso die Zahl derer, die nur sehr geringe Energie haben. Dagegen ist die Zahl der Elektronen gross, die mit mit - lerer Energie austreten. Diese Umstände scheinen doch zu beweisen, dass die angegebene Verteilung der Geschwindigkeit schon bei dem Austritt aus dem Kern vorliegt. Ist einerseits anzunehmen, dass dieselbe Energie bei jedem β-Zerfall frei wird, und ist andererseits die Energie, die der β-Strahl mitnimmt, nach einer Wahrscheinlichkeitskurve auf die β-Teilchen verteilt und stets geringer als bei A, so liegt die Annahme nahe, dass die dem einzelnen β-Teilchen fehlende Energie einem anderen Korpuskel mitgegeben wird, das gleichzeitig austritt, sich aber der Beobachtung entzieht. Ein solches Korpuskel könnte es geben. Es müsste ungeladen sein, denn ungeladene Korpuskeln rufen keine Ionisation hervor und Ionisation ist das Mittel, mit dem man Korpuskeln nachweist. So hat man die Hypothese aufgestellt, die aber bisher noch durchaus unbewiesen ist, dass bei der Aussendung eines β-Teilchens gleichzeitig vom Kern ein neutrales Korpuskel von etwa gleicher Masse wie das Elektron ausgestossen wird, das man Neutrino nennt. Verlassen Neutrino und β-Teilchen das Atom in demselben Elementarakt, so ist möglich, aber wenig wahrscheinlich, das eines der beiden Korpuskeln die gesamte Energie enthält, aber sehr wahrscheinlich, dass ein mittlerer Wert auf beide entfällt. Damit erklärt sich der Verlauf der Kurve.

Die Materie

Grundlegende Begriffe und Masse. Der Materielle Körper

Wenn wir eine möglichst anschauliche, wissenschaftlich einwandfreie Darstellung des physikalischen Begriffssystems, seines Aufbaus und seines Zusammenhangs geben wollen, so haben wir zunächst die Grundlagen zu erörtern, auf denen sich das System aufbaut. Bei der Vielseitigkeit der zu betrachtenden Vorgänge ist es aber nicht möglich, eine abgeschlossene Übersicht über die Grundlagen zu geben. Wir müssen uns zunächst darauf beschränken, ein bestimmtes Gebiet herauszugreifen und in ihm die für dieses Gebiet wesentlichen Begriffe zu entwickeln. Je mehr eine Wissenschaft an Umfang und Tiefe der vermittelten Einsicht zunimmt, desto mehr erfahren gerade die grundlegenden Begriffe eine schärfere Abgrenzung gegeneinander und eine Vertiefung. Dem Gang der Entwicklung folgend, lassen sich Grundbegriffe nicht abschliessend einführen, sondern nur nach und nach entwickeln.

Wir wollen im folgenden zunächst die am physikalischen Körper beobachtbaren Vorgänge betrachten. Wir können dabei voraussetzen, dass bekannt ist, was ein mathematischer Körper ist und haben uns nur darüber zu verständigen, was wir unter einem physikalischen Körper verstehen wollen. Er hat mit dem mathematischen Körper das Merkmal der räumlichen Ausdehnung gemeinsam. Er muss aber überdies noch sinnlich wahrnehmbar sein, denn er muss irgendein Stück oder ein Teil der Natur sein, auf die unsere Erkenntnis gerichtet ist. Das, was den physikalischen Körper von dem mathematischen verschieden erscheinen lässt und die Möglichkeit der sinnlichen Wahrnehmung gewährleistet, nennen wir "Stoff" oder "Materie". Wir sprechen daher anstatt von physikalischen Körpern meist von "materiellen Körpern". Sagen wir dabei, der Körper bestehe aus Materie, so bedeutet das keine Begriffsbestimmung. Es ist nur damit gesagt, dass ihm ausser der räumlichen Ausdehnung noch mindestens ein zweites Merkmal zukommt. Aus der vorwissenschaftlichen Erfahrung wissen wir, dass an materiellen Körpern viele Eigentümlichkeiten zu beobachten sind. Sie können fest oder flüssig, blau oder grün, elastisch oder plastisch usw. sein. Wollen wir den Begriff materieller Körper so abgrenzen, dass wir genau wissen, wann wir es mit einem solchen zu tun haben und wann nicht, so müssen wir ein Merkmal angeben, das unbedingt vorhanden sein muss. Dieses Kennzeichen für den Begriff können wir willkürlich wählen, und so nehmen wir dafür, im Bewusstsein, dass wir möglicherweise auch ein anderes hätten wählen können, das Merkmal, dass materielle Körper ausnahmslos schwer sind. Besser gesagt: Wir gehen so vor, dass wir einen Körper, der schwer ist, einen materiellen Körper nennen. Wir kommen so zu der Begriffsbestimmung: Ein materieller Körper ist räumlich ausgedehnt und schwer. Ein Körper, der nicht schwer ist, ist damit kein materieller Körper. Dies trifft auf den mathematischen Körper, aber auch z. B. auf ein räumlich begrenztes elektrisches Feld zu.

Es ist begrifflich ein Unterschied zwischen einem materiellen Körper mit vielen Merkmalen und einem, dem nur das Merkmal der Schwere zukommt. Man bezeichnet den letztgenannten Begriff mit dem Wort "Masse", um ihn gegenüber den anderen herauszuheben. Die Masse besitzt das Merkmal der Schwere.

Das Wort "Masse" wird oft für Materie gebraucht. Man sagt dann: ein materieller "Körper enthält oder besitzt Masse. Man kann aber auch das Wort für den Körper als Ganzes benutzen und spricht dann von einer Masse im Sinne eines räumlich ausgedehnten Körpers. Unser Begriffe formender Verstand hat sogar noch einen weiteren Begriff geschaffen, der sich auf eine Masse bezieht, deren Ausdehnung so gering ist, dass sie sich wie ein Punkt darbietet. Man nennt diesen Körper einen Massenpunkt. Als wichtiges Ergebnis dieser Erörterung über den Begriff materieller Körper sei festgestellt, dass unsere Begriffsbestimmung ihn auf zwei grundlegende und messbare Begriffe zurückführt: die Masse, deren Grösse durch die Schwere gemessen werden kann, die räumliche Ausdehnung, die in Raummassen gemessen wird.

Der Massendefekt des Atomkerns

Wenn sich zwei Atome zu einem Molekül vereinigen, wenn wir also aus zwei Elementen eine chemische Verbindung herstellen, so ist der Vorgang entweder mit Wärmeabgabe oder Wärmeverbrauch verbunden. Die dabei frei werdende oder verbrauchte Energie nennt man die Wärmetönung des Prozesses. Die entwickelte Wärme ist ein Mass für die Stabilität der gebildeten Moleküle. Ebenso können wir den Unterschied zwischen der Summe der Massen aller Protonen, Neutronen und Elektronen, die in einem Atom eingebaut sind, und dem Isotopengewicht des Atoms als diejenige Energie auffassen, die bei der Bildung eines stabilen Atoms frei wird und damit ein Mass für seine Stabilität gibt.

Betrachten wir als Beispiel einen aus 2 Protonen und 2 Neutronen bestehenden Heliumatomkern. Die Masse des Heliumatoms setzt sich zusammen aus der Masse von 2 Neutronen mit 2,0180, 2 Protonen mit 2,0152 und 2 Elektronen der Hülle mit 0,0011 atomaren Masseneinheiten. Insgesamt würde, wenn kein Energieumsatz erfolgt, die Masse gleich 4,0343, der Summe aller Massen, sein. Das Heliumatom besitzt aber nach experimentellen Messungen die Masse 4,00386. Die Masse der Bestandteile ist grösser als die Masse der im Kern verbundenen Teile. Der Massenunterschied beträgt 0,0304 atomare Masseneinheiten. Er hat oben im Beispiel des Stickstoffatomkerns 0,1161 betragen. Wir können daraus schliessen, dass bei der Bildung des Heliums aus Protonen und Neutronen Energie in einem Betrage frei wird, der dem Massenschwund oder Massendefekt 0,0304 entspricht. Betrachten wir 4 g Helium, so werden bei seiner Bildung 0,0304 g in Energie umgewandelt. Auf 1 g Helium entfallen 0,0076 g.

ATOM UND MOLEKÜL—ATOMTHEORIE†

Die Frage, ob eine chemisch wohldefinierte Substanz ein Element oder eine Verbindung verschiedener Elemente repräsentiert, und wieviel im letzten Falle von jedem Elemente in der Gewichtseinheit der Verbindung enthalten ist, bietet ein Problem rein experimenteller Natur, welches sich im gegebenen Falle ohne Zuziehung theoretischer Spekulationen mittels des Rüstzeuges der chemischanalytischen Methoden mit mehr oder weniger grosser Sicherheit und Genauigkeit beantworten lässt. Die Elementaranalyse einer Verbindung gehört ja zu den haüfigsten Operationen des Laboratoriums, und ein Eingehen auf die rein chemischen Methoden der Forschung liegt ausserhalb des Rahmens dieses Werkes.

Ganz anders liegt die Frage in betreff des Zahlenverhältnisses der Atome, die das Molekül der Verbindung bilden. Um hierauf eine Antwort zu geben, bedarf man neben der Kenntnis der durch das Experiment unmittelbar zu erlangenden Verbindungsgewichte noch derjenigen der relativen Gewichte der Atome, welche zur betreffenden Verbindung zusammengetreten sind, und diese Kenntnis lässt sich ohne neue theoretische Einblicke nicht erhalten. Aus den S. 39 dargelegten Prinzipien der Atomtheorie folgt zwar, dass die Atom-und Verbindungsgewichte in einfachen rationalen Zahlenverhältnissen stehen; aber die Grösse dieser Zahlenverhältnisse blieb zunächst unbestimmt. Die Wahrscheinlichkeit dafür, dass die theoretischen Betrachtungen zu einem sicheren Resultate geführt haben, steigt nun natürlich ausserordentlich, sobald man auf ganz verschiedenen Wegen zu dem gleichen Ergebnis kommt. Bei der Frage nach den relativen Atomgewichten der Elemente ist das nun in solchem Masse der Fall gewesen, dass über ihre Richtigkeit heute bereits nicht mehr diskutiert wird; um so lehrreicher ist die Betrachtung der verschiedenen Pfade, auf denen man, allerdings nicht ohne vielfach auf Irrwege geraten zu sein, schliesslich zu dem gewünschten Endziele gelangte.

Wenn man eine empirisch gefundene Tatsache durch eine Hypothese erklären will, wie wir hier zur Veranschaulichung des Gesetzes der konstanten und multiplen Proportionen die atomistische Hypothese zu Hilfe nehmen, so darf als leitendes Prinzip der rationellen Naturforschung nicht dasjenige übersehen werden, welches unter den möglichen Erklärungsweisen die einfachste zu wählen fordert. Von diesem darf man erst dann abgehen, wenn weitere Erfahrungstatsachen uns zwingen, zu komplizierteren Auffassungen zu greifen. So verfuhr denn auch Dalton (1808), als er die erste Atomgewichtstabelle aufstellte; bei denjenigen Verbindungen, die nur aus zwei Elementen bestehen, ist offenbar die Annahme am einfachsten, dass die gleiche Anzahl von Atomen zur Verbindung sich vereinigt, dass also z. B. bei der Bildung des Kohlenoxyds gleich viel Sauerstoff- wie Wasserstoffatome usw. zusammengetreten sind. Auf diese Weise suchte Dalton sich die Kenntnis der relativen Atomgewichte der wichtigsten Elemente zu verschaffen, und in derselben Weise weitergehend dann auch die Zahl der Atome in aus mehr als zwei Elementen bestehenden Verbindungen festzusetzen, um so ein in sich abgeschlossenes System der Atomgewichte zu erlangen.

Allein dasselbe war keineswegs frei von Willkür aufgestellt; denn mit gleichem Rechte, wie das Kohlenoxyd als aus gleicher Anzahl Atome Kohlenstoff und Sauerstoff, die Kohlensäure hingegen als aus der doppelten Anzahl

†W. Nernst, **Theoretische Chemie**

Atome Sauerstoff wie Kohlenstoff bestehend angesehen wurde, hätte Dalton auch die Kohlensäure als aus ebensoviele Atomen Kohlenstoff wie Sauerstoff und dementsprechend das Kohlenoxyd aus der doppelten Anzahl Atome Kohlenstoff wie Sauerstoff sich entstanden denken und demgemäss die Wahl der Atomgewichte treffen können; dass gerade in diesem Falle seine Wahl eine glückliche war, muss als lediglich zufällig angesehen werden; beim Wasser traf er bekanntlich nicht das Richtige. Es bedurfte der Zuziehung neuer Erfahrungstatsachen und einer Deutung derselben auf Grund eines weiteren Ausbaues der Atomhypothese, um zu einer von Willkür freien Aufstellung der Atomgewichte zu gelangen.

Zur historischen Beurteilung der Fruchtbarkeit atomistischer Anschauungen ist der vor einiger Zeit erbrachte Nachweis von hohem Interesse, dass Dalton nicht zur Erklärung des Gesetzes der konstanten und multiplen Proportionen die Atomtheorie nachträglich hinzugezogen hat, wie man früher annahm, sondern umgekehrt durch molekular-theoretische Betrachtungen zur Entdeckung des Fundamentalsatzes der Chemie geführt worden ist. Vgl. hierzu Roscoe und Harden, Daltons Atomtheorie, übersetzt von G. W. A. Kahlbaum, Leipzig 1898.

Regel von Avogadro

Eine solche Erfahrungstatsache wurde in dem Gay-Lussacschen Gesetze gefunden, wonach die Volumina der Gase, die sich miteinander verbinden, in einem einfachen rationalen Verhältnis stehen, und auch das Volum der entstandenen Verbindung, wenn selbst gasförmig, ein einfaches rationales Zahlenverhältnis zu denen der Bestandteile aufweist. Die theoretische Deutung im Sinne der atomistischen Hypothese erfuhr dies Gesetz durch die von Avogadro aufgestellte Hypothese, nach der die verschiedenen einfachen wie zusammengesetzten Gase in der Raumeinheit die gleiche Anzahl Moleküle enthalten.

Die atomistische Theorie der Elektrizität

Allgemeines. In den vorhergehenden beiden Kapiteln haben wir uns mit den Eigenschaften der freien Ione, d. h. der positiv oder negativ elektrisch geladenen Moleküle, beschäftigt; im Buch III werden wir erfahren, wie die Theorie der freien Ionen für das Verständnis zahlreicher chemischer Prozesse von grösster Bedeutung ist.

Damit werden wir von selbst zu der Frage nach dem Wesen der Elektrizität selber geführt, einem Problem, das, obwohl mehr in das Gebiet der reinen Physik gehörig, doch auch für den theoretischen Chemiker von so gewaltiger Wichtigkeit ist, dass ein Eingehen darauf auch hier am Platze erscheint, um so mehr, als sich in neuerer Zeit eine geradezu chemische Auffassung der Elektrizität entwickelt hat.

Es wird nicht überflüssig sein, vor einer offenbar missverständlichen Deutung der neueren, vornehmlich an die Namen von Maxwell und Hertz anknüpfenden Entwicklung der Elektrizitätslehre zu warnen, die ziemlich verbreitet ist und das Verständnis des Folgenden sehr erschweren würde. Es ist allgemein bekannt, dass die Physik der neueren Zeit sich sehr eingehend mit den elektrischen Schwingungen beschäftigt hat; offenbar unter dem Einfluss dieser Arbeiten hat der Glaube Platz gegriffen, dass die sogenannte Fluidumstheorie der Elektrizität, die in ihr ein körperliches Agens erblickt, beseitigt sei, und man findet sogar häufig die ganz unmotivierte Behauptung, die Elektrizität sei ein "Schwingungszustand." Allerdings hat die elektromagnetische Lichttheorie einen in jeder Hinsicht bündigen Beweis dafür geliefert, dass die Erscheinungen des Lichts, die man ja bekanntlich seit langem auf Wellenbewegungen zurückführt, ihrem Wesen nach elektrische Phänomene sind, oder dass mit anderen Worten ein prinzipieller Unterschied zwischen den Lichtschwingungen und den elektrischen Schwingungen nicht besteht. Damit ist nun in der Tat die Optik geradeso ein Spezialkapitel der Elektrizitätslehre geworden, wie es der Magnetismus seit langem war. Die Frage nach dem Wesen der Elektrizität bleibt trotzdem aber im grossen und ganzen dieselbe wie vorher.

Ein Beispiel mag die Sache uns verdeutlichen. Die Physik hat gelehrt, dass die Tonempfindungen sich auf Schwingungen der Luft zurückführen lassen, die Akustik wird dadurch zu einem Spezialgebiete der Hydrodynamik, speziell der Theorie der Schwingungen gasförmiger Substanzen. Wenn jemand, gestützt auf die Erfolge der Akustik, etwa sagen wollte, die Luft wäre ein Schwingungszustand, so würde man sofort das Ungegründete dieser Behauptung erkennen; und doch hat man in neuester Zeit der Elektrizität gegenüber genau den entsprechenden Fehlschluss bisweilen begangen. Ueber das Wesen der Luft selber haben uns bekanntlich hauptsächlich Forschungen rein chemischer Natur Aufschluss gegeben, der Ausbau der Akustik hat dazu nicht eben sonderlich mitgeholfen. Aehnlich versprechen allem Anschein nach über das Wesen der Elektrizität und vielleicht auch des Lichtäthers uns Forschungen Auskunft zu geben, die mit den von der Chemie benutzten Methoden die allergrosste Aehnlichkeit besitzen.

Theorie der Radioaktivität

Es ist, wie schon oben bemerkt, Rutherford gelungen, die Erscheinungen der Radioaktivität durch eine einfache Hypothese zusammenzufassen, nach welcher dieselben durch einen explosionsartigen Zerfall des Atoms eines chemischen Elementes bedingt sind.

Wenn dies sehr oft passiert, so wird das betreffende Element instabil oder überhaupt gar nicht existenzfähig sein; passiert dies im Gegenteile nur ganz ungeheuer selten, so wird das Element praktisch völlig unveränderlich sein, und dies würde also der Zustand sein, in welchem sich die früher bekannten chemischen Elemente, mit Ausnahme höchstens von Uran und Thorium, befinden.

Besitzt hingegen das Atom eines Elementes weder eine ungeheuer kleine noch eine ungeheuer grosse Stabilität, so werden nach den Gesetzen der Wahrscheinlichkeit fortwährend einzelne Atome zerfallen und somit wird eine Strahlung in Gestalt der mit grosser lebendiger Kraft fortgeschleuderten Bruchstücke des Atoms unterhalten werden können; in diesem Zustande befinden sich nach der obigen Hypothese die radioaktiven Elemente (Uran, Thor und besonders Radium). Offenbar ist also im Sinne dieser Auffassung die Radioaktivität eine ganz allgemeine Erscheinung; der Beobachtung zugänglich kann sie nach obigem aber nur werden, wenn der Atomzerfall weder zu oft noch zu selten stattfindet. Dass in diesem Zustande relativ wenige Elemente sich befinden, kann nicht wundernehmen; vielmehr muss es geradezu als ein glücklicher Zufall bezeichnet werden, dass stark radioaktive Elemente der Forschung zugänglich wurden. Jetzt, nachdem die Forschung auf diese Erscheinungen aufmerksam gemacht worden ist, steht zu hoffen, dass bei der ausserordentlichen Verfeinerung, welcher insbesondere die elektrostatischen Methoden fähig sind, auch ein ungeheuer seltener Atomzerfall, d. h. eine ungeheuer schwache Radioaktivität, der Messung einst zugänglich werden wird.

Durch Hinzuziehung der Auffassungen über die Konstitution der Atome, die wir S. 196 besprochen haben, lässt sich die Atomzerfalltheorie noch weiter spezialisieren; negative Elektronen, die mit so ungeheurer Geschwindigkeit fortgeschleudert werden, können nicht aus den Elektronenringen stammen und ebenso sicher müssen die α-Teilchen von dem Kerne selber abgegeben werden. Mit anderen Worten, der Sitz der Radioaktivität ist im Atomkern zu suchen, eine Auffassung, die wir in allen ihren Konsequenzen bestätigt finden werden.

Konstitution der Atome

Nachdem wir in den vorhergehenden Abschnitten gesehen haben, wie das relative Gewicht der Atome einer vielseitigen und sicheren Bestimmung zugänglich gemacht worden ist, entsteht die Frage nach der Beschaffenheit der Atome.

Die einfachste Annahme, dass sie nämlich lediglich sehr kleine kugelförmige Massenpunkte seien, liess sich zwar in vielen Betrachtungen der kinetischen Theorie der Materie durchführen, aber andere Erscheinungen, insbesondere die Äusserung der chemischen Valenz und die Spektra der Elemente, liessen schon früh einen wesentlich komplizierteren Aufbau vermuten. Zahlreiche Beobachtungen deuteten auf die Tendenz der Atome, den Ionenzustand anzunehmen, d. h. postiv oder negativ geladen aufzutreten und schliesslich lehrten die Erscheinungen der Radioaktivität den Atomzerfall kennen, als endgültigen Beweis des komplizierten Aufbaus der Atome.

Alle diese ganz verschiedenartigen Phänomene liessen sich durch die Auffassung deuten, dass die Atome aus einem äusserst kleinen positiv geladenen Kerne bestehen, der fast ausschliesslich die Masse des Atoms (Atomgewicht) repräsentiert, und dass um diesen Kern eine Anzahl negativer Elektronen (die nur wenig Masse besitzen) kreisen. Beim elektrisch neutralen Atom wird die positive Ladung des Kernes gerade durch die Summe der negativen Ladungen der kreisenden Elektronen kompensiert; durch Aufnahme weiterer Elektronen bekommt das Atom negative Ladung, durch Abgabe derselben erhält es im Gegenteil einen Ueberschuss an positiver Elektrizität, d. h. so entstehen aus dem gewöhnlichen elektrisch neutralen Atom negative oder positive Ionen.

Die negativen Elektronen sind unter sich gleichartig, wie die Atome eines gewöhnlichen Elements, d. h. sie sind gleich schwer (ihre Masse wurde zu 1/1850 derjenigen des Wasserstoffatoms bestimmt) und ihre elektrische Ladung ist stets die gleiche; die Existenz dieser negativen Elektronen war übrigens schon lange nachgewiesen.

Dass diese Auffassung der Konstitution der Atome als gesichert gelten kann, verdankt man im wesentlichen ausser den Arbeiten von Rutherford denen von Bohr; auf die experimentelle Begründung dieser Auffassung wollen wir hier im einzelnen nicht eingehen, wir werden sie aber sehr häufig benutzen und von ihrer logischen Kraft uns überzeugen.

Die weitere Spezialisierung dieser Anschauungen werden wir im nachfolgenden Abschnitt kennen lernen, ferner auch bei der Besprechung der Quantentheorie und der Radioaktivität, immerhin wird es nützlich sein, wenn auch zunächst ohne nähere Begründung, jetzt schon folgende Erläuterungen zu geben.

Der Kern des Wasserstoffatoms, des leichtesten der Elemente, hat eine positive Ladung, die ebenso gross ist wie die eines negativen Elektrons; derselbe kann daher durchaus als das Gegenstück zum negativen Elektron angesehen werden, man bezeichnet es daher passend als das "positive Elektron." Lediglich die sehr viel grössere Masse unterscheidet das positive Elektron vom negativen, aber doch nur quantitativ, ein Wesensunterschied ist nicht zu konstatieren. Warum freilich die Masse des positiven Elektrons so viel grösser ist, dafür haben wir keine Erklärung; zurzeit können wir darin, aber auch nur darin, den Unterschied zwischen positiver und negativer Elektrizität überhaupt erblicken.

Die positiven Elektronen vermögen sich untereinander und mit negativen Elektronen zu einem neuen Kern zu polymerisieren; vier positive und zwei negative Elektronen bilden z. B. den doppelt positiv geladenen Kern des Heliumatoms, dessen Masse also nahe viermal so gross ist als die des Wasserstoffatoms. Derartige Polymerisationen sind mit gewaltigen Energieänderungen verknüpft, die nach der S. 44 mitgeteilten Gleichung Massenänderungen, allerdings, wie es scheint, von relativ nicht sehr hohem Grade, bedingen. So erklärt sich der Umstand, dass die Masse des Kernes der Elemente zwar nicht ein genaues Multiplum derjenigen des Wasserstoffkernes plus der Summe der Massen der aufgenommenen negativen Elektronen ist, dass aber immerhin bei vielen Elementen ganzzahlige Verhältnisse auftreten. Grössere Abweichungen von der Ganzzahligkeit dürften auf Isotopie zurückzuführen sein.

Die Zahl der positiven Kernladungen bedingt nicht nur, was selbstverständlich ist, die Zahl der negativen Elektronen, die im gewöhnlichen nicht ionisierten, d. h. elektrisch neutralen Atom vorhanden sind, indem sie den Kern umkreisen, sondern, was höchst merkwürdig erscheint, eindeutig auch die Art und Weise, wie die kreisenden Elektronen angeordnet sind und mit welcher Geschwindigkeit sie ihre Umlaufszeit vollenden. Höchstwahrscheinlich sind es die Bedingungen der Quantentheorie, welche hier bestimmend wirken, wenn wir zurzeit auch nur in den allereinfachsten Fällen diese Bedingungen anzugeben in der Lage sind.

Wenn die Kerne also auch sämtlich aus positiven und negativen Elektronen aufgebaut gedacht werden können, so spielt der Heliumkern als sekundärer Baustein doch eine ganz besondere Rolle, wie unter anderem auch aus den Erscheinungen der Radioaktivität (Zerfall des Kernes in einfachere Bausteine) mit Sicherheit folgt.

Die Anordnung der negativen Elektronen bedingt fast alle physikalischen und chemischen Eigenschaften der Atome; der Bau des Kernes bedingt im wesentlichen das Atomgewicht des Elementes und seine Masse überhaupt also auch die Gravitationswirkungen. Ferner hat das radioaktive Verhalten der Elemente seinen Sitz im Kern. Mit anderen Worten, die grosse Mehrzahl der physikalischen und die Gesamtheit der chemischen Probleme wird gelöst sein, sobald es gelungen sein wird, die Gesetze aufzudecken, nach denen die Kernladung die Anordnung der kreisenden negativen Elektronen und ihre Austauschfähigkeit bei chemischen Vorgängen bestimmt. Bisher ist diese Aufgabe nur beim Wasserstoffatom gelöst.

Osmotischer Druck†

Die Bakterienzelle stellt, wie die Zelle der höheren Pflanzen, ein osmotisches System vor, das im wesentlichen aus einer protoplasmatischen Grenzschicht besteht, die der Zellwand anliegt, und aus einem oder mehreren innen im Protoplasma liegenden Safträumen. Ausserdem muss die äussere Grenzschicht zwar eine unbegrenzte Durchlässigkeit für Wasser, aber eine beschränkte für die im Wasser gelösten Verbindungen (Salze) besitzen. Die Zelle kann nur als osmotisches System wirken, wenn sie sich in Wasser oder wässerigen Lösungen befindet, was ja bei Bakterien immer zutrifft. Mit Alfred Fischer können wir sagen:

"Das Wesen des osmotischen Zellsystems beruht also darauf, dass in das Lösungsmittel Wasser eine von Wasser durchsetzte Blase (der Protoplasmabauch) eingetaucht ist und dass diese Blase eine Lösung verschiedener Stoffe umschliesst, die nach Diffusionsgesetzen in das umgebende Wasser sich ausbreiten möchten, daran aber durch die mehr oder weniger grosse Impermeabilitat der Blase verhindert werden."

Auf diese Weise entsteht im Innern der Zelle ein Druck, der osmotische Druck, der abhängig ist vom Grade der Impermeabilität oder Undurchlässigkeit der Grenzschichte für die druckerzeugenden gelösten Verbindungen und von der Menge und Qualität der letzteren. Die Summe aller dieser von den verschiedenen Stoffen im Innern der Zelle erzeugten Teildrucke oder Partialdrucke ist die Grösse des osmotischen Druckes. Dieser Druck lastet auf der Zellwand, die also als resistente Stütze des Protoplasten aufzufassen ist. Die lebende Zelle befindet sich normal ständig in einem solchen Spannungszustande, den man als ihren Turgor bezeichnet. Die Grösse des Turgors ist gleich der Grösse des osmotischen Druckes, der in toto gemessen oder für jeden Stoff auch einzeln bestimmt werden kann.

Man hat festgestellt, dass z. B. eine 1/10 normale Kalisalpeterlösung auf eine für dieses Salz impermeable Wand einen Druck von 3,5 Atmosphären ausübt. Die physikalische Chemie lehrt uns weiter, dass alle äquimolekularen Lösungen der Alkalisalze einbasischer Säuren den gleich grossen osmotischen Druck entwickeln, also in 1/10 Normal- oder Molekularlösungen 3,5 Atmosphären; denselben Druck erzeugen 0,075 normale Lösungen von Alkalisalzen mit zweibasischen Säuren und 0,15 normale Lösungen von organischen Substanzen ohne Metall. Man bezeichnet alle gleich osmotisch wirksamen Lösungen als isomatisch oder isotonisch; werden zwei Lösungen mit verschiedenem osmotischen Druck miteinander verglichen, so heisst diejenige mit grösserer osmotischer Wirksamkeit hyperosmotisch oder hypertonisch gegenüber jener mit geringerem osmotischen Druck, die als hypotonisch oder hyposmotisch anzusprechen ist.

Da sich die Bakterien stets in osmotisch wirksamen Lösungen befinden, so wird auch von aussen her auf die Zellwand ein gewisser Druck herrschen, dessen Grösse wieder die Summe der Partialdrucke der einzelnen gelösten Stoffe entspricht. Normal werden aussen immer niedere Drucke herrschen als im Innern der Bakterienzelle. Die Druckgrösse wird also im Innern das positive Vorzeichen aufweisen.

Wenn nun der umgekehrte Fall eintritt, indem die Bakterienzellen plötzlich in eine hyperosmotische Lösung gebracht werden, so entsteht im Innern ein negativer Druck, der sich dadurch bemerkbar machen wird, dass der Protoplast von der Zellwand abrückt und unter Wasserabgabe sich zusammenzieht. Diese Schrumpfung geht so lange weiter, bis durch die Wasserabgabe die Konzentration im Innern so gross geworden ist, als dem aussen wirkenden osmotischen Druck entspricht. Man bezeichnet diese Zusammenziehung des Protoplasmas als Plasmolyse, weil sich dabei dasselbe von der Zellwand abhebt.

Man kann nun mit Hilfe der Plasmolyse den osmotischen Innerdruck bei allen plasmolysierbaren Bakterien messen. Diese Messungen ergeben sehr grosse Werte für den Turgor. Nach Fischer besitzt der Choleravibrio bei der Zucht auf Nähragar, dessen Stoffe selbst den osmotischen Druck einer 0,04-Normal-Chlornatriumlösung aufweisen, einen Turgor von 1,4—2,1 Atmosphären, was auf 1 μ Wandfläche 0, 018 Milligramm ergibt.

Die osmotisch wirksamen Lösungen verhalten sich gegenüber den Bakterien verschieden. Hyperosmotische Lösungen werden die Bakterienzellen nur dann plasmolysieren können, wenn der Protoplast für sie einen gewissen Grad von Impermeabilität oder Undurchlässigkeit besitzt. Ist dies nicht der Fall, ist die Zelle für den betreffenden Stoff also vollkommen permeabel oder durchlässig, dann wird jede plasmolytische Erscheinung ausbleiben. Der Stoff geht ungehindert durch die Zelle hindurch. Irgendeine Beeinflussung des Innendruckes ist daher ausgeschlossen. Die Impermeabilität der Zelle für gewisse Stoffe ist aber keine konstante Eigenschaft, auch die Grösse derselben unterliegt nennenswerten Schwankungen, die im Alter der Zellen und in ihrer Ernährung ihren hauptsächlichsten Grund haben. Auch das Zurückgehen der Plasmolyse nach einiger Zeit beim längeren Verweilen der Bakterienzellen in hyperosmotischen Lösungen ist auf ein Nachlassen der Impermeabilität zurückzuführen. Es liegt hierin eine grosse Anpassungsfähigkeit der Mikroorganismen an Konzentrationsänderungen in den sie umgebenden Lösungen. Dadurch sind sie auch in der Lage, trotz plötzlich eingreifender starker Konzentrationsänderungen ihr Protoplasma vor zu grossen Aussen- und Innendrucken bis zu einem gewissen Grade zu schützen. Dies gilt besonders für den plötzlichen Übergang von Zellen aus hyperosmotischen in hyposmotische Lösungen.

Geschichte der technischen Mykologie

Man wird nicht fehlgehen, wenn man die ersten Anfänge des bewussten Gebrauches von Gärungen bei der Herstellung von verschiedenen Nahrung- und Genussmitteln in das graue Altertum verlegt. Die durch Gärung bewerkstelligte Wein- und Bierbereitung ist beispielsweise eine der ältesten Erfindungen der Menschheit, zurückgeführt auf Götter. So haben die alten Ägypter ihren Gott Osiris unter anderem auch dafür verehrt, dass er sie die Herstellung des Bieres gelehrt hat. Die Griechen weihte Gott Bacchus in die Geheimnisse der Weinkelterei ein. Man kennt also die praktische Einleitung und Durchführung solcher geistige Getränke haltbar und gar machenden Gärungen schon sehr lange, ohne aber sich über die dabei auftretenden Vorgänge irgendeine Vorstellung zu bilden und die Ursache dieser Umsetzung richtig zu deuten.

Der Begriff "Gärung" umfasst ursprünglich jene Vorgänge, durch die spontan eine Verbesserung und Fertigstellung, Garmachung von Nahrungs- und Genussmitteln erreicht wird. In der Gelehrtensprache bürgerte sich dafür der Name Fermentatio ein, der später durch die Alchemisten eine sehr weite Fassung bekommen hat und zu

†F. Fuhrmann, **Einführung in die Grundlagen der technischen Mykologie**

ganz widersinnigen Begriffsverwirrungen führen musste. So arteten im 15. und 16. Jahrhundert Meinungsverschiedenheiten über das Wesen der Gärung in müssige Wortgefechte aus, was schliesslich zu einem Zusammenwerfen von Fermentatio (Gärung) und Digestio (Verdauung) führte und unter den Begriffen dieser beiden alles fallen liess, was überhaupt bei stofflicher Umsetzung der organischen und unorganischen Welt irgendwie in Erscheinung tritt.

Man beschrieb ganz richtig zahlreiche bei der Gärung sich einstellende Erscheinungen, z. B. das Auftreten von starken Schaumbildungen beim Einsetzen der Gärung von Traubensaft, das Nachlassen des Schäumens unter gleichzeitiger Abscheidung eines Bodensatzes in beträchtlicher Menge. Darnach verursachte die Gärung eine Reinigung, durch die die in Gärung geratene Flüssigkeit wesentlich verbessert, von Schmutz befreit und rein und geistig geworden ist. Der Alchimist und Mönch Basilius Valentinus bezeichnet den bei der Wein- und Biergärung sich bildenden Bodensatz im obigen Sinne geradezu als faeces vini, bzw. cerevisiae, um damit die Gärung geradezu als Reinigungsprozess zu charakterisieren. Zu Beginn des 16. Jahrhunderts finden wir auch schon als Namen für die Körper, welche angeblich die Gärung verursachen, das Wort "Ferment", womit man im weitesten Sinne des Wortes jeden Stoff bezeichnete, welcher irgendwelche chemischen Reaktionen auszulösen imstande ist.

Kopp schildert in seiner "Geschichte der Chemie" ausführlich das trostlose Durcheinander in der Lehre von der Gärung zur damaligen Zeit.

Im 17. Jahrhundert haben deutsche Alchimisten neue Gedanken in die Lehre von der Gärung hineingebracht und wenigstens eine reinliche Scheidung von "fermentatio" und "putrefactio" (Fäulnis) herbeizuführen gesucht, indem sie unter ersterer nur das Gärungsprodukt verbessernde und unter letzterer verschlechternde Vorgänge zusammenfassten. J. Becker unterscheidet übrigens schon zwischen einer wallenden, geistigen (also alkoholischen) und saueren Gärung.

Ungefähr in dieselbe Zeit fällt auch die Entstenung einer mechanischen Gärungstheorie, die aber mit unserer heutigen energetischen Auffassung solcher Vorgänge nicht das geringste zu tun hat. Der englische Chemiker Th. Willis definierte im 17. Jahrhundert das Ferment als einen innerlich bewegten Körper, der seine Bewegung auf gärungsfähige Stoffe überträgt und dadurch die Gärung durchführt. Fast die gleiche Erklärung der Gärung findet man in der Zymotechnia fundamentalis von Georg Ernst Stahl aus der zweiten Hälfte des 17. Jahrhunderts, worin nach der im Jahre 1748 erschienenen deutschen Übersetzung steht: "Die Fermentation ist eine innerliche Bewegung, wodurch verschiedene, nicht gar zu fest verknüpfte Zusammensetzungen, vermittelst einer dahin dienlichen Feuchtigkeit ergriffen und durch langwieriges Untereinandertreiben an einander getrieben und gestossen werden, wesfalls die Verknüpfungen des gegenwärtigen Zusammenhanges voneinander gerissen werden, die abgerissenen Teilchen aber durch das stetige Reiben verdünnet und in eine neue und zwar stärkere Verbindung versetzt werden."

Am 24. Oktober 1632 wurde zu Delft in Holland Antoni van Leeuwenhoek geboren. Als Sechzehnjähriger trat er in ein Schnittwarengeschäft zu Amsterdam als Lehrling ein, wo er es in Kürze bis zum Kassierer brachte. Er gab dann seine Stelle auf und lebte einige Zeit als Privatmann in Delft, um später ein Amt in der Stadtverwaltung anzunehmen. Schon als Lehrling befasste er sich in seinen freien Stunden mit der mühevollen und schwierigen Herstellung kleinster Glaslinsen, die er passend in Gold- und Silberplättchen fasste und dann zur Untersuchung der verschiedensten Substrate verwendete. Die besten seiner Linsen hatte eine ungefähr hundertsechzigfache lineare Vergrösserung und waren leistungsfähiger als die damals schon erfundenen zusammengesetzten Mikroskope, die nur für die Beobachtung im auffallenden Lichte eingerichtet waren. Leeuwenhoek untersuchte damit zahlreiche Substrate, wie Regenwasser, Zahnschleim und beobachtete darin kleinste "Tierchen" von verschiedener Grösse, Gestalt und Beweglichkeit.

Bildung, Bau und Keimung der Hefesporen

Bei der Beschreibung des Kernes der Hefezelle wurden die wahrend der Sporulation an demselben sich abspielenden Vorgänge bereits erörtert. Im allgemeinen ist die Sporulation bei der Hefe wie bei den Bakterien als eine freie Zellbildung aufzufassen. Die Sporen sind Endosporen und entstehen in der unmittelbar sich zur Sporenmutterzelle oder dem Askus umwandelnden vegetativen Hefezelle.

Die Sporenbildung setzt nun bei der Hefe dann ein, wenn in voller Entwicklung stehende Zellen durch äussere Bedingungen an der Sprossung verhindert werden. Wir haben uns also zwischen der Sprossung und Sporulation eine Art Kampf vorzustellen. Solange es irgend möglich ist, bleibt die Hefe bei der Vermehrung durch Sprossung. Auch ist die Neigung der einzelnen Hefearten zur Sporulation eine verschiedene. Ganz allgemein können wir sagen, dass zur Sporenbildung ausser dem guten Ernahrungszustand noch reichlich Sauerstoff, Feuchtigkeit and relativ hohe Temperaturen unbedingt notwendig sind.

Die zahlreichen experimentellen Untersuchungen Emil Christian Hansens über die Bedingungen der Sporenbildung bei der Hefe haben zu Ergebnissen geführt, die wir in folgenden Sätzen kurz wiedergeben können.

1. Nur junge, kräftige, gut ernährte Zellen bilden in typischer Weise ihre Sporen aus.

2. Die Sporenbildung geht nur unter Luftzutritt vor, ist also ein streng aërober Prozess, für dessen Zustandekommen eine genügende Sauerstoffmenge unerlässlich ist.

3. Die Unterlage, auf der die Zellen sich bei der Sporenbildung befinden, muss reichliche Mengen von Feuchtigkeit aufweisen.

4. Das Optimum der Temperatur für die Sporulation liegt bei den meisten Hefearten um 25° C.

5. Die Zeitdauer der Sporenbildung ist unmittelbar von der Temperatur in dem Sinne abhängig, dass dieselbe für die betreffende Art am kürzesten ist, je mehr sich die herrschende Temperatur dem Optimum derselben für die Sporulation nähert.

6. Das Temperaturmaximum der Sporenbildung liegt niedriger als dasjenige der Sprossung, während das Minimum für die Sporulation höher ist als für die Sprossung.

Endlich ist gewiss ein die Sporulation wesentlich beeinflussender Faktor der Gehalt an Nährstoffen und die Art derselben im Nahrsubstrat. Je kleiner der Vorrat an Nährstoffen in der Nährflüssigkeit im allgemeinen wird, desto sicherer und rascher setzt die Sporenbildung ein. Besonders günstig scheinen erfahrungsmässig Übergänge von üppigster Ernährung zu mangelhafter zu wirken, worauf man bei den Sporulationsversuchen besonders zu achten hat.

Über die Einwirkung der Art der Nährstoffe auf die Sporenbildung wissen wir noch nicht viel. Nach den vorliegenden wenigen in dieser Richtung angestellten Versuchen scheint besonders gewissen Zuckern eine günstige Beeinflussung der Sporenerzeugug zuzukommen, während andere direkt jede Sporulation unterdrücken. Am schnellsten setzt letztere bei der Anwendung von Laktose und Rhamnose als Kohlenstoffquelle in der Nährlösung ein; Saccharose und auch Maltose wirken hemmend, so dass jede Sporenproduktion bei ihrer Anwesenheit ausbleibt.

Entsprechend den eben mitgeteilten Erkenntnissen über die Bedingungen der Sporenbildung hat man eine besondere Methode der Untersuchung der Sporulation ausgearbeitet, die allen obigen Anforderungen gerecht wird und in bezug auf die Kardinalpunkte der Sporenbildung hinsichtlich der Zeitdauer und Temperatur Ergebnisse liefert, die für die Unterscheidung der Arten von grösster Wichtigkeit sind.

Wir verwenden dabei Zellen, die sich in höchster Spross- und Gärtätigkeit befinden. Deshalb überimpfen wir dieselben vor der Anlage der Sporenkultur in gut nährende und leicht vergärbare Substrate, wie frische sterile Bierwürze, in der wir einige Tage bei Zimmer-temperatur züchten. Von der in dieser Zeit gebildeten Bodensatzhefe überimpft man dann in eine neue Portion steriler Bierwürze und züchtet durch 24 Stunden bei 25° C. Die nunmehr entstandene Satzhefe wird nach vorsichtiger Entfernung der überstehenden Nährflüssigkeit auf eine für die Sporulation geeignete Unterlage gebracht. Als solche erweist sich am zweckmässigsten der Gipsblock in der Form, wie es Figur 86 zeigt, wenn im grossen gearbeitet werden soll, oder in ein Hansenkölbchen eingegossen, wie aus Figur 87 ersichtlich ist. Auf die Oberfläche der sterilen, trockenen Gipsblöcke wird von der Satzhefe nach der oben geschilderten Vorbehandlung eine Portion ausgestrichen und in das Glasgefäss eine etwa bis zur Hälfte der Blockhöhe reichende Menge sterilen Wassers eingegossen, damit der Block sich mit Wasser von unten her vollsaugen kann und ständig feucht gehalten ist. Der nur lose schliessende Deckel oder beim Hansenkölbchen der lockere Wattepfropf gestattet einen genügenden Luftzutritt. Unter diesen Verhältnissen tritt die Sporenbildung unter Erhaltung der geeigneten Temperaturen alsbald ein, und die erhaltenen Kardinalpunkte in bezug auf die Temperatur sind für die einzelnen Arten als sehr konstant anzusehen.

Folgendes Beispiel für die Kardinalpunkte der Temperaturen für die Sporenbildung von Saccharomyces cerevisiae nach Hansen sei hier aufgeführt.

Für die Sporenbildung von Saccharomyces cerevisiae ergibt sich somit ein Optimum von 30° C, ein Minimum zwischen 11 und 12° und ein Maximum zwichen 36 und 37°. Die Sporulationsweite erstreckt sich für diese Hefeart also von ca. 12 bis 37° C.

Abgrenzung der Psychologie†

Die Psychologie ist die wissenschaftliche Lehre von den Bewusstseinserscheinungen. Wenn diese Worte richtig verstanden werden, ist die Definition völlig scharf, weder zu weit noch zu eng. Erläutern wir sie daher etwas näher.

Die Bewusstseinserscheinungen sind uns als unmittelbare Erlebnisse gegeben. Empfindungen, Vorstellungen, Gedanken, Gefühle, Wünsche, Entschlüsse usw. sind Beispiele solcher Erlebnisse, die jedermann bekannt sind. Die erwähnten sowie alle übrigen im Bewusstsein zu beobachtenden Erscheinungen, die wir auch als seelische oder psychische Phänomeme bezeichnen, sind die Objekte der Psychologie.

Die Psychologie als wissenschaftliche Lehre von den genannten Objekten hat drei verschiedene Aufgaben zu lösen: 1. die Beschreibung der beobachteten Erscheinungen; 2. die Feststellung der gesetzmässigen Beziehungen, die diese Erscheinungen einerseits zueinander und andererseits zu andern damit in Verbindung stehenden Erscheinungen aufweisen; 3. die Erklärung dieser Beziehungen, indem sie, soweit es zu gegebener Zeit möglich ist, auf allgemeinere, umfassendere Gesetze zurückgeführt werden.

Die Lösung der ersten dieser Aufgaben ist eine unvermeidliche Vorstufe der zweiten; die Erscheinungen müssen zuvörderst so genau beschrieben werden, dass Verwechslung unmöglich ist, ehe eine nähere Untersuchung ihrer Beziehungen sich überhaupt durchführen lässt. Die zweite, in praktischer Hinsicht wichtigste Aufgabe führt uns bald zu der Erkenntnis, dass die psychischen Erscheinungen nicht nur voneinander und von äusseren physischen Vorgängen, sondern auch von etwas kaum näher Bestimmbarem abhängig sind, das zwar denselben Gesetzen wie die Bewusstseinserscheinungen zu unterliegen scheint, sich aber im Bewusstsein nicht nachweisen lässt. Man nennt es daher das Unbewusste oder Unterbewusste (subliminale). Die Beziehungen der psychischen Erscheinungen zu diesem unbekannten Unbewussten sind selbstverständlich auch festzustellen, und eine Untersuchung derselben ist also durch unsere Definition der Psychologie nicht ausgeschlossen.

Wie die Definition sich mithin, recht verstanden, genügend weit erweist, ist sie auch hinreichend eng. Tatsächlich ist uns alles, auch die physische Welt, nur als Bewusstseinserscheinungen gegeben, und man hat daraus gefolgert, dass sämtliche Wissenschaften nur verschiedene Zweige der Psychologie wären. Dieser Schluss ist entschieden unrichtig. Mit demselben Rechte könnte fast behauptet werden, dass alle Wissenschaften nur Grammatik seien, weil sie alle unvermeidlich mit Wörtern operieren.

Die Methode der Psychologie

Da die Bewusstseinserscheinungen nicht wie äussere Objekte wahrgenommen, sondern nur innerlich erlebt werden können, gibt es tatsächlich nur eine Methode zur Erforschung dieses Gebietes, nämlich die der Selbstbeobachtung. Die Methode leidet indes, solange sie nicht auf eine ganz bestimmte Weise systematisch betrieben wird, an zahlreichen schwerwiegenden Übelständen; ihre Ergebnisse sind daher keineswegs so zuverlässig, wie nach dem unmittelbaren Verhältnis des Beobachters zum Gegenstand seiner Beobachtung zu erwarten stand. Erstens kann die Selbstbeobachtung uns nur über die psychischen Erlebnisse des einzelnen Beobachters belehren.

†A. G. L. Lehmann, **Grundzüge der Psychophysiologie**

die Beobachtungen zahlreicher Individuen verglichen werden, damit das allgemein Gültige aus den verschiedenen individuellen Eigentümlichkeiten ausgeschieden werden kann. Zweitens wird das Material, die zur Verfügung stehenden Tatsachen, dadurch beschränkt, dass der Beobachter seine Erfahrungen nur gelegentlich, unter gegebenen äusseren oder inneren Umständen, ernten kann; und die zu vergleichenden Erfahrungen sind keineswegs immer unter denselben Umständen zustande gekommen, so dass ihre Vergleichbarkeit zweifelhaft wird. Drittens kann die Selbstbeobachtung nur die gegenseitigen Beziehungen der seelischen Erscheinungen nachweisen, während sowohl ihre Abhängigkeit von äusseren Reizen als die physischen Begleiterscheinungen der seelischen Erlebnisse sich schwerlich konstatieren lassen. Viertens schliesslich sind die zu beobachtenden Bewusstseinserscheinungen manchmal so kompliziert, dass die einzelnen Glieder derselben nicht festzuhalten sind; in der hieraus resultierenden lückenhaften Beschreibung können somit sehr wesentliche Umstände vergessen sein.

Dass die Hindernisse, die die erwähnten Schwierigkeiten dem Fortschritte der Wissenschaft in den Weg legen, keineswegs gering sind, geht aus der Tatsache hervor, dass fast überall, wo es auf die Beobachtung feinerer Einzelheiten ankommt, Ansicht gegen Ansicht steht. Was der eine Psychologe behauptet, unmittelbar beobachten zu können, kann der andere schlechterdings nicht konstatieren; was dem einen als Regel erscheint, kennt der andere nur als seltene Ausnahme. Solche Widersprüche können zwar manchmal auf individuellen Unterschieden beruhen, manchmal lassen sie sich aber viel leichter dadurch erklären, dass der eine Psychologe ein guter, der andere ein schlechter Beobachter ist. Da wir aber leider kein Mass der Fähigkeit des Selbstbeobachtens besitzen, können wir in jedem gegebenen Falle durchaus nicht entscheiden, ob durch die verschiedenen Angaben wirklich existierende individuelle Differenzen konstatiert seien, oder ob vielleicht die eine Beobachtung richtig, die andere falsch sei. Hieraus folgt dann, dass feinere Einzelheiten des seelischen Geschehens durch einfache Selbstbeobachtung nicht bestimmt werden können.

Theorien von den wechselseitigen Beziehungen

Während die beiden ersten Aufgaben der Phychologie, die Beschreibung der Erscheinungen und die Festellung der gesetzmässigen Beziehungen derselben, nur auf dem Wege der Erfahrung, durch Beobachtung, zu lösen sind, erfordert die dritte Aufgabe, die Erklärung der gefundenen Tatsachen, eine ganz andere Behandlung. Wie die physikalischen und chemischen Gesetze nur auf die Weise zu erklären sind, dass man von gewissen Annahmen über die Natur der Materie ausgeht und dann die betreffenden Gesetze als notwendige Folgerungen dieser Annahmen ableitet, so kann eine Erklärung der psychologischen Gesetze nur durch ein analoges Verfahren erreicht werden. Man muss von einer Theorie über die Natur der psychischen Erscheinungen ausgehen und den Nachweis führen, dass die gefundenen Gesetze einfache Folgerungen der Theorie sind. Je vollständiger eine Theorie solche Ableitungen gestattet, um so grösser ist ihre Bedeutung und die Wahrscheinlichkeit ihrer Richtigkeit.

An Seelentheorien haben wir keinen Mangel. Dieser Umstand aber, dass es deren mehrere gibt, zeigt deutlich, wie keine derselben imstande ist, die Forderungen zu erfüllen, die an eine solche Theorie zu stellen sind. Die Möglichkeit ist zwar nicht ausgeschlossen, dass mehrere Theorien gleichzeitig eine gewisse Gruppe von Tatsachen gleich gut zu erklären vermögen; je zahlreicher aber die zu erklärenden Tatsachen sind, um so grösser wird die Wahrscheinlichkeit, dass eine der um die Herrschaft ringenden Theorien sich den anderen überlegen erweist. Handelt es sich daher um so umfassende Theorien wie diejenigen, die die Beziehungen zwischen Seele und Leib zu erklären haben, so ist es kaum denkbar, dass mehrere verschiedene den Tatsachen gleich gut gerecht werden können. Wenn dennoch keine der historisch gegebenen Seelentheorien sich als die einzig mögliche erwiesen hat, liegt es einfach darin, dass keine dieser Theorien überhaupt etwas zu erklären imstande ist. Darüber kann man sich auch nicht wundern, weil diese Theorien als Resultat philosophischer Spekulationen in alten Zeiten entstanden sind, wo nur die unmittelbaren Ergebnisse der Selbstbeobachtung bekannt waren. Der Zweck der Theorien konnte folglich nicht derjenige sein, eine Reihe festgestellter gesetzmässiger Beziehungen zu erklären; in der Tat haben die Theorien ganz anders zum Teil recht verschiedene Ziele gehabt.

Analyse psychischer Erscheinungen

Die Psychophysik ist die Lehre von den Beziehungen zwischen Seele und Leib, zwischen den Bewusstseinszuständen und den physischen und physiologischen Verhältnissen, mit welchen sie einhergehen. Damit aber diese Beziehungen dargelegt werden können, muss eine andere Aufgabe vorher gelöst werden. Wie schon früher hervorgehoben, treten die Bewusstseinserscheinungen fast immer massenhaft auf. Ein Blick auf die Strasse gibt uns eine überwältigende Menge Bilder von Häusern, Menschen, Tieren, Wagen usw., und gleichzeitig hören wir einen Lärm, der von den Fusstritten und Stimmen der Gehenden, dem Bellen der Hunde, dem Rollen der Wagen, dem Sausen des Windes usw, hervorgebracht wird. In diesem und in ähnlichen Fällen sind uns also äusserst komplizierte Bewusstseinszustände gegeben, und es würde entschieden eine unlösbare Aufgabe sein, die Beziehungen zwischen solchen psychischen Komplexen und ihren äusseren Ursachen festzustellen. Die Aufgabe muss daher vereinfacht werden, indem der zusammengesetzte Bewusstseinsinhalt zuvörderst in Teile zerlegt wird, die sich einzeln untersuchen lassen. Eine solche Zerlegung, Analyse, unserer komplizierten Bewusstseinszustände kommt schon teilweise durch die täglichen Erlebnisse zustande. Indem uns nämlich häufig bestimmte Gruppen von Bewusstseinserscheinungen in verschiedenen Verbindungen gegeben sind, treten diese Gruppen als etwas Zusammengehöriges und, im Vergleich mit den wechselnden Nebenerscheinungen, als etwas relativ Selbständiges hervor. Und da sie ferner in mannigfachen Verbindungen vorkommen können, sind sie auch etwas relativ Einfaches.

Es gibt zwei Arten solcher relativ einfachen psychischen Gebilde, nämlich die Wahrnehmungen von den Dingen der Aussenwelt und die Gemütsbewegungen. Die ersteren werden von den Sinnesorganen vermittelt, und sie verschwinden, wenn die betreffenden Organe sich vor den äusseren Reizen verschliessen. Aus diesem Umstande folgert man, dass die Wahrnehmungen von äusseren Ursachen herrühren, und diese Ursachen müssen relativ unveränderlich sein, weil eine bestimmte Wahrnehmung in sehr verschiedenen Verbindungen vorkommen kann. Diese konstanten Ursachen der Wahrnehmungen nennt man die Dinge, die Gegenstände. Die Wahrnehmungen beziehen sich mithin stets auf Gegenstände; die Psychologie des Alltagslebens macht überhaupt keinen Unterschied zwischen den Dingen und unsern Wahrnehmungen der Dinge. Wie die Wahrnehmungen sind auch die Gemütsbewegungen relativ konstante Erscheinungen, was einfach aus der Tatsache hervorgeht, dass die Sprache eine ganze Reihe Namen solcher Gebilde hat. Schreck, Verwunderung, Erstaunen, Spannung, Hoffnung, Furcht, Zorn, Scham, Ärger, Freude, Kummer, Wehmut, Schadenfreude, Mitleid, Neid, Dankbarkeit, Achtung, Bewunderung, Reue usw. sind Beispiele solcher Zustände, die jedermann aus eigener Erfahrung kennt und zu benennen weiss. Von den Wahrnehmungen unterscheiden sich die Gemütsbewegungen zuvörderst dadurch, dass sie sich nicht auf Dinge beziehen.

Einteilung der Empfindungen

Die herkömmliche Einteilung der Empfindungen ist eine rein physiologische. Da es bei oberflächlicher Betrachtung fünf verschiedene Sinnesorgane gibt, so besitzen wir mithin fünf Sinne: das Gesicht, das Gehör, den Geruch, den Geschmack und das Gefühl. Die Anzahl unserer Empfindungsgruppen oder Modalitäten ist indes in neuerer Zeit durch die gemeinsame Arbeit der physiologischen und psychologischen Forschung bedeutend vermehrt worden. Es konnte der psychologischen Beobachtung nicht entgehen, dass die Empfindungen, die unter dem Namen Gefühl zusammengefasst wurden, so verschiedenartig waren, dass sie kaum durch ein einzelnes Sinnesorgan vermittelt werden konnten. Einige derselben, wie die Druck- und Temperaturempfindungen, rühren von äusseren Reizen her, während andere dagegen von inneren Zuständen des Organismus erregt werden; es konnte somit kaum zweifelhaft sein, dass hier verschiedene Sinnesgebiete vorlagen. Die eingehende physiologische Untersuchung wies denn auch bald mehrere verschiedene Sinnesorgane nach, die je ihrer besonderen Modalität der Empfindungen entsprachen. Bezüglich der in der Haut liegenden Sinnesorgane, die der experimentellen Untersuchung leicht zugänglich sind, besteht jetzt kaum ein Zweifel; unsicherer sind dagegen die Ergebnisse in bezug auf die Arten der Sinne und die Lage ihrer Organe im Inneren des Körpers. Der physiologische Nachweis der Sinnesorgane genügt somit nicht um eine vollständige Bestimmung sämtlicher Empfindungsmodalitäten zu gewährleisten.

Es scheint denn auch natürlicher, eine Einteilung der Empfindungen von einem psychologischen Gesichtspunkte aus durchzuführen. Die Empfindungen sind uns als Tatsachen der inneren Erfahrung, unabhängig von jeder Kenntnis der Sinnesorgane, gegeben, und sie müssen daher auch nach ihrer psychischen Verwandtschaft eingeteilt werden können. Die Verwandschaft z. B. von zwei beliebigen Farbenempfindungen zeigt sich dadurch, dass sich immer eine ganze Reihe anderer Farbenempfindungen nachweisen lässt, die einen allmählichen Übergang zwischen den beiden Aussengliedern bilden. Solche Übergabe gibt es aber nicht z. B. zwischen Farbenempfindungen und Tonempfindungen, während diese letzteren ihrerseits wiederum stetige Übergänge zwischen beliebigen Gliedern aufweisen. Jede Gruppe von Empfindungen, deren einzelne Glieder durch stetige Übergänge miteinander verbunden sind, bildet eine besondere Empfindungsmodalität. Es gibt mithin ebenso viele verschiedene Modalitäten, wie sich kontinuierliche Mannigfaltigkeiten von Empfindungen nachweisen lassen.

Die Gefühle

Wie schon oben hervorgehoben, sind sowohl die einfachen Empfindungen als die davon zusammengesetzten Wahrnehmungen und Vorstellungen meistens von besonderen Zuständen der Lust und der Unlust begleitet. Wir bezeichnen diese Begleiterscheinungen, im Gegensatz zu den erwähnten intellektuellen Zuständen, als die emotionellen Elemente, die Gefühlselemente oder Gefühlstöne, während die aus Empfindungen und Gefühlselementen zusammengesetzten Zustände Gefühle heissen. Es wurde ebenfalls früher hervorgehoben, dass dem Anschein nach recht einfache Gefühle keineswegs immer als nur lust- oder unlustbetont auftreten, indem die Gefühle Modifikationen aufweisen, die sich durch die Gegensätze erregend-deprimierend, heiter-ernst, beruhigend-beunruhigend usw. bezeichnen lassen. Wenn wir hier zur Erklärung dieser Modifikationen des Gefühls neben Lust und Unlust keine neuen Gefühlselemente annehmen, beruht es hauptsächlich darauf, dass die intellektuellen Elemente des Gefühls in allen solchen Fällen sich als recht kompliziert erweisen, was später im einzelnen nachgewiesen werden soll.

Begründung der Bakteriologie

Die Lehre von den Bakterien ist fast gänzlich ein Produkt der Neuzeit. Allerdings hatte man schon früher teils kleine Lebewesen als Schmarotzer in Pflanzen, im Menschen und Tierleib beobachtet und teils eine Ahnung davon, dass diese auch die Ursachen von Krankheiten sein könnten. Zu einer eigentlichen naturwissenschaftlichen, fest und exakt begründeten Disziplin wurde die Bakteriologie aber erst in den letzten 25 Jahren ausgebaut und als ihr Vater muss Robert Koch (geb. 1843 in Berlin) angesehen werden, dem zugleich das Verdienst zukommt, eine grosse Reihe ungeahnter Funde ermittelt zu haben, die von epochemachender Bedeutung geworden sind und tatsächlich auf die Lehre von den Ursachen der anstekkenden Krankheiten neues Licht geworfen haben.

Um die Funde recht zu verstehen, sei ein kurzes erklärendes Wort über die Bakterien eingefügt. Die Bakterien oder Spaltpilze sind kleinste pflanzliche einzellige Lebewesen, die sich durch Zweiteilung, durch Querspaltung vermehren. Der Hauptsache nach* unterscheidet man: Kokken (kugelige Individuen), Bazillen (gerade zylindrische Stäbchen) und Spirillen (gekrümmte Formen). Die krankheiterregende Wirkung der sogenannten pathogenen Bakterien beruht auf der Hervorbringung von dem Organismus schädlichen Giften (Toxinen), die, je nachdem jener ein guter oder schlechter Nährboden für die betreffende Bakterienart ist, in verschiedenem Grade erzeugt werden.

In neuster Zeit ist es teilweise gelungen, die Giftbildung der pathogenen Pilze durch geeignete Methoden abzuschwächen. Impft man mit dem abgeschwächten und wirksamen Parasiten, so entwickelt er sich zwar auch, ohne jedoch eine so schwere Krankheit als bei voller Virulenz hervorzurufen, d. h. Fähigkeit zur Ausscheidung giftiger Produkte. Wunderbarerweise wird dagegen der geimpfte Organismus durch das Überstehen der schwächeren spezifischen Krankheit immun, d. h. widerstandsfähig gegen stärkere Infektionen. Hierauf beruhen die sogenannten Schutzimpfungen.

Koch ging von der Milzbrandfrage aus. Als praktischer Arzt in Wollstein hatte er oft Gelegenheit, Tiere, die an dieser Krankheit starben, zu untersuchen. Die Übertragbarkeit des Milzbrandes war nun zwar lang bekannt, auch dass Bazillen im ursächlichen Zusammenhang damit standen und dabei eine Rolle spielten, wusste man; aber es fehlte der genaue Nachweis, und diesen lieferte Koch.

Mit Hilfe der Anilinfärbemethode sowie eines verbesserten Mikroskopes entdeckte er 1876 die längst vermuteten Milzbrand-Bazillensporen, deren Widerstandsfähigkeit sowie ihre Neigung zu Bazillen auszuwachsen, er nachwies. Er setzte seine Forschungen fort und tat in einer Schrift (1878) auf Grund von Versuchen an Tieren in ebenso exakter wie überzeugender Weise den Zusammenhang zwischen den sogenannten akzidentellen Wundkrankheiten mit gewissen Bakterien dar. Dasselbe gelang ihm bald auch für zwei andere Krankheiten; für die Tuberkulose durch Auffindung des Tuberkelbazillus (1882, in welchem Jahre er auch als Geheimer Regierungsrath berufen wurde) und für die Cholera durch Nachweis des sog. Kommabazillus (1883). Damit waren Tatsachen von umwälzender Tragweite gewonnen. Durch Annahme seiner Methoden, der Herstellung von "Reinkulturen", gewisser Färbeflüssigkeiten u. s. w., begann man nun für eine ganze Reihe von Krankheiten, wie Diphtherie, Lungenentzündung, Wundstarrkrampf, Scharlach, die Blattern oder Pocken, sowie die Maul- und Klauenseuche den pathogenen Bazillus aufzufinden, und toxin- oder bakteriengifthaltiges Blutwasser (Serum) in abgeschwächter Form dem an der betreffenden Krankheit leidenden Menschen einzuspritzen.

Chemische Beschaffenheit der Zellmembran

Über die chemische Beschaffenheit der Bakterienmembran ist noch wenig bekannt, doch dürfte im allgemeinen aus den bisherigen Forschungsergebnissen hervorgehen, dass sie nach Arten und Nährböden verschiedene Zusammensetzung besitzt.

Am häufigsten ist wohl Sarcina ventriculi auf die Beschaffenheit der Zellmembran untersucht worden. Während aber Hasse, Virchow und Schlossberger bei ihren Versuchen, eine Zellulosemembran nachzuweisen, keinen Erfolg hatten, glaubt Pokels eine solche annehmen zu können, und Suringar gibt mit aller Bestimmtheit an, dass er die Zellulosereaktion beobachtet habe. Die Annahme Halliers, dass sie ähnlich den Diatomeen eine Kieselmembran ausscheide, wurde von Suringar widerlegt. Die späteren Forscher, auch Zopf und de Bary geben stets das Vorhandensein einer Cellulosemembran für Sarcina ventriculi an. Auch Sarcina aurea Mace soll Zellulosereaktion zeigen. Gruber konnte bei keiner der von ihm untersuchten und beschriebenen Sarcina-Arten Zellulose nachweisen, auch bei Sarcina ventriculi nicht.

Ich selbst habe die von Gruber beschriebenen Arten nachgeprüft und fand ebenfalls niemals Zellulosereaktion. Bei Sarcina ventriculi konnte ich 2 mal Zellulosereaktion nachweisen. 3 mal dagegen gelang mir dies in keiner Weise, und obgleich alle 5 Fälle sich auf Untersuchungen von erbrochenem Mageninhalt bezogen, in welchem sich die Sarcina in grosser Menge und in ganz typischen Paketen vorfand, glaubte ich doch anfangs, zwei verschiedene Arten vor mir zu haben. Es gelang mir wiederholt, Sarcina ventriculi aus dem Erbrochenen zu züchten, und in einem Falle, wo sie sich in ausserordentlich zahlreichen Kolonien entwickelt hatte, gab sie in dem Erbrochenen deutlich die Zellulosereaktion, Material aus den Kulturen dagegen wurde mit Chlorzinkjod gelb, mit Jod und Schwefelsäure bräunlich. Kultiviert man sie dagegen in neutralem Stärkekleister, so färben sich die Zellen, auch wenn keine Spur des Stärkekleisters anhaftet, mit Jod und Schwefelsäure blau. Ich habe die Versuche nicht weiter fortgesetzt, glaube aber hieraus schon schliessen zu dürfen, dass sich die chemische Beschaffenheit der Membran bei dieser Art ändert, wenn der Nährboden eine andere Zusammensetzung zeigt. Ob es sich übrigens bei Sarcina ventriculi um echte Zellulose handelt oder um irgend einen andern die Zellulosereaktion gebenden Körper, ist zunächst noch sehr fraglich und durch die Untersuchungen Wintersteins neuerdings zweifelhaft geworden.

Die chemische Beschaffenheit der Zellmembran bei Bakterien ist wiederholt Gegenstand der Untersuchung gewesen, sehr oft handelte es sich dabei aber um Bakteriengemenge und nicht um eine einheitliche Art. Für Bakterium aceti geben beispielsweise Nägeli und Loew 98,3 Proz. Wasser und 1,7 Proz. Trockensubstanz an; die letztere enthielt 3,37 Proz. Asche und 1,82 Proz. Stickstoff. Daraus zieht Nägeli den Schluss, dass neben dem eiweisshaltigen Zellinhalt noch etwa 84 Proz. aschefrei Zellulose vorhanden seien. Ebenso soll auch Leuconostoc ein Kohlehydrat in grossen Mengen enthalten.

Für Fäulnisbakterien wiesen Nencki und Schaffer nach, dass sie zum weitaus grössten Teil aus Proteinstoffen bestehen, dass aber nach Bestimmung dieser, der Fettstoffe, und Aschebestandteile noch ein unbestimmter Rest bleibt, der von den Autoren der Hauptsache nach als Zellulose gedeutet wird. Die Zusammensetzung der Bakterien stellt sich hiernach folgendermassen.

Bei den reifen, d. h. den auf der Höhe der Entwickelung stehenden Bakterien, ist also der Gehalt an Zellulose nach Nencki und Schaffer am grössten.

Erste Entdeckungsfahrt des Columbus

Nachdem Columbus mit all seinen Gefährten die heil. Kommunion empfangen hatte, ging er am Freitag den 3. August 1492 in See. Wenn wir nun verstehen wollen, welchen Reiseplan Columbus verfolgte, so müssen wir nicht unsere heutigen Karten zur Hand nehmen, sondern einen Blick auf diejenigen werfen, welche kurz vor der Entdeckung von Amerika angefertigt wurden; denn nach ihnen richtete Columbus den Kurs seiner Schiffe. Auf diesen Karten ist die Erde viel kleiner als in Wirklichkeit dargestellt. Die neue Welt fehlt auf ihnen gänzlich, jenseit des Ozeans liegt die Ostküste von Asien, das Ziel der grossen Entdecker jener Zeit. Die Azoren, die Kanarien und die Capverdischen Inseln waren die äussersten bekannten Punkte der Alten Welt. Westlich von denselben sind auf den Karten und auf dem ersten Globus von Martin Benaim zwei Inseln eingetragen: südlich die Insel des heiligen Brandan und nördlich die Insel Antilia, hinter welcher in nicht mehr weiter Ferne die asiatische Insel Cipango (Japan) liegt.

Nach diesen Karten war also der günstigste Ausgangspunkt zur Erreichung der Ostküste von Asien eine der Kanarischen Inseln; von hier musste man nach der Insel Antilia segeln und von dieser Cipango erreichen. Nach unseren Karten ist dagegen dieser Weg der weiteste nach Amerika; Irland und Neufundland und Südamerika liegen weit näher aneinander. Die Wahl der Fahrt über die Azoren oder die Capverdischen Insel hätte Columbus viel eher nach Amerika geführt, die Dauer der Fahrt wäre etwa um die Hälfte gekürzt worden. Aber die Spanier hätten auch zunächst Florida oder Guyana entdeckt, sie wären nicht sofort in die goldreichen Länder gelangt und die Besiedlungsgeschichte hätte vielleicht einen ganz anderen Verlauf genommen.

Columbus hielt sich also sofort in westlicher Richtung und immer im Breitengrade der Kanarischen Inseln, nach dem damals herrschenden Brauch der Seefahrer, welcher erst mit der Einführung des Chronometers abkam, auf ein und demselben Breitengrade zu steuern, und hatte den Vorteil eines beständig günstigen Windes. Am 12. August lief er in den Hafen von St. Sebastian auf der Insel Gomer ein und verblieb daselbst vier Wochen, um sich frisch zu verproviantieren. Er schilderte seinen Gefährten die im Westen liegenden Wunderländer in den glühendsten Farben und versprach ihnen Gold und Schätze. Er hielt das Schiffsvolk von nun an im Irrtum über die Entfernung, indem er in der offen ausgestellten Berechnung den zurückgelegten Weg viel geringer angab, als er in Wirklichkeit war, bemerkte den wahren Lauf aber in einem geheimen Schiffstagebuch.

Die Fahrt erfolgte bei günstigem Wetter und milder Luft, so dass man vierunddreissig Tage lang nichts als Himmel und Wasser erblickte. Je mehr der Raum wuchs, der die Segler von der Heimat trennte, desto grösser wurde ihre Aufregung und Unruhe. Die Abweichung der Magnetnadel in nordwestlicher Richtung, welche Columbus am Abend des 11. September zum erstenmal sah, erfüllte sie mit Furcht und Schrecken: es schien ihnen, als ob sie in eine Welt einträten, wo die Grundgesetze der Natur sich veränderten und unbekannte Einflüsse regierten. Columbus suchte sie zu beruhigen, indem er die Ursache der Abweichung auf die Umdrehung des Polarsterns zurückführte. Selbst die günstigen Winde, welche, von Osten wehend, die Schiffe in der zweiten Hälfte des September sanft über die ruhige, hie und da mit grünen Seepflanzen bedeckte Wasserfläche dahingleiten liessen, erregten Sorge.

Am 14. September stellten sich Anzeichen von der Nähe von Land ein, und zwar in Gestalt eines Reihers und eines im Spanischen Rabo de Junco, im Englischen water-wagtail genannten Vogels, zweier sich niemals weit vom Lande entfernenden Vogelarten. Dann umschwebte die Schiffe ein weisser Vogel der Tropen, welcher nicht auf dem Meere zu ruhen vermag. Am 25. September hielten die aufgeregten Offiziere und Mannschaften eine Wolkenbank im Norden, die bei Sonnenuntergang die Gestalt einer Insel annahm, für Land und begrüssten die Botschaft mit einem Lobgesang, bis das Nebelbild am folgenden Morgen sich als eine Sinnestäuschung erwies.

In den ersten Tagen des Oktober mehrten sich die Anzeichen, dass Land in der Nähe sein müsse. Züge von kleinen bunten Vögeln schwärmten um die Schiffe her und flogen dann weiter nach Südwest; frische grüne Gewächse, vom Lande gelöst, trieben auf dem Wasser umher, ein Rohr, ein kleines Brett, ein künstlich geschnitzter Stab wurden aufgefischt. Am 11. Oktober abends um 10 Uhr nahm der spähende Admiral in der klaren Herbstnacht ein sich bewegendes Licht wahr und machte auch andere darauf aufmerksam. Um 2 Uhr in der Frühe, Freitag den 12. Oktober, erspähte Rodrigo de Triana, ein Matrose auf der Pinta, in der Entfernung von zwei Meilen im Mondenglanz den schimmernden Saum eines vorspringenden Gestades. Unter dem freudigen Rufe "Land! Land!" stürzte er auf das nächste Geschütz, um das Signal zu geben.

Sobald der Tag graute, legten die Schiffe an und Columbus bestieg, in scharlachrote Admiralsuniform gekleidet und das königliche Banner von Castilien schwingend, das neuentdeckte Land. Es war die heutige Watlings-Insel von der Bahama-Gruppe, welche die Einwohner Guanahani nannten, der aber Columbus zu Ehren des Erlösers den Namen San Salvador beilegte.

Als Columbus die Watlings-Insel betrat und an den folgenden Tagen einige andere kleine Inseln aus der Gruppe der Bahama-Inseln entdeckte und mit neuen Namen belegte, lebte er in dem Glauben, dass er sich vor dem ostasiatischen Küstenlande befinde und dass die aus dem Reisewerke Marco Polos berühmten und auf der Seekarte Toscanellis verzeichneten Landschaften Cipango (Japan) und Kithai (China) in der Nähe sein müssten. Diese aufzusuchen war sein eifrigstes Bestreben. Er liess einige von den harmlosen Naturmenschen einfangen, und sogleich auf die Schiffe bringen und in der spanischen Sprache unterrichten, um sie als Führer gebrauchen zu können. Sobald sie an Bord waren, lichtete er die Anker und fuhr weiter in südwestlicher Richtung; am 28. Oktober gelangte er nach der grossen Insel Cuba, welche er für Cipango hielt. Da hier ein mächtiger Fürst residieren sollte, so entsandte er sofort zwei Boten; sie kehrten indessen nach mehreren Tagen bitter enttäuscht zurück, da sie nur einen nackten Häuptling mit seinem ebenso bekleidungslosen Volke in einem armseligen Dorfe, das aus mit Palmblättern gedeckten Hütten bestand, aufgefunden hatten. Von Gold und anderen Kostbarkeiten war nichts zu finden.

Er verliess mit den beiden Schiffen Cuba, nachdem er seine sämtlichen Leute schwören liess, dass sie wirklich das Festland Asiens betreten hätten und dass sie glaubten, man könne von dort zu Fuss nach Spanien gelangen. Am 6. Dezember landete er auf dem reizenden, mit Wäldern, Bergen und fruchtbaren Ebenen durchzogenen Haiti, welches er wegen der Ähnlichkeit mit andalusischen Landschaften Hispaniola nannte. Auch die hier empfangenen Eindrücke bestärkten die Spanier in dem Wahne, dass sie das gepriesene glückliche Indien gefunden hätten.

Goethe

Johann Wolfgang Goethe wurde geboren den 28. Aug. 1749 zu Frankfurt am Main. Von seinem Vater Johann Kaspar, einem wohlhabenden Privatmanne mit dem Titel "kaiserlicher Rat" erbte er "die Statur," jene Ordnungsliebe und ernste Ruhe, welche die Grundlage der Kunst ist; von seiner Mutter die lebhafteste Phantasie und das ausgezeichnete Erzählungstalent. Was der Dichter beiden verdankt, hat er ausgesprochen in den Worten: "Vom Vater hab' ich die Statur, des Lebens ernstes Führen, vom Mütterchen die Frohnatur und Lust zu fabulieren."

Seine Geburtsstadt mit dem ausgebreiteten Handel, den jährlichen Messen, den geschichtlichen Denkmälern bot dem Knaben die vielseitigste Gelegenheit zu objektiver Anschauung und enthielt so unendlich vieles, um den Dichtergenius des Knaben zu wecken. Neue Anschauungen wurden dem Knaben zugeführt, als Frankfurt während des siebenjährigen Krieges eine französische Besatzung erhielt und ein Teil des Goethe'schen Hauses vom Königslieutenant, Graf Thoranc, bezogen wurde. Da der kunstliebende Graf eine Reihe von Bildern von den geschicktesten Malern unter seinen Augen ausführen liess, kam der Knabe mit diesen Künstlern in nahe Berührung und wurde so auf das Gebiet der Malerei hingewiesen.

Den Unterricht leitete der Vater selbst, der namentlich die Selbsttätigkeit des Knaben zu wecken suchte. Eine Art Roman in Briefen, die der junge Goethe in sieben Sprachen verfasste, gab ihm Gelegenheit sich im schriftlichen Ausdruck des Lateinischen, Griechischen, Französischen, Englischen, Italienischen, Deutschen und des Frankfurter jüdischen Dialektes zu üben. Dieses Judendeutsch führte ihn zum Studium des Hebräischen und zu einer fleissigen Beschäftigung mit dem alten Testament und der Bibel. Unter den deutschen Dichtern war es namentlich Klopstock, dessen "Messias" ihn mächtig ergriff. Er selbst dichtete in seiner Jugend eine Anzahl geistlicher Oden und Lieder, unter denen das "die Höllenfahrt Christi" betitelte das älteste ist, was in Goethes Werken sich findet. Ausserdem entstand als die Frucht seiner hebräischen Studien ein biblisches Gedicht über Joseph und seine Brüder.

Nachdem so der Knabe bei äusserem Wohlstande unter günstigen Verhältnissen und unter der sorgfältigen Pflege der Eltern herangewachsen war, bezog er 1765 die Universität Leipzig, um die Rechte zu studieren. Doch fand er zunächst an den juristischen Vorlesungen kein Interesse, ebensowenig an den philosophischen. Dagegen brachte ihm die feine städtische Sitte der Leipziger Gesellschaft, in die er eingeführt worden war, grossen Gewinn. Ausserdem studierte er mit dem grössten Eifer die Kunst, wofür schon im Vaterhause durch allerhand Abbildungen von Roms Denkmälern der Sinn geweckt worden war. Sein Lehrer, Oeser, der Direktor der Leipziger Kunstschule, führte ihn in die Kunstgeschichte ein und erschloss ihm das Verständnis von Winkelmanns Werken und Lessings Laokoon.

Zwei von seinen ersten Lustspielen sind noch in französischem Geschmack und französischer Form gedichtet. Aber wenn auch Goethe damals noch an den überlieferten Formen und Regeln festhielt, so zeigte sich doch schon hier die Eigentümlichkeit seiner Dichternatur, insofern er den Quell seiner Dichtung im Gemüt fand. Beide Stücke geben davon Zeugnis, wie Goethe schon damals bestrebt war, alles was ihn freute oder quälte, poetisch zu erfassen, in ein Gedicht zu verwandeln. Weil Goethe so nur dem Selbsterlebten einen poetischen Ausdruck gab, in diesem Sinne nennt er alle seine Gedichte Gelegenheitsgedichte oder "Bruchstücke einer grossen Konfession."

Ende des Sommers 1768 kehrte Goethe krank von Leipzig nach Frankfurt zurück, um im elterlichen Hause seine Gesundheit wiederherzustellen. Während seiner Genesung wurde er durch eine Freundin seiner Mutter, Fräulein von Klettenberg, sowie durch seinen Arzt mit allerlei alchemistischen Büchern bekannt und machte auf diesem Gebiete allerhand Experimente, deren Spuren sich noch im Faust erkennen lassen. Nachdem er seine volle Gesundheit und Jugendkraft erlangt, begab er sich im Frühling des Jahres 1770 nach Strassburg, um hier nach dem Willen seines Vaters die juristischen Studien zu vollenden.

Doch hörte er neben den juristischen auch allerhand medizinische und naturwissenschaftliche Vorlesungen, denn seine Tischgenossen waren vorzugsweise Mediziner. Zu seinen Strassburger Freunden gehörten ausser dem unglücklichen Lenz und dem liebenswürdigen Lerse der kindlich fromme Jung-Stilling. Von dem bedeutendsten Einfluss aber auf Goethe war die Bekanntschaft mit Herder, der ihm, obgleich nur um fünf Jahre älter, doch an Erfahrung, Selbstständigkeit und Reife weit überlegen war. Goethe selbst bezeichnet die Verbindung mit Herder als das bedeutendste Ereignis, welches für seine Geistes- und Charakterentwickelung die wichtigsten Folgen haben sollte. Er lernte nun verstehen, dass die Dichtkunst eine Welt- und Völkergabe sei, nicht das Erbteil einiger feingebildeter Männer. Durch Herder wurde er auf die Volksdichtung, auf die Poesie der Hebräer, auf Homer und auf die Genialität Shakespeares hingewiesen.

Einen gewaltigen Eindruck auf Goethe machte der Strassburger Münster und war er bisher von Vorurteilen

---

Note: How many of the eleven Rules of this system are included on this page? How many prefixes are there? "zu" verbs? After you have gone over the page, reread it in order that you become accustomed to the German word order, and of course the Rules you have learned.

gegen die gotische Architektur befangen gewesen, so erfüllte ihn dieser Bau mit Staunen; er lernte jetzt den Geist der altdeutschen Baukunst erfassen und legte die Eindrücke, die er damals empfangen hatte, in einem Aufsatze: "Von deutscher Baukunst" nieder. Inzwischen hatte er sich den juristischen Doktorgrad erworben und ging nun auf kurze Zeit nach Frankfurt, wo er seinen Freund Schlosser, den er schon in Leipzig kennen gelernt, seinen nachmaligen Schwager, wiederfand. Durch ihn wurde er dem Kriegsrat Merck in Darmstadt zugeführt, der auf Goethes Entwickelung von bedeutendem Einflusse war. Um sich mit dem deutschen Staats- und Zivilrecht bekannt zu machen, ging Goethe im Frühjahr 1772 nach Wetzlar, und arbeitete hier vier Monate am Reichskammergericht. Von da kehrte er nach Frankfurt zurück und hier erschien 1773 das Schauspiel "Götz von Berlichingen," womit Goethe seinen Ruhm als Dichter begründete. Darauf folgte dann 1774 der grösstenteils in Briefform verfasste Roman "Die Leiden des jungen Werther."

Götz von Berlichingen ist ein Produkt der Sturm- und Drangperiode, zu dem er den Stoff aus einer Selbstbiographie des alten fränkischen Ritters aus dem 16. Jahrhundert nahm. In der Form ahmt er Shakespeare nach. Schon in Strassburg hatte er sich mit dem Stoff beschäftigt und die Geschichte des Ritters mit eiserner Hand dramatisiert. Diese erste Bearbeitung wurde dann von neuem umgearbeitet unter dem Titel "Götz von Berlichingen, ein Schauspiel," wobei er die Einsicht, die er am Reichskammergericht in Wetzlar über die Schwäche und Zerrüttung des Deutschen Reiches gewonnen, verwertete. Daran reihte sich später in Weimar eine dritte Bearbeitung für die Bühne.

Das Stück stellt den Konflikt der alten selbstständigen Reichsritterschaft mit der neuen Ordnung der Dinge dar. In Götz tritt uns das scheidende Mittelalter mit seiner ritterlichen Treue und Tugend, in dem bischöflichen Hof zu Bamberg die hereinbrechende Kulturwelt mit ihrer Falschheit und Tücke entgegen. Götz ist ein Ritter nach alter Art, dem die kürzlich aufgekommenen Reichsgerichte ein Greuel sind, der durch eigene Kraft die Bedrängten schützt und jede Übeltat rächt.

Der Ruhm des Verfassers von Götz und Werther zog mancherlei bedeutende Persönlichkeiten nach Frankfurt, die als Gäste in Goethes Hause willkommen waren. Zu ihnen gehörten zunächst Klopstock und Lavater. Lavater, ein Prediger in Zürich, war ein tief christlicher Charakter: als Dichter setzte er die religiöse und patriotische Richtung Klopstocks weiter fort in seinen christlichen Gesängen und Schweizerliedern. Dazu kamen auch die beiden Grafen Stolberg, mit denen Goethe seine erste Reise in die Schweiz unternahm. Mit Friedrich Heinrich Jacobi, Philosoph und Romanschriftsteller, der jüngere Bruder von Joh. Georg Jacobi, den er in Düsseldorf kennen lernte, schloss er einen innigen Freundschaftsbund. Die wichtigste und erfolgreichste Bekanntschaft, die ihm aber zu teil wurde, war die des Erbprinzen Karl August von Weimar, der ihn zuerst in Frankfurt, dann in Karlsruhe sah. Sobald derselbe zur Regierung gelangt war, erhielt Goethe von dem jungen Herzog eine Einladung nach Weimar, der er auch folgte.

Napoleons Feldzug nach Russland 1812

Before you begin to translate a paragraph, spot each of the breaks and notice carefully the part of speech on the breaks. Remove or become conscious of such obstacles as: 1. prefixes, 2. verbs with "zu." If nouns are on the break, work toward the nouns. If verbs are there, use Rules 4, 5, 6 to remove the verbs. After all, the sentence must end with a word.

How many **breaks** are there in the paragraph? how many **nouns** are on the breaks? verbs? adjectives? prefixes? and if you are careful you cannot make an error.

Grenzen waren dem Herrscher Europas, Napoleon, im Osten gesetzt. Russland war dem Mächtigen nicht untertan. Der russische Kaiser Alexander hatte die Festlandssperre aufgehoben. Nicht länger konnte sein Volk den Zwang und den Druck ertragen. Überall brachen schon Aufstände aus. Der russische Bauer wusste nicht, was er mit den riesigen Mengen von Roggen und Flachs, von Häuten und Leder machen könnte. Das russische Reich war nach allen Seiten abgeschlossen. Nach Süden sperrten die Dardanellen den freien Zugang zum Meere, von Norden waren nur in eisfreien Monaten die Häfen mit dem Schiffe zu erreichen. Nach Westen war die Zu- und Ausfuhr für englische Schiffe verboten, und aus dem Osten war der Bezug der Waren unmöglich.

Mit einem gewaltigen Heere zieht Napoleon nach Osten. Nie hat die Welt ein glänzenderes Heer gesehen: 500,000 Krieger mit fast 200,000 Pferden. Bei der letzten Heerschau erscheinen der König von Österreich, die Könige von Preussen und von Sachsen, dem fremden Herrscher zu dienen. Während der Kaiser und die Fürsten in der sächsischen Hauptstadt spielen und tanzen, und frohe Feste feiern, fahren die Heere auf verschiedenen Strassen ostwärts nach einem dunkeln Schicksal. Der Sommer vergeht und das Heer marschiert immer noch durch die weite Unendlichkeit der russischen Ebene. Regen hat die Felder ersäuft und die Hitze des russischen Sommers die Truppen erschöpft. Immer weiter schleppt sich das Heer. Erst vor Smolensk trifft es auf Russen. Endlich steht der Winter vor der Türe; und die Armee ist noch nicht vor der alten Hauptstadt Russlands angelangt.

Das heilige Moskau mit seinen Kirchen and Türmen grüsst die ankommenden Soldaten. "Hier werden wir bleiben und im Frühjahr weiterziehen" hat der Feldherr seinen Soldaten verheissen. Wie sehnen sich die Müden nach Ruhe und Rast. Als die flinken Husaren in Moskau einreiten, ist die Stadt menschenleer. Leer sind auch die Lagerhäuser und die Vorratskammern, die Keller, die Scheunen und Schuppen. Nirgends sind Lebensmittel, nirgends Futtervorräte zu finden.

Hier züngelt eine Flamme, da schlägt sie aus Fenstern heraus, dort steigt sie schon naushoch über die Dächer empor. Moskau in Flammen. Die ganze Stadt brennt in allen Ecken und Enden. Vergeblich versuchen die Soldaten die Flammen zu löschen. 38,000 opfern sich im Brande. Machtlos steht der Grosse dem wütenden Feuer gegenüber. Dunkle Ahnungen steigen in ihm auf. Er schaudert vor allem dunklen Schicksal. Entfliehen will er diesem Geschick.

Der Feldherr zieht mit seiner Truppe den langen Weg durch das verwüstete Land zurück. Von rechts und von links springen die russischen Verfolger aus den Verstecken und von rückwärts drängen die wilden Kosaken. Die Schnee-und Eisfelder sind plötzlich lebendig geworden. Napoleons Soldaten fallen, bleiben am Wege in der Winterkälte liegen und erfrieren oder werden die Beute der hungernden Wölfe. Eine Brücke bricht und Tausend lassen ihr Leben in den eisigen Fluten des Flusses. Im Schlitten ist Napoleon davon gereist. Der Grosse, Gewaltige auf der Flucht nach Frankreich. Endlich kommen auch die Reste des einst so stolzen Heeres.

Die Unabhängigkeits-Erklärung

Die Vereinigten Staaten begehen am 4. Juli 1876 die hundertjährige Jubelfeier ihrer politischen Selbstständigkeit. Seit jener berühmten Unabhängigkeits-Erklärung vom 4. Juli 1776 ist aus den schwachen staatlichen Anfängen am Rande des Atlantischen Ozeans ein mächtiges Reich erwachsen, welches reichend im Westen bis an das Stille Weltmeer, und im Norden und Süden fast von dem Pol und den Tropen begrenzt, mit seinen vierzig Millionen Einwohnern einen stolzen Platz unter den Völkern der Erde einnimmt.

Die Amerikaner haben volle Ursache, am 4. Juli mit Stolz und Dank auf den Tag ihrer nationalen Geburt zurückzublicken, und ebenso hat die übrige Welt nicht allein das Recht, sondern auch reichliche Veranlassung, in ihren Jubel einzustimmen, und sich der Erfolge des jüngsten Kulturvolkes zu erfreuen. Der kleinste Ansiedler der westlichsten Einöde, der ärmste Bergmann des abgelegensten Gebirgstales, der niedrigste Fischer oder Schiffer eines der zahlreichen Gewässer lässt am 4. Juli die gewohnte Arbeit ruhen und wetteifert, wenn auch in bescheidener Weise, mit seinen besser gestellten Mitbürgern in der Feier des Tages, welcher das zweite Säkulum der amerikanischen Geschichte einläutet.

An die Nichtamerikaner aber tritt mit der hundertjährigen Wiederkehr des 4. Juli die Aufforderung heran, sich über seine Bedeutung in der Geschichte der Vereinigten Staaten klar zu werden. Es ist eine der schönsten Eigentümlichkeiten solcher grosser welthistorischer Gedenktage, dass sie selbst in Kreisen, welche sich sonst um die Geschichte wenig oder gar nicht kümmern, das Bedürfnis erwecken, sich in den Geist der sie erzeugenden Zeiten zu versetzen. Ich will versuchen, diesem Bedürfnis zu dienen und die treibenden Interessen, Ideen und Ereignisse zu schildern, welche in ihrem Endergebnis zu der Unabhängigkeits-Erklärung geführt haben.

Die amerikanische Revolution war keine innere Staatsumwälzung in dem Sinne, in welchem wir den gewaltsamen Umschwung in England und Frankreich zu bezeichnen pflegen, sondern eine nationale Erhebung, wie sie ihrer Zeit die Schweiz und die Niederlande durchgefochten hatten. Also weder das Verhältnis der Kolonien unter einander, noch die Ordnung innerer staatlicher Angelegenheiten, noch die Erledigung lokaler Streitfragen, sondern die politischen Beziehungen zum Mutterlande bedingten den sich langsam vorbereitenden, gewaltsamen Bruch und führten schliesslich zur Unabhängigkeit. Durch diesen Unterschied und durch diese Beschränkung wird die Stärke der amerikanischen Erhebung und auch ihr endlicher glücklicher Ausgang bedingt.

Als England im Anfang des siebenzehnhnten Jahrhunderts in die Reihe der kolonisierenden Mächte eintrat, waren Süd- und Mittel-Amerika, ja sogar ein Teil des nördlichen Kontinentes schon von den romanischen Völkern besetzt, so dass es sich mit den mittleren Breitengraden des Nordens begnügen musste. Nicht freie Wahl wies also die Engländer in diese damals unwirtbaren Gegenden, sondern die Unmöglichkeit, anderswo festen Fuss zu fassen. Ihre Seefahrer und ersten Entdecker hätten gerade so gern Gold gesucht wie Spanier und Portugiesen; sie suchten es auch, allein sie fanden keins: das war ihr grosses Glück. So wurden sie gezwungen, sich der Bebauung des Bodens zuzuwenden, und Ackerbau-Kolonien zu gründen.

Bekannte Persönlichkeiten aus der Geschichte
Wolfgang Amadeus Mozart

Die Zeit Mozarts ist es, die man als die Blütezeit, die idealste, die wahrhaft klassische Zeit der deutschen Musik anzusehen pflegt. Zu ihr gehört auch noch Beethoven bis zu den Werken, deren Reihe die siebente Symphonie eröffnet.

In früher Kindheit offenbarte sich in Mozart der musikalische Genius schon in bewunderswerter Klarheit; der hochentwickelte Musiksinn des Knaben und des Jünglings, seine pianistische Virtuosität, seine Kompositionen versetzten die Welt in staunende Bewunderung. Kunstreisen durch Deutschland, England, Frankreich und Italien füllten die Jugend des Salzburger Musikersohnes aus. Früh schon wirkte das Leben, oft bedrückend, mit Leid und Freud, mit Erfolgen und Enttäuschungen auf seine Seele ein. Er war schon im Jünglingsalter eine europäische Berümtheit, während Haydns Name erst im Alter, nach seinen englischen Triumphen, sich Geltung erringen konnte. In jungen Jahren war er bereits eine geschlossene Künstler-Individualität, während Haydn erst im letzten Drittel seines Lebens dazu gelangte.

David Straus sagte einmal: ob Goethe einem Homer, Sophokles, Shakespeare gleich stehe, darüber lässt sich streiten, dass aber Mozart in aller Welt nicht seinesgleichen hat, unterliegt wohl keinem Zweifel. Er gehört zu jenen grossen Genies, deren Werke sich auch ohne den Kommentar des Verstandes geniessen lassen und zu dem einfachsten, naivsten Empfinden mit ebenso unmittelbarer Frische sprechen, wie sie dem gereiften Hörer, dem feingebildeten Kenner immer neues Entzücken, immer tiefere Einblicke in einen wunderbaren Künstlerorganismus gewähren.

Das Schaffen dieses herrlichen, erhabenen und uns doch so menschlich nahe stehenden Meisters umfasste alle Gebiete der Tonkunst vom Lied bis zur Oper und Oratorium, vom einfachen Klavierstück bis zur Symphonie; sein Bestes gab er uns jedoch in den Opern. Im Andante und Adagio entfaltet er den Zauber seiner herrlichen Melodien am schönsten, hier ist sein ureigenstes Gebiet, wie sich uns Haydn am charakteristischsten in seinen Menuettsätzen und Beethoven am grössten in seinen gewaltigen Allegros zu erkennen gibt. Auf dem Gebiet der Symphonie und der Kammermusik, auf dem wir ihm eine Reihe schöner Werke verdanken, stellt er den Übergang von Haydn zu Beethoven dar. Auf dem Gebiet der Oper war er es, der diese Kunstform zu einer für seine Zeit als vollendet geltenden Höhe emporführte, zu einer Höhe, auf die ihm niemand hat folgen können. In Deutschland fand Mozart wohl viele Nachahmer, aber keine Nachfolger, die sich mit ihren Schöpfungen auch nur im entferntesten an seine Grösse hätten anreihen können.

Mozart genoss das Glück, eine treue, besorgte Gattin zu besitzen, während Haydns Ehe tiefunglücklich war, und Beethoven niemals seine Sehnsucht nach einer gleichgestimmten Lebensgefährtin zu stillen vermochte.

Franz Schubert

Der nächste geistige Nachfolger Beethovens, der ihn nur um ein Jahr überlebte und der den Übergang vom Klassizismus zu den Romantikern bildet, war der Wiener Franz Schubert. Obschon er nur 31 Jahre alt wurde, schuf er doch auf den meisten Gebieten der Tonkunst, in der Symphonie, im Quartett, in seinen Klavierwerken ganz hervorragende Werke und errang sich vor allem als der grösste Meister des deutschen Liedes Unsterblichkeit. Sein Vater war an der Pfarrschule in der Wiener Vorstadt Lichtental als Lehrer angestellt, und erteilte auch seinem am 31. Januar 1797 geborenen "Franzl" den ersten Musikunterricht.

Mit elf Jahren wurde dieser unter die Schüler aufgenommen und erhielt nun Unterricht im Violinspiel und in der Kompositionslehre durch den Dirigenten Ruczizka und den Kapellmeister Salieri. 1814 wurde er auf drei Jahre der Schulgehilfe seines Vaters, ohne seine musikalische Tätigkeit zu unterbrechen, in der Haydn, Mozart und Beethoven seine Leitsterne waren.

Es war dem bescheidenen und anspruchslosen Manne überhaupt beschieden, seine Tage in stetem Kampf mit der kleinlichen Not und Sorge des Daseins zu verbringen. Nur in engerem Kreise wusste man den Genius des Meisters zu würdigen. Treue Freunde sammelten sich um ihn, zu denen unter anderen der Maler Moritz, der Dichter Mayrhofer, der nachmalige bayerische Hofkapellmeister Franz Lachner, und der Sänger Vogl gehörten. Häufig kam man bei dem Wiener Kunstfreunde Ritter v. Spaun zusammen, wo dann die neusten Schöpfungen des Tondichters vorgeführt wurden.

Er starb bereits am 19. November 1828 und wurde auf dem Währinger Friedhof in der Nähe von Beethovens Grab bestattet. Gradezu erstaunlich ist die Menge von Kompositionen der verschiedensten Gattungen, die Schubert in seinem leider so kurzen Leben geschaffen hat. Er wurde vor allem der Schöpfer des modernen Liedes mit Klavierbegleitung; etwa 700 Lieder hat er hinterlassen. Dann hat er auch der Entwickelung der Instrumentalmusik (C Dur-Symphonie und die unvollendete in H Moll) und den übrigen Vokalformen eine neue Richtung gegeben. Von seinen zahlreichen Bühnenwerken hat keines festen Fuss zu fassen vermocht, manche haben niemals das Lampenlicht erblickt.

Franz Liszt und Richard Wagner

Auf die grosse deutsche Glanzzeit der Musik im ersten Viertel des 19. Jahrhunderts, die sich an die Namen Mozart und Beethoven knüpft und auf die Triumphzeit der italienisch-französischen Richtung eines Meyerbeer in den vierziger und fünfziger Jahren folgte in der zweiten Hälfte des Jahrhunderts eine neue deutsche Glanzzeit der Musik, deren Führer Richard Wagner war. Den Übergang zu ihr, die Verbindung zwischen den beiden Musikheroen Beethoven und Wagner stellt Hector Berlioz her; er war Wagners Vorläufer, wies und ordnete ihm den Weg, indem er mit seinen symphonischen Schöpfungen in die festen Mauern des Orchesterstils eine Bresche legte und die Fahne des Fortschritts aufpflanzte. Sein Haupt-und Lebenselement war das Orchester, dessen Leistungs- und Darstellungsvermögen er auf eine vorher ungeahnte Höhe erhob, und mit dem er es verstand, eine poetische Idee musikalisch zu verkörpern. Er wurde dadurch der eigentliche Vater der neueren Programmmusik und des Leitmotivs.

Ehe wir nun zu Wagner übergehen, müssen wir eines Mannes gedenken, der Freund und Geistesgenosse Wagners wurde, der aber vorher schon als Klaviervirtuose aufgetreten war, und als solcher nach dem Urteil der ganzen gebildeten Welt das Höchste erreicht hat,—Franz Liszt. Er war geboren am 22. October 1811 zu Railing bei Odenburg (Ungarn), trat als neunjähriger Knabe als Klavierspieler öffentlich auf und entwickelte sich zum ersten Klaviervirtuosen der Welt. Auch die bedeutendsten unter seinen Nachfolgern, wie Tausig, Rubenstein, Bülow, Paderewski, haben ihn nicht ganz erreicht. 1847 gab Liszt die unruhige Virtuosenlaufbahn auf und ging als Hofkapellmeister nach Weimar, wo er ganz seinem musikalischen Schaffen lebte und in selbstlosester Weise bemüht war, Wagner, Berlioz und andere Komponisten zur Geltung zu bringen. Während Wagner sich im Sinne seines "Gesamtkunstwerkes" beinahe ausschliesslich auf das dramatische Gebiet beschränkte, bezeichnen den Höhepunkt von Liszts Schaffen als Komponist seine "Symphonischen Dichtungen." "Man findet in ihnen," wie F. Brendel sagt, "als charakteristisches Unterscheidungsmaterial den Bruch mit der bisherigen Form der Instrumentalmusik, die ebenfalls zur Schablone zu werden drohte."

Bedeutendes hat Frank Liszt aber auch als Klavier- und Liederkomponist, wie als musikalischer Schriftsteller geleistet. Er war 1859 nach Rom gegangen und in den geistlichen Stand getreten, verbrachte seine letzten Lebensjahre abwechselnd in Pest und Weimar und starb am 31. Juli 1886.

Was Beethoven in seinem "Fidelio" ersehnt, was die Romantiker nicht erreichten und die französisch-italienische grosse "Oper" noch viel weniger hervorbringen konnte: die Schöpfung eines musikalischen Dramas, in welchem Wort und Ton zu einer Einheit verschmolzen und alle Künste als gleichberechtigte Schwestern mitwirken sollten, das gelang Richard Wagner.

Er war am 21. Mai 1813 in Leipzig geboren. Seine Neigung zog ihn frühzeitig zum Theater hin. In der Musik suchte er sich vorwiegend autodidaktisch zu bilden, fand aber in dem in den Traditionen Joh. Seb. Bachs auf gewachsenen Thomaskantor Weinlich einen trefflichen Kompositionslehrer, der ihn mit den Geheimnissen des Kontrapunktes aufs beste vertraut machte.

Wagner war kein musikalisches Wunderkind, doch begann er frühzeitig Opernentwürfe zu verfassen, ja ganze Opern zu schreiben. Aus dieser Zeit haben sich "die Feen" — aufgeführt in München 1888 — und "das Liebesverbot" erhalten, die aber den künftigen Meister des Musikdramas noch nicht ahnen lassen. In den Jahren 1836-1837 war er in Königsberg und in Riga als Kapellmeister angestellt. Hier fasste er den Entschluss, eine historisch grosse Oper zu schreiben, die so gross und so schwer zu bewältigen sei, dass sie an Provinzbühnen unmöglich aufgeführt werden könne. So entstand "Rienzi," der ganz und gar noch im Stil Meyerbeers gehalten und mit riesigen äusseren Effektmitteln ausgestattet ist. In der Hoffnung, den "Rienzi" an der "grossen Oper" anzubringen, begab er sich unter den grössten Schwierigkeiten nach Paris. Er reiste auf einem Segler von Riga ab und erlebte in den Scheeren einen Sturm, während dessen er die Idee zum "Fliegenden Holländer" bekam. In Paris erlebte er Enttäuschung auf Enttäuschung und geriet in die bitterste Not. Er suchte, sich mit Schriftstellerei und mit Arrangieren von Potpouris seinen kärglichen Lebensunterhalt zu erwerben. Dennoch wurde während dieser Zeit der "Rienzi" vollendet und ebenso der "Fliegende Holländer.

Endlich im Jahre 1842 nahte die Erlösung. Durch die Bemühungen des Sängers Tischatscheck war der "Rienzi" angenommen worden und Wagner siedelte nach der sächsischen Residenz über. Der "Rienzi" hatte einen kolossalen Erfolg, so dass die dadurch ermutigte Intendanz gleich im nächsten Jahr zur Inszenierung des "Holländers" schritt. Im "Fliegenden Holländer" hatte aber Wagner sich von dem Stil der grossen Oper abgewandt, und an den Schöpfer des "Freischütz" Weber, den er schon in seiner Jugend abgöttisch verehrte, und an Marschner angeknüpft.

Ludwig von Beethoven

Er wurde am 16. Dezember 1770 zu Bonn geboren, wo sein Vater Tenorist in der Kapelle des Kurfürsten von Köln war, und verlebte eine ziemlich freudlose Jugend. 1792 siedelte er für immer nach Wien über, wo er zuerst Haydns und dann Albrechtsbergers Unterricht genoss. Um die Wende des Jahrhunderts machte sich schon hin und wieder eine Schwerhörigkeit bemerkbar, die später in vollständige Taubheit ausarten sollte; damit begann aber auch sein fruchtbarstes und grossartigstes Schaffen. Vorher war bei seinen Kompositionen noch deutlich der Einfluss Haydns und Mozarts wahrzunehmen gewesen, während sie fortan nur noch die Offenbarungen seines eigenen gewaltigen Geistes wurden, der sich gedrungen fühlte, das Höchste und Heiligste, das Unaussprechliche zu offenbaren.

Nach schweren körperlichen wie seelischen Leiden, die bei dem Mangel an häuslichem Glück oft in verzweifelten Schmerzensausbrüchen zum Ausdruck kamen, starb er am 26. März 1827. Beethovens Werke sind erlebt; die Seelenzustände, die er schildert, sind seine eigenen; seine ganze Künstler Persönlichkeit ist darin. Sein Schaffen war universal wie dasjenige Mozarts; weltliche und kirchliche Musik umspannte es, Vokal- und Instrumentalmusik, Lied, Chor, Oper, Oratorium, Sonate, und Symphonie; die Instrumentalmusik stand dabei im Vordergrund. Seine Klaviersonaten, seine Symphonien, vornehmlich die aus seiner letzten Periode, zeigen ihn auf der unerreichten Höhe seiner Kunst. Wir erinnern bloss, an das wunderbare Adagio seiner "Sonate pathetique" oder an seinen "Fidelio," dieses Hohelied der Gattenliebe und Gattentreue. Die Symphonie erweiterte sich bei ihm ebenso wie die Sonate und das Quartett zum grossangelegten instrumentalen Drama.

Die instrumentale Tonsprache erreichte durch ihn eine bis dahin ungeahnte Ausdrucksfähigkeit und Tiefe, eine bis dahin ungekannte Mannigfaltigkeit. Von seinen Symphonien gehört die dritte, die sogenannte "Eroica" die er Napoleon widmen wollte, sowie die übermenschlich grosse neunte mit dem weltumfassenden Freudenchore zu den erhabensten Schöpfungen, die jemals dem Menschengeiste gelungen sind. Die neunte Symphonie hat Richard Wagner als den höchsten, nicht mehr zu übersteigenden Gipfelpunkt symphonischer Kunst bezeichnet.

Beethoven war mehr als der reine Musiker. Er ging in seinen Werken zurück auf den Ursprung menschlichen Strebens, den Blick stets gerichtet auf das Ewig-Göttliche. Er erfasste es als Dichter zugleich und als Philosoph und stellte es in seiner Muttersprache dar, der Musik. In seinen Werken vermählte sich die Poesie mit der Musik, und aus der Vermählung entstand das allgemein menschliche Kunstwerk. Darin ist der fortwirkende Einfluss Beethovens auf die Musik unseres Jahnhunderts und die Bedeutung seiner kulturgeschichtlichen Mission begründet.

Sir Joseph Lister

Der Vater der antiseptischen Wundbehandlung ist der Londoner Chirurg Sir Joseph Lister (geb. 1827), der von den Pasteurschen Beobachtungen ausging und einen neuen Modus ersann, bei der Operation alle verderblichen Luftkeime von dem Operationsgebiete fern zu halten. Fast mit einem Schlage gelang es ihm dadurch, das ganz Heer der accidentellen Wundkrankheiten, die früher jede Verletzung und jeden scheinbar harmlosesten chirurgischen Eingriff zu einem gefährlichen Unternehmen stempelten, zu beseitigen.

Die chirurgischen Hospitäler, früher eine wahre Brutstätte und der permanente Sitz von Affektionen, wie Eiter-Faulfieber, Wundstarrkrampf, Delirium, verwandelten sich in Orte von grösster Salubrität. Wo zur Vermeidung der gefährlichen Folgezustände von Verletzungen früher möglichst schleunige Amputationen in grösserem Massstabe erforderlich erschienen, konnte jetzt die konservierende Behandlungsmethode in ihre Rechte treten. Noch mehr: Operationen und Eingriffe, die früher wegen der Gefahr der Sepsis undenkbar waren, wie die chirurgische Beseitigung krankhafter Zustände innerlicher Organe, beispielsweise mittels Bauchschnittes, gehören heute, besonders seitdem aus der Antisepsis dank den Ergebnissen der Kochschen Lehren eine Asepsis, d. h. eine sichere vorbeugende Fernhaltung aller ansteckenden Keime geworden ist, zu den gewöhnlichen Ereignissen. Die anti- oder aseptische Wundbehandlung hat denn auch einen unaufhaltsamen Triumphzug durch die ganze Welt angetreten und gehört in der Gegenwart zu den Grundbedingungen jeder chirurgischen Tätigkeit.

Charles Jackson führt Narkose ein

Endlich ist noch zu erwähnen die Einführung der chirurgischen Narkose, einer der grössten und segensreichsten Entdeckungen, die je für das menschliche Leben gemacht wurden. Das Bestreben, Patienten vor und während der Operation in den Zustand der Betäubung zu versetzen, bzw. darin zu erhalten, fand zwar bereits im Mittelalter eine, wenn auch sehr unvollkommene und primitive Art der Verwirklichung. Man tränkte Schwämme mit betäubenden Flüssigkeiten, liess die Schwämme an der Sonne trocknen und hielt sie dann, vor der Operation angefeuchtet, den Patienten vor Mund und Nase. Indessen wurde später dieses Verfahren wegen seiner völligen Nutzlosigkeit aufgegeben.

In den vierziger Jahren des 19. Jahrhunderts wurde die Narkose von dem Bostoner Arzt Charles Jackson eingeführt. Geboren zu Plymouth, hatte er sich 1833 als Arzt in Boston niedergelassen. Bei chemischen Versuchen zerbrach er im Winter 1841 einen mit Chlor gefüllten Behälter. Das Erstickungsgefühl, das ihn bei der Einatmung dieses Gases überkam, suchte er durch Aetherdampf mit Erfolg zu bekämpfen. Er nahm dabei eine Lähmung der Empfindung wahr, die ihn auf den Gedanken brachte, dass sich Aethereinatmungen möglicherweise auch als Mittel gegen den Schmerz auch bei chirurgischen Operationen bewähren würden.

Ludwig Traube

Auf dem Gebiet der innern Medizin ist ferner auch noch Ludwig Traube zu nennen, der Begründer der experimentellen Pathologie durch berühmte Versuche, die er mit Durchschneidung des Lungenmagennerven zur Erforschung gewisser Ursachen der Lungenentzündung anstellte. Traube gebührt auch das Verdienst, das Thermometer am Krankenbette zur Fieberbestimmung wieder eingeführt zu haben.

Georg Washington

Schon seit drei Generationen verehrt ihn die gebildete Welt als edlen Patrioten, als erfolgreichen General und als bedeutenden Staatsmann. Angehörige der verschiedensten Parteien sind gezwungen, seinem Genius zu huldigen.

Geboren am 22. Februar 1732 auf einer Pflanzung in Virginien als der Sprössling einer reichen, der dortigen Pflanzeraristokratie angehörigen Familie, verlor er schon im elften Jahre seinen Vater, erhielt jedoch von seiner Mutter eine tüchtige Erziehung, die ihn befähigte, sich das im praktischen Leben anzueignen, was der Unterricht ihm nicht bieten konnte. Nach dem Tode seines ältern Bruders bewirtschaftete Washington das Gut Mount Vernon am Potomac, bis der genannte Krieg ihn ebenso in das öffentliche Leben hineinzog, wie Franklin, mit dem er damals eine erste Begegnung hatte. 1759, nachdem der Krieg durch die Schlacht bei Quebec zu Gunsten der Engländer entschieden worden war, verheiratete er sich mit der schönen Witwe, Martha Custis und lebte nun fünfzehn Jahre in ungestörter Ruhe auf seinem Gute inmitten eines grossen Kreises gesellschaftlich gebildeter Männer, aber ohne mehr als nötig sich an den politischen Ereignissen zu beteiligen.

Er ging 1774 als einer der virginischen Abgesandten nach Philadelphia zu dem allgemeinen Kongresse, wo er seine Pflicht geräuschlos, ohne jedes Hervordrängen seiner Person erfüllte, bis ihn Adams zum Oberbefehlshaber vorschlug. Seine Wahl erwies sich als die beste und war einer der glücklichsten Griffe, welchen der Kongress getan zu haben sich rühmen darf. Unabhängig, reich, Vertrauen erweckend, war Washington der Mann, unter den schwierigen, durch die Indolenz und den bösen Willen der einzelnen Kolonien und die Furcht des Kongresses vor der Militärherrschaft hervorgerufenen Verhältnissen eine auf Grund absoluter Freiheit zusammengebrachte Armee zu beseelen und zu lenken.

Der Kongress beschloss ferner am 23. Juni, auf seinen Kredit vorläufig zwei Millionen Dollarnoten auszugeben, zu deren Einlösung die Vereinigten Kolonien, eine jede nach ihrer Quote, verpflichtet sein sollten, und fügte alsdann noch eine dritte Million hinzu, indem er zugleich ein Schatzamt mit zwei Chefs einrichet und ein Department für die indianischen Angelegenheiten ins Leben rief. Zu derselben Zeit erliess er ein Manifest an das öffentliche Urteil aller Völker unter Darlegung der Ursachen, welche die Amerikaner zwangen, die Waffen zu ergreifen, und verwarf am 31. Juli einstimmig einen Vergleichsvorschlag, den Lord North an die Gouverneure geschickt hatte.

Nachdem Washington von John Adams vorgeschlagen worden war und später einstimmig gewählt wurde, richtete er an die hohe Körperschaft folgende Worte:

"Herr Vorsitzender: Obwohl ich ganz und voll die hohe Ehre empfinde, welche mir durch diese Ernennung gegeben wird, so fühle ich mich doch sehr beklemmt bei dem Bewusstsein, dass meine Fähigkeiten und meine militärischen Erfahrungen einem so ausgedehnten und wichtigen Vertrauen nicht entsprechen dürften. Indess, da der Kongress es wünscht, so werde ich ohne Säumen mich meiner Pflicht unterziehen und alle Kräfte, die mir zu Gebote stehen, im Dienste unserer rühmreichen Sache ausüben.

Was die Bezahlung anbelangt, so erlaube ich mir, dem Kongress zu versichern, dass keinerlei pekuniäre Erwägung mich veranlasst haben könnte, diese schwierige Stellung gegen den Verlust häuslicher Bequemlichkeit und die Entbehrung häuslichen Glückes einzutauschen; ich will keinen Gewinn daraus ziehen. Ich werde genaue Rechnung über meine Ausgaben führen und das ist alles, was ich wünsche."

Benjamin Franklin

Franklin war aus einer Familie hervorgegangen, welche seit Jahrhunderten die volle Gesundheit des Geistes und des Körpers auf ihn vererbt hatte. Seine ihm bekannt gewordenen Vorfahren, ehrbare Schmiede und Bauern in Northhampshire, dem Herzen Englands, erreichten alle ein hohes Alter: einige seiner Onkel und Grossonkel brachten es auf 90 Jahre und darüber. Sein Vater Josua starb 89 Jahre alt und war bis an sein Ende nie krank gewesen; ebensowenig seine Mutter, welche ihre zehn Kinder selbst genährt hatte. Die Familie, welche gleich zu Anfang der Reformation protestantisch geworden war und stets in bescheidenen, aber auskömmlichen Verhältnissen gelebt zu haben scheint, muss schon mit den Sachsen ins Land gekommen sein. Der Name Franklin bedeutet Freisasse und wird in diesem Sinne sogar noch von Chaucer und Spenser gebraucht.

Die Verhältnisse, in welchen Franklin aufwuchs, waren gleichfalls einfache und gesunde. Boston, wo er geboren wurde, zählte damals kaum 8000 Einwohner und bot durch seine herrliche Bay und schönen ländlichen Umgebungen einen willkommenen Tummelplatz für die ersten Kraftanstrengungen des heranwachsenden Knaben, der sich früh als ein vortrefflicher Schwimmer, Schlittschuhläufer und Ruderer auszeichnete. Die Eltern waren fleissige und verständige Menschen, welche sich durch eigene Kraft zu einer geachteten Stellung im Leben emporgearbeitet hatten. Das gute Beispiel, welches sie ihren Kindern durch ein inniges, eheliches Verhältnis und ein wohlgeordnetes häusliches Leben gaben, machten seinen bleibenden Eindruck auf den empfänglichen Geist ihres jüngsten Sohnes, welcher im Kreise zahlreicher Geschwister sich unterordnen lernte, aber auch seine häuslichen Pflichten und Rechte erkennen lernen durfte.

APPENDIX

HOW TO START YOUR STUDY OF GERMAN

The graduate student who is pressed for time and does not have the desire to spend two or three **semesters** in acquiring sufficient grammar to read German in his particular field of interest will profit by the helpful suggestions and hints given in the pages of this section. The object is to introduce a few of the most essential tables that are indispensable for reading purposes and which the student should learn before any attempt is made to read material of major difficulty.

An attempt has been made to include only those forms that are most essential to enable the student to begin with advanced reading as early as possible, namely the article tables, the personal and relative pronoun tables and the possessive adjectives. The declension of these forms is highly important in order to recognize subjects, indirect and direct objects and other case forms.

This book may be used in any class that has had instruction in elementary grammar. In some schools classes for advanced students have been organized who have had no formal grammar training. This section is particularly intended for them. If some teachers feel that more grammar forms should be given than those listed here, they may, of course, supplement any amount they care to. The author has had also those students in mind who are studying the book by themselves and who want to begin to read as soon as possible. His experience with Ph.D. students over a score of years has shown that these are the bare essentials for the beginner. By learning carefully these tables, the student should have little difficulty in attacking the more difficult style of scientific literature and should benefit early in the use of the rules of this system.

Part One

1.

The Definite Article

1. Study thoroughly the declension of the definite article—der die das (the). This is the basic declension and most of the other declensions are similar to this table. Put each of these tables on small cards and in your spare time during the day refer to them as many times as possible until they are learned.

	Masculine	Feminine	Neuter	Plural	
the	d **er**	d **ie**	d **as**	d **ie**	Note that the plural forms of **der die das are the same for all genders.**
of the	d **es**	d **er**	d **es**	d **er**	
to (for) the	d **em**	d **er**	d **em**	d **en**	
the	d **en**	d **ie**	d **as**	d **ie**	

Except for minor changes, the bold-faced endings are the same for all "der" words:

dieser—this, the latter	jeder—each, every	jener—that, the former
welcher—which	solcher—such	mancher—many a

Illustration of the declension of a "der" word: **dieser diese dieses** plural **diese.**

this	dies **er**	dies **e**	dies **es****	dies **e**	
of this	dies **es**	dies **er**	dies **es**	dies **er**	**Here the endings are dieses—not diesas.
to (for) this	dies **em**	dies **er**	dies **em**	dies **en**	
this	dies **en**	dies **e**	dies **es****	dies **e**	

Keep constantly in mind that the endings of this table are exactly like the endings of the definite article except in two places marked with **. Here the ending is not diesas but dieses.

How would you then decline jener? jeder? welcher? solcher?

What would be the meaning of jedem, solchem, jenes, welche?

Some Helpful Hints to Remember

a) As a general rule a "DES" or "DER" **after a noun** means "of", also a word with **es** or **er** endings when following another noun would mean "of".

Examples: Das Buch des Mannes; die Hand der Frau; die Studenten dieser Schule.
Die Hilfe mehrerer Studenten; die Geschichte aller Wissenschaften.

b) The "den" form can only mean the or "to" or "for" the. (Occasionally "from".)

Examples: Wir sehen den Lehrer; wir geben den Hunden das Fleisch.
Wir nehmen den Männern das Geld ab. We take the money from the men.

c) The "der" form can mean the, of the, and to or for the. (Occasionally "from" as in b.)

Examples: Der Lehrer ist in dem Zimmer.
Das Buch **der** Dame liegt auf dem Tisch.
Er gibt **der** Frau das Papier. Er nimmt der Frau das Geld ab.

d) The "dem" form can mean **the** or **to the**; diesem can mean **this** or **to this**; **jedem each** or **to each**; **jenem that** or **to that**; solchem **such** or **to such**. (Occasionally also **from** as in b, c.)

Examples: In dem Hause, in jenem Hause, in diesem Hause, nach dem Dorf, nach diesem Dorf.
Ich sende jedem Lehrer einen Brief, er gibt jenem or diesem Manne das Papier.
Ich nehme jenem Manne das Geld ab.

2.

The Indefinite Article

When you learned the declension of the definite article, you also learned the declension of the indefinite article, for the endings are practically the same.

	mas.	fem.	neut.	
a	**ein***	ein **e**	**ein***	
of a	ein **es**	ein **er**	ein **es**	**NO PLURAL FORM**
to or for a	ein **em**	ein **er**	ein **em**	
a	ein **en**	ein **e**	**ein***	

Compare the endings of this table with the endings of the definite article. Except for the three forms marked with an asterisk, the endings are exactly like the endings of the definite article. What can the "es" form mean? the "er" form? the "e"? the "em"?

ALL POSSESSIVE ADJECTIVES DISCUSSED UNDER "4" **are declined just like this table.**

3.

The Relative Pronouns

The endings of the relative pronouns are almost exactly like the endings of the definite article. The variations are shown in bold-face forms. Note the change in meanings.

	mas.	fem.	neut.	plural
which or who	d **er**	d ie	d **as**	d ie
of which or whose	d **essen**	d **eren**	d **essen**	d **eren**
to which or to whom	d em	d er	d em	d **enen**
which or whom	d en	d ie	d **as**	d ie

There is one other relative form that is often used: **welcher, welche, welches, welche.**

which or who	welch er	welch e	welch es	welch e
of which or whose	**dessen**	**deren**	**dessen**	**deren**
to which or to whom	welch em	welch er	welch em	welch en **or denen**
which or whom	welch en	welch e	welch es	welch e

NOTE THAT THE **WELCHER** FORM DOES NOT HAVE A GENITIVE; THEREFORE THE GENITIVE OF the "DER" FORM IS USED How to recognize a relative.

a) Relative pronouns are almost invariably preceded by commas. There may be an exception to this when the relative follows und, aber, oder, denn and sondern.

b) as a rule relatives are not followed by a noun.

c) THE CONJUGATED VERB IS PLACED AT THE END OF THE CLAUSE WHEN RELATIVES ARE USED.

More information on the use of the relative is given in the discussion of Rule 5.

4.

The Personal Pronouns

Learn the personal pronouns for the third person singular and plural. Your reading will be almost entirely in the third person of the verb. You may learn later the pronouns for the first and second person if need arises. Refer to any elementary grammar for these forms. The genitive form of the declension of the personal pronoun is intentionally omitted as it may not be encountered at all in your reading work. The genitive form is indicated by the dash.

Nom.	Dat.	Acc.		Corresponding Possessive Adjectives			
er* —	ihm	ihn	(he, to him, him)	**sein (M)	seine (F)	sein (N)	seine (Pl)
sie* —	ihr	sie	(she, to her, her)	ihr	ihre	ihr	ihre
es —	ihm	es	(it, to it, it)	sein	seine	sein	seine
wir —	uns	uns	(we, to us, us)	unser	unsere	unser	unsere
sie —	ihnen	sie	(they, to them, them)	ihr	ihre	ihr	ihre
Sie —	Ihnen	Sie	(You, to you, you)	Ihr	Ihre	Ihr	Ihre

*The "er" and "sie" forms may also mean "it" if they take the place of masculine and feminine nouns. Examples: der Arm — er, die Feder — sie, der Tisch — er, die Tinte—sie.

In case the "er" in this line means "it", the translation would then be:

it —	to it,	it	**its M	its F	its N	its Pl.

Take the "sie" form across the table and give the meanings. Also "wir", "Sie", "es".
Note the difference between sie and Sie, Ihnen and ihnen, Ihr and ihr.
**These are possessive adjective forms for the corresponding personal pronouns.

5.

Give special attention to the possessive adjectives. These are declined also like the indefinite article. Compare the endings of this table with the endings shown in table 2. Note that except for the letter "s" (sein instead of 'ein') this word is identical with **ein.**

his*	**sein**	sein e	**sein**	sein e
of his	**sein es**	**sein er**	**sein es**	**sein er**
to his	**sein em**	**sein er**	**sein em**	**sein en**
his	**sein en**	**sein e**	**sein**	sein e

*) This his could also mean "its".
Go through the table with 'its' as the meaning.

Observations: There is no ending on the **three** bold-face forms. Except for these three places the endings of this table are the same as the endings of the indefinite article. Practice on these forms by writing them out a number of times.

Take any "4" of the forms in the table above (Corresponding Possessive Adjectives) and attach the endings according to the table under number 5. For example:

Ihr	Ihre	Ihr	Ihre	or	unser	unsere	unser	unsere
Ihres	Ihrer	Ihres	Ihrer	or	unseres	unserer	unseres	unserer
etc.	etc.	etc.	etc.		etc.	etc.	etc.	etc.

(THE USE OF THESE FORMS WILL BECOME CLEAR AFTER YOU BEGIN TO READ.)

6.

How to Find a Troublesome Verb in the Dictionary

Students who have not had courses in German and have not learned the various parts of the verb will have difficulty at first in finding some irregular verbs in the dictionary. Even regular verbs will often be puzzling to the student who does not know how to find the infinitive. The purpose of this section is to show how to look up a verb without knowing the principal parts of it. It is important to find the root verb or the form that is given in the dictionary. Drill work, as supplied in these illustrations, will be very valuable later.

Verbs, as a rule, follow certain patterns and after some skill is acquired in recognizing the various parts of them, it should not be difficult to find any verb form. Students with some grammar training will find benefit by following the discussion of this section. This is true in particular if students wish to review verb forms.

Have before you for the present time a list of the irregular verbs. This list is found in the last few pages of this book. Such a list, including perhaps all of the irregular verbs, will also be found in Cassell's dictionary.

If you encounter in your reading the verbs "griff, wies, riss, gab, warf," refer to the verb list — NOT THE DICTIONARY. If you find "gelungen, geschossen, verdorben, geflogen," refer again to the verb list — in the participle column — not the dictionary. In ordinary tables of the irregular verbs you will find the various forms listed as follows:

Infinitive	3rd person singular	past or imperfect	past subjunctive	past participle
sehen	sieht	sah	sähe	gesehen

Characteristics of these verb forms:

The Infinitive always ends with **en** or **n**. The third person singular ends with **t** or **et**.

If the verb form has no ending it is very probably the past tense.

Most of the verbs in the past tense are monosyllables.
If the verb has a -te ending, it is usually the imperfect tense. The past subjunctive form usually has a modified vowel (umlaut) and ends with **e** .

THE PAST PARTICIPLE HAS USUALLY A "GE" PREFIX; it ends with t or **en**.

By following the steps listed below, you should have little trouble in finding the infinitive of any German verb. There are four steps to take in looking up a verb form. As you become more skillful, you will be able to reduce these steps to three and later on to two or one.

1. Vernommen: perceived

a) remove the prefix ver; b) refer to the list of verbs under n and look for the verb form "nommen"; c) drop back to the infinitive; d) tack on what you took off and look up in the dictionary the verb form "vernehmen". How would you look up the following verbs? Write out their meanings: bezog, empfand, hinterliess, vorging, ergaben, verwarf, besah, zerbrach, entwich, entgangen.

2. hinaufstieg: climbed up

If after you remove the prefix you cannot find the verb form in the verb list, you must then **remove more of the prefix.** In this verb you would then:

a) remove the prefix hin. Since aufstieg is not listed in the verb list, remove also the "auf" and then: b) refer to the verb list and look for "stieg". c) drop back to the infinitive; d) tack on the entire prefix hinauf and look up hinaufsteigen. In some verbs the entire verb form may not be given in the dictionary. In this case look up steigen and then look up **hinauf.**

How would you then look up the following verbs? Write out the meanings:
Zusammenzog, entgegenkam, emporstieg, anbehielt, versah.

3. aufgestanden: arisen

a) Remove the auf; this is a prefix.

b) Refer to the verb list and look up under the **participle** column the form **gestanden.**

c) Drop back to the infinitive. d) Tack on what you took off and look up **aufstehen.**

Note: **Past participles appear generally with "ge" prefix. This is not always the case, however, as there are about a dozen inseparable prefixes which remain attached to the verb stem. In such cases the participles have no "ge". On many participles you may save time by looking for the verb in the participle column of the verb table. If the participle does not have a "ge" prefix, follow the four steps given under numbers 1 and 2. How would you look up the following verbs:**

zusammengehalten, hingewiesen, vorgelesen, erfunden, zerbrochen, ausgenommen, bezogen, abgehalten, empfunden, emporgekommen, hingezogen, hinausgefahren, zurückgezogen?

4. If a "zu" appears in the verb, as in anzukommen to arrive,

a) remove the "zu"; b) look up the entire verb with the prefix attached **ankommen.**

How would you look up the following: anzuhören, vorzukommen, hinaufzuziehen, beizustehen?
(Be careful with "hinzu;" this may be a prefix: hinzufügen.)

5. There are two participial endings in German. The past participle of the strong verb ends with **en.** The participle of the regular verb ends with **t.** There are a few irregular verbs in the strong verb list which change the stem vowel and also add the weak ending. For example: gewusst (wissen), gesandt (senden), genannt (nennen).

If you look up the past participle according to the four steps given under 3 and you see that you cannot find a verb like "ausgeführt" in the verb list or in the dictionary, then you must realize that you are dealing with a regular verb. These are the steps you must then take:

ausgeführt: carried out, performed

a) Remove the prefix as you have been doing heretofore.

b) When you find that the participle begins with ge and ends with t, you may be almost sure that you are dealing with a regular or weak verb. Hence, leave the "ge" and the "t" off and put the prefix back on and then look up the complete verb in the infinitive form—ausführen.

Practice on these verb forms: **durchgemacht, abgenutzt, vorgerückt, angemerkt, heruntergesetzt.**

6. If the prefix cannot be removed from the verb, then look up the verb with the prefix attached. If you look up the verb form "vereinigt", simply change the verb to the infinitive form by dropping the t and adding **en—vereinigen.** How would you look up the following verbs?

bestellt, erwählt, erfolgt, versucht, versagt, bestätigt, beschämt, bedeutet, bedrückt.

7. Helpful hints to remember:

a) If a verb has a t or et on it, after the prefix is removed, it will usually be found in the second column of the verb list. Check the following:

vorliest, annimmt, behilft, zerbricht, versieht, beträgt, gilt, besteht.

b) If a verb has one syllable after the prefix is removed, it will be found in the third column of the verb list. Note these forms:

anrief, entging, vorlas, zerschnitt, aufwuchs, aufschrieb, besah, beschloss.

c) If a verb has a modified vowel, check the fifth column of the verb list.

bestünde, bezöge, würfe, stürbe, behülfe, ankäme, besähe, empfände, abnähme.

IT IS HIGHLY ADVISABLE TO LOOK UP ALL OF THE VERBS IN THIS SECTION IN ORDER TO ACQUIRE SKILL IN FINDING ODD VERB FORMS. Practice with groups of students has shown that with some drill with forms like those given from 1-7 they are able to look up a verb in ten to fifteen seconds.

7.

The Auxiliary Verbs (See also Rule 6.)

It would be rather difficult to do any reading without first knowing the auxiliary verbs in all tenses. The verbs "sein," "haben" and "werden" offer difficulty even to students who have had two or more semesters of German grammar. For the time being, go through each one of these verbs in the various tenses and learn their meanings. You will find later in your reading work that a large percentage of German sentences are connected in one way or the other with one of these verbs.

Observe that only the third person singular and plural are given here. In case other forms should be encountered in your reading, reference may be made to any elementary grammar.

REFER TO THESE VERBS WHENEVER DIFFICULTY ARISES.

1. SEIN— to be (is, are, was, were, has or had been, will be.)

a)	er, sie, es sie	ist sind	he, she, it is they are
b)	er, sie, es sie	war waren	he, she, it was they were
c)	er, sie sie	ist*—gewesen sind*—gewesen	he, she has been they have been
d)	er, sie sie	war*—gewesen waren*—gewesen	he, she had been they had been
e)	er, sie sie	wird—sein werden—sein	he, she, will be they will be
f)	er, sie sie	würde—sein würden—sein	he would be they would be
g)	er, sie sie	würde—gewesen*sein würden—gewesen*sein	he, she, would have been they would have been

2. HABEN—to have (has, had, etc.)

a)	er, sie, es sie	hat haben	he, she, it has they have
b)	er, sie, es sie	hatte hatten	he, she it had they had
c)	er, sie, es sie	hat—gehabt haben—gehabt	he, she, has had they have had
d)	er, sie sie	hatte—gehabt hatten—gehabt	he, she had had they had had
e)	er, sie sie	wird—haben werden—haben	he, she, will have they will have
f)	er, sie sie	würde—haben würden—haben	he would have they would have
g)	er, sie sie	würde—gehabt haben würden—gehabt haben	he would have had they would have had

*** Note that "sein" in these tenses means "have".**

WERDEN

3. **Werden** is the most important verb in German and most American students have difficulty with it. You need to become thoroughly familiar with this verb in its various tenses and uses. The use of "werden" will become clear to you with practice. Adequate references are made to this section (and to Sections 4, 5 and 6) to enable you to acquire thorough mastery of this verb.

Werden means TO BECOME when it is used **without a verb.** The tenses of **werden** to become:

a) er wird sie werden	he becomes they become		e) er wird—werden sie werden—werden	he will become they will become
b) er wurde sie wurden	he became they became		f) er würde—werden sie würden—werden	he would become they would become
c) er ist*—geworden sie sind*—geworden	he has become they have become		g) er würde—geworden sein* sie würden—geworden sein*	he would have become they would have become
d) er war*—geworden sie waren*—geworden	he had become they had become			

*Forms marked with the asterisk are translated with **have.** Note that the future perfect (seldom used) is intentionally omitted.

4. WERDEN — WITH A VERB FORM.

When **werden is** used with a verb form, the verb form will be either the **infinitive** or the past participle. **Werden cannot be used with any other verb form.**

The present tense of **werden,** when used with the **infinitive** means **shall** or **will.**

Illustrations: (Note the position of the infinitive.)

1. Er **wird** nächstes Jahr eine Reise **machen.** He will take a trip next year.
2. Sie **werden** jetzt das Buch lesen **können.** You will now be able to read the book.
3. Sie **wird** ihren Vater besuchen. She will visit her father.

5. WERDEN — used with a **past participle** means "be" and is used passively. Here the subject suffers the action of the verb. Tenses of **werden** meaning "be" are as follows:

a) er wird sie werden	(von mir) (von mir)	gesehen gesehen		he is seen by me they are seen by me
b) er wurde sie wurden	(von mir) (von mir)	gesehen gesehen		he was seen by me they were seen by me
c) er ist* sie sind*	(von mir) (von mir)	gesehen gesehen	worden** worden**	he has been seen by me they have been seen by me
d) er war* sie waren*	(von mir) (von mir)	gesehen gesehen	worden** worden**	he had been seen by me they had been seen by me
e) er wird sie werden	(von mir) (von mir)	gesehen gesehen	werden werden	he will be seen by me they will be seen by me
f) er würde sie würden	(von mir) (von mir)	gesehen gesehen	werden werden	he would be seen by me they would be seen by me
g) er würde sie würden	(von mir) (von mir)	gesehen gesehen	worden sein* worden sein*	he would have been seen by me they would have been seen by me

*Note that ist, sind, war, waren mean **have** in these tenses.

**Observe the absence of the "ge" in this participle form. This is one way to recognize the passive use of the verb.

"Worden" — always means some form of "been".

The participle form (gesehen) never changes.

6. Note the passive use of "werden" when used with a modal auxiliary.

a) Das Buch muss heute gelesen werden. The book must be read today.

b) Es kann wahrscheinlich dargestellt werden. It can probably be prepared.

c) Er glaubt nicht, dass es dargestellt werden kann. He does not believe that it can be manufactured. Here werden is found on the other side of the participle form.

d) Die Studenten in der Klasse wollten nicht geprüft sein.
The students in the class did not want **to be** tested.
Forms of "sein" are also common after modal auxiliaries.

7. The MODAL AUXILIARIES— See also Rule 6.

The auxiliary verbs used in Rule 6 are listed here. Learn the third person singular and plural of these verbs. The first person singular and plural of the first six modal verbs are exactly like the third person:

a)								
kann	will	muss	darf	soll	mag	lässt**	bleibt**	
können	wollen	müssen	dürfen	sollen	mögen	lassen	bleiben	present
b)								
konnte	wollte	musste	durfte	sollte	mochte	liess	blieb	
konnten	wollten	mussten	durften	sollten	mochten	liessen	blieben	past
c)								
gekonnt	gewollt	gemusst	gedurft	gesollt	gemocht	gelassen	geblieben	past
können*	wollen*	müssen*	dürfen*	sollen*	mögen*	lassen*	———	participles

d)
*These infinitives may appear instead of the past participle form WHEN ANOTHER VERB IS EXPRESSED.

Examples: Er hat nicht kommen können (not gekonnt) Er hat den Doktor kommen lassen. Ich habe gewollt would simply mean "I have wanted to" — the moment you express another verb, then gewollt is changed to the infinitive form. Ich habe das Buch **lesen** wollen. **Note that "lassen and bleiben" are used like modal auxiliaries.

8.
Brief Hints on the Verb Endings

While it is advantageous to learn the verb endings for all persons and for all types of verbs, for reading purposes it is particularly important to watch the third person of the verb. The first and second person singular and the second person plural are seldom encountered in the reading of a scientific text.

The German verb is on the whole much easier to master than the verb in some of the other foreign languages. Keep these points in mind:

PRESENT TENSE ENDINGS: (all types of verbs—except the modal auxiliaries discussed under 7, 7)

1)

	singular		plural
er	t	wir	en
sie	t	sie	en
es	t	Sie	en

Illustrations:

er	gibt	wir	geben
sie	sieht	wir	sehen
es	steht	wir	stehen

PAST TENSE:

Weak verbs — 2a)

	singular	plural
er	te	ten
sie	te	ten
es	te	ten

Strong Verbs — 2b)

singular	plural
——	en
——	en
——	en

3. SUMMARY—HELPFUL POINTS TO REMEMBER:

a) A verb in the present tense ends with **t** in the singular and **en** in the plural.

b) A regular verb in the past tense ends with **te** in the singular and **ten** in the plural.

c) If there is no ending on the verb, it is probably the past tense of a strong verb.

d) NOTE THAT ALL VERBS END WITH EN OR TEN IN THE PLURAL.

For practice indicate what the tense is for the following verbs: Cite the reason according to a, b, c, d.

konnte	sieht	sandten	hilft	ergab	erfand	reisst
griff	stahl	wusste	brauchte	besah	nahm	nimmt

e) The past participles have two endings: **t** or **en.** The sign of the past participle is the prefix **"ge"** and almost invariably they have also an auxiliary verb, a form of **sein, haben** or **werden.**
Examples of past participles; note the position of them:

1. Die Amerikaner **haben** die Kenntnis von den Engländern **erhalten.**
The Americans have received the knowledge from the English.

2. Er **hat** die Antwort **bekommen.** He has received the answer.

3. Wir **haben** die Wissenschaften unter anderen **Punkten** betrachtet. We have considered the sciences under other aspects.

4. Die Entwicklung der Pflanze **wird** in verschiedener Weise **beeinflusst.** (App. 7, 5, a)
The development of the plant is influenced in a different way.

5. **Ihre** chemischen Unterschungen **waren** auf die Bereitung der Arzneien **gerichtet.**

Their chemical investigations were directed at (toward) the preparation of medicines.

f) Some of these participles may assume the form of infinitives. (See also 7, 7, d)

1. Er **hat** kein Wort **verstehen können.** He has not been able to understand a word.
2. Wir **haben** den Doktor **kommen lassen.** We have had the doctor come.

When used with **haben,** both **lassen** and **können** should appear in the participle form. However, when the participle is used with another infinitive, they both assume the infinitive form. (See also App. 7, 7, c)

Part Two

This section is designed to help students and others over some of the major obstacles which they may encounter in the reading of involved material. References will be made constantly to this section. It is not imperative that beginners know all of the points discussed in this section before they start to read. It is, however, advisable to go over them and to have them at their finger tips so that they may know where to refer when difficulty arises. After reference is made to them a number of times, the points discussed will become clear.

9.

How to Find the Subject

The rules of our system almost invariably lead the translator to the subject of the sentence. If difficulty should arise, it would be helpful to keep these points in mind:

1. The German sentence MAY NOT BEGIN WITH THE SUBJECT. The sentence may begin with any word, **phrase,** or clause, depending on how much emphasis the writer wishes to put on any of these elements. The verb occupies **the key** position. The subject will be found on either side of it, either before it or after it. The following illustrations will bring more light to bear on this point:

a) Die Naturwissenschaft gibt hierauf die Antwort. Natural science gives the answer to this.

b) Die Antwort hierauf **gibt die Naturwissenschaft.** Here the emphasis is on "die Antwort".

c) In **diesem Falle gibt die Naturwissenschaft** die Antwort.
The subject is in bold face in these illustrations. Note that the verb is always SECOND.

d) Wärmekonvektion **spielt** eine grosse Rolle bei den Winden.
Heat convection plays a big role with the winds. Here the subject is first, the verb is next.

e) **Eine grosse** Rolle **spielt die Wärmekonvektion bei den Winden.** The subject now follows the verb.

f) Bei den Winden **spielt** die Wärmekonvektion eine grosse Rolle. With the prepositional phrase beginning the sentence, the subject must now follow the verb. Translate it.

g) Wie ich in dem Buche lese, **spielt** die Konvektion eine grosse Rolle.
As I read in the book, convection plays a great role. Even a dependent clause at the first of the sentence will cause the subject to appear after the verb.

KEEP CONSTANTLY IN MIND THAT THE VERB OCCUPIES ALWAYS THE SECOND POSITION IN **THE SENTENCE.** Only one grammatical element may precede the verb. This grammatical element may **be one word, a phrase, a clause (or several clauses).** In illustrations a, b, c, the subject appears in bold face type. In illustrations d, e, f, g, the verb is in bold-face type. Frequently it is difficult to tell whether the first or third element is the subject; hence you must get this from the context.

h) **Eine eigentümliche Vorgeschichte hat** die Schilddrüse.
Either the element before the verb is the subject or it is the first nominative form after the verb. Let the context tell you, for this time the grammar will not aid you. Both article forms are identical in the nominative and accusative.

10.

The Troublesome ES, DAS or DIES

Inasmuch as the subject does not always begin the German sentence, it is common to find "es" as the introductory word. The "es" corresponds to some extent to the English "there". It is often advisable to use "there" for "es" in translation work until the subject is announced. When "es" is used to introduce the sentence, there may be two subjects in the sentence: the grammatical subject "es" and the logical subject that follows the verb. Reference will be made to these illustrations throughout the text.

1. Es kommt **ein Student.** A student is coming or there comes a student. (The subject is boldfaced)

   a) Es kommen **zwei Studenten.** Two students are coming or there are two students coming.

   b) Es mag **das** der Grund sein. That may be the reason. (Here "es" is not translated at all.)

   c) The "es" may be translated with "there" or the "es" may be discarded entirely if a nominative (subject) form follows the verb: **Always discard the "es" if the verb is plural.**

   d) Es kommen **zwei Kinder** in die Schule. Two children are coming to school.

   e) Es war **dies** ein Teil der Infanterie. This was a part of the infantry.

2. The "es" may be translated as the indefinite "it".

   a) Es ist möglich diese Bücher zu kaufen. It is possible to buy these books.

   b) Es macht mir grosse Freude, die Studenten wieder zu sehen.
   It gives me great joy to see these students again.

3. Other types:

   c) Es gibt viele Worte in diesem Buch. There are many words in this book.

   d) Es hat überall gute Studenten gegeben. There have been good students everywhere.

   e) Es könnte noch eine andere Möglichkeit geben. There might be still another possibility.

   f) Es darf in diesem Zimmer nicht geraucht werden. There must be no smoking in this room.

   g) Es sind keine Mädchen in dieser Schule. There are no girls in this school.

   h) Es waren damals gute Könige. There were good kings at that time.

   i) Es werden **viele Bücher** gelesen. Many books are being read.

   j) Es hat viel Lärm gegeben. There has been much noise.

   k) Das sind andere schwere Stoffe. Those are other heavy substances.

   l) Es wurde ihm **ein Buch** gegeben. A book was given to him.

   m) Es wird ihm viel Neues gesagt. He is told many new things or Many new things are told to him.

   n) Das sind auch wahre Berichte. Those are also true reports.

11.
The Reflexive Pronoun "sich"

One of the most troublesome words for the American student of German is "sich". The meanings given in the dictionary only add to the student's confusion. It is natural for the student to turn to the dictionary when "sich" is encountered. There he learns that it means "itself, herself, himself, each other, themselves".

The reflexive verb has a much broader range of application than in English. For translation purposes certain specific points must be observed. Adequate illustrations follow in this section to help you with most of the difficulties connected with this verb. Become thoroughly familiar with the model sentences, for they will be referred to throughout the book.

1. Where reflexive pronouns are used the SUBJECT AND OBJECT are the same.
   a) Er lobt sich. He praises himself. Sie loben sich. They praise themselves.

   b) Since most of the reading material is in the third person of the verb, it is the third person reflexive pronoun "sich" that is most often encountered.

2. Some verbs that are not reflexive in English may be used reflexively in German. These verbs then have special meanings. In the dictionary you will find two meanings for many verbs: 1. the meaning without "sich" and 2. the meaning with "sich".

   a) Es handelt sich um. It deals with. We are dealing with. Er freut sich. He rejoices. Not reflexive in English.

3. It is a good habit NOT TO TRANSLATE SICH unless you find that it is a reflexive pronoun that means some form of "self". For example: He amuses himself. Er amüsiert sich.

4. **WHEN SICH IS ENCOUNTERED, UNDERLINE IT, BUT DO NOT TRANSLATE IT UNTIL YOU FIND OUT HOW IT IS USED.**

As a general rule the "sich" is most often used when the English would use some form of the passive (or to be). The following model sentences will show how the **sich** is used as a passive substitute. Reference will be made constantly **to these model sentences in the reading material of this book.**

a) Die Ansicht gründet sich in der Chemie auf das Gesetz der konstanten Proportionen.
The view (is based) in chemistry on the law of constant proportions.
Die Thermometer befinden sich unterhalb des Kondensationsrohres.
The thermometers are found below the condensation tube.

b) Der Schwefel verbindet (verband) sich mit Natrium.
Sulphur is (was) combined with sodium.

c) Beim Eintauchen in die Flüssigkeit löste sich die Farbe auf.
On immersion in the liquid the color was dissolved.

d) Es hat sich zur Grundlage der modernen Forschung entwickelt. Es hatte sich—entwickelt.

It has been developed as a basis of modern study. (Note has been.) It had been—developed.

e) Der Raum wird sich mit Rauch füllen. The room will be filled with smoke.
Der Raum würde sich mit Rauch füllen. The room would be filled with smoke.

Part Three

For the benefit of graduate students as well as other students who desire to read highly complicated material, specific points are discussed in Part Three which tend to confuse students of German. It is not necessary to memorize these points at this time, for reference will be made to them at any time difficulty may arise in the reading material of this text.

12.

1. Infinitives with "zu" when used with forms of "sein" (often also "bleiben") are translated with **to be.**

 a) Viele Bücher sind in der Stadt zu haben. Many books are **to be had** in the city.

 b) Es waren viele in dem Theater zu sehen. There were many **to be** seen in the theater.

 c) Es bleibt noch viel zu tun. Much still remains **to be done.**

2. Present participles (any infinitive with an added d—singend, tanzend) when used with "zu" are translated with "to be". They indicate an action which is **to be done.**

 a) Eine anzufangende Arbeit. A work which is **to be started.**

 b) Das ist eine zu prüfende Säure. That is an acid which is **to be tested.**

 c) Dies ist ein leicht zu erreichendes Ziel. This is a goal which is **to be attained easily.**

 d) Die immer zu gehorchenden Gesetze. The laws which are **to be obeyed** always.
 Compare the English: **The girl to arrive tomorrow is Elizabeth** and **The laws to be obeyed** always.

 e) Sein in diesem Jahrhundert zu vollendendes Werk wird willkommen sein.
 His work, which is to be completed in this century, will be welcome.
 See more on this sentence in the discussion of Rule 3—type 2.

13.

What to do with SELBST (or selber)

1. **Selbst** is an intensifying pronoun, meaning himself, herself, themselves, itself. In such cases the **selbst** is usually found immediately after the noun or pronoun.

 a) Der Mann selbst the man himself; er selbst, er selber he himself; wir selbst we ourselves.

2. Or selbst may be used as an adverb. It then usually precedes the noun or pronoun.

 a) Selbst die Studenten in dieser Schule lernen Deutsch. Even the students in this school learn German.

 b) Selbst die platonische und aristotelische Philosophie kennt man meist aus Übersetzungen.
 Even the Platonic and Aristotelian philosophy one knows mostly from translations.

SELBST (or selber) MAY MEAN HIMSELF; HERSELF, **etc. even though it does not follow the noun immediately.**

 c) Er tat es selbst. He did it himself. Er tat es selber.

d) Ich habe die Briefe selbst gelesen. I have read the letters myself.

SELBST may also mean "even" if it **follows** a noun or pronoun (but it precedes the noun it modifies).

e) Die Worte selbst des Feindes waren freundlich. The words of **even** the enemy were friendly.

THE BEST RECOMMENDATION WOULD BE TO TRY "SELBST" AS AN INTENSIFYING PRONOUN TO MEAN SOME FORM OF **self** and if the meaning is not clear, to realize that **selbst** may mean **even.**

f) DO NOT PICK UP SELBST IF YOU ARE MOVING BACKWARD TOWARD A NOUN. The **selbst** may be intensifying the noun or pronoun in front of it.

1. Merkwürdiger ist es, dass ähnliche Ansichten auch auf die Philosophie selbst zurückführten.
   It is more remarkable that similar views led back to philosophy **itself.**

14.

Derselbe, dieselbe, dasselbe the same

1. **Derselbe** (meaning the **same,** the **latter** is declined just like the definite article. See also the definite article table, this section 1, 1.)

	masculine	feminine	neuter	plural
the same	**derselbe**	**dieselbe**	**dasselbe**	**dieselben**
of the same	**desselben**	**derselben**	**desselben**	**derselben**
to the same	**demselben**	**derselben**	**demselben**	**denselben**
the same	**denselben**	**dieselbe**	**dasselbe**	**dieselben**

2. **Derjenige** (the one, that one, he who, she who, those, etc.). Also declined just like the article.

that one	derjenige	diejenige	dasjenige	diejenigen
of that one	desjenigen	derjenigen	desjenigen	derjenigen
to that one	demjenigen	derjenigen	demjenigen	denjenigen
that one	denjenigen	diejenige	dasjenige	diejenigen

3. Dieser (See declension section 1, table 2.) this one, the latter, he
   Jener (See table 2, section 1.) that one, the former

15.

Troublesome Prepositions

Beginning students have always complained about the "little" words and the many meanings they may have. The difficulty generally clears up after some reading is done. Most of the prepositions may be interpreted correctly without knowing that they are used with certain cases. It is not necessary to know that "trotz", in spite of, or "gemäss", according to, are used with the genitive and dative respectively in order to translate them correctly. There are about nine prepositions which do cause some confusion. These are considered and explained in this section. The most common are:

1. nach to, after, toward, according to
   entgegen against, contrary to
   gegenüber opposite to, vis-à-vis
   zuwider contrary to
   wegen on account of
   halber on account of
   zufolge as a result of, according to
   gemäss according to
   entsprechend corresponding to

2. As a general rule these prepositions precede the noun or pronoun. In such cases they do not offer any particular difficulty as then they are just like any other prepositions. The difficulty arises from the fact that very often they follow nouns or pronouns. Observe carefully these model sentences:

a) Er nannte das Kind nach seinem Vater. He named the child after his father.

b) Sie liefen zusammen nach der Stadt. They ran together to the city.

c) Gegenüber diesem Dorf liegt eine Festung. Opposite this (or to this) village lies a fortress.

d) Gemäss dem Wunsche meiner Mutter muss er hier bleiben.
   According to the wish of my mother he must remain here.

e) Entgegen meinen Wünschen kam er. He came contrary to my wishes.

3. IF ONE OF THESE PREPOSITIONS FOLLOWS THE NOUN OR PRONOUN, BE MORE CAUTIOUS. If in following the rules of this system these prepositions are found in a clause or sentence **after** a noun, stop and survey the situation. Rephrase the sentence and in so doing begin the particular phrase with the preposition that is causing the difficulty. Usually it will be one of those listed in this section.

a) Den Worten Ihres letzten Briefes zufolge schicke ich Ihnen den Bericht.
Inasmuch as you have a noun on the break, you are to proceed directly to this noun. On the way you encounter "zufolge" (one of the words listed in 15, 1), hence you must stop and rephrase the sentence; this time begin with "zufolge": According to the words of your last letter, I am sending you the report.

b) Der Verabredung **gemäss** kamen sie. They came according to the agreement.

c) Röntgenstrahlen erweisen sich den Enzymen **gegenüber** als ziemlich indifferent.
X-rays prove (themselves) vis-à-vis the enzymes as rather indifferent.

d) Dem früheren Friedensvertrag **nach** musste Deutschland das Gebiet aufgeben.
According to the earlier peace treaty Germany had to give up the territory.

e) Very often the preposition falls into place by following the rules. Note these sentences:

1. **Da beide Welten ihrem Inhalte nach völlig geschieden sind,** so kann die Philosophie ebensowenig **bestimmte Gesetze** geben.

Since both worlds are separated completely **according to their content**, philosophy can give just as little definite laws. (Note how "nach" falls into place.)

f) Translate this sentence word for word, then rephrase it after you encounter "nach".

1. **Aller Wahrscheinlichkeit nach handelt es sich um** bestimmte Teile.

All probability according to . . . According to all probability we are dealing with certain parts.

g) For the sake of practice, translate the following sentences. (The prepositions are bold-faced)

1. **Dem frühen Tode Rohrschachs zufolge konnte dies nur von Römer durchgeführt werden.**
2. **Der Einfachheit halber** nehmen wir an, **die Geschwindigkeit ist gleichmässig verteilt.**
3. Diesem Verhalten **entsprechend** bezeichnet man die Bakterien als Pilze.
4. Dem **Luftsauerstoff gegenüber** verhalten sich **die meisten Bakterien sehr verschieden.**

16.

Words that cause Trouble

Because mässig is defined in the dictionary as moderate, temperate, etc., students try to use this meaning even **if mässig is attached to another word. The best meaning for mässig when it is attached to another word is according to — whatever word precedes it. Examples:**

1. Planmässig	**according to plan, systematic**	**erfahrungsmässig**	**according to experience**
naturmässig	**according to nature, natural**	**vernunftmässig**	**according to reason, reasonable**
regelmässig	**according to rule, regular**	**verhältnismässig**	**according to proportion, proportional**

2. Once in a while mässig is used as an adjective, particularly as a predicate adjective. It then has the dictionary meaning of **moderate, temperate**, etc. The best advice is to try to deduce the meaning of a word like "erfahrungsmässig" by looking up "Erfahrung". Then if you do not get the meaning by adding "mässig" to it (according to) look up the entire word.

17.

Indem while, in that, by —ing

1. Inasmuch as this word frequently introduces a dependent clause, students attempt to translate this word with "in which". No matter where this word may be found, it is best to translate it with "while", inasmuch as, in that, by —ing, but not as a relative.

a) Ein Geldeinkommen wird verwendet, nur indem es zur Bezahlung eines Realeinkommens dient.
A money income is used only in that it serves for the payment of real income.

b) Indem sich General Pierce **Bethel** näherte, zog sich der **Feind zurück.**
While (or inasmuch as) General Pierce was approaching Bethel, the enemy withdrew.

c) Die Energielehre bewährte sich hier als eine sehr nützliche Dienerin, **indem** sie uns den Überblick über das Material erleichtert. The energy theory proved here a useful servant, in that it facilitates (for us) the survey over the material. Or, even better, . . . **by** facilitating for us the survey over the material.

18.

Bei at, in the case of, in the vicinity of, in connection with

a) Sie wohnen jetzt bei Dallas. They live now in the vicinity of Dallas.

b) Bei diesen Krankheiten gebrauchte man eine neue Medizin.
In the case of these diseases one used a new medicine. Try also "in connection with" or just "with".

c) Bei der nächsten Gelegenheit möchte ich ihn sehen. I would like to see him at the next opportunity.
d) Bei dem Theaterspiel traf ich sie. I met her at the play.
e) bei hohem Druck at high pressure; bei den Säuren in the case of acids (or with acids)
f) bei Sonnenaufgang at sun rise; bei uns in our country, at our home

19.

Wenn auch (or wenn ——— auch)

1. Wenn by itself would mean "whenever" or "if". If "auch" is also used either with it or somewhere in the clause, it will likely mean **even if** or **even though.**

a) Er wird wahrscheinlich kommen, wenn es auch heute regnet.
He will probably come, even though it rains today.

b) Wenn auch die Zahl der chemischen Umsetzungen gering ist, so wächst die Zahl von Tag zu Tag.
Even though the number of chemical changes is slight, the number increases from day to day.

c) Note that the AUCH may occupy another position in the sentence; the translation is the same.
Wenn die Zahl der chemischen Umsetzungen **auch** gering ist, so wächst die Zahl von Tag zu Tag.

20.

Um —willen for the sake of, on account of

1. These are two words that are seldom found together. They may be separated by one word or several.

a) Plato nannte ihn um seines Studierens willen "den Leser."
Plato called him on account of his studying "the reader."

b) Um seines Vaters willen wird er noch ein Jahr bleiben.
He will remain another year for the sake of his father.

21.

How to Treat "aus" and Some extra Prepositions or Adverbs.

1. "Aus" and a few words like "hin, her, hinaus, an, zu, herum", must often be omitted in translation.

a) von dem Standpunkt aus from this point of view
b) von der Seite des Gerichts aus on the part of the court
c) von Grund aus basically von einer Flasche aus from a bottle
d) von der Schule aus originating from or at school
e) von Anfang an from the beginning on von alters her from olden times
nach der Stadt hin toward the city
f) nach dem Fenster zu toward the window
g) über diesen Standpunkt hinaus over (and beyond) this standpoint
h) um die Achse herum around (about) the axis
i) von dieser Quelle an from this source (onward)
j) durch die Wand hindurch through (and through) the wall
k) nach allen Richtungen hin in all directions

22.

Demonstrative Pronouns

1. The definite articles have different uses: They are declined much like the relative pronouns. (sec. 3) They are used:

a) As articles, in which case the nouns follow directly or after one or more adjectives.
Examples: der Knabe; der gute Knabe; der gute, fleissige Knabe

b) As relatives (with a slight change in declension) (see also section 3 and rule 5). When used as relatives the articles are generally preceded by commas and call for a verb at the end.
1. Der Student, der heute in der Stadt ist, ist krank.

2. c) AS DEMONSTRATIVE PRONOUNS. If so used keep these points in mind:
1. If der, die, das are used as demonstrative pronouns, they do not affect the word order; i.e., the verb will not be placed at the end of a clause as is the case when they are used as relatives.
2. If the articles are used as demonstrative pronouns, these pronouns mean **the one, that one, that, he, she, those (plural) it, this.**

c) **Denen darf man keine Aufmerksamkeit geben. Man darf denen keine Aufmerksamkeit geben.**
One must give them no attention. Or one must not give them any attention.

d) **Von der kannst du nichts erwarten. You cannot expect anything from her.**

e) **Der angenehmste Tag ist der, an dem kein Regen fällt.**
The most pleasant day is the one on which no rain falls.

3. DO NOT **CONFUSE THE GENITIVE FORMS DESSEN AND DEREN WITH THE CORRESPONDING FORMS OF THE RELATIVE PRONOUNS. The relative pronouns dessen and deren mean which, of which or whose.**

4. When used as demonstratives **dessen** and **deren** mean its, or his or her, its and their respectively.

a) **Ich traf den Mann und dessen Gemahlin. I met the man and his wife.**

b) **Ich sah die Frau und deren Tochter. I saw the woman and her daughter.**

c) **Ich sprach viel von meiner Mutter und erzählte von deren Erfahrungen.**
I spoke much of my mother and told of her experiences.

d) **Er hat dem Manne und dessen Sohn alles erzählt. He told the man and his son everything.**

e) **Die Mädchen und deren Eltern waren im Theater. The girls and their parents were in the theater.**

f) die Schule und deren Lehrkörper the school and its faculty

5. **The plural genitive form differs slightly from the relative pronoun in the genitive.**

a) **Hier sind die Namen derer, die sich an dem Spiel beteiligen.**
Here are the names of those who are taking part in the play.

b) **Das Schicksal derer, die an keinen Gott glauben, ist bekannt.**
The fate of those who do not believe in God is known.

c) **Das Glück derer, die sich ihrem Gotte nähern, ist unser Ziel.**
The happiness of those who get near to their God is our goal.

5. See also the discussion of **derselbe** and **derjenige.** (App. 14, 1 and 2)

23.

The "da"-Words

1. When the personal pronouns have reference to things or inanimate objects, they are often replaced by a "da"-word. Most prepositions may be used with "da". Observe the following examples: the "da" in this construction usually means it or **that.**

a) **Was tun Sie mit dem Bleistfit? Ich schreibe damit.**
What are you doing with the pencil. I am writing with it.

b) Wir öffnen den Brief und sprechen davon. We open the letter and speak **about it.**

c) **Er nimmt einen Stuhl und setzt sich darauf.** He takes a chair and sits down upon it.

d) **Jeden Abend nehmen wir die Zeitung und lesen darin.** Every evening we take the paper and read **in it.**

e) Meine Mutter gibt mir ein Glas und ich trinke daraus.
My mother gives me a glass and I drink out of it or from it.

WHEN REFERRING TO PERSONS, THE PERSONAL PRONOUNS ARE USED, NOT THE "DA"-WORD.

f) **Ich traf die Kinder und spielte mit ihnen. I met the children and played with them.**

g) **Ich gehe zu dem Lehrer und spreche mit ihm. I go to the teacher and speak with him.**

2. It is often helpful and possible to translate the "da" word with "by the fact that".

a) Er wies plötzlich darauf him, dass es sich um wenige Säuren handelte.
He pointed suddenly **to the fact that** few acids were involved.

b) **Eine Stütze dieser Annahme kann dadurch bewiesen werden, dass die Substanz brennbare Dämpfe entwickelt.**
A support of this assumption can be proved by the fact that the substance develops combustible vapors.

3. The "da"-word often calls for infinitives used with "zu".

a) Aristoteles ist nur **darauf** ausgegangen, die logischen Tatsachen in **Beziehung zu** bringen.
Aristotle proceeded only to that point to bring the logical facts in relation (. . . of bringing the . . .).

b) Das Bestreben geht hier **darauf** hinaus, die Bedürfnisse von **Anfang** an zu beschränken.
The tendency here endeavors (do not translate **darauf**) to limit the wants from the beginning (on).

c) Trotz der Bewegungen in den Kolonien dachte niemand **daran**, das Band mit **England** zu lösen.
In spite of the movements in the colonies no one thought **(there-of)** to dissolve the union with England.

d) Der Nutzen einer Hypothese besteht wesentlich darin, unsere Kenntnisse zu erweitern.
The utility of a hypothesis consists essentially **(therein)** to broaden (in broadening) our knowledge.

SEE MORE ON THIS POINT IN THE DISCUSSION OF RULE 7.

24.

The "wo"-Words

1. **The "wo" words frequently take the place of relative pronouns when referring to inanimate objects. In this sense they are like the** "da"-words. The "wo" now means **"which** or **what"**. Compare the following: womit—with which; worin—in which; worauf—upon which; wodurch—through which.

Illustrations:

a) Pope richtete einen Brief an ihn, worin er ihm die Stellung der Armee klarlegte.
Pope directed a letter to him in which he explained the position of the army.

b) Wir finden das Wort "Ferment", womit man jeden Stoff bezeichnete.
We find the word "ferment", with which one designated every material.

c) Es gibt eine Gesellschaft, worin die Gesamtheit die ganze Bedürfnisbefriedigung reguliert.
There is a society in which the totality regulates the entire want-satisfaction.

d) Der absolute Gegensatz zum Kostenprinzip ist das "Gratisprinzip", wonach wirtschaftliche Güter den Konsumenten ohne spezielles Entgelt dargeboten werden.
The absolute contrast to the cost principle is the gratis-principle **according to which** economic **goods are offered** to the consumers without special compensation.

See more on discussion of the "wo"-words in the discussion of Rule 5, b.

25.

The troublesome "da"— there, then, as, when, since

Inasmuch as the dictionary lists so many meanings for "da", students find some difficulty in deciding which one to use. These model sentences will clear up this difficulty.

1. **Da** will likely mean "there" or "then" when the verb is **beside** it.

a) Da schien es nicht wichtig. Then it did not seem important.

b) Da bestieg Lyon das Pferd. Then Lyon mounted the horse.

c) Da sitzen die Freunde des Generals. The friends of the general are sitting there.

d) Da herrschen aber noch Besonderheiten. Peculiarities still prevail there, however.

2. **Da** will probably mean "since" when the **verb is not** by it.

a) Da er nur eine geringe Meinung von der **Miliz** hatte, verwarf er den Plan.
Since he had only a poor opinion of the militia, he rejected the plan.

b) Da nun zwei Planeten zwischen Mars und Jupiter existierten, so kam Olbers auf einen sonderbaren Gedanken.
Now since two planets existed between Mars and Jupiter a strange thought occurred to Olbers.

3. When "da" means "since", **when** and **as** may also be used to translate it.

26.

je — je; je — desto; je — umso the — the; je — nachdem according as

1. Je is best omitted in translation.

a) je nach der Art und Weise je nach der Zusammensetzung je nach dem Vorherrschen der Gruppe
according to the type (and manner) according to the composition according to the predominance of the group

b) Die Nickelstähle zeigen je nach ihrer Zusammensetzung thermische Nachwirkungen.
The nickelsteels show according to their composition thermal after-effects.

2. Je—desto and je—umso—both mean **the—the** or **so much the.**

a) Je beträchtlicher diese sind, desto (or umso) rascher ist die Bewegung.
The more considerable these are, the more rapid is the movement.

b) Je mehr Bilder wir von einer Region besitzen, desto (or umso) breiter ist unser Urteil.
The more pictures we possess of a region, the broader is our judgment.

3. The 'umso' or 'desto' may appear at the first of the sentence.

a) Umso eingehender werden wir uns mit diesen Sedimenten beschäftigen.
All the more thoroughly we will concern ourselves with these sediments.

b) Desto mächtiger tritt sie an der Küste von Alaska auf.
All the more (or so much the more) thick does it appear on the coast of Alaska.

4. Je—nachdem according as, in proportion as.

a) **Der Mann arbeitet je nachdem die Umstände sind. The man works according as the conditions are.**

b) **Je nachdem die Arbeit ist, nach dem wird der Lohn sein.**
According as the work is, according to that will be the reward.

c) **Die Wirkung der Bakterien beruht auf der Hervorbringung von Giften, die, je nachdem jener ein guter oder** schlechter Nährboden für die Bakterienart ist, **in verschiedenem Grade erzeugt werden.**
The effect of bacteria depends upon the production of poisons, which, (according as the former is a good or bad nutrient base for the type of bacteria,) are produced in different degree.

d) **Sie verraten die Neigungen der Verfasser, je nachdem dieselben reimlose Verse nach antikem Muster einführen. They reveal the inclinations of the writers according as the same introduce rhymless verses according to ancient pattern.**

5. **je—je the–the**

a) **Je mehr er arbeitet, je mehr lernt er. The more he works, the more he learns.**

b) Je länger ich lebe, je mehr verstehe ich deine Herzensgüte.
The longer I live, the more I understand your kindness.

27.

The Subjunctive for Translation Purposes

The purpose of this book is to train the student to translate from German to English. The emphasis has been brought to bear, therefore, on the recognition of the forms and the arrangement of the words in the sentence. In this process a complete knowledge of the subjunctive is not as imperative as it would be if the student were translating from English to German.

The fear of the subjunctive which haunts most students in their attempt to learn a new language should be dispelled, for the German, no less than the English, is gradually getting away from the subjunctive. This is particu-larly true with respect to scientific German articles. In fact in some books very few subjunctive forms appear.

Certain subjunctive forms are found in certain fields, for example the optative subjunctive in mathematics and physics. More subjunctive forms are used in poetry than in prose, more in imaginative literature than in the sciences. It is suggested to master certain patterns of the subjunctive and refer to these patterns whenever difficulty arises in the reading material.

1. The identification of the subjunctive forms of the verb is of paramount importance. Subjunctive forms are on the whole quite regular. A glance at the fourth column of a verb list in Cassell's dictionary, or at the verb list at the end of this book, shows the most distinctive feature of the subjunctive—namely the modified (umlaut) vowel. If the verb should not have an **a, o, u** root vowel, there is still an **e** on the ending which indicates the use of the subjunctive. This applies even in the present tense where **e** may also appear while in this same person of the indicative there would be a **t.**

Note: Present **subjunctive** 3rd person sg.: habe, lese, halte, mache, gebe, sehe, kenne, höre, sage
Present **indicative** 3rd person sg.: hat, liest, hält, macht, gibt, sieht, kennt, hört, sagt
Past **subjunctive** 3rd person sg.: führe, gäbe, läge, stünde, bräche, brächte, läse, sähe
Past **indicative** 3rd person sg.: fuhr, gab, lag, stand, brach, brachte, las, sah

2. Since the subjunctive is after all a mood of doubt or probability, the object should be to tranlate the subjunctive forms with a word in English that will admit of possibility or uncertainty. One way to do this is to supply a word like might, should or would (often may). For the auxiliary verbs **sein, haben and werden, the words that most often apply are were and had.**

PRACTICE ON THESE FORMS:

a) **sei may or might be; wäre would or should be (were); habe may or might have**
hätte—should or would have (had)

b) **Note how should or would, may or might apply for the past subjunctive forms:**
fände would or should find (found) gäbe should or would give (gave)
stünde would or should stand (stood) spräche would or should speak (spoke)

c) **NOTE THAT THE PAST OF THE WEAK VERB IN THE SUBJUNCTIVE IS THE SAME AS THE PAST INDICATIVE.**
machte would or should make (made) folgte would or should follow (followed)

d) **What could the following mean? täte, zöge, verlöre, erzählte, sänge, trüge, vergässe, träte, wüsste**

e) **NOTE THE PERFECT TENSES and their meanings:**

1. wäre geblieben had or would have remained; hätte gegeben had or would have given
wäre gegangen had or would have gone; hätte gesagt had or would have said
wäre gestohlen worden had or would have been stolen; wäre geworden had or would have become
2. Note that wäre may mean **had** or **would have** with some verbs.
3. What could then these mean?
wäre gestorben; hätte geschlagen; wäre gestiegen; hätte gesprochen; wäre gekommen

28.

Patterns of the Most Common Subjunctive Forms

These are the patterns of the subjunctive uses occuring most frequently in scientific and advanced German readings. Reference will be made to these patterns whenever difficult subjunctive forms occur.

1. The following examples express commands:

   a) Man nehme folgendes Beispiel. Let one take the following example.

   b) Es sei S die Sonne. **Let** S be the sun.

   c) Es sei hier ausdrücklich betont. Let it be expressly emphasized here.

   d) Man zeige einem Beobachter zwei Papierscheiben. Let one show an observer two paper discs.

   e) Man frage den Beobachter wieviel Töne es enthält. Let one ask an observer how many tones it has.

2. These are contrary-to-fact sentences:

   a) Wenn das Kind krank wäre, käme der Doktor zu ihm. If the child were ill the doctor would come to him.

   b) Wenn dies die einzige Anschauung wäre, würden wir sie annehmen.
   If this were the only viewpoint, we would accept it.

   c) Wenn der Jäger den Wolf gesehen hätte, hätte er ihn geschossen.

   d) Wäre der Leser nach der Definition der Psychologie gefragt worden, so hätte er wahrscheinlich erklärt, sie sei die Wissenschaft der Seele.
   If the reader had been asked for a definition of psychology, he would probably have explained that it was the science of the mind.

   e) Wäre er durstig gewesen, so hätte er mehr Wasser getrunken. If he had been thirsty, he would have drunk more water.

NOTE THAT IN MOST OF THESE SENTENCES THE WORDS **were, had** fit well for the auxiliary verbs and that the result clauses readily admit of either **should** or **would, may** or **might.**

3. Potential Subjunctive, of which there are many types, admits also of a possibility or doubt.

   In some instances a sentence may be toned down by the use of the subjunctive, i.e., stated more politely and not as abrubtly as in the case of the indicative. Note that in this type of the subjunctive the words "were" (for sein) and had (for haben) are applicable almost always for the auxiliary verbs, and that in the case of the other verbs the words **should** or **would, may** or **might** are almost always correct and acceptable.

   a) Das wäre dann zwecklos. That **would be** without purpose. If this were stated: Das ist zwecklos, then the meaning would be **That is** without purpose. The first sentence is more polite, not as abrupt.

   b) Wir könnten die Pflanzen als eine Bedingung des Lebens nennen. We **might designate** the plants as a condition of life. This type is similar to the result clauses in 28, 2.

   c) Es stünde auch mit der genetischen Definition im Einklang.
   It **would stand** also in harmony with the genetic definition. (Not **stands.**)

   d) Hierzu wäre die Arbeit erforderlich.
   For this the work **would be** necessary. What would the sentence mean if the verb were "ist"?

   e) Das geologische Bild des Eiszeitalters wäre unvollständig, wollten wir nicht noch einer Ablagerung gedenken.
   The geologic picture of the glacial age **would be** incomplete, if we would not be mindful of one more deposit.

4. Other practice sentences which might well fit in with sentences under 1, 2, 3, but where you would likely be correct if you would use **may** or **might, should** or **would, had** or **were,** are:

   a) Einige kurze Bemerkungen seien hinzugefügt. Some brief remarks may be added.

   b) Es sei hier gestattet, auf diese einen Blick zu werfen.
   It **may be** permissible to throw a glance upon these.

   c) Wenn der Sand wirklich über das ganze Feld von Oklahoma reichen sollte, hätte er eine Ausdehnung, die diejenige der ganzen Schweiz überträfe.
   If the sand should reach really over the whole field of Oklahoma, it **would have** an extension that **would exceed** that of entire Switzerland.

   d) Erwähnt seien hier noch die genannten Verbindungen. Es seien hier noch die g.Verbindungen erwähnt.
   There may be mentioned here still the compounds mentioned. Let there be mentioned in addition . . .

   e) Hier könnte besonders auf die Fette hingewiesen werden.
   Here particularly the fats might be referred to.

Word Formation

With syntactic difficulties well in hand, students have renewed incentive to acquire as rapidly as possible a broad vocabulary in their respective fields. In the following pages are given a few suggestions which will help them in bringing this about.

Inasmuch as the results of this system tell the student "where to go next", he senses very early the necessity of a vocabulary and as a rule he seeks every possible aid in the acquisition of it. The aim should be to analyze words in order to use the dictionary as little as possible. The use of the dictionary on too many words will make translation slow and laborious. Furthermore, many words which do not carry meaning in isolation will clear up of themselves when used in context.

A thorough knowledge of the most common suffixes will aid greatly in arriving at the meaning of a word. After a suffix has been added to an adjective, another suffix may be added to form a noun. Thus in the word Sichtbarkeit three divisions are to be noted: Sicht—sight, sichtbar—visible, Sichtbarkeit—visibility. Follow the illustrations and give the meanings of the nouns:

1. **-bar** -able,-ible (occasionally -ful)

Almost all of these adjectives may be changed into nouns by adding the suffix **-keit**, the English **-ty**, or **-ness.**

Adjective	English	Noun	Adjective	English	Noun
teilbar	divisible	Teilbarkeit	brennbar	inflammable	Brennbarkeit
dankbar	thankful	Dankbarkeit	hörbar	audible	Hörbarkeit
lesbar	legible	Lesbarkeit	schmelzbar	fusible	Schmelzbarkeit
anwendbar	applicable	Anwendbarkeit	vergleichbar	comparable	Vergleichbarkeit
fruchtbar	fertile, fruitful	Fruchtbarkeit	ausführbar	executable	Ausführbarkeit

NOTE: Most of these adjectives will admit of an **un** to make them mean just the opposite. For example: teilbar unteilbar Unteilbarkeit fruchtbar unfruchtbar Unfruchtbarkeit

2. **-los** -less

The noun (if present) is formed by adding **ig** before attaching the suffix **keit.**

farblos	colorless	Farblosigkeit	fruchtlos	fruitless	Fruchtlosigkeit
gottlos	godless	Gottlosigkeit	nutzlos	useless	Nutzlosigkeit
sinnlos	senseless	Sinnlosigkeit	zweifellos	doubtless	Zweifellosigkeit
hilflos	helpless	Hilflosigkeit	grundlos	baseless	Grundlosigkeit
hoffnungslos	hopeless	Hoffnungslosigkeit	wertlos	valueless	Wertlosigkeit

3. **-lich** -ly (like) The nouns are formed by adding **-keit.** Give their meanings.

mütterlich	**motherly**	Mütterlichkeit	schädlich	harmful(ly)	Schädlichkeit
glücklich	happ(il)y	Glücklichkeit	hässlich	ugly	Hässlichkeit
herzlich	heart(il)y	Herzlichkeit	göttlich	godly	Göttlichkeit
männlich	manly	Männlichkeit	sterblich	mortal(ly)	Sterblichkeit
weiblich	wife(ly), female	Weiblichkeit	feindlich	hostile(ly)	Feindlichkeit

NOTE: Many of these words may be used with **un** to form the negative: sterblich unsterblich Unsterblichkeit

4. **-haft** having the quality (of the word expressed in the stem) For example: zweifelhaft having the quality of doubt, doubtful. The noun is formed as in number 2. Only the meaning of the stem is listed here. Give the meaning of the nouns.

zweifelhaft	doubt	Zweifelhaftigkeit	boshaft	wicked	Boshaftigkeit
mangelhaft	fault	Mangelhaftigkeit	tadelhaft	blame	Tadelhaftigkeit
riesenhaft	giant	Riesenhaftigkeit	rätselhaft	puzzle	Rätselhaftigkeit
vorteilhaft	advantage		fabelhaft	fable	

5. **-ung** -ing (or -tion) These nouns are usually formed from verbs, have a feminine gender and plural ending **-en.** Determine the meaning of the noun from the meaning of the verb. In the following illustrations, recite the meaning of the noun after you note the English verb meaning:

Verb	English	Noun	Verb	English	Noun
führen	lead	Führung	retten	save	Rettung
teilen	divide	Teilung	zeichnen	draw	Zeichnung
zählen	count	Zählung	bezahlen	pay	Bezahlung
enden	end	Endung	behandeln	treat	Behandlung
einladen	invite	Einladung	beschreiben	describe	Beschreibung

6. **-ig** sometimes the English -y: eisig icy, völlig fully
Usually comes from an adjective or a noun.

Adjective or **Noun**	**English**	**Adjective** or **noun**	**English**
zornig	angry	holzig	woody
steinig	stony	geduldig	patiently
kräftig	powerful	sandig	sandy
mächtig	mighty	völlig	fully
flüssig	fluid	feuchtig	moist

NOTE: The noun, if present, is formed as in number 2.

7. **-heit** (or the more common **-keit**) corresponds to the English -hood, -ty, -ness. See also the discussion and illustrations of 1, 2, 3, 4.

Adjective	**English**	**Noun**	**Adjective**	**English**	**Noun**
dumm	stupid	Dummheit	rein	pure	**Reinheit**
frei	free	Freiheit	wahr	true	**Wahrheit**
neu	new	Neuheit	wirklich	real	**Wirklichkeit**
ewig	eternal	Ewigkeit	traurig	sad	**Traurigkeit**
möglich	possible	Möglichkeit	krank	sick	**Krankheit**

NOTE: Some of these will admit of the negative "un" in both the adjective and the noun. As for example: unmöglich Unmöglichkeit.

8. **-schaft** -ship

Freund	friend	Freundschaft	Verwandte	relative	Verwandtschaft
Herr	ruler, master	Herrschaft	**Nachbar**	neighbor	Nachbarschaft
Bruder	brother	Bruderschaft			

9. **-mässig** (sometimes **-gemäss**) according to (whatever the word is that precedes it). See also Appendix 16. Planmässig —according to plan; naturmässig—according to nature. Usually comes from nouns. Note that nouns are formed as in number 2.

regelmässig	regular	Regelmässigkeit	verhältnismässig	relatively	**Verhältnismässigkeit**
zweckmässig	suitable	Zweckmässigkeit	erfahrungsmässig erfahrungsgemäss	according to experience	
vernunftmässig	reasonable	Vernunftmässigkeit			
heldenmässig	hero-like	—	zahlenmässig	**according to numbers, numerically**	
gesetzmässig	legal	Gesetzmässigkeit	verfassungsmässig	**according to the constitution**	
lehrmässig	dogmatic, according to theory		gedankenmässig	**according to thought**	
zeitgemäss	seasonable, up to date		schulmässig	**classic, according to the school**	
			kunstgemäss	**according to the rules of art**	

10. **er** corresponds to the -er on English nouns, as for example: hunt, hunter. If the English will admit of an -er, in all probability the German noun will also. If the -er is used, it denotes the agent expressed by the verb. Try to gain the meaning of the noun by tracing it back to the verb form. The feminine forms end with **-in** as in Leser Leserin, Tänzer Tänzerin. The vowels a, o, u in the stem are regularly umlauted.

backen	**bake**	Bäcker	sprechen	speak	Sprecher
finden	**find**	Finder	fischen	fish	Fischer
tragen	**carry**	Träger	führen	lead	Führer
rauben	**rob**	Räuber	schlafen	sleep	Schläfer
jagen	**hunt**	Jäger	besitzen	possess	Besitzer
kaufen	**buy**	Käufer	schreiben	write	Schreiber

11. An-e attached to an adjective. Recite the meaning of the nouns.

gut	Güte	good	schwach	Schwäche	weak
heiss	Hitze	hot	stark	Stärke	strong
kalt	Kälte	cold	treu	Treue	true
hart	Härte	hard	hoch	Höhe	high
kurz	Kürze	short	scharf	Schärfe	sharf
gross	Grösse	large	lang	Länge	long
breit	Breite	broad, wide	warm	Wärme	warm

How to Multiply Your Vocabulary

A large percentage of German words are traced to verb forms. If you are familiar with 50 of the more common verbs in your field of study, you may multiply these fifty verbs in several different ways.

1. These 50 infinitives may be capitalized and used as nouns. They form then what is generally known as verbal nouns. Some of these infinitives have been used so often as nouns that they are now accepted as common nouns and are found in the dictionary as such. They are always neuter.

leben	das Leben	living, life	hören	das Hören	hearing
schreiben	das Schreiben	writing, letter	sieden	das Sieden	boiling
gehen	das Gehen	walking	singen	das Singen	singing
lesen	das Lesen	reading	fahren	das Fahren	traveling, driving

2. You would have 50 more words if the verbs will accept of an -er in English. See also number 10 above. Illustrations:

führen	Führer	leader	verkaufen	Verkäufer	seller	Other illustrations under
lehren	Lehrer	teacher	zuhören	Zuhörer	listener	Number 10 above.

3. You would have 50 more words if you add a 'd' to the infinitive. This is the present participle form that may be translated with 'ing'. (See also Rule 11.)

singen	singend	singing—or while singing (Rule 11)
sprechen	sprechend	speaking—or while speaking (Rule 11)
sieden	siedend	boiling—or while boiling
beschränken	beschränkend	limiting—or while limiting
verbringen	verbringend	spending—or while spending

4. You can add 50 more words to your vocabulary by capitalizing the present participle form. This noun would then mean "the one who". For example: der Fahrende the one who travels, the traveler.

fahren	der Fahrende	the one who travels, traveler	the one who is doing the traveling
schreiben	der Schreibende	the one who writes, writer	Do not confuse with number 3.
tragen	der Tragende	the one who carries, carrier	the one who is doing the carrying
finden	der Findende	the one who finds, finder	Do not confuse with number 2 and
schlafen	der Schlafende	the one who sleeps, sleeper	10 above.

5. Out of the original 50 infinitives you can make 50 more words by capitalizing the past participle form. See also Rule 3 C-3. Try to translate the past participles with "that which", plural "those which".

schreiben	geschrieben	das Geschriebene	that which is written, was written, has been written
sagen	gesagt	das Gesagte	that which is said, was said, etc.
lesen	gelesen	das Gelesene	that which is read, was read, etc.
sehen	gesehen	das Gesehene	that which is seen, was seen, etc.
kochen	gekocht	das Gekochte	that which is boiled, was boiled, etc.

6. Many nouns are derived from the verb stem, i.e., the infinitive stem, the imperfect stem, the third person singular stem, or the past participle stem. Acquire the habit of tracing the noun to a verb form which you may know. Usually if a noun comes from a verb stem it is masculine gender. (See column six of the verb list on pp. 24-26.)

kaufen	kaufte	gekauft	kauft	Kauf	to buy
springen	sprang	gesprungen	springt	Sprung	jump
greifen	griff	gegriffen	greift	Griff	grasp
fallen	fiel	gefallen	fällt	Fall	fall
treten	trat	getreten	tritt	Tritt	step
laufen	lief	gelaufen	läuft	Lauf	run
schneiden	schnitt	geschnitten	schneidet	Schnitt	cut
graben	grub	gegraben	gräbt	Grab, Grube	dig
streiten	stritt	gestritten	streitet	Streit	quarrel
pfeifen	pfiff	gepfiffen	pfeift	Pfiff	whistle
sein	war	gewesen	ist	Wesen	be
wachsen	wuchs	gewachsen	wächst	Wuchs	grow
finden	fand	gefunden	findet	Fund	find
binden	band	gebunden	bindet	Binde, Band, Bund	bind
schlagen	schlug	geschlagen	schlägt	Schlag	strike
raten	riet	geraten	rät	Rat	advise
rufen	rief	gerufen	ruft	Ruf	call
sitzen	sass	gesessen	sitzt	Sitz	sit
schreiten	Schritt	geschritten	schreitet	Schritt	stride
beissen	biss	gebissen	beisst	Biss	bite
fangen	fing	gefangen	fängt	Fang	catch

NOTE: Many of these nouns may also appear in compounds. For example:

Wesen	Lebewesen	Kleinwesen	Rat	Ratgeber	Kaufpreis
Bund	Völkerbund		Wuchs	Pflanzenwuchs	Regierungssitz
Schlag	Donnerschlag		Schnitt	Abschnitt	Rathaus

7. **Many nouns come from adjectives and from these adjectives verbs are formed. These verbs may in turn be changed into nouns. Frequently they are compounded with other** nouns. This list shows how this is done. **Adverbs may also operate the same way. Try to derive the meaning from the "inside word" without paying too much attention to the prefix or the suffix.**

English	German	Verb	Noun	English
warm	warm	erwärmen	Erwärmung	heating
cold	kalt	erkälten	Erkältung	cooling
slow	langsam	verlangsamen	Verlangsamung	retardation
small	klein	verkleinern	Verkleinerung	diminishment, diminution
large	gross	vergrössern	Vergrösserung	enlargement
easy	leicht	erleichtern	Erleichterung	facilitation, relief
difficult	schwer	erschweren	Erschwerung	aggravation
possible	möglich	ermöglichen	Ermöglichung	making possible
more	mehr	vermehren	Vermehrung	reproduction, increase
high	hoch	erhöhen	Erhöhung	increase, elevation
long	lang	verlängern	Verlängerung	lengthening, elongation
bad	schlecht	verschlechtern	Verschlechterung	worsening
yes	ja	bejahen	Bejahung	affirmation
no	nein	verneinen	Verneinung	negation
far	fern	entfernen	Entfernung	removal, remoteness, distance
sharp	scharf	verschärfen	Verschärfung	sharpening, growing critical
low	niedrig	erniedrigen	Erniedrigung	lowering
short	kurz	verkürzen	Verkürzung	shortening
good	gut	vergüten	Vergütung	making good, indemnification

Note these compound nouns, coming from these adjective forms:

Vergrösserungsglas	microscope		
Volksvermehrung	increase in population	Siedepunktserniedrigung	lowering of the boiling point
Lichtverbreitung	spreading of light	Preiserhöhung	increase in price
Verkleinerungsmasstab	scale of reduction	Strahlungsverstärkung	intensification of rays
Zinsvergütung	payment by way of interest	Zustandsverschlechterung	worsening of conditions
Verlängerungsgurt	lengthening strap		

Compound Nouns

German forms compound nouns more readily than English. It is impossible to give in this limited discussion any accurate listing of the various ways compounds can be formed. It is sufficient in this chapter to note some of the peculiarities of compound nouns and to learn how to analyze them. Frequently the entire noun will not appear in the dictionary and in that case the individual parts must be looked up separately. Observe the following points:

1. **Very often it is possible (and preferable) to translate the noun from beginning to end:**

Bindegewebe	connective tissue	Zuckergehalt	sugar content	Vollmond?
Blutgefäss	blood vessel	Luftdruck	air pressure	Salzgehalt?
Wärmeentwicklung	heat development	Sehnerv	optic nerve	Heizfläche?
Tageslicht	day light	Schulhaus	school house, school	Vorwort?
Muttersprache	mother tongue	Lesebuch	reading book, reader	Schwefelsäure?

2. **If an "s" appears inside of the noun, let the "s" divide the word. Try the last part first and say "of" as you come back through the noun. You are most generally correct by saying "of" when an "s" is inside of the word, for the "s" is a genitive form.** Practice on these nouns:

Bildungsart	manner of formation	Entstehungsweise	manner of origination
Angriffspunkt	point of attack	Ernährungsorgan	organ of nutrition
Gefühlssinn	sense of feeling	Geschmacksempfindung	sensation of taste
Kriegsbrauch	custom of war	Atmungsapparat	organ of breathing
Kriegsgesetz	law of war	Entdeckungsreihe	series of discoveries

NOTE: There is no reason why you cannot go straight forward through the noun as in number 1 if the English does not sound stilted. For example: breathing apparatus, taste sensation, but do not say origination manner.

3. Notice that the noun may be composed of several words. It is often advisable to start with the last word and go backward through the noun. Use "of" where difficulty arises.

Wasserdichtigkeitsbestimmung	determination of the density of water
Wärmeentwicklungsvermögen	power of development of heat
Zuckergehaltsmesser	meter for content of sugar
Tuberkel-bazillen-färbungsmittel	means for staining tubercle bacilli
Erziehungsanstaltsverwalter	administrator of institution of learning
Erdentstehungslehre	theory of origin of the earth
Lebenserhaltungstrieb	instinct for preservation of life
Pflanzenentstehungslehre	theory of origin of plants
Sättigungspunktsbestimmung	determination of point of saturation

Look up the meaning for these nouns:

Bindegewebesentzündung
Vaterlandsverteidigungsplan
Wasserversorgungsgesellschaft
Wollreinigungsmaschine
Volksschullehrerseminar

Wasserstandsanzeiger
Lebensrettungsapparat
Wasserleitungsröhre
Unfallsversicherungsgesellschaft

4. If there is no "s", you will probably be correct in going forward through the noun as shown in number 1. However, once in a while it is best to do as shown in number 3, namely go back through the noun using "of" or "for" whichever sounds best. (Which do you prefer in the following illustrations?)

Wahrsagekunst	art of fortune telling	or	fortune telling art
Tonsetzkunst	art of writing music	or	music writing art
Wärmekraftlehre	theory of force of heat	or	heat-power-theory
Erdnaturbeschreibung	description of the nature of the earth	or	earth nature description
Versteinerungskunde	science of fossils	or	fossil science
Schädelkenntnislehre	theory of knowledge of the skull	or	skull recognition theory
Erziehungsanstalt	institution of learning	or	educational institution
Herzentzündung	inflamation of the heart	or	heart inflammation

---

How to Handle Prefixes

There are two kinds of prefixes in German—separable and inseparable. The separable verbs are taken care of by Rule 2, for the prefix is usually found at the end of the main clauses. (Review illustrations of Rule 2). Although some texts have attempted to define the meanings for the inseparable prefixes, the author feels that no general rules can be formulated for them. In most cases it is best to look up the verb in the dictionary in order to avoid error and confusion. There are a few prefixes which follow certain rules and meanings. A careful study of these may prove to be helpful.

1. **un-** corresponds to the English un-, im-, mis-, dis-, in-.

unmöglich	impossible	Unmöglichkeit	impossibility	Unglücksfall	misfortune
unglücklich	unhappy	Unglücklichkeit	unhappiness	Ungnade	disgrace
undenkbar	inconceivable	Undenkbarkeit	inconceivableness	Unruhe	unrest
unglaubwürdig	untrustworthy	Unglaubwürdigkeit	untrustworthiness	Unsicherheit	unsafeness
unanwendbar	inapplicable	Unanwendbarkeit	inapplicability	Ungleichheit	inequality
unbegreiflich	incomprehensible	Unbegreiflichkeit	incomprehensibility		

2. **miss-** corresponds to the English mis-, dis-, ill-, mal-.

Missverständnis	misunderstanding	Missbildung	malformation
Misstrauen	distrust	Missbilligung	disapproval
Misserfolg	ill success	Missdeutung	misinterpretation
Misshandlung	maltreatment	Missverhältnis	disproportion

Verbs

missbrauchen	misuse	misshandeln	ill-treat	missdeuten	misconstrue
missbilligen	disapprove	missverstehen	misunderstand	missachten	disregard
missbehagen	displease	missleiten	mislead	missfallen	displease

3. **zer-** corresponds to the English meaning of 'broken up,' 'shatter' or destroy in some way

reissen	tear	zerreissen	tear up or destroy by ripping
brechen	break	zerbrechen	break or destroy by breaking
stören	disturb	zerstören	destroy
kochen	boil	zerkochen	destroy by boiling
schneiden	cut	zerschneiden	destroy by cutting
legen	put, lay	zerlegen	break up, analyze, lay out in sections
klopfen	knock	zerklopfen	to knock to pieces
mahlen	grind	zermahlmen	to grind to pieces, pulverize

4. **ent-** corresponds to the English un-, dis-, away, off (subject to exceptions).
Try and deduce the word with these English prefixes and the aid you get from the context. If you are in doubt, refer to the dictionary. The 'ent' may sometimes mean to begin, start, separate.

entdecken	uncover, discover	entkleiden	undress, disrobe, take off clothes
enthaupten	take off the head, behead	entspringen	originate, begin, start
entkorken	uncork, take away the cork	entziehen	take away, withdraw, remove
entwaffnen	disarm, take away the arms	entnehmen	take away, take off from

5. **be-** is often used to make a transitive verb and then has an object. In case **be-** is attached to a verb, try to derive the meaning by the context. Intensify the verb as is the case in English: moan about something or bemoan something; stride over something or bestride something. Any attempt to define fully this prefix will lead to difficulty. Some help may be gained from the following examples:

treten	step	betreten	enter	drohen	threaten	bedrohen	**threaten**
folgen	follow	befolgen	follow	dienen	serve	bedienen	**make use of**
gehen	go	begehen	celebrate, commit	weinen	cry	beweinen	**mourn**
kommen	come	bekommen	get, come by	handeln	handle, act	behandeln	**treat**

6. **You may arrive at the meaning of some verbs which have "separable prefixes", as discussed in Rule 2, by staying as near as possible to the meaning of the prefix.** Hence a verb like **aufstehen** would have to mean "up" in some **way—arise, get up, stand up, etc.** A verb with the prefix "zurück" must indicate "back" because of the meaning **of the prefix. The verb "übertragen" would mean "over" in some way; i.e., there must be a "transfer" implied in the verb. These suggestions are, of course, subject to exception.** Note the following examples:

lassen	let	durchlassen	let through	nehmen	take	unternehmen	undertake
wirken	work	mitwirken	work with, cooperate	steigen	climb	hinaufsteigen	climb up
treten	step	eintreten	step in, enter	stehen	stand	beistehen	stand by, assist
nehmen	take	zurücknehmen	take back, withdraw	legen	lay	niederlegen	lay down
halten	hold	zusammenhalten	hold together	segeln	sail	umsegeln	sail around
gehen	go	übergehen	go over	schliessen	close	einschliessen	enclose
teilen	part	mitteilen	impart, inform	schweissen	weld	zusammenschweissen	weld together
fliegen	fly	nachfliegen	fly after,	prägen	stamp	aufprägen	imprint on
setzen	set	aussetzen	set out, expose				

Words That Need Special Attention

brechen	brach	gebrochen	to break
bringen	brachte	gebracht	to bring
brauchen	brauchte	gebraucht	to use, need

denken	dachte	gedacht	to think, imagine

Sometimes used with the past participle, as: Wir denken es durch eine Wand getrennt. We imagine (that) it is separated by a wall.

einige	some
einzig	single, alone
einzeln	single, individual

hören	hörte	gehört	to hear
gehören	gehörte	gehört	to belong

gelingen	gelang	gelungen	to succeed
gelangen	gelangte	gelangt	to arrive, come

handeln	handelte	gehandelt	to deal, act, treat

Often used with "um". Es handelt sich—um. It deals with, is a question of, we are dealing with.

gelten	galt	gegolten	is of value, valid

es gilt   it is true, is of value, the object is

können	konnte	gekonnt	can, be able,
kennen	kannte	gekannt	know (a person)

nehmen	nahm	genommen	to take,
nennen	nannte	genannt	to name

gewähren	gewährte	gewährt	afford, guaranteed,
gewahren	gewahrte	gewahrt	perceive,

fahren	fuhr	gefahren	travel, drive
führen	führte	geführt	lead, guide

A List of German Irregular Verbs

The stem from which the noun is formed is in bold-face type.

Infinitive	3rd Sing.	Imperfect	Past Participle	Imp. Subj.	Noun and its Gender		English
backen	bäckt	buk	gebacken	büke			bake
befehlen	befiehlt	befahl	befohlen	beföhle	Befehl	M	command
beginnen	beginnt	begann	begonner	begönne	Beginn	M	begin
beissen	beisst	biss	gebissen	bisse	Biss	M	bite
bergen	birgt	barg	geborgen	bärge			conceal
bersten	birst	barst	geborsten	bärste			burst
betrügen	betrügt	betrog	betrogen	betröge	Betrug	M	deceive
bewegen	bewegt	bewog	bewogen	bewöge			move, induce
biegen	biegt	bog	gebogen	böge	Bug	M	bend (bow)
bieten	bietet	bot	geboten	böte	(An)gebot	N	offer
bitten	bittet	bat	gebeten	bäte	Bitte	F	beg, request
blasen	bläst	blies	geblasen	bliese			blow
bleiben	bleibt	blieb	geblieben	bliebe			remain
braten	brät	briet	gebraten	briete	Braten	M	fry (roast)
brechen	bricht	brach	gebrochen	bräche	Bruch	M	break
brennen	brennt	brannte	gebrannt	brennte	(Brennpunkt)	M	burn
bringen	bringt	brachte	gebracht	brächte			bring
denken	denkt	dachte	gedacht	dächte	Gedanke	M	think (thought)
dringen	dringt	drang	gedrungen	dränge	Drang	M	press, push
dürfen	darf	durfte	gedurft	dürfte			be permitted
empfangen	empfängt	empfing	empfangen	empfinge	Empfang	M	receive
empfehlen	empfiehlt	empfahl	empfohlen	empfähle	Empfehlung	F	recommend
empfinden	empfindet	empfand	empfunden	empfände	Empfindung	F	sense, feel
essen	isst	ass	gegessen	ässe	Essen	N	eat
fahren	fährt	fuhr	gefahren	führe	Fahrt	F	travel
fallen	fällt	fiel	gefallen	fiele	Fall	M	fall
fangen	fängt	fing	gefangen	finge	Fang	M	catch
fechten	ficht	focht	gefochten	föchte	Gefecht	N	fence, fight
finden	findet	fand	gefunden	fände	Fund	M	find
flechten	flicht	flocht	geflochten	flöchte	Flechte	F	braid, plait
fliegen	fliegt	flog*	geflogen	flöge	Flug	M	fly
fliehen	flieht	floh	geflohen	flöhe	Flucht	F	flee
fliessen	fliesst	floss*	geflossen	flösse	Fluss	M	flow
frieren	friert	fror	gefroren	fröre			freeze
gären	gärt	gor or gärte	gegoren	göre			ferment
gebären	gebärt	gebar	geboren	gebäre	Geburt	F	bear
geben	gibt	gab	gegeben	gäbe	Gabe	F	give
gedeihen	gedeiht	gedieh	gediehen	gediehe			prosper
gehen	geht	ging	gegangen	ginge	Gang	M	go, proceed
gelingen	gelingt	gelang	gelungen	gelänge			succeed
gelten	gilt	galt	gegolten	gälte			to be valid
genesen	genest	genas	genesen	genäse			recover
geniessen	geniesst	genoss	genossen	genösse	Genuss	M	enjoy
geraten	gerät	geriet	geraten	geriete			fall into
geschehen	geschieht	geschah	geschehen	geschähe	Geschichte	F	happen (history)
gewinnen	gewinnt	gewann	gewonnen	gewänne	Gewinn	M	gain
giessen	giesst	goss	gegossen	gösse	Guss	M	pour, cast
gleichen	gleicht	glich	geglichen	gliche			be similar
gleiten	gleitet	glitt	geglitten	glitte			glide
graben	gräbt	grub	gegraben	grübe	Grab N, Grube	F	dig (grave, ditch)
greifen	greift	griff	gegriffen	griffe	Griff	M	grasp
halten	hält	hielt	gehalten	hielte	Halt	M	hold, keep
hangen	hängt	hing	gehangen	hinge	Hang	M	hang (incline)
heben	hebt	hob	gehoben	höbe	Hub	M	lift
heissen	heisst	hiess	geheissen	hiesse			to be called
helfen	hilft	half	geholfen	hülfe	Hilfe	F	help

ADDITIONAL VERBS AND NOTES:

kennen	**kennt**	**kannte**	**gekannt**	kennte	Kenntnis	F	know
klingen	**klingt**	**klang**	**geklungen**	klänge	Klang	M	ring, sound
kommen	kommt	kam	gekommen	käme			come
können	kann	konnte	gekonnt	könnte	Kunst	F	can, be able (art)
kriechen	kriecht	kroch	gekrochen	kröche	(Kriechtier)	N	crawl
laden	lädt	lud	geladen	lüde	Ladung	F	load
lassen	lässt	liess	gelassen	liesse			let, allow
laufen	läuft	lief	gelaufen	liefe	Lauf	M	run
leiden	leidet	litt	gelitten	litte	Leid	N	suffer
leihen	leiht	lieh	geliehen	liehe			lend
lesen	liest	las	gelesen	läse			read
liegen	liegt	lag	gelegen	läge	Lage	F	lie (location)
lügen	lügt	log	gelogen	löge	Lüge	F	lie (tell)
meiden	meidet	mied	gemieden	miede			avoid
melken	melkt	melkte, molk	gemolken	mölke	Milch	F	to milk
messen	misst	**mass**	gemessen	mässe	Mass	N	measure
mögen	mag	mochte	gemocht	möchte			like, may
müssen	muss	musste	gemusst	müsste			must
nehmen	nimmt	nahm	genommen	nähme			take
nennen	nennt	nannte	genannt	nennte	(Nennwert)	M	name
pfeifen	pfeift	**pfiff**	gepfiffen	pfiffe	Pfiff	M	whistle
pflegen	pflegt	pflegte, pflog	**gepflegt**	pflöge	Pflege	F	care for
preisen	preist	pries	gepriesen	priese	Preis	M	praise
quellen	quillt	quoll	gequollen	quölle	Quell(e)	M, F	gush forth
raten	rät	riet	geraten	riete	Rat	M	advise
reiben	reibt	rieb	gerieben	riebe	(Reibfläche)	F	rub
reissen	reisst	**riss**	gerissen	risse	Riss	M	tear
reiten	reitet	ritt	geritten	ritte	Ritt	M	ride
rennen	rennt	rannte	gerannt	rennte	Rennpferd	N	run, race
riechen	riecht	roch	gerochen	röche	Geruch	M	smell
ringen	ringt	rang	gerungen	ränge			struggle
rinnen	rinnt	rann	geronnen	ränne	Rinne	F	trickle
rufen	ruft	rief	gerufen	riefe	Ruf	M	call
säen	sät	säte	gesät	säte	Saat	F	sow
schaffen	schafft	schuf	geschaffen	schüfe			create
scheiden	scheidet	schied	geschieden	schiede	Scheide	F	divide
scheinen	scheint	schien	geschienen	schiene	Schein	M	seem, appear
schelten	schilt	schalt	gescholten	schälte			scold
schieben	schiebt	schob	geschoben	schöbe	Schub	M	geschoben
schiessen	schiesst	**schoss**	geschossen	schösse	Schuss	M	shot
schlafen	schläft	schlief	geschlafen	schliefe	Schlaf	M	sleep
schlagen	schlägt	schlug	geschlagen	schlüge	Schlag	M	strike
schleichen	schleicht	schlich	geschlichen	schliche			crawl, creep
schliessen	schliesst	**schloss**	geschlossen	schlösse	Schluss	M	close
schmeissen	schmeisst	schmiss	geschmissen	schmisse	Schmiss	M	throw, fling
schmelzen	schmilzt	schmolz	geschmolzen	schmölze	(Schmelzpunkt)	M	melt, fuse
schneiden	schneidet	**schnitt**	geschnitten	schnitte	Schnitt	M	cut
schreiben	schreibt	schrieb	geschrieben	schriebe	(Schreibfeder)	F	write
schreien	schreit	schrie	geschrieen	schriee	Schrei	M	cry
schreiten	schreitet	**schritt**	geschritten	schritte	Schritt	M	step, stride
schweigen	schweigt	schwieg	geschwiegen	schwiege			be silent
schwimmen	schwimmt	schwamm	geschwommen	schwämme			swim
schwinden	schwindet	**schwand**	**geschwunden**	schwände	Schwund	M	disappear
schwingen	schwingt	schwang	**geschwungen**	schwänge	Schwung	M	swing
schwören	schwört	**schwor**	geschworen	schwöre	Schwur	M	swear
sehen	sieht	sah	gesehen	sähe	Sicht	F	see
sein	ist	war	**gewesen**	wäre	Wesen	N	be
senden	sendet	sandte	gesandt	sendete			send
sieden	siedet	siedete	gesotten	sötte	(Siedepunkt)	M	boil
singen	singt	sang	gesungen	sänge	Gesang	M	sing
sinken	sinkt	sank	gesunken	sänke			sink
sinnen	sinnt	sann	gesonnen	sänne	Sinn	M	think
sitzen	sitzt	sass	gesessen	sässe	Sitz	M	sit
sollen	soll	sollte	gesollt	sollte			is to, shall

ADDITIONAL VERBS AND NOTES:

spalten	spaltet	spaltete	gespaltet	spaltete	Spalt	M	split
spinnen	spinnt	spann	gesponnen	spänne	Spinne	F	spin
sprechen	spricht	sprach	gesprochen	spräche	Sprache	F	speak
spriessen	spriesst	spross	gesprossen	sprösse	Spross	M	sprout
springen	springt	sprang	gesprungen	spränge	Sprung	M	spring
stechen	sticht	stach	gestochen	stäche	Stich	M	pierce
stehen	steht	stand	gestanden	stünde	Stand	M	stand
stehlen	stiehlt	stahl	gestohlen	stähle	Diebstahl	M	steal
steigen	steigt	stieg	gestiegen	stiege	Steig	M	climb
sterben	stirbt	starb	gestorben	stärbe, stürbe			die
stossen	stösst	stiess	gestossen	stiesse	Stoss	M	push
streichen	streicht	strich	gestrichen	striche	Strich	M	stretch
streiten	streitet	stritt	gestritten	stritte	Streit	M	dispute
tragen	trägt	trug	getragen	trüge	Tracht	F	carry, wear
treffen	trifft	traf	getroffen	träfe	(Treffpunkt)	M	meet,
treiben	treibt	trieb	getrieben	triebe	Trieb	M	drive
treten	tritt	trat	getreten	träte	Tritt	M	step
trinken	trinkt	trank	getrunken	tränke	Trank, Trunk	M	drink
tun (thun)	tut (thut)	tat	getan	täte	Tat	F	do, act
verderben	verdirbt	verdarb	verdorben	verdärbe			ruin
verdriessen	verdriesst	verdross	verdrossen	verdrösse	Verdruss	M	grieve
vergessen	vergisst	vergass	vergessen	vergässe			forget
verhehlen	verhehlt	verhehlte	verhehlt, verhohlen	verhehlte			conceal
verlieren	verliert	verlor	verloren	verlöre	Verlust	M	lose
verwirren	verwirrt	verwirrte	verwirrt, verworren	verwirrte			confuse
wachsen	wächst	wuchs	gewachsen	wüchse	Wuchs	M	grow
wägen	wägt	wog, wägte	gewogen	wöge	Waage	F	consider
waschen	wäscht	wusch	gewaschen	wüsche	Wäsche	F	wash
weben	webt	wob, webte	gewoben, gewebt	wöbe, webte	Gewebe	N	weave
weichen	weicht	wich	gewichen	wiche	Weiche	F	soften, yield
weisen	weist	wies	gewiesen	wiese	Beweis	M	show
wenden	wendet	wendete, wandte	gewandt, gewendet	wendete	Wende	F	turn
werben	wirbt	warb	geworben	wärbe			acquire
werden	wird	wurde	geworden	würde			become, be
werfen	wirft	warf	geworfen	wärfe	Wurf	M	throw
wiegen	wiegt	wog	gewogen	wöge	Wiege	F	weigh
winden	windet	wand	gewunden	wände	Winde	F	wind, reel
wissen	weiss	wusste	gewusst	wüsste	Bewusstsein	N	know
wollen	will	wollte	gewollt	wollte	Wille	M	will
ziehen	zieht	zog	gezogen	zöge	Zug	M	pull, draw
zwingen	zwingt	zwang	gezwungen	zwänge	Zwang	M	force, compel

ADDITIONAL VERBS AND NOTES:

THE GERMAN NOUN

Perhaps no one principle of German grammar gives the American student more trouble than the noun. It is an almost endless task to learn the five classes of nouns, for each of them is subject to numerous exceptions. In the most recent grammars students are advised to learn the plural of each noun separately.

Many of the students in my classes have derived much benefit from the rules given below. These are tips on recognition of the plural noun. These rules are, of course, not without exception, but they are particularly valuable for reading purposes as here it is necessary to recognize the plural forms.

The plural of nouns in German is formed by adding either **e** or **en**, sometimes **er.** Most nouns end with **e** or **en** in the plural. Nouns ending with **es** or **s** are genitive singular and are **never** plural, unless you are dealing with a foreign noun such as: Radios, Autos.

The singular of a noun will most generally be preceded by some kind of a qualifying word to indicate that the noun is singular. You may say in English: "We saw loads of melons" or "We saw flocks of birds." The same is true in German. You are not likely to say: "We saw load of melons" or "We saw flock of birds." In English it is necessary to put down the indefinite article (a) to indicate the singular form of the noun. This is also the case in German. This does not mean that a noun in German cannot appear without an "ein". It simply means that:

THE ABSENCE OF THE "EIN" indicates that the writer probably intends it to be plural. As a double check, see if the noun **ends** with **e, en,** or **er;** if it does the noun is in all probability plural. How would you recognize that the nouns in the first column below are plural and those in the second column singular? What is the number of the nouns in the third column.

chemische Prozesse	Lösung	Erklärung
Atome	eine Eigenschaft	Ringe
Vorgänge	Darstellung	Aufgaben
Grundlagen	Gegenstand	Zustände
Molekülen	diese Arbeitsbedingung	Götter
wichtige Worte	Fluss	Bedingungen
einige Bestandteile	Schritt	Vorschläge
anerkannte Sätze	langsame Nebenreaktion	Temperatur
Dampfströme	heisser Dampfstrom	Gesteine

WATCH THE VERB FORMS

The verb form will also tell you the number of the noun. If the subject is plural the verb will END with an **en** or **n.** If the subject is singular the verb will END with **t** or **et.** This is always true except for the modal auxiliaries, sein, haben, werden, wissen and perhaps two or three irregular verbs. (If the first or second person is used, the verb will END with **e** or **st.**)

Since you are reading in the third person about 95% of the time, only the endings **t** or **et** need to be observed in the present tense. If the verb is used in the past tense, the endings will be **te** for the regular verbs and no ending at all for the irregular verbs (fiel, gab, half, schlug). The irregular verbs will also end with **n** or **en** in the plural.

The modal auxiliaries and SEIN, HABEN and WERDEN must be learned separately. These are taken care of in Rule 6.

TIPS FROM THE ADJECTIVES

The adjective that precedes the noun will tell you now to recognize the plural form. If the adjective stands alone before the noun—that is, without a qualifying word—the endings of the adjective will be the same as the plural endings of **dieser,** (e, er, en, e.) Example: wichtige Worte.

If the article "die" is used, the adjective will end with **e** in the singular and **en** in the plural. For example: die einzige Aufgabe — die einzige**n** Aufgaben.

If the article "den" is used, this article is either the accusative masculine or dative plural. If it is dative plural the noun will always end with **n** or **en.**

If the article "der" is used, chances are the noun is genitive singular or dative singular or genitive plural. Close observation of these forms in reading will help you determine the number of the noun. The nominative masculine form is also "der."

VERBS IN RELATIVE CLAUSES

If the verb in the relative clause is plural, the antecedent of the relative pronoun will also be plural. (Alle Gesetze, welche den Handel **regulierten,** wurden vom Kongress gemacht.) Whereas if the verb in the relative clause is singular (that is, ends with t, te, or nothing as in gab, half), then the antecedent of the relative is singular. (Es ist dieselbe **Kraft, die** einen fallenden Apfel in der Richtung zum Mittelpunkt der Erde **zieht.**

Most Common Abbreviations

a.a.O.	am angegebenen Ort am andern Ort	loc. cit. or elsewhere
Abb.	Abbildung	illustration, figure
Abk.	Abkürzung	abbreviation
Abt.	Abteilung	department, division
Anm.	Anmerkung	foot-note, remark
Bd.	Band	volume
bes.	besonders	particular, especial
betr.	betreffend	said, concerned, in question
bisw.	bisweilen	at times, sometimes
b.w.	bitte wenden	please turn (page), over
b.z.w. **or** bzw.	beziehungsweise	respectively, or
ca.	circa	about, nearly, approximate
dergl., desgl.	dergleichen, desgleichen	the like, such, same, similar
DIN	Deutsche Industrie Norm	German Industry Standard(s)
ebd.	ebenda	in the same place
entspr.	entsprechend	corresponding
ev., event., evtl.	eventuell	perhaps
ff.	und folgend	and following
folg.	folgend	following
Hg.; hrsg.	Herausgeber; herausgegeben	editor; edited
inkl.	inklusive	inclusive, including
i.J.	im Jahre	in the year
Kap.	Kapitel	chapter
lfd.	laufend	current, consecutive, regular
mögl.	möglich(st)	possibly, as (if) possible
N.F., n. F.	neue Folge	new series
P.S., PS	Pferdestärke	horsepower
rd.	rund	approximate, about
resp.	respektive	respectively, rather, or
s.a.	siehe auch	see also, cf. also
S.	Seite	page
S.A.	Soderabdruck	separate, reprint
sog.	sogenannt	so-called
s.o.; s.u.	siehe oben; siehe unten	see above; see below
SS.	Säuren	acids
t., T.	Tonne(n)	ton(s)
Tab.	Tabelle	table
u.	und; unten	and; below
u.a.	unter andern (anderm)	among others, among other considerations
u.E.	unsers Erachtens	in our opinion
U./M., U.p.M.	Umdrehungen (Umlaufungen) pro Minute	revolutions per minute
ung., ungef.	ungefähr	about, approximate(ly)
u.s.f., u.s.w.	und so fort, und so weiter	and so forth, and so on
u.U.	unter Umständen	under certain circumstances
v.	von	from, of
v.Chr.	vor Christo	B.C.
Verf.	Verfasser	author
vergr.; verkl.	vergrössert; verkleinert	magnified; reduced
vergl.	vergleiche	compare, cf., see
v.H.	von Hundert	per cent
Z.	Zeile; Zeitschrift	line; journal
z.B.	zum Beispiel	for example, e.g.
z.T.	zum Teil	in part, partly
zus.	zusammen	together, totaling

Much more inclusive lists of abbreviations may be found in Louis DeVries' **German-English Science Dictionary** and in **The New Cassell German and English Dictionary.** The above dictionaries also give information on glossaries and specialized dictionaries.